8TH EDITION

[CRIMINAL JUSTICE] IN ACTION

THE CORE

LARRY K. GAINES

California State University
San Bernardino

ROGER LeROY MILLER

Institute for University Studies
Arlington, Texas

CENGAGE
Learning

Australia • Brazil • Mexico • Singapore • United Kingdom • United States

CENGAGE
Learning

Criminal Justice in Action, The Core,
Eighth Edition
Larry K. Gaines and Roger LeRoy Miller

VP for Social Science and Qualitative Business:
Erin Joyner

Product Director: Marta Lee-Perriard

Sr. Product Manager: Carolyn Henderson Meier

Sr. Content Developer: Shelley Murphy

Media Developer: Andy Yap

Product Assistant: Stephen Lagos

Content Coordinator: Casey Lozier

Marketing Director: Jennifer Levanduski

Marketing Manager: Kara Kindstrom

Marketing Coordinator: Angeline Low

Production Director: Brenda Ginty

Sr. Content Project Manager: Ann Borman

Sr. Content Digitization Project Manager:
Lezlie Light

Manufacturing Planner: Judy Inouye

IP Analyst: Deanna Ettinger

IP Project Manager: Anne Sheroff

Art Director: Brenda Carmichael

Interior and Cover Design: Lumina Datamatics

Copyeditor: Jeanne Yost

Proofreader: Susan Bradley

Indexer: Teresa Casey

Production Service: Lachina Publishing Services

Compositor: Lachina Publishing Services

Cover Image: seraficus/Getty Images

Design Credit Lines: Chapter opening
stories, background: © Gray wall studio/
Shutterstock.com; Comparative Criminal
Justice: © saicle/Shutterstock.com; Policy.cj:
© MPFphotography/Shutterstock.com;
Discretion in Action: © somchai rakin/
Shutterstock.com; CJ & Technology:
Shutterstock.com; CJ Controversy:
© HomeStudio/Shutterstock.com; Landmark
Cases: © kentoh/Shutterstock.com; A Question
of Ethics: © manfredxy/Shutterstock.com

Unless otherwise noted, all content is copyright
Cengage Learning.

For product information and technology assistance, contact us at
Cengage Learning Customer & Sales Support, 1-800-354-9706

For permission to use material from this text or product,
submit all requests online at **cengage.com/permissions**
Further permissions questions can be emailed to
permissionrequest@cengage.com

Library of Congress Control Number: 2014949707

Student Edition:
ISBN: 978-1-305-26107-5

Cengage Learning
20 Channel Center Street
Boston, MA 02210
USA

Cengage Learning is a leading provider of customized learning solutions with
office locations around the globe, including Singapore, the United Kingdom,
Australia, Mexico, Brazil, and Japan. Locate your local office at **www.cengage
.com/global.**

Cengage Learning products are represented in Canada by Nelson Education, Ltd.

To learn more about Cengage Learning Solutions, visit **www.cengage.com.**

Purchase any of our products at your local college store or at our preferred
online store **www.cengagebrain.com.**

Printed in the United States of America
Print Number: 01   Print Year: 2014

Contents in Brief

Hyoung Chang/*Denver Post*/Getty Images

AP Photo/*Atlanta Journal-Constitution*, John Spink

PART TWO: The Police and Law Enforcement

T.J. Kirkpatrick/Getty Images

RJ Sangosti/*The Denver Post*/Getty Images

6 POLICE AND THE CONSTITUTION: THE RULES OF LAW ENFORCEMENT 168

PART THREE: Criminal Courts

7 COURTS AND THE QUEST FOR JUSTICE 200

8 PRETRIAL PROCEDURES AND THE CRIMINAL TRIAL 230

Ethan Miller/Getty Images

9 PUNISHMENT AND SENTENCING 268

PART FOUR: Corrections

10 PROBATION, PAROLE, AND INTERMEDIATE SANCTIONS 304

11 PRISONS AND JAILS 332

Getty Images

12 THE PRISON EXPERIENCE AND PRISONER REENTRY 362

Khue Bui/*The New York Times*/Redux

PART FIVE: Special Issues

13 THE JUVENILE JUSTICE SYSTEM 392

Joe Raedle/Getty Images

FEATURES OF SPECIAL INTEREST

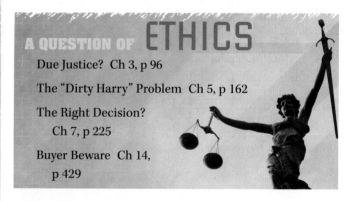

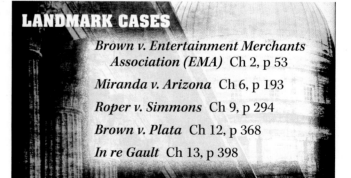

In Chapter 12 of this Eighth Edition of *Criminal Justice in Action, The Core,* Julie Howe, a halfway house program manager, tells students that her favorite part of her job is that she "has an impact on people's lives." In Chapter 4, FBI Agent Arnold Bell describes a "particularly interesting time" that he spent in Los Angeles solving bank robberies. In Chapter 10, Peggy McCarthy, a probation officer, says that, although her duties can be demanding, when she helps a client make a "positive change" in his or her life, she realizes that "what I'm doing day in and day out is 100 percent worthwhile."

Impactful. Interesting. Worthwhile. In their own words, Howe, Bell, and McCarthy capture the essence of a career in the American criminal justice system. As in previous editions, each chapter of *Criminal Justice in Action, The Core, Eighth Edition,* includes a **Careers in CJ feature** in which a criminal justice practitioner presents a personal account of his or her profession. Combining this first-person insight with a solid pedagogical foundation and numerous real-world examples, *Criminal Justice in Action, The Core* offers students unmatched insight into the world of crime and justice that goes well beyond the clichés of Hollywood or the rhetoric of politicians. With the help and advice of the many criminal justice professors who have adopted this best-selling textbook over the years, we believe we have created an invaluable introduction to the field.

Focus on Critical Thinking and Analysis

Even more so than in previous editions, the Eighth Edition of *Criminal Justice in Action, The Core,* focuses on developing critical thinking skills. To this end, two new features require students to research a given topic on the Internet, and then use their research to come to a conclusion regarding specific aspects about that topic and its place in the American criminal justice system. These two new writing assignment features are:

- **CJ Controversy.** Each chapter of the textbook includes one of these new features, which start with a short summary of a controversial criminal justice topic, followed by general "for" and "against" arguments concerning that topic. Then, students are asked to go online and research a specific issue, event, or policy related to the controversy surrounding the topic. Finally, students have the opportunity to analyze the results of their research in a short writing assignment of at least two paragraphs. These features not only help students improve writing and critical thinking skills, but also they act as a review of important material in the chapter.

- **Policy.cj.** Also included in each chapter of the textbook, this new margin feature introduces students to many of the most pressing policy issues in criminal justice today. Again, students must go online to research a crucial aspect of the relevant policy, and then either make a short list or complete a one-paragraph writing assignment in which they give their views on the policy and its ramifications.

In addition to these new features, we have added three critical analysis questions to the introductory page of each chapter. These questions relate back to the chapter opening vignette and introduce themes crucial to the coming pages. As these changes show, our commitment to developing students' abilities to think critically about criminal justice permeates *Criminal Justice in Action, The Core.* Indeed, each of our approximately ninety features and most photograph captions end with a question that requires an innovative, inquisitive response. Other critical thinking tools in this edition include:

- **Learning Objectives.** At the beginning of each chapter, students are introduced to up to eight learning objectives (LOs) for that chapter. For example, in Chapter 3, "Inside Criminal Law," Learning Objective 6 (LO6) asks students to "Discuss a common misperception concerning the insanity defense in the United States." The area of text that furnishes the information is marked with an LO6 graphic, and, finally, the correct answer is found in the chapter-ending materials. This constant active learning greatly expands students' understanding of dozens of crucial criminal justice topics.

- **Self-Assessment Boxes.** Students are not, however, required to wait until they have finished reading a chapter to engage in self-assessment. We have placed a self-assessment box at the end of each major section of each chapter. Three to five sentences long, these items require students to fill in the blanks, thereby reinforcing the most important points in the section they have just read. (All answers are found at the end of each chapter.)

Further Changes to the Eighth Edition

As in previous editions of *Criminal Justice in Action, The Core,* each chapter in the Eighth Edition begins with a new "ripped from the headlines" vignette that introduces the themes to be covered in the pages that follow. Furthermore, the text continues to reflect the ever-changing nature of our topic with approximately **140 new references to recent research involving crime and criminal behavior** and **110 new real-life examples of actual crimes.** The Eighth Edition also includes about **fifty new features and fifteen new figures, as well as discussions of twenty new United States Supreme Court cases and nearly eighty new photos.** Additionally, we allow both expert and lay witnesses to give their opinions of criminal justice matters, with **more than sixty new quotes from professionals and twenty new quotes from "ordinary" citizens in the text.**

Two other extensive changes to the Eighth Edition involve topics crucial to the American criminal justice system:

- **Victims.** For much of the history of American criminal justice, the role of the crime victim was limited to taking the witness stand in court. This is no longer the case, and we have **greatly expanded our coverage of victims' rights and responsibilities** in today's crime picture. Six of the chapters of *Criminal Justice in Action, The Core,* now include in-depth discussions of victims, covering a variety of issues relating to the legal and ethical aspects of victim participation in the criminal justice system.

- **Gun Control.** As the result of a number of high-profile mass shootings that have plagued the nation over the past several years, the issue of gun control has returned to the forefront of American criminal justice policy and politics. Consequently, in a revamped Chapter 14, we have added an entire section on this topic. In this new section, students will learn about **existing regulations on gun ownership in the United States, the challenges of keeping firearms out of the hands of the mentally ill, and the present state of the national debate over gun control.**

In addition, **we have remodeled the popular feature You Be the _____,** which now goes by the name **Discretion in Action.** As before, the feature asks students to step into the shoes of a criminal justice professional or other CJ participant and make a difficult decision. As revised, the feature enhances the emphasis on the pivotal role that discretion plays in the criminal justice system, a subject that was expanded upon over the past several editions of *Criminal Justice in Action, The Core.*

CHAPTER-BY-CHAPTER ORGANIZATION OF THE TEXT

This edition's fourteen chapters blend the principles of criminal justice with current research and high-interest examples of what is happening in the world of crime and crime prevention right now. What follows is a summary of each chapter, along with a description of some of the revisions to the Eighth Edition.

Part One: The Criminal Justice System

Chapter 1 provides an introduction to the criminal justice system's three major institutions: law enforcement, the courts, and corrections. The chapter also answers conceptual questions such as "what is crime?" and "what are the values of the American criminal justice system?"

- The chapter has been expanded with a **new section** entitled "Homeland Security and Domestic Terrorism," which focuses on law enforcement efforts to combat the problems posed by homegrown extremists who may not fit the "young, Islamic, male" profile.

- A **new** Discretion in Action feature ("Duty vs. Family") addresses the dilemma facing an off-duty police officer who must decide whether to disregard a family member's low-level criminal behavior.

Chapter 2 furnishes students with an understanding of two areas fundamental to criminal justice: (1) the various methods of measuring crime, including the FBI's Uniform Crime Report and the U.S. Department of Justice's National Crime Victimization Survey, and (2) criminology, providing students with insight into why crime occurs before they shift their attention, in later chapters, toward combating it.

- A **new** discussion of **women as crime victims** focuses on criminal activity that exhibits a gender bias such as domestic violence, sexual violence, and stalking.

- A **new** CJ Controversy feature ("Legalizing Marijuana") asks students to research the topic of marijuana legalization in Colorado and Washington and then decide whether they believe marijuana legalization to be a positive or negative development in the United States.

Chapter 3 lays the foundation of criminal law. It addresses constitutional law, statutory law, and other sources of American criminal law before shifting its focus to the legal framework that allows the criminal justice system to determine and punish criminal guilt.

- A **new** Policy.cj margin feature asks the student to research hate crime legislation online and give his or her opinion of this form of "penalty enhancement" legislation.

- An **updated** discussion of state stand your ground laws in the context of George Zimmerman's 2013 acquittal on murder charges for killing Trayvon Martin, which includes a **new** CJ Controversy feature asking students whether these laws benefit society.

Part Two: The Police and Law Enforcement

Chapter 4 acts as an introduction to law enforcement in the United States today. This chapter offers a detailed description of the country's numerous local, state, and federal law enforcement agencies and examines the responsibilities and duties that come with a career in law enforcement.

- As part of a **new** consideration of intelligence-led policing and the need for law enforcement agencies to do "more with less," students will learn about police strategies such as using Predpol, which is software that attempts to predict when and where crimes are most likely to occur.

- A **new** discussion describes the cooperative efforts of the U.S. Border Patrol and the Drug Enforcement Administration to combat the flow of illegal drugs into the United States from Mexico.

Chapter 5 puts students on the streets and gives them a gritty look at the many challenges of being a law enforcement officer. It starts with a discussion of the importance of discretion in law enforcement and then moves on to policing strategies and issues in modern policing, such as use of force, corruption, and the "thin blue line."

- Students' understanding of split-second decision making with life-or-death consequences is enhanced by a **new** Discretion in Action feature ("High-Speed Force") that puts them behind the wheel during a high-speed pursuit.

- A **new** discussion of how aggressive investigative strategies such as **informants and undercover agents** are used to combat **domestic terrorism** includes an in-depth examination of the **pros and cons of preventive policing.**

Chapter 6 examines the sometimes uneasy relationship between law enforcement and the U.S. Constitution by explaining the rules of being a police officer. Particular emphasis is placed on the Fourth, Fifth, and Sixth Amendments, giving students an understanding of crucial concepts such as probable cause, reasonableness, and custodial interrogation.

- An **updated** section entitled "Electronic Surveillance" illuminates the constitutional issues surrounding law enforcement use of closed-circuit television (CCTV) cameras as crime-fighting tools. The section includes a **new** discussion of the controversy surrounding the National Security Agency's seemingly unchecked policy of collecting information about the telephone habits of Americans.

- In the context of racial profiling, we have added a **new** discussion of the Supreme Court's decision regarding Arizona's "papers, please" law that requires local police officers, "when practicable," to check the legal status of potential undocumented immigrants.

Part Three: Criminal Courts

Chapter 7 takes a big-picture approach in describing the American court system, giving students an overview of the basic principles of our judicial system, the state and federal court systems, and the role of judges, prosecutors, and defense attorneys in the criminal justice system.

- The court system's ability to live up to societal expectations of truth and justice, a running theme of the third part of this textbook, is explored in the chapter's **new** opening vignette ("A Long Time Ago . . .") concerning the wrongful conviction of David Bryant, who was recently freed after spending nearly forty years behind bars for the murder of an eight-year-old girl in New York in 1975.

- A **new** Policy.cj margin feature requires students to critique "no drop policies," which force prosecutors to press charges against domestic violence suspects even if the alleged victim of the domestic violence refuses to cooperate.

Chapter 8 provides students with a rundown of pretrial procedures and highlights the role that these procedures play in America's adversarial system. Chapter materials also place the student in the courtroom and give her or him a comprehensive understanding of the steps in the criminal trial.

- The section on plea bargaining now includes a **new** analysis of the United States Supreme Court's potentially "game-changing" recent decision providing defendants with a constitutional right to effective representation during plea negotiations.
- The student's understanding of constitutional protections against double jeopardy will be enhanced by a **new** Comparative Criminal Justice feature ("Double Trouble") describing the plight of Amanda Knox, a former American exchange student who has been charged a second time for murder by Italian judicial officials.

Chapter 9 links the many different punishment options for those who have been convicted of a crime with the theoretical justifications for those punishments. The chapter also examines punishment in the policy context, weighing the public's desire for ever-harsher criminal sanctions against the consequences of such governmental strategies.

- As part of our continuing exploration of the underlying concepts of **restorative justice,** this chapter offers a **new** discussion of the **practical aspects of restitution** and of **victim-offender dialogue programs** that provide convicts with the opportunity to apologize in person to the victims of their crimes.
- A **new** CJ Controversy feature ("The Morality of the Death Penalty") asks students to give their opinion of the death penalty in the context of a United States Supreme Court ruling limiting capital punishment to cases involving murder.

Part Four: Corrections

Chapter 10 makes an important point, and one that is often overlooked in the larger discussion of the American corrections system: not all of those who are punished need to be placed behind bars. This chapter explores the community corrections options, from probation to parole to intermediate sanctions such as intensive supervision and home confinement.

- A **new** section **comparing probation and parole** is designed to help the student distinguish between these two forms of community corrections, whose similarities can tend to obscure very important conceptual differences.
- Continuing our focus on crime victims, we have added a **new** discussion of the sometime murky **role of the victim** in determining an offender's chances of being **granted parole.**

Chapter 11 focuses on prisons and jails. High rates of incarceration have pushed these institutions to the forefront of the criminal justice system, and this chapter explores the various issues—such as overcrowding and the emergence of private prisons—that have resulted from the prison population boom.

- An **updated** section on the many problems facing jail administrators and inmates in the United States, including mental illness, poor physical health, substance abuse, and overcrowded facilities.
- A **new** discussion of the future of incarceration in the United States recognizes the historical significance of recent small drops in America's prison population and raises the question: do these decreases only reflect a desire to cut costs, or has there been a sea change in the values of the American criminal justice system?

Chapter 12 is another example of our efforts to get students "into the action" of the criminal justice system, this time putting them in the uncomfortable position of being behind bars. It also answers the question, "What happens when the inmate is released back into society?"

- A **new** Landmark Cases feature ("*Brown v. Plata*") explores the United States Supreme Court's ruling that overcrowding in California prisons had become so egregious that it denied inmates acceptable levels of health care and therefore constituted cruel and unusual punishment.
- A **new** CJ & Technology feature ("Contraband Cell Phones") considers the difficulties facing prison administrators when it comes to keeping cell phones out of the hands of inmates and the consequences of cell phone use behind bars.

Part Five: Special Issues

Chapter 13 examines the juvenile justice system, giving students a comprehensive description of the path taken by delinquents from first contact with police to trial and punishment. The chapter contains a strong criminological component as well, scrutinizing the various theories of why certain juveniles turn to delinquency and what steps society can take to stop them from doing so before it is "too late."

- A **new** discussion examines the United States Supreme Court's 2012 ruling that juveniles who are convicted of murder may not be automatically sentenced to life in prison without the possibility of parole.
- A **new** Policy.cj margin feature asks students to research and evaluate "zero tolerance" policies in American schools, particularly as these policies are applied to members of minority groups.

Chapter 14 concludes the text by taking an expanded look at four crucial criminal justice topics: (1) white-collar crime, (2) cyber crime, (3) gun control policy, and (4) international terrorism.

- A **new** Question of Ethics feature ("Buyer Beware") examines whether practices by employees at auto companies such as General Motors and Toyota that lead to the deaths of drivers should be considered white-collar crimes and punished accordingly.
- A **new** CJ Controversy feature ("The Debate over Gun Control") requires students to support their own opinions on whether federal and state government should make it more difficult for people to purchase and own guns in the United States.

SPECIAL FEATURES

Supplementing the main text of *Criminal Justice in Action, The Core, Eighth Edition,* are numerous eye-catching, instructive, and penetrating special features. These features, described below with examples, have been designed to enhance the student's understanding of a particular criminal justice issue.

CAREERS IN CJ As stated before, many students reading this book are planning a career in criminal justice. We have provided them with an insight into some of these careers by offering first-person accounts of what it is like to work as a criminal justice professional. Each Career in CJ feature also includes a **Social Media Career Tip** to help students succeed in today's competitive labor market for criminal justice professionals.

- In Chapter 13, Carl McCullough, a former professional football player, provides an inside look at his duties as a resident youth worker at a juvenile detention center in Hennepin County, Minnesota.

MASTERING CONCEPTS Some criminal justice topics require additional explanation before they become crystal clear in the minds of students. This feature helps students to master many of the essential concepts in the textbook.

- In Chapter 6, this feature helps students understand the legal differences between a police stop and a police arrest.

DISCRETION IN ACTION This **revised** feature puts students into the position of a criminal justice actor in a hypothetical case or situation that is based on a real-life event. The facts of the case or situation are presented with alternative possible outcomes, and the student is asked to take the part of the criminal justice professional or lay participant and make a decision. Students can then consult Appendix B at the end of the text to learn what actually happened in the offered scenario.

- "Murder or Manslaughter?" (Chapter 3), a **new** feature, requires students to play the role of prosecutor and charge a defendant who killed his girlfriend under opaque circumstances with first degree murder, second degree murder, or involuntary manslaughter.

CJ & TECHNOLOGY Advances in technology are constantly transforming the face of criminal justice. In these features, which appear in nearly every chapter, students learn of one such emergent technology and are asked to critically evaluate its effects.

- This **new** feature in Chapter 6 describes how airborne drones may soon become crime-fighting tools and, in the process, change the face of law enforcement.

COMPARATIVE CRIMINAL JUSTICE The world offers a dizzying array of different criminal customs and codes, many of which are in stark contrast to those accepted in the United States. This feature provides dramatic and sometimes perplexing examples of foreign criminal justice practices in order to give students a better understanding of our domestic ways.

- "The Great Firewall of China" (Chapter 14), a **new** feature, describes China's recent efforts to limit and control the use of the Internet through criminal laws to an extent that is unimaginable to most Americans.

A QUESTION OF ETHICS Ethical dilemmas occur in every profession, but the challenges facing criminal justice professionals often have repercussions beyond their own lives and careers. In this feature, students are asked to place themselves in the shoes of police officers, prosecutors, defense attorneys, and other criminal justice actors facing ethical dilemmas. Will they do the right thing?

- In "The 'Dirty Harry' Problem" (Chapter 5), a police detective is trying to save the life of a young girl who has been buried alive with only enough oxygen to survive for a few hours. Is he justified in torturing the one person—the kidnapper—who knows where the girl is buried?

LANDMARK CASES Rulings by the United States Supreme Court have shaped every area of the criminal justice system. In this feature, students learn about and analyze the most influential of these cases.

- In Chapter 9's *"Roper v. Simmons"* (2005), the Supreme Court ruled that the execution of offenders who were under the age of eighteen when they committed the crimes is cruel and unusual punishment and therefore unconstitutional.

MYTH VS REALITY Nothing endures like a good myth. In this feature, we try to dispel some of the more enduring myths in the criminal justice system while at the same time asking students to think critically about their consequences.

- "Are Too Many Criminals Found Not Guilty by Reason of Insanity?" (Chapter 3) dispels the notion that the criminal justice is "soft" because it lets scores of "crazy" defendants go free due to insanity.

Extensive Study Aids

Criminal Justice in Action, The Core, Eighth Edition, includes a number of pedagogical devices designed to complete the student's active learning experience.

- Concise **chapter outlines** appear at the beginning of each chapter. The outlines give students an idea of what to expect in the pages ahead, as well as a quick source of review when needed.

- Dozens of **key terms and a running glossary** focus students' attention on major concepts and help them master the vocabulary of criminal justice. The chosen terms are boldfaced in the text, allowing students to notice their importance without breaking the flow of reading.

On the same page where a key term is highlighted, a margin note provides a succinct definition of the term. For further reference, a glossary at the end of the text provides a full list of all the key terms and their definitions. This edition includes over forty new key terms.

- Each chapter has at least four **figures,** which include graphs, charts, and other forms of colorful art that reinforce a point made in the text. This edition includes fifteen new figures.

- Hundreds of **photographs** add to the overall readability and design of the text. Each photo has a caption, and most of these captions include a critical-thinking question dealing with the topic at hand. This edition includes more than eighty new photos.

- At the end of each chapter, students will find five **Questions for Critical Analysis.** These questions will help the student assess his or her understanding of the just-completed chapter, as well as develop critical-thinking skills.

- Our teaching/learning package offers numerous opportunities for using **online technology** in the classroom. In the margins of each chapter, students will find links to various Web sites that illuminate a particular subject in the corresponding text.

Ancillary Materials

To access additional course materials, including CourseMate, please visit **www.cengagebrain.com.** At the CengageBrain.com home page, search for the ISBN of your title (from the back cover of your book) using the search box at the top of the page. This will take you to the product page where these resources can be found.

An extensive pack of supplemental aids accompanies this edition. Many separate items have been developed to enhance the course and to assist instructors and students. Available to qualified adopters. Please consult your local sales representative for details.

FOR THE INSTRUCTOR Instructor's Resource Manual and Lesson Plans with Test Bank. The manual, written by Janine Kremling of California State University at San Bernardino, includes learning objectives, key terms, a detailed chapter outline, a chapter summary, discussion topics, student activities, and a Test Bank. Each chapter's Test Bank contains questions in multiple-choice, true-false, fill-in-the-blank, and essay formats, with a full answer key. The Test Bank is coded to the section headings and learning objectives for each chapter of the text. Finally, each question in the Test Bank has been carefully reviewed by experienced criminal justice instructors for quality, accuracy, and content coverage. Our Instructor Approved seal, which appears on the front cover, is our assurance that you are working with an assessment and grading resource of the highest caliber.

Online PowerPoint® Lectures. These handy Microsoft PowerPoint slides, developed by Samantha Carlo of Miami-Dade Community College, which outline the chapters of the main text in a classroom-ready presentation, will help you in making your lectures engaging and in reaching your visually oriented students. The presentations are available for download on the password-protected Web site and can also be obtained by e-mailing your local Cengage Learning representative.

Cengage Learning Testing Powered by Cognero. Cognero is a flexible online system that allows you to author, edit, and manage test bank content from multiple Cengage Learning solutions; create multiple test versions in an instant; and deliver tests from your LMS, your classroom, or wherever you want.

FOR THE STUDENT *MindTap Criminal Justice for Criminal Justice in Action, The Core.* MindTap from Cengage Learning represents a new approach to a highly personalized, online learning platform. A fully online learning solution, MindTap combines all of a student's learning tools—readings, multimedia, activities, and assessments—into a singular Learning Path that guides the student through the curriculum. Instructors personalize the experience by customizing the presentation of these learning tools for their students, allowing instructors to seamlessly introduce their own content into the Learning Path via "apps" that integrate into the MindTap platform. Additionally, MindTap provides interoperability with major Learning Management Systems (LMS) via support for open industry standards and fosters partnerships with third-party educational application providers to provide a highly collaborative, engaging, and personalized learning experience.

ACKNOWLEDGMENTS

Throughout the creation of the eight editions of this text, we have been aided by hundreds of experts in various criminal justice fields and by professors throughout the country, as well as by numerous students who have used the text. We list below the reviewers for this Eighth Edition, followed by the class-test participants and reviewers for the first seven editions. We sincerely thank all who participated on the revision of *Criminal Justice in Action, The Core.* We believe that the Eighth Edition is even more responsive to the needs of today's criminal justice instructors and students alike because we have taken into account the constructive comments and criticisms of our reviewers and the helpful suggestions of our survey respondents.

Reviewers for the Eighth Edition

The following individuals contributed valuable comments and suggestions for this edition:

Desire' J.M. Anastasia
Metropolitan State University
of Denver

Andre L. Barnes
City College of San Francisco

Robert Barnes
SUNY Westchester Community College

Curt Blakely
Truman State University

Kristen K. Bowen
Florida A&M University

Kenton J. Burns
South Plains College

Mark A. Byington
Jefferson College

Brian E. Cranny
Greenville Technical College

Barbara A. Crowson
Norwich University

Anthony Dangelantonio
Keene State College

Melchor C. de Guzman
The College at Brockport, SUNY

Peter Fenton
Kennesaw State University

Colin P. Gallagher
Wichita Area Technical College

Brian J. Gorman
Towson University

Michele Grillo
Monmouth University

Brittany Hayes
John Jay College

John E. Hertel
St. Louis Community College

Carly Hilinski-Rosick
Grand Valley State University

Susan S. Hodge
University of North Carolina at
Charlotte

Daniel L. Lawson
City College of San Francisco

John Mabry
University of Central Oklahoma

Tamara D. Madensen
University of Nevada, Las Vegas

Shana Mell
Virginia Commonwealth University

Eric Metchik
Salem State University

Nathan Moran
Midwestern State University

Barry "Lynn" Parker
Palo Alto College

Rebecca Pfeffer
University of Houston–Downtown

Melissa L. Ricketts
Shippensburg University
of Pennsylvania

Marny Rivera
University of Alaska, Anchorage

Martin D. Schwartz
George Washington University

Patrick L. Shade
Edison Community College

Susan Thomas
University of Tennessee, Chattanooga

Suzanne Youngblood
Lancaster Campus, Harrisburg Area
Community College

CLASS-TEST PARTICIPANTS

We also want to acknowledge the participation of the professors and their students who agreed to class-test portions of the text. Our thanks go to:

Tom Arnold
College of Lake County

Paula M. Broussard
University of Southwestern Louisiana

Mike Higginson
Suffolk Community College

Andrew Karmen
John Jay College of Criminal Justice

Fred Kramer
John Jay College of Criminal Justice

Anthony P. LaRose
Western Oregon University

Anne Lawrence
Kean University

Jerry E. Loar
Walters State Community College

Phil Reichel
University of Northern Colorado

Albert Sproule
Allentown College

Gregory B. Talley
Broome Community College

Karen Terry
John Jay College of Criminal Justice

Angelo Tritini
Passaic County Community College

Gary Uhrin
Westmoreland County Community
College

Robert Vodde
Fairleigh Dickinson University

REVIEWERS OF THE FIRST, SECOND, THIRD, FOURTH, FIFTH, SIXTH, AND SEVENTH EDITIONS

We appreciate the assistance of the following reviewers whose guidance helped create the foundation for this best seller. We are grateful to all.

Lorna Alvarez-Rivera
Ohio University

Angela Ambers-Henderson
Montgomery County Community
College

Gaylene Armstrong
Southern Illnois University

Judge James Bachman
Bowling Green State University

Tom Barclay
University of South Alabama

Julia Beeman
University of North Carolina at
Charlotte

Lee Roy Black
California University of Pennsylvania

Anita Blowers
University of North Carolina at
Charlotte

Stefan Bosworth
Hostos Community College

John Bower
Bethel College

Michael E. Boyko
Cuyahoga Community College

Steven Brandl
University of Wisconsin–Milwaukee

Scott Brantley
Chancellor University

Charles Brawner III
Heartland Community College

Timothy M. Bray
University of Texas–Dallas

Susan Brinkley
University of Tampa

Paula Broussard
University of Southwestern Louisiana

Michael Brown
Ball State College

Patrick Buckley
San Bernardino Valley College

Joseph Bunce
Montgomery College–Rockville

James T. Burnett
SUNY, Rockland Community College

Ronald Burns
Texas Christian University

Theodore Byrne
California State University, Dominguez
Hills

Paul Campbell
Wayne State College

Dae Chang
Wichita State University

Sheri Chapel
Ridley-Lowell Business and Technical
Institute and Keystone College

Steven Chermak
Indiana University

Charlie Chukwudolue
Northern Kentucky University

Monte Clampett
Asheville-Buncombe Community
College

John Cochran
University of South Florida

Ellen G. Cohn
Florida International University

Corey Colyer
West Virginia University

Mark Correia
University of Nevada–Reno

Theodore Darden
College of Du Page

John del Nero
Lane Community College

Richard H. De Lung
Wayland Baptist University

John Dempsey
Suffolk County Community College

Tom Dempsey
Christopher Newport University

Joyce Dozier
Wilmington College

Frank J. Drummond
Modesto Junior College

M. G. Eichenberg
Wayne State College

Frank L. Fischer
Kankakee Community College

Linda L. Fleischer
The Community College of Baltimore
County

Aric Steven Frazier
Vincennes University

Frederick Galt
Dutchess Community College

Phyllis Gerstenfeld
California State University Stanislaus

James Gilbert
University of Nebraska–Kearney

Dean Golding
West Chester University of
Pennsylvania

Debbie Goodman
Miami-Dade Community College

Cecil Greek
Florida State University

Donald Grubb
Northern Virginia Community College

Sharon Halford
Community College of Aurora

Michael Hallett
Middle Tennessee State University

Mark Hansel
Moorhead State University

Pati Hendrickson
Tarleton State University

Michelle Heward
Weber State University

Gerald Hildebrand
Austin Community College

Dennis Hoffman
University of Nebraska–Omaha

Richard Holden
Central Missouri State University

Ronald Holmes
University of Louisville

Marilyn Horace-Moore
Eastern Michigan University

Matrice Hurrah
Shelby State Community College

Nicholas Irons
County College of Morris

Michael Israel
Kean University

J. D. Jamieson
Southwest Texas State University

James Jengeleski
Shippensburg University

Robert Jerin
Endicott College

Paul Johnson
Weber State University

Jason R. Jolicoeur
Cincinnati State Technical and
Community College

Casey Jordan
Western Connecticut State University

Matthew Kanjirathinkal
Texas A & M University–Commerce

Bill Kelly
University of Texas–Austin

Paul Klenowski
Clarion University

David Kotajarvi
Lakeshore Technical College

John H. Kramer
Pennsylvania State University

Janine Kremling
California State University at
San Bernardino

Kristen Kuehnle
Salem State University

Karl Kunkel
Southwest Missouri State

James G. Larson
National University

Barry Latzer
John Jay College of Criminal Justice

Deborah Laufersweiler-Dwyer
University of Arkansas at Little Rock

Paul Lawson
Montana State University

Nella Lee
Portland State University

Walter Lewis
St. Louis Community
College–Meramec

Larry Linville
Northern Virginia Community College

Faith Lutze
Washington State University

Richard Martin
Elgin Community College

Richard H. Martin
University of Findlay

William J. Mathias
University of South Carolina

Janet McClellan
Southwestern Oregon Community
College

Pat Murphy
State University of New York–Geneseo

Rebecca Nathanson
Housatonic Community Technical
College

Ellyn Ness
Mesa Community College

Kenneth O'Keefe
Prairie State College

Michael Palmiotto
Wichita State University

Rebecca D. Petersen
University of Texas–San Antonio

Gary Prawel
Monroe Community College

Mark Robarge
Mansfield University

Matt Robinson
Appalachian State University

Debra Ross
Buffalo State College

William Ruefle
University of South Carolina

Gregory Russell
Washington State University

John Scheb II
University of Tennessee–Knoxville

Melinda Schlager
University of Texas at Arlington

Ed Selby
Southwestern College

Larry Snyder
Herkimer County Community College

Ronald Sopenoff
Brookdale Community College

Domenick Stampone
Raritan Valley Community College

Katherine Steinbeck
Lakeland Community College

Hallie Stephens
Southeastern Oklahoma State
University

Kathleen M. Sweet
St. Cloud State University

Gregory Talley
Broome Community College

Karen Terry
John Jay College of Criminal Justice

Amy B. Thistlethwaite
Northern Kentucky University

Rebecca Titus
New Mexico Junior College

Lawrence F. Travis III
University of Cincinnati

Kimberly Vogt
University of Wisconsin–La Crosse

Robert Wadman
Weber State University

Ron Walker
Trinity Valley Community College

John Wyant
Illinois Central College

Others were instrumental in bringing this Eighth Edition to fruition. We continue to appreciate the extensive research efforts of Shawn G. Miller and the additional legal assistance of William Eric Hollowell. Shelley Murphy, our Content Developer, provided equal parts elbow grease and creative energy; it was a pleasure to work with her. Product Manager Carolyn Hendersen Meier supplied crucial guidance to the project through her suggestions and recommendations. At the production end, we once again feel fortunate to have enjoyed the services of our tireless content project manager, Ann Borman, who oversaw virtually all aspects of this book. Additionally, we wish to thank the designer of this new edition, Lumina Datamatics, who has created what we believe to be the most dazzling and student-friendly design of any text in the field. We are also thankful for the services of all those at Lachina Publishing Services who worked on the Eighth Edition, particularly Molly Montanaro. The eagle eyes of Jeanne Yost and Sue Bradley, who shared the duties of copy editing and proofreading, were invaluable. A special word of thanks must also go to the team responsible for the extensive multimedia package included in this project, including Media Developer for Criminal Justice, Andy Yap, and writer Robert C. De Lucia of John Jay College of Criminal Justice. In addition, we appreciate the work of Janine Kremling of California State University at San Bernardino, who revised the Instructor's Resource Manual and Lesson Plans with Test Bank, and Samantha Carlo of Miami-Dade Community College, who revised the PowerPoints. We are also grateful for the aid of Product Assistant Stephen Lagos and Associate Content Developer Jessica Alderman for ensuring the timely publication of supplements. A final thanks to all of the great people in marketing and advertising who helped to get the word out about the book, including marketing manager Kara Kindstrom, who has been tireless in her attention to this project.

Any criminal justice text has to be considered a work in progress. We know that there are improvements that we can make. Therefore, write us with any suggestions that you may have.

L. K. G.
R. L. M.

Dedication

This book is dedicated to my good friend and colleague, Lawrence Walsh, of the Lexington, Kentucky, Police Department. When I was a rookie, he taught me about policing. When I became a researcher, he taught me about the practical applications of knowledge. He is truly an inspiring professional in our field.

L.K.G.

To Lorraine and Richard,

Every moment counts.

R.L.M.

CHAPTER

1 Criminal Justice Today

To target your study and review, look for these numbered Learning Objective icons throughout the chapter.

Hyoung Chang/*Denver Post*/Getty Images

Green WEDNESDAY

"IT MAKES YOU giddy to say it: I went into a store and bought pot," said Linda Walmsley as she walked out of the Denver Kush Club. Walmsley was not the only person feeling "giddy" in Colorado on January 1, 2014. That day, thousands participated in the first state-regulated sale of recreational marijuana in United States history. At about forty shops around the state, buyers paid as much as $70 for an eighth of an ounce of the drug, which had been selling for about $25 per eighth on the black market. Despite the higher prices, sales of pot on "Green Wednesday" were so brisk that sellers worried about running out of product by the end of the week.

Thirteen months earlier, residents in Colorado and Washington set the stage for legalized marijuana by voting to regulate the drug like alcohol within state lines. (Washington would open its pot stores later in 2014.) Supporters predict that the new laws will significantly reduce public costs associated with the criminal justice system by removing low-level drug offenders from state courtrooms and prisons. They also highlight economic benefits of taxing marijuana, which was expected to generate about $70 million of extra revenue for Colorado in its first year as a legal commodity.

Critics of the measures, including many politicians and parents' groups, countered that the new measures would lead to a spike in underage marijuana use, with disastrous public health consequences. Law enforcement officials pointed out that police in Colorado and Washington are now required to determine whether the marijuana being offered for sale is indeed state licensed, which may increase their workload. It will likely take months, if not years, to determine the overall consequences of legalizing marijuana in the two states. "We are floating in uncharted waters here," admitted Denver mayor Michael B. Hancock.

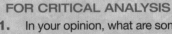

FOR CRITICAL ANALYSIS

1. In your opinion, what are some the positive consequences of legalizing the sale of small quantities of marijuana?

2. What might be some of the negative consequences of legal marijuana sales?

3. Why might some people be willing to pay significantly higher prices for legal marijuana instead of purchasing cheaper black market marijuana, which is still available in both Colorado and Washington?

Bloomberg/Getty Images

On January 9, 2014, an employee at the Evergreen Apothecary in Denver, Colorado, measures out a portion of newly legalized marijuana.

WHAT IS CRIME?

The recreational use of marijuana in Colorado, though now legal, is heavily regulated.[1] All sellers must be licensed by a state regulatory agency. As with alcohol, buyers must be at least twenty-one years old, and locals cannot purchase more than one ounce of the drug in a single transaction. (For those who live out of state, the limit is a quarter-ounce per transaction.) It remains illegal to smoke the drug in public, as well as transport it across state lines.

Consequently, a thirty-year-old from Fort Collins, Colorado, who buys a half-ounce of pot from a licensed seller and smokes it in his apartment does not have to worry about being arrested by state law enforcement officers. If that same person drives to Cheyenne, Wyoming, and shares the pot with a friend, he has committed a crime, according to Colorado's criminal code. As this example shows, a **crime** is not simply an act that seems dishonest or dangerous or taboo. It is a wrong against society that is *proclaimed by law* and that, if committed under specific circumstances, is punishable by the criminal justice system.

Determining Criminal Behavior

One problem with the definition of crime just provided is that it obscures the complex nature of societies. A society is not static—it evolves and changes, and its concept of criminality evolves and changes as well. Our nation's inconsistent treatment of marijuana shows that different communities can have vastly different ideas about what constitutes a crime. As we just noted, Colorado and Washington recently legalized recreational use of the drug in small quantities. In twenty states and the District of Columbia, marijuana can be used for medicinal purposes. Under most circumstances, however, the sale or possession of pot is illegal in the United States, and as we will discuss later in the chapter, the federal government still considers it a dangerous drug.

Different countries often have differing ideas of criminal behavior, as well. Several years ago, for example, police in West Sumatra, Indonesia, arrested Alexander Aan for writing "God is not great" on Facebook. An Indonesian court sentenced Aan to two and a half years in prison for violating a criminal prohibition against "inciting religious hatred." Such legislation would not be allowed in the United States because of our country's long traditions of freedom of speech and religion. (See the feature *Comparative Criminal Justice—Speech Crime* that follows to learn about another foreign criminal law that runs counter to America's legal traditions.)

To more fully understand the concept of crime, it will help to examine the two most common models of how society decides which acts are criminal: the consensus model and the conflict model.

LEARNING **1** OBJECTIVE

Describe the two most common models of how society determines which acts are criminal.

THE CONSENSUS MODEL The term *consensus* refers to general agreement among the majority members of any particular group. Thus, the **consensus model** rests on the assumption that as people gather together to form a society, its members will naturally come to a basic agreement with regard to shared norms and values. Those individuals whose actions deviate from the established norms and values are considered to pose a threat to the well-being of society as a whole and must be sanctioned (punished). The society passes laws to control and prevent unacceptable behavior, thereby setting the boundaries for acceptable behavior within the group.[2]

COMPARATIVE CRIMINAL JUSTICE

Central Intelligence Agency

Speech Crime

Travel on the cramped, overcrowded London subway system is often unpleasant. For those riders stuck in the same car as Jacqueline Williams on a recent October afternoon, however, the trip was nearly unbearable. At that time, Williams, who is white, unleashed a verbal rant against black commuters on the train, saying, "Go home where you belong. . . . You might have been born here, but I bet your grandparents weren't." Williams continued, "You make me sick. If you belonged here, you'd be pink-skinned, blonde-haired, blue eyes, green eyes." She also told one black passenger that she walked "like a monkey."

Williams's actions were ugly and offensive, but were they criminal? In the United States, no. As interpreted by American courts, the First Amendment to the U.S. Constitution does not allow laws punishing speech unless that speech is likely to provoke immediate violence. England's Crime and Disorder Act, in contrast, prohibits "threatening, abusive, or insulting words" within the "hearing or sight" of someone "likely to be caused harassment, alarm, or distress which was racially aggravated." Consequently, British Transport Police identified Williams using a YouTube video of the incident and arrested her for committing a racially aggravated public order offense.

If convicted, Williams faced a significant punishment. Six months earlier, another Londoner, Jacqueline Woodhouse, was found guilty of similarly insulting black passengers on a subway car. In sentencing Woodhouse to twenty-one weeks behind bars, a British judge lamented that "our citizens could be subject to such behavior."

FOR CRITICAL ANALYSIS

Do you think that the United States should criminalize "threatening, abusive, or insulting words" aimed at members of a minority group? What would be the consequences—both intended and unintended—of such a law?

Morals Principles of right and wrong behavior, as practiced by individuals or by society.

Conflict Model A criminal justice model in which the content of criminal law is determined by the groups that hold political power in a community.

The consensus model, to a certain extent, assumes that a diverse group of people can have similar **morals.** In other words, they share an ideal of what is "right" and what is "wrong." Consequently, as public attitudes toward morality change, so do laws. In seventeenth-century America, a person found guilty of *adultery* (having sexual relations with someone other than one's spouse) could expect to be publicly whipped, branded, or even executed. Furthermore, a century ago, one could walk into a pharmacy and purchase heroin. Today, social attitudes have shifted to consider adultery a personal issue, beyond the reach of the state, and to consider the sale of heroin a criminal act.

THE CONFLICT MODEL Some people reject the consensus model on the ground that moral attitudes are not constant or even consistent. In large democratic societies such as the United States, different groups of citizens have widely varying opinions on controversial issues of morality and criminality such as abortion, the war on drugs, immigration, and assisted suicide. These groups and their elected representatives are constantly coming into conflict with one another. According to the **conflict model,** then, the most politically powerful segments of society—based on class, income, age, and race—have the most influence on criminal laws and are therefore able to impose their values on the rest of the community.

Consequently, what is deemed criminal activity is determined by whichever group happens to be holding power at any given time. Because certain groups do not have access to political power, their interests are not served by the criminal justice system. To give one example, with the exception of Oregon, Vermont, and Washington, physician-assisted suicide for the terminally ill is illegal in the United States. Although opinion polls show that the general public is evenly divided on the issue,[3] highly motivated individuals and special interest groups have been able to convince lawmakers that the practice goes against America's shared moral and religious values.

An Integrated Definition of Crime

Considering both the consensus and the conflict models, we can construct a definition of crime that will be useful throughout this textbook. For our purposes, crime is an action or activity that is

LEARNING **2** OBJECTIVE   Define *crime*.

1. Punishable under criminal law, as determined by the majority or, in some instances, by a powerful minority.
2. Considered an *offense against society as a whole* and prosecuted by public officials, not by victims and their relatives or friends.
3. Punishable by sanctions based on laws that bring about the loss of personal freedom or life.

At this point, it is important to understand the difference between crime and **deviance,** or behavior that does not conform to the norms of a given community or society. Deviance is a subjective concept. For example, some segments of society may think that smoking marijuana or killing animals for clothing and food is deviant behavior. Deviant acts become crimes only when society as a whole, through its legislatures, determines that those acts should be punished—as is the situation today in the United States with using illegal drugs but not with eating meat. Furthermore, not all crimes are considered particularly deviant—little social disapprobation is attached to those who fail to follow the letter of parking laws. In essence, criminal law reflects those acts that we, as a society, agree are so unacceptable that steps must be taken to prevent them from occurring.

E-cigarettes, such as the one shown in this photo, deliver the drug nicotine to users without some of the tobacco-related health risks of traditional cigarettes. Nicotine is, however, highly addictive. Why might e-cigarette use be considered deviant behavior by minors, but not by adults?

Joe Raedle/Getty Images

//// **SELF** ASSESSMENT

Fill in the blanks, and check your answers on page 29.

The consensus model of crime assumes that diverse members of society share similar _____, or ideals of right and wrong. The _____ model, in contrast, focuses on dissimilarities of such attitudes within society. A criminal act is a wrong against _____ and therefore is "avenged," or prosecuted, by _____ _____, not by the individual victims of a crime. A crime is not the same as an act of _____, the term for behavior that is nonconformist but not necessarily criminal.

THE PURPOSE OF THE CRIMINAL JUSTICE SYSTEM

Defining which actions are to be labeled "crimes" is only the first step in safeguarding society from criminal behavior. Institutions must be created to apprehend alleged wrongdoers, to determine whether these persons have indeed committed crimes, and to punish those who are found guilty according to society's wishes. These institutions combine to form the **criminal justice system.** As we begin our examination of the American criminal justice system in this introductory chapter, it is important to have an idea of its purpose.

Maintaining Justice

As its name implies, the explicit goal of the criminal justice system is to provide *justice* to all members of society. Because **justice** is a difficult concept to define, this goal can be challenging, if not impossible, to meet. Broadly stated, justice means that all individuals are equal before the law and that they are free from arbitrary arrest or seizure as defined by the law. In other words, the idea of justice is linked with the idea of fairness. Above all, we want our laws and the means by which they are carried out to be fair.

Justice and fairness are subjective terms, which is to say that people may have different concepts of what is just and fair. If a woman who has been beaten by her husband retaliates by killing him, what is her just punishment? Reasonable persons could disagree, with some thinking that the homicide was justified and that she should be treated leniently. Others might insist that she should not have taken the law into her own hands. Police officers, judges, prosecutors, prison administrators, and other members of the criminal justice system must decide what is "fair." Sometimes, their course of action is obvious, but often, as we shall see, it is not.

Protecting Society

Within the broad mandate of "maintaining justice," Megan Kurlychek of the University at Albany, New York, has identified four specific goals of our criminal justice system:

1. To protect society from potential future crimes of the most dangerous or "risky" offenders.
2. To determine when an offense has been committed and provide the appropriate punishment for that offense.
3. To rehabilitate those offenders who have been punished so that it is safe to return them to the community.
4. To support crime victims and, to the extent possible, return them to their pre-crime status.[4]

Again, though these goals may seem straightforward, they are fraught with difficulty. Take the example of James Holmes, who was charged with twenty-four counts of murder and 116 counts of attempted murder by law enforcement officials on July 30, 2012. Ten days earlier, Holmes—armed with an assault rifle and three other guns—had apparently opened fire on the audience at a late-night screening of a Batman movie in Aurora, Colorado. Following the incident, authorities at the University of Colorado, where Holmes had been a graduate student, came under heavy criticism for not reacting more forcefully to staff concerns about his behavior. In the next chapter, we will study the challenges of predicting criminality.

On June 4, 2013, a Colorado judge allowed Holmes to plead not guilty by reason of insanity for the shooting. As a result, many of his victims and their family members have stated publicly that they fear he will not receive an appropriate punishment for his actions.[5] In Chapter 3, you will learn how insanity can be used as a defense to criminal wrongdoing. Furthermore, regardless of his mental state, should Holmes ever be set free? In Chapters 9 and 12, we will discuss the concept of rehabilitation and the role that victims play in the eventual return of offenders to the community. Throughout this textbook, you will come to better understand the criminal justice system by exposure to differing opinions on these topics and many others.

POLICY.CJ

Forty-one states ban texting while driving, and another twelve states prohibit drivers from using a handheld cell phone. Now, many policy makers are suggesting a similar crackdown on "distracted walking"—the use of electronic devices by pedestrians that poses a risk to public safety. To learn more about this topic, go online and search for the terms **distracted walking**, **regulation**, and **statistics**. Make two lists describing the pros and cons of criminal laws prohibiting distracted walking. Then, write a full paragraph explaining why you think such laws would or would not be in your community's best interests.

////SELF ASSESSMENT

Fill in the blanks, and check your answers on page 29.

The concept of _____ is closely linked with ideas of fairness and equal treatment for all, and it is a primary goal of American police officers, judges, and prison administrators. Other goals include _____ society from criminal behavior, _____ those who are guilty of criminal wrongdoing, and supporting the _____ of crime.

THE STRUCTURE OF THE CRIMINAL JUSTICE SYSTEM

Society places the burden of maintaining justice and protecting our communities on those who work for the three main institutions of the criminal justice system: law enforcement, the courts, and corrections. In this section, after discussing the concept of federalism, we take an introductory look at these institutions and their roles in the criminal justice system as a whole.

The Importance of Federalism

To understand the structure of the criminal justice system, you must understand the concept of **federalism,** which means that government powers are shared by the national (federal) government and the states. The framers of the U.S. Constitution, fearful of tyranny and a too-powerful central government, chose the system of federalism as a compromise.

The appeal of federalism was that it established a strong national government capable of handling large-scale problems while allowing for state powers and local traditions. For example, earlier in the chapter we noted that physician-assisted suicide, though banned in most of the country, is legal in three states. In 2006, the federal government challenged the decision made by voters in two of those states—Oregon and Washington—to allow the practice. The United States Supreme Court sided with the states, ruling that the principle of federalism supported their freedom to differ from the majority viewpoint in this instance.[6] In general, however, federal criminal law takes priority over local and state criminal law, as we will see throughout this textbook.

The Constitution gave the national government certain express powers, such as the power to coin money, raise an army, and regulate interstate commerce. All other powers

Federalism A form of government in which a written constitution provides for a division of powers between a central government and regional governments.

F. W. GILL

GANG INVESTIGATOR

Photo Courtesy of F. W. Gill

The problem, for most of these kids, is that nobody cares. Their parents don't, or can't, get involved in their children's lives. (How many times have I heard parents deny that their son or daughter is a gang banger, even though it's obvious?) Teachers are in the business of teaching and don't, or can't, take the time to get to know their most troubled students. So, when I'm dealing with gang members, the first thing I do is listen. I don't lecture them, I don't tell them that they are throwing away their lives. I just listen. You'd be amazed how effective this can be—these kids, who look so tough on the outside, just want an adult to care.

Not that there is any magic formula for convincing a gang member to go straight. It is very difficult to get someone to change his or her lifestyle. If they don't want to change—really want to change—then nothing I can say or do is going to make much of a difference. Unfortunately, there are many lost causes. I've even had a couple of cases in which a juvenile was afraid to leave the gang because his father was a gang member, and he insisted that the boy stay in the gang. I have had some success in convincing gang members to turn their lives around by joining the military. The military provides discipline and a new outlook on life, things that these kids badly need. The way I look at it, in some cases, war is the best shot these kids have at saving their own lives.

Social Media Career Tip When you are posting on Facebook, assume that your post will be published in your local newspaper and read by a potential employer. So, if you think the post might reflect poorly on you as a potential employee, keep it offline.

were left to the states, including police power, which allows the states to enact whatever laws are necessary to protect the health, morals, safety, and welfare of their citizens. As the American criminal justice system has evolved, the ideals of federalism have ebbed somewhat. Specifically, the powers of the national government have expanded significantly. In the early 1900s, only about one hundred specific activities were illegal under federal criminal law. Today, there are more than 4,500 federal criminal statutes, meaning that Americans are increasingly likely to come in contact with the federal criminal justice system.[7]

LAW ENFORCEMENT The ideals of federalism can be clearly seen in the local, state, and federal levels of law enforcement. Though agencies from the different levels cooperate if the need arises, they have their own organizational structures and tend to operate independently of one another. We briefly introduce each level of law enforcement here and cover them in more detail in Chapters 4, 5, and 6.

Local Law Enforcement On the local level, the duties of law enforcement agencies are split between counties and municipalities. The chief law enforcement officer of most counties is the county sheriff. The position of sheriff is usually an elected post, with a two- or four-year term. In some areas, where city and county governments have merged, there is a county police force, headed by a chief of police. As Figure 1.1 that follows shows, the bulk of all police officers in the United States are employed on a local level.

Outline the three levels of law enforcement.

LEARNING **3** OBJECTIVE

The majority of these work in departments that consist of fewer than 10 officers, though a large city such as New York may have a police force of about 36,000.

Local police are responsible for the "nuts and bolts" of law enforcement work. They investigate most crimes and attempt to deter crime through patrol activities. They apprehend criminals and participate in trial proceedings, if necessary. Local police are also charged with "keeping the peace," a broad set of duties that includes crowd and traffic control and the resolution of minor conflicts between citizens. In many areas, local police have the added obligation of providing social services, such as dealing with domestic violence and child abuse.

State Law Enforcement Hawaii is the only state that does not have a state law enforcement agency. Generally, there are two types of state law enforcement agencies—those designated simply as "state police," and those designated as "highway patrols." State highway patrols concern themselves mainly with infractions on public highways and freeways. Other state law enforcers include fire marshals, who investigate suspicious fires and educate the public on fire prevention, and fish, game, and watercraft wardens, who police a state's natural resources and often oversee its firearms laws.

Federal Law Enforcement The enactment of new national antiterrorism, gun, drug, and violent crime laws over the past forty years has led to an expansion in the size and scope of the federal government's participation in the criminal justice system. The Department of Homeland Security, which we will examine in detail in Chapter 4, combines the police powers of twenty-four federal agencies to protect the United States from terrorist attacks. Other federal agencies with police powers include the Federal Bureau of Investigation (FBI), the Drug Enforcement Administration (DEA), the U.S. Secret Service, and the Bureau of Alcohol, Tobacco, Firearms and Explosives (ATF). In fact, almost every federal agency, including the postal and forest services, has some kind of police power.

Federal law enforcement agencies operate throughout the United States and often work in cooperation with their local and state counterparts. There can be tension between the different branches of law enforcement, however, when state and federal

FIGURE 1.1 Local, State, and Federal Employees in Our Criminal Justice System

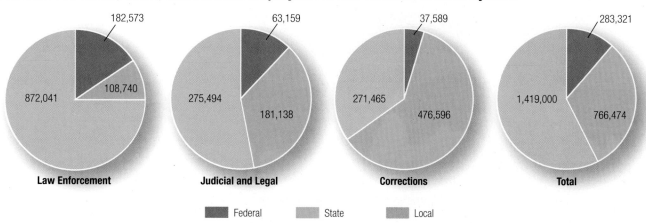

Source: Bureau of Justice Statistics, *Justice Expenditure and Employment in the United States, 2010* (Washington, D.C.: U.S. Department of Justice, July 2013), Table 2.

criminal law is incompatible. For example, even though Colorado and Washington have legalized the sale and possession of small amounts of marijuana, as noted at the beginning of this chapter, the drug is still illegal under federal law. Consequently, federal officers are authorized to make marijuana arrests in those states, regardless of any changes to the states' criminal codes.

THE COURTS The United States has a *dual court system*, which means that we have two independent judicial systems, one at the federal level and one at the state level. In practice, this translates into fifty-two different court systems: one federal court system and fifty different state court systems, plus that of the District of Columbia. In general, defendants charged with violating federal criminal law will face trial in federal court, while defendants charged with violating state law will appear in state court.

The *criminal court* and its work group—the judge, prosecutors, and defense attorneys—are charged with the weighty responsibility of determining the innocence or guilt of criminal suspects. We will cover these important participants, their roles in the criminal trial, and the court system as a whole in Chapters 7, 8, and 9.

List the essential elements of the corrections system. **LEARNING** **4** **OBJECTIVE**

CORRECTIONS Once the court system convicts and sentences an offender, she or he is relegated to the corrections system. (Those convicted in a state court will be under the control of that state's corrections system, and those convicted of a federal crime will find themselves under the control of the federal corrections system.) Depending on the seriousness of the crime and their individual needs, offenders are placed on probation, incarcerated, or transferred to community-based correctional facilities.

At midyear 2013, America's jails held approximately 744,000 inmates, including these residents of the Orange County Men's Jail in Santa Ana, California. What are the basic differences between jails and prisons?

1. *Probation,* the most common correctional treatment, allows the offender to return to the community and remain under the supervision of an agent of the court known as a probation officer. While on probation, the offender must follow certain rules of conduct. When probationers fail to follow these rules, they may be incarcerated.

2. If the offender's sentence includes a period of *incarceration,* he or she will be remanded to a correctional facility for a certain amount of time. *Jails* hold those convicted of minor crimes with relatively short sentences, as well as those awaiting trial or involved in certain court proceedings. *Prisons* house those convicted of more serious crimes with longer sentences. Generally speaking, counties and municipalities administer jails, while prisons are the domain of federal and state governments.

3. *Community-based corrections* have increased in popularity as jails and prisons have been plagued with problems of funding and overcrowding. Community-based correctional facilities include halfway houses, residential centers, and work-release centers. They operate on

Lucy Nicholson/Reuters/Landov

the assumption that all convicts do not need, and are not benefited by, incarceration in jail or prison.

The majority of those inmates released from incarceration are not finished with the corrections system. The most frequent type of release from a jail or prison is *parole,* in which an inmate, after serving part of his or her sentence in a correctional facility, is allowed to serve the rest of the term in the community. Like someone on probation, a parolee must conform to certain conditions of freedom, with the same consequences if these conditions are not followed. Issues of probation, incarceration, community-based corrections, and parole will be covered in Chapters 10, 11, and 12.

Formal Criminal Justice Process The model of the criminal justice process in which participants follow formal rules to create a smoothly functioning disposition of cases from arrest to punishment.

The Criminal Justice Process

In its 1967 report, the President's Commission on Law Enforcement and Administration of Justice asserted that the criminal justice system

> is not a hodgepodge of random actions. It is rather a continuum—an orderly progression of events—some of which, like arrest and trial, are highly visible and some of which, though of great importance, occur out of public view.[8]

The commission's assertion that the criminal justice system is a "continuum" is one that many observers would challenge.[9] Some liken the criminal justice system to a sports team, which is the sum of an indeterminable number of decisions, relationships, conflicts, and adjustments.[10] Such a volatile mix is not what we generally associate with a "system." For most, the word *system* indicates a certain degree of order and discipline. That we refer to our law enforcement agencies, courts, and correctional facilities as part of a system may reflect our hopes rather than reality. Still, it will be helpful to familiarize yourself with the basic steps of the *criminal justice process,* or the procedures through which the criminal justice system meets the expectations of society. These basic steps are provided in Figure 1.2 that follows.

In his classic study of the criminal justice system, Herbert Packer, a professor at Stanford University, compared the ideal criminal justice process to an assembly line "down which moves an endless stream of cases, never stopping."[11] In Packer's image of assembly-line justice, each step of the **formal criminal justice process** involves a series of "routinized operations" with the end goal of getting the criminal defendant from point A (his or her arrest by law enforcement) to point B (the criminal trial) to point C (if guilty, her or his punishment).[12] As Packer himself often pointed out, the daily operations of criminal justice rarely operate so smoothly. In this textbook, the criminal justice process will be examined as the end product of many different decisions made by many different criminal justice professionals in law enforcement, the courts, and corrections.

//// SELF ASSESSMENT

Fill in the blanks, and check your answers on page 29.

To protect against a too-powerful central government, the framers of the U.S. Constitution relied on the principle of _____ to balance power between the national government and the states. Consequently, the United States has a _____ court system—one at the federal level and one at the _____ level. One expert has compared the _____ criminal justice process to an assembly line involving a series of routine operations.

FIGURE 1.2 The Criminal Justice Process

This diagram provides a simplified overview of the basic steps of the criminal justice process, from criminal act to release from incarceration. Next to each step, you will find the chapter of this textbook in which the event is covered.

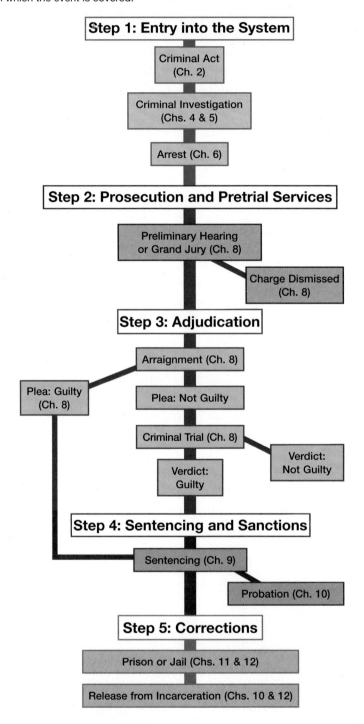

DISCRETION AND ETHICS

Practically, the formal criminal justice process suffers from a serious drawback: it is unrealistic. Law enforcement agencies do not have the staff or funds to investigate *every* crime, so they must decide where to direct their limited resources. Increasing caseloads and a limited amount of time in which to dispose of them constrict many of our nation's courts. Overcrowding in prisons and jails affects both law enforcement agencies and the courts—there is simply not enough room for all convicts.

The criminal justice system relies on *discretion* to alleviate these pressures. By **discretion,** we mean the authority to choose between and among alternative courses of action, based on individual judgment and conscience. Collectively, the discretionary decisions made by criminal justice professionals are said to produce an **informal criminal justice process** that does not operate within the rigid confines of formal rules and laws.

LEARNING **5** OBJECTIVE Explain the difference between the formal and informal criminal justice processes.

Informal Decision Making

By its nature, the informal criminal justice process relies on the discretion of individuals to offset the rigidity of criminal statutes and procedural rules. For example, even if a prosecutor believes that a suspect is guilty, she or he may decide not to bring charges against the suspect if the case is weak or the police erred during the investigative process. In many instances, prosecutors will not squander the scarce resource of court time on a case they might not win. Some argue that the informal process has made our system more just. Given the immense pressure of limited resources, the argument goes, only rarely will an innocent person end up before a judge and jury.[13]

LAW ENFORCEMENT DISCRETION The use of discretion in law enforcement is also widespread, and this informal decision making often directly impacts the public. For example, both New York and Los Angeles have local ordinances prohibiting pedestrians from *jaywalking,* or crossing the street outside of a crosswalk or against a traffic light.

Although jaywalking is quite common in New York, police rarely issue tickets to sanction such behavior. In Los Angeles, however, where an automobile culture dominates, police handed out more than 31,000 jaywalking citations from January 2013 to November 2013 in the downtown area alone.[14] Evidently, New York police officers are using their discretion to ignore this form of law breaking, while their counterparts in Los Angeles have decided to expend considerable resources in an effort to reduce it.

In Chapters 4, 5, and 6, we will examine many other circumstances that call for discretionary decision making by law enforcement officers. (See Figure 1.3 that follows for a description of some of the important discretionary decisions that make up the informal criminal justice process.)

Discretion The ability of individuals in the criminal justice system to make operational decisions based on personal judgment instead of formal rules or official information.

Informal Criminal Justice Process A model of the criminal justice system that recognizes the informal authority exercised by individuals at each step of the criminal justice process.

FIGURE 1.3 Discretion in the Criminal Justice System

Criminal justice officials must make decisions every day concerning their duties. The officials listed below, whether they operate on a local, state, or federal level, rely heavily on discretion when meeting the following responsibilities.

test question

Police	Judges
• Enforce laws. • Investigate specific crimes. • Search people or buildings. • Arrest or detain people.	• Set conditions for pretrial release. • Accept pleas. • Dismiss charges. • Impose sentences.
Prosecutors	**Correctional Officials**
• File charges against suspects brought to them by the police. • Drop cases. • Reduce charges.	• Assign convicts appropriate housing in prison or jail. • Punish prisoners who misbehave. • Reward prisoners who behave well.

THE PITFALLS OF DISCRETION Unfortunately, the informal criminal justice process does not always benefit from measured, rational decision making. Individual judgment can be tainted by personal bias, erroneous or irrational thinking, and plain ill will. When this occurs, discretion becomes "the power to *get away* with alternative decisions [emphasis added]."[15] Indeed, many of the rules of the formal criminal justice process are designed to keep its employees from substituting their own judgment for that of the general public, as expressed by the law.

In 2013, the American Civil Liberties Union of Michigan accused police officers in Saginaw of improperly using their discretion to racially profile recipients of jaywalking citations.[16] As you will learn in Chapter 6, racial profiling is the police practice of improperly targeting members of minority groups based on personal characteristics such as race or ethnicity. Furthermore, associate Supreme Court justice Antonin Scalia has criticized discretion in the courts for its tendency to cause discriminatory and disparate criminal sentences, a subject we will discuss in Chapter 9. According to Scalia, the need for fairness and certainty in the criminal justice system outweighs the practical benefits of widespread and unpredictable discretionary decision making.[17]

Ethics and Justice

How can we reconcile the need for some sort of discretion in criminal justice with the ever-present potential for abuse? Part of the answer lies in our initial definition of *discretion,* which mentions not only individual judgment but also *conscience.* Ideally, actors in the criminal justice system will make moral choices about what is right and wrong based on the norms that have been established by society. In other words, they will behave *ethically.*

Ethics in criminal justice is closely related to the concept of justice. Because criminal justice professionals are representatives of the state, they have the power to determine whether the state is treating its citizens fairly. If some law enforcement officers in fact make the decision to arrest a jaywalker based on that person's race, then they are not only acting unethically but also unjustly.

ETHICS AND THE LAW The line between ethics and justice is often difficult to discern, as ethical standards are usually not written into criminal statutes. Consequently, individuals must often "fill in" the ethical blanks. To make this point, ethics expert John Kleinig uses the real-life example of a police officer who refused to arrest a homeless person for sleeping in a private parking garage. A local ordinance clearly prohibited such behavior.

The officer, however, felt it would be unethical to arrest a homeless person under those circumstances unless he or she was acting in a disorderly manner. The officer's supervisors were unsympathetic to this ethical stance, and he was suspended from duty without pay.[18] (To consider another ethical dilemma that can arise for police officers, see the feature *Discretion in Action—Duty vs. Family* that follows.)

ETHICS AND CRITICAL THINKING Did the police officer in the above example behave ethically by inserting his own beliefs into the letter of the criminal law? Would an officer who arrested peaceful homeless trespassers be acting unethically? In some cases, the ethical decision will be *intuitive,* reflecting an automatic response determined by a person's background and experiences. In other cases, however, intuition is not enough. *Critical thinking* is needed for an ethical response. Throughout this textbook, we will use the principle of critical thinking—which involves developing analytical skills and reasoning—to address the many ethical challenges inherent in the criminal justice system.

Fill in the blanks, and check your answers on page 29.

At every level, the criminal justice system relies on the _____ of its employees to keep it from being bogged down by formal rules. Some critics think that this freedom to make decisions leads to the dominance of an _____ criminal justice system, which can, in some cases, result in unequal treatment and even discrimination. Ideally, to avoid this kind of injustice, criminal justice professionals will incorporate _____ in their decision-making process.

Crime Control Model A criminal justice model that places primary emphasis on the right of society to be protected from crime and violent criminals.

Due Process Model A criminal justice model that places primacy on the right of the individual to be protected from the power of the government.

CRIMINAL JUSTICE TODAY

In describing the general direction of the criminal justice system as a whole, many observers point to two models introduced by Professor Herbert Packer: the *crime control model* and the *due process model*.[19] The underlying value of the **crime control model** is that the most important function of the criminal justice process is to punish and repress criminal conduct. The system must be quick and efficient, placing as few restrictions as possible on the ability of law enforcement officers to make discretionary decisions in apprehending criminals.

Although not in direct conflict with crime control, the underlying values of the **due process model** focus more on protecting the rights of the accused through formal, legal restraints on the police, courts, and corrections. That is, the due process model relies on the courts to make it more difficult to prove guilt. It rests on the belief that it is more desirable for society that ninety-nine guilty suspects go free than that a single

LEARNING **7** OBJECTIVE
Contrast the crime control and due process models.

DISCRETION in Action

DUTY VS. FAMILY

THE SITUATION Ray, a third-year police officer, goes to a party hosted by his sister Sally on a Friday night, when he is off duty. During the party, Ray sees one man and two women snorting cocaine in the kitchen. Sally is in her backyard talking to other guests and seems oblivious to the illegal drug use.

THE LAW According to the rules of search and seizure, which you will learn more about in Chapter 6, if a police officer is legally in a position to see illegal activity, he or she is authorized to immediately seize any evidence of that illegal activity.

WHAT WOULD YOU DO? Ray's duty is clear: as an officer of the law, he must uphold the law. At the same time, if he reports the crime, he exposes his sister Sally to possible punishment, as the cocaine is in her home. Ray is sure that Sally has no knowledge of this illegal activity. He also wonders, given the vast amount of casual illegal drug use that goes undetected by the police in this country every day, if it would be so unethical for him to "look the other way." If you were Ray, how would you handle this situation?

Define *ethics*, and describe the role that it plays in discretionary decision making. LEARNING **6** OBJECTIVE

To learn how police officers generally approach this sort of ethical dilemma, go to Example 1.1 in Appendix B.

innocent person be condemned.[20] (The *Mastering Concepts* feature that follows provides a further comparison of the two models.)

Crime and Law Enforcement: The Bottom Line

It is difficult to say which of Packer's two models has the upper hand today. As we will see later in this section, homeland security concerns have brought much of the criminal justice system in line with crime control values. At the same time, decreasing arrest and imprisonment rates suggest that due process values are strong, as well. Indeed, despite the fact that most Americans believe our crime problem to be worsening,[21] national rates of violent and property crimes are at historically low levels.[22] In Chapter 2, we will discuss some of the reasons for this phenomenon, as well as some experts' concerns that crime rates in the United States have "plateaued" and are likely to rise in the near future.[23]

SMARTER POLICING Just as law enforcement inevitably gets a great deal of the blame when crime rates are high, American police forces have received much credit for the apparent decline in criminality. The consensus is that the police have become smarter and more disciplined over the past two decades, putting into practice strategies that allow them to more effectively prevent crime. For example, the widespread use of *proactive policing* promotes more rigorous enforcement of minor offenses—such as drunkenness

MASTERING CONCEPTS
CRIME CONTROL MODEL VERSUS DUE PROCESS MODEL

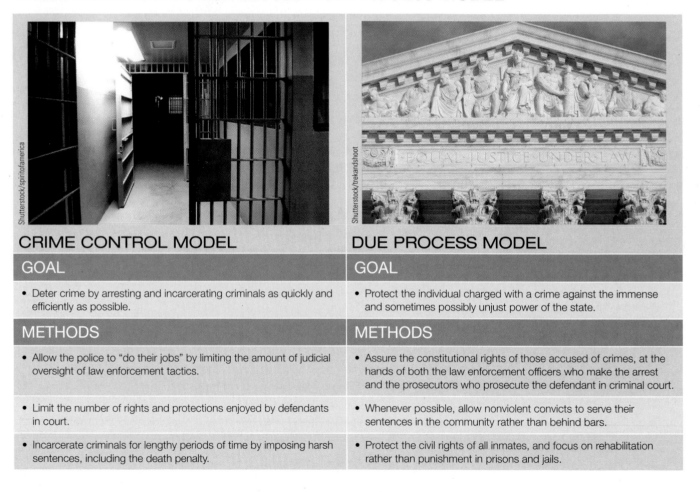

CRIME CONTROL MODEL	DUE PROCESS MODEL
GOAL	**GOAL**
• Deter crime by arresting and incarcerating criminals as quickly and efficiently as possible.	• Protect the individual charged with a crime against the immense and sometimes possibly unjust power of the state.
METHODS	**METHODS**
• Allow the police to "do their jobs" by limiting the amount of judicial oversight of law enforcement tactics.	• Assure the constitutional rights of those accused of crimes, at the hands of both the law enforcement officers who make the arrest and the prosecutors who prosecute the defendant in criminal court.
• Limit the number of rights and protections enjoyed by defendants in court.	• Whenever possible, allow nonviolent convicts to serve their sentences in the community rather than behind bars.
• Incarcerate criminals for lengthy periods of time by imposing harsh sentences, including the death penalty.	• Protect the civil rights of all inmates, and focus on rehabilitation rather than punishment in prisons and jails.

Shutterstock/spiritofamerica

Shutterstock/trekandshoot

EQUAL JUSTICE UNDER LAW

and public disorder—with an eye toward preventing more serious wrongdoing.[24] In addition, *hot-spot policing* has law enforcement officers focusing on high-crime areas rather than spreading their resources evenly throughout metropolitan areas.[25] These and other innovative policing strategies will be explored more fully in Chapter 5.

IDENTIFYING CRIMINALS Technology has also played a significant role in improving law enforcement efficiency. Police investigators are enjoying the benefits of perhaps the most effective new crime-fighting tool since fingerprint identification: *DNA profiling*. This technology allows law enforcement agents to identify a suspect from body fluid evidence (such as blood, saliva, or semen) or biological evidence (such as hair strands or fingernail clippings). As we will also see in Chapter 5, by collecting DNA from convicts and storing the information in databases, investigators have been able to reach across hundreds of miles and back in time to catch wrongdoers.

Law enforcement's ability to identify criminal suspects is set to receive another boost with the increased use of **biometrics.** The term refers to the process by which various technological devices read a person's unique physical characteristics and report his or her identity to authorities. The most common biometric devices record a suspect's fingerprints, but hand geometry, facial features, and the minute details of the human eye can also provide biometric identification.

Already, some banks are using biometrics in the form of voice recognition software to confirm clients' identities. Before long, smartphones and other electronic devices will be activated by facial recognition, and drivers will be able to start their cars with their fingerprints. In law enforcement, the FBI is consolidating all of its biometric information, such as fingerprints and mug shots, into a single database that will allow local police departments to verify the identities of more than 100 million Americans.[26] We will address the consequences—intended and unintended—of the spread of this technology in Chapter 6.

CJ & TECHNOLOGY — BOSS (Biometric Optical Surveillance System)

iStockphoto.com/labsas

As far back as the 2001 Super Bowl, the federal government has been experimenting with facial recognition software that would allow video cameras to identify individuals within large crowds of people. Finally, it seems, the technology is close to becoming operational. The Biometric Optical Surveillance System (BOSS) uses 3-D cameras mounted on the top of two towers to take photos of a subject from different angles. A computer then reads the features of the subject's face and matches those features against those stored in a database.

The goal, according to researchers, is for BOSS to provide a near-instant match at a range of more than three hundred feet. The technology is being developed primarily for counterterrorism purposes. For example, BOSS could be used to search for terrorist suspects at a presidential inaugural parade or in an airport lounge.

Thinking about BOSS

How could local police departments implement BOSS to identify and apprehend criminal suspects or fugitives? Should law enforcement agencies wait until BOSS's successful match rate is close to 100 percent, or would an 80 percent certainty be acceptable? Explain your answer.

CONTINUING CHALLENGES FOR LAW ENFORCEMENT Not every policing trend is positive. Due to economic concerns, according to one recent survey, about half of the nation's local law enforcement agencies have been subject to budget cuts in recent years.[27] The impact of these cuts, which include officer layoffs and resource reductions, could seriously hamper efforts to combat three of the major challenges facing today's police: gangs, guns, and illegal drugs.

The Scourge of Street Gangs For many local law enforcement agencies, particularly those in large metropolitan areas, success is measured by their ability to control **street gangs.** These gangs are often identified as groups of offenders who band together to engage in violent, unlawful, or criminal activity. According to the most recent data, about 30,000 gangs, with approximately 780,000 members, are criminally active in the United States. The same study estimates that the number of gangs has grown by nearly one-third since 2003 and are responsible for 12 percent of homicides in the United States.[28] The topic of youth gangs and efforts to combat their criminal activity will be covered more extensively in Chapter 13.

Gun Use and Crime Even though gangs are heavily involved in criminal activity, most gang-related homicides are not crime related. That is, the killings do not occur during drug deals or robberies "gone bad." Rather, according to data collected by the federal government, the great majority of gang deaths involve the deadly mix of inter-gang conflict (such as territorial or personal disputes) and firearms.[29] Overall, about 475,000 violent crimes are committed each year using a firearm, including over 10,000 homicides,[30] and illegally obtained firearms are a constant concern for law enforcement officials.

At the same time, legal ownership of guns is widespread, with about one-third of American households possessing at least one gun.[31] In 2008, the United States Supreme Court further solidified the legal basis for gun ownership by ruling that the U.S. Constitution protects an individual's right to "bear arms."[32] The Court's decision has done little to lessen the debate over **gun control,** the policies that the government implements to keep firearms out of the hands of the wrong people.

The clamor surrounding this debate has intensified in recent years as a result of several high-profile, multiple-victim incidents involving firearms. On December 14, 2012, Adam Lanza shot and killed twenty first-graders and six adults at an elementary school in Newtown, Connecticut. Then, on September 16, 2013, Aaron Alexis went on a shooting spree that left twelve people dead at a military base in Washington, D.C. We will take a closer look at mass shootings in the next chapter, and we will cover gun control extensively in Chapter 14.

The Illegal Drugs Problem One area in which the nation's crime outlook has not been particularly encouraging involves illegal drugs. Over the past two decades, while arrests for most criminal behavior declined, the arrest rate for illegal drug possession and use increased by 80 percent.[33] Today, more than six of every ten arrestees test positive for at least one illegal drug in their systems at the time of arrest.[34]

The broadest possible definition of a **drug,** which includes alcohol, is any substance that modifies biological, psychological, or social behavior. In popular terminology, however, the word *drug* has a more specific connotation. When people speak of the drug problem, or the war on drugs, or drug abuse, they are referring specifically to illegal **psychoactive drugs,** which affect the brain and alter consciousness or perception. Almost all of the drugs that we will be discussing in this textbook, such as marijuana, cocaine, heroin, and amphetamines, are illegal and psychoactive.

Drug Use in the United States The main source of drug use data is the National Survey on Drug Use and Health, conducted annually by the National Institute on Drug Abuse (see Figure 1.4). According to the survey, only 9.2 percent of those questioned had used an illegal drug in the past month. Even so, this means that a significant number of Americans—about 23.9 million—are regularly using illegal drugs, and the figure mushrooms when users of legal substances such as alcohol (136 million users) and tobacco (70 million users) are included.[35]

It is too early to determine how the legalization of small amounts of marijuana in Colorado and Washington, discussed at the beginning of the chapter, is going to impact illegal drug use in this country. One trend in those states that experts will certainly focus on is the change in marijuana abuse rates among young people. Drug abuse in any form often leads to further criminal behavior in adolescents, as we will see when we look at the juvenile justice system in Chapter 13. In general, the massive market for illegal drugs causes significant damage both in the United States and in countries such as Mexico that supply America with its "fix."

Homeland Security and Domestic Terrorism

Without question, the attacks of September 11, 2001— when terrorists hijacked four commercial airlines and used them to kill nearly three thousand people in New York City, northern Virginia, and rural Pennsylvania—were the most significant events of the first decade of the 2000s as far as crime fighting is concerned. As we will see throughout this textbook, the resulting **homeland security** movement has touched nearly every aspect of criminal justice. This movement has the ultimate goal of protecting America from **terrorism,** which can be broadly defined as the random use or threat of violence to achieve political goals.

COUNTERTERRORISM AND CIVIL LIBERTIES "September 11 is the day that never ends," wrote journalist Richard Cohen on the occasion of its tenth anniversary in 2011.[36] Certainly, the memory of that day's events has lingered in the public consciousness. In an April 2013 survey, more than half of the respondents thought that a future terrorist attack was "very" or "somewhat" likely, and 40 percent worried about terrorism directly impacting themselves or their families.[37] Mobilized by such fears, federal, state, and local governments spent about $600 billion from 2002 to 2011 to bolster the nation's homeland security apparatus.[38]

The Patriot Act The need to respond to the terrorist threat led American politicians and police officials to turn sharply toward crime control principles, as discussed on page 17. In particular, the Patriot Act,[39] passed six weeks after the 9/11 attacks, strengthened the

FIGURE 1.4 **Drug Use in the United States**

According to the National Survey on Drug Use and Health, about 23.9 million Americans, or 9.2 percent of those over twelve years old, can be considered "illicit drug users." As you can see, most of these people used marijuana exclusively. Furthermore, eighteen- to twenty-five-year-olds were more likely to have used illegal drugs than any other segment of the population.

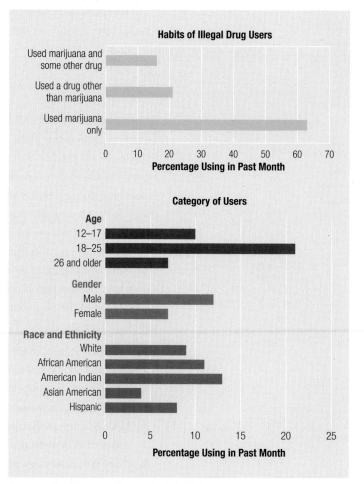

Source: National Survey on Drug Use and Health, 2013.

Homeland Security
A concerted national effort to prevent terrorist attacks within the United States and reduce the country's vulnerability to terrorism.

Terrorism The use or threat of violence to achieve political objectives.

ability of federal law enforcement agents to investigate and incarcerate suspects. The 342-page piece of legislation is difficult to summarize, but some of its key provisions include the following:

1. An expansion of the definition of what it means to "engage in terrorist activity" to include providing "material support" through such activities as fund-raising or operating Web sites for suspected terrorist organizations.
2. Greater leeway for law enforcement agents to track Internet use, access private financial records, and wiretap those suspected of terrorist activity.
3. A reduction in the amount of evidence that law enforcement agents need to gather before taking a terrorist suspect into custody.

Homeland Security and Civil Liberties In 2013, disclosures that the federal government had secretly acquired the phone records of millions of Americans caused many to reassess their views on privacy and national security. Following these revelations, which we will explore in Chapter 6, a national poll showed that 47 percent of Americans said that the federal government had gone too far in restricting *civil liberties* in its efforts to fight terrorism.[40] The term **civil liberties** refers to the personal freedoms guaranteed to all Americans by the U.S. Constitution, particularly the first ten amendments, known as the Bill of Rights.

Concerns about balancing personal freedoms and personal safety permeate our criminal justice system. In fact, an entire chapter of this textbook—Chapter 6—discusses the rules that law enforcement must follow to protect the civil liberties of crime suspects. Many of the issues that we will address in that chapter are particularly relevant to counterterrorism efforts. For example,

1. The First Amendment to the U.S. Constitution states that the government shall not interfere with citizens' "freedom of speech." Does this mean that individuals should be allowed to support terrorist causes on the Internet?
2. The Fourth Amendment protects against "unreasonable searches and seizures." Does this mean that law enforcement agents should not be able to seize the computer of a terrorist suspect unless they have actual proof of wrongdoing?
3. The Sixth Amendment guarantees a trial by jury to a person accused of a crime. Does this mean that the U.S. military can find a suspect guilty of terrorist actions without providing a jury trial?

Critics of counterterrorism measures that include increased surveillance of Internet activity (including e-mails), phone records, and citizens' daily movements believe that limits should be placed on the government's ability to collect "Big Data." Supporters counter that, for the most part, such tactics have been effective and therefore are worth any minimal privacy intrusions.

DOMESTIC TERRORISM For most of the past decade, America's counterterrorism strategies have focused on international terrorism, represented by foreign terrorist organizations that possess the resources to carry out large-scale, coordinated attacks. According to James Comey, director of the FBI, because of these strategies, "the risk of that spectacular attack in the homeland is significantly lower than it was before 9/11." At the same time, Comey warned against the "risk of smaller attacks" by *domestic terrorists*.[41] Though the label covers a variety of illegal activities, **domestic terrorism** generally refers to acts of terror that are carried out within one's own country, against one's own people, and with little or no direct foreign involvement.

Domestic terrorists are often alienated individuals who become emboldened after meeting others who share their extreme views. In many instances, these views involve outrage over American military excursions against Muslims in the Middle East, as well as contempt for Western cultural norms at home. For example, Dzhokhar Tsarnaev told investigators that he and his brother, Tamerlan, planted pressure-cooker bombs near the finish line of the 2013 Boston Marathon as a protest against U.S.-led wars in Iraq and Afghanistan.[42] The bombs killed three people and injured more than 260 spectators at that event.

The Tsarnaev brothers neatly fit the domestic terrorist stereotype of the "self-radicalized extremist" with roots in a faraway Muslim land. (In 2012, Tamerlan Tsarnaev spent six months in Dagestan, a republic of Russia that is considered a training ground for Islamic militants.) Many domestic terrorists have no connection whatsoever to Islamic fundamentalism, however. According to one study, 25 percent of all known terrorist incidents in this country since 2001 have involved antigovernment extremists or white supremicists.[43] The FBI devotes significant resources to thwarting domestic threats such as the "sovereign citizens" movement, whose members reject government authority and plot to kill police officers as a form of protest.[44]

AP Images/Las Vegas Review-Journal/Chase Stevens

In August 2013, David Brutsche (second from the right) appeared in Las Vegas, Nevada, Justice Court to face charges related to his plans to kidnap and murder a law enforcement agent. Why is Brutsche, a member of the "sovereign citizens" movement described in the text, considered a domestic terrorist?

The Emergence of Victims' Rights

In August 2013, lawyers for James Holmes—whose violent rampage in an Aurora, Colorado, movie theater was described earlier in the chapter—requested that survivors of the attack not be allowed in court during Holmes's trial. The lawyers asserted that the presence of the survivors would prejudice the proceedings against their client. Somewhat predictably, District Court Judge Carlos A. Samour denied the request.

"There has been a huge movement in criminal law toward giving victims a voice in what happens—which provides both some solace and closure," says Chicago Kent College of Law professor Doug Godfrey.[45] For our purposes, a **victim** is any person against whom a crime has been committed or who is directly or indirectly harmed by a criminal act.

ADVOCACY FOR CRIME VICTIMS Widespread recognition of crime victims is a relatively recent phenomenon. It was not until the 1970s that victims' rights advocates began addressing what they perceived to be an imbalance in favor of criminal defendants in the criminal justice system. These activists pointed out that crime victims had virtually no rights under state or federal law. Therefore, they were forced to deal with the physical, emotional, and financial consequences of victimization on their own. As a presidential task force concluded in 1982, "The victims of crime have been transformed into a group oppressively burdened by a system designed to protect them. This oppression must be redressed."[46]

LEGISLATIVE EFFORTS Over the past twenty years, all fifty states have redressed the situation by providing legal rights to victims in their statutory codes or state constitutions. Furthermore, in 2004, the U.S. Congress passed the Crime Victims' Rights Act.[47]

Victim Any person who suffers physical, emotional, or financial harm as the result of a criminal act.

These legislative actions have given victims a much greater presence in criminal proceedings, including the right to be heard in criminal court.[48] Various government agencies also provide a broad range of services to crime victims, from crisis intervention to emotional support to financial compensation.

Not all observers believe that the emergence of victims' rights has had a positive impact. In many instances, these critics point out, the various legislative efforts have failed to protect victims' rights as promised. Furthermore, some, such as James Holmes's lawyers, feel that that the presence of victims in the courtroom adds an element of bias to criminal proceedings.[49] Throughout this textbook, we will examine the growing role of the victim in the criminal justice system to determine whether such criticisms are justified.

During the 2014 trial of Tyler Savage for raping and murdering twenty-one-year-old Kimberly Daily in South Hill, Washington, Kiasa Sims, shown here, expressed her sorrow over the victim's death and suffering. What are the consequences—positive and negative—of allowing a murder victim's friends and family to speak in court?

Inmate Population Trends

After increasing by 500 percent from 1980 to 2008, the inmate population in the United States has leveled off and, as you can see in Figure 1.5 that follows, has even decreased slightly over the past several years. Certainly, these decreases have been small, and the American corrections system remains immense. More than 2.2 million offenders are in prison or jail in this country, and another 4.8 million are under community supervision.[50] Still, the new trend reflects a series of crucial changes in the American criminal justice system.

CHANGING INCARCERATION POLICIES For many years, the growing prison population was fed by a number of "get tough on crime" laws passed by politicians in response to the crime wave of the late 1980s and early 1990s. These sentencing laws—discussed in Chapter 9—made it more likely that a person arrested for a crime would wind up behind

FIGURE 1.5 Prison and Jail Populations in the United States, 1985–2012

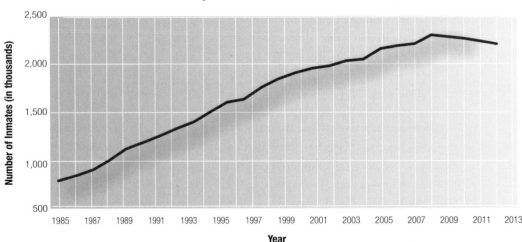

Sources: Bureau of Justice Statistics, *Correctional Populations in the United States, 1995* (Washington, D.C.: U.S. Department of Justice, June 1997), Table 1.1, page 12; and Bureau of Justice Statistics, *Correctional Populations in the United States, 2012* (Washington, D.C.: U.S. Department of Justice, December 2013), Table 2, page 3.

bars and that, once there, he or she would not be back in the community for a long while. The recent reversal of this pattern has led some experts to suggest that the due process model, which favors rehabilitation over incarceration, has started to play a larger role in American criminal justice policy. "This is the beginning of the end of mass incarceration," predicts Natasha Frost of Northeastern University.[51]

There is no question that economic considerations have played a role in the nation's shrinking inmate population. Federal, state, and local governments spend $80 billion a year on prisons and jails, and many corrections officials are under pressure to decrease costs.[52] Increasingly, however, downsizing efforts reflect "the message that locking up a lot of people doesn't necessarily bring public safety," says Joan Petersilia, co-director of Stanford University's Criminal Justice Center.[53] To reduce prison populations, therefore, federal and state correctional officials are

1. Granting early release to nonviolent offenders, particularly low-level drug offenders,
2. Diverting offenders from jail and prison through special courts that promote rehabilitation rather than punishment, and
3. Implementing a number of programs to reduce the *recidivism rate* of ex-convicts. **Recidivism** refers to the act of committing another crime (and possibly returning to incarceration) after a person has already been punished for previous criminal behavior.

We will examine these policies and the ramifications for the nation's prisons and jails in Chapters 10, 11, and 12.

DECLINING USE OF THE DEATH PENALTY Another interesting corrections trend involves death row inmates, who are in prison awaiting execution after having been found guilty of committing a **capital crime.** In April 2013, the death row population in American prisons stood at 3,108, down from 3,653 in 2000.[54] During that same time period, the number of annual executions in this country dropped from 85 to 39.

Judges and juries, it seems, have become less willing to sentence the "worst of the worst" criminals to death. In 2013, only 80 convicts were sentenced to death, down from 315 in 1996, and Maryland became the sixth state in six years to abolish the death penalty.[55] We will further explore *capital punishment,* one of the most controversial areas of the criminal justice system, in Chapter 9.

INCARCERATION AND RACE One troublesome aspect of capital punishment is that a black defendant is much more likely to be sentenced to death for killing a white victim than a white defendant is for killing a black victim.[56] Indeed, looking at the general statistics, a bleak picture of minority incarceration emerges. Even though African Americans make up only 13 percent of the general population in the United States, the number of black men in state prisons (510,000) is larger than the number of white men (465,200).[57] (We should note, however, that this disparity has been shrinking during the recent decrease in overall prison populations.)

In federal prisons, one in every three inmates is Hispanic,[58] a ratio that has increased dramatically over the past decade as law enforcement and homeland security agencies have focused on immigration law violations, a subject we will consider in Chapter 4. The question of whether these figures reflect purposeful bias on the part of certain members of the criminal justice community will be addressed at various points in this textbook.

The Social Media Revolution

LEARNING
List the major issues in
criminal justice today. **8**
OBJECTIVE

Two days after several bombs went off near the finish of the 2013 Boston Marathon—an event described earlier in the chapter—several media outlets incorrectly reported that a suspect had been arrested. Immediately, news of the nonexistent arrest spread across the Internet. Within an hour, however, the Boston Police Department (BPD) posted a tweet that, in fact, no arrest had been made. Thanks to more than nearly 10,500 re-tweets, the false report was refuted in relatively short period of time.[59]

The BPD's corrective tweeting is just one example of the influence that social media can have in the criminal justice arena. *Social media* is the popular term for Internet-based technologies that allow users to interact with each other and a larger online community. The most popular social media outlets are Facebook, through which users can create and share personal files; Instagram, which allows users to circulate photos and videos; and microblogs such as Twitter, where they can post short comments. According to the Pew Research Center, almost three-quarters of all Internet users regularly access at least one social networking site.[60]

SOCIAL MEDIA AND LAW ENFORCEMENT The high level of social media use offers law enforcement agencies numerous opportunities to interact with the communities they serve. Consequently, over 75 percent of the largest police departments in the United States have a social media presence.[61] As we will discuss in Chapter 4, law enforcement agents are benefiting from using social media as crime-fighting tool. For example, the BPD posted surveillance camera photos of the Tsarnaev brothers taken in the aftermath of the marathon bombing. The images were immediately and repeatedly reposted, leaving the suspects with few places in the city to hide.

Law enforcement agencies often use social media for public relations purposes, such as congratulating an officer for solving a crime. Also, a social networking site can helpful in passing along "tips" to the community. When officials at the Los Angeles Police Department decided to crack down on jaywalking—as discussed earlier in the chapter—the department posted relevant sections of the state vehicle code on its Facebook page. (To further explore the online relationship between the public and law enforcement, see the feature *CJ Controversy—Crowdsourcing and Crime* that follows.)

THE DARK SIDE OF SOCIAL MEDIA As a rule, any technology that helps law enforcement provides new opportunities for criminal behavior, as well. Social media are no exception. Before being shut down by authorities, for example, an anonymous Instagram account posted photos and police statements identifying thirty witnesses to violent crimes in Philadelphia. The site's stated purpose was to "expose rats" and keep them from testifying in criminal court.[62] As we will see in Chapter 14, international terrorist groups are also able to raise money, recruit, and spread propaganda via social media.

Finally, because of the anonymity they provide, social media are natural outlets for stalking, bullying, and harassment, topics we address in Chapter 14's section on cyber crime. "The fascinating thing about technology is that once we open the door, it's going to move in ways that we can't always predict and are slow to control," says Scott Decker, a criminal justice professor at Arizona State University.[63]

//// SELF ASSESSMENT

Fill in the blanks, and check your answers on page 29.

The _____ _____ model of criminal justice places great importance on high rates of apprehension and conviction of criminal suspects. In contrast, the _____ _____ model emphasizes the rights of the _____ over the powers of the government. The ability of law enforcement to identify criminal suspects will continue to be improved by its use of _____, technology that reads and recognizes physical characteristics. America's homeland security apparatus, designed to protect the nation from _____, has raised questions concerning the proper balance between security and _____ _____.

CJ CONTROVERSY

CROWDSOURCING AND CRIME

Following the Boston Marathon bombings on April 15, 2013, law enforcement agents asked the public for help solving the case. In particular, the police were interested in any photos or videos taken at the scene of the crime. This tactic of soliciting the input of large groups of people via the Internet is called "crowdsourcing," and its presence in criminal investigations is increasing—for better or worse.

CROWDSOURCING CAN HELP CRIME INVESTIGATIONS BECAUSE . . .

- It places the efforts of thousands of computer-savvy civilians at the disposal of law enforcement.

- It creates networks where participants can quickly and easily share massive amounts of information concerning crimes.

CROWDSOURCING CAN HURT CRIME INVESTIGATIONS BECAUSE . . .

- Untrained "cybersleuths" are unskilled at interpreting all the information that can be gathered on the Internet.

- There is a high potential for an innocent person to be targeted as a suspect based on evidence that would never be accepted in a criminal court of law.

Your Assignment

To learn more about crowdsourcing and criminal justice, go to the Web sites of the **Reddit Bureau of Investigation** and **Websleuths**. Also, investigate the case of **Sunil Tripathi** online. After doing whatever further Internet research you feel is necessary, write at least two full paragraphs describing why you feel crowdsourcing should or should not be encouraged by criminal justice officials.

CHAPTER SUMMARY

For more information on these concepts, look back to the Learning Objective icons throughout the chapter.

 Describe the two most common models of how society determines which acts are criminal. The consensus model argues that the majority of citizens will agree on which activities should be outlawed and punished as crimes. It rests on the assumption that a diverse group of people can have similar morals. In contrast, the conflict model argues that in a diverse society, the dominant groups exercise power by codifying their value systems into criminal laws.

 Define *crime*. Crime is any action punishable under criminal statutes and is considered an offense against society. Therefore, alleged criminals are prosecuted by the state rather than by victims. Crimes are punishable by sanctions that bring about a loss of personal freedom or, in some cases, fines.

 Outline the three levels of law enforcement. Because we have a federal system of government, law enforcement occurs at the (a) national, or federal, level, (b) state level, and (c) local levels within the states. Because crime is mostly a local concern, most employees in the criminal justice system work for local governments. State police are often designated as "highway patrols." Agencies at the federal level include the FBI, the DEA, and the U.S. Secret Service, among others.

 List the essential elements of the corrections system. Criminal offenders are placed on probation, incarcerated in a jail or prison, or transferred to community-based corrections facilities. After serving a partial sentence in a jail or prison, many inmates are released on parole.

 Explain the difference between the formal and informal criminal justice processes. The formal criminal justice process involves the somewhat mechanical steps that are designed to guide criminal defendants from arrest to possible punishment. For every step in the formal process, though, someone has discretion, and such discretion leads to an informal process. Even when prosecutors believe that a suspect is guilty, they have the discretion not to prosecute, for example.

 Define *ethics*, and describe the role that it plays in discretionary decision making. Ethics is a system of moral principles that guides a person's perception of right and wrong. Most criminal justice professionals have a great deal of discretionary leeway in their day-to-day decision making, and their ethical beliefs can help ensure that they make such decisions in keeping with society's established values.

 Contrast the crime control and due process models. The crime control model assumes that the criminal justice system is designed to protect the public from criminals. Thus, its most important function is to punish and repress criminal conduct. The due process model presumes that the accused are innocent and provides them with the most complete safeguards, usually within the court system.

 List the major issues in criminal justice today. (a) Maintaining low violent and property crime rates; (b) continually improving policing strategies; (c) street gangs; (d) gun sales and gun control; (e) use of illegal drugs; (f) homeland security; (g) the Patriot Act and civil liberties; (h) the proper role of victims in the criminal justice system; (i) America's shrinking, though still massive, inmate population; (j) cost-cutting measures in the corrections system; (k) possible bias against minorities in the criminal justice system; and (l) social media in the criminal justice system.

QUESTIONS FOR CRITICAL ANALYSIS

1. How is it possible to have a consensus about what should or should not be illegal in a country with several hundred million adults from all races, religions, and walks of life?

2. What would be some of the drawbacks of having the victims of a crime, rather than the state (through its public officials), prosecute criminals?

3. Are you worried about being the victim of a terrorist attack? If so, why? If not, why not?

4. Refer back to this chapter's discussion of ethics and the police officer who refused to arrest the nonviolent homeless person. Did the officer act properly in this situation, or should he have carried out the law regardless of his personal ethical beliefs? Explain your answer.

5. As noted earlier in the chapter, corrections officials are reducing prison budgets by releasing nonviolent offenders before their sentences are finished. What is your opinion of this strategy? What might be some of the consequences of large-scale early-release programs for drug dealers and those convicted of property crimes?

KEY TERMS

biometrics   19
capital crime   25
civil liberties   22
conflict model   6
consensus model   5
crime   5
crime control model   17
criminal justice system   8
deviance   7

discretion   15
domestic terrorism   22
drug   20
due process model   17
ethics   16
federalism   9
formal criminal justice process   13
gun control   20
homeland security   21

informal criminal justice process   15
justice   8
morals   6
psychoactive drugs   20
recidivism   25
street gang   20
terrorism   21
victim   23

SELF-ASSESSMENT ANSWER KEY

Page 7: i. morals; **ii.** conflict; **iii.** society; **iv.** public officials/ the government; **v.** deviance

Page 9: i. justice; **ii.** protecting; **iii.** punishing; **iv.** victims

Page 13: i. federalism; **ii.** dual; **iii.** state; **iv.** formal

Page 17: i. discretion; **ii.** informal; **iii.** ethics

Page 27: i. crime control; **ii.** due process; **iii.** accused; **iv.** biometrics; **v.** terrorism; **vi.** civil liberties

NOTES

1. Colorado Constitutional Amendment LXIV (2012), available at **www.fcgov.com /mmj/pdf/amendment64.pdf.**

2. Herman Bianchi, *Justice as Sanctuary: Toward a New System of Crime Control* (Bloomington: Indiana University Press, 1994), 72.

3. Lydia Saad, "U.S. Support for Euthanasia Hinges on How It's Described," *Gallup Politics* (May 29, 2013), at **www.gallup.com /poll/162815/support-euthanasia -hinges-described.aspx.**

4. Megan Kurlychek, "What Is My Left Hand Doing? The Need for Unifying Purpose and Policy in the Criminal Justice System," *Criminology & Public Policy* (November 2011), 909.

5. Tracy Connor, "Judge OK's Insanity Defense for Aurora Massacre Suspect James Holmes," *NBCNEWS.com* (June 4, 2013), at **usnews.nbcnews.com /_news/2013/06/04/18749073-judge -oks-insanity-defense-for-aurora -massacre-suspect-james-holmes?lite.**

6. *Gonzales v. Oregon,* 546 U.S. 243 (2006). Many United States Supreme Court cases will be cited in this book, and it is important to understand these citations. *Gonzales v. Oregon* refers to the parties in the case that the Court is reviewing. "U.S." is the abbreviation for *United States Reports,* the official publication of United States Supreme Court decisions. "546" refers to the volume of the *United States Reports* in which the case appears, and "243" is the

page number. The citation ends with the year the case was decided, in parentheses. Most, though not all, Supreme Court case citations in this book will follow this formula.

7. Steve Nelson, "Bipartisan Task Force Looks to Cut List of 4,500 Federal Crimes," *U.S. News & World Report* (June 14, 2013), at **www.usnews.com/news/newsgram /articles/2013/06/14/bipartisan-task -force-looks-to-cut-list-of-4500-federal -crimes.**

8. President's Commission on Law Enforcement and Administration of Justice, *The Challenge of Crime in a Free Society* (Washington, D.C.: Government Printing Office, 1967), 7.

9. John Heinz and Peter Manikas, "Networks among Elites in a Local Criminal Justice System," *Law and Society Review* 26 (1992), 831–861.

10. James Q. Wilson, "What to Do about Crime: Blaming Crime on Root Causes," *Vital Speeches* (April 1, 1995), 373.

11. Herbert Packer, *The Limits of the Criminal Sanction* (Stanford, Calif.: Stanford University Press, 1968), 154–173.

12. *Ibid.*

13. Daniel Givelber, "Meaningless Acquittals, Meaningful Convictions: Do We Reliably Acquit the Innocent?" *Rutgers Law Review* 49 (Summer 1997), 1317.

14. Donna Evans, "Police Crackdown on Jaywalking Means Tickets of Up to $250," *DT News* (December 9, 2013), at **www.la downtownnews.com/news/police -crackdown-on-jaywalking-means -tickets-of-up-to/article_f7ebf922-5ec6 -11e3-b537-001a4bcf887a.html.**

15. George P. Fletcher, "Some Unwise Reflections about Discretion," *Law & Contemporary Problems* (Autumn 1984), 279.

16. "ACLU Asks Justice Department to Investigate Racially-Biased Police Practices in Saginaw," *aclu.org* (September 19, 2013), at **www.aclu.org/criminal-law-reform -prisoners-rights-racial-justice/aclu -asks-justice-department-investigate.**

17. Antonin Scalia, "The Rule of Law as a Law of Rules," *University of Chicago Law Review* 56 (1989), 1178–1180.

18. John Kleinig, *Ethics and Criminal Justice: An Introduction* (New York: Cambridge University Press, 2008), 33–35.

19. Packer, *op. cit.*

20. Givelber, *op. cit.*

21. Andrew Dugan, "More Say Crime Is Serious Problem in U.S. than Locally," *Gallup Politics* (November 1, 2013), at **www.gallup .com/poll/165677/say-crime-serious -problem-locally.aspx.**

22. Federal Bureau of Investigation, *Crime in the United States 2012* (Washington, D.C.: U.S. Department of Justice, 2013), at **www.fbi.gov/about-us/cjis/ucr /crime-in-the.u.s/2012/crime-in-the -u.s.-2012.**

23. James Alan Fox, quoted in Donna Leinwand Leger, "Violent Crime Rises for 2nd Year," *USA Today* (October 25–27, 2013), 1A.

24. Charis E. Kubrin et al., "Proactive Policing and Robbery Rates across U.S. Cities," *Criminology* (February 2010), 57–91.

25. James Q. Wilson, "Hard Times, Fewer Crimes," *Wall Street Journal* (May 31, 2011), 9.

26. The Federal Bureau of Investigation, "Next Generation Identification," at **www .fbi.gov/about-us/cjis/fingerprints _biometrics/ngi.**

27. *Policing and the Economic Downturn: Striving for Efficiency Is the New Normal* (Washington, D.C.: Police Executive Research Forum, February 2013), 1.

28. National Gang Center, *2011 National Youth Gang Survey Analysis* (January 15, 2014), at **www.nationalgangcenter.gov /Survey-Analysis.**

29. Centers for Disease Control and Prevention, "Gang Homicides—Five Cities, 2003 to 2008," *Morbidity and Mortality Weekly Report* (January 27, 2012), at **www.cdc.gov/mmwr /preview/mmwrhtml/mm6103a2.htm.**

30. Michael Planty and Jennifer L. Truman, *Firearm Violence, 1993–2011* (Washington, D.C.: U.S. Department of Justice, May 2013), 1.

31. National Opinion Research Center, *General Social Survey Cumulative Datafile 1972–2012* (Chicago, IL: University of Chicago, 2013), 3.

32. *District of Columbia v. Heller,* 554 U.S. 570 (2008).

33. Howard Snyder, *Arrests in the United States, 1990–2010* (Washington, D.C.: Bureau of Justice Statistics, October 2012), 12.

34. Office of National Drug Control Policy, *ADAM II: 2012 Annual Report* (Washington, D.C.: Executive Office of the President, May 2013), x.

35. Substance Abuse and Mental Health Services Administration, *Results from the 2012 National Survey on Drug Use and Health: Summary of National Findings* (Washington, D.C.: National Institute on Drug Abuse, 2012), 1–4.

36. Quoted in "9/11: Ten Years Later, How America Has Changed," *The Week* (September 16, 2011), 18.

37. Lydia Saad, "Post-Boston, Half in U.S. Anticipate More Terrorism Soon," *Gallup Politics* (April 26, 2013), at **www.gallup .com/poll/162074/post-boston-half -anticipate-terrorism-soon.aspx.**

38. Scott Shane, "Shifting Mood May End Blank Check for U.S. Security Efforts," *New York Times* (October 25, 2012), A1.

39. Uniting and Strengthening America by Providing Appropriate Tools Required to Intercept and Obstruct Terrorism (USA PATRIOT) Act of 2001, Pub. L. No. 107-56, 115 Stat. 272 (2001).

40. Pew Research Center for the People & the Press, "Few See Adequate Limits on NSA Surveillance Program" (July 26, 2013), at **www.people-press.org/2013/07/26 /few-see-adequate-limits-on-nsa -surveillance-program.**

41. Quoted in Timothy M. Phelps, "Terrorist Threat in U.S. Declining, FBI Directory Says," *Arizona Daily Star* (November 15, 2013), A15.

42. Greg Miller and Sari Horwitz, "Blasts Point to Gaps in U.S. Counterterror System," *Chicago Tribune* (May 6, 2013), 12.

43. "Terrorism: Are We Ignoring the Biggest Threat?" *The Week* (August 24–31, 2012), 19.

44. Federal Bureau of Investigation, "Domestic Terrorism: The Sovereign Citizen Movement" (April 13, 2010), at **www .fbi.gov/news/stories/2010/april /sovereigncitizens_041310.**

45. Quoted in Daniel B. Wood, "James Holmes Hearing: At Last, A Chance for Victims to Testify," *Christian Science Monitor* (January 7, 2013), at **www.csmonitor.com/USA /Justice/2013/0107/James-Holmes -hearing-At-last-a-chance-for-victims -to-testify.**

46. Lois Haight Herrington et al., *President's Task Force on Victims of Crime: Final Report* (1982), at **www.ojp.usdoj.gov/ovc/public ations/presdntstskforcrprt/87299.pdf.**

47. 18 U.S.C. Section 3771 (2006).

48. Susan Herman, *Parallel Justice for Victims of Crime* (Washington, D.C.: The National Center for Victims of Crime), 46–47.

49. Danielle Levine, "Public Wrongs and Private Rights: Limiting the Victim's Role in a System of Public Prosecution," 104 *Northwestern University Law Review* (2010), 335–362.

50. Bureau of Justice Statistics, *Correctional Populations in the United States, 2012* (Washington, D.C.: U.S. Department of Justice, December 2013), Table 2, page 3.

51. Quoted in Erica Goode, "U.S. Prison Populations Decline, Reflecting New Approach to Crime," *New York Times* (July 26, 2013), A11.

52. "One Nation, Behind Bars," *The Economist* (August 17, 2013), 12.

53. Quoted in Goode, *op. cit.*

54. Death Penalty Information Center, "Death Row Inmates by State and Size of Death Row by Year," at **www.deathpenaltyinfo .org/death-row-inmates-state-and-size -death-row-year.**

55. Death Penalty Information Center, "The Death Penalty in 2013: Year End Report," at **deathpenaltyinfo.org/YearEnd2013.**

56. Death Penalty Information Center, "National Statistics on Death Penalty and Race," at **www.deathpenaltyinfo.org/race -death-row-inmates-executed-1976.**

57. Bureau of Justice Statistics, *Prisoners in 2012—Advance Counts* (Washington, D.C.: U.S. Department of Justice, July 2013), Table 9, page 10.

58. Federal Bureau of Prisons, "Inmate Ethnicity," at **www.bop.gov/about/statistics /statistics_inmate_ethnicity.jsp.**

59. Michael Chertoff and Dallas Lawrence, "Investigating Terror in the Age of Twitter," *Wall Street Journal* (April 24, 2013), 18.

60. Joanna Brenner, "Pew Internet: Social Networking (full detail)" (December 31, 2013), at **pewinternet.org/Commentary /2012/March/Pew-Internet-Social -Networking-full-detail.aspx.**

61. Joel D. Lieberman, Deborah Koetzle, and Mari Sakiyama, "Police Departments' Use of Facebook: Patterns and Policy Issues," *Police Quarterly* (December 2013), 439.

62. "Philadelphia Police Find Online List of Witnesses," *Associated Press* (November 10, 2013).

63. Quoted in Patrik Jonsson, "'Flash Robs': How Twitter Is Being Twisted for Criminal Gain," *Christian Science Monitor* (August 3, 2011), at **www.csmonitor.com/USA/2011/0803/Flash-robs-How-Twitter-is-being-twisted-for-criminal-gain-VIDEO.**

CHAPTER ONE APPENDIX

How to Read Case Citations and Find Court Decisions

Many important court cases are discussed throughout this book. Every time a court case is mentioned, you will be able to check its citation using the endnotes on the final pages of the chapter. Court decisions are recorded and published on paper and on the Internet. When a court case is mentioned, the notation that is used to refer to, or to *cite,* the case denotes where the published decision can be found.

Decisions of state courts of appeals are usually published in two places: the state reports of that particular state and the more widely used *National Reporter System* published by West Group. Some states no longer publish their own reports. The *National Reporter System* divides the states into the following geographic areas: Atlantic (A. or A.2d), North Eastern (N.E. or N.E.2d), North Western (N.W. or N.W.2d), Pacific (P., P.2d, or P.3d), Southern (So., So.2d, or So.3d), and South Western (S.W., S.W.2d, or S.W.3d). The 2d and 3d in these abbreviations refer to the *Second Series* and *Third Series,* respectively.

Federal trial court decisions are published unofficially in West's *Federal Supplement* (F.Supp. or F.Supp.2d), and opinions from the circuit courts of appeals are reported unofficially in West's *Federal Reporter* (F., F.2d, or F.3d). Opinions from the United States Supreme Court are reported in the *United States Reports* (U.S.), the *Lawyers' Edition of the Supreme Court Reports* (L.Ed.), West's *Supreme Court Reporter* (S.Ct.), and other publications. The *United States Reports* is the official publication of United States Supreme Court decisions. It is published by the federal government. Many early decisions are missing from these volumes. The citations of the early volumes of the *United States Reports* include the names of the actual reporters, such as Dallas, Cranch, or Wheaton. *McCulloch v. Maryland,* for example, is cited as 17 U.S. (4 Wheat.) 316. Only after 1874 did the present citation system, in which cases are cited based solely on their volume and page numbers in the *United States Reports,* come into being. The *Lawyers' Edition of the Supreme Court Reports* is an unofficial and more complete edition of Supreme Court decisions. West's *Supreme Court Reporter* is an unofficial edition of decisions dating from October 1882. These volumes contain headnotes and numerous brief editorial statements of the law involved in a given case.

Citations to decisions of state courts of appeals give the name of the case; the volume, name, and page number of the state's official report (if the state publishes its own reports); and the volume, unit, and page number of the *National Reporter.* Federal court citations also give the name of the case and the volume, name, and page number of the reports. In addition to the citation, this textbook lists the year of the decision in parentheses. Consider, for example, the case *Miranda v. Arizona,* 384 U.S. 436 (1966). The Supreme Court's decision in this case may be found in volume 384 of the *United States Reports* on page 436. The case was decided in 1966.

CHAPTER

2 Measuring and Explaining Crime

Matt McClain/The Washington Post/Getty Images

CHAPTER OUTLINE		CORRESPONDING LEARNING OBJECTIVES
Types of Crime		Identify the six main categories of crime.
Measuring Crime in the United States		Identify the publication in which the FBI reports crime data, and list the two main ways in which the data are reported.
		Distinguish between the National Crime Victimization Survey (NCVS) and self-reported surveys.
Crime Trends		Discuss the prevailing explanation for the rising number of women being incarcerated in the United States.
What Causes Crime?		Discuss the difference between a hypothesis and a theory in the context of criminology.
		Explain how brain-scanning technology is able to help scientists determine if an individual is at risk for criminal offending.
		Describe the importance of early childhood behavior for those who subscribe to self-control theory.
Victims of Crime		Explain the routine activities theory of victimization.
The Link between Drugs and Crime		Discuss the connection between the learning process and the start of an individual's drug use.

To target your study and review, look for these numbered Learning Objective icons throughout the chapter.

33

Warning
SIGNS?

ON SEPTEMBER 16, 2013, a contractor named Aaron Alexis smuggled a shotgun onto the grounds of the U.S. Navy Yard command complex in Washington, D.C. After fatally shooting twelve civilian employees and contractors, the gunman was himself killed by local police, leaving his motives a mystery. Digging into Alexis's past, authorities did find a number of red flags. Within the past decade, he had twice been investigated—though not charged—for firearms offenses. Just a month before the carnage in Washington, D.C., Alexis told police in Rhode Island that he was hearing voices and being controlled by low-frequency radio waves.

Senseless acts such as Alexis's shooting spree inevitably cause us to look for clues in the offender's personal history that may have predicted the violence to come. Before James Holmes killed twelve moviegoers and wounded fifty-eight others in Aurora, Colorado, in July 2012,

a University of Colorado psychiatrist expressed concerns about Holmes's mental well-being to the school's threat assessment team. Adam Lanza—who shot and killed twenty first-graders, six faculty members, his mother, and himself in Newtown, Connecticut, on December 14, 2012—had amassed an arsenal of 1,600 rounds of ammunition, 11 knives, a starter pistol, a bayonet, and 3 samurai swords. Lanza apparently suffered from a form of autism that had led to his being bullied at school.

There is one significant problem with working backward in this manner. For practical purposes, it is almost impossible to predict violent behavior. Jeffrey W. Swanson, a psychiatry professor at Duke University, points out that "tens of thousands" of "troubled, isolated young men" with mental health problems will never commit any crime. Consequently, the challenges facing the criminal justice system when it comes to protecting society from mass violence are quite daunting. As one observer asked after the Navy Yard shootings, "Who knows how many other . . . Aaron Alexises are out there?"

Win McNamee/Getty Images

FOR CRITICAL ANALYSIS

1. One psychiatrist has suggested that hospitals offer "mental health ambulances" that police could call when they encounter someone like Aaron Alexis. How might this strategy help avoid tragedies such as the shootings at the Navy Yard in Washington, D.C.?

2. Should psychiatrists be required to report patients who exhibit possible signs of future violent behavior to the police? Why or why not?

3. Why were parents of children diagnosed with autism upset when the national media speculated that Adam Lanza may have suffered from this disorder?

On September 25, 2013, police chief Cathy Lanier of Washington, D.C., listens to a question from a reporter regarding Washington Navy Yard shooter Aaron Alexis.

TYPES OF CRIME

Shooting rampages such as the one carried out by Aaron Alexis focus national attention on violent crime and generally lead Americans to make two assumptions: (1) gun murders are rising, and (2) there are now more mass killings in the United States than there were in the past. In fact, neither assumption is correct. First, the rate of firearm murders dropped by half between 1981 and 2011.[1] Second, the number of mass killings, defined by the federal government as four or more murders without a "cooling-off" period by the guilty party, is relatively constant from year to year.[2]

As you will see later in this chapter, measurements of crime are important tools that the criminal justice community can use for crime prevention and victim assistance. We start our discussion of measuring and explaining crime, however, with a description of the six basic categories of criminal behavior in American law: violent crime, property crime, public order crime, white-collar crime, organized crime, and high-tech crime. The following overview of these categories will cover most of the criminal activity discussed in this textbook.

LEARNING OBJECTIVE **1** Identify the six main categories of crime.

Violent Crime

Crimes against persons, or *violent crimes,* have come to dominate our perspectives on crime. There are four major categories of violent crime:

1. **Murder,** or the unlawful killing of a human being.
2. **Sexual assault,** or *rape,* which refers to coerced actions of a sexual nature against an unwilling participant.
3. **Assault** and **battery,** two separate acts that cover situations in which one person physically attacks another (battery) or, through threats, intentionally leads another to believe that he or she will be physically harmed (assault).
4. **Robbery,** or the taking of funds, personal property, or any other article of value from a person by means of force or fear.

As you will see in Chapter 3, these violent crimes are further classified by *degree,* depending on the circumstances surrounding the criminal act. These circumstances include the intent of the person committing the crime, whether a weapon was used, and (in cases other than murder) the level of pain and suffering experienced by the victim.

Property Crime

The most common form of criminal activity is *property crime,* or those crimes in which the goal of the offender is some form of economic gain or the damaging of property. There are three major forms of property crime:

1. Pocket picking, shoplifting, and the stealing of any property that is not accomplished by force are covered by laws against **larceny,** also known as *theft.*
2. **Burglary** refers to the unlawful entry of a structure with the intention of committing a serious crime such as theft.
3. *Motor vehicle theft* describes the theft or attempted theft of a motor vehicle. Motor vehicles include any vehicle commonly used for transportation, such as a motorcycle or motor scooter, but not farm equipment or watercraft.

Arson is also a property crime. It involves the willful and malicious burning of a home, automobile, commercial building, or any other construction.

Murder The unlawful killing of one human being by another.

Sexual Assault Forced or coerced sexual intercourse or other sexual acts.

Assault A threat or an attempt to do violence to another person that causes that person to fear immediate physical harm.

Battery The act of physically contacting another person with the intent to do harm, even if the resulting injury is insubstantial.

Robbery The act of taking property from another person through force, threat of force, or intimidation.

Larceny The act of taking property from another person without the use of force with the intent of keeping that property.

Burglary The act of breaking into or entering a structure (such as a home or office) without permission for the purpose of committing a felony.

A female member of the Prince George's County Police Department poses as a prostitute as part of an operation to crack down on the illegal activity in College Park, Maryland. Do you agree with the characterization of prostitution as a victimless crime? Why or why not?

Public Order Crime

The concept of **public order crime** is linked to the consensus model discussed in Chapter 1. Historically, societies have always outlawed activities that are considered contrary to public values and morals.

Today, the most common public order crimes include public drunkenness, prostitution, gambling, and illicit drug use. These crimes are sometimes referred to as *victimless crimes* because they often harm only the offender. As you will see throughout this textbook, however, that term is rather misleading. Public order crimes may create an environment that gives rise to property and violent crimes.

White-Collar Crime

Business-related crimes are popularly referred to as **white-collar crime.** The term *white-collar crime* is broadly used to describe an illegal act or series of acts committed by an individual or legal business entity using some nonviolent means to obtain a personal or business advantage.

As you will see in Chapter 14, when we consider the topic in much greater detail, certain property crimes fall into this category when committed in a business context. Although the extent of this criminal activity is difficult to determine with any certainty, the Association of Certified Fraud Examiners estimates that white-collar crime costs businesses worldwide as much as $3.5 trillion a year.[3]

Organized Crime

In contrast to white-collar crime, which involves the use of legal business facilities and employees to commit illegal acts, **organized crime** describes illegal acts by illegal organizations, usually geared toward satisfying the public's demand for unlawful goods and services. Organized crime broadly implies a conspiratorial and illegal relationship among any number of persons engaged in unlawful acts. More specifically, groups engaged in organized crime employ criminal tactics such as violence, corruption, and intimidation for economic gain.

The hierarchical structure of organized crime operations often mirrors that of legitimate businesses. Like other corporations, these groups attempt to capture a sufficient percentage of any given market to make a profit. Preferred markets for organized crime are gambling, prostitution, and illegal narcotics, among others.

High-Tech Crime

The newest variation on crime is directly related to the increased presence of computers in everyday life. The Internet, with approximately 2.8 billion users worldwide, is the site of numerous *cyber crimes,* such as selling pornographic materials, soliciting minors, and defrauding consumers through bogus financial investments. Corporate dependence on computer operations has left businesses vulnerable to sabotage, fraud, embezzlement,

Public Order Crime Behavior that has been labeled criminal because it is contrary to shared social values, customs, and norms.

White-Collar Crime Nonviolent crimes committed by business entities or individuals to gain a personal or business advantage.

Organized Crime Illegal acts carried out by illegal organizations engaged in the market for illegal goods or services, such as illicit drugs or firearms.

and theft of proprietary data. We will address this particular criminal activity in much greater detail in Chapter 14.

////SELF ASSESSMENT

Fill in the blanks, and check your answers on page 65.

Murder, assault, and robbery are labeled _____ crimes because they are committed against persons. The category of crime that includes larceny, motor vehicle theft, and arson is called _____ crime. When a person acts to gain an illegal business advantage, he or she has committed what is commonly known as a _____-_____ crime.

MEASURING CRIME IN THE UNITED STATES

The six general categories of criminal behavior act as a frame for this country's crime picture. To fill in the frame's interior, experts rely on numerous measurements and studies of criminality, carried out by an array of government agencies, academic institutions, and individual researchers. The most widespread and best known of these surveys tries to answer the broadest of questions: How much crime is there in the United States?

The Uniform Crime Report

Suppose that a firefighter dies while fighting a fire at an office building. Later, police discover that the building manager intentionally set the fire. All of the elements of the crime of arson have certainly been met, but can the manager be charged with murder? In some jurisdictions, the act might be considered a form of murder, but according to the U.S. Department of Justice, arson-related deaths and injuries of police officers and firefighters due to the "hazardous natures of their professions" are not murders.[4]

The distinction is important because the Department of Justice provides us with the most far-reaching and oft cited set of national crime statistics. Each year, the department releases the **Uniform Crime Report (UCR).** Since its inception in 1930, the UCR has attempted to measure the overall rate of crime in the United States by organizing "offenses known to law enforcement."[5] To produce the UCR, the Federal Bureau of Investigation (FBI) relies on the voluntary participation of local law enforcement agencies. These agencies—approximately 18,300 in total, covering 95 percent of the population—base their information on three measurements:

1. The number of persons arrested.
2. The number of crimes reported by victims, witnesses, and the police themselves.
3. Police employee data.[6]

Once this information has been sent to the FBI, the agency presents the crime data in two important ways:

1. As a *rate* per 100,000 people. So, for example, suppose the crime rate in a given year is 3,500. This means that, for every 100,000 inhabitants of the United States, 3,500 *Part I offenses* (explained on the following page) were reported to the FBI by local police departments. The crime rate is often cited by media sources when discussing the level of crime in the United States.

LEARNING OBJECTIVE **2** Identify the publication in which the FBI reports crime data, and list the two main ways in which the data are reported.

Uniform Crime Report (UCR)
An annual report compiled by the FBI to give an indication of criminal activity in the United States.

2. As a *percentage* change from the previous year or other time periods. For example, from 2003 to 2012, there was a 12.2 percent decrease in violent crime and a 14.1 percent decrease in property crime.[7]

The Department of Justice publishes these data annually in *Crime in the United States*. Along with the basic statistics, this publication offers an exhaustive array of crime information, including breakdowns of crimes committed by city, county, and other geographic designations and by the demographics (gender, race, age) of the individuals who have been arrested for crimes.

PART I OFFENSES The UCR divides the criminal offenses it measures into two major categories: Part I and Part II offenses. **Part I offenses** are those crimes that, due to their seriousness and frequency, are recorded by the FBI to give a general idea of the level of crime in the United States each year. For a description of the seven Part I offenses, see Figure 2.1 that follows.

Part I violent offenses are those most likely to be covered by the media and, consequently, inspire the most fear of crime in the population. These crimes have come to dominate crime coverage to such an extent that, for most Americans, the first image that comes to mind at the mention of "crime" is one person physically attacking another person or a robbery taking place with the use or threat of force.[8] Furthermore, in the stereotypical crime, the offender and the victim usually do not know each other.

Given the trauma of violent crimes, this perception is understandable, but it is not accurate. According to UCR statistics, a relative or other acquaintance of the victim commits at least 43 percent of the homicides in the United States.[9] Furthermore, as is

FIGURE 2.1 Part I Offenses

Every month, local law enforcement agencies voluntarily provide information on serious offenses in their jurisdiction to the FBI. These serious offenses, known as Part I offenses, are listed here along with their definitions, as provided by the UCR. (Arson is not included in the national crime report data, but it is sometimes considered a Part I offense nonetheless, so its definition is included here.) As the graph shows, most Part I offenses reported by local police departments in any given year are property crimes.

Murder. The willful (nonnegligent) killing of one human being by another.

Forcible rape. The carnal knowledge of a female forcibly and against her will.*

Robbery. The taking or attempting to take of anything of value from the care, custody, or control of a person or persons by force or threat of force or violence and/or by putting the victim in fear.

Aggravated assault. An unlawful attack by one person on another for the purpose of inflicting severe or aggravated bodily injury. This type of assault is usually accompanied by the use of a weapon or by means likely to produce death or great bodily harm.

Burglary—breaking or entering. The unlawful entry of a structure to commit a felony or a theft. Attempted forcible entry is included.

Larceny/theft (except motor vehicle theft). The unlawful taking, carrying, leading, or riding away of property from the possession or constructive possession of another.

Motor vehicle theft. The theft or attempted theft of a motor vehicle.

Arson. Any willful or malicious burning or attempt to burn, with or without intent to defraud, a dwelling house, public building, motor vehicle or aircraft, personal property of another, and the like.

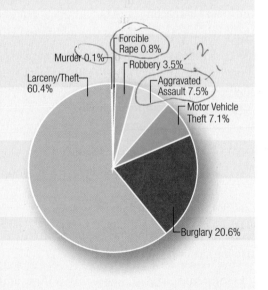

Murder 0.1%
Forcible Rape 0.8%
Robbery 3.5%
Aggravated Assault 7.5%
Motor Vehicle Theft 7.1%
Larceny/Theft 60.4%
Burglary 20.6%

*Future versions of the UCR will use a more expanded definition of *rape* to include offenses involving male victims and a wider range of nonconsensual sexual activity.

Sources: Federal Bureau of Investigation, *Crime in the United States, 2012* (Washington, D.C.: U.S. Department of Justice, 2013), at **www.fbi.gov/about-us/cjis/ucr /crime-in-the-u.s/2012/crime-in-the-u.s.-2012/resource-pages/offense-definitions/offensedefinitions.pdf**, and Table 1, at **www.fbi.gov/about-us/cjis/ucr/crime -in-the-u.s/2012/crime-in-the-u.s.-2012/cius_home.**

evident from Figure 2.1, the majority of Part I offenses committed are property crimes. Notice that 60 percent of all reported Part I offenses are larceny/thefts, and another 21 percent are burglaries.[10]

PART II OFFENSES Not only do violent crimes represent the minority of Part I offenses, but Part I offenses are far outweighed by **Part II offenses,** which include all crimes recorded by the FBI that do not fall into the category of Part I offenses. In general, Part II offenses are less serious than Part I offenses and carry lighter punishments. Of the nineteen categories that make up Part II offenses, the most common are drug abuse violations, simple assaults (in which no weapons are used and no serious harm is done to the victim), driving under the influence, and disorderly conduct.[11]

Information gathered on Part I offenses reflects those offenses "known," or reported to the FBI by local agencies. Part II offenses, in contrast, are measured only by arrest data. In 2012, the FBI recorded about 2.2 million arrests for Part I offenses in the United States. That same year, about 10 million arrests for Part II offenses took place.[12] In other words, a Part II offense was about four and one-half times more common than a Part I offense. Such statistics have prompted Marcus Felson, a professor at Texas State University, to comment that "most crime is very ordinary."[13]

The National Incident-Based Reporting System

About three decades ago, the Department of Justice began seeking ways to improve its data-collecting system. The result was the National Incident-Based Reporting System (NIBRS). In the NIBRS, local agencies collect data on each single crime occurrence within twenty-two offense categories made up of forty-six specific crimes called Group A offenses. These data are recorded on computerized record systems provided—though not completely financed—by the federal government.

The NIBRS became available to local agencies in 1989. Twenty-five years later, thirty-two states have been NIBRS certified, with about 40 percent of the agencies in those states using the updated system.[14] Even in its limited form, however, criminologists have responded enthusiastically to the NIBRS because the system provides information about four "data sets"—offenses, victims, offenders, and arrestees—unavailable through the UCR. The NIBRS also presents a more complete picture of crime by monitoring all criminal "incidents" reported to the police, not just those that lead to an arrest.[15] Furthermore, because jurisdictions involved with the NIBRS must identify bias motivations of offenders, these data are very useful in studying hate crimes, a topic we will address in the next chapter. (See Figure 2.2 that follows to get a clearer sense of the differences between the UCR and the NIBRS.)

Victim Surveys

One alternative method of data collecting attempts to avoid the distorting influence of the "intermediary," or the local police agency. In **victim surveys,** criminologists or other researchers ask the victims of crime directly about their experiences, using techniques such as interviews or e-mail and phone surveys. The first large-scale victim survey took place in 1966, when members of ten thousand households answered questionnaires as part of the President's Commission on Law Enforcement and the Administration of Justice. The results indicated a much higher victimization rate than had been previously expected, and researchers felt the process gave them a better understanding of the **dark figure of crime,** or the actual amount of crime that occurs in the country.

Part II Offenses All crimes recorded by the FBI that do not fall into the category of Part I offenses. These crimes include both misdemeanors and felonies.

Victim Surveys A method of gathering crime data that directly surveys participants to determine their experiences as victims of crime.

Dark Figure of Crime A term used to describe the actual amount of crime that takes place. The "figure" is "dark," or impossible to detect, because a great number of crimes are never reported to the police.

FIGURE 2.2 Comparing the UCR and the NIBRS

As the following scenario shows, the process of crime data collection under the NIBRS is much more comprehensive than the reporting system of the UCR.

At approximately 9:30 p.m. on March 22, 2014, two young males approach a thirty-two-year-old African American woman in the parking garage of a movie theater. The first man, who is white, puts a knife to the woman's throat and grabs her purse, which contains $150. The second man, who is Hispanic, then puts a gun to the woman's temple and rapes her. When he is finished, he shoots her in the chest, a wound that does not prove to be fatal. The two men flee the scene and are not apprehended by law enforcement.

	UCR	NIBRS
Crime reported to FBI	One rape. Under the UCR, when more than one crime is involved in a single incident, only the most serious is reported. Also, attempts are not recorded.	One rape, one robbery, and one attempted murder.
Age, sex, and race of the victim	Not recorded.	Recorded.
Age, sex, and race of the offenders	Not recorded.	Recorded.
Location and time of the attack	Not recorded.	Recorded.
Type and value of lost property	Not recorded.	Recorded.

Source: U.S. Department of Justice.

Criminologists were so encouraged by the results of the 1966 experiment that the federal government decided to institute an ongoing victim survey. The result was the National Crime Victimization Survey (NCVS), which started in 1972. Administered by the U.S. Bureau of the Census in cooperation with the Bureau of Justice Statistics of the Justice Department, the NCVS conducts an annual survey of over 92,000 households with about 163,000 occupants over twelve years of age. Participants are interviewed twice a year concerning their experiences with crimes in the prior six months. As you can see in Figure 2.3 that follows, the questions are quite detailed in determining the experiences of crime victims.

Self-Reported Surveys

Based on many of the same principles as victim surveys, but focusing instead on offenders, **self-reported surveys** are a third source of data for criminologists. In this form of data collection, persons are asked directly—through personal interviews, telephone interviews, or questionnaires—about specific criminal activity to which they may have been a party. Self-reported surveys are most useful in situations in which the group to be studied is already gathered in an institutional setting, such as a juvenile facility or a prison. One of the most widespread self-reported surveys in the United States, the Drug Use Forecasting Program, collects information on narcotics use from arrestees who have been brought into booking facilities.

Because there is no penalty for admitting to criminal activity in a self-reported survey, subjects tend to be more forthcoming in discussing their behavior. Researchers interviewing a group of male students at a state university, for example, found that a significant number of them admitted to committing minor crimes for which they had never been arrested.[16] This fact points to the most striking finding of self-reported surveys: the dark figure of crime, referred to earlier as the *actual* amount of crime that takes place, appears to be much larger than the UCR or NCVS suggests.

Self-Reported Survey A method of gathering crime data from offenders that relies on participants to reveal and detail their own criminal or delinquent behavior.

31a. What were the injuries you suffered, if any?
- a. None
- b. Raped
- c. Attempted rape
- d. Sexual assault other than rape or attempted rape
- e. Knife or stab wounds
- f. Gun shot, bullet wounds
- g. Broken bones or teeth knocked out
- h. Internal injuries
- i. Knocked unconscious
- j. Bruises, black eye, cuts, scratches, swelling, chipped teeth

37. Still thinking about your distress associated with being a victim of this crime, did you feel any of the following ways for A MONTH OR MORE?
- a. Worried or anxious?
- b. Angry?
- c. Sad or depressed?
- d. Vulnerable?
- e. Violated?
- f. Like you couldn't trust people?
- g. Unsafe?

63. How old would you say the offender was?
- a. Under 12
- b. 12–14
- c. 15–17
- d. 18–20
- e. 21–29
- f. 30 or older
- g. Don't know

78a. Were any of the offenders a member of a street gang?
- a. Yes.
- b. No.
- c. Don't know.

78b. Were any of the offenders drinking or on drugs?
- a. Yes
- b. No.
- c. Don't know.

104b. What was the value of the PROPERTY that was taken?
- a. $ _____.

Source: Adapted from U.S. Department of Justice, *National Crime Victimization Survey 2009* (Washington, D.C.: Bureau of Justice Statistics, 2011).

///▨SELF▨ ASSESSMENT

Fill in the blanks, and check your answers on page 65.

To produce its annual _____ _____ _____ , the FBI relies on the cooperation of local law enforcement agencies. _____ surveys rely on those who have been the subject of criminal activity to discuss the incidents with researchers, while _____ - _____ surveys ask participants to detail their own criminal behavior. These two methods show that the _____ _____ of crime, or the actual amount of crime that takes place in this country, is much _____ than official crime data suggest.

CRIME TRENDS

According to the UCR and the NCVS, the two most extensive measurements of national crime rates, the United States is presently enjoying historically low levels of crime. Since the early 1990s, the violent crime rate has declined by more than 70 percent (see Figure 2.4 that follows) and the property crime rate has dropped about 40 percent.[17] Experts have put forth a number of theories to explain this fall in crime, including

1. Improvements in law enforcement, particularly DNA fingerprinting and information-based policing techniques that focus crime prevention tactics on "hot spots" of criminal activity.
2. An aging population: the median age in the United States is around thirty-seven years, the oldest of any time in the nation's history.[18] In general, older people commit fewer crimes than younger people.
3. The end of a crack-cocaine epidemic that shook the nation in the late 1980s and is blamed, in part, for that decade's relatively high crime rates.
4. The gentrification of many former high-crime neighborhoods, which has contributed significantly to a 64 percent crime-rate reduction in America's largest cities.[19]

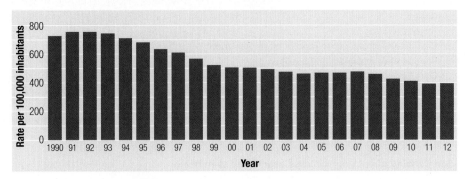

FIGURE 2.4 Violent Crime in the United States, 1990–2012

According to statistics gathered each year by the FBI, American violent crime rates rose slightly in 2012 after declining for the previous several years.

Source: Federal Bureau of Investigation.

Another possible factor in the decline in crime may be the large number of offenders who have been locked up in prison over the past two decades. The relationship between inmate populations and crime rates is controversial, however, and we will look at it more closely in Chapter 11.

Leveling Off: Crime in the 2010s

While the UCR and NCVS generally mirror each other, a recent divergence in the two surveys has raised some interesting questions about the immediate future of crime in the United States. In 2012, the UCR showed essentially no change in the nation's violent and property crime rates. That same year, however, the NCVS measured a 15 percent increase in violent crime and a 12 percent increase in property crime.[20]

This discrepancy seems to be driven by crimes not reported to the police, which are included in the NCVS but not the UCR. Indeed, according the NCVS, victims notify police of only 44 percent of all violent crimes.[21] Still, most of these unreported crimes are less-serious offenses such as simple assault, and experts are generally unsurprised by the slight uptick in the statistics. "We've plateaued," says James Alan Fox of Northeastern University in Boston. "The challenge will be making sure crime rates don't go back up."[22]

Crime, Race, and Poverty

Although crime and victimization rates have decreased across racial lines over the past twenty years, the trends have been less positive for African Americans than for whites. For example, blacks are 6.3 times more likely to be homicide victims than are whites,[23] and almost 20 percent more likely to be homicide offenders.[24] African Americans are particularly susceptible to gun violence, with firearm murder rates of 14.6 per 100,000 adults, compared to 1.9 for whites and 4.0 for Hispanics.[25] A large part of this violence is taking place within the African American community—nationwide, most murder victims are killed by someone of the same race (91 percent for blacks and 84 percent for whites).[26]

RACE AND CRIME Homicide rates are not the only area in which there is a divergence in crime trends between the races. Official crime data seem to indicate a strong correlation between minority status and crime: African Americans—who make up 13 percent of the population—constitute 39 percent of those arrested for violent crimes and 29 percent of those arrested for property crimes.[27] A black man is almost twelve times more likely than a white man to be sent to prison for a drug-related conviction, while black women are about five times more likely than white women to be incarcerated for a drug offense.[28] (See the feature *Myth vs Reality—Race Stereotyping and Drug Crime* that follows.) Furthermore, a black juvenile in the United States is about twice as likely as a white juvenile to end up in delinquency court.[29]

CLASS AND CRIME The racial differences in the crime rate represent one of the most controversial areas of the criminal justice system. At first glance, crime statistics seem to support the idea that the subculture of African Americans in the United States is disposed toward criminal behavior.

Not all of the data, however, support that assertion. A recent research project led by sociologist Ruth D. Peterson of Ohio State University gathered information on nearly 150 neighborhoods in Columbus, Ohio. Peterson and her colleagues separated the neighborhoods based on race and on levels of disadvantage such as poverty, joblessness, lack of college graduates, and high levels of female-headed families. She found that whether the

MYTH VS REALITY
Race Stereotyping and Drug Crime

THE MYTH African Americans are sent to prison for drug crimes in greater numbers than whites because more of them buy, sell, and use drugs.

THE REALITY The use of illegal drugs by blacks and whites in the United States is roughly equal. According to data gathered by the federal government, about 11 percent of African Americans and about 9 percent of whites admit to using drugs within the previous month. A study conducted by Duke University researchers showed that black adolescents are about only half as likely as their white counterparts to become dependent on illegal drugs and alcohol.

These figures are not reflected in criminal justice trends. African Americans who use drugs are arrested at about three times the rate of whites who use drugs. Furthermore, although blacks account for only 31 percent of all drug arrests, they represent 44 percent of those convicted of drug crimes and 40 percent of all Americans sent to prison for drug crimes. Finally, more than four out of every five drug arrests are for possession of the banned substance, not for its sale or manufacture. Thus, the racial disparity in arrests cannot be due to a large class of African American drug dealers.

Although these statistics leave the criminal justice system open to charges of institutionalized racism, the disparities are possibly the result of practical considerations. Several years ago, criminologists Robin Engel, Michael Smith, and Francis Cullen compared police deployment patterns and drug arrests in Seattle. They found that, as police presence is necessarily greater in crime-prone areas, the numbers of drug arrests in those areas were higher than normal. Because crime-prone areas have large concentrations of minority residents, that population is subject to greater law enforcement scrutiny. The authors concluded, therefore, that citizens' demand for protection played a much more significant role than possible police bias in the disproportionate drug arrest rates for African Americans in the city.

FOR CRITICAL ANALYSIS
Heather Mac Donald, a crime expert at the Manhattan Institute in New York, suggests that the racial disparities in the "war on drugs" make sense because the urban street trade often leads to violence and other crimes that harm inner-city communities. Drug use by whites, in contrast, generally takes place in suburban homes, hidden from view, without the same level of negative side effects. What is your opinion of Mac Donald's theory?

By some measures, black citizens are twice as likely as whites to live in poverty and hold low-wage jobs. What is your opinion of the theory that economic disadvantage, rather than skin color, accounts for the disproportionate number of African Americans in U.S. prisons, such as these inmates at Florida's Dade County Correctional Facility?

Visions of America/UIG/Getty Images

neighborhoods were predominantly white or predominantly black had little impact on violent crime rates. Those neighborhoods with higher levels of disadvantage, however, had uniformly higher violent crime rates.[30]

Peterson's research suggests that, regardless of race, a person is at a much higher risk of violent offending or being a victim of violence if he or she lives in a disadvantaged neighborhood. Given that African Americans are two times more likely than whites to live in poverty and hold low-wage-earning jobs, they are, as a group, more susceptible to the factors that contribute to criminality.[31]

ETHNICITY AND CRIME Statistical studies of minority offenders and victims tend to focus on race, which distinguishes groups based on physical characteristics such as skin color, rather than *ethnicity,* which denotes national or cultural background. Thus, the bulk of criminological research in this area has focused on the differences between European Americans and African Americans, both because the latter have been the largest minority group in the United States for most of its history and because the racial differences between the two groups are easily identifiable.

Americans of Hispanic descent have been either excluded from many crime studies or linked with whites or blacks based on racial characteristics. Other minority groups, such as Asian Americans, Native Americans, and immigrants from the South Pacific or Eastern Europe, have been similarly underreported in crime studies.

This state of affairs is in the process of changing. At present rates of growth, the Hispanic population will triple by 2050, when it will account for approximately one-third of the total U.S. population. Hispanics are also the fastest-growing minority group in the U.S. prison population.[32] Because of an increased emphasis on immigration law enforcement, more than one-third of the inmates in federal prisons in this country today are Hispanic.[33]

Women and Crime

To put it bluntly, crime is an overwhelmingly male activity. More than 68 percent of all murders involve a male victim and a male perpetrator, and in only 2.2 percent of homicides are both the offender and the victim female.[34] Only 13 percent of the national jail population and 7 percent of the national prison population are female, and in 2012 only 26 percent of all arrests involved women.[35]

The statistics cited above fail to convey the startling rate at which the female presence in the criminal justice system has been increasing. For example, the male arrest rate for aggravated assault was about the same in 2009 as it was in 1980. During that same time period, the female arrest rate for aggravated assault doubled.[36] In 1970, there were about 6,000 women in federal and state prisons. In 2012, even after four years of decreases, there were almost 109,000.[37] There are two possible explanations for these increases. Either (1) the life circumstances and behaviors of women have changed dramatically in the past forty years, or (2) the criminal justice system's attitude toward women has changed over that time period.[38]

LEARNING OBJECTIVE **4** Discuss the prevailing explanation for the rising number of women being incarcerated in the United States.

In the 1970s, when female crime rates started surging upward, many observers accepted the former explanation. "You can't get involved in a bar fight if you're not allowed in the bar," said criminologist and feminist theorist Freda Adler in 1975.[39] It has become clear, however, that a significant percentage of women arrested are involved in a narrow band of wrongdoing, mostly drug- and alcohol-related offenses or property crimes.[40] Research shows that as recently as the 1980s, many of the women now in prison would not have been arrested or would have received lighter sentences for their crimes.[41] Consequently, more scholars are convinced that rising female criminality is the result of a criminal justice system that is "more willing to incarcerate women."[42]

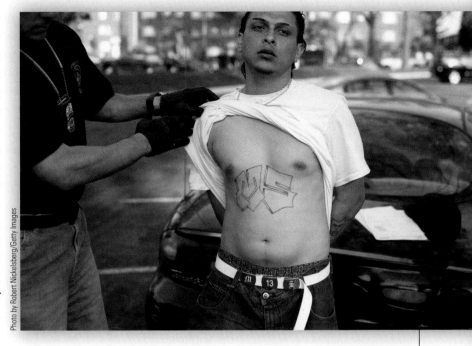

Photo by Robert Nickelsberg/Getty Images

A member of Prince George's County's Anti-Gang Unit makes an arrest during a crackdown on Hispanic gangs in Langley Park, Maryland. Why is it likely that crime experts will increase their focus on issues of Hispanic offenders and victims in the United States over the next few decades?

//// SELF ASSESSMENT

Fill in the blanks, and check your answers on page 65.

According to crime experts, some possible reasons for declining crime rates in the United States include improvements in _____ _____ and the _____ of America's population. In general, the crime trends have been less positive for _____ _____ than for whites, a situation that appears to be more directly linked to _____ level than to race or ethnicity. The number of women in prison has _____ dramatically over the past four decades.

WHAT CAUSES CRIME?

Several years ago, a judge in Cook County, Illinois, found that Janet Thies-Keogh was not legally responsible for suffocating her infant son to death. During the trial, mental health professionals testified that Thies-Keogh was suffering from *postpartum depression* at the time of the killing. This temporary illness, believed to be caused partly by bodily changes that women experience after childbirth, triggers abnormal behavior in a small percentage of new mothers.[43]

The study of crime, or **criminology,** is rich with different reasons as to why people commit crimes. They range from mental illness to violent video games to low self-control. In this section, we discuss the most influential of these explanations put forth by *criminologists,* or researchers who study the causes of crime.

Correlation and Causation

In the study of criminology, it is important to first understand the difference between *correlation* and *causation*. **Correlation** between two variables means that they tend to vary together. **Causation,** in contrast, means that one variable is responsible for the change in the other. In a number of cases, new mothers who kill their children have been found to suffer from postpartum depression. Therefore, statistically, there may be a correlation between postpartum depression and infanticide. The condition does not, however, *cause* violent behavior. Indeed, very few of the millions of mothers with postpartum

Criminology The scientific study of crime and the causes of criminal behavior.

Correlation The relationship between two measurements or behaviors that tend to move together in the same direction.

Causation The relationship in which a change in one measurement or behavior creates a recognizable change in another measurement or behavior.

Theory An explanation of a happening or circumstance that is based on observation, experimentation, and reasoning.

Hypothesis A possible explanation for an observed occurrence that can be tested by further investigation.

Rational Choice Theory A school of criminology that holds that wrongdoers weigh the possible benefits of criminal or delinquent activity against the expected costs of being apprehended.

Discuss the difference between a hypothesis and a theory in the context of criminology. **LEARNING OBJECTIVE 5**

depression pose a threat to their children. Rather, it is one variable that may contribute to violent behavior when combined with other variables.[44]

So, correlation does not equal causation. Such is the quandary for criminologists. We can say that there is a correlation between many factors and criminal behavior, but it is quite difficult to prove that the factors directly cause criminal behavior. Consequently, the question that is the underpinning of criminology—what causes crime?—has yet to be definitively answered.

The Role of Theory

Criminologists have uncovered a wealth of information concerning a different, and more practically applicable, inquiry: Given a certain set of circumstances, why do individuals commit criminal acts? This information has allowed criminologists to develop a number of *theories* concerning the causes of crime.

Most of us tend to think of a *theory* as some sort of guess or a statement that is lacking in credibility. In the academic world, and therefore for our purposes, a **theory** is an explanation of a happening or circumstance that is based on observation, experimentation, and reasoning. Scientific and academic researchers observe facts and their consequences to develop *hypotheses* about what will occur when a similar fact pattern is present in the future. A **hypothesis** is a proposition that can be tested by researchers or observers to determine if it is valid. If enough authorities find the hypothesis valid, it will be accepted as a theory. See Figure 2.5 alongside for an example of this process, known as the *scientific method,* in action.

Criminological theories are primarily concerned with attempting to determine the reasons for criminal behavior, but they also provide practical guidance for law enforcement, the courts, and corrections officials. In the remainder of this section, we examine the mostly widely recognized of these theories, starting with one that relies on freedom of choice.

The Brain and the Body

Perhaps the most basic answer to the question of why a person commits a crime is that he or she makes a willful decision to do so. This is the underpinning of the **rational choice theory** of crime, summed up by criminologist James Q. Wilson (1931–2012) as follows:

> At any given moment, a person can choose between committing a crime and not committing it. The consequences of committing a crime consist of rewards (what psychologists call "reinforcers") and punishments; the consequences of not committing the crime also entail gains and losses. The larger the ratio of the net rewards of crime to the net rewards of [not committing a crime], the greater the tendency to commit a crime.[45]

FIGURE 2.5 **The Scientific Method**

The scientific method is a process through which researchers test the accuracy of a hypothesis. This simple example provides an idea of how the scientific method works.

 Observation: I left my home at 7:00 this morning, and I was on time for class.

 Hypothesis: If I leave home at 7:00 every morning, then I will never be late for class.
(Hypotheses are often presented in this "If . . . , then . . ." format.)

 Test: For three straight weeks, I left home at 7:00 every morning. Not one time was I late for class.

 Verification: Four of my neighbors have the same morning class. They agree that they are never late if they leave by 7:00 A.M.

 Theory: As long as I leave home at 7:00 A.M., I don't have to worry about being late for class.

 Prediction: Tomorrow morning I'll leave at 7:00, and I will be on time for my class.

Note that even a sound theory supported by the scientific method, such as this one, does not *prove* that the prediction will be correct. Other factors not accounted for in the test and verification stages, such as an unexpected traffic accident, may disprove the theory. Predictions based on complex theories, such as the criminological ones we will be discussing in this chapter, are often challenged in such a manner.

In other words, a person, before committing a crime weighs (perhaps subconsciously) the benefits (which may be money, in the case of a robbery) against the costs (the possibility of being caught and going to prison or jail). If the perceived benefits are greater than the potential costs, the person is more likely to commit the crime.

"THRILL OFFENDERS" Expanding on rational choice theory, sociologist Jack Katz has stated that the "rewards" of crime may be sensual as well as financial. The inherent danger of criminal activity, according to Katz, increases the "rush" a criminal experiences on successfully committing a crime. Katz labels the rewards of this "rush" the *seduction of crime*.[46] For example, one of the three teenagers charged with randomly and fatally shooting a jogger in Duncan, Oklahoma, on August 16, 2013, told police that he and his friends were "bored and didn't have anything to do, so we killed somebody."[47] (See photo alongside.) Katz believes that such seemingly "senseless" crimes can be explained by rational choice theory only if the intrinsic (inner) reward of the crime itself is considered.

AP Images/Sue Ogrocki

Chancey Luna, standing, and Michael Jones, sitting, are two of the three "bored" teenagers charged with fatally shooting Australian Christopher Lane in Duncan, Oklahoma, on August 16, 2013. How is the assumption that some people commit crimes for the "thrill of it" consistent with rational choice theory?

RATIONAL CHOICE THEORY AND PUBLIC POLICY The theory that wrongdoers choose to commit crimes is a cornerstone of the American criminal justice system. Because crime is seen as the end result of a series of rational choices, policymakers have reasoned that severe punishment can deter criminal activity by adding another variable to the decision-making process. Supporters of the death penalty—now used by thirty-two states and the federal government—emphasize its deterrent effects, and legislators historically have used harsh mandatory sentences in their attempts to reduce illegal drug use and trafficking.

TRAIT THEORIES OF CRIME If society is willing to punish crimes that are the result of a rational decision-making process, what should be its response to criminal behavior that is irrational or even unintentional? What if, for example, a schoolteacher who made sexual advances to young girls, including his stepdaughter, could prove that his wrongdoing was actually caused by an egg-sized tumor in his brain?[48]

Somewhat in contrast to rational choice theory, *trait theories* suggest that certain *biological* or *psychological* traits in individuals could incline them toward criminal behavior given a certain set of circumstances. **Biology** is a very broad term that refers to the scientific study of living organisms, while **psychology** pertains more specifically to the study of the mind and its processes. "All behavior is biological," pointed out geneticist David C. Rowe. "All behavior is represented in the brain, in its biochemistry, electrical activity, structure, and growth and decline."[49]

Biology The science of living organisms, including their structure, function, growth, and origin.

Psychology The scientific study of mental processes and behavior.

Genetics and Crime Criminologists who study biological theories of crime often focus on the effect that *genes* have on human behavior. Genes are coded sequences of DNA that control every aspect of our biology, from the color of our eyes and hair to the type of emotions we have. Every person's genetic makeup is determined by genes inherited from his or her parents. Consequently, when scientists study ancestral or evolutionary developments, they are engaging in **genetics,** a branch of biology that deals with traits that are passed from one generation to another through genes.

Research has shown a genetic basis for such traits as attention deficit hyperactivity disorder (ADHD) and low self-control, both of which have been linked to antisocial behavior and crime.[50] Keep in mind, however, that no single gene or trait has been proved to *cause* criminality. As a result, the best that genetics can do is raise the possibility for a predisposition toward aggression or violence in an individual based on her or his family background.

Hormones and Aggression One trait theory holds that *biochemistry,* or the chemistry of living matter, can influence criminal behavior. For example, chemical messengers known as **hormones** have been the subject of much criminological study. Criminal activity in males has been linked to elevated levels of hormones—specifically, **testosterone,** which controls secondary sex characteristics and has been associated with traits of aggression. Testing of inmate populations shows that those incarcerated for violent crimes exhibit higher testosterone levels than do other prisoners.[51] Elevated testosterone levels have also been used to explain the age-crime relationship, as the average testosterone level of men under the age of twenty-eight is double that of men between thirty-one and sixty-six years old.[52]

The Brain and Crime The study of the nervous system and brain activity, or *neurophysiology,* has also found a place in criminology. Indeed, Jessica Wolpaw Reyes, an economist at Amherst College in Massachusetts, uses neurophysiology to help explain the drop in crime rates over the past two decades (discussed earlier in the chapter).

Numerous studies have shown that exposure to lead damages the brains of children, causing them to have lower IQs, less impulse control, and a propensity for violent behavior. In the late 1970s, the federal government banned lead in gasoline and many types of paint. A generation of lead-free children has reached adulthood since then, and, Reyes believes, its nonviolent tendencies are responsible for half of the recent drop in violent crime rates.[53]

Mental Illness and Crime More than half of all prison and jail inmates in the United States have mental health problems, with smaller percentages suffering from severe brain disorders.[54] Many experts believe that Aaron Alexis, whose shooting rampage at the Washington, D.C., Navy Yard we discussed at the beginning of this chapter, should have been diagnosed with *schizophrenia,* a chronic brain disorder that can lead to erratic, uncontrollable behavior.[55] Persons suffering from this disease are at an unusually high risk for committing suicide or harming others. Psychiatrist E. Fuller Torrey estimates that schizophrenics commit about a thousand homicides each year.[56]

Further research shows that even moderate use of alcohol or drugs increases the chances that a schizophrenic will behave violently.[57] Still, it is important to note that about 2.4 million Americans—1 percent of the adult population—have been diagnosed with schizophrenia, and the vast majority of them will never become criminal offenders. That is, there may be a correlation between schizophrenia and violence, but the brain disorder cannot be said to cause violence.

Explain how brain-scanning technology is able to help scientists determine if an individual is at risk for criminal offending.

Using various techniques, from X-ray technology to magnetic resonance imaging (MRI) to measuring oxygen flow, specialists have become quite skilled at mapping the human brain. Among other uses, these approaches can identify functional abnormalities and physical deformities in the brain that correlate with violent behavior.

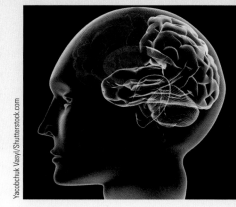

For example, violent criminals tend to have impaired prefrontal cortexes—the part of the brain that manages our impulses and emotions. Furthermore, brain scanning has shown that criminal behavior is often associated with a smaller-than-average amygdala, a cranial region that has been linked to moral decision making. Finally, Kent Kiehl of the University of New Mexico recently mapped the brains of ninety-six offenders in New Mexico's prison system. Kiehl found that, in the four years after these men had been released from prison, those with low activity in the anterior cingulate cortex were twice as likely to commit a crime as those with high activity in this area of the brain.

Thinking about Brain Science and Crime

Brain scans cannot *predict* future criminal offending. They can only indicate that a *possibility* exists for future criminal offending. With this proviso in mind, what use should the criminal justice system make of brain-mapping technology, if any?

PSYCHOLOGY AND CRIME Like biological theories of crime, psychological theories of crime operate under the assumption that individuals have traits that make them more or less predisposed to criminal activity. To a certain extent, however, psychology relies more heavily on abstract ideas than does biology. Even Sigmund Freud (1856–1939), perhaps the most influential of all psychologists, considered the operations of the mind to be, like an iceberg, mostly hidden.

One influential branch of psychology—*social psychology*—focuses on human behavior in the context of how human beings relate to and influence one another. Social psychology rests on the assumption that the way we view ourselves is shaped to a large degree by how we think others view us. Generally, we act in the same manner as those we like or admire because we want them to like or admire us. Thus, social psychology tries to explain the influence of crowds on individual behavior.

About three decades ago, psychologist Philip Zimbardo highlighted the power of group behavior in dramatic fashion. Zimbardo randomly selected some Stanford University undergraduate students to act as "guards" and other students to act as "inmates" in an artificial prison environment. Before long, the students began to act as if these designations were real, with the "guards" physically mistreating the "inmates," who rebelled with equal violence. Within six days, Zimbardo was forced to discontinue the experiment out of fear for its participants' safety.[58] One of the basic assumptions of social psychology is that people are able to justify improper or even criminal behavior by convincing themselves that it is actually acceptable behavior. This delusion, researchers have found, is much easier to accomplish with the support of others behaving in the same manner.[59]

Yacobchuk Vasyl/Shutterstock.com

Stuart Isett/Bloomberg via Getty Images

TRAIT THEORIES AND PUBLIC POLICY Whereas rational choice theory justifies punishing wrongdoers, biological and psychological views of criminality suggest that antisocial behavior should be identified and treated before it manifests itself in first-time or further criminal activity. Though the focus on treatment diminished slightly in the 1990s, rehabilitation practices in corrections have made somewhat of a comeback over the past few years. The primary motivation for this new outlook, as we will see in Chapters 10 through 12, is the pressing need to divert nonviolent offenders from the nation's overburdened prison and jail system.

Police struggle to control anticapitalism protesters in Seattle, Washington. How does social psychology help explain acts of violence or disorder by large groups of people?

Bad Neighborhoods and Other Economic Disadvantages

After the bodies of three murdered women were found in East Cleveland on July 22, 2013, observers seemed to draw a connection between the crime and the neighborhood where it took place. The suburb lost 40 percent of its population between 1990 and 2011, and nearly one in three of its homes is boarded up and abandoned. The area is also racked by unemployment and high levels of gang activity. "This is what happens when you have poverty," said Ohio governor John R. Kasich.[60] Indeed, for decades, criminologists focusing on **sociology** have argued that neighborhood conditions are perhaps the most important variable in predicting criminal behavior.

SOCIAL DISORGANIZATION THEORY In the early twentieth century, juvenile crime researchers Clifford Shaw and Henry McKay popularized sociological explanations for crime with their **social disorganization theory.** Shaw and McKay studied various high-crime neighborhoods in Chicago and discovered certain "zones" that exhibited high rates of crime. These zones were characterized by "disorganization," or a breakdown of the traditional institutions of social control such as family, school systems, and local businesses. In contrast, in the city's "organized" communities, residents had developed certain agreements about fundamental values and norms.

Shaw and McKay found that residents in high-crime neighborhoods had to a large degree abandoned these basic values and norms. Also, a lack of social controls had led to increased levels of antisocial, or criminal, behavior.[61] According to social disorganization theory, factors that lead to crime in these neighborhoods are

1. High levels of high school dropouts,
2. Chronic unemployment,
3. Deteriorating buildings and other infrastructures, and
4. Concentrations of single-parent families.

(See Figure 2.6 that follows for an illustration of social disorganization theory.)

STRAIN THEORY Another self-perpetuating aspect of disorganized neighborhoods is that once residents gain the financial means to leave a high-crime community, they usually do so. Most Americans have similar life goals, which include gaining a certain measure of wealth and financial freedom. **Strain theory** suggests that the means of

Sociology The study of the development and functioning of groups of people who live together within a society.

Social Disorganization Theory The theory that deviant behavior is more likely in communities where social institutions such as the family, schools, and the criminal justice system fail to exert control over the population.

Strain Theory The theory that crime is the result of frustration and anger felt by individuals who cannot reach their financial and personal goals through legitimate means.

attaining these goals, however, are not universally available. Many citizens do not have access to the education or training necessary for financial success. This often results in frustration and anger, or *strain*. Sociologist Robert K. Merton (1910–2003) believed that strain is caused by a social structure in which all citizens have similar goals without equal means to achieve them.[62] One way to alleviate this strain is to gain wealth by the means that are available to the residents of disorganized communities: drug trafficking, burglary, and other criminal activities.

In the 1990s, Robert Agnew of Emory University in Atlanta, Georgia, updated this line of thinking with his *general strain theory*, or GST.[63] Agnew reasoned that of all "strained" individuals, very few actually turn to crime to relieve the strain. GST tries to determine what factors, when combined with strain, actually lead to criminal activity. By the early 2000s, Agnew and other criminologists had settled on the factor of *negative emotionality*, a term used to cover personality traits of those who are easily frustrated, quick to lose their tempers, and disposed to blame others for their own problems.[64] Thus, GST mixes strain theory with this aspect of psychological theories of crime.

SOCIAL CONFLICT THEORIES Strain theory suggests that the unequal structure of our society is, in part, to blame for criminal behavior. This argument forms the bedrock of

POLICY.CJ

The link between unemployment and crime is one that criminologists have long studied and debated. After searching online for **unemployment and crime rates**, write a full paragraph giving your own opinion on the subject. Then, use the Internet to find one example of a government policy to reduce unemployment that would also impact crime rates.

FIGURE 2.6 The Stages of Social Disorganization Theory

Social disorganization theory holds that crime is related to the environmental pressures that exist in certain communities or neighborhoods. These areas are marked by the desire of many of their inhabitants to "get out" at the first possible opportunity. Consequently, residents tend to ignore the important institutions in the community, such as businesses and education, causing further erosion of social controls and an increase in the conditions that lead to crime.

The Problem: Poverty
The Consequences:
Formation of isolated impoverished areas, racial and ethnic discrimination, lack of legitimate economic opportunities.

Leads to

The Problem: Social Disorganization
The Consequences:
Breakdown of institutions such as school and the family.

Leads to

The Problem: Breakdown of Social Controls
The Consequences:
Replacement of family and educators by peer groups as primary influences on youth; formation of gangs.

Leads to

The Problem: Criminal Careers
The Consequences:
The majority of youths "age out" of crime, start families, and, if they can, leave the neighborhood. Those who remain still adhere to the norms of the impoverished-area culture and may become career criminals.

Leads to

The Problem: Cultural Transmission
The Consequences:
The younger juveniles follow the model of delinquent behavior set by their older siblings and friends, establishing a deep-rooted impoverished-area culture.

Leads to

The Problem: Criminal Areas
The Consequences:
Rise of crime in poverty-stricken neighborhood; social acceptance of delinquent behavior by youths; shunning of area by outside investment and support.

Source: Adapted from Larry J. Siegel, *Criminology*, 10th ed. (Belmont, CA: Thomson/Wadsworth, 2009), 180.

Two law enforcement officers investigate a murder in the Desire neighborhood of New Orleans. How would a criminologist who advocates social conflict theories of criminal behavior explain high crime rates in low-income neighborhoods such as Desire?

social conflict theories of crime. These theories, which entered mainstream criminology in the 1960s, hold capitalism responsible for high levels of violence and crime because of the disparity of income that it encourages.

According to social conflict theory, the poor commit property crimes for reasons of need, and because, as members of a capitalist society, they desire the same financial rewards as everybody else. They commit violent crimes because of the frustration and rage they feel when these rewards seem unattainable. Laws, instead of reflecting the values of society as a whole, reflect only the values of the segment of society that has achieved power and is willing to use the criminal justice system as a tool to keep that power.[65] Thus, the harsh penalties for "lower-class" crimes such as burglary can be seen as a means of protecting the privileges of the "haves" from the aspirations of the "have-nots."

Life Lessons and Criminal Behavior

Some criminologists find class theories of crime overly narrow. Surveys that ask people directly about their criminal behavior have shown that the criminal instinct is pervasive in middle- and upper-class communities, although it may be expressed differently. Anybody, these criminologists argue, has the potential to act out criminal behavior, regardless of class, race, or gender.

SOCIAL PROCESS THEORIES Philip Zimbardo conducted a well-known, if rather unscientific, experiment to show the broad potential for misbehavior. The psychologist placed an abandoned automobile with its hood up on the campus of Stanford University. The car remained in place, untouched, for a week. Then, Zimbardo smashed the car's window with a sledgehammer. Within minutes, passersby had joined in the destruction of the automobile, eventually stripping its valuable parts.[66]

Social process theories function on the same basis as Zimbardo's "interdependence of decisions experiment": the potential for criminal behavior exists in everyone and will be realized depending on an individual's interaction with various institutions and processes of society. Social process theories include (1) learning theory and (2) control theory.

Social Conflict Theories
A school of criminology that views criminal behavior as the result of class conflict.

Social Process Theories A school of criminology that considers criminal behavior to be the predictable result of a person's interaction with his or her environment.

Learning Theory The theory that delinquents and criminals must be taught both the practical and the emotional skills necessary to participate in illegal activity.

Learning Theory Popularized by Edwin Sutherland in the 1940s, **learning theory** contends that criminal activity is a learned behavior. In other words, a criminal is taught both the practical methods of crime (such as how to pick a lock) and the psychological aspects of crime (how to deal with the guilt of wrongdoing).

Sutherland's *theory of differential association* holds that individuals are exposed to the values of family and peers such as school friends or co-workers. If the dominant values that a person is exposed to favor criminal behavior, then that person is more likely to mimic such behavior.[67] Sutherland's focus on the importance of family relations in this area is underscored by more recent research showing that sons of fathers who have been incarcerated are at an increased risk of delinquency and arrest.[68]

More recently, learning theory has been expanded to include the growing influence of the media. In the latest in a long series of studies, researchers released data in 2013 showing that children or adolescents who watch "excessive" amounts of violent television content face an elevated risk of exhibiting antisocial behavior such as criminality in early adulthood.[69] Such findings have spurred a number of legislative attempts to curb violence on television. Washington, D.C., Navy Yard gunman Aaron Alexis was, according to acquaintances, an avid player of violent "zombie" video games.[70] Three years prior to Alexis's shooting spree, discussed at the beginning of this chapter, the issue of whether such games can be blamed for violent behavior was addressed by the United States Supreme Court, as shown in the feature *Landmark Cases—Brown v. EMA* that follows.

LANDMARK CASES:
Brown v. Entertainment Merchants Association (EMA)

Reacting to studies linking violent video games to violent behavior in children, in 2006 then–California governor Arnold Schwarzenegger signed a bill prohibiting the sale or rental of games that portray "killing, maiming, dismembering or sexually assaulting an image of a human being" to people younger than eighteen years old. The law imposed a $1,000 fine on violators. Immediately, video game sellers sued the state, saying it had violated their constitutional right to freedom of speech. After two lower courts accepted this argument and invalidated California's law, the issue finally arrived before the United States Supreme Court.

Brown v. EMA
United States Supreme Court
559 S.Ct. 1448 (2010)

IN THE WORDS OF THE COURT . . .
JUSTICE SCALIA, MAJORITY OPINION

＊　＊　＊　＊

Like the protected books, plays, and movies that preceded them, video games communicate ideas—and even social messages—through many familiar literary devices (such as characters, dialogue, plot, and music) and through features distinctive to the medium (such as the player's interaction with the virtual world). That suffices to confer First Amendment protection. Under our Constitution, "esthetic and moral judgments about art and literature * * * are for the individual to make, not for the Government to decree, even with the mandate or approval of a majority."

＊　＊　＊　＊

No doubt a State possesses legitimate power to protect children from harm, but that does not include a free-floating power to restrict the ideas to which children may be exposed.

＊　＊　＊　＊

California relies primarily on * * * research psychologists whose studies purport to show a connection between exposure to violent video games and harmful effects on children. These studies have been rejected by every court to consider them, and with good reason: They do not prove that violent video games *cause* minors to act aggressively (which would at least be a beginning). Instead, "[n]early all of the research is based on correlation, not evidence of causation * * * ." They show at best some correlation between exposure to violent entertainment and minuscule real-world effects, such as children's feeling more aggressive or making louder noises in the few minutes after playing a violent game than after playing a nonviolent game.

DECISION
In the absence of any provable negative effects on minors from violent video games, the Court ruled that California's ban was unconstitutional and therefore could not be enforced.

FOR CRITICAL ANALYSIS
If states have the "legitimate power" to "protect children from harm," why did the Court invalidate California's violent video game law? How did Justice Scalia use the concepts of *causation* and *correlation* to support the Court's decision? (You can review those terms in our discussion earlier in the chapter.)

Control Theory Criminologist Travis Hirschi focuses on the reasons why individuals do not engage in criminal acts, rather than why they do. According to Hirschi, social bonds promote conformity to social norms. The stronger these social bonds—which include attachment to, commitment to, involvement with, and belief in societal values—the less likely that any individual will commit a crime.[71] **Control theory** holds that although we all have the potential to commit crimes, most of us are dissuaded from doing so because we care about the opinions of our family and peers.

Janet Lauritsen, a criminologist at the University of Missouri–St. Louis, believes that familial control factors are more important than sociological disadvantages when it comes to criminal behavior. Lauritsen found that adolescents residing in two-parent households were victims of crime at similar rates, regardless of the levels of disadvantage in the neighborhoods in which they lived. By contrast, adolescents from single-parent homes who lived in highly disorganized neighborhoods were victimized at much higher rates than their counterparts in more stable locales. In Lauritsen's opinion, the support of a two-parent household offers crucial protection for children, whatever the condition of their neighborhood.[72]

LIFE COURSE THEORIES OF CRIME If crime is indeed learned behavior, some criminologists are asking, shouldn't we be focusing on early childhood—the time when humans do the most learning? Practitioners of **life course criminology** believe that lying, stealing, bullying, and other conduct problems that occur in childhood are the strongest predictors of future criminal behavior and have been seriously undervalued in the examination of why crime occurs.[73]

Self-Control Theory Focusing on childhood behavior raises the question of whether conduct problems established at a young age can be changed over time. Michael Gottfredson and Travis Hirschi, whose 1990 publication *A General Theory of Crime* is one of the foundations of life course criminology, think not.[74] Gottfredson and Hirschi believe that criminal behavior is linked to "low self-control," a personality trait that is formed before a child reaches the age of ten and can usually be attributed to poor parenting.[75]

In general, someone who has low self-control is

1. Impulsive,
2. Thrill-seeking, and
3. Likely to solve problems with violence rather than her or his intellect.

Gottfredson and Hirschi think that once low self-control has been established, it will persist. In other words, childhood behavioral problems are not "solved" by positive developments later in life, such as healthy personal relationships or a good job.[76] Thus, these two criminologists ascribe to what has been called the *continuity theory of crime*, which essentially says that once negative behavior patterns have been established, they cannot be changed.

The Possibility of Change Not all of those who subscribe to life course criminology follow the continuity theory. Robert Sampson and John Laub have gathered a great deal of data showing, in their opinion, that offenders may experience "turning points," when they are able to veer off the road from a life of crime.[77]

Describe the importance of early childhood behavior for those who subscribe to self-control theory. **LEARNING OBJECTIVE 7**

A good deal of research in this area has concentrated on the positive impact of getting married, having children, and finding a job,[78] but other turning points are also being explored. John F. Frana of Indiana State University and Ryan D. Schroeder of the University of Louisville argue that military service can act as a "rehabilitative agent."[79] Several researchers have studied the role that religion and spirituality can play as "hooks for change."[80] Furthermore, particularly for drug abusers, the death of a loved one or friend from shared criminal behavior can provide a powerful incentive to discontinue that behavior. (See *Mastering Concepts* that follows for a review of theories discussed in this chapter so far.)

MASTERING CONCEPTS
THE CAUSES OF CRIME

RATIONAL CHOICE THEORY

Key Concept: Crime is the result of rational choices made by those who decide to engage in criminal activity for the rewards—financial and otherwise—that it offers.

Example: A Texas judge sentenced Jimmy Billingsley to fifteen years in prison for knowingly infecting a woman with the HIV virus. The victim testified that Billingley "insisted on having unprotected sex."

TRAIT THEORIES

Key Concept: Criminal behavior is explained by the biological and psychological attributes of an individual.

Example: A Polk County, Tennessee, jury acquitted Bradley Waldroup of first degree murder after hearing testimony that he suffered from a genetic mutation that predisposed him to violence. This finding allowed Waldroup to avoid a life sentence in prison.

SOCIOLOGICAL THEORIES

Key Concept: Crime is not something one is "born to do." Rather, crime is the result of the social conditions such as poverty, poor schools, unemployment, and discrimination with which a person lives.

Example: Researchers at Boston's Northeastern University estimate that, on any given day, about one in ten young male high school dropouts is in prison or jail, whereas only one in thirty-five young male high school graduates is incarcerated.

SOCIAL CONFLICT THEORIES

Key Concept: Through criminal laws, the dominant members of society control the minority members, using institutions such as the police, courts, and prisons as tools of oppression.

Example: In 2011, of the 684,330 people stopped and searched by New York City police officers, 87 percent were African American or Hispanic. As those groups comprise only about 25 percent and 28 percent of the city's population, respectively, the police force opened itself to charges of racial profiling, covered in Chapter 6.

SOCIAL PROCESS THEORIES

Key Concept: Family, friends, and peers have the greatest impact on an individual's behavior, and the interactions with these groups ultimately determine whether a person will become involved in criminal behavior.

Example: According to the U.S. Department of Justice, nearly 50 percent of inmates in state prisons have relatives who have also been incarcerated.

LIFE COURSE THEORIES

Key Concept: Criminal and antisocial behavior is evident at each stage of a person's life. By focusing on such behavior in early childhood, criminologists may be able to better understand and predict the offending patterns that emerge as a person grows older.

Example: After interviewing 261 inmates serving time for violent crimes in state prison, criminologists found that more than half had behaved with cruelty toward animals when they were children.

VICTIMS OF CRIME

Since its founding, criminology has focused almost exclusively on one-half of the crime equation: the offender. If you review our discussion of criminology up to this point, you will find little mention of the other half: the victim. Indeed, only in the past several decades has *victimology* become an essential component of criminology. This growing emphasis on the victim has had a profound impact on the police, the courts, and corrections administrators in this country. Accordingly, Andrew Karmen, a professor of sociology at the John Jay College of Criminal Justice in New York City, has defined **victimology** as the study of "relationships between victims and offenders [and] the interactions between victims and the criminal justice system."[81]

The Risks of Victimization

Anybody can be a victim of crime. This does not mean, however, that every person is at an equal risk of being victimized. For instance, residents of neighborhoods with heavy concentrations of payday lending businesses are targeted by criminals at unusually high rates.[82] To better explain the circumstances surrounding this type of victimization, criminologists Larry Cohen and Marcus Felson devised the *routine activities theory*. According to Cohen and Felson, most criminal acts require the following:

Explain the routine activities theory of victimization. LEARNING **8** OBJECTIVE

1. A likely offender.
2. A suitable target (a person or an object).
3. The absence of a capable guardian—that is, any person (not necessarily a law enforcement agent) whose presence or proximity prevents a crime from happening.[83]

When these three factors are present, the likelihood of crime rises. Cohen and Felson cite routine activities theory in explaining the link between payday lenders and crime. People who use payday lenders often leave those establishments with large sums of cash, late at night or during weekends when there is less street traffic. Consequently, they act as suitable targets, attracting likely offenders to neighborhoods where the payday lenders are located.[84]

REPEAT VICTIMIZATION Cohen and Felson also hypothesize that offenders attach "values" to suitable targets. The higher the value, the more likely that target is going to be the subject of a crime.[85] A gold watch, for example, would obviously have a higher value for a thief than a plastic watch and therefore is more likely to be stolen. Similarly, people who are perceived to be weak or unprotected can have high value for criminals. Law enforcement officials in southern Florida, for example, believe that undocumented immigrants in the area have high victimization rates because criminals know they are afraid to report crimes to authorities for fear of being removed from the country.

Victimology A school of criminology that studies why certain people are the victims of crimes and the optimal role for victims in the criminal justice system.

Resources such as the National Crime Victimization Survey provide criminologists with an important tool for determining which types of people are most valued as potential victims. Statistics clearly show that a relatively small number of victims are involved in a disproportionate number of crimes. These findings support an approach to crime analysis known as **repeat victimization.** This theory is based on the premise that certain populations—mostly low-income residents of urban areas—are more likely to be victims of crimes than are others and, therefore, past victimization is a strong predictor of future victimization.[86]

THE VICTIM-OFFENDER CONNECTION Not only does past victimization seem to increase the risk of future victimization, but so does past criminal behavior. "The notion that [violent crimes] are random bolts of lightning, which is the commonly held image, is not the reality at all," says David Kennedy, a professor at New York's John Jay College of Criminal Justice.[87]

Kennedy's point is made by Figure 2.7 that follows, which identifies young African American males from urban neighborhoods as the most common victims of crimes. This demographic, as we have discussed, is also at the highest risk for criminal behavior. Increasingly, law enforcement agencies are applying the lessons of repeat victimization and other victim studies to concentrate their attention on "hot spots" of crime, a strategy we address in Chapter 5.

Women as Crime Victims

The most striking aspect of women as victims of crime is the extent to which such victimization involves a prior relationship. According to the National Crime Victimization Survey, a male is twice as likely as a female to experience violence at the hands of a stranger.[88] With regard to intimate partner violence—involving a spouse, ex-spouse, boyfriend, girlfriend, ex-boyfriend, or ex-girlfriend—the gender difference is even more pronounced. Women are about five times more likely than men to be victims of intimate partner violence.[89]

SEXUAL VIOLENCE In general, about six of every ten crimes in the United States are committed by someone known to the victim. Those crimes that usually involve strangers, such as robbery and assault, most often target male victims. In contrast, women have a greater chance of being victimized in nonstranger crimes, such as sexual assault.[90] Indeed, women are the victims in 86 percent of all intimate partner violence prosecutions.[91] The highest rate of victimization occurs among women between the ages of twelve and thirty-four, and one study estimates that between one-fifth and one-quarter of female college students have experienced a rape or attempted rape.[92]

OTHER COMMON CRIMES AGAINST WOMEN Statistically, women are also at a greater risk than men of being

FIGURE 2.7 Crime Victims in the United States

According to the U.S. Department of Justice, African Americans, residents of urban areas, and people between the ages of eighteen and twenty-four are most likely to be victims of violent crime in this country.

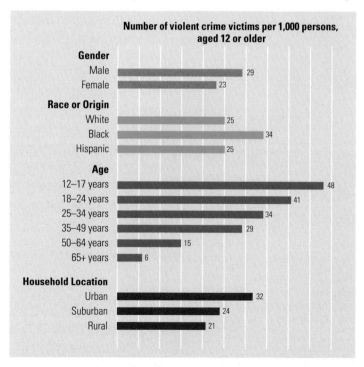

Source: Bureau of Justice Statistics, *Criminal Victimization, 2012* (Washington, D.C.: U.S. Department of Justice, October 2013), 8, 9.

Photo Courtesy of Anne Seymour

ANNE SEYMOUR

NATIONAL VICTIM ADVOCATE

The aspect of my job that I enjoy the most is my direct work with crime victims and survivors. These are people who have been severely traumatized by pain and suffering and loss, and I consider it a true honor to be able to assist them. I'll never forget the day I met a young survivor who had been abducted, beaten within an inch of her life, raped, and then left to die in the forest. This young woman became one of my closest friends, and I helped her to speak out in her state and at the national level. Every time she does so, she has a powerful impact on our society. So my help in turning a victim/survivor into a stellar victim advocate/activist began on the day I met her, and it continues.

Victim advocacy is one of the most exciting and rewarding careers you could ever embark on, though it is not one that you should get into because of the money. (Few victim advocates become rich doing this work!) Every day is unique and different, reflecting the people I assist and the colleagues with whom I interact. I am never, ever bored and never will be. AND I go to bed every single day knowing that I have done at least one thing—and often many more than one!—to promote social justice and to help someone who is hurting. It's an amazing feeling!

Social Media Career Tip Social media technologies are about connecting and sharing information—which means privacy is an important issue. Make sure you understand who can see the material you post and how you can control it. Facebook has numerous privacy settings, for example, as does Google+.

victims of **domestic violence.** This umbrella term covers a wide variety of maltreatment, including physical violence and psychological abuse, inflicted among family members and others in close relationships. Though government data show that women are significantly more likely to be victims of domestic violence than are men, these findings are not unquestioned. Men, many observers assume, are less likely to report abuse because of the social stigma surrounding female-on-male violence.[93]

Another crime that appears to mainly involve female victims is **stalking,** or a course of conduct directed at a person that would reasonably cause that person to feel fear. Such behavior includes unwanted phone calls, following or spying, and a wide range of online activity that we will address in Chapter 14. Stalkers target women at about three times the rate that they target men, and seven out of ten stalking victims have had some prior relationship with their stalkers.[94]

Mental Illness and Victimization

Those who suffer from mental illness are much more likely to be victims of crime than perpetrators. There are several reasons for this high victimization risk:

1. Mental illness often interferes with a person's ability to find and keep employment, and therefore leads to poverty, which, as we have seen, correlates with victimization.

2. The mentally ill are more likely to be homeless, a circumstance that leaves them particularly susceptible to crime.[95]

Domestic Violence
Maltreatment, including physical violence and psychological abuse, that occurs within a familial or other intimate relationship.

Stalking The criminal act of causing fear in a person by repeatedly subjecting that person to unwanted or threatening attention.

3. Mental illness can interfere with a person's ability to make prudent decisions in potentially dangerous situations, increasing her or his chances of being assaulted.[96]

A recent review of the subject found that rates of victimization among people with mental illnesses are up to 140 times higher than in the general population.[97]

Mental health advocates insist that increasing services such as treatment and temporary housing for American's mentally ill will reduce the harm they cause themselves and others. The prohibitive costs of such services, however, seem to guarantee that mental illness will continue to be a problem for the criminal justice system, and for society at large.

///// SELF ASSESSMENT

Fill in the blanks, and check your answers on page 65.

The _____ _____ theory predicts that a combination of factors concerning a victim's environment make that victim more susceptible to crime. The theory of _____ victimization holds that past victimization is a strong predictor of future victimization. Men are more likely than women to be victims of crimes committed by a _____. More so than other segments of society, the _____ _____ are more likely to be victims of crime than offenders.

THE LINK BETWEEN DRUGS AND CRIME

Earlier in this chapter, we discussed the difference between correlation and causation. As you may recall, criminologists are generally reluctant to declare that any one factor causes a certain result. Richard B. Felson of Penn State University and Keri B. Burchfield of Northern Illinois University, however, believe that alcohol consumption has a causal effect on crime victimization under certain circumstances.[98] Felson and Burchfield found that "frequent and heavy" drinkers are at a great risk of assault when they are drinking, but do not show abnormal rates of victimization when sober. They hypothesize that consuming alcohol leads to aggressive and offensive behavior, particularly in men, which in turn triggers violent reactions from others.

As we discussed in Chapter 1, about 24 million Americans regularly use illegal drugs such as marijuana and cocaine, with another 206 million using legal drugs such as alcohol and nicotine. In the following section, we will discuss why people use drugs, and what the consequences of drug use are for the criminal justice system.

The Criminology of Drug Use

At first glance, the reason people use drugs, including legal drugs such as alcohol, is obvious: such drugs give the user pleasure and provide a temporary escape for those who may feel tension or anxiety. Ultimately, though, such explanations are unsatisfactory because they fail to explain why some people use drugs while others do not.

THEORIES OF DRUG USE Several of the theories we discussed earlier in the chapter have been used by experts to explain drug use. *Social disorganization theory* holds that a lack of institutions of social control can cause people to become disaffiliated from mainstream society, causing them to turn to drugs. *Control theory* suggests that a lack of social controls, as provided by entities such as the family or school, can lead to antisocial behavior.

Discuss the connection between the learning process and the start of an individual's drug use.

LEARNING **9** OBJECTIVE

DRUGS AND THE LEARNING PROCESS Focusing on the question of why first-time drug users become habitual users, sociologist Howard Becker sees three factors in the learning process. He believes that first-time users

1. Learn the techniques of drug use.
2. Learn to perceive the pleasurable effects of drug use.
3. Learn to enjoy the social experience of drug use.[99]

Becker's assumptions are evident in the widespread belief that positive images of drug use in popular culture "teach" adolescents that such behavior is not only acceptable but desirable. The entertainment industry, in particular, has been criticized for glamorizing various forms of drug use.

Drug Addiction and Dependency

Another theory rests on the assumption that some people possess overly sensitive drug receptors in their brains and are therefore biologically disposed toward drug use.[100] Though there is little conclusive evidence that biological factors can explain initial drug experimentation, scientific research has provided a great deal of insight into patterns of long-term drug use.

Drug Abuse The use of drugs that results in physical or psychological problems for the user, as well as disruption of personal relationships and employment.

DRUG USE VS. DRUG ABUSE In particular, science has aided our understanding of the difference between drug *use* and drug *abuse*. **Drug abuse** can be defined as the use of any drug—licit or illicit—that causes either psychological or bodily harm to the abuser or to third parties. Just as most people who drink beer or wine avoid abusing alcohol, most users of illegal substances are not abusers. For most drugs except nicotine, only between 7 and 20 percent of all users suffer from compulsive abuse.[101]

Despite their relatively small numbers, drug abusers have a disparate impact on the drug market. The 20 percent of Americans, for example, who drink the most consume more than 80 percent of all alcoholic beverages sold in the United States. The data are similar for illicit substance abusers, leading to the conclusion that, to a large extent, abusers and addicts sustain the market for illegal drugs.

A young woman prepares to use heroin under a bridge in Portland, Maine. Do you think that drug abusers should be treated as criminals to be punished or as ill people in need of treatment? Explain your answer.

Cheryl Senter/The New York Times/Redux

ADDICTION BASICS The most extreme abusers are addicted to, or physically dependent on, a drug. To understand the basics of addiction and physical dependence, you must understand the role of *dopamine* in the brain. Dopamine is a neurotransmitter responsible for delivering pleasure signals to brain nerve endings in response to behaviors that make us feel good—such as eating good food or engaging in sex. The bloodstream delivers drugs to the area of the brain that produces dopamine, thereby triggering the production of a large amount of the substance in the brain.

Over time, the continued use of drugs physically changes the nerve endings, called *receptors*. To continue operating in the presence of large amounts of dopamine, the receptors become less sensitive, meaning that greater amounts of any particular drug are required to create the amount of dopamine needed for the same levels of pleasure. When the drug supply is cut off, the brain strongly feels the lack of dopamine stimulation, and the abuser suffers symptoms of withdrawal until the receptors readjust.[102]

Prescription Drugs Medical drugs that require a physician's permission for purchase.

The Drug-Crime Relationship

Of course, because many drugs are illegal, anybody who sells, uses, or in any way promotes the use of these drugs is, under most circumstances, breaking the law. The drug-crime relationship goes beyond the language of criminal drug statutes, however. As we will see throughout this textbook, the prosecution of illegal drug users and suppliers has been one of the primary factors in the enormous growth of the American correctional industry.

PRESCRIPTION DRUG ABUSE Although marijuana continues to be the most widely abused drug in the United States, **prescription drugs** are next on the list. These powerful drugs—which include pain relievers, tranquilizers, stimulants, and sedatives—are not available for sale "over the counter." Rather, they can be obtained only with the permission of a licensed healthcare professional.

According to the National Survey on Drug Use and Health, 2.4 million people over the age of twelve used prescription drugs for nonmedical purposes for the first time in 2012.[103] In total, the number of people addicted to painkillers increased from 936,000 in 2002 to 2.1 million in 2011. Prescription drugs are also implicated in more than half of the nearly 40,000 fatal overdoses that occur in the country each year.[104]

METH AND HEROIN Legal over-the-counter substances are the main ingredients in the manufacture of *methamphetamine (meth),* a highly addictive stimulant of the central nervous system. Meth is relatively easy to make in home laboratories using the ingredients of common cold medicines and farm chemicals. Consequently, the drug provides a "cheap high" and has become the scourge of many poor rural areas, particularly in the western half of the United States.

Even when law enforcement efforts to reduce prescription drug abuse prove successful, unintended consequences can temper the accomplishment. For example, over the past decade, painkiller abuse has dropped dramatically in New England, thanks to restrictions on sales of the products. As a consequence, however, drug abusers have turned to *heroin,* a highly addictive narcotic that, according to one observer, is easier to get in some parts of the region than "a UPS delivery."[105] In 2012, twenty-one people died from heroin overdoses in Maine (up from seven in 2011), and forty people suffered a similar fate in New Hampshire (up from seven in 2002).[106]

An employee at Colorado's Dixie Elixir fills a jar with watermelon-flavored cannabis drops.

■ Why might such fruit-flavored "edibles"—which are eaten rather than smoked—make legal marijuana products more attractive to underage users?

Andrew Hetherington/Redux

MARIJUANA LEGALIZATION How would the link between certain illegal drugs and crime change if those drugs were legalized? That is, what if a particular illegal drug was treated in the same manner as alcohol and tobacco—heavily regulated but available to persons over the age of twenty-one? While this question is not being asked with regard to "hard" drugs such as heroin and cocaine, the legalization of marijuana—America's most-used illicit drug—has become an important policy issue. Indeed, as we saw at the beginning of Chapter 1, Colorado and Washington recently became the first states to legalize the sale, possession, and use of small amounts of marijuana.

The idea of marijuana legalization has certainly gained a certain amount of acceptance by the American public. A recent poll showed that 52 percent of adults favor legalization, compared to only 17 percent in 1991.[107] Politicians in Mexico, where drug-related violence claimed about sixty thousand lives between 2006 and 2013, have also urged their northern counterparts to engage in a "national debate about legalization."[108]

In the end, whether or not the legalization movement spreads beyond Colorado and Washington depends to a large extent on what happens in those states. If they see a dramatic increase in underage pot use or drugged driving, or experience an unexpected rise in marijuana-related health problems, then the drug's movement toward mainstream acceptance could come to a halt. If, however, marijuana legalization has a primarily positive impact, particularly in areas such as tax revenue and crime reduction, then, in the words of one supporter, other states will "want to get rid of their prohibition laws, too."[109] (See the feature *CJ Controversy—Legalizing Marijuana* that follows for more information on this subject.)

///// SELF ASSESSMENT

Fill in the blanks, and check your answers on page 65.

Drug _____ is defined as the use of any drug that causes physical or psychological harm to the user or a third party. People who are _____, meaning that they desire the drug long after use has stopped, need greater amounts of the drug to stimulate a neurotransmitter in the brain called _____. Harms associated with the abuse of _____ drugs, which require a physician's permission, have increased over the past decade. The recent legalization of _____ in certain parts of the country could dramatically change the nation's antidrug policy in the near future.

CJ CONTROVERSY

LEGALIZING MARIJUANA

The popularity of marijuana, the most commonly used illegal drug in the United States, is growing. Over the past six years, the number of regular users has swollen from about 15 million to about 19 million. If, as some observers believe, the reason for this increase is a "get soft" movement regarding marijuana, then we can expect the trend to continue. Due to recent developments in Colorado and Washington, marijuana may be positioned to join alcohol and tobacco as a socially acceptable—and legal—drug of choice for adult Americans.

MARIJUANA SHOULD BE LEGALIZED NATIONWIDE BECAUSE . . .

- It would put the black market for marijuana—estimated at $15 to $30 billion a year—out of business, ending violent crime associated with the pot trade and depriving thousands of criminals of their livelihood.

- It would result in a more efficient criminal justice system, as scarce law enforcement resources would be diverted away from marijuana offenses and the pressure on both overloaded courts and overcrowded prisons would be alleviated.

MARIJUANA SHOULD NOT BE LEGALIZED NATIONWIDE BECAUSE . . .

- Frequent marijuana use has been linked to mental disorders such as depression and anxiety. It is also associated with respiratory problems, IQ reduction, and immune system weakness, particularly for young people.

- Minors can often easily obtain legal but controlled drug products such as cigarettes and alcohol. If marijuana is legalized, we can expect minors to have greater access to it, as well.

Your Assignment

To learn more about this topic, visit the **Drug Policy Alliance's Marijuana and Legalization Regulation** Web site, as well as the Web site of the **Office of National Drug Control Policy's Marijuana Resource Center**. Also, search online for **Uruguay Legalizes Pot**. After doing whatever further Internet research you feel is necessary, write at least two full paragraphs describing your opinion of widespread marijuana legalization in the United States.

CHAPTER SUMMARY

For more information on these concepts, look back to the Learning Objective icons throughout the chapter.

 Identify the six main categories of crime. The six main categories of crime are (a) violent crime—murder, rape, assault and battery, and robbery; (b) property crime—pocket picking, shoplifting, larceny/theft, burglary, motor vehicle theft, and arson; (c) public order crime—public drunkenness, prostitution, gambling, and illicit drug use; (d) white-collar crime—business-related crimes such as fraud and embezzlement; (e) organized crime—illegal acts undertaken by illegal organizations, usually to satisfy the public's demand for unlawful goods and services; and (f) high-tech crime—theft of data from computer systems, as well as cyber crimes, such as selling child pornography over the Internet.

 Identify the publication in which the FBI reports crime data, and list the two main ways in which the data are reported. Every year, the FBI releases the Uniform Crime Report (UCR), in which it presents different crimes as (a) a rate per 100,000 people and (b) a percentage change from the previous year or other time periods.

 Distinguish between the National Crime Victimization Survey (NCVS) and self-reported surveys. The NCVS involves an annual survey of more than 92,000 households conducted by the Bureau of the Census along with the Bureau of Justice Statistics. The survey queries citizens about crimes that were committed against them in the previous six months. As such, the NCVS includes crimes not necessarily reported to police. Self-reported surveys, in contrast, involve asking individuals about criminal activity to which they may have been a party.

 Discuss the prevailing explanation for the rising number of women being incarcerated in the United States. Experts believe that many women today are arrested and given harsh punishment for activity that would not have put them behind bars several decades ago. For the most part, this activity is nonviolent: the majority of female arrestees are involved in drug- and alcohol-related offenses or property crimes.

 Discuss the difference between a hypothesis and a theory in the context of criminology. A hypothesis is a proposition, usually presented in an "If . . . , then . . ." format, that can be tested by researchers. If enough different authorities are able to test and verify a hypothesis, it will usually be accepted as a theory. Because theories can offer explanations for behavior, criminologists often rely on them when trying to determine the causes of criminal behavior.

 Explain how brain-scanning technology is able to help scientists determine if an individual is at risk for criminal offending. Brain-scanning technologies provide scientists with detailed depictions of brain structure and brain activity. When these depictions show disease or dysfunction that is correlated with violent behavior, the subject is at greater risk of criminal offending.

 Describe the importance of early childhood behavior for those who subscribe to self-control theory. Advocates of self-control theory believe that violent and antisocial behavior in adulthood can be predicted, to a large extent, by low levels of self-control in early childhood. Therefore, a child who is impulsive and tends to solve problems with violence is at risk for adult offending.

 Explain the routine activities theory of victimization. The routine activities theory holds that victimization becomes more likely to occur when the following three factors are present: (a) a likely offender; (b) a suitable target, in the form of either a person or an object to be stolen; and (c) the absence of a person who could prevent the crime, such as a law enforcement agent.

 Discuss the connection between the learning process and the start of an individual's drug use. One criminologist believes that first-time illegal drug users go through a learning process in taking up the habit. That is, more experienced users teach them the techniques of drug use, they learn to perceive the pleasurable aspects of drug use, and they learn to enjoy the social experience of drug use.

QUESTIONS FOR **CRITICAL ANALYSIS**

1. Do you agree that public order crimes such as prostitution and illegal gambling are "victimless" crimes? Why or why not?

2. Assume that you are a criminologist who wants to determine the extent to which high school students engage in such risky behavior as abusing alcohol and illegal drugs, carrying weapons, and contemplating suicide. How would you go about gathering these data?

3. Research shows that when levels of single-family mortgage foreclosures rise in a neighborhood, so do levels of violent crime. Explain the correlation between these two sets of statistics. Why is it false to say that single-family mortgage foreclosures cause violent crimes to occur?

4. Why might someone who subscribes to rational choice theory believe that increasing the harshness of a penalty for a particular crime would necessarily lead to fewer such crimes being committed?

5. Research shows that female college students who have been the victim of rape or attempted rape are at an unusually high risk of repeat victimization if they engage in binge alcohol drinking. What victim services should colleges provide to reduce the chances that this group of women will be revictimized?

KEY **TERMS**

assault   35
battery   35
biology   47
burglary   35
causation   45
control theory   54
correlation   45
criminology   45
dark figure of crime   39
domestic violence   58
drug abuse   60
genetics   48
hormone   48
hypothesis   46

larceny   35
learning theory   52
life course criminology   54
murder   35
organized crime   36
Part I offenses   38
Part II offenses   39
prescription drugs   61
psychology   47
public order crime   36
rational choice theory   46
repeat victimization   57
robbery   35
self-reported survey   40

sexual assault   35
social conflict theories   52
social disorganization theory   50
social process theories   52
sociology   50
stalking   58
strain theory   50
testosterone   48
theory   46
Uniform Crime Report (UCR)   37
victimology   56
victim surveys   39
white-collar crime   36

SELF-ASSESSMENT **ANSWER KEY**

Page 37: i. violent; **ii.** property; **iii.** white-collar

Page 41: i. Uniform Crime Report; **ii.** Victim; **iii.** self-report; **iv.** dark figure; **v.** greater/larger

Page 45: i. law enforcement; **ii.** aging; **iii.** African Americans; **iv.** income; **v.** increased

Page 56: i. Rational choice; **ii.** Social disorganization; **iii.** social process; **iv.** life; **v.** childhood

Page 59: i. routine activities; **ii.** repeat; **iii.** stranger; **iv.** mentally ill

Page 62: i. abuse; **ii.** addicted; **iii.** dopamine; **iv.** prescription; v. marijuana

NOTES

1. "Mass Shootings," *The Economist* (September 21, 2013), 30.

2. William M. Welch and Meghan Hoyer, "30 Mass Killings, 137 Victims: A Typical Year," *USA Today* (December 16, 2013), 1A.

3. *2012 Report to the Nations: Occupational Fraud and Abuse* (Austin, TX: Association of Certified Fraud Examiners, 2012), 2.

4. Federal Bureau of Investigation, *Uniform Crime Reporting Handbook* (Washington, D.C.: U.S. Department of Justice, 2004), 74.

5. Federal Bureau of Investigation, *Crime in the United States 2012* (Washington, D.C.: U.S. Department of Justice, 2013), at **www.fbi.gov/about-us/cjis/ucr /crime-in-the-u.s/2012/crime-in-the -u.s.-2012.**

6. *Ibid.*

7. *Ibid.,* Table 1.

8. Jeffrey Reiman, *The Rich Get Richer and the Poor Get Prison,* 4th ed. (Boston: Allyn & Bacon, 1995), 59–60.

9. *Crime in the United States 2012, op. cit.,* Expanded Homicide Data Table 10.

10. *Ibid.,* Table 1.

11. *Ibid.,* Table 29.

12. *Ibid.*

13. Marcus Felson, *Crime in Everyday Life* (Thousand Oaks, Calif.: Pine Forge Press, 1994), 3.

14. *Crime in the United States 2012, op. cit.,* "About CIUS."

15. David Hirschel, "Expanding Police Ability to Report Crime: The National Incident-Based Reporting System," *In Short: Toward Criminal Justice Solutions* (Washington, D.C.: National Institute of Justice, July 2009), 1–2.

16. Peter B. Wood, Walter R. Grove, James A. Wilson, and John K. Cochran, "Nonsocial Reinforcement and Criminal Conduct: An Extension of Learning Theory," *Criminology* 35 (May 1997), 335–366.

17. *Crime in the United States 2012, op. cit.,* Table 1.

18. Andrew Mach, "Violent Crime Rates in the U.S. Drop, Approach Historical Lows," *msnbc. com* (June 11, 2012), at **usnews.nbcnews .com/_news/2012/06/11/12170947 -fbi-violent-crime-rates-in-the-us-drop -approach-historic-lows?lite.**

19. "Where Have All the Burglars Gone?" *The Economist* (July 20, 2013), 21–23.

20. Bureau of Justice Statistics, *Crime Victimization, 2012* (Washington, D.C.: U.S. Department of Justice, October 2013), 1.

21. *Ibid.,* 4.

22. Quoted in Donna L. Leger, "Violent Crime Rises for 2nd Year," *USA Today* (October 25–27, 2013), 1A.

23. Erica L. Smith and Alexia Cooper, *Homicide in the U.S. Known to Law Enforcement,* *2011* (Washington, D.C.: U.S. Department of Justice, December 2013), 1.

24. *Crime in the United States 2012, op. cit.,* Expanded Homicide Data Table 3.

25. Michael Planty and Jennifer L. Truman, *Firearm Violence, 1993–2011* (Washington, D.C: U.S. Department of Justice, May 2013), 5.

26. *Crime in the United States 2012, op. cit.,* Expanded Homicide Data Table 6.

27. *Crime in the United States 2012, op. cit.,* Table 43A.

28. *Targeting Blacks: Drug Law Enforcement and Race in the United States* (New York: Human Rights Watch, May 2008), 3.

29. Charles Puzzanchera and Sarah Hockenberry, *Juvenile Court Statistics 2010* (Pittsburgh, Pa.: National Center for Juvenile Justice, June 2013), 20.

30. Ruth D. Peterson, "The Central Place of Race in Crime and Justice—The American Society of Criminology's 2011 Sutherland Address," *Criminology* (May 2012), 303–327.

31. Patricia Y. Warren, "Inequality by Design: The Connection between Race, Crime, Victimization, and Social Policy," *Criminology & Public Policy* (November 2010), 715.

32. Marguerite Moeller, *America's Tomorrow: A Profile of Latino Youth* (New York: National Council of La Raza, 2010).

33. Federal Bureau of Prisons, *Inmate Ethnicity,* at **www.bop.gov/about/statistics /statistics_inmate_ethnicity.jsp.**

34. Alexia Cooper and Erica L. Smith, *Homicide Trends in the United States, 1980–2008* (Washington, D.C.: Bureau of Justice Statistics, November 2011), Table 4, page 9.

35. Bureau of Justice Statistics, *Jail Inmates at Midyear 2012—Statistical Tables* (Washington, D.C.: U.S. Department of Justice, May 2013), Table 2, page 5; Bureau of Justice Statistics, *Prisoners in 2012—Advance Counts* (Washington, D.C.: U.S. Department of Justice, July 2013), Table 1, page 2; and *Crime in the United States 2012, op. cit.,* Table 33.

36. Howard Snyder, *Arrest in the United States 1980–2009* (Washington, D.C.: U.S. Department of Justice, September 2011), 1.

37. *Prisoners in 2012—Advance Counts, op. cit.,* Table 1, page 2.

38. Jennifer Schwartz and Bryan D. Rookey, "The Narrowing Gender Gap in Arrests: Assessing Competing Explanations Using Self-Report, Traffic Fatality, and Official Data on Drunk Driving, 1980–2004," *Criminology* (August 2008), 637–638.

39. Quoted in Barry Yeoman, "Violent Tendencies: Crime by Women Has Skyrocketed in Recent Years," *Chicago Tribune* (March 15, 2000), 3.

40. *Crime in the United States 2012, op. cit.,* Table 42.

41. Schwarz and Rookey, *op. cit.,* 637–671.

42. Meda Chesney-Lind, "Patriarchy, Prisons, and Jails: A Critical Look at Trends in Women's Incarceration," *Prison Journal* (Spring/Summer 1991), 57.

43. Benjamin J. Sadock, Harold I. Kaplan, and Virginia A. Sadock, *Kaplan & Sadock's Synopsis of Psychiatry* (Philadelphia: Lippincott Williams & Wilkins, 2007), 865.

44. Cindy-Lee Dennis and Simone N. Vigod, "The Relationship between Postpartum Depression, Domestic Violence, Childhood Violence, and Substance Use: Epidemiologic Study of a Large Community Sample," *Violence against Women* (April 2013), 503–517.

45. James Q. Wilson and Richard J. Hernstein, *Crime and Human Nature: The Definitive Study of the Causes of Crime* (New York: Simon & Schuster, 1985), 44.

46. Jack Katz, *Seductions of Crime: Moral and Sensual Attractions of Doing Evil* (New York: Basic Books, 1988).

47. Quoted in Matt Pearce, "Police: 'Bored' Oklahoma Teens Randomly Kill Australian Student," *Los Angeles Times* (August 20, 2013), A5.

48. Jeffrey M. Burns and Russell H. Swerdlow, "Right Orbifrontal Tumor with Pedophilia Symptom and Constructional Apraxia Sign," *Archives of Neurology* (March 2003), 437.

49. David C. Rowe, *Biology and Crime* (Los Angeles: Roxbury, 2002), 2.

50. Gail S. Anderson, *Biological Influences on Criminal Behavior* (Boca Raton, Fla.: CRC Press, 2007), 105–118.

51. L. E. Kreuz and R. M. Rose, "Assessment of Aggressive Behavior and Plasma Testosterone in Young Criminal Population," *Psychosomatic Medicine* 34 (1972), 321–332.

52. H. Persky, K. Smith, and G. Basu, "Relation of Psychological Measures of Aggression and Hostility to Testosterone Production in Men," *Psychosomatic Medicine* 33 (1971), 265, 276.

53. Jessica Wolpaw Reyes, *Environmental Policy as Social Policy? The Impact of Childhood Lead Exposure on Crime* (Cambridge, Mass.: National Bureau of Economic Research, May 2007), at **www.nber.org /papers/w13097.pdf.**

54. Bureau of Justice Statistics, *Health Problems of Prison and Jail Inmates* (Washington, D.C.: U.S. Department of Justice, September 2006), 1.

55. "How Did Aaron Alexis Get Security Clearance to Be a Defense Contractor?" *PBS Newshour* (September 17, 2013), at **www .pbs.org/newshour/bb/nation/july -dec13/shooting2_09-17.html.**

56. Quoted in Eileen Sullivan, "Loners Like Tucson Gunman 'Fly below the Radar,'" *Associated Press* (January 17, 2011).

57. Herman Bianchi, *Justice as Sanctuary: Toward a New System of Crime Control* (Bloomington: Indiana University Press, 1994), 72.

58. Philip Zimbardo, "Pathology of Imprisonment," *Society* (April 1972), 4–8.

59. David Canter and Laurence Alison, "The Social Psychology of Crime: Groups, Teams, and Networks," in *The Social Psychology of Crime: Groups, Teams, and Networks,* eds. David Canter and Laurence Alison (Hanover, N.H.: Dartmouth, 2000), 3–4.

60. Quoted in Trip Gabriel, "Welcome Mat for Crime as Neighborhoods Crumble," *New York Times* (July 25, 2013), A12.

61. Clifford R. Shaw and Henry D. McKay, *Report on the Causes of Crime,* Vol. 2: *Social Factors in Juvenile Delinquency* (Washington, D.C.: National Commission on Law Observance and Enforcement, 1931).

62. Robert K. Merton, *Social Theory and Social Structure* (New York: Free Press, 1957). See the chapter on "Social Structure and Anomie."

63. Robert Agnew, "Foundation for a General Strain Theory of Crime and Delinquency," *Criminology* 30 (1992), 47–87.

64. Robert Agnew, Timothy Brezina, John Paul Wright, and Francis T. Cullen, "Strain, Personality Traits, and Delinquency: Extending General Strain Theory," *Criminology* (February 2002), 43–71.

65. Robert Meier, "The New Criminology: Continuity in Criminology Theory," *Journal of Criminal Law and Criminology* 67 (1977), 461–469.

66. Philip G. Zimbardo, "The Human Choice: Individuation, Reason, and Order versus Deindividuation, Impulse, and Chaos," in *Nebraska Symposium on Motivation,* eds. William J. Arnold and David Levie (Lincoln, Neb.: University of Nebraska Press, 1969), 287–293.

67. Edwin H. Sutherland, *Criminology,* 4th ed. (Philadelphia: Lippincott, 1947).

68. Michael E. Roettger and Raymond Swisher, "Associations of Fathers' History of Incarceration with Sons' Delinquency and Arrest among Black, White, and Hispanic Males in the United States," *Criminology* (November 2011), 1109–1147.

69. Lindsay A. Robertson, Helena M. McAnally, and Robert J. Hancox, "Childhood and Adolescent Television Viewing and Antisocial Behavior in Early Adulthood," *Pediatrics* (March 2013), 439–446.

70. Nick Allen, "Washington Navy Yard Gunman 'Obsessed with Violent Video Games,'" *The Telegraph* (London, UK) (September 17, 2013), at **www.telegraph.co.uk/news /worldnews/northamerica/usa /10314585/Aaron-Alexis-Washington -navy-yard-gunman-obsessed-with -violent-video-games.html.**

71. Travis Hirschi, *Causes of Delinquency* (Berkeley: University of California Press, 1969).

72. Janet L. Lauritsen, *How Families and Communities Influence Youth Victimization* (Washington, D.C.: Office of Juvenile Justice and Delinquency Prevention, 2003).

73. Francis T. Cullen and Robert Agnew, *Criminological Theory, Past to Present: Essential Readings,* 2d ed. (Los Angeles: Roxbury Publishing Co., 2003), 443.

74. Michael R. Gottfredson and Travis Hirschi, *A General Theory of Crime* (Stanford, Calif.: Stanford University Press, 1990).

75. *Ibid.,* 90.

76. *Ibid.*

77. Robert J. Sampson and John H. Laub, *Crime in the Making: Pathways and Turning Points through Life* (Cambridge, Mass.: Harvard University Press, 1993), 11.

78. *Ibid.;* John H. Laub and Robert J. Sampson, *Shared Beginnings, Divergent Lives: Delinquent Boys to Age 70* (Cambridge, Mass.: Harvard University Press, 2003); and Derek A. Kreager, Ross L. Matsueda, and Elena A. Erosheva, "Motherhood and Criminal Desistance in Disadvantaged Neighborhoods," *Criminology* (February 2010), 221–257.

79. John F. Frana and Ryan D. Schroeder, "Alternatives to Incarceration," *Justice Policy Journal* (Fall 2008), available at **www .cjcj.org/files/alternatives_to.pdf.**

80. Peggy C. Giordano, Monica A. Longmore, Ryan D. Schroeder, and Patrick M. Seffrin, "A Life-Course Perspective on Spirituality and Desistance from Crime," *Criminology* (February 2008), 99–132.

81. Andrew Karmen, *Crime Victims: An Introduction to Victimology* (Belmont, Calif.: Wadsworth, 2003).

82. Charis E. Kubrin et al., "Does Fringe Banking Exacerbate Neighborhood Crime Rates?" *Criminology and Public Policy* (May 2011), 437–464.

83. Larry Cohen and Marcus Felson, "Social Change and Crime Rate Trends: A Routine Activity Approach," *American Sociological Review* (1979), 588–608.

84. Kubrin et al., *op. cit.,* 441.

85. Cohen and Felson, *op. cit.*

86. Susan Herman, *Parallel Justice for Victims of Crime* (Washington, D.C.: The National Center for Victims of Crime, 2010), 13–16.

87. Quoted in Kevin Johnson, "Criminals Target Each Other, Trend Shows," *USA Today* (August 31, 2007), 1A.

88. Erika Harrell, *Violent Victimization Committed by Strangers, 1993–2010* (Washington, D.C.: U.S. Department of Justice, December 2012), 2.

89. Shannan Catalano, *Intimate Partner Violence, 1993–2010* (Washington, D.C.: U. S. Department of Justice, November 2012), Table 1, page 2.

90. Harrell, *op. cit.,* Table 1, page 2.

91. Bureau of Justice Statistics, *Female Victims of Violence* (Washington, D.C.: U.S. Department of Justice, September 2009), Table 2, page 5.

92. Bonnie S. Fisher, Francis T. Cullen, and Michael G. Turner, *The Sexual Victimization of College Women* (Washington, D.C.: U.S. Department of Justice, December 2000), 10.

93. Eve S. Buzawa, "Victims of Domestic Violence," in Robert C. Davis, Arthur Lurigio, and Susan Herman, eds., *Victims of Crime,* 4th ed. (Los Angeles: Sage, 2013), 36–37.

94. Shannan Catalano, *Stalking Victims in the United States—Revised* (Washington, D.C.: U.S. Department of Justice, September 2012), 1, 5.

95. Arthur J. Lurigio, Kelli E. Canada, and Matthew W. Epperson, "Crime Victimization and Mental Illness," in *Victims of Crime,* 216–217.

96. *Ibid.,* 217–218.

97. Roberto Maniglio, "Severe Mental Illness and Criminal Victimization: A Systematic Review," *Acta Psychiactra Scandinavica* 119 (2009), 180–191.

98. Richard B. Felson and Keri B. Burchfield, "Alcohol and the Risk of Physical and Sexual Assault Victimization," *Criminology* (November 1, 2004), 837.

99. Becker, *op. cit.*

100. Myers, *op. cit.,* 75–76.

101. Peter B. Kraska, "The Unmentionable Alternative: The Need for and Argument against the Decriminalization of Drug Laws," in *Drugs, Crime, and the Criminal Justice System,* ed. Ralph Weisheit (Cincinnati, Ohio: Anderson Publishing, 1990).

102. Anthony A. Grace, "The Tonic/Phasal Model of Dopamine System Regulation," *Drugs and Alcohol* 37 (1995), 111.

103. Substance Abuse and Mental Health Services Administration, *Results from the 2012 National Survey on Drug Use and Health: Summary of National Findings* (Washington, D.C.: National Institute on Drug Abuse, September 2013), 58.

104. Centers for Disease Control and Prevention, "Drug Overdose in the United States: Fact Sheet," at **www.cdc.gov/homeand recreationalsafety/overdose/facts.html.**

105. Quoted in Katharine Q. Seelye, "Heroin in New England, More Abundant and Deadly," *New York Times* (July 19, 2013), A11.

106. *Ibid.*

107. Patrick Radden Keefe, "Buzzkill," *The New Yorker* (November 18, 2013), 43; and "By the Numbers," *Arizona Daily Star* (June 30, 2013), A11.

108. Quoted in "Burn-Out and Battle Fatigue," *The Economist* (March 17, 2012), 24.

109. Quoted in Matt Ferner, "Recreational Marijuana Shops Open in Colorado," *The Huffington Post* (January 1, 2014), at **www.huffingtonpost.com/2014/01/01 /marijuana-shops-open-colorado_n _4519506.html.**

CHAPTER

3 Inside Criminal Law

CHAPTER OUTLINE		CORRESPONDING LEARNING OBJECTIVES
Written Sources of American Criminal Law		List the four written sources of American criminal law.
The Purposes of Criminal Law		Explain the two basic functions of criminal law.
Classification of Crimes		Discuss the primary goals of civil law and criminal law, and explain how these goals are realized.
The Elements of a Crime		Delineate the elements required to establish *mens rea* (a guilty mental state).
Defenses under Criminal Law		List and briefly define the most important excuse defenses for crimes.
		Discuss a common misperception concerning the insanity defense in the United States.
		Describe the four most important justification criminal defenses.
Procedural Safeguards		Explain the importance of the due process clause in the criminal justice system.

To target your study and review, look for these numbered Learning Objective icons throughout the chapter.

AP Images/*Atlanta Journal-Constitution*, John Spink

ONE UNLUCKY PUNCH

ACCORDING TO a family friend, James Malecek is "a real gentleman, a sweet kid, not a big kid, not a brawler." Several years ago, however, Malecek—then nineteen years old—did get involved in a brawl, with deadly consequences. The altercation initially involved Malecek's sister, who got into a physical confrontation with a young man at a Fourth of July lakeside party in Long Beach, Indiana. When Malecek came to his sister's aid, seventeen-year-old Kevin Kennelly stepped in to break up the fight. Malecek then accidentally punched Kennelly in the right ear. Two days later, Kennelly died from blunt-force trauma to the head.

By all accounts, Malecek had no intention of harming Kennelly. "When confronted with a situation in which he felt compelled to help, protect, defend, and remain loyal, he acted, and his actions resulted in this terrible accident," said Malecek's mother. In court, Malecek apologized, telling Kennelly's parents, "Every day I think about the pain and suffering you're experiencing." Understandably, the apology fell on somewhat deaf ears. "How can we forgive when the destruction is so complete?" asked Kennelly's mother.

Following an unlawful killing, criminal justice professionals turn to the law to determine the proper course of action. Under Indiana's criminal code, when one person strikes another without the intent to kill and that action results in death, the offender has committed the crime of involuntary manslaughter. After pleading guilty to this crime in May 2013, Malecek was sentenced by an Indiana judge to spend 145 days in jail, to be followed by four years of court surveillance. Angered at what he considered lenient treatment, Kennelly's father called the punishment a "slap on the wrist."

FOR CRITICAL ANALYSIS

1. Do you agree with Kevin Kennelly's father that James Malecek should have been punished more severely? Why or why not?

2. Can you make the argument that even though Malecek did not intend to kill Kennelly, he should have been punished as if he did? Explain your answer.

3. Why do you think the issue of intent is so crucial to criminal law?

M. Spencer Green/AP Images

Long Beach, Indiana, a popular vacation destination for residents of nearby Chicago, was the site of James Malecek's accidental killing of Kevin Kennelly during a lakeside Fourth of July party.

WRITTEN SOURCES OF AMERICAN CRIMINAL LAW

LEARNING OBJECTIVE 1 List the four written sources of American criminal law.

Originally, American criminal law was *uncodified*. That is, it relied primarily on judges following precedents, and the body of the law was not written down in any single place. Uncodified law, however, presents a number of drawbacks. For one, if the law is not recorded in a manner or a place in which the citizenry has access to it, then it is difficult, if not impossible, for people to know exactly which acts are legal and which acts are illegal. Furthermore, citizens have no way of determining or understanding the procedures that must be followed to establish innocence or guilt. Consequently, U.S. history has seen the development of several written sources of American criminal law, also known as "substantive" criminal law. These sources include

1. The U.S. Constitution and the constitutions of the various states.
2. Statutes, or laws, passed by Congress and by state legislatures, plus local ordinances.
3. Regulations, created by regulatory agencies, such as the federal Food and Drug Administration.
4. Case law (court decisions).

We describe each of these important written sources of law in the following pages. (For a preview, see Figure 3.1 that follows.)

Constitutional Law

The federal government and the states have separate written constitutions that set forth the general organization and powers of, and the limits on, their respective governments. **Constitutional law** is the law as expressed in these constitutions.

The U.S. Constitution is the supreme law of the land. As such, it is the basis of all law in the United States. Any law that violates the Constitution, as ultimately determined by the United States Supreme Court, will be declared unconstitutional and will not be enforced. The Tenth Amendment, which defines the powers and limitations of the federal government, reserves to the states all powers not granted to the federal government. Under our system of federalism (see Chapter 1), each state also has its own constitution. Unless they conflict with the U.S. Constitution or a federal law, state constitutions are

> **Constitutional Law** Law based on the U.S. Constitution and the constitutions of the various states.

FIGURE 3.1 Sources of American Law

Constitutional law	**Definition:** The law as expressed in the U.S. Constitution and the various state constitutions.	**Example:** The Fifth Amendment to the U.S. Constitution states that no person shall "be compelled in any criminal case to be a witness" against himself or herself.
Statutory law	**Definition:** Laws and *ordinances* created by federal, state, and local legislatures and governing bodies.	**Example:** Texas state law considers the theft of cattle, horses, or exotic livestock or fowl a felony.
Administrative law	**Definition:** The rules, orders, and decisions of federal or state government administrative agencies.	**Example:** The federal Environmental Protection Agency's rules criminalize the use of lead-based paint in a manner that causes health risks to the community.
Case law	**Definition:** Judge-made law, including judicial interpretations of the other three sources of law.	**Example:** A federal judge overturns a Nebraska state law making it a crime for sex offenders to use social networking sites on the ground that the statute violated the constitutional right of freedom of speech.

Statutory Law The body of law enacted by legislative bodies.

Supremacy Clause A clause in the U.S. Constitution establishing that federal law is the "supreme law of the land" and shall prevail when in conflict with state constitutions or statutes.

Ballot Initiative A procedure through which the citizens of a state, by collecting enough signatures, can force a public vote on a proposed change to state law.

supreme within their respective borders. (You will learn more about how constitutional law applies to our criminal justice system throughout this textbook.)

Statutory Law

Statutes enacted by legislative bodies at any level of government make up another source of law, which is generally referred to as **statutory law**. *Federal statutes* are laws that are enacted by the U.S. Congress. *State statutes* are laws enacted by state legislatures, and statutory law also includes the ordinances passed by cities and counties. A federal statute, of course, applies to all states. A state statute, in contrast, applies only within that state's borders. City or county ordinances (statutes) apply only to those jurisdictions where they are enacted.

LEGAL SUPREMACY It is important to keep in mind that there are essentially fifty-two different criminal codes in this country—one for each state, the District of Columbia, and the federal government. Originally, the federal criminal code was quite small. The U.S. Constitution mentions only three federal crimes: treason, piracy, and counterfeiting. Today, federal law includes about 4,500 offenses that carry criminal penalties.[1] Inevitably, these federal criminal statutes are bound to overlap or even contradict state statutes. In such cases, thanks to the **supremacy clause** of the Constitution, federal law will almost always prevail. Simply put, the supremacy clause holds that federal law is the "supreme law of the land."

As an example of the supremacy clause in action, at least 330 individuals have been charged with violating federal law for possessing or selling medical marijuana in states where such use is legal under state law.[2] As we discussed earlier in the textbook, marijuana use—for medicinal purposes or otherwise—remains illegal under federal law, and, in the words of one federal judge, "we are all bound by federal law, like it or not."[3] Along the same lines, any statutory law—federal or state—that violates the Constitution will be overturned. In the late 1980s, for example, the United States Supreme Court ruled that any state laws banning the burning of the American flag were unconstitutional because they impinged on the individual's right to freedom of expression.[4]

In Oregon, because of a ballot initiative, any person who fails a field sobriety test, such as the one shown here, and is convicted of drunk driving for a third time must spend ninety days in jail. What are some of the pros and cons of using ballot initiatives to create criminal law?

Joe Raedle/Getty Images

BALLOT INITIATIVES On a state and local level, voters can write or rewrite criminal statutes through a form of direct democracy known as the **ballot initiative**. In this process, a group of citizens draft a proposed law and then gather a certain number of signatures to get the proposal on that year's ballot. If a majority of the voters approve the measure, it is enacted into law. Currently, twenty-four states and the District of Columbia accept ballot initiatives, and these special elections have played a crucial role in shaping criminal law in those jurisdictions.

In the mid-1990s, for example, California voters approved a "three-strikes" measure (discussed in Chapter 9) that increases penalties for third-time felons, transforming the state's criminal justice system in the process. In 2012, when Colorado and Washington decided to legalize the sale and possession of small amounts of marijuana, voters in those states approved this dramatic legal change through ballot initiatives. As we just noted, however, ballot initiatives do not supplant federal law, and marijuana sellers and users in these states are still subject to arrest under federal drug laws.

Administrative Law

A third source of American criminal law consists of **administrative law**—the rules, orders, and decisions of *regulatory agencies.* A regulatory agency is a federal, state, or local government agency established to perform a specific function. The Occupational Safety and Health Administration (OSHA), for example, oversees the safety and health of American workers. The Environmental Protection Agency (EPA) is concerned with protecting the natural environment, and the Food and Drug Administration (FDA) regulates food and drugs produced in the United States.

Disregarding certain laws created by regulatory agencies can be a criminal violation. Federal statutes, such as the Clean Water Act, authorize a specific regulatory agency, such as the EPA, to enforce regulations to which criminal sanctions are attached.[5] So, in 2013, following a criminal investigation led by the EPA, a North Carolina dairy farm was found guilty of discharging waste into the French Broad River. As punishment, a federal judge sentenced the company to pay $80,000 in fines and open its facilities to government inspectors for a four-year probationary period.

Case Law

Another basic source of American law consists of the rules of law announced in court decisions, or **precedents.** These rules of law include interpretations of constitutional provisions, of statutes enacted by legislatures, and of regulations created by administrative agencies. Today, this body of law is referred to as the common law, judge-made law, or **case law.**

Case law relies to a certain extent on how courts interpret a codified law. If you wanted to learn about the coverage and applicability of a particular statute, for example, you would need to locate the statute and study it. You would also need to see how the courts in your jurisdiction have interpreted the statute—in other words, what precedents have been established in regard to that statute. The use of precedent means that case law varies from jurisdiction to jurisdiction.

////▰SELF ASSESSMENT

Fill in the blanks, and check your answers on page 100.

The U.S. _____ is the supreme law of this country. Any law that violates this document will be declared _____ by the United States Supreme Court. Laws enacted by legislative bodies are known as _____, while the body of law created by judicial decisions is known as _____ law.

Administrative Law The body of law created by administrative agencies (in the form of rules, regulations, orders, and decisions) in order to carry out their duties and responsibilities.

Precedent A court decision that furnishes an example of authority for deciding subsequent cases involving similar facts.

Case Law The rules of law announced in court decisions.

THE PURPOSES OF CRIMINAL LAW

Why do societies need laws? Many criminologists believe that criminal law has two basic functions: one relates to the legal requirements of a society, and the other pertains to the society's need to maintain and promote social values.

LEARNING

2

OBJECTIVE

Explain the two basic functions of criminal law.

Protect and Punish:
The Legal Function of the Law

The primary legal function of the law is to maintain social order by protecting citizens from *criminal harm.* This term refers to a variety of harms that can be generalized to fit into two categories:

1. Harms to individual citizens' physical safety and property, such as the harm caused by murder, theft, or arson.
2. Harms to society's interests collectively, such as the harm caused by unsafe foods or consumer products, a polluted environment, or poorly constructed buildings.[6]

Because criminal law has the primary goal of protecting people from harm, new criminal laws are often passed in response to specific acts. So, following the fatal shooting of twenty children and six adults at an elementary school in Newtown, Connecticut, on December 14, 2012, many states moved to tighten their gun laws.

CJ & TECHNOLOGY Revenge Porn

iStockphoto.com/Yuri_Arcurs

Consider the following scenario: Jasmine, a graduate student, exchanges intimate photos with Josh, her boyfriend. Then they break up. Several months later, Josh begins posting nude pictures of Jasmine online. Although she is mortified, there is little Jasmine can do to stop Josh, because such behavior is not illegal in most of the United States. For the most part, Web site operators are not responsible for content provided by others, unless that content happens to be in violation of federal law, such as child pornography.

Technology often moves faster than criminal law, allowing for behavior that would seem to be illegal but is not. In 2013, California became only the second state—along with New Jersey—to ban "revenge porn," or the posting of pornographic material without the subject's consent and "with the intent to cause serious emotional distress." Under the new California law, a person convicted of publishing such material online faces six months in jail or a $1,000 fine.

Thinking about Revenge Porn

The California law does not apply if the pornographic material is a "selfie." That is, if the alleged victim of the revenge porn took the video or photograph of himself or herself, then no criminal charges can be brought against the person who posted it online. Why do you think the law was written this way? Are revenge porn victims who took the photographs themselves less deserving of protection under the law? Why or why not?

Maintain and Teach:
The Social Function of the Law

If criminal laws against acts that cause harm or injury to others are almost universally accepted, the same cannot be said for laws that criminalize "morally" wrongful activities that may do no obvious physical harm outside the families of those involved. Why criminalize gambling or prostitution if the participants are consenting?

EXPRESSING PUBLIC MORALITY The answer lies in the social function of criminal law. Many observers believe that the main purpose of criminal law is to reflect the values and norms of society, or at least of those segments of society that hold power. Legal scholar Henry Hart has stated that the only justification for criminal law and punishment is "the judgment of community condemnation."[7]

Take, for example, the misdemeanor of bigamy, which occurs when someone knowingly marries a second person without terminating her or his marriage to an original husband or wife. Apart from moral considerations, there would appear to be no victims of criminal harm in a bigamous relationship, and indeed many societies have allowed and continue to allow bigamy to exist. In the American social tradition, however, as John L. Diamond of the University of California's Hastings College of the Law points out:

> Marriage is an institution encouraged and supported by society. The structural importance of the integrity of the family and a monogamous marriage requires unflinching enforcement of the criminal laws against bigamy. The immorality is not in choosing to do wrong, but in transgressing, even innocently, a fundamental social boundary that lies at the core of social order.[8]

Of course, public morals are not uniform across the entire nation, and a state's criminal code often reflects local responses to local circumstances. In Kentucky, for example, someone who uses a reptile as part of a religious service is subject to up to $100 in fines, and New Hampshire prohibits any person or agency from introducing a wolf into the state's wilds.[9] Sometimes, local values and federal law will conflict with one another. In South Carolina, operating a cockfighting operation is a misdemeanor, and violators are often let off with a fine. Under federal animal welfare laws, however, the same activity carries a potential five-year prison term.[10] In 2012, five South Carolinians arrested by federal agents for cockfighting claimed—unsuccessfully—in court that their convictions were illegitimate because the federal government has no authority to regulate the "sport" within state borders.[11]

TEACHING SOCIETAL BOUNDARIES Some scholars believe that criminal laws not only express the expectations of society, but "teach" them as well. Professor Lawrence M. Friedman of Stanford University thinks that just as parents teach children behavioral norms through punishment, criminal justice "'teaches a lesson' to the people it punishes, and to society at large." Making burglary a crime, arresting burglars, putting them in jail—each step in the criminal justice process reinforces the idea that burglary is unacceptable and is deserving of punishment.[12]

Al Bello/Staff/Getty Images

Some state laws are more lenient than federal animal welfare law when it comes to cockfighting. Why does the supremacy clause make it unlikely that residents of these states would be able to avoid the harsher punishments of the federal laws that prohibit the practice?

Civil Law The branch of law dealing with the definition and enforcement of all private or public rights, as opposed to criminal matters.

Plaintiff The person or institution that initiates a lawsuit in civil court proceedings by filing a complaint.

Defendant In a civil court, the person or institution against whom an action is brought. In a criminal court, the person or entity who has been formally accused of violating a criminal law.

Liability In a civil court, legal responsibility for one's own or another's actions.

This teaching function can also be seen in traffic laws. There is nothing "natural" about most traffic laws: Americans drive on the right side of the street, the British on the left side, with no obvious difference in the results. These laws, such as stopping at intersections, using headlights at night, and following speed limits, do lead to a more orderly flow of traffic and fewer accidents—certainly socially desirable goals. The laws can also be updated when needed. Over the past few years, several states have banned the use of handheld cell phones while driving because of the safety hazards associated with that behavior. Various forms of punishment for breaking traffic laws teach drivers the social order of the road.

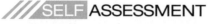 //// SELF ASSESSMENT

Fill in the blanks, and check your answers on page 100.

The _____ function of the law is to protect citizens from _____ harm by assuring their physical safety. The _____ function of the law is to teach citizens proper behavior and express public _____ by codifying the norms and values of the community.

CLASSIFICATION OF CRIMES

The huge body of the law can be broken down according to various classifications. Three of the most important distinctions are those between (1) civil law and criminal law, (2) felonies and misdemeanors, and (3) crimes *mala in se* and *mala prohibita.*

Civil Law and Criminal Law

All law can be divided into two categories: civil law and criminal law. These two categories of law are distinguished by their primary goals. The criminal justice system is concerned with protecting society from harm by preventing and prosecuting crimes. A crime is an act so reprehensible that it is considered a wrong against society as a whole, as well as against the individual victim. Therefore, the state prosecutes a person who commits a criminal act. If the state is able to prove that a person is guilty of a crime, the government will punish her or him with imprisonment or fines, or both.

Civil law, which includes all types of law other than criminal law, is concerned with disputes between private individuals and between entities. Proceedings in civil lawsuits are normally initiated by an individual or a corporation (in contrast to criminal proceedings, which are initiated by public prosecutors). Such disputes may involve, for example, the terms of a contract, the ownership of property, or an automobile accident. Under civil law, the government provides a forum for the resolution of *torts*—or private wrongs—in which the injured party, called the **plaintiff,** tries to prove that a wrong has been committed by the accused party, or the **defendant.** (Note that the accused party in both criminal and civil cases is known as the *defendant.*)

GUILT AND RESPONSIBILITY A criminal court is convened to determine whether the defendant is *guilty*—that is, whether the defendant has, in fact, committed the offense charged. In contrast, civil law is concerned with responsibility, a much more flexible concept. For example, when James Morrin committed suicide after fatally shooting his wife, a civil court in Waterbury, Connecticut, blamed Morrin's doctor, Carl Koplin, for the tragedy. Apparently, Koplin had failed to properly evaluate Morrin's deteriorating mental state and refer him to a qualified psychiatrist or psychologist for treatment. Even though Koplin was never charged with any crime, the civil court decided that he was **liable,** or legally responsible, for the murder-suicide because of his carelessness.

Discuss the primary goals LEARNING
of civil law and criminal law, **3**
and explain how these goals
are realized. OBJECTIVE

Most civil cases involve a request for monetary damages to compensate for the wrong that has been committed. Thus, in 2014, the civil court had Carl Koplin and his employers pay $8 million to the Morrins's two daughters to help compensate them for the trauma of their parents' deaths.

THE BURDEN OF PROOF Although criminal law proceedings are completely separate from civil law proceedings in the modern legal system, the two branches of law do have some similarities. Both attempt to control behavior by imposing sanctions on those who violate society's definition of acceptable behavior. Furthermore, criminal and civil law often supplement each other. In certain instances, a victim may file a civil suit against an individual who is also the target of a criminal prosecution by the government.

Because the burden of proof is much greater in criminal trials than civil ones, it is almost always easier to win monetary damages than a criminal conviction. During a criminal trial, the prosecution must prove **beyond a reasonable doubt** that the defendant has committed the crime with which he or she has been charged. In a civil trial, the plaintiff must establish by a **preponderance of the evidence** only that the defendant is responsible for the harm that has been alleged.

In other words, in a criminal trial, a judge or jury must be *practically certain* that a crime has occurred to convict. In a civil trial, the plaintiff need only show that her or his explanation of events is *more likely than not* the truth to win damages or some other form of compensation. (See the *Mastering Concepts* feature that follows for a comparison of civil and criminal law.)

Felonies and Misdemeanors

Depending on their degree of seriousness, crimes are classified as *felonies* or *misdemeanors*. **Felonies** are crimes punishable by death or by imprisonment in a federal or state penitentiary for one year or longer (though some states, such as North Carolina, consider felonies to be punishable by at least two years' incarceration). The Model Penal Code, a general guide for criminal law, provides for four degrees of felony:

1. Capital offenses, for which the maximum penalty is death.
2. First degree felonies, punishable by a maximum penalty of life imprisonment.
3. Second degree felonies, punishable by a maximum of ten years' imprisonment.
4. Third degree felonies, punishable by a maximum of five years' imprisonment.

Beyond a Reasonable Doubt The degree of proof required to find the defendant in a criminal trial guilty of committing the crime. The defendant's guilt must be the only reasonable explanation for the criminal act before the court.

Preponderance of the Evidence The degree of proof required to decide in favor of one side or the other in a civil case. In general, this requirement is met when a plaintiff proves that an explanation more likely than not is true.

Felony A serious crime, usually punishable by death or imprisonment for a year or longer.

MASTERING CONCEPTS
CIVIL LAW VERSUS CRIMINAL LAW

ISSUE	CIVIL LAW	CRIMINAL LAW
Area of concern	Rights and duties between individuals	Offenses against society as a whole
Wrongful act	Harm to a person or business entity	Violation of a statute that prohibits some type of activity
Party who brings suit	Person who suffered harm (plaintiff)	The state (prosecutor)
Party who responds	Person who supposedly caused harm (defendant)	Person who allegedly committed a crime (defendant)
Standard of proof	Preponderance of the evidence	Beyond a reasonable doubt
Remedy	Damages to compensate for the harm	Punishment (fine or incarceration)

In August 2013, Chris Bucchere, wearing the red tie, pleaded guilty to felony vehicular manslaughter for killing a pedestrian while riding his bicycle in San Francisco. Bucchere was sentenced to three years of probation and 1,000 hours of community service. Under what circumstances do you think a bicyclist should be incarcerated for accidentally causing the death of a pedestrian?

Michael Macor/San Francisco Chronicle/Corbis

For the most part, felonies involve crimes of violence such as armed robbery or sexual assault, or other "serious" crimes such as stealing a large amount of money or selling illegal drugs.

TYPES OF MISDEMEANORS Under federal law and in most states, any crime that is not a felony is considered a **misdemeanor**. Misdemeanors are crimes punishable by a fine or by confinement for up to a year. If imprisoned, the guilty party goes to a local jail instead of a prison. Disorderly conduct and trespassing are common misdemeanors. Most states distinguish between *gross misdemeanors,* which are offenses punishable by thirty days to a year in jail, and *petty misdemeanors,* or offenses punishable by fewer than thirty days in jail. Probation and community service are often imposed on those who commit misdemeanors, especially juveniles. In rare cases, a homicide can be considered a misdemeanor if the offender was taking part in a generally harmless activity when an accidental death occurred. (See photo alongside.)

INFRACTIONS The least serious form of wrongdoing is often called an **infraction** and is punishable only by a small fine. Even though infractions such as parking tickets or traffic violations technically represent illegal activity, they generally are not considered "crimes." Therefore, infractions rarely lead to jury trials and are deemed to be so minor that they do not appear on the offender's criminal record. In some jurisdictions, the terms *infraction* and *petty offense* are interchangeable. In others, however, they are different. Under federal guidelines, for example, an infraction can be punished by up to five days of prison time, while a petty offender is only liable for a fine.[13] Finally, those who string together a series of infractions (or fail to pay the fines that come with such offenses) are in danger of being criminally charged. In Illinois, having three or more speeding violations in one year is considered criminal behavior.[14]

Mala in Se and *Mala Prohibita*

Criminologists often express the social function of criminal law in terms of *mala in se* or *mala prohibita* crimes. A criminal act is referred to as **mala in se** if it would be considered wrong even if there were no law prohibiting it. *Mala in se* crimes are said to go against "natural" laws—that is, against the "natural, moral, and public" principles of a society. Murder, rape, and theft are examples of *mala in se* crimes. These crimes are generally the same from country to country or culture to culture.

In contrast, the term **mala prohibita** refers to acts that are considered crimes only because they have been codified as such through statute—"human-made" laws. A *mala prohibita* crime is considered wrong only because it has been prohibited. It is not inherently wrong, though it may reflect the moral standards of a society at a given time. Thus, the definition of a *mala prohibita* crime can vary from country to country and even from state to state. Bigamy, or the offense of having two legal spouses, could be considered a *mala prohibita* crime.[15]

Misdemeanor A criminal offense that is not a felony; usually punishable by a fine and/or a jail term of up to one year.

Infraction In most jurisdictions, a noncriminal offense for which the penalty is a fine rather than incarceration.

Mala in Se A descriptive term for acts that are inherently wrong, regardless of whether they are prohibited by law.

Mala Prohibita A descriptive term for acts that are made illegal by criminal statute and are not necessarily wrong in and of themselves.

Some observers question the distinction between *mala in se* and *mala prohibita*. In many instances, it is difficult to define a "pure" *mala in se* crime. That is, it is difficult to separate a crime from the culture that has deemed it a crime.[16] Even murder, under certain cultural circumstances, is not considered a criminal act. In a number of poor, traditional areas of the Middle East and Asia, the law excuses "honor killings" in which men kill female family members suspected of sexual indiscretion. Our own legal system excuses homicide in extreme situations, such as self-defense or when a law enforcement agent kills in the course of upholding the law. Therefore, "natural" laws can be seen as culturally specific. Similar difficulties occur in trying to define a "pure" *mala prohibita* crime. More than 150 countries, including most members of the European Union, have legalized prostitution. With the exception of seven rural counties of Nevada, prostitution is illegal in the United States.

Corpus Delicti The body of circumstances that must exist for a criminal act to have occurred.

///// SELF ASSESSMENT

Fill in the blanks, and check your answers on page 100.

_____ law is concerned with disputes between private individuals and other entities, whereas criminal law involves the _____'s duty to protect society by preventing and prosecuting crimes. A _____ is a serious crime punishable by more than a year in prison or the death penalty, while a person found guilty of a _____ will usually spend less than a year in jail and/or pay a fine.

THE ELEMENTS OF A CRIME

In fictional accounts of police work, the admission of guilt is often portrayed as the crucial element of a criminal investigation. Although an admission is certainly useful to police and prosecutors, it alone cannot establish the innocence or guilt of a suspect. Criminal law normally requires that the *corpus delicti,* a Latin phrase for "the body of the crime," be proved before a person can be convicted of wrongdoing.

Corpus delicti can be defined as "proof that a specific crime has actually been committed by someone."[17] It consists of the basic elements of any crime, which include

1. The *actus reus,* or guilty act,
2. The *mens rea,* or guilty intent,
3. Concurrence, or the coming together of the criminal act or the guilty mind,
4. Causation, a link between the act and the legal definition of the crime,
5. Any attendant, or accompanying, circumstances, and
6. The harm done by the crime.

An explanation of each of these basic elements follows.

Criminal Act: *Actus Reus*

Suppose Mr. Smith walks into a police department and announces that he just killed his wife. In and of itself, the confession is insufficient for conviction unless the police find Mrs. Smith's corpse, for example, with a bullet in her brain and establish through evidence that Mr. Smith fired the gun. (This does not mean that an actual dead body has to be found in every homicide case. Rather, it is the fact of the death that must be established in such cases.)

Most crimes require an act of *commission,* meaning that a person must *do* something in order to be accused of a crime. The prohibited act is referred to as the

CRIME SCENE PHOTOGRAPHER JOB DESCRIPTION:

- Photograph physical evidence and crime scenes related to criminal investigations.
- Must be able to compose reports, testify in court, and understand basic computer software and terminology.

WHAT KIND OF TRAINING IS REQUIRED?

- One year in law enforcement or commercial photography OR a degree or certificate in photography and darkroom techniques OR some combination of the above training and experience totaling one year.

ANNUAL SALARY RANGE?

- $45,780–$53,290

DIANA TABOR

CRIME SCENE PHOTOGRAPHER

Photo Courtesy of Diana Tabor

iStockphoto.com/Vozks

A crime scene photographer's job is invaluable to those who are not present at the scene, yet need to be able to observe the scene as accurately as possible. I like the variety of my work. No two scenes are exactly alike, and the conditions pose different challenges. I have photographed scenes in cramped mobile homes, spacious homes, and out in the woods where we had to hike because there were no roads leading directly to the scene. I've been really hot and sweaty, fogging up the viewfinder. Then I have been so cold that I had to go sit in the van to let my hands and the camera warm up because they had stopped working.

I do wonder what the people at the gas stations think when we come in there after we're done to clean up and get something to drink. Fingerprint powder gets everywhere—I have found that nothing less than a shower really gets rid of it completely. It is sometimes difficult to accept that there is nothing to prevent the crime that has already happened, but I take pride in representing the victim when he or she cannot speak.

Social Media Career Tip Don't forget about your phone! Every week, call at least three people from your social media networks and talk with them about your career interests. This kind of personal contact can be far more useful than an exchange of posts.

---

actus reus, or guilty act. Furthermore, the act of commission must be voluntary. For example, if Mr. Smith had an epileptic seizure while holding a hunting rifle and accidentally shot his wife, he normally would not be held criminally liable for her death.

What if Mr. Smith was aware that he was susceptible to epileptic seizures and still decided to handle a hunting rifle near Mrs. Smith? Under those circumstances, he might have acted with guilt. In one well-known case, a driver killed four pedestrians in Buffalo, New York, after having a seizure and losing control of his car. Because the driver knew that he was subject to seizures, a court found that the *actus reus* was not the accident, but the decision to get behind the wheel in the first place. Because that decision was voluntary, the driver could be charged for causing the four deaths.[18]

A LEGAL DUTY In some cases, an act of *omission* can be a crime, but only when a person has a legal duty to perform the omitted act. One such legal duty is assumed to exist based on a "special relationship" between two parties, such as that between a parent and child, adult children and their aged parents, and spouses.[19] Those persons involved in contractual relationships with others, such as physicians and lifeguards, must also perform legal duties to avoid criminal penalty. Hawaii, Minnesota, Rhode Island, Vermont, and Wisconsin have even passed "duty to aid" statutes, requiring their citizens to report criminal conduct and help victims of such conduct if possible.[20] Another example of a criminal act of omission is failure to file a federal income tax return when required by law to do so.

Actus Reus (pronounced *ak*-tus *ray*-uhs). A guilty (prohibited) act.

A PLAN OR ATTEMPT The guilty act requirement is based on one of the premises of criminal law—that a person is punished for harm done to society. Planning to kill someone or to steal a car may be wrong, but the thoughts do no harm and are therefore not criminal until they are translated into action. Of course, a person can be punished for *attempting* murder or robbery, but normally only if he or she took substantial steps toward the criminal objective and the prosecution can prove that the desire to commit the crime was present. Furthermore, the punishment for an **attempt** normally is less severe than if the act had succeeded.

Mental State: *Mens Rea*

A wrongful mental state—*mens rea*—is usually as necessary as a wrongful act in determining guilt. The mental state, or requisite *intent,* required to establish guilt of a crime is indicated in the applicable statute or law. For theft, the wrongful act is the taking of another person's property, and the required mental state involves both the awareness that the property belongs to another and the desire to deprive the owner of it.

THE CATEGORIES OF *MENS REA* A guilty mental state includes elements of purpose, knowledge, negligence, and recklessness.[21] A defendant is said to have *purposefully* committed a criminal act when he or she desires to engage in certain criminal conduct or to cause a certain criminal result. For a defendant to have *knowingly* committed an illegal act, he or she must be aware of the illegality, must believe that the illegality exists, or must correctly suspect that the illegality exists but fail to do anything to dispel (or confirm) his or her belief.

Negligence Criminal **negligence** involves the mental state in which the defendant grossly deviates from the standard of care that a reasonable person would use under the same circumstances. The defendant is accused of taking an unjustified, substantial, and foreseeable risk that resulted in harm. Several years ago, for example, a San Diego County, California, man named Richard Fox killed his girlfriend by accidentally shooting her with a homemade cannon. The fireworks enthusiast obviously did not intend for his girlfriend to die. At the same time, there is certainly a foreseeable risk inherent in operating homemade cannons around other people. Eventually, Fox was arrested for negligently discharging an explosive instead of murder.

Recklessness A defendant who commits an act recklessly is more blameworthy than one who is criminally negligent. The Model Penal Code defines criminal **recklessness** as "consciously disregard[ing] a substantial and unjustifiable risk."[22] A Waldo County, Maine, jury recently found Luke Bryant guilty of criminal recklessness in the death of his friend Tyler Seaney. Bryant killed Seaney while the two were playing a game that involved pointing unloaded shotguns at each other and pulling the trigger.

Even though Bryant was unaware that the gun was actually loaded in this instance, the risk of harm associated with this game was so great that the jury felt he should have taken greater safety measures. (As you can see, the difference between negligence and recklessness is not always clear. One could certainly argue that Richard Fox's behavior in causing the death of his girlfriend, described above, rose to the level of recklessness.)

DEGREES OF CRIME Earlier in this chapter, you learned that crimes are graded by degree. Generally speaking, the degree of a crime is a reflection of the seriousness of that crime and is used to determine the severity of any subsequent punishment.

Attempt The act of taking substantial steps toward committing a crime while having the ability and the intent to commit the crime, even if the crime never takes place.

Mens Rea (pronounced mehns ray-uh). A wrongful mental state or intent, which is usually as necessary as a wrongful act to establish criminal liability.

Negligence A failure to exercise the standard of care that a reasonable person would exercise in similar circumstances.

Recklessness The state of being aware that a risk does or will exist and nevertheless acting in a way that consciously disregards this risk.

 LEARNING OBJECTIVE **4** Delineate the elements required to establish *mens rea* (a guilty mental state).

With many crimes, degree is a function of the criminal act itself, as determined by statute. For example, most criminal codes consider a burglary that involves a nighttime forced entry into a home to be a burglary in the first degree. If the same act takes place during the day and involves a nonresidential building, then it is burglary in the second degree. As you might expect, burglary in the first degree carries a harsher penalty than burglary in the second degree.

Willful Murder With murder, the degree of the crime is, to a large extent, determined by the *mens rea* of the offender. Murder is generally defined as the willful killing of a human being. It is important to emphasize the word *willful,* as it precludes homicides caused by accident or negligence. A death that results from negligence or accident generally is considered a private wrong and therefore a matter for civil law.

In addition, criminal law punishes those who plan and intend to do harm more harshly than it does those who act wrongfully because of strong emotions or other extreme circumstances. First degree murder—usually punishable by life in prison or the death penalty—occurs under two circumstances:

1. When the crime is premeditated, or contemplated beforehand by the offender, instead of being a spontaneous act of violence.
2. When the crime is deliberate, meaning that it was planned and decided on after a process of decision making. Deliberation does not require a lengthy planning process. A person can be found guilty of first degree murder even if she or he made the decision to kill only seconds before committing the crime.

Second degree murder, usually punishable by a minimum of fifteen to twenty-five years in prison, occurs when no premeditation or deliberation was present, but the offender did have *malice aforethought* toward the victim. In other words, the offender acted with wanton disregard for the consequences of his or her actions. (*Malice* means "wrongful intention" or "the desire to do evil.")

The difference between first and second degree murder is illustrated in a case involving a California man who beat a neighbor to death with a partially full brandy bottle. The crime took place after Ricky McDonald, the victim, complained to Kazi Cooksey, the offender, about the noise coming from a late-night barbecue Cooksey and his friends were holding. The jury could not find sufficient evidence that Cooksey's actions were premeditated, but he certainly acted with wanton disregard for his victim's safety. Therefore, the jury convicted Cooksey of second degree murder rather than first degree murder.

Types of Manslaughter A homicide committed without malice toward the victim is known as *manslaughter* and is commonly punishable by up to fifteen years in prison. **Voluntary manslaughter** occurs when the intent to kill may be present, but malice is lacking. Voluntary manslaughter covers crimes of passion, in which the emotion of an argument between two friends may lead to a homicide. Voluntary manslaughter can also occur when the victim provoked the offender to act violently.

As you saw at the opening of this chapter, **involuntary manslaughter** covers incidents in which the offender's acts may have been careless, but he or she had no intent to kill. In 2013, for example, Sharon Moore was convicted of involuntary manslaughter in the death of her friend Nadia Williams. Moore and Williams were part of a group that got involved in a scuffle with other customers at a fast food restaurant in Cleveland Heights,

Ohio. When a security guard tried to break up the fight, his firearm accidentally discharged, fatally injuring Williams.

Though Moore had certainly not intended for her friend to die, because of her participation in the fight she was held criminally responsible for Williams's death and sentenced to nine months in prison. (As the feature *Discretion in Action—Murder or Manslaughter?* that follows shows, the distinction between various homicide charges is not always clear and often rests on the issue of intent.)

STRICT LIABILITY For certain crimes, criminal law holds the defendant to be guilty even if intent to commit the offense is lacking. These acts are known as **strict liability crimes** and generally involve endangering the public welfare in some way.[23] Drug-control statutes, health and safety regulations, and traffic laws are all strict liability laws.

Protecting the Public To a certain extent, the concept of strict liability is inconsistent with the traditional principles of criminal law, which hold that *mens rea* is required for an act to be criminal. The goal of strict liability laws is to protect the public by eliminating the possibility that wrongdoers could claim ignorance or mistake to absolve themselves of criminal responsibility.[24] Thus, a person caught dumping waste in a protected pond or driving 70 miles per hour in a 55 miles-per-hour zone cannot plead a lack of intent in his or her defense.

Protecting Minors One of the most controversial strict liability crimes is **statutory rape**, in which an adult engages in a sexual relationship with a minor. In most states, even if the minor consents to the sexual act, the crime still exists because, being underage, he

DISCRETION in Action

MURDER OR MANSLAUGHTER?

THE SITUATION It is after midnight and George, drunk and angry, decides to pay a visit to Yeardley, his ex-girlfriend. When Yeardley refuses to let George into her apartment, he kicks the door down, grabs Yeardley by the neck, and wrestles her to the floor before leaving. Several hours later, Yeardley's roommate finds her dead, lying face down on a pillow soaked with blood.

THE LAW George can be charged with one of three possible crimes: (1) first degree murder, which is premeditated and deliberate; (2) second degree murder, which means he acted with wanton disregard for the consequences of his actions; or (3) involuntary manslaughter, which involves extreme carelessness but no intent to kill.

WHAT WOULD YOU DO? Further investigation shows that, two years prior to Yeardley's death, a jealous George put her in a chokehold in public. Furthermore, just days before breaking into her apartment, George sent Yeardley an e-mail in which he reacted to news that she was dating someone else by threatening, "I should have killed you." In his defense, George says that although he did have a physical confrontation with Yeardley, she did not seem injured when he left the apartment. George's lawyer claims that Yeardley died from suffocation, not from any wound caused by George. If it were your decision, would you charge George with first degree murder, second degree murder, or involuntary manslaughter?

To see how prosecutors in Mecklenburg County, Virginia, handled a similar situation, go to Example 3.1 in Appendix B.

Felony-Murder An unlawful homicide that occurs during the attempted commission of a felony.

or she is considered incapable of making a rational decision on the matter.[25] Therefore, statutory rape has been committed even if the adult was unaware of the minor's age or was misled to believe that the minor was older.

ACCOMPLICE LIABILITY Under certain circumstances, a person can be charged with and convicted of a crime that he or she did not actually commit. This occurs when the suspect has acted as an *accomplice,* helping another person commit the crime. Generally, to be found guilty as an accomplice, a person must have had "dual intent." This level of *mens rea* includes both

1. The intent to aid the person who committed the crime, and
2. The intent that such aid would lead to the commission of the crime.[26]

So, assume that Jerry drives Jason to a bank that Jason intends to rob. If Jerry had no knowledge of Jason's criminal plan, he would not fulfill the second prong of the "dual intent" test. As for the *actus reus,* the accomplice must have helped the primary actor in either a physical sense (for example, by providing the getaway car) or a psychological sense (for example, by encouraging her or him to commit the crime).[27]

In some states, a person can be convicted as an accomplice even without intent if the crime was a "natural and probable consequence" of his or her actions.[28] This principle has led to a proliferation of **felony-murder** legislation. Felony-murder is a form of first degree murder that applies when a person participates in any of a list of serious felonies that results in the death of a human being. Under felony-murder law, if two men rob a bank, and the first man intentionally kills a security guard, the second man can be convicted of first degree murder as an accomplice to the bank robbery, even if he had no intent to hurt anyone. Along these same lines, if a security guard accidentally shoots and kills a customer during a bank robbery, the bank robbers can be charged with first degree murder because they committed the underlying felony.

Concurrence

According to criminal law, there must be *concurrence* between the guilty act and the guilty intent. In other words, the guilty act and the guilty intent must occur together. Suppose, for example, that a woman intends to murder her husband with poison in order to collect his life insurance. Every evening, this woman drives her husband home from work. On the night she plans to poison him, however, she swerves to avoid a cat crossing the road and runs into a tree. She survives the accident, but her husband is killed. Even though her intent was realized, the incident would be considered an accidental death because she had not planned to kill him by driving the car into a tree.

Causation

Criminal law also requires that the criminal act cause the harm suffered. In 1989, for example, nineteen-year-old Mike Wells shook his two-year-old daughter, Christina, so violently that she suffered brain damage. Soon after the incident, Wells served prison time for aggravated child abuse. Seventeen years later, in 2006, Christina died. When a coroner ruled that the cause of death was the earlier brain injury, Pasco County, Florida, authorities decided that, despite the passage of time, Wells was criminally responsible for his daughter's death. In 2010, Wells pleaded guilty to second degree murder and received a fifteen-year prison sentence.

Attendant Circumstances

In certain crimes, **attendant circumstances**—also known as accompanying circumstances—are relevant to the *corpus delicti*. Most states, for example, differentiate between simple assault and the more serious offense of aggravated assault depending on the attendant circumstance of whether the defendant used a weapon such as a gun or a knife while committing the crime. Criminal law also classifies degrees of property crimes based on the attendant circumstance of the amount stolen. According to federal statutes, the theft of less than $1,000 from a bank is a misdemeanor, while the theft of any amount over $1,000 is a felony.[29] (To get a better understanding of the role of attendant circumstances in criminal statutes, see Figure 3.2 that follows.)

REQUIREMENTS OF PROOF AND INTENT Attendant circumstances must be proved beyond a reasonable doubt, just like any other element of a crime.[30] Furthermore, the *mens rea* of the defendant regarding each attendant circumstance must be proved as well. Consider the case of Christopher Jones, who was convicted of third degree rape in a South Dakota criminal court. Under state law, third degree rape occurs when the victim is incapable of giving consent to the sex act due to severe intoxication.

A South Dakota appeals court overturned Jones's conviction, ruling that prosecutors did not prove beyond a reasonable doubt that the defendant knew of his victim's drunken state and, thus, her inability to give consent. The court added that if the state legislature wanted to remove such knowledge from the definition of the crime, it must say so in the statute, thus making awareness of the victim's intoxication a *strict liability* (see the previous discussion) attendant circumstance.[31]

HATE CRIME LAWS In most cases, a person's motive for committing a crime is irrelevant—a court will not try to read the accused's mind. Over the past few decades, however, nearly every state and the federal government have passed *hate crime laws* that make the suspect's motive an important attendant circumstance to his or her criminal act. In general, **hate crime laws** provide for greater sanctions against those who commit crimes motivated by bias against a person or group based on race, ethnicity, religion, gender, sexual orientation, disability, or age.

In 2013, for example, Michal Gunar pleaded guilty to violating federal hate crime law as a result of his behavior during an attack on two men of Egyptian descent in Sayreville, New Jersey. Gunar had shouted anti-Arab slurs at his victims before the attack, which he carried out while wearing brass knuckles. Because his criminal act was obviously motivated by bias, Gunar was sentenced to three years in prison, a tougher punishment than he would have received if he had committed assault without the element of hate.

Attendant Circumstances The facts surrounding a criminal event that must be proved to convict the defendant of the underlying crime.

Hate Crime Law A statute that provides for greater sanctions against those who commit crimes motivated by bias against an individual or a group based on race, ethnicity, religion, gender, sexual orientation, disability, or age.

FIGURE 3.2 Attendant Circumstances in Criminal Law

Most criminal statutes incorporate three of the elements we have discussed in this section: the intent (*mens rea*), the act (*actus reus*), and attendant circumstances. This diagram of the federal false imprisonment statute should give you an idea of how these elements combine to create the totality of a crime.

Intent	Act	Attendant Circumstances

Whoever intentionally confines, restrains, or detains another against that person's will is guilty of felony false imprisonment.

Harm

For most crimes to occur, some harm must have been done to a person or to property. A certain number of crimes are actually categorized depending on the harm done to the victim, regardless of the intent behind the criminal act. Take two offenses, both of which involve one person hitting another in the back of the head with a tire iron. In the first instance, the victim dies, and the offender is charged with murder. In the second, the victim is only knocked unconscious, and the offender is charged with battery. Because the harm in the second instance was less severe, so was the crime with which the offender was charged, even though the act was exactly the same. Furthermore, most states have different degrees of battery depending on the extent of the injuries suffered by the victim.

Many acts are deemed criminal if they could do harm that the laws try to prevent. Such acts are called **inchoate offenses.** They exist when only an attempt at a criminal act was made. If Jenkins solicits Peterson to murder Jenkins's business partner, this is an inchoate offense on the part of Jenkins, even though Peterson fails to carry out the act. *Conspiracies* also fall into the category of inchoate offenses. The United States Supreme Court has ruled that a person working with another person or group could be convicted of criminal **conspiracy** even though police intervention made the completion of the illegal plan impossible.[32]

///SELF ASSESSMENT

Fill in the blanks, and check your answers on page 100.

Proof that a crime has been committed is established through the elements of the crime, which include the _____ _____, or the physical act of the crime; the _____ _____, or the intent to commit the crime; and the _____ of the guilty act and the guilty intent. With _____ _____ crimes, the law determines that a defendant is guilty even if he or she lacked the _____ to perform a criminal act. _____ circumstances are those circumstances that accompany the main criminal act in a criminal code, and they must be proved _____ _____ _____ _____, just like any other elements of a crime.

DEFENSES UNDER CRIMINAL LAW

On the night of June 15, 2013, sixteen-year-old Ethan Couch, driving with a blood-alcohol level three times the legal limit, killed four pedestrians in Burleson, Texas. During Couch's trial, a psychiatrist testified that the teenager should receive a lenient sentence because he suffered from "affluenza," a condition that "afflicts" irresponsible children of rich, lenient parents.

Although legal experts do not expect American judges to embrace the "spoiled brat" excuse,[33] defendants can raise a number of other, established defenses for wrongdoing in our criminal courts. These defenses generally rely on one of two arguments: (1) the defendant is not responsible for the crime, or (2) the defendant was justified in committing the crime.

Inchoate Offenses Conduct deemed criminal without actual harm being done, provided that the harm that would have occurred is one the law tries to prevent.

Conspiracy A plot by two or more people to carry out an illegal or harmful act.

Criminal Responsibility and the Law

The idea of responsibility plays a significant role in criminal law. In certain circumstances, the law recognizes that even though an act is inherently criminal, society will not punish the actor because he or she does not have the requisite mental condition. In other words, the law "excuses" the person for his or her behavior. Insanity, intoxication, and mistake are the most important excuse defenses today, but we start our discussion of the subject with one of the first such defenses recognized by American law: infancy.

LEARNING **5** OBJECTIVE List and briefly define the most important excuse defenses for crimes.

INFANCY Under the earliest state criminal codes of the United States, children younger than seven years of age could never be held legally accountable for crimes. Those between seven and fourteen years old were presumed to lack the capacity for criminal behavior, while anyone over the age of fourteen was tried as an adult. Thus, early American criminal law recognized **infancy** as a defense in which the accused's wrongdoing is excused because he or she is too young to fully understand the consequences of his or her actions.

With the creation of the juvenile justice system in the early 1900s, the infancy defense became redundant, as youthful delinquents were automatically treated differently from adult offenders. Today, most states either designate an age (eighteen or under) under which wrongdoers are sent to juvenile court or allow prosecutors to decide whether a minor will be charged as an adult on a case-by-case basis. We will explore the concept of infancy as it applies to the modern American juvenile justice system in much greater detail in Chapter 13.

INSANITY After Miguel Renteria stabbed and suffocated his daughter and his granddaughter to death, he told police investigators that his victims were possessed by devils and he killed them to save their souls. In 2013, a Cook County, Illinois, judge found that Renteria suffered from schizophrenia and therefore could not appreciate the criminality of his actions. As a result, Renteria was sent to a psychiatric hospital rather than prison. Thus, **insanity** may be a defense to a criminal charge when the defendant's state of mind is such that she or he cannot claim legal responsibility for her or his actions.

Measuring Sanity The general principle of the insanity defense is that a person is excused for his or her criminal wrongdoing if, as a result of a mental disease or defect, he or she

1. Does not perceive the physical nature or consequences of his or her conduct,
2. Does not know that his or her conduct is wrong or criminal, or
3. Is not sufficiently able to control his or her conduct so as to be held accountable for it.[34]

Although criminal law has traditionally accepted the idea that an insane person cannot be held responsible for criminal acts, society has long debated what standards should be used to measure sanity for the purposes of a criminal trial. This lack of consensus is reflected in the diverse tests employed by different American jurisdictions to determine insanity. The tests include the following:

1. *The* M'Naghten *rule.* Derived from an 1843 British murder case, the **M'Naghten rule** states that a person is legally insane and therefore not criminally responsible if, at the time of the offense, he or she was not able to distinguish between right and wrong.[35] As Figure 3.3 on the following page shows, half of the states still use a

Infancy A condition that, under early American law, excused young wrongdoers of criminal behavior because presumably they could not understand the consequences of their actions.

Insanity A defense for criminal liability that asserts a lack of criminal responsibility due to mental instability

M'Naghten Rule A test of criminal responsibility, derived from *M'Naghten's* Case in 1843, that relies on the defendant's inability to distinguish right from wrong.

version of the *M'Naghten* rule. One state, New Hampshire, uses a slightly different version of this rule called the "product test." Under this standard, a defendant is not guilty if the unlawful act was the product of a mental disease or defect.

2. *The ALI/MPC test.* In the early 1960s, the American Law Institute (ALI) included an insanity standard in its exhaustive criminal law guidebook called the Model Penal Code (MPC). Also known as the **substantial-capacity test,** the **ALI/MPC test** requires that the defendant lack "substantial capacity" to either "appreciate the wrongfulness" of his or her conduct or to conform that conduct "to the requirements of the law."[36]

3. *The irresistible-impulse test.* Under the **irresistible-impulse test,** a person may be found insane even if he or she was aware that a criminal act was "wrong," provided that some "irresistible impulse" resulting from a mental deficiency drove him or her to commit the crime.[37]

Public backlash against the insanity defense has caused seven state legislatures to pass "guilty but mentally ill" statutes. Under these laws, a jury can determine that a defendant is "mentally ill" rather than insane, and therefore responsible for her or his actions.[38] Defendants who are found guilty but mentally ill generally spend the early part of their sentences in a psychiatric hospital and the rest of the time in prison, or they receive treatment while in prison.

FIGURE 3.3 Insanity Defenses

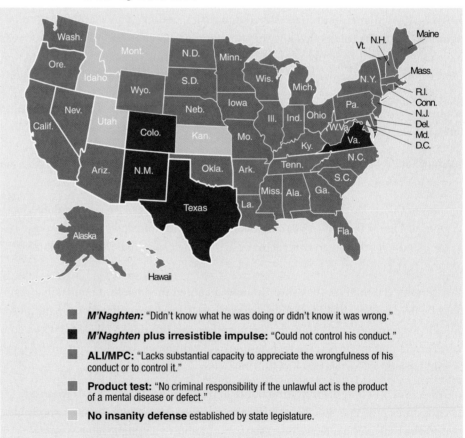

■ *M'Naghten:* "Didn't know what he was doing or didn't know it was wrong."

■ *M'Naghten* **plus irresistible impulse:** "Could not control his conduct."

■ **ALI/MPC:** "Lacks substantial capacity to appreciate the wrongfulness of his conduct or to control it."

■ **Product test:** "No criminal responsibility if the unlawful act is the product of a mental disease or defect."

■ **No insanity defense** established by state legislature.

Source: Bureau of Justice Statistics, *The Defense of Insanity: Standards and Procedures,* State Court Organization, 1998 (Washington, D.C.: U.S. Department of Justice, June 2000).

Determining Competency Whatever the standard, the insanity defense is rarely entered and is even less likely to result in an acquittal, as it is difficult to prove.[39] (See the feature *Myth vs Reality—Are Too Many Criminals Found Not Guilty by Reason of Insanity?* that follows.) Psychiatry is far more commonly used in the courtroom to determine the "competency" of a defendant to stand trial. If a judge believes that the defendant is unable to understand the nature of the proceedings or to assist in his or her own defense, the trial will not take place.

When **competency hearings** (which may also take place after the initial arrest and before sentencing) reveal that the defendant is in fact incompetent, criminal proceedings come to a halt. For example, in January 2013, an Alameda County, California, judge ruled that because One L. Goh suffered from paranoid schizophrenia, he was not fit to stand trial. Goh had been charged with seven counts of murder resulting from a shooting rampage on the campus of Oikos University in Oakland. As a result of the judge's decision, Goh would receive psychiatric treatment to restore his competency. When this goal was achieved, the criminal proceedings would continue.

INTOXICATION The law recognizes two types of **intoxication,** whether from drugs or from alcohol: *voluntary* and *involuntary.* Involuntary intoxication occurs when a person is physically forced to ingest or is injected with an intoxicating substance, or is unaware that a substance contains drugs or alcohol. Involuntary intoxication is a viable defense to a crime if the substance leaves the person unable to form the mental state necessary to understand

Competency Hearing A court proceeding to determine whether the defendant is mentally well enough to understand the charges filed against him or her and cooperate with a lawyer in presenting a defense.

Intoxication A defense for criminal liability in which the defendant claims that the taking of intoxicants rendered him or her unable to form the requisite intent to commit a criminal act.

MYTH VS REALITY
Are Too Many Criminals Found Not Guilty by Reason of Insanity?

LEARNING OBJECTIVE 6 Discuss a common misperception concerning the insanity defense in the United States.

THE MYTH The American system of criminal justice generally holds that a person may not be tried for an offense if that person cannot be held legally responsible for her or his actions. Because of the publicity surrounding the insanity defense, many people are under the impression that it is a major loophole in our system, allowing criminals to be "let off" no matter how heinous their crimes.

THE REALITY In fact, the insanity defense is raised in only about 1 percent of felony trials, and it is successful only one out of every four times it is raised. The reason: it is extremely difficult to prove insanity under the law. For example, Andre Thomas cut out the hearts of his wife, their young son, and her thirteen-month-old daughter. Before his murder trial, Thomas pulled his right eye out of its socket. (Several years later, while

on death row, he ripped out the other eye and apparently ate it.) Nonetheless, prosecutors were able to convince a Texas jury that Brown understood the difference between right and wrong at the time of the murders, and an appeals court upheld the conviction. Thomas is "clearly 'crazy,'" said one of the appellate judges who heard his case, "but he is also 'sane' under Texas law."

Even if Thomas had succeeded with the insanity defense, he would not have been "let off" in the sense that he would have been set free. Many defendants found not guilty by reason of insanity spend more time in mental hospitals than criminals who are convicted of similar acts spend in prison.

FOR CRITICAL ANALYSIS
What do the relatively limited use and success rate of the insanity defense indicate about the impact of public opinion on criminal law?

that the act committed while under the influence was wrong.[40] Several years ago, for example, Montana's Supreme Court ruled that a woman had wrongly been denied the ability to present the involuntary intoxication defense to counter a drunken driving charge. The defendant claimed that she had unwittingly consumed a drink laced with GHB, known as the "date rape drug," before being arrested during her drive home from a bar.[41]

Voluntary drug or alcohol intoxication is also used to excuse a defendant's actions, though it is not a defense in itself. Rather, it is used when the defense attorney wants to show that the defendant was so intoxicated that *mens rea* was negated. In other words, the defendant could not possibly have had the state of mind that a crime requires. Many courts are reluctant to allow voluntary intoxication arguments to be presented to juries, however. After all, the defendant, by definition, voluntarily chose to enter an intoxicated state. Twelve states have eliminated voluntary intoxication as a possible defense, a step that has been criticized by many legal scholars but was upheld by the United States Supreme Court in *Montana v. Egelhoff* (1996).[42]

MISTAKE Everyone has heard the saying, "Ignorance of the law is no excuse." Ordinarily, ignorance of the law or a *mistaken idea* about what the law requires is not a valid defense.[43] For example, several years ago retired science teacher Eddie Leroy Anderson and his son dug for arrowheads near their favorite campground site in Idaho, unaware that the land was a federally protected archaeological site. Facing two years in prison for this mistake, they pleaded guilty and were given a year's probation and a $1,500 fine each. "Folks need to pay attention to where they are," said U.S. attorney Wendy Olson.[44]

Mistake of Law As the above example suggests, strict liability crimes specifically preclude the *mistake of law* defense, because the offender's intent is irrelevant. For practical reasons, the mistake of law defense is rarely allowed under any circumstances. If "I didn't know" was a valid defense, the courts would be clogged with defendants claiming ignorance of all aspects of criminal law. In some rare instances, however, people who claim that they honestly did not know that they were breaking a law may have a valid defense if (1) the law was not published or reasonably known to the public, or (2) the person relied on an official statement of the law that was erroneous.[45]

Mistake of Fact A *mistake of fact,* as opposed to a mistake of law, operates as a defense if it negates the mental state necessary to commit a crime. If, for example, Oliver mistakenly walks off with Julie's briefcase because he thinks it is his, there is no theft. Theft requires knowledge that the property belongs to another. The mistake-of-fact defense has proved very controversial in rape and sexual assault cases, in which the accused claims a mistaken belief that the sex was consensual, while the victim insists that he or she was coerced.

Justification Criminal Defenses and the Law

In certain instances, a defendant will accept responsibility for committing an illegal act, but contend that—given the circumstances— the act was justified. In other words, even though the guilty act and the guilty intent are present, the particulars of the case relieve the defendant of criminal liability. In 2012, for example, there were 720

In July 2013, John Spooner, right, was convicted of fatally shooting his thirteen-year-old neighbor. Spooner mistakenly thought that the boy had broken into his home and stolen four firearms. Why do you think this mistake-of-fact defense failed to keep Spooner from being sentenced to life in prison for his crime?

Kristyna Wentz-Graff/Milwaukee Journal Sentinel/MCT/Landov

"justified" killings of those who were in the process of committing a felony: 410 by law enforcement officers and 310 by private citizens.[46] Four of the most important justification defenses are duress, self-defense, necessity, and entrapment.

LEARNING
7 Describe the four most important justification criminal defenses.
OBJECTIVE

DURESS Duress exists when the *wrongful* threat of one person induces another person to perform an act that she or he would otherwise not perform. In such a situation, duress is said to negate the *mens rea* necessary to commit a crime. For duress to qualify as a defense, the following requirements must be met:

1. The threat must be of serious bodily harm or death.
2. The harm threatened must be greater than the harm caused by the crime.
3. The threat must be immediate and inescapable.
4. The defendant must have become involved in the situation through no fault of his or her own.[47]

Note that some scholars consider duress to be an excuse defense, because the threat of bodily harm negates any guilty intent on the part of the defendant.[48]

When ruling on the duress defense, courts often examine whether the defendant had the opportunity to avoid the threat in question. Two narcotics cases illustrate this point. In the first, the defendant claimed that an associate threatened to kill him and his wife unless he participated in a marijuana deal. Although this contention was proved true during the course of the trial, the court rejected the duress defense because the defendant made no apparent effort to escape, nor did he report his dilemma to the police. In sum, the drug deal was avoidable—the defendant could have made an effort to extricate himself, but he did not, thereby surrendering the protection of the duress defense.[49]

In the second case, a taxi driver in Bogotá, Colombia, was ordered by a passenger to swallow cocaine-filled balloons and take them to the United States. The taxi driver was warned that if he refused, his wife and three-year-old daughter would be killed. After a series of similar threats, the taxi driver agreed to transport the drugs. On arriving at customs at the Los Angeles airport, the defendant consented to have his stomach X-rayed, which led to discovery of the contraband and his arrest. During his trial, the defendant told the court that he was afraid to notify the police in Colombia because he believed them to be corrupt. The court accepted his duress defense, on the grounds that it met the four requirements listed above and the defendant had notified American authorities when given the opportunity to do so.[50]

JUSTIFIABLE USE OF FORCE—SELF-DEFENSE A person who believes he or she is in danger of being harmed by another is justified in defending himself or herself with the use of force, and any criminal act committed in such circumstances can be justified as **self-defense.** Other situations that also justify the use of force include the defense of another person, the defense of one's dwelling or other property, and the prevention of a crime. In all of these situations, it is important to distinguish between deadly and nondeadly force. Deadly force is likely to result in death or serious bodily harm.

The Amount of Force Generally speaking, people can use the amount of nondeadly force that seems necessary to protect themselves, their dwellings, or other property or to prevent the commission of a crime. Deadly force can be used in self-defense if there is a *reasonable belief* that imminent death or bodily harm will otherwise result, if the attacker is using unlawful force (an example of lawful force is that exerted by a police officer), if

Duress Unlawful pressure brought to bear on a person, causing the person to perform an act that he or she would not otherwise perform.

Self-Defense The legally recognized privilege to protect one's self or property from injury by another.

the defender has not initiated or provoked the attack, and if there is no other possible response or alternative way out of the life-threatening situation.[51]

Deadly force normally can be used to defend a dwelling only if the unlawful entry is violent and the person believes deadly force is necessary to prevent imminent death or great bodily harm. In some jurisdictions, it is also a viable defense if the person believes deadly force is necessary to prevent the commission of a felony (such as arson) in the dwelling.

The Duty to Retreat

When a person is outside the home or in a public space, the rules for self-defense change somewhat. Until relatively recently, almost all jurisdictions required someone who is attacked under these circumstances to "retreat to the wall" before fighting back. In other words, under this **duty to retreat** one who is being assaulted may not resort to deadly force if she or he has a reasonable opportunity to "run away" and thus avoid the conflict. Only when this person has run into a "wall," literally or otherwise, may deadly force be used in self-defense.

Recently, however, several states have changed their laws to eliminate this duty to retreat. For example, a Florida law did away with the duty to retreat outside the home, stating that citizens have "the right to stand [their] ground and meet force with force, including deadly force," if they "reasonably" fear for their safety.[52] Florida's "stand your ground" law also allows a person to use deadly force against someone who unlawfully intrudes into her or his house (or vehicle), even if that person does not fear for her or his safety.[53]

The George Zimmerman Case

Ironically, the case that brought stand your ground laws to national attention was not decided on the basis of a stand your ground statute. On February 26, 2012, George Zimmerman shot and killed unarmed seventeen-year-old Trayvon Martin in Sanford, Florida. Zimmerman told police that he had encountered Martin during his rounds as a neighborhood watchman, and that he had pulled the trigger only after being attacked by the younger man. Initially, local police accepted this version of events and did not arrest Zimmerman, who appeared to have acted within the limits of the state's stand your ground law.

After a national outcry, Zimmerman eventually was arrested and a special prosecutor charged him with second degree murder. During the trial, Zimmerman's lawyers did not need to rely on the state's stand your ground law. Rather, they only had to prove "classic self-defense"—that he feared great bodily harm or death when he pulled out his gun and shot Martin.[54] Photographs of injuries that Zimmerman sustained during the confrontation, including a bloody nose and cuts on the back of his head, created sufficient doubt in the minds of the jurors, and he was acquitted.

The verdict did not, however, end the controversy surrounding these laws. Of particular concern are statistics showing that the stand your ground defense is much more likely to succeed when the defendant is white or Hispanic (as is Zimmerman) and the homicide victim is African American (as was Martin).[55] (See the feature *CJ Controversy— Stand Your Ground Laws* that follows to explore this topic more thoroughly.)

NECESSITY

The **necessity** defense requires courts to weigh the harm caused by the crime actually committed against the harm that would have been caused by the criminal act avoided. If the avoided harm is greater than the committed harm, then the defense has a chance of succeeding. The necessity defense often is raised by drunk driving defendants who point to extenuating circumstances—such as the need to flee a domestic abuser or get a sick cat to the hospital—to justify getting behind the wheel while

STAND YOUR GROUND LAWS

In the five years after Florida passed the nation's first stand your ground law in 2005, the number of justifiable homicides in the state tripled. Depending on one's perspective, such statistics show that the statute is having the intended impact or, conversely, that it has turned Florida into "the Wild West." Given that more than thirty states now have passed legislation that removes the duty to retreat before using force in self-defense, such laws have become a matter of national debate.

STAND YOUR GROUND LAWS BENEFIT SOCIETY BECAUSE . . .

- They strengthen the concept of self-defense. That is, they allow people who face serious bodily harm or death the opportunity to defend themselves without first having to retreat as far as possible.
- It is difficult to define an "appropriate retreat." These laws remove the possibility that someone defending himself or herself from deadly force will be charged with a crime because he or she did not make a reasonable attempt to run away.

STAND YOUR GROUND LAWS HARM SOCIETY BECAUSE . . .

- They encourage violence and are creating a "nation where disputes are settled by guns instead of gavels, and where suspects are shot by civilians instead of arrested by the police."
- They require only that a person *believe or imagine* that he or she is in danger of bodily harm or death, not that the person *actually is* facing such dangers. This increases the likelihood of violence based on misunderstanding or prejudice.

Your Assignment

Go online and learn the facts about the incident in which **Joe Hendrix** fatally shot **Ronald Westbrook** in Chickamauga, Georgia. According to traditional concepts of self-defense, was Hendrix justified in using deadly force against Westbrook? Under Florida's stand your ground law, would Hendrix have a valid claim to self-defense? What is your opinion of stand your ground laws with regard to home intruders? Write at least two full paragraphs to explain your answers.

---

impaired. (This use of the necessity defense rarely succeeds.) Murder is the one crime for which the necessity defense is not applicable under any circumstances.[56]

ENTRAPMENT **Entrapment** is a justification defense that criminal law allows when a police officer or government agent deceives a defendant into wrongdoing. Although law enforcement agents can legitimately use various forms of subterfuge—such as informants or undercover agents—to gain information or apprehend a suspect in a criminal act, the law places limits on these strategies. Police cannot persuade an innocent person to commit a crime, nor can they coerce a suspect into doing so, even if they are certain she or he is a criminal. (For an overview of justification and excuse defenses, see Figure 3.4 that follows.)

> **Entrapment** A defense in which the defendant claims that he or she was induced by a public official—usually an undercover agent or police officer—to commit a crime that he or she would otherwise not have committed.

///// SELF ASSESSMENT

Fill in the blanks, and check your answers on page 100.

Criminal law recognizes that a defendant may not be _____ for a criminal act if her or his mental state was impaired, by either _____—the psychological inability to separate right from wrong—or _____ due to drugs or alcohol. Defendants may also claim that they were _____ in committing an act either because they were under _____ to perform an act that they would not otherwise have performed or because they were acting in _____-_____ to protect themselves from serious bodily harm. _____ occurs when a government agent deceives a defendant into committing a crime.

FIGURE 3.4 Excuse and Justification Defenses

Excuse Defenses: Based on a defendant admitting that she or he committed the criminal act, but asserting that she or he cannot be held criminally responsible for the act due to lack of criminal intent.

	The defendant must prove that . . .	Example
INFANCY	Because he or she was under a statutorily determined age, he or she did not have the maturity to make the decisions necessary to commit a criminal act.	A thirteen-year-old takes a handgun from his backpack at school and begins shooting at fellow students, killing three. (In such cases, the offender is often processed by the juvenile justice system rather than the criminal justice system.)
INSANITY	At the time of the criminal act, he or she did not have the necessary mental capacity to be held responsible for his or her actions.	A man with a history of mental illness pushes a woman in front of an oncoming subway train, which kills her instantly.
INTOXICATION	She or he had diminished control over her or his actions due to the influence of alcohol or drugs.	A woman who had been drinking malt liquor and vodka stabs her boyfriend to death after a domestic argument. She claims to have been so drunk as to not remember the incident.
MISTAKE	He or she did not know that his or her actions violated a law (this defense is very rarely even attempted), or that he or she violated the law believing a relevant fact to be true when, in fact, it was not.	A woman, thinking that her divorce in another state has been finalized when it has not, marries for a second time, thereby committing bigamy.

Justification Defenses: Based on a defendant admitting that he or she committed the particular criminal act, but asserting that, under the circumstances, the criminal act was justified.

	The defendant must prove that . . .	Example
DURESS	She or he performed the criminal act under the use or threat of use of unlawful force against her or his person that a reasonable person would have been unable to resist.	A mother assists her boyfriend in committing a burglary after he threatens to kill her children if she refuses to do so.
SELF-DEFENSE	He or she acted in a manner to defend himself or herself, others, or property, or to prevent the commission of a crime.	A husband awakes to find his wife standing over him, pointing a shotgun at his chest. In the ensuing struggle, the firearm goes off, killing the wife.
NECESSITY	The criminal act he or she committed was necessary in order to avoid a harm to himself or herself or another that was greater than the harm caused by the act itself.	Four people physically remove a friend from her residence on the property of a religious cult, arguing that the crime of kidnapping was justified in order to remove the victim from the damaging influence of cult leaders.
ENTRAPMENT	She or he was encouraged by agents of the state to engage in a criminal act she or he would not have engaged in otherwise.	The owner of a boat marina agrees to allow three federal drug enforcement agents, posing as drug dealers, to use his dock to unload shipments of marijuana from Colombia.

PROCEDURAL SAFEGUARDS

To this point, we have focused on **substantive criminal law,** which defines the acts that the government will punish. It brings the force of the state, with all its resources, to bear against the individual. We will now turn our attention to **procedural criminal law.** (The section that follows will provide only a short overview of criminal procedure. In later chapters, many other constitutional issues will be examined in more detail.) Criminal procedures, drawn from the ideals stated in the Bill of Rights, are designed to protect the constitutional rights of individuals and to prevent the arbitrary use of power by the government.

The Bill of Rights

Substantive Criminal Law
Law that defines the rights and duties of individuals with respect to one another.

Procedural Criminal Law
Law that defines the manner in which the rights and duties of individuals may be enforced.

For various reasons, proposals related to the rights of individuals were rejected during the framing of the U.S. Constitution in 1787. The need for a written declaration of rights of individuals eventually caused the first Congress to draft twelve amendments to the Constitution and submit them for approval by the states. Ten of these amendments, commonly known as the **Bill of Rights,** were adopted in 1791. Since then, seventeen more amendments have been added.

The Bill of Rights, as interpreted by the United States Supreme Court, has served as the basis for procedural safeguards of the accused in this country. These safeguards include the following:

1. The Fourth Amendment protection from unreasonable searches and seizures.
2. The Fourth Amendment requirement that no warrants for a search or an arrest can be issued without probable cause.
3. The Fifth Amendment requirement that no one can be deprived of life, liberty, or property without "due process" of law.
4. The Fifth Amendment prohibition against *double jeopardy* (trying someone twice for the same criminal offense).
5. The Fifth Amendment guarantee that no person can be required to be a witness against (incriminate) himself or herself.
6. The Sixth Amendment guarantees of a speedy trial, a trial by jury, a public trial, the right to confront witnesses, and the right to a lawyer at various stages of criminal proceedings.
7. The Eighth Amendment prohibitions against excessive bails and fines, and cruel and unusual punishments. (For the full text of the Bill of Rights, see Appendix A.)

The Bill of Rights initially offered citizens protection only against the federal government. Over the years, however, the procedural safeguards of most of the provisions of the Bill of Rights have been applied to the actions of state governments through the Fourteenth Amendment.[57] Furthermore, the states, under certain circumstances, have the option to grant even more protections than are required by the federal Constitution. As these protections are crucial to criminal justice procedures in the United States, they will be afforded much more attention in Chapter 6, with regard to police action, and in Chapter 8, with regard to the criminal trial.

Due Process

Both the Fifth and the Fourteenth Amendments provide that no person should be deprived of "life, liberty, or property without due process of law." This **due process clause** basically requires that the government not act unfairly or arbitrarily. In other words, the government cannot rely on individual judgment and impulse when making decisions, but must stay within the boundaries of reason and the law. Of course, disagreements as to the meaning of this clause have plagued courts, politicians, and citizens since this nation was founded, and will undoubtedly continue to do so.

To understand due process, it is important to consider its two types: procedural due process and substantive due process.

PROCEDURAL DUE PROCESS According to **procedural due process,** the law must be carried out by a *method* that is fair

Bill of Rights The first ten amendments to the U.S. Constitution.

Due Process Clause The provisions of the Fifth and Fourteenth Amendments to the Constitution that guarantee that no person shall be deprived of life, liberty, or property without due process of law.

Procedural Due Process A provision in the Constitution that states the law must be carried out in a fair and orderly manner.

■ Why do most Americans accept certain precautions taken by the federal government—such as full body scans at airports—that restrict our individual freedom or compromise our privacy?

John Moore/Getty Images

LEARNING
8
OBJECTIVE

Explain the importance of the
due process clause in the
criminal justice system.

and orderly. It requires that certain procedures be followed in administering and executing a law so that an individual's basic freedoms are not violated.

The American criminal justice system's adherence to due process principles is evident in its treatment of the death penalty. To ensure that the process is fair, a number of procedural safeguards have been built into capital punishment, as we will see in Chapter 9. Much to the dismay of many victims' groups, these procedures make the process expensive and lengthy. In California, for example, the average time between conviction for a capital crime and execution is twenty-five years.[58] (Concepts of due process can become muddied when it comes to fighting terrorism, as is detailed in the feature *A Question of Ethics—Due Justice?* that follows.)

SUBSTANTIVE DUE PROCESS Fair procedures would obviously be of little use if they were used to administer unfair laws. For example, suppose a law requires everyone to wear a red shirt on Mondays. You wear a blue shirt on Monday, and you are arrested, convicted, and sentenced to one year in prison. The fact that all proper procedures were followed and your rights were given their proper protections would mean very little because the law that you broke was unfair and arbitrary.

Thus, **substantive due process** requires that the laws themselves be reasonable. The idea is that if a law is unfair or arbitrary, even if properly passed by a legislature, it must be declared unconstitutional. In 1935, for example, Oklahoma instituted the

Substantive Due Process
The constitutional requirement that laws used in accusing and convicting persons of crimes must be fair.

A QUESTION OF ETHICS: Due JUSTICE?

THE SITUATION The U.S. government has learned the precise location of an Islamist cleric in the Middle Eastern country of Yemen. This cleric has been linked to more than a dozen terrorist operations, including a failed plot to blow up cargo airplanes bound for the United States, and his online sermons in English contain numerous threats to Americans. Using a Predator drone—a remote-controlled unmanned aircraft armed with missiles—the U.S. military has the ability to target and kill the cleric. There is one problem, however: the target was born in New Mexico and is therefore a citizen of the United States.

THE ETHICAL DILEMMA The U.S. Constitution forbids the conviction and execution of American citizens without due process of law, which usually means a criminal trial.

WHAT IS THE SOLUTION? In 2011, an American Predator drone missile killed Anwar al-Awlaki, the U.S. citizen Islamist cleric described above. Legal expert Glenn Greenwald echoed the sentiments of a number of critics by arguing that this action was inherently unfair. Awlaki had not been charged with any crime, and he had not been afforded a trial to prove his innocence. "[Awlaki] was simply ordered

killed by [President Barack Obama]: his judge, jury, and executioner," Greenwald said.

Federal counterterrorism officials defended the drone strike as "'legal,' 'ethical,' and 'wise.'" According to the Obama administration, Awlaki was no ordinary American citizen. Rather, he was a member of terrorist organizations that were, essentially, at war with the United States. Furthermore, in 2013, federal lawyers justified targeted assassinations of suspected terrorists—including U.S. citizens—as "lawful acts of self-defense." After reviewing our discussion of self-defense earlier in this chapter, what is your opinion of this argument? Do you think that the assassination of U.S. citizens without due process is acceptable? Explain your answer.

Habitual Criminal Sterilization Act. Under this statute, a person who had been convicted of three felonies could be "rendered sexually sterile" by the state (that is, the person would no longer be able to produce children). The United States Supreme Court held that the law was unconstitutional, as there are "limits to the extent to which a legislatively represented majority may conduct biological experiments at the expense of the dignity and personality and natural powers of a minority."[59]

THE JUDICIAL SYSTEM'S ROLE IN DUE PROCESS As the last example suggests, the United States Supreme Court often plays the important role of ultimately deciding when due process has been violated and when it has not. (See Figure 3.5 that follows for a list of important Supreme Court due process cases.)

The Court is also called on from time to time to determine whether a due process right exists in the first place. For example, in Figure 3.3 on page 88, you will notice that four states—Idaho, Kansas, Montana, and Utah—do not provide defendants with access to the insanity defense. In 2007, John Delling killed two men in Idaho whom he believed had conspired to steal his soul. Because Idaho does not allow the insanity defense, Delling pleaded guilty to the murders and was sentenced to life in prison. Several years ago, his lawyers asked the Supreme Court to rule that the insanity defense was a constitutional right that should be available to all defendants in the United States. The Court refused to do so, allowing individual states to prohibit the insanity defense if they so wish.[60]

Victims' Rights in the Criminal Justice System

In 2012, several members of Congress proposed a Victims' Rights Amendment to the U.S. Constitution.[61] Indeed, victims' rights supporters have been trying, without success, to amend the Constitution in favor of victims for nearly two decades. The problem, according to these activists, is that once a crime has occurred, the victim is relegated to a single role: being a witness against the suspect in court. Legally, he or she has no say in the

FIGURE 3.5 Important United States Supreme Court Due Process Decisions

YEAR	ISSUE	AMENDMENT INVOLVED	COURT CASE
1948	Right to a public trial	VI	*In re Oliver*, 333 U.S. 257
1952	Police searches cannot be so invasive as to "shock the conscience"	IV	*Rochin v. California*, 342 U.S. 165
1961	Exclusionary rule	IV	*Mapp v. Ohio*, 367 U.S. 643
1963	Right to a lawyer in all criminal felony cases	VI	*Gideon v. Wainwright*, 372 U.S. 335
1964	No compulsory self-incrimination	V	*Malloy v. Hogan*, 378 U.S. 1
1964	Right to have counsel when taken into police custody and subjected to questioning	VI	*Escobedo v. Illinois*, 378 U.S. 478
1965	Right to confront and cross-examine witnesses	VI	*Pointer v. Texas*, 380 U.S. 400
1966	Right to an impartial jury	VI	*Parker v. Gladden*, 385 U.S. 363
1966	Confessions of suspects not notified of due process rights ruled invalid	V	*Miranda v. Arizona*, 384 U.S. 436
1967	Right to a speedy trial	VI	*Klopfer v. North Carolina*, 386 U.S. 21
1967	Juveniles have due process rights, too	V	*In re Gault*, 387 U.S. 1
1968	Right to a jury trial ruled a fundamental right	VI	*Duncan v. Louisiana*, 391 U.S. 145
1969	No double jeopardy	V	*Benton v. Maryland*, 395 U.S. 784

AP Images/Press of Atlantic City/Danny Drake

Family members of murder victim Martin Caballero address a criminal court in Mays Landing, New Jersey. Should crime victims and their families have the "right" to participate in the criminal justice system? Why or why not?

prosecution of the offender, or even whether such a prosecution is to take place. Such powerlessness can be extremely frustrating, particularly in the wake of a traumatic, life-changing event.

LEGISLATIVE ACTION To remedy this situation, all states have passed legislation creating certain rights for victims. On a federal level, such protections are encoded in the Crime Victims' Rights Act of 2004, which gives victims "the right to participate in the system."[62] This participation primarily focuses on three categories of rights:

1. *The right to be informed,* which includes receiving information about victims' rights in general, as well as specific information such as the dates and time of court proceedings relating to the relevant crime.

2. *The right to be present,* which includes the right to be present at those court hearings involving the case at hand, so long as the victim's presence does not interfere with the rights of the accused.

3. *The right to be heard,* which includes the ability to consult with prosecutorial officials before the criminal trial (addressed in Chapter 8), to speak during the sentencing phase of the trial (Chapter 9), and to offer an opinion when the offender is scheduled to be released from incarceration (Chapter 10).[63]

Some jurisdictions also provide victims with the right of law enforcement protection from the offender during the time period before a criminal trial. In addition, most states require restitution, or monetary payment, from offenders to help victims repay any costs associated with the crime and rebuild their lives.

ENFORCEABILITY Although many victims have benefited from the legislation described above, advocates still find fault with the manner in which the legislation is applied. The main problem, they say, is that the federal and state laws do not contain sufficient enforcement mechanisms. That is, if a victim's rights are violated in some way, the victim has little recourse. Indeed, almost all victims' rights legislation gives criminal justice officials the discretion to deny the very protections they contain. Consequently, according to one observer, victims' rights are often more illusion than reality, a situation that can only be remedied by the proposed amendment to the Constitution mentioned above.[64]

////SELF ASSESSMENT

Fill in the blanks, and check your answers on page 100.

The basis for procedural safeguards for the accused is found in the _____ _____ _____ of the U.S. Constitution. According to these safeguards, no person shall be deprived of life or liberty without _____ _____ of law. This means that the _____ by which the law is carried out must be fair and orderly and the laws themselves must be _____. The _____ _____ _____ _____ ultimately decides whether these rights have been violated.

CHAPTER **SUMMARY**

For more information on these concepts, look back to the Learning Objective icons throughout the chapter.

 List the four written sources of American criminal law. (a) The U.S. Constitution and state constitutions; (b) statutes passed by Congress and state legislatures (plus local ordinances); (c) administrative agency regulations; and (d) case law.

 Explain the two basic functions of criminal law. The primary legal function is to protect citizens from physical harms to their safety and property and from such harms to society's interest collectively. The social function is to maintain and teach social values as well as social boundaries—for example, speed limits and laws against bigamy.

 Discuss the primary goals of civil law and criminal law, and explain how these goals are realized. Civil law is designed to resolve disputes between private individuals and between other entities, such as corporations. In these disputes, one party, called the plaintiff, tries to gain monetary damages by proving that the accused party, the defendant, is to blame for a tort, or wrongful act. In contrast, criminal law exists to protect society from criminal behavior. To that end, the government prosecutes defendants, or persons who have been charged with committing a crime.

 Delineate the elements required to establish *mens rea* **(a guilty mental state).** (a) Purpose, (b) knowledge, (c) negligence, or (d) recklessness.

 List and briefly define the most important excuse defenses for crimes. Insanity—different tests of insanity can be used, including (a) the *M'Naghten* rule (right-wrong test); (b) the ALI/MPC test, also known as the substantial-capacity test; and (c) the irresistible-impulse test. **Intoxication**—classifications are voluntary and involuntary, the latter being a possible criminal defense. **Mistake**—a mistake of law defense is sometimes valid if the law was not published or reasonably known or if the alleged offender relied on an official statement of the law that was erroneous. Also, a mistake of fact may negate the mental state necessary to commit a crime.

 Discuss a common misperception concerning the insanity defense in the United States. Contrary to popular opinion, the insanity defense is not an often-used loophole that allows criminals to avoid responsibility for committing heinous crimes. Insanity defenses are difficult to mount and very rarely succeed. Even when a defendant is found not guilty by reason of insanity, she or he does not "go free." Instead, such defendants are sent to mental health care institutions and may spend more time there than they would have in prison.

 Describe the four most important justification criminal defenses. Duress—requires that (a) the threat is of serious bodily harm or death, (b) the harm is greater than that caused by the crime; (c) the threat is immediate and inescapable; and (d) the defendant became involved in the situation through no fault of his or her own. **Self-defense**—asserts justifiable use of force in the defense of one's person, dwelling, or property, or the prevention of a crime. **Necessity**—requires courts to determine if the harm sought to be avoided is greater than that sought to be prevented by the law defining the offense charged. **Entrapment**— claims that the criminal action was induced by certain governmental persuasion or trickery.

 Explain the importance of the due process clause in the criminal justice system. The due process clause—which states that no person shall be deprived of life, liberty, or property without due process of law—acts to limit the power of government. In the criminal justice system, the due process clause requires that certain procedures be followed to ensure the fairness of criminal proceedings and that all criminal laws be reasonable and in the interest of the public good.

QUESTIONS FOR **CRITICAL ANALYSIS**

1. Give an example of a criminal law whose main purpose seems to be teaching societal boundaries rather than protecting citizens from harm. By searching the Internet, can you find examples of other countries where this behavior is *not* considered criminal? How is the behavior perceived in those countries?

2. Why is murder considered a *mala in se* crime? What argument can be made that murder is not a *mala in se* crime?

3. Nine-year-old Savannah lies to her grandmother Jessica about eating candy bars. As punishment, Jessica forces Savannah to run for three hours without a rest. Severely dehydrated, the girl has a seizure and dies. What should be the criminal charge against Jessica, and why?

4. Keith lends his car to Jermaine, who drives with two other friends to the home of a marijuana dealer. The three men break into the home, intending to steal a safe full of cash. The drug dealer is unexpectedly at home, however, and in a struggle Jermaine winds up murdering him. What rule allows local prosecutors to charge Keith with first degree murder? Why?

5. Suppose that Louisiana's legislature passes a law allowing law enforcement officers to forcibly remove residents from their homes in the face of an imminent hurricane. Why might a court uphold this law even though, in most circumstances, such forcible removal would violate the residents' due process rights? If you were a judge, would you uphold Louisiana's new law?

KEY TERMS

actus reus   80
administrative law   73
attempt   81
attendant circumstances   85
ballot initiative   72
beyond a reasonable doubt   77
Bill of Rights   95
case law   73
civil law   76
competency hearing   89
conspiracy   86
constitutional law   71
corpus delicti   79
defendant   76
due process clause   95
duress   91
duty to retreat   92
entrapment   93

felony   77
felony-murder   84
hate crime law   85
inchoate offenses   86
infancy   87
infraction   78
insanity   87
intoxication   89
involuntary manslaughter   82
irresistible-impulse test   88
liability   76
mala in se   78
mala prohibita   78
mens rea   81
misdemeanor   78
M'Naghten rule   87
necessity   92
negligence   81

plaintiff   76
precedent   73
preponderance of the evidence   77
procedural criminal law   94
procedural due process   95
recklessness   81
self-defense   91
statutory law   72
statutory rape   83
strict liability crimes   83
substantial-capacity test
   (ALI/MPC test)   88
substantive criminal law   94
substantive due process   96
supremacy clause   72
voluntary manslaughter   82

SELF-ASSESSMENT ANSWER KEY

Page 73: i. Constitution; **ii.** unconstitutional; **iii.** statutes; **iv.** case

Page 76: i. legal; **ii.** criminal; **iii.** social; **iv.** morality

Page 79: i. Civil; **ii.** state/government; **iii.** felony; **iv.** misdemeanor

Page 86: i. *actus reus;* **ii.** *mens rea;* **iii.** concurrence; **iv.** strict liability; **v.** intent/*mens rea*/mental state; **vi.** Attendant; **vii.** beyond a reasonable doubt

Page 93: i. responsible; **ii.** insanity; **iii.** intoxication; **iv.** justified; **v.** duress; **vi.** self-defense; **vii.** Entrapment

Page 98: i. Bill of Rights; **ii.** due process; **iii.** procedures; **iv.** reasonable/fair; **v.** United States Supreme Court

NOTES

1. John S. Baker, Jr., *Measuring the Explosive Growth of Federal Crime Legislation* (Washington, D.C.: The Federalist Society for Law and Public Policy Studies, 2008), 1.

2. "US Court Records Show Nearly 500 Years in Prison Time for Medical Marijuana Offenses," *California NORML* (June 13, 2013), at **www.canorml.org/costs /Nearly_500_Years_Prison_Time_for _Medical_Marijuana_Offenses.**

3. Quoted in "Judge: Federal Law Trumps Montana's Medical Pot Law," *Associated Press* (January 23, 2012).

4. *Texas v. Johnson*, 491 U.S. 397 (1989).

5. Clean Water Act Section 309, 33 U.S.C.A. Section 1319 (1987).

6. Joel Feinberg, *The Moral Limits of the Criminal Law: Harm to Others* (New York: Oxford University Press, 1984), 221–232.

7. Henry M. Hart, Jr., "The Aims of the Criminal Law," *Law & Contemporary Problems* 23 (1958), 405–406.

8. John L. Diamond, "The Myth of Morality and Fault in Criminal Law Doctrine," *American Criminal Law Review* 34 (Fall 1996), 111.

9. Kentucky Statutes Section 437.060; and New Hampshire Revised Statutes Section 207:61.

10. The Humane Society of the United States, "Ranking of State Cockfighting Laws," June 2010, at **www.humanesociety.org /assets/pdfs/animal_fighting/cock fighting_statelaws.pdf;** and Animal Welfare Act Amendments of 2007, Pub. L. No. 110-246, 122 Statute 223 (2007).

11. John Monk, "Cockfighters Take Fight to Federal Appeals Court," *The State* (Columbia, SC) (December 4, 2011), A1.

12. Lawrence M. Friedman, *Crime and Punishments in American History* (New York: Basic Books, 1993), 10.

13. *Federal Criminal Rules Handbook*, Section 2.1 (West 2008).

14. 625 Illinois Compiled Statutes Annotated Section 5/16-104 (West 2002).

15. William F. Wieczorek, "Criminal Justice and Public Health Policies to Reduce the Negative Impacts of DUI," *Criminology & Public Policy* (May 2013), 195.

16. Johannes Andenaes, "The Moral or Educative Influence of Criminal Law," *Journal of Social Issues* 27 (Spring 1971), 17, 26.

17. *Hawkins v. State*, 219 Ind. 116, 129, 37 N.E.2d 79 (1941).

18. *People v. Decina*, 138 N.E.2d 799 (1956).

19. David C. Biggs, "'The Good Samaritan Is Packing': An Overview of the Broadened Duty to Aid Your Fellowman, with the Modern Desire to Possess Concealed Weapons," *University of Dayton Law Review* 22 (Winter 1997), 225.

20. Terry Halbert and Elaine Ingulli, *Law and Ethics in the Business Environment*, 6th ed. (Mason, Ohio: South-Western Cengage Learning, 2009), 8.

21. Model Penal Code Section 2.02.

22. Model Penal Code Section 2.02(c).

23. *Black's Law Dictionary*, 1423.

24. *United States v. Dotterweich*, 320 U.S. 277 (1943).

25. *State v. Stiffler*, 763 P.2d 308, 311 (Idaho Ct.App. 1988).

26. *State v. Harrison*, 425 A.2d 111 (1979).

27. Richard G. Singer and John Q. LaFond, *Criminal Law: Examples and Explanations* (New York: Aspen Law & Business, 1997), 322.

28. *State v. Linscott*, 520 A.2d 1067 (1987).

29. Federal Bank Robbery Act, 18 U.S.C.A. Section 2113.

30. *In re Winship*, 397 U.S. 358, 364, 368–369 (1970).

31. *State v. Jones*, 2011 S.D. 60 (2011).

32. *United States v. Jiminez Recio*, 537 U.S. 270 (2003).

33. Yamiche Alcindor, "'Affluenza' Defense Won't Last, Experts Say," *USA Today* (December 17, 2013), 3A.

34. Paul H. Robinson, *Criminal Law Defenses* (St. Paul, Minn.: West, 2008), Section 173, Ch. 5Bl.

35. *M'Naghten's* Case, 10 Cl.&F. 200, Eng.Rep. 718 (1843). Note that the name is also spelled M'Naughten and McNaughten.

36. Model Penal Code Section 401 (1952).

37. Joshua Dressler, *Cases and Materials on Criminal Law*, 2d ed. (St. Paul, Minn.: West Group, 1999), 599.

38. South Carolina Code Annotated Section 17-24-20(A) (Law. Co-op. Supp., 1997).

39. Ronald Schouten, "The Insanity Defense: An Intersection of Morality, Public Policy, and Science," *Psychology Today* (August 16, 2012), at **www.psychologytoday.com /blog/almost-psychopath/201208/the -insanity-defense.**

40. Lawrence P. Tiffany and Mary Tiffany, "Nosologic Objections to the Criminal Defense of Pathological Intoxication: What Do the Doubters Doubt?" *International Journal of Law and Psychiatry* 13 (1990), 49.

41. *City of Missoula v. Paffhausen*, 289 P.3d 149–150 (Mont. 2012).

42. 518 U.S. 37 (1996).

43. Kenneth W. Simons, "Mistake and Impossibility, Law and Fact, and Culpability: A Speculative Essay," *Journal of Criminal Law and Criminology* 81 (1990), 447.

44. Quoted in Gary Fields and John R. Emshwiller, "As Criminal Laws Proliferate, More Are Ensnared," *Wall Street Journal* (July 23, 2011), at **online.wsj.com/article/SB1000 14240527487037495045761727141846046 1654.html.**

45. *Lambert v. California*, 335 U.S. 225 (1957).

46. Federal Bureau of Investigation, *Crime in the United States 2012* (Washington, D.C.: U.S. Department of Justice, Expanded Homicide Data Tables 14 and 15, at **www .fbi.gov/about-us/cjis/ucr/crime-in -the-u.s/2012/crime-in-the-u.s.-2012 /cius_home.**

47. Craig L. Carr, "Duress and Criminal Responsibility," *Law and Philosophy* 10 (1990), 161.

48. Arnold N. Enker, "In Supporting the Distinction between Justification and Excuse," *Texas Tech Law Review* 42 (2009), 277.

49. *United States v. May*, 727 F.2d 764 (1984).

50. *United States v. Contento-Pachon*, 723 F.2d 691 (1984).

51. *People v. Murillo*, 587 N.E.2d 1199, 1204 (Ill. App.Ct. 1992).

52. Florida Statutes Section 776.03 (2005).

53. *Ibid.*

54. Lizette Alvarez, "In Zimmerman Case, Self-Defense Was Too Hard to Topple," *New York Times* (July 15, 2013), A1.

55. John K. Roman, *Race, Justifiable Homicide, and Stand Your Ground Laws: Analysis of FBI Supplementary Homicide Report Data* (Washington, D.C.: Urban Institute, July 2013).

56. *People v. Petro*, 56 P.2d 984 (Cal.Ct.App. 1936); and *Regina v. Dudley and Stephens*, 14 Q.B.D. 173 (1884).

57. Henry J. Abraham, *Freedom and the Court: Civil Liberties in the United States*, 7th ed. (New York: Oxford University Press, 1998), 38–41.

58. Arthur L. Alarcon and Paula M. Mitchell, "Executing the Will of the Voters? A Legislature's Multi-Billion Dollar Death Penalty Debacle," *Loyola of Los Angeles Law Review* 44 (2011), S109.

59. *Skinner v. Oklahoma*, 316 U.S. 535, 546–547 (1942).

60. Jonathan Stempel, "Supreme Court Declines to Review Insanity Defense Appeal," *Reuters* (November 26, 2012).

61. House Joint Resolution 106, 112th Congress (2012).

62. 18 U.S.C. Section 3771 (2006).

63. Susan Herman, *Parallel Justice for Victims of Crime* (Washington, D.C.: The National Center for Victims of Crime, 2010), 45–48.

64. Douglas E. Beloof, "The Third Wave of Crime Victims' Rights: Standing, Remedy, and Review," *Brigham Young University Law Review* 2 (2005), 258.

CHAPTER

4 Law Enforcement Today

To target your study and review, look for these numbered Learning Objective icons throughout the chapter.

Reuters/Richard Carson

"Ask Me ANYTHING"

WHEN THE content-sharing community Web site Reddit arranges an "Ask Me Anything" (AMA) session, it usually involves a celebrity such as Bill Gates, Ice Cube, or President Barack Obama. In August 2013, however, an anonymous Seattle police officer caused a similar stir by hosting an AMA, giving the public a rare chance to interact directly with law enforcement. The officer, who went by GoHawks206, candidly answered questions about being watched on the job ("Between people with cell phones, my in-car camera, the news, and security cameras, I'm pretty much always on tape"), gun control ("I've never had a problem with concealed carry"), and police pay ("I'm happy with what I make").

Technically, GoHawks206 overstepped his or her bounds. Like nearly two-thirds of all law enforcement agencies in the United States, the Seattle Police Department has a policy that requires employees to keep their personal opinions off social media sites. In general, these policies threaten disciplinary action against officers who make any online statement that embarrasses or discredits the department. For example, about the same time GoHawks206 went on Reddit, a Daytona Beach, Florida, officer was being fired for a post on his Facebook page that said of Trayvon Martin (discussed in Chapter 3), "Another thug gone. Pull up your pants and be respectful." A few years earlier, an Albuquerque, New Mexico, gang unit officer was suspended for listing his occupational field online as "human waste disposal."

Given GoHawks206's more thoughtful responses to nearly four hundred questions, his or her superiors actually seemed pleased by the AMA. "It represents a shift in police culture," said Seattle Police Department spokesman Sergeant Sean Whitcomb. "We've been working towards this: having a model of open access and understanding that our department is full of people who are good ambassadors." Indeed, Whitcomb indicated that, rather than face any disciplinary action, GoHawks206 would be encouraged to keep the online conversation going—as long as he or she stayed within the rules.

iStockphoto.com/Jacom Stephens

FOR CRITICAL ANALYSIS

1. Can you make the argument that a police officer should be able to say anything she or he wants online, regardless of how it reflects on her or his department? Why or why not?

2. The New York City Police Department prohibits its officers from posting photos of themselves in uniform online, unless the photo was taken at an official police ceremony. What might be the reasoning behind this policy?

3. The Denver Police Department recently hosted an AMA regarding marijuana legalization. If your local police department were to host an AMA, what topics would you like to see covered? Why?

Many police departments in the United States have implemented guidelines to prevent their officers from giving personal opinions about law enforcement matters on social media.

THE RESPONSIBILITIES OF THE POLICE

Whether they are expressing their views on social media or not, police officers are the most visible representatives of our criminal justice system. Indeed, they symbolize the system for many Americans who may never see the inside of a courtroom or a prison cell. The general perception of a "cop's life" is often shaped by television dramas such as the *CSI* and *Law and Order* series. In reality, police spend a great deal of time on such mundane tasks as responding to noise complaints, confiscating firecrackers, and poring over paperwork. Indeed, in his "Ask Me Anything" session, GoHawks206 called paperwork the "real enemy" of effective police work.[1]

Sociologist Egon Bittner warned against the tendency to see the police primarily as agents of law enforcement and crime control. A more inclusive accounting of "what the police do," Bittner believed, would recognize that they provide "situationally justified force in society."[2] In other words, the function of the police is to solve any problem that may *possibly,* though not *necessarily,* require the use of force.

Within Bittner's rather broad definition of "what the police do," we can pinpoint four basic responsibilities of the police:

1. To enforce laws.
2. To provide services.
3. To prevent crime.
4. To preserve the peace.

LEARNING OBJECTIVE 1 List the four basic responsibilities of the police.

As will become evident in the next two chapters, there is a great deal of debate among legal and other scholars and law enforcement officers over which responsibilities deserve the most police attention and what methods should be employed by the police in meeting those responsibilities.

Enforcing Laws

In the public mind, the primary role of the police is to enforce society's laws—hence, the term *law enforcement officer.* In their role as "crime fighters," police officers have a clear mandate to seek out and apprehend those who have violated the law. The crime-fighting responsibility is so dominant that all police activity—from the purchase of new automobiles to a plan to hire more minority officers—must often be justified in terms of its law enforcement value.[3]

Police officers also see themselves primarily as crime fighters, or "crook catchers," a perception that often leads people into what they believe will be an exciting career in law enforcement. Although the job certainly offers challenges unlike any other, police officers normally do not spend the majority of their time in law enforcement duties. After surveying a year's worth of dispatch data from the Wilmington (Delaware) Police Department, researchers Jack Greene and Carl Klockars found that officers spent only about half of their time enforcing the law or dealing with crimes. The rest of their time was spent on order maintenance, service provision, traffic patrol, and medical assistance.[4]

Furthermore, information provided by the Uniform Crime Report shows that most arrests are made for "crimes of disorder" or public annoyances rather than violent or property crimes. In 2012, for example, police made about 10 million arrests for drunkenness, liquor law violations, disorderly conduct, vagrancy, loitering, and other minor offenses, but only about 520,000 arrests for violent crimes.[5]

Providing Services

The popular emphasis on crime fighting and law enforcement tends to overshadow the fact that a great deal of a police officer's time is spent providing services for the community. The motto "To Serve and Protect" has been adopted by thousands of local police departments, and the *Law Enforcement Code of Ethics* recognizes the duty "to serve the community" in its first sentence.[6] The services that police provide are numerous—a partial list would include directing traffic, performing emergency medical procedures, counseling those involved in domestic disputes, providing directions to tourists, and finding lost children.

As we will see in the next section, a majority of police departments have adopted a strategy called *community policing,* which requires officers to provide assistance in areas that are not, at first glance, directly related to law enforcement. Often, regardless of policy, the police are forced into providing certain services. For example, law enforcement officers are often first on the scene when a person has been seriously injured. As a result, some cities allow police officers to take these patients to the hospital in a squad car rather than wait for an ambulance.[7]

Also, because of changes in national health-service policy, law enforcement agents find themselves on the front lines when it comes to dealing with mental illness and substance abuse. The Tucson (Arizona) Police Department, for example, receives more calls about mental illness than about stolen cars or burglaries.[8] Of all contacts that police officers have with members of the public, an estimated 20 percent involve those who are mentally ill or intoxicated.[9]

Preventing Crime

Perhaps the most controversial responsibility of the police is to *prevent* crime. According to Jerome Skolnick, co-director of the Center for Research in Crime and Justice at the New York University School of Law, there are two predictable public responses when crime rates begin to rise in a community. The first is to punish convicted criminals with stricter laws and more severe penalties. The second is to demand that the police "do something" to prevent crimes from occurring in the first place. Is it, in fact, possible for the police to "prevent" crimes? The strongest response that Professor Skolnick is willing to give to this question is "maybe."[10]

On a limited basis, police can certainly prevent some crimes. If a rapist is dissuaded from attacking a solitary woman because a patrol car is cruising the area, then the police officer behind the wheel has prevented a crime. Furthermore, exemplary police work can have a measurable effect. "Quite simply, cops count," says William Bratton, who has directed police departments in Boston, Los Angeles, and New York. "[T]he quickest way to impact crime is with a well-led, [well-]managed, and appropriately resourced police force."[11] In Chapter 5, we will study a number of policing strategies that have been credited, by some, for decreasing crime rates in the United States.

In general, however, the deterrent effects of police presence are unclear. Carl Klockars has written that the "war on crime" is a war that the police cannot win because they cannot control the factors—such as unemployment, poverty, immorality, inequality, political change, and lack of educational opportunities—that contribute to criminal behavior in the first place.[12]

Preserving the Peace

To a certain extent, the fourth responsibility of the police, that of preserving the peace, is related to preventing crime. Police have the legal authority to use the power of arrest, or even force, in situations in which no crime has yet occurred, but might occur in the immediate future.

In the words of James Q. Wilson, the police's peacekeeping role (which Wilson believed to be the most important role of law enforcement officers) often takes on a pattern of simply "handling the situation."[13] For example, when police officers arrive on the scene of a loud late-night house party, they may feel the need to disperse the party and even arrest some of the partygoers for disorderly conduct. By their actions, the officers have lessened the chances of serious and violent crimes taking place later in the evening. The same principle is often used when dealing with domestic disputes, which, if escalated, can lead to homicide. Such situations are in need of "fixing up," to use Wilson's terminology, and police can use the power of arrest, threat, coercion, or sympathy to do just that.

The basis of Wilson and George Kelling's zero-tolerance theory is similar: street disorder—such as public drunkenness, urination, and loitering—signals to both law-abiding citizens and criminals that the law is not being enforced and therefore leads to more violent crime. Hence, if police preserve the peace and "crack down" on the minor crimes that make up street disorder, they will in fact be preventing serious crimes that would otherwise occur in the future.[14]

A Los Angeles police officer oversees community efforts to clean up trash and graffiti. What are the benefits and drawbacks of having law enforcement agents provide services that do not directly involve preventing and solving crimes?

Monica Almeida/The New York Times/Redux

//// SELF ASSESSMENT

Fill in the blanks, and check your answers on page 131.

Both the public and law enforcement officers themselves believe that the police's primary job is to _____ laws. A large and crucial part of policing, however, involves providing _____, such as directing traffic. The ability of the police to actually _____ crime is a matter of great debate, and some experts believe that the most important role of a police officer is to _____ the peace.

A SHORT HISTORY OF THE AMERICAN POLICE

Although modern society relies on law enforcement officers to control and prevent crime, in the early days of this country police services had little to do with crime control. The policing efforts in the first American cities were directed toward controlling certain groups of people (mostly slaves and Native Americans), delivering goods, regulating activities such as buying and selling in the town market, maintaining health and sanitation, controlling gambling and vice, and managing livestock and other animals.[15] Furthermore, these police services were for the most part performed by volunteers, as a police force was an expensive proposition. Often, the volunteers were organized using the **night watch system,** brought over from England by colonists in the seventeenth century. Under this system, all physically fit males were required to offer their services to protect the community on a rotating nightly basis.[16]

The Evolution of American Law Enforcement

The night watch system did not ask much of its volunteers, who were often required to do little more than loudly announce the time and the state of the weather. Furthermore, many citizens avoided their duties by hiring others to "go on watch" in their place, and those who did serve frequently spent their time on watch sleeping and drinking.[17] Eventually, as the populations of American cities grew in the late eighteenth and early nineteenth centuries, so did the need for public order and the willingness to devote public resources to the establishment of formal police forces. The night watch system was insufficient to meet these new demands, and its demise was inevitable.

EARLY POLICE DEPARTMENTS In 1833, Philadelphia became the first city to employ both day and night watchmen. Five years later, working from a model established by British home secretary Sir Robert "Bobbie" Peel in London, Boston officials formed the nation's first organized police department, consisting of six full-time officers. In 1844, New York City laid the foundation for the modern police department by combining its day and night watches under the control of a single police chief. By the onset of the Civil War in 1861, a number of American cities, including Baltimore, Boston, Chicago, Cincinnati, New Orleans, and Philadelphia, had similarly consolidated police departments, modeled on the Metropolitan Police of London.[18]

THE POLITICAL ERA Like their modern counterparts, many early police officers were hard working, honest, and devoted to serving and protecting the public. On the whole, however, in the words of historian Samuel Walker, "The quality of American police service in the nineteenth century could hardly have been worse."[19] This poor quality can be attributed to the fact that the recruitment and promotion of police officers were intricately tied to the politics of the day. Police officers received their jobs as a result of political connections, not because of any particular skills or knowledge. Whichever political party was in power in a given city would hire its own cronies to run the police department. Consequently, the police were often more concerned with serving the interests of the political powers than with protecting the citizens.[20]

A horse-drawn police wagon used by the New York City Police Department, circa 1886.
■ Why might this new form of transportation have represented a "revolution" for early American police forces?

Corruption was rampant during this *political era* of policing, which lasted roughly from 1840 to 1930. Police salaries were relatively low, and many police officers saw their positions as opportunities to make extra income through any number of illegal activities. Bribery was common, as police would use their close proximity to the people to request "favors," which went into the police officers' own pockets

Bettmann/Corbis

POLICE PATROL
35 PRECINCT

or into the coffers of the local political party as "contributions."[21] This was known as the **patronage system,** or the "spoils system," because to the political victors went the spoils.

THE REFORM ERA The abuses of the political era of policing did not go unnoticed. Led by August Vollmer, the police chief of Berkeley, California, from 1905 to 1932, advocates of dramatic changes to American law enforcement initiated the *reform era* in American policing.[22] Along with his protégé O. W. Wilson, Vollmer promoted a style of policing known as the **professional model.** Under the professional model, police chiefs, who had been little more than figureheads during the political era, took more control over their departments. A key to these efforts was the reorganization of police departments in many major cities. To improve their control over operations, police chiefs began to add midlevel positions to the force. These new officers, known as majors or assistant chiefs, could develop and implement crime-fighting strategies and more closely supervise individual officers. Police chiefs also tried to consolidate their power by bringing large areas of a city under their control so that no local ward, neighborhood, or politician could easily influence a single police department.

The professionalism trend benefited law enforcement agents in a number of ways. Salaries and working conditions improved, and for the first time, women and members of minority groups were given opportunities—albeit limited—to serve.[23] At the same time, police administrators controlled officers to a much greater extent than in the past, expecting them to meet targets for arrests and other numerical indicators that were seen as barometers of effectiveness. Any contact with citizens that did not explicitly relate to law enforcement was considered "social work" and discouraged.[24] As police expert Chris Braiden puts it, American police officers were expected to "park their brains at the door of the stationhouse" and simply "follow orders like a robot."[25] The isolation of officers from the public was made complete by an overreliance on the patrol car, a relatively new technological innovation at the time. In the political era, officers walked their beats, interacting with citizens. In the reform era, they were expected to stay inside their "rolling fortresses," driving from one call to the next without wasting time or resources on public relations.[26]

CJ & TECHNOLOGY   High-Tech Cop Cars

When patrol cars came into common use by police departments in the 1930s, they changed the face of American policing. Nine decades later, the technology associated with patrol cars continues to evolve. Today, approximately 80 percent of all police cars in the United States are equipped with on-board computers. Specialized software for these computers allows law enforcement agents to turn cars into mobile offices. So, for example, if a patrol officer receives a call concerning an incident involving a known suspect, he or she can use the in-car computer to immediately access the suspect's criminal files. In Tampa, Florida, patrol officers have access to NC4 Safecop software, which allows them to analyze neighborhood crime data from the driver's seat.

Other recent innovations include Automatic License Plate Recognition, a three-camera computer-operated system that performs a "20-millisecond" background check on every license plate it sees, and the StarChase launcher, a small, laser-guided cannon that shoots a small, sticky radio transmitter at a fleeing vehicle. Once the offending car has been "tagged" with this device, police can track the fugitive at a safe distance without the need for a dangerous, high-speed pursuit. *(Continued on the next page)*

Michael Hanson/The New York Times/Redux

Thinking about Police Automobile Technology

In Austin, Texas, police cars are equipped with digital cameras to record "critical events" involving officers. These cameras automatically begin operating when triggered by seven different actions, including the driver's door being opened and the car's flashing lights or siren being activated. What do you think is the reason for these automatic triggers?

The Community Era The drawbacks of the professional model became evident in the 1960s, one of the most turbulent decades in American history. Unrest associated with the civil rights movement and protests against the Vietnam War (1965–1975) led to a series of clashes—often violent—between police and certain segments of society. By the early 1970s, many observers believed that poor policing was contributing to the national turmoil. The National Advisory Commission on Civil Disorders stated bluntly that poor relations between the police and African American communities were partly to blame for the violence that plagued many of those communities.[27] In striving for professionalism, the police appeared to have lost touch with the citizens they were supposed to be serving. To repair their damaged relations with a large segment of the population, police would have to rediscover their community roots.

The result of this rediscovery was the *community* era of American policing. Starting in the 1970s, most large-city police departments established entire units devoted to community relations, implementing programs that ranged from summer recreation activities for inner-city youths to "officer-friendly" referral operations that encouraged citizens to come to the police with their crime concerns.

At the same time, the country was hit by a crime wave. Thus, police administrators were forced to combine efforts to improve community relations with aggressive and innovative crime-fighting strategies. As we will see in Chapter 5, when we discuss these strategies in more depth, the police began to focus on stopping crimes before they occurred, rather than concentrating only on solving crimes that had already been committed. A dedication to such proactive strategies led to widespread acceptance of community policing in the 1980s and 1990s. Community policing is based on the notion that meaningful interactions between officers and citizens will lead to a partnership in preventing and fighting crime. (See Figure 4.1 that follows for an overview of the three eras of policing described in this section.)

Policing Today: Intelligence, Terrorism, and Technology

Many law enforcement experts believe that the events of September 11, 2001, effectively ended the community era of policing.[28] Though police departments have not, in general, abandoned the idea of partnering with the community, their emphasis has shifted toward developing new areas of expertise, including counterterrorism and surveillance through technology. In particular, the process of collecting, analyzing, and mapping crime data has become a hallmark of law enforcement in the twenty-first century.

FIGURE 4.1 The Three Eras of American Policing

George L. Kelling and Mark H. Moore have separated the history of policing in the United States from 1840 to 2000 into three distinct periods. Below is a brief summarization of these three eras.

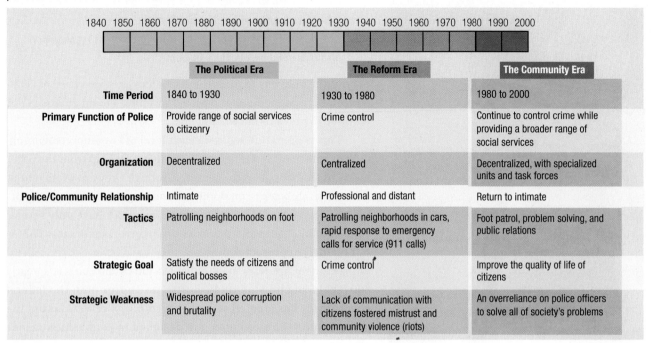

	The Political Era	The Reform Era	The Community Era
Time Period	1840 to 1930	1930 to 1980	1980 to 2000
Primary Function of Police	Provide range of social services to citizenry	Crime control	Continue to control crime while providing a broader range of social services
Organization	Decentralized	Centralized	Decentralized, with specialized units and task forces
Police/Community Relationship	Intimate	Professional and distant	Return to intimate
Tactics	Patrolling neighborhoods on foot	Patrolling neighborhoods in cars, rapid response to emergency calls for service (911 calls)	Foot patrol, problem solving, and public relations
Strategic Goal	Satisfy the needs of citizens and political bosses	Crime control	Improve the quality of life of citizens
Strategic Weakness	Widespread police corruption and brutality	Lack of communication with citizens fostered mistrust and community violence (riots)	An overreliance on police officers to solve all of society's problems

Sources: Adapted from George L. Kelling and Mark H. Moore, "From Political to Reform to Community: The Evolving Strategy of Police," in *Community Policing: Rhetoric or Reality*, ed. Jack R. Greene and Stephen D. Mastrofski (New York: Praeger Publishers, 1991), 14–15, 22–23; plus authors' updates. Reproduced with permission of Greenwood Publishing Group, Inc., Westport, Connecticut.

INTELLIGENCE-LED POLICING "Humans are not nearly as random as we think," says Jeff Brantingham, an anthropologist at the University of California, Los Angeles. "Crime is a physical process, and if you can explain how offenders move and how they mix with victims, you can understand an incredible amount."[29] Relying on this basic principle, Brantingham and several colleagues developed PredPol, a software program that strives to predict when and where crimes are most likely to occur. The software relies on a basic truism of criminal behavior: most crime is local. That is, offenders tend to commit crimes close to home, and they tend to victimize the same people and neighborhoods repeatedly.[30] (Remember, from Chapter 2, the concept of repeat victimization.)

The PredPol approach is known as predictive policing, or **intelligence-led policing** (ILP), because it relies on data—or intelligence—concerning past crime patterns to predict future crime patterns. In theory, ILP is relatively simple. Just as commercial fishers are most successful when they concentrate on the areas of the ocean where the fish are, law enforcement does well to focus its scarce resources on the areas where the most crime occurs. With programs such as PredPol and other "hot spot" technologies that we will discuss in the next chapter, police administrators are able to deploy small forces to specific locations, rather than blanketing an entire city with random patrols. Doing "more with less" in this manner is a particularly important consideration as police budgets shrink around the country.[31]

THE CHALLENGES OF COUNTERTERRORISM Applying basic ILP principles, it quickly becomes clear that terrorists, like other criminals, are likely to choose targets close to their homes. At the same time, when terrorist attacks occur great distances from those homes, the attacks are more deadly. Consequently, counterterrorism provides three specific challenges for American law enforcement:

LEARNING OBJECTIVE **2** Explain how intelligence-led policing works and how it benefits modern police departments.

Intelligence-Led Policing
An approach that measures the risk of criminal behavior associated with certain individuals or locations so as to predict when and where such criminal behavior is most likely to occur in the future.

On April 19, 2013, Boston Marathon bombing suspect Tamerlan Tsarnaev (shown here participating in a Golden Gloves boxing tournament several years earlier) was killed during a confrontation with six Watertown, Massachusetts, police officers. Although Tsarnaev and his brother Dzokhar were identified as suspects by the FBI, why was it more likely that they would be apprehended by local police officers?

Glenn DePriest/Getty Images

1. The need to focus scarce resources to prevent and fight crimes that are relatively uncommon,

2. Dealing with the scrutiny that comes with crimes that often have international implications, and

3. The difficult task of gathering information, or *intelligence,* about crimes before they happen.[32]

Clearly, the only way to meet these challenges is for a level of cooperation between federal and local law enforcement that was not required in previous eras of policing.

This cooperation relies on each level of law enforcement taking advantage of its strengths while relying on help from the other levels to shore up its weaknesses. Although they are proficient at gathering intelligence on domestic and, especially, foreign terrorist suspects, federal law enforcement agencies have only several thousand agents available for counterterrorism duties. This is not enough to protect Americans on a local level. So, the federal antiterrorism agencies must enlist the aid of the country's nearly 800,000 local and state police officers. To this end, the federal government has created seventy-seven *fusion centers* across the United States. These centers are designed to enable intelligence sharing among all levels of law enforcement on homeland security matters.

Financial support from the federal government has also helped create more than one hundred local and state police intelligence units, with at least one in each state.[33] The New York Police Department, in a class by itself, has more than one thousand personnel assigned to homeland security and has stationed agents in six foreign countries. Furthermore, that city's 2,500 subway police conduct tens of thousands of random bag checks each year and watch for commuters walking in a stiff manner and talking to themselves—potential signs of a suicide bomber.[34] Indeed, all police officers in the country are now expected to prepare for a terrorist attack in their communities, and counterterrorism has become part of the day-to-day law enforcement routine.

LAW ENFORCEMENT 2.0 Fortunately, just as more intelligence has become crucial to police work, the means available to gather such intelligence have also increased greatly. Nearly every successful antiterrorism investigation has relied on information gathered from the Internet.

Online Investigations and Intelligence Just like the rest of American society, criminals are active on social networking sites, providing police officers with a wealth of potential evidence, including messages, chat logs, tweets, photos, videos, tags, "likes," profiles, lists of friends, locations, and more.[35] At least 90 percent of law enforcement agencies monitor social media to find leads on criminal activity.[36]

Several years ago, the New York Police Department set up a new unit dedicated to preventing violence between groups of neighborhood adolescents knows as "crews." Because most of these youths use social media to communicate with each other, police officers monitoring Facebook and Twitter are often able to learn about potential conflicts before they take place. New York officials credit Operation Crew Cut with contributing to a record-low number of murders in the city in 2013.[37] (The feature *CJ Controversy—Facebook Undercover* that follows examines a particular form of online investigating that has raised concerns among privacy advocates.)

Technology on the Beat As the leaders of the reform movement envisioned, technology also continues to improve the capabilities of officers in the field. Using special applications on smartphones or tablet computers, police can instantly access the addresses of wanted persons, registered sex offenders, gang members, and recent crime locations. As we saw earlier in this section, the modern police car is quickly evolving into a command center on wheels, and police officers also enjoy the use of mobile fingerprint readers, less lethal weapons such as laser beams, and dozens of other technological innovations.

Some law enforcement veterans are concerned that the "art" of policing is being lost in an era of intelligence-led policing and increased reliance on technology. "If it becomes all about the science," says Los Angeles Police Department deputy chief Michael Downing, "I worry we'll lose the important nuances."[38] As the remainder of this chapter and the two chapters that follow show, however, the human element continues to dominate all aspects of policing in America.

CJ CONTROVERSY

FACEBOOK UNDERCOVER

As part of Operation Crew Cut, New York Police Department (NYPD) officers routinely pretend to be young women in order to "friend" suspects on Facebook. Using these fake identities, the officers are able to avoid the social media site's privacy settings and gain valuable information about crew members' illegal activities. This practice is hardly limited to the NYPD. Hundreds of federal, state, and local law enforcement agencies encourage their agents to go undercover in this manner, raising legal and ethical questions about respect for users' online privacy—or lack thereof.

POLICE SHOULD USE FAKE IDENTITIES ON FACEBOOK BECAUSE . . .

- Undercover officers routinely use fake identities in the "real world" to fool criminal suspects. As long as entrapment (see Chapter 3) does not occur, using fake identities on Facebook is no different.
- Police investigators have legal access to *all* information on Facebook, as stated in the company's privacy policy.

POLICE SHOULD NOT USE FAKE IDENTITIES ON FACEBOOK BECAUSE . . .

- Facebook provides users with a number of controls to restrict information to "friends," and it is unethical for police officers to circumvent these privacy settings with false information.
- In many instances, targets of these undercover operations have not committed any crime and do not deserve such intrusions on their privacy.

Your Assignment

Using the Internet, research the case of **Lori Drew** and the role she played in the suicide of **Megan Meier**. Do you think that Drew should have been punished by the criminal justice system for her actions? If you were to make up a set of rules for police officers who were creating fake profiles on Facebook, what lessons would you take from Meier's suicide? Explain your answers in two full paragraphs.

Fill in the blanks, and check your answers on page 131.

During the _____ era of American policing, which lasted roughly from 1840 to 1930, police officers used the _____ system to enrich themselves. The _____ era, which followed, saw the modernization of our nation's law enforcement system through innovations like Vollmer and Wilson's _____ model of policing. Following the national turmoil of the 1960s and early 1970s, _____ era strategies encouraged a partnership between citizens and the police. Today, _____-led policing efforts attempt to make law enforcement agencies more efficient and better able to prevent future _____ attacks.

RECRUITMENT AND TRAINING: BECOMING A POLICE OFFICER

In 1961, police expert James H. Chenoweth commented that the methods used to hire police officers had changed little since the days of the first American police forces.[39] The past half-century, however, has seen a number of improvements in the way that police administrators handle the task of **recruitment,** or the development of a pool of qualified applicants from which to select new officers. Efforts have been made to diversify police rolls, and recruits in most police departments undergo a substantial array of tests and screens—discussed below—to determine their aptitude. Furthermore, annual starting salaries that can exceed $50,000, along with the opportunities offered by an interesting profession in the public service field, have attracted a wide variety of applicants to police work.

Basic Requirements

The selection process involves a number of steps, and each police department has a different method of choosing candidates. Most agencies, however, require at a minimum that a police officer:

1. Be a U.S. citizen.
2. Not have been convicted of a felony.
3. Have or be eligible to have a driver's license in the state where the department is located.
4. Be at least twenty-one years of age.
5. Meet weight and eyesight requirements.

In addition, few departments will accept candidates older than forty-five years of age.

BACKGROUND CHECKS AND TESTS Beyond these minimum requirements, police departments usually engage in extensive background checks, including drug tests; a review of the applicant's educational, military, and driving records; credit checks; interviews with spouses, acquaintances, and previous employers; and a background search to determine whether the applicant has been convicted of any criminal acts.

Furthermore, more than one-third of American police agencies now review an applicant's social media activity on sources such as Facebook, Instagram, and Twitter.[40] "A single posting on Facebook in poor taste won't automatically eliminate someone from our hiring process," explains Arlington, Texas, deputy chief Lauretta Hill. "But if we see a pattern of behavior or something that raises a red flag, it lets us know that we need to dig a little deeper during our background investigation."[41] Police agencies generally

Recruitment The process by which law enforcement agencies develop a pool of qualified applicants from which to select new employees.

also require certain physical attributes in applicants: normally, they must be able to pass a physical agility or fitness test. (For an example of one such test, see Figure 4.2 that follows.)

Probationary Period A period of time at the beginning of a police officer's career during which she or he may be fired without cause.

EDUCATIONAL REQUIREMENTS One of the most dramatic differences between today's police recruits and those of several generations ago is their level of education. In the 1920s, when August Vollmer began promoting the need for higher education in police officers, few had attended college. Today, 82 percent of all local police departments require at least a high school diploma, and 9 percent require a degree from a two-year college.[42] Recruits with college or university experience are generally thought to have an advantage in hiring and promotion.

Not all police observers believe that education is a necessity for police officers, however. In the words of one police officer, "Effective street cops learn their skills on the job, not in a classroom."[43] By emphasizing a college degree, say some, police departments discourage those who would make solid officers but lack the education necessary to apply for positions in law enforcement.

Training

If an applicant successfully navigates the application process, he or she will be hired on a *probationary* basis. During this **probationary period,** which can last from six to eighteen months depending on the department, the recruit is in jeopardy of being fired without cause if he or she proves inadequate to the challenges of police work. Almost every state requires that police recruits pass through a training period while on probation. During this time, they are taught the basics of police work and are under constant supervision by superiors. The training period usually has two components: the police academy and field training. On average, local police departments serving populations of 250,000 or more require 1,648 hours of training—972 hours in the classroom and 676 hours in the field.[44]

LEARNING 3 OBJECTIVE Identify the differences between the police academy and field training as learning tools for recruits.

ACADEMY TRAINING The *police academy,* run by either the state or a police agency, provides recruits with a controlled, militarized environment in which they receive their introduction to the world of the police officer. They are taught the laws of search, seizure, arrest, and interrogation; how and when to use weapons; the procedures of securing a crime

FIGURE 4.2 **Physical Agility Exam for the Henrico County (Virginia) Division of Police**

Those applying for the position of police officer must finish this physical agility exam within 3 minutes, 30 seconds. During the test, applicants are required to wear the equipment (with a total weight of between 9 and 13 pounds) worn by patrol officers, which includes the police uniform, leather gun belt, firearm, baton, portable radio, and ballistics vest.

1. Applicant begins test seated in a police vehicle, door closed, seat belt fastened.
2. Applicant must exit vehicle and jump or climb a six-foot barrier.
3. Applicant then completes a one-quarter mile run or walk, making various turns along the way, to simulate a pursuit run.
4. Applicant must jump a simulated five-foot culvert/ditch.
5. Applicant must drag a "human simulator" (dummy) weighing 175 pounds a distance of 50 feet (to simulate a situation in which an officer is required to pull or carry an injured person to safety).
6. Applicant must draw his or her weapon and fire five rounds with the strong hand and five rounds with the weak hand.

Getty Images

scene and interviewing witnesses; first aid; self-defense; and other essentials of police work. Nine in ten police academies also provide terrorism-related training to teach recruits how to respond to terrorist incidents, including those involving weapons of mass destruction.[45] Academy instructors evaluate the recruits' performance and send intermittent progress reports to police administrators.

IN THE FIELD Field training takes place outside the confines of the police academy. A recruit is paired with an experienced police officer known as a field training officer (FTO). The goal of field training is to help rookies apply the concepts they have learned in the academy "to the streets," with the FTO playing a supervisory role to make sure that nothing goes awry. While the academy introduces recruits to the formal rules of police work, field training gives the rookies their first taste of the informal rules. In fact, the initial advice to recruits from some FTOs is often along the lines of "O.K., kid. Forget everything you learned in the classroom. You're in the real world now." Nonetheless, the academy is a critical component in the learning process, as it provides rookies with a road map to the job.

A recruit performs pushups under duress at the Cleveland Police Academy. Why are police academies an important part of the learning process for a potential police officer?

Marvin Fong / The Plain Dealer/Landov

/// SELF ASSESSMENT

Fill in the blanks, and check your answers on page 131.

Most police agencies require that recruits be at least _____-_____ years of age and have no prior _____ convictions. During the _____ period, which can last as long as eighteen months, a recruit will attend a _____ _____ to learn the rules of police work in an institutional setting. Then, she or he will leave the classroom and partner with an experienced officer for _____ _____.

WOMEN AND MINORITIES IN POLICING TODAY

For many years, the typical American police officer was white and male. As recently as 1968, African Americans represented only 5 percent of all sworn officers in the United States, and the percentage of "women in blue" was even lower.[46] Only within the past thirty years has this situation been addressed, and only within the past twenty years have many police departments actively tried to recruit women, African Americans, Hispanics, Asian Americans, and members of other minority groups. The result, as you will see, has been a steady though not spectacular increase in the diversity of the nation's police forces. When it comes to issues of gender, race, and ethnicity, however, mere statistics rarely tell the entire story.

Field Training The segment of a police recruit's training in which he or she is removed from the classroom and placed on the beat, under the supervision of a senior officer.

Antidiscrimination Law and Affirmative Action

To a certain extent, external forces have driven law enforcement agencies to increase the number of female and minority recruits. The 1964 Civil Rights Act and its 1972 amendments guaranteed members of minority groups and women equal access to jobs in law enforcement, partly by establishing the Equal Employment Opportunity Commission (EEOC) to ensure fairness in hiring practices. The United States Supreme Court has also ruled on several occasions that **discrimination** by law enforcement agencies violates federal law.[47] In legal terms, discrimination occurs when hiring and promotion decisions are based on individual characteristics such as gender or race, and not on job-related factors.

Since the early 1970s, numerous law enforcement agencies have instituted **affirmative action** programs to increase the diversity of their employees. These programs are designed to give women and members of minority groups certain advantages in hiring and promotion to remedy the effects of past discrimination and prevent future discrimination. Often, affirmative action programs are established voluntarily. Sometimes, however, they are the result of lawsuits brought by employees or potential employees who believe that the employer has discriminated against them.

In such instances, if the court finds that discrimination did occur, it will implement a *consent decree* to remedy the situation. Under a consent decree, the law enforcement agency often agrees to meet certain numerical goals in hiring women and members of minority groups. If it fails to meet these goals, it is punished with a fine or some other sanction.[48]

Discrimination The illegal use of characteristics such as gender or race by employers when making hiring or promotion decisions.

Affirmative Action A hiring or promotion policy favoring those groups, such as women, African Americans, or Hispanics, who have suffered from discrimination in the past or continue to suffer from discrimination.

Working Women: Gender and Law Enforcement

In 1987, about 7.6 percent of all local police officers were women. By 2012, that number had risen to only 11.9 percent.[49] This small increase seems even less impressive when one considers that women make up more than half of the population of the United States, meaning that they are severely underrepresented in law enforcement.

ADDED SCRUTINY There are several reasons for the low levels of women serving as police officers. First, relatively few women hold positions of high rank in American police departments,[50] and only about 3 percent of the police chiefs in the United States are women.[51] Consequently, female police officers have few superiors who might be able to mentor them in what can be a hostile work environment.

In addition to the dangers and pressures facing all law enforcement agents, which we will discuss in the next chapter, women must deal with an added layer of scrutiny. Many male police officers feel that their female counterparts are mentally soft, physically weak, and generally unsuited for the rigors of the job. At the same time, male officers often try to protect female officers by keeping them out of hazardous situations, thereby denying the women the opportunity to prove themselves.[52]

TOKENISM Women in law enforcement also face the problem of *tokenism,* or the belief that they have been hired or promoted to fulfill diversity requirements and have not earned their positions. Tokenism creates pressure to prove the stereotypes wrong. When comparing the arrest patterns of male and female officers over a twelve-month period in Cincinnati, Ohio, for example, researchers noted several interesting patterns. Although overall arrest rates were similar, female officers were much more likely than their male counterparts to arrest suspects who were "non-deferential," or hostile. Also, the presence of a supervisor greatly increased the likelihood that a female officer would make an arrest.

Such patterns, the researchers concluded, show that female officers feel pressure to demonstrate that they are "good cops" who cannot be intimidated because of their gender.[53] Similarly, women who rise through the law enforcement ranks often face questions concerning their worthiness. According to Tampa, Florida, police chief Jane Castor, "No matter how qualified you are or how much experience you have, . . . people will say that you were promoted—in part, if not fully—because you're a woman."[54]

In fact, most of the negative attitudes toward women police officers are based on prejudice rather than actual experience. A number of studies have shown that there is very little difference between the performances of men and women in uniform.[55] (For more on this topic, see the feature *Myth vs Reality—Women Make Bad Cops* that follows.)

MYTH VS REALITY
Women Make Bad Cops

LEARNING **4** OBJECTIVE

Describe some of the benefits that female police officers bring to law enforcement.

THE MYTH The perception that women are not physically strong enough to be effective law enforcement officers prevails both in the public mind and within police forces themselves. Criminologist Susan Martin has found that policewomen are under "constant pressure to demonstrate their competence and effectiveness vis-à-vis their male counterparts." One female police officer describes her experience:

> I was the smallest person. . . . They [male officers] didn't feel I could do the job. They tried to get me into fighting situations to see if I would back down. They told me, "You know, if you aren't strong enough or are going to be a coward, we have to find out fast and get you out of here."

THE REALITY In fact, a number of studies have shown that policewomen can be as effective as men in most situations, and often more so. Citizens appear to prefer dealing with a female police officer rather than a male during service calls—especially those that involve domestic violence. In general, policewomen are less aggressive and more likely to reduce the potential for a violent situation by relying on verbal skills rather than their authority as law enforcement agents. According to a study conducted by the National Center for Women and Policing, payouts in lawsuits for claims of brutality and misconduct involving male officers exceed those involving females by a ratio of 43 to 1. Furthermore, female police officers are certainly capable of acts of bravery and physical prowess—the names of hundreds of women are included on the National Law Enforcement Officers Memorial in Washington, D.C.

FOR CRITICAL ANALYSIS
Do you believe that female police officers can be just as effective as men in protecting citizens from criminal behavior? Why or why not?

Joe Raedle/Getty Images

A female member of the Miami (Florida) Police Department provides security during a public event.

Minority Report: Race and Ethnicity in Law Enforcement

As Figure 4.3 that follows shows, like women, members of minority groups have been slowly increasing their presence in local police departments since the late 1980s. Specifically, in 2007, African American officers comprised about 12 percent of the nation's police officers; Hispanic officers, about 10 percent; and other minority groups such as Asians, American Indians, and Pacific Islanders, about 3 percent.[56] By some measures, members of minority groups are better represented than women in policing. Cities such as Detroit and Washington have local police departments that closely match their civilian populations in terms of diversity, and in recent years, a majority of police recruits in New York City have been members of minority groups. On other measures, such as promotion, minorities in law enforcement continue to seek parity.[57]

DOUBLE MARGINALITY According to Peter C. Moskos, a professor at the John Jay College of Criminal Justice in New York, "Black and white police officers remain two distinct shades of blue, with distinct attitudes toward each other and the communities they serve."[58] While that may be true, minority officers generally report that they have good relationships with their white fellow officers.[59] Often, though, members of minority groups in law enforcement—particularly African Americans and Hispanics—do face the problem of **double marginality.** This term refers to a situation in which minority officers are viewed with suspicion by both sides:

1. White police officers believe that minority officers will give members of their own race or ethnicity preferential treatment on the streets.
2. Those same minority officers face hostility from members of their own community who are under the impression that black and Hispanic officers are traitors to their race or ethnicity.

FIGURE 4.3 Members of Minority Groups in Local Law Enforcement

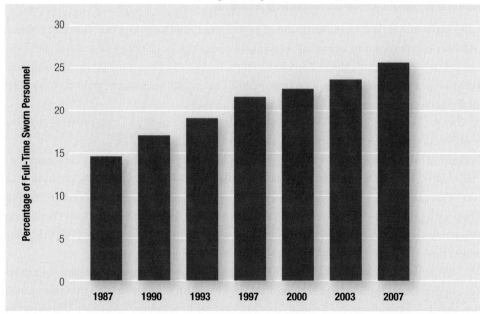

Note: Includes blacks or African Americans, Hispanics or Latinos, Asians, Native Hawaiians or other Pacific Islanders, American Indians, Alaska Natives, and persons identifying two or more races.

Source: Bureau of Justice Statistics, *Local Police Departments, 2007* (Washington, D.C.: U.S. Department of Justice, December 2010), Figure 9, page 14.

In response, minority officers may feel the need to act more harshly toward minority offenders to prove that they are not biased in favor of their own racial or ethnic group.[60]

Identify the main advantage of a racially and ethnically diverse police force.

LEARNING
5
OBJECTIVE

THE BENEFITS OF A DIVERSE POLICE FORCE In 1986, Supreme Court justice John Paul Stevens spoke for many in the criminal justice system when he observed that "an integrated police force could develop a better relationship [with a racially diverse citizenry] and therefore do a more effective job of maintaining law and order than a force composed of white officers."[61] Indeed, despite the effects of double marginality, African American officers may have more credibility in a predominantly black neighborhood than white police officers, leading to better community-police relations and a greater ability to solve and prevent crimes.

Certainly, in the Mexican American communities typical of border states such as Arizona, Texas, and California, many Hispanic officers are able to gather information that would be very difficult for non–Spanish-speaking officers to collect. Finally, however, the best argument for a diverse police force is that members of minority groups represent a broad source of talent in this country, and such talent can only enhance the overall effectiveness of American law enforcement.

/// SELF ASSESSMENT

Fill in the blanks, and check your answers on page 131.

In the past, women and members of minority groups in law enforcement have suffered from _____, or hiring practices that exclude potential employees based on their gender, race, or ethnicity. To remedy this situation, many law enforcement agencies have instituted _____ _____ programs to diversify their workforces. In some instances, a court will issue a _____ _____, under which an agency agrees to reach certain numerical hiring goals or be penalized.

PUBLIC AND PRIVATE LAW ENFORCEMENT

Americans are served by a multitude of police organizations. Overall, there are about 18,000 law enforcement agencies in the United States, employing about 880,000 officers.[62] For the most part, these agencies operate on three different levels: local, state, and federal. Each level has its own set of responsibilities, which we shall discuss starting with local police departments.

Municipal Law Enforcement Agencies

According to federal statistics, there is one local or state police officer for every four hundred residents of the United States.[63] About two-thirds of all *sworn officers,* or those officers with arrest powers, work in small- and medium-sized police departments serving cities with populations from ten thousand to 1 million.[64] While the New York City Police Department employs about 37,000 police personnel, 50 percent of all local police departments have ten or fewer law enforcement officers.[65]

Of the three levels of law enforcement, municipal agencies have the broadest authority to apprehend criminal suspects, maintain order, and provide services to the community. Whether the local officer is part of a large force or the only law enforcement officer in the community, he or she is usually responsible for a wide spectrum of duties, from responding to noise complaints to investigating homicides.

Sheriffs and County Law Enforcement

The **sheriff** is a very important figure in American law enforcement. Almost every one of the more than three thousand counties in the United States (except those in Alaska) has a sheriff. In every state except Rhode Island and Hawaii, sheriffs are elected by members of the community for two- or four-year terms and are paid a salary set by the state legislature or county board.

As elected officials who do not necessarily need a background in law enforcement, modern sheriffs resemble their counterparts from the political era of policing in many ways. Simply stated, the sheriff is also a politician. When a new sheriff is elected, she or he will sometimes repay political debts by appointing new deputies or promoting those who have given her or him support.

SIZE AND RESPONSIBILITY OF SHERIFFS' DEPARTMENTS Like municipal police forces, sheriffs' departments vary in size. The largest is the Los Angeles County Sheriff's Department, with more than nine thousand deputies. Of the 3,063 sheriffs' departments in the country, thirteen employ more than one thousand officers, while forty-five have only one.[66]

Keep in mind that cities, which are served by municipal police departments, often exist within counties, which are served by sheriffs' departments. Therefore, police officers and sheriffs' deputies often find themselves policing the same geographical areas. Police departments, however, are generally governed by a local political entity such as a mayor's office, while most sheriffs' departments are assigned their duties by state law. About 80 percent of all sheriffs' departments have the primary responsibility for investigating violent crimes in their jurisdictions. Other common responsibilities of a sheriff's department include the following:

1. Investigating drug crimes.
2. Maintaining the county jail.
3. Carrying out civil and criminal processes within county lines, such as serving eviction notices and court summonses.
4. Keeping order in the county courthouse.
5. Collecting taxes.
6. Enforcing orders of the court, such as overseeing the isolation of a jury during a trial.[67]

It is easy to confuse sheriffs' departments and local police departments. Both law enforcement agencies are responsible for many of the same tasks, including crime investigation and routine patrol. There are differences, however. Sheriffs' departments are more likely to be involved in county court and jail operations, and to perform certain services such as search and rescue. Local police departments, for their part, are more likely to perform traffic-related functions than are sheriffs' departments.[68]

Lane County, Oregon, sheriff's deputies take part in an "active shooter" training exercise to protect local grade schools students. Why do sheriffs' departments and municipal police agencies often find themselves policing the same geographical areas?

AP Images/*The Register-Guard*, Brian Davies

Coroner The medical examiner of a county, usually elected by popular vote.

THE COUNTY CORONER Another elected official on the county level is the **coroner**, or medical examiner. Duties vary from county to county, but the coroner has a general mandate to investigate all sudden, unexplained, unnatural, or suspicious deaths reported to the office. The coroner is ultimately responsible for determining the cause of death in these cases. Coroners also perform autopsies and assist other law enforcement agencies in homicide investigations. For example, after actor Philip Seymour Hoffman died in February 2014 of an apparent heroin overdose, the New York City medical examiner needed to determine the exact cause of death. After a four-week investigation, the medical examiner announced that Hoffman had died because he mixed heroin with a number of other drugs, including cocaine and amphetamines.

State Police and Highway Patrols

The most visible state law enforcement agency is the state police or highway patrol agency. Historically, state police agencies were created for three reasons:

1. To assist local police agencies, which often did not have adequate resources or training to handle their law enforcement tasks.

2. To investigate criminal activities that crossed jurisdictional boundaries (such as when bank robbers committed a crime in one county and then fled to another part of the state).

3. To provide law enforcement in rural and other areas that did not have local or county police agencies.

Today, there are twenty-three state police agencies and twenty-six highway patrols in the United States. State police agencies have statewide jurisdiction and are authorized to perform a wide variety of law enforcement tasks. Thus, they provide the same services as city or county police departments and are restricted only by the boundaries of the state. In contrast, highway patrols have limited authority. Their duties are generally defined either by their jurisdiction or by the specific types of offenses they have the authority to control. As their name suggests, most highway patrols concentrate primarily on regulating traffic. Specifically, they enforce traffic laws and investigate traffic accidents. Furthermore, they usually limit their activity to patrolling state and federal highways.

Federal Law Enforcement Agencies

Statistically, employees of federal agencies do not make up a large part of the nation's law enforcement force. In fact, the New York City Police Department has about one-third as many employees as all of the federal law enforcement agencies combined. Nevertheless, the influence of these federal agencies is substantial.

Unlike local police departments, which must deal with all forms of crime, federal agencies have been authorized, usually by Congress, to enforce specific laws or attend to specific situations. Members of the U.S. Coast Guard, for example, patrol the nation's waterways, while U.S. postal inspectors investigate and prosecute crimes perpetrated through the use of the U.S. mail system. In this section, you will learn the elements and duties of the most important federal law enforcement agencies, which are grouped according to the federal department or bureau to which they report. (See Figure 4.4 that follows for the current federal law enforcement "lineup.")

FIGURE 4.4 Federal Law Enforcement Agencies

A number of federal agencies employ law enforcement officers who are authorized to carry firearms and make arrests. The most prominent of these agencies are under the control of the U.S. Department of Homeland Security, the U.S. Department of Justice, and the U.S. Department of the Treasury.

Department of Homeland Security

AGENCY NAME	APPROXIMATE NUMBER OF OFFICERS	MAIN RESPONSIBILITIES
U.S. Customs and Border Protection (CBP)	37,000	(1) Prevent the illegal flow of people and goods across America's international borders; (2) facilitate legal trade and travel.
U.S. Immigration and Customs Enforcement (ICE)	12,500	Uphold public safety and homeland security by enforcing the nation's immigration and customs laws.
U.S. Secret Service	5,000	(1) Protect the president, the president's family, former presidents and their families, and other high-ranking politicians; (2) combat currency counterfeiters.

Department of Justice

AGENCY NAME	APPROXIMATE NUMBER OF OFFICERS	MAIN RESPONSIBILITIES
Federal Bureau of Investigation (FBI)	13,000	(1) Protect national security by fighting international and domestic terrorism; (2) enforce federal criminal laws such as those dealing with cyber crime, public corruption, and civil rights violations.
Drug Enforcement Administration (DEA)	4,500	Enforce the nation's laws regulating the sale and use of drugs.
Bureau of Alcohol, Tobacco, Firearms and Explosives (ATF)	2,500	(1) Combat the illegal use and trafficking of firearms and explosives; (2) investigate the illegal diversion of alcohol and tobacco products.
U.S. Marshals Service	3,500	(1) Provide security at federal courts; (2) protect government witnesses; (3) apprehend fugitives from the federal court or corrections system.

Department of the Treasury

AGENCY NAME	APPROXIMATE NUMBER OF OFFICERS	MAIN RESPONSIBILITIES
Internal Revenue Service (IRS)	2,500	Investigate potential criminal violations of the nation's tax code.

Source: Bureau of Justice Statistics, *Federal Law Enforcement Officers, 2008* (Washington, D.C.: U.S. Department of Justice, June 2012), Table 1, page 2.

THE DEPARTMENT OF HOMELAND SECURITY Comprising twenty-two federal agencies, the Department of Homeland Security (DHS) coordinates national efforts to protect the United States against international and domestic terrorism. While most of the agencies under DHS control are not specifically linked with the criminal justice system, the department does oversee three agencies that play an important role in counterterrorism and fighting crime: U.S. Customs and Border Protection, U.S. Immigration and Customs Enforcement, and the U.S. Secret Service.

LEARNING **6** OBJECTIVE Indicate some of the most important law enforcement agencies under the control of the Department of Homeland Security.

U.S. Customs and Border Protection (CBP) Each year, the federal government spends about $18 billion on enforcing immigration law.[69] A large chunk of these funds go to

U.S. Customs and Border Protection (CBP), which polices the flow of goods and people across the United States' international borders. In general terms, this means that the agency has two primary goals:

1. To keep undocumented immigrants, illegal drugs, and drug traffickers from crossing our borders; and
2. To facilitate the smooth flow of legal trade and travel.

Consequently, CBP officers are stationed at every port of entry and exit to the United States. The officers have widespread authority to investigate and search all international passengers, whether they arrive on airplanes, ships, or other forms of transportation.

To ensure that those coming into the United States from abroad have permission to do so, CBP officers check documents such as passports and *visas*. (A **visa** is a document issued by the U.S. State Department that indicates the conditions under which the holder can enter and travel within the United States.) The officers also have the responsibility of inspecting luggage and cargo to ensure compliance with immigration and trade laws.

Under the Office of Biometric Identity Management (OBIM) program, most foreigners entering the United States on visas are subject to fingerprinting and a facial scan using digital photography. Their names are also checked against criminal records and watch lists for suspected terrorists. Although the program has been effective in recording the entry of foreigners, it has been less successful in following their movements once they are in the United States. Without the cooperation of the visitor, OBIM is unable to confirm when, or if, she or he has left the country. As a result, about 200,000 non–U.S. citizens intentionally overstay their visas each year.[70]

Unregulated Border Entry The U.S. Border Patrol, a branch of the CBP, has the burden of policing the Mexican and Canadian borders between official ports of entry. Every year, hundreds of thousands of non–U.S. citizens, unable to legally obtain visas, attempt to enter the country illegally by crossing these large, underpopulated, mostly unregulated regions, particularly in the southern part of the United States. In 2013, Border Patrol agents apprehended about 420,000 illegal border crossers, down from a high of more than 1.6 million in 2000.[71]

To a certain extent, this large decrease reflects the recent economic downturn, which removed some of the monetary incentives for illegal crossers looking for jobs in the United States. In addition, the DHS has "tightened" the border, deterring potential crossers with the increased threat of apprehension. In Arizona, for example, the Border Patrol uses helicopters, surveillance towers, reconnaissance planes with infrared radar, and highly-sensitive cameras to spot undocumented immigrants attempting to enter from Mexico. As a result, apprehensions in that state dropped 78 percent from 2005 to 2012.[72] Another result is that the new "hot spot" for illegal crossers is now Texas's Rio Grande Valley, which has fewer Border Patrol resources and has seen a "demoralizing" increase in apprehensions.[73]

U.S. Immigration and Customs Enforcement (ICE) The CBP shares responsibility for locating and apprehending those persons illegally in the United States with special agents from **U.S. Immigration and Customs Enforcement (ICE).** While the CBP focuses almost exclusively on the nation's borders, ICE has a broader mandate to investigate and to enforce our country's immigration and customs laws. Simply stated, the CBP covers the borders, and ICE covers everything else. The latter agency's duties include detaining undocumented immigrants and deporting (removing) them from the United States, ensuring that those without permission do not work or gain other benefits in this country, and disrupting human trafficking operations.

Recently, ICE has become more aggressive in its efforts to apprehend and remove undocumented immigrants with criminal records. In 2013, it removed about 370,000 undocumented immigrants from the United States. Approximately 60 percent of these immigrants had been convicted of felonies or misdemeanors.[74]

The U.S. Secret Service When it was created in 1865, the U.S. Secret Service was primarily responsible for combating currency counterfeiters. In 1901, the agency was given the added responsibility of protecting the president of the United States, the president's family, the vice president, the president-elect, and former presidents. These duties have remained the cornerstone of the agency, with several expansions. After a number of threats against presidential candidates in the 1960s and early 1970s, including the shootings of Senator Robert Kennedy of New York and Governor George Wallace of Alabama, in 1976 Secret Service agents became responsible for protecting those political figures as well.

In addition to its special plainclothes agents, the agency also directs two uniformed groups of law enforcement officers. The Secret Service Uniformed Division protects the grounds of the White House and its inhabitants, and the Treasury Police Force polices the Treasury Building in Washington, D.C. In addition, the Secret Service investigates threats against visiting heads of state. To aid its battle against counterfeiters and forgers of government bonds, the agency has the use of a laboratory at the Bureau of Engraving and Printing in the nation's capital.

Additional DHS Agencies Besides the three already discussed—CBP, ICE, and the U.S. Secret Service—three other DHS agencies play a central role in preventing and responding to crime and terrorist-related activity:

1. The *U.S. Coast Guard* defends the nation's coasts, ports, and inland waterways. It also combats illegal drug shipping and enforces immigration law at sea.

2. The *Transportation Security Administration* is responsible for the safe operation of our airline, rail, bus, and ferry services. It also operates the Federal Air Marshals program that places undercover federal agents on commercial flights.

3. The *Federal Emergency Management Agency* holds a position as the lead federal agency in preparing for and responding to disasters such as hurricanes, floods, terrorist attacks, and *infrastructure* concerns. Our national **infrastructure** includes all of the facilities and systems that provide the daily necessities of modern life, such as electric power, food, water, transportation, and telecommunications.

THE DEPARTMENT OF JUSTICE The U.S. Department of Justice, created in 1870, is still the primary federal law enforcement agency in the country. With the responsibility of enforcing federal criminal law and supervising the federal prisons, the Justice Department plays a leading role in the American criminal justice system. To carry out its responsibilities to prevent

Joshua Lott/The New York Times/Redux

In Douglas, Arizona, Border Patrol agents detain a man suspected of smuggling marijuana across the U.S. border from Mexico. What is the difference between U.S. Customs and Border Protection, which oversees the Border Patrol, and U.S. Immigration and Customs Enforcement?

U.S. Secret Service A federal law enforcement organization with the primary responsibility of protecting the president, the president's family, the vice president, and other important political figures.

Infrastructure The services and facilities that support the day-to-day needs of modern life, such as electricity, food, transportation, and water.

Federal Bureau of Investigation (FBI) The branch of the Department of Justice responsible for investigating violations of federal law.

Drug Enforcement Administration (DEA) The federal agency responsible for enforcing the nation's laws and regulations regarding narcotics and other controlled substances.

Identify the duties of the FBI.

LEARNING 7 OBJECTIVE

and control crime, the department has a number of law enforcement agencies, including the Federal Bureau of Investigation; the federal Drug Enforcement Administration; the Bureau of Alcohol, Tobacco, Firearms and Explosives; and the U.S. Marshals Service.

The Federal Bureau of Investigation (FBI) Initially created in 1908 as the Bureau of Investigation, this agency was renamed the **Federal Bureau of Investigation (FBI)** in 1935. One of the primary investigative agencies of the federal government, the FBI has jurisdiction over nearly two hundred federal crimes, including white-collar crimes, espionage (spying), kidnapping, extortion, interstate transportation of stolen property, bank robbery, interstate gambling, and civil rights violations. With its network of agents across the country and the globe, the FBI is also uniquely positioned to combat worldwide criminal activity such as terrorism and drug trafficking. In fact, since 2001, the agency has shifted its focus from traditional crime to national security. Over a recent two-year period, more than half of all FBI investigations have focused on groups or individuals suspected of terrorist activity as opposed to "ordinary" crimes.[75]

The FBI is also committed to providing valuable support for local and state law enforcement agencies. Its Identification Division maintains a large database of fingerprint information and offers assistance in finding missing persons and identifying the victims of fires, airplane crashes, and other disfiguring disasters. The services of the FBI Laboratory, the largest crime laboratory in the world, are available at no cost to other agencies. Finally, the FBI's National Crime Information Center (NCIC) provides lists of stolen vehicles and firearms, missing license plates, vehicles used to commit crimes, and other information to local and state law enforcement officers.

The Drug Enforcement Administration (DEA) The mission of the **Drug Enforcement Administration (DEA)** is to enforce domestic drug laws and regulations and to assist other federal and foreign agencies in combating illegal drug manufacture and trade on an international level. The agency also enforces the provisions of the Controlled Substances Act, which governs the manufacture, distribution, and dispensing of legal drugs, such as prescription drugs.

Because the main conduit for illegal drugs entering the country is our border with Mexico, the DEA often operates on the same turf as the U.S. Border Patrol. Indeed, as that agency has become more efficient at apprehending illegal crossers who also happen to be drug smugglers, the DEA has had to respond to more creative plots to funnel contraband into the United States. In November 2013, for example, DEA agents discovered a six-hundred-foot-long tunnel that stretched from Mexico into a San Diego warehouse, designed to get cocaine and marijuana "under" the border.[76] The DEA also partners with the Mexican military to combat that country's powerful drug cartels.

The Bureau of Alcohol, Tobacco, Firearms and Explosives (ATF) As its name suggests, the Bureau of Alcohol, Tobacco, Firearms and Explosives (ATF) is primarily concerned with the illegal sale, possession, and use of firearms and the control of untaxed tobacco and liquor products.

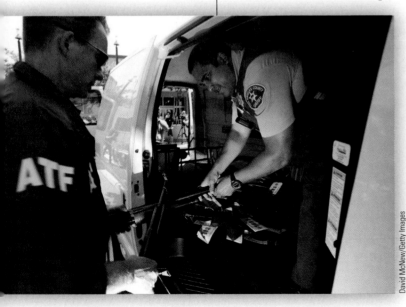

A sheriff's deputy transfers confiscated firearms to an ATF agent in Los Angeles. Some law enforcement experts have suggested that the ATF could do its job more effectively if handguns sold in the United States were listed in a national database. What would be the benefits and drawbacks of such a database?

David McNew/Getty Images

Photo Courtesy of Arnold E. Bell

FASTFACTS

**FBI AGENT
JOB DESCRIPTION:**

- Primary role is to oversee intelligence gathering and investigate crimes.

- Special agent careers are divided into five career paths: intelligence, counterintelligence, counterterrorism, criminal, and cyber.

WHAT KIND OF TRAINING IS REQUIRED?

- Bachelor's and/or master's degree, plus three years of work experience. U.S. citizen, 23–36 years old.

- A written and oral examination, medical and physical examinations, a psychological assessment, and an exhaustive background investigation.

ANNUAL SALARY RANGE?

- $61,100–$69,900 (for new agents)

ARNOLD E. BELL

FEDERAL BUREAU OF INVESTIGATION (FBI) AGENT

I came to the FBI from the U.S. Army, where I worked as a crewman on a UH-1 helicopter and subsequently as a special agent with the U.S. Army Criminal Investigation Command. My work experience in the U.S. Army and degree from St. Leo College (now University) provided the educational foundation that allowed entry into the FBI. After graduating from the FBI Academy in Quantico, Virginia, I was assigned to our Los Angeles division, where I spent the next twelve years. It was a particularly interesting time to be working in Los Angeles, which was experiencing a boom in bank robberies. During the most intense stretches, we were averaging between five and seven bank robberies a day! When I wasn't chasing down a bank robber, I had my hands full with hunting down fugitives, working against organized crime, and dealing with public corruption.

I am currently assigned to the FBI's cyber division as an assistant section chief. The primary mission of my division is to combat cyber-based terrorism and hostile-intelligence operations conducted via the Internet, and to address general cyber crime. Since September 11, 2001, our primary focus has shifted from criminal work to counterterrorism. This has been a difficult transformation for many of us "old-timers" because we grew up in the Bureau doing criminal work. We all recognize, however, the importance of this new challenge, and, despite the difficulties, I believe we have been successful in fulfilling both missions.

fbi.gov

Social Media Career Tip Be aware of your e-mail address/screen name/login name and what it represents. Stay away from nicknames. Use a professional and unique name to represent yourself consistently across social media platforms.

The Firearms Division of the agency has the responsibility of enforcing the Gun Control Act of 1968, which sets the circumstances under which firearms may be sold and used in this country. The bureau also regulates all gun trade between the United States and foreign nations, and collects taxes on all firearm importers, manufacturers, and dealers. In keeping with these duties, the ATF is also responsible for policing the illegal use and possession of explosives. Furthermore, the ATF is charged with enforcing federal gambling laws.

The U.S. Marshals Service The oldest federal law enforcement agency is the U.S. Marshals Service. In 1789, President George Washington assigned thirteen U.S. Marshals agents to protect his attorney general. That same year, Congress created the office of the U.S. Marshals and Deputy Marshals. Originally, U.S. Marshals agents acted as the main law enforcement officers in the western territories. Following the Civil War (1861–1865), when most of these territories had become states, these agents were assigned to work for the U.S. district courts, where federal crimes are tried. The relationship between the U.S. Marshals Service and the federal courts continues today and forms the basis for the officers' main duties, which include

1. Providing security at federal courts for judges, jurors, and other courtroom participants.
2. Controlling property that has been ordered seized by federal courts.
3. Protecting government witnesses who put themselves in danger by testifying against the targets of federal criminal investigations. This protection is sometimes accomplished by relocating the witnesses and providing them with different identities.
4. Transporting federal prisoners to detention institutions.
5. Investigating violations of federal fugitive laws.[77]

THE DEPARTMENT OF THE TREASURY The Department of the Treasury, formed in 1789, is mainly responsible for all financial matters of the federal government. It pays all the federal government's bills, borrows funds, collects taxes, mints coins, and prints paper currency. The largest bureau of the Treasury Department, the Internal Revenue Service (IRS), is concerned with violations of tax laws and regulations. The bureau has three divisions, only one of which is involved in criminal investigations. The examination branch of the IRS audits the tax returns of corporations and individuals. The collection division attempts to collect taxes from corporations or citizens who have failed to pay the taxes they owe. Finally, the criminal investigation division investigates cases of tax evasion and tax fraud.

Analyze the importance of private security today.

LEARNING **8** OBJECTIVE

Private Security

Even with increasing numbers of local, state, and federal law enforcement officers, the police do not have the ability to prevent every crime. Recognizing this, many businesses and citizens have decided to hire private guards for their properties and homes. In fact, according to the United States Security Industry Survey, demand for **private security** generates revenues of nearly $350 billion a year.[78] More than 10,000 firms employing around 2 million people provide private security services in this country, compared with about 880,000 public law enforcement agents.

PRIVATIZING LAW ENFORCEMENT As there are no federal regulations regarding private security, each state has its own rules for this form of employment. In several states, including California and Florida, prospective security guards must have at least forty hours of training. Ideally, a security guard—lacking the extensive training of a law enforcement agent—should only observe and report criminal activity unless use of force is needed to prevent a felony.[79]

As a rule, private security is not designed to replace law enforcement. It is intended to deter crime rather than stop it.[80] A uniformed security guard patrolling a shopping mall parking lot or a bank lobby has one primary function—to convince a potential criminal to search out a shopping mall or bank that does not have private security. For the same reason, many citizens hire security personnel to drive marked cars through their neighborhoods, making them a less attractive target for burglaries, robberies, vandalism, and other crimes.

CONTINUED HEALTH OF THE INDUSTRY Indicators point to continued growth for the private security industry. *The Hallcrest Report II,* a far-reaching overview of private security trends funded by the National Institute of Justice, identifies four factors driving this growth:

A private security guard patrols the Manhattan Mall in New York City. Why is being visible such an important aspect of many private security jobs?

Mario Tama/Getty Images News/Getty Images

1. An increase in fear on the part of the public triggered by media coverage of crime.

2. The problem of crime in the workplace. According to the University of Florida's National Retail Security Survey, American retailers lose about $35 billion a year because of shoplifting and employee theft.

3. Budget cuts in states and municipalities that have forced reductions in the number of public police, thereby raising the demand for private ones.

4. A rising awareness of private security products (such as home burglar alarms) and services as cost-effective protective measures.[81]

Another reason for the industry's continued health is terrorism. Private security is responsible for protecting more than three-fourths of the nation's likely terrorist targets, such as power plants, financial centers, dams, malls, oil refineries, and transportation hubs.

//// SELF ASSESSMENT

Fill in the blanks, and check your answers on page 131.

Municipal police departments and _____ departments are both considered "local" organizations and have many of the same responsibilities. On the state level, the authority of the _____ _____ is usually limited to enforcing traffic laws. Nationally, the _____ has jurisdiction over all federal crimes, while the _____ focuses on federal drug laws and the _____ regulates the sale and possession of guns. Private security is designed to _____ crime rather than prevent it.

CHAPTER SUMMARY

For more information on these concepts, look back to the Learning Objective icons throughout the chapter.

 List the four basic responsibilities of the police. (a) To enforce laws, (b) to provide services, (c) to prevent crime, and (d) to preserve the peace.

 Explain how intelligence-led policing works and how it benefits modern police departments. Intelligence-led policing uses past crime patterns to predict when and where crime will occur in the future. In theory, intelligence-led policing allows police administrators to use fewer resources because it removes costly and time-consuming "guesswork" from the law enforcement equation.

 Identify the differences between the police academy and field training as learning tools for recruits. The police academy is a controlled environment where police recruits learn the basics of policing from instructors in classrooms. In contrast, field training takes place in the "real world": the recruit goes on patrol with an experienced police officer.

 Describe some of the benefits that female police officers bring to law enforcement. Apart from bravery and prowess, female police officers seem to put citizens at ease and are therefore often more effective during service calls. Policewomen are also more likely to use verbal skills rather than force when placed in situations of potential violence, leading to fewer claims of brutality than is the case with their male counterparts.

 Identify the main advantage of a racially and ethnically diverse police force. Particularly in communities that are themselves racially and ethnically diverse, police officers who are members of minority groups are often more easily able to communicate with citizens. This trust enables the officers to do a better job maintaining order, as well as solving and preventing crimes.

 Indicate some of the most important law enforcement agencies under the control of the Department of Homeland Security. (a) U.S. Customs and Border Protection, which polices the flow of goods and people across the United States' international borders and oversees the U.S. Border Patrol; (b) U.S. Immigration and Customs Enforcement, which investigates and enforces our nation's immigration and customs laws; and (c) the U.S. Secret Service, which protects high-ranking federal government officials and federal property, as well as investigates currency counterfeiting.

 Identify the duties of the FBI. The FBI has jurisdiction to investigate hundreds of federal crimes, including white-collar crimes, kidnapping, bank robbery, and civil rights violations. The FBI is also heavily involved in combating terrorism and drug-trafficking operations in the United States and around the world. Finally, the agency provides support to state and local law enforcement agencies through its crime laboratories and databases.

 Analyze the importance of private security today. In the United States, businesses and citizens spend billions of dollars each year on private security. Heightened fear of crime and increased crime in the workplace have fueled the growth in spending on private security.

QUESTIONS FOR CRITICAL ANALYSIS

1. Which of the four basic responsibilities of the police do you think is most important? Why?

2. Some law enforcement agencies have the same physical agility and fitness requirements for male and female applicants, while others do not hold women to the same physical standards as men. Which approach do you favor, and why?

3. Review the discussion of double marginality in this chapter. Why would members of a minority community think that police officers of the same race or ethnicity

were "traitors"? What can police departments do to dispel this misperception?

4. One of the major differences between a local police chief and a sheriff is that the sheriff is elected, while the police chief is appointed. What are some of the possible problems with having a law enforcement official who, like any other politician, is responsible to voters? What are some of the possible benefits of this situation?

5. Twenty-nine states do not require any specific training for private security personnel. What are the arguments for and against requiring at least forty hours of training, as is the case in California and Florida?

KEY TERMS

affirmative action   117
coroner   122
discrimination   117
double marginality   119
Drug Enforcement Administration
    (DEA)   126
Federal Bureau of Investigation
    (FBI)   126
field training   116

infrastructure   125
intelligence-led policing   111
night watch system   108
patronage system   109
private security   128
probationary period   115
professional model   109
recruitment   114
sheriff   121

U.S. Customs and Border Protection
    (CBP)   124
U.S. Immigration and Customs
    Enforcement (ICE)   124
U.S. Secret Service   125
visa   124

SELF-ASSESSMENT ANSWER KEY

Page 107: i. enforce; **ii.** services; **iii.** prevent; **iv.** preserve

Page 114: i. political; **ii.** patronage; **iii.** reform; **iv.** professional; **v.** community; **vi.** intelligence; **vii.** terrorist

Page 116: i. twenty-one; **ii.** felony; **iii.** probationary; **iv.** police academy; **v.** field training

Page 120: i. discrimination; **ii.** affirmative action; **iii.** consent decree

Page 129: i. sheriffs'; **ii.** highway patrol; **iii.** FBI (Federal Bureau of Investigation); **iv.** DEA (Drug Enforcement Administration); **v.** ATF (Bureau of Alcohol, Tobacco, Firearms and Explosives); **vi.** deter

NOTES

1. "IamA SPD Officer AMAA," at **www.reddit.com/r/Seattle/comments/1jp0hu/iama_spd_officer_amaa.**

2. Egon Bittner, *The Functions of Police in a Modern Society,* Public Health Service Publication No. 2059 (Chevy Chase, Md.: National Institute of Mental Health, 1970), 38–44.

3. Carl Klockars, "The Rhetoric of Community Policing," in *Community Policing: Rhetoric or Reality,* eds. Jack Greene and Stephen Mastrofski (New York: Praeger Publishers, 1991), 244.

4. Jack R. Greene and Carl B. Klockars, "What Do Police Do?" in *Thinking about Police,* 2d ed., eds. Carl B. Klockars and Stephen D. Mastrofski (New York: McGraw-Hill, 1991), 273–284.

5. Federal Bureau of Investigation, *Crime in the United States 2012* (Washington, D.C.: U.S. Department of Justice, 2013), Table 29, at **www.fbi.gov/about-us/cjis/ucr/crime-in-the-u.s/2012/crime-in-the-u.s.-2012.**

6. Reprinted in *The Police Chief* (January 1990), 18.

7. Jason Busch, "Shots Fired: When a Police Car Becomes an Ambulance," *Law Enforcement Technology* (September 2013), 8–10.

8. Darren DaRonco and Carli Brosseau, "Hundreds in Mental Crisis Call Police," *Arizona Daily Star* (April 14, 2013), C1.

9. Robert J. Kaminski, Clete DiGiovanni, and Raymond Downs, "The Use of Force between the Police and Persons with Impaired Judgment," *Police Quarterly* (September 2004), 311–338.

10. Jerome H. Skolnick, "Police: The New Professionals," *New Society* (September 5, 1986), 9–11.

11. Quoted in Nancy Ritter, ed., "LAPD Chief Bratton Speaks Out: What's Wrong with Criminal Justice Research—and How to Make It Right," *National Institute of Justice Journal* 257 (2007), 29.

12. Klockars, *op. cit.,* 250.

13. James Q. Wilson, *Varieties of Police Behavior: The Management of Law and Order in Eight Communities* (Cambridge, Mass.: Harvard University Press, 1968).

14. James Q. Wilson and George L. Kelling, "Broken Windows," *Atlantic Monthly* (March 1982), 29.

15. M. K. Nalla and G. R. Newman, "Is White-Collar Crime Policing, Policing?" *Policing and Society* 3 (1994), 304.

16. Mitchell P. Roth, *Crime and Punishment: A History of the Criminal Justice System,* 2d ed. (Belmont, Calif.: Wadsworth Cengage Learning, 2011), 65.

17. *Ibid.*

18. Mark H. Moore and George L. Kelling, "'To Serve and Protect': Learning from Police History," *Public Interest* 70 (1983), 53.

19. Samuel Walker, *The Police in America: An Introduction* (New York: McGraw-Hill, 1983), 7.

20. Moore and Kelling, *op. cit.,* 54.

21. Mark H. Haller, "Chicago Cops, 1890–1925," in *Thinking about Police,* eds. Carl Klockars and Stephen Mastrofski (New York: McGraw-Hill, 1990), 90.

22. Roger G. Dunham and Geoffrey P. Alpert, *Critical Issues in Policing: Contemporary Issues* (Prospect Heights, Ill.: Waveland Press, 1989).

23. Ken Peak and Emmanuel P. Barthe, "Community Policing and CompStat: Merged, or Mutually Exclusive?" *The Police Chief* (December 2009), 73.

24. *Ibid.,* 74.

25. Quoted in *ibid.*

26. Peter K. Manning, "The Police: Mandate, Strategies, and Appearances," in *Crime and Justice in American Society,* ed. Jack D. Douglas (Indianapolis, Ind.: Bobbs-Merrill, 1971), 149–163.

27. National Advisory Commission on Civil Disorder, *Report* (Washington, D.C.: U.S. Government Printing Office, 1968), 157–160.

28. Jason Vaughn Lee, "Policing after 9/11: Community Policing in an Age of Homeland Security," *Police Quarterly* (November 2010), 351–353.

29. Quoted in Ronnie Garrett, "Predict and Serve," *Law Enforcement Technology* (January 2013), 19.

30. *Ibid.*

31. Charlie Beck and Colleen McCue, "Predictive Policing: What Can We Learn from Wal-Mart and Amazon about Fighting Crime in a Recession?" *The Police Chief* (November 2009), 19.

32. Gary LaFree, *Policing Terrorism* (Washington, D.C.: The Police Foundation, 2012), 1.

33. "Spies among Us," *U.S. News & World Report* (May 8, 2006), 41–43.

34. Tom Hays, "Post-9/11, Biggest Terror Threat Is Underground," *Associated Press* (July 18, 2011).

35. Adrian Fontecilla, "The Ascendance of Social Media as Evidence," *Criminal Justice* (Spring 2013), 55.

36. *How Are Innovations in Technology Transforming Policing?* (Washington, D.C.: Police Executive Research Forum, January 2012), 2.

37. Joseph Goldstein and J. David Goodman, "Frisking Tactic Yields to a Focus on Youth Gangs," *New York Times* (September 13, 2013), A1.

38. Quoted in Joel Rubin, "Stopping Crime before It Starts," *Los Angeles Times* (August 21, 2010), A17.

39. James H. Chenoweth, "Situational Tests: A New Attempt at Assessing Police Candidates," *Journal of Criminal Law, Criminology and Police Science* 52 (1961), 232.

40. D. P. Hinkle, "College Degree: An Impractical Prerequisite for Police Work," *Law and Order* (July 1991), 105.

41. Quoted in *How Are Innovations in Technology Transforming Policing?,* 10.

42. Bureau of Justice Statistics, *Local Police Departments, 2007* (Washington, D.C.: U.S. Department of Justice, December 2010), Table 5, page 11.

43. Hinkle, *op. cit.,* 105.

44. *Local Police Departments, 2007, op. cit.,* 12.

45. Bureau of Justice Statistics, *State and Local Law Enforcement Training Academies, 2006* (Washington, D.C.: U.S. Department of Justice, February 2009), 7.

46. National Advisory Commission on Civil Disorder, *Report* (Washington, D.C.: U.S. Government Printing Office, 1968), Chapter 11.

47. *Griggs v. Duke Power Co.,* 401 U.S. 424 (1971); and *Abermarle Paper Co. v. Moody,* 422 U.S. 405 (1975).

48. Gene L. Scaramella, Steven M. Cox, and William P. McCamey, *Introduction to Policing* (Thousand Oaks, Calif.: Sage Publications, 2011), 30–31.

49. Federal Bureau of Investigation, *Crime in the United States* (Washington, D.C.: U.S. Department of Justice, 2013), Table 74, at **www.fbi.gov/about-us/cjis/ucr/crime -in-the-u.s/2012/crime-in-the-u.s.-2012 /cius_home.**

50. Marisa Silvestri, "Doing Time: Becoming a Police Leader," *International Journal of Police Science & Management* (November 2005), 266–281.

51. Dorothy Shulz, quoted in Talk of the Nation, "What Changes as Women Rise through Law Enforcement Ranks," *NPR* (April 2, 2013), at **www.npr.org/2013/04/02/176037643 /what-changes-as-women-rise-through -law-enforcements-ranks.**

52. Robin N. Haarr and Merry Morash, "The Effect of Rank of Police Women Coping with Discrimination and Harassment," *Police Quarterly* (December 2013), 403.

53. Kenneth J. Novak, Robert A. Brown, and James Frank, *Women on Patrol: An Analysis of Differences in Officer Arrest Behavior* (Bingley, United Kingdom: Emerald Group, 2011).

54. Quoted in Talk of the Nation, *op. cit.*

55. Katherine Stuart van Wormer and Clemens Bartollas, *Women and the Criminal Justice System,* 3d ed. (Upper Saddle River, N.J.: Pearson Education, 2011), 318–319.

56. *Local Police Departments, 2007, op. cit.,* 14.

57. David Alan Sklansky, "Not Your Father's Police Department: Making Sense of the New Demographics of Law Enforcement," *Journal of Criminal Law and Criminology* (Spring 2006), 1209–1243.

58. Peter C. Moskos, "Two Shades of Blue: Black and White in the Blue Brotherhood," *Law Enforcement Executive Forum* (2008), 57.

59. Scaramella, Cox, and McCamey, *op. cit.,* 324.

60. John S. Dempsey and Linda S. Forst, *An Introduction to Policing,* 6th ed. (Clifton Park, N.Y.: Delmar Cengage Learning, 2012), 183.

61. *Wygant v. Jackson Board of Education,* 476 U.S. 314 (1986).

62. Bureau of Justice Statistics, *Census of State and Local Law Enforcement Agencies, 2008* (Washington, D.C.: U.S. Department of Justice, July 2011), 1; and Bureau of Justice Statistics, *Federal Law Enforcement Officers, 2008* (Washington, D.C.: U.S. Department of Justice, June 2012), 1.

63. *Census of State and Local Law Enforcement Agencies, 2008, op. cit.,* 3.

64. *Local Police Departments, 2007, op. cit.,* Table 3, page 9.

65. *Census of State and Local Law Enforcement Agencies, 2008, op. cit.,* 4.

66. *Ibid.,* Table 4, page 5.

67. Bureau of Justice Statistics, *Sheriffs' Offices, 2003* (Washington, D.C.: U.S. Department of Justice, May 2006), 15–18.

68. Bureau of Justice Statistics, *Sheriffs' Departments, 1997* (Washington, D.C.: U.S. Department of Justice, February 2000) 14.

69. Doris Meissner et al., *Immigration Enforcement in the United States: The Rise of a Formidable Machinery* (Washington, D.C.: Migration Policy Institute, January 2013), 2.

70. James C. McKinley, Jr., and Julia Preston, "U.S. Can't Trace Foreign Visitors on Expired Visas," *New York Times* (October 12, 2009), A1.

71. United States Border Patrol, "Nationwide Illegal Alien Apprehensions Fiscal Years 1925–2013," at **www.cbp.gov/xp /cgov/border_security/border_patrol /usbp_statistics/usbp_fy13_stats.**

72. Julia Preston, "Arizona Borders Quiets after Gains in Security," *New York Times* (March 16, 2013), A1.

73. Eric Lipton and Julia Preston, "As U.S. Plugs Border in Arizona, Crossings Shift to South Texas," *New York Times* (June 17, 2013), A1.

74. U.S. Immigration and Customs Enforcement, "FY 2013: ICE Announces Year-End Removal Numbers" (December 19, 2013), at **www.ice.gov/news/releases/1312/13 1219washingtondc.htm.**

75. Charlie Savage, "F.B.I. Focusing on Security Over Ordinary Crime," *New York Times* (August 24, 2011), A15.

76. Liam Dillon and Ian Lovett, "Tunnel for Smuggling Found under U.S.-Mexico Border; Tons of Drugs Seized," *New York Times* (November 1, 2013), A14.

77. United States Marshals Service, "Fact Sheet," at **www.justice.gov/marshals /duties/factsheets/general-1209.html.**

78. ASIS International and the Institute of Finance and Management, "Groundbreaking Study Finds U.S. Security Industry to Be $350 Billion Market" (August 12, 2013), at **www.asisonline.org/News/Press -Room/Press-Releases/2013/Pages /Groundbreaking-Study-Finds-U.S. -Security-Industry-to-be-$350-Billion -Market.aspx.**

79. John B. Owens, "Westec Story: Gated Communities and the Fourth Amendment," *American Criminal Law Review* (Spring 1997), 1138.

80. National Retail Federation, "Retail Fraud, Shoplifting Rates Decrease, According to National Retail Security Survey," at **www.nrf.com/modules.php?name =News&op=viewlive&sp_id=945.**

81. William C. Cunningham, John J. Strauchs, and Clifford W. Van Meter, *The Hallcrest Report II: Private Security Trends, 1970 to 2000* (Boston: Butterworth-Heinemann, 1990), 236.

CHAPTER

5
Problems and Solutions
in Modern Policing

CHAPTER OUTLINE	CORRESPONDING LEARNING OBJECTIVES
Police Organization and Field Operations	List the three primary purposes of police patrol.
	Indicate some investigation strategies that are considered aggressive.
	Describe how forensic experts use DNA fingerprinting to solve crimes.
Police Strategies: What Works	Explain why differential response strategies enable police departments to respond more efficiently to 911 calls.
	Explain why reactive arrest strategies might be incompatible with problem-oriented policing.
"Us versus Them": Issues in Modern Policing	Determine when police officers are justified in using deadly force.
Police Misconduct and Ethics	Explain why police officers are allowed discretionary powers.
	8 Explain what an ethical dilemma is, and name four categories of ethical dilemmas that a police officer typically may face.

To target your study and review, look for these numbered Learning Objective icons throughout the chapter.

T.J. Kirkpatrick/Getty Images

135

The Big
QUESTION

WHEN TWO Nassau County, New York, police officers arrived at the house early on the morning of May 17, 2013, they had little idea of what was happening inside. They were responding to a 911 call that described a robbery in progress at the given address, with few additional details. As they approached the property, someone screaming, "He's got a gun!" ran past them. Thinking that they were dealing with a lone offender only, the officers split up, with the first taking a position by the front door and the second entering the house. Both had their weapons drawn.

Inside, the second officer found himself face to face with a man wearing a ski mask. With one arm, the masked man had a young woman in a chokehold. With the other, he was holding a gun to the woman's head. "I'm going to kill her," the masked man yelled and then pointed his gun at the officer. In response, the officer fired eight rounds. Seven struck the intruder, a career criminal named Dalton Smith. The eighth hit the young woman, Andrea Rebello, a twenty-one-year-old student at nearby Hofstra University. Neither Smith nor Rebello survived.

Following the incident, Rebello's family was critical of the police officer's actions. "If he's [a] professional, he should have tried negotiation," said Rebello's godfather. As a number of law enforcement experts pointed out, however, when the officer entered the house, he was unaware that the intruder had a hostage. The experts also cautioned against second-guessing the officer's decision making in such a stressful, high-risk situation. "The big question is, how do you know, when someone's pointing a gun at you, whether you should keep talking to them or shoot?" said Michele Galietta, a professor of psychology at New York's John Jay College of Criminal Justice. "That's what makes the job of an officer amazingly difficult."

FOR CRITICAL ANALYSIS

1. Do you think that the Nassau County police officer acted correctly in this situation? Why or why not?

2. In January 2014, Andrea Rebello's family filed a wrongful death civil suit against Nassau County, claiming that the officer should have waited for the arrival of a hostage negotiator before entering the home. What is your opinion of this claim?

3. After retiring, one thirty-year police veteran said, "Although my gun left its holster on [many] occasions, I am grateful that I never had to shoot anyone." In your opinion, what types of crime would justify a law enforcement officer's decision to shoot a suspect?

James Keivom/*New York Daily News*/Getty Images

■ Mourners embrace during the funeral of Andrea Rebello, who was accidentally shot to death by a police officer responding to a robbery call at Rebello's residence in Uniondale, New York.

POLICE ORGANIZATION AND FIELD OPERATIONS

Nassau County police administrators placed the officer involved in Andrea Rebello's death on *administrative leave*, pending an investigation into the incident. In other words, the officer was temporarily relieved of his duties, with pay. This step does not imply that he was suspected of any wrongdoing. Most law enforcement agencies react similarly when a firearm is fired in the line of duty, both to allow for a full investigation of the event and to give the officer a chance to recover from what can be a traumatic experience.

Administrative leave is a *bureaucratic* response to an officer-involved shooting. In a **bureaucracy**, formal rules govern an individual's actions and relationships with co-employees. The ultimate goal of any bureaucracy is to reach its maximum efficiency—in the case of a police department, to provide the best service for the community within the confines of its limited resources, such as staff and budget. Although some police departments are experimenting with alternative structures based on a partnership between management and the officers in the field, most continue to rely on the hierarchical structure described below.

The Structure of the Police Department

Each police department is organized according to its environment: the size of its jurisdiction, the type of crimes it must deal with, and the demographics of the population it must police. The Metropolitan Police Department of Washington, D.C., operates an Asian Liaison Unit that works within that city's Asian community, while the Evansville (Indiana) Police Department has set up a "No Meth" task force. Geographic location also influences police department organization. The San Diego Police Department has a Harbor Patrol Unit, which would be unproductive in Grand Forks, North Dakota—as would be the Grand Forks Police Department's snowmobile patrol in Southern California.

CHAIN OF COMMAND Whatever the size or location of a police department, it needs a clear rank structure and strict accountability to function properly.[1] One of the goals of the police reformers, especially beginning in the 1950s, was to lessen the corrupting influence of politicians. The result was a move toward a militaristic organization of police.[2] As you can see in Figure 5.1 to the right, a typical police department is based on a "top-down" chain of command that leads from the police chief down to detectives and patrol officers. In this formalized structure, all persons are aware of their place in the chain and of their duties and responsibilities within the organization.

Delegation of authority is a critical component of the chain of command, especially in larger departments. The chief of police delegates authority to deputy chiefs, who delegate authority to assistant chiefs, and on down through the organization. This structure creates a situation in which nearly every member of a police department is directly accountable to a superior. As was the original goal of police reformers, these links encourage discipline and control, and lessen the possibility that any individual police employee will have the unsupervised freedom to abuse her or his position.[3]

ORGANIZING BY AREA AND TIME In most metropolitan areas, police responsibilities are divided according to zones known as *beats* and *precincts*. A beat is the smallest stretch

Bureaucracy A hierarchically structured administrative organization that carries out specific functions.

Delegation of Authority The principles of command on which most police departments are based, in which personnel take orders from and are responsible to those in positions of power directly above them.

FIGURE 5.1 A Typical Police Department Chain of Command

Most American police departments follow this model of the chain of command, though smaller departments with fewer employees often eliminate several of these categories.

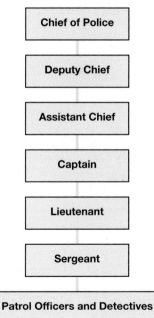

Chief of Police

Deputy Chief

Assistant Chief

Captain

Lieutenant

Sergeant

Patrol Officers and Detectives

A lieutenant (in the white shirt) gives instructions to two sergeants. On his left, a patrol officer appears to be awaiting instructions. How do the delegation of authority and the chain of command contribute to police efficiency?

that a police officer or a group of police officers regularly patrol. A precinct—also known as a *district* or a *station*—is a collection of beats. A precinct commander, or captain, is held responsible by his or her superiors at police headquarters for the performance of the officers in that particular precinct.[4]

Police administrators must also organize their personnel by time. Most departments separate each twenty-four-hour day into three eight-hour *shifts,* also called *tours* or *platoons.* The night shift generally lasts from midnight to 8 A.M., the day shift from 8 A.M. to 4 P.M., and the evening shift from 4 P.M. to midnight. Officers either vary their hours by, say, working days one month and nights the next, or they have fixed tours in which they consistently take day, night, or evening shifts. A number of police departments have implemented compressed work-weeks, in which officers work longer shifts (ten or twelve hours) and fewer days. Such schedules are believed to improve the officers' quality of life by providing more substantial blocks of time off the job to recover from the stresses of police work.[5]

LAW ENFORCEMENT IN THE FIELD To a large extent, the main goal of any police department is the most efficient organization of its *field services.* Also known as "operations" or "line services," field services include patrol activities, investigations, and special operations. According to Henry M. Wrobleski and Karen M. Hess, most police departments are "generalists." Thus, police officers are assigned to general areas and perform all field service functions within the boundaries of their beats.

Larger departments may be more specialized, with personnel assigned to specific types of crime, such as illegal drugs or white-collar crime, rather than geographic locations. Smaller departments, which make up the bulk of local law enforcement agencies, rely almost exclusively on general patrol.[6]

Police on Patrol:
The Backbone of the Department

Every police department has a patrol unit, and patrol is usually the largest division in the department. More than two-thirds of the sworn officers, or those officers authorized to make arrests and use force, in local police departments in the United States have patrol duties.[7]

"Life on the street" is not easy. Patrol officers must be able to handle any number of difficult situations, and experience is often the best and, despite training programs, the only teacher. As one patrol officer commented:

> You never stop learning. You never get your street degree. The person who says . . . they've learned it all is the person that's going to wind up dead or in a very compromising position. They've closed their minds.[8]

It may take a patrol officer years to learn when a gang is "false flagging" (trying to trick rival gang members into the open) or what to look for in a suspect's eyes to sense if he or she is concealing a weapon. This learning process is the backdrop to a number of different general functions that a patrol officer must perform on a daily basis.

THE PURPOSE OF PATROL In general, patrol officers do not spend most of their shifts chasing, catching, and handcuffing suspected criminals. The vast majority of patrol shifts are completed without a single arrest.[9] Officers spend a great deal of time meeting with other officers, completing paperwork, and patrolling with the goal of preventing crime in general rather than focusing on any specific crime or criminal activity.

List the three primary purposes of police patrol.

As police accountability expert Samuel Walker has noted, the basic purposes of the police patrol have changed very little since 1829, when Sir Robert Peel founded the modern police department in London, England. These purposes include

1. The deterrence of crime by maintaining a visible police presence.
2. The maintenance of public order and a sense of security in the community.
3. The twenty-four-hour provision of services that are not crime related.[10]

The first two goals—deterring crime and keeping order—are generally accepted as legitimate police functions. The third, however, has been more controversial. As noted in Chapter 4, the community era saw a resurgence of the patrol officer as a provider of community services, many of which have little to do with crime. The extent to which noncrime incidents dominate patrol officers' time is evident in the Police Services Study, a survey of 26,000 calls to police in sixty different neighborhoods. The study found that only one out of every five calls involved the report of criminal activity.[11] (See Figure 5.2 that follows for the results of another survey of crime calls.)

PATROL ACTIVITIES To recap, the purposes of police patrols are to prevent and deter crime, to maintain order in the community, and also to provide social services. How can the police best accomplish these goals? Of course, each department has its own methods and strategies, but William Gay, Theodore Schell, and Stephen Schack divide routine patrol activity into four general categories:

1. *Preventive patrol.* By maintaining a presence in a community, either in a car or on foot, patrol officers attempt to prevent crime from occurring. This strategy, which O. W. Wilson called "omnipresence," was a cornerstone of early policing philosophy and still takes up roughly 40 percent of patrol time.
2. *Calls for service.* Patrol officers spend nearly a quarter of their time responding to 911 calls for emergency service or other citizen problems and complaints.
3. *Administrative duties.* Paperwork takes up nearly 20 percent of patrol time.
4. *Officer-initiated activities.* Incidents in which the patrol officer initiates contact with citizens, such as stopping motorists and pedestrians and questioning them, account for 15 percent of patrol time.[12]

The category estimates made by Gay, Schell, and Schack are not universally accepted. Professor of law enforcement Gary W. Cordner argues that administrative duties account for the largest percentage of patrol officers' time. According to

Given that most patrol shifts end without an officer making a single arrest, what activities take up most of a patrol officer's time?

Rod Lamkey Jr/AFP/Getty Images

FIGURE 5.2 Calls for Service

Over a period of two years, the Project on Policing Neighborhoods gathered information on calls for service in Indianapolis, Indiana, and St. Petersburg, Florida. As you can see, the largest portion of these calls involved disputes where no violence or threat of violence existed. Be aware also that nearly two-thirds of the nonviolent dispute calls and nearly half of the assault calls answered by police dealt with domestic confrontations.

Description of Violation	Percentage of Total Calls
NONSERIOUS CRIME CALLS	
Nonviolent disputes	42
Public disorder (examples: drunk, disorderly, begging, prostitution)	22
Assistance (examples: missing persons, traffic accident, damaged property)	10
Minor violations (examples: shoplifting, trespassing, traffic/parking offense, refusal to pay)	4
SERIOUS CRIME CALLS	
Assaults (examples: using violence against a person, kidnapping, child abuse)	26
Serious theft (examples: motor vehicle theft, burglary, purse snatching)	5
General disorder (examples: illicit drugs, fleeing police, leaving the scene of an accident)	2

Source: Adapted from Stephen D. Mastrofski, Jeffrey B. Snipes, Roger B. Parks, and Christopher D. Maxwell, "The Helping Hand of the Law: Police Control of Citizens on Request," *Criminology 38* (May 2000), Table 5, page 328.

Detective The primary police investigator of crimes.

Cordner, when officers are not consumed with paperwork and meetings, they are either answering calls for service (which takes up 67 percent of the officers' time on the street) or initiating activities themselves (the remaining 33 percent).[13]

Police Investigations

Investigation is the second main function of police, along with patrol. Whereas patrol is primarily preventive, investigation is reactive. After a crime has been committed and the patrol officer has gathered the preliminary information from the crime scene, the responsibility of finding "whodunnit" is delegated to the investigator, generally known as the **detective.** The most common way for someone to become a detective is to be promoted from patrol officer. Detectives have not been the focus of nearly as much reform attention as their patrol counterparts, mainly because the scope of the detective's job is limited to law enforcement, with less emphasis given to social services or order maintenance.

The detective's job is not quite as glamorous as it is sometimes portrayed by the media. Detectives spend much of their time investigating common crimes such as burglaries and are more likely to be tracking down stolen property than a murderer. They must also prepare cases for trial, which involves a great deal of time-consuming paperwork. Furthermore, a landmark RAND Corporation study estimated that more than 97 percent of cases that are "solved" can be attributed to a patrol officer making an arrest at the scene, witnesses or victims identifying the perpetrator, or detectives undertaking routine investigative procedures that could easily be performed by clerical personnel.[14]

Aggressive Investigation Strategies

LEARNING 2 OBJECTIVE Indicate some investigation strategies that are considered aggressive.

Detective bureaus also have the option of implementing aggressive strategies. For example, if detectives suspect that a person was involved in the robbery of a Mercedes-Benz parts warehouse, one of them might pose as a "fence"—or purchaser of stolen goods. In what is known as a "sting" operation, the suspect is deceived into thinking that the detective (fence) wants to buy stolen car parts. After the transaction takes place, the suspect can be arrested.

UNDERCOVER OPERATIONS Perhaps the most dangerous and controversial operation that a law enforcement agent can undertake is to go *undercover,* or to assume a false identity in order to obtain information concerning illegal activities. Though each department has its own guidelines on when undercover operations are necessary, all that is generally required is the suspicion that illegal activity is taking place. Today, undercover officers are commonly used to infiltrate large-scale narcotics operations or operations run by organized crime.

New York City detective Debra Lawson has worked undercover as part of an elite unit devoted to seizing illegal firearms. Recently, a New York state legislator proposed a bill that would limit the amount of time that a law enforcement officer would be allowed to go undercover. What might be the reasoning behind this legislation?

In some situations, a detective bureau may not want to take the risk of exposing an officer to undercover work or may believe that an outsider cannot infiltrate an organized crime network. When the police need access and information, they have the option of turning to a **confidential informant (CI).** A CI is a person who is involved in criminal activity and gives information about that activity and those who engage in it to the police. As many as 80 percent of all illegal drug cases in the United States involve confidential informants. "They can get us into places we can't go," says one police administrator. "Without them, narcotics cases would practically cease to function."[15]

PREVENTIVE POLICING AND DOMESTIC TERRORISM Aggressive investigation strategies also play a crucial role in the federal government's efforts to combat domestic terrorism. Because would-be terrorists often need help to procure the weaponry necessary for their schemes, they are natural targets for well-placed informants and undercover agents. According to the Center on Law and Security at New York University, about two-thirds of the federal government's major terrorism prosecutions have relied on evidence provided by informants.[16]

The recent arrest of Terry Lee Loewen provides an example of *preventive policing,* which has become a popular strategy for American law enforcement when it comes to potential domestic terrorists. On December 13, 2013, federal agents apprehended Loewen as he attempted to drive a van of what he thought were explosives onto the tarmac of the Mid-Continent Airport in Wichita, Kansas. About six months earlier, while online, Loewen had shared his desire to engage in terrorist acts with an undercover Federal Bureau of Investigation (FBI) agent.[17] A second FBI undercover agent sold Loewen a fake car bomb and accompanied him to the airport on the morning of his arrest.

With preventive policing, then, the goal is not to solve the crime after it has happened, but rather to prevent it from happening in the first place. Inevitably, such tactics raise the issue of entrapment. As you learned in Chapter 3, entrapment is a possible

Confidential Informant (CI) A person who provides police with information concerning illegal activity in which he or she is involved.

Clearance Rate A comparison of the number of crimes cleared by arrest and prosecution with the number of crimes reported during any given time period.

Cold Case A criminal investigation that has not been solved after a certain amount of time.

Forensics The application of science to establish facts and evidence during the investigation of crimes.

Trace Evidence Evidence such as a fingerprint, blood, or hair found in small amounts at a crime scene.

defense for criminal behavior when a government agent plants the idea of committing a crime in the defendant's mind. Although the entrapment defense has often been raised in domestic terrorism cases involving undercover agents, it has yet to succeed. The government has been uniformly successful in proving that these defendants were predisposed to commit the crime regardless of any outside influence. Often, as happened with Loewen, the undercover agent explicitly gives the suspect ample opportunity to "back out at any time," which counteracts the entrapment claim.[18]

Clearance Rates and Cold Cases

The ultimate goal of all law enforcement activity is to *clear* a crime, or secure the arrest and prosecution of the offender. Even a cursory glance at **clearance rates,** which show the percentage of reported crimes that have been cleared, reveals that investigations succeed only part of the time. In 2012, just 63 percent of homicides and 47 percent of total violent crimes were solved, while police cleared only 19 percent of property crimes.[19] For the most part, the different clearance rates for different crimes reflect the resources that a law enforcement agency expends on each type of crime. The police generally investigate a murder or a rape more vigorously than the theft of an automobile or a computer.

As a result of low clearance rates, police departments are saddled with an increasing number of **cold cases,** or criminal investigations that are not cleared after a certain amount of time. (The length of time before a case becomes "cold" varies from department to department. In general, a cold case must be "somewhat old" but not "so old that there can be no hope of ever solving it".[20]) Even using various technologies that we will explore in the next section, cold case investigations rarely succeed. A RAND study found that only about one in twenty cold cases results in an arrest, and only about one in a hundred results in a conviction.[21]

Forensic Investigations and DNA

Although the crime scene typically offers a wealth of evidence, some of it is incomprehensible to a patrol officer or detective without assistance. For that aid, law enforcement officers rely on experts in **forensics,** or the practice of using scientific knowledge and methods to investigate crimes. Forensic experts apply their knowledge to items found at the crime scene to determine crucial facts, such as

1. The cause of death or injury.
2. The time of death or injury.
3. The type of weapon or weapons used.
4. The identity of the crime victim, if that information is unavailable.
5. The identity of the offender (in the best-case scenario).[22]

To assist forensic experts, many police departments operate or are affiliated with approximately four hundred publicly funded crime laboratories in the United States. As we noted in the previous chapter, the FBI also offers the services of its crime lab to agencies with limited resources. The FBI's aid in this area is crucial, given that the nation's crime labs are burdened with a backlog of nearly 1 million requests for forensic services.[23]

CRIME SCENE FORENSICS The first law enforcement agent to reach a crime scene has the important task of protecting any **trace evidence** from contamination. Trace evidence is generally very small—often invisible to the naked human eye—and often requires technological aid for detection. Hairs, fibers, blood, fingerprints, broken glass,

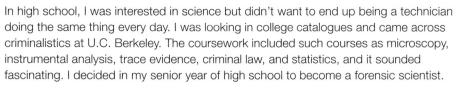

and footprints are all examples of trace evidence. A National Institute of Justice study confirms that when police are able to link such evidence to a suspect, the likelihood of a conviction rises dramatically.[24]

Police will also search a crime scene for bullets and spent cartridge casings. These items can provide clues as to how far the shooter was from the target. They can also be compared with information stored in national firearms databases to determine, under some circumstances, the gun used and its most recent owner. The study of firearms and its application to solving crimes goes under the general term **ballistics.**

For more than a century, the most important piece of trace evidence has been the human fingerprint. Because no two fingerprints are alike, they are considered reliable sources of identification. Forensic scientists compare a fingerprint lifted from a crime scene with that of a suspect and declare a match if there are between eight and sixteen "points of similarity." This method of identification is not infallible, however. It is often difficult to lift a suitable print from a crime scene, and researchers have uncovered numerous cases in which innocent persons were convicted based on evidence obtained through faulty fingerprinting procedures.[25]

THE DNA REVOLUTION The technique of **DNA fingerprinting,** or using a suspect's DNA to match the suspect to a crime, emerged in the mid-1990s and has now all but replaced fingerprint evidence in many types of criminal investigations. The shift has been a boon to crime fighters: one law enforcement agent likened DNA fingerprinting to "the finger of God pointing down" at a guilty suspect.[26]

DNA, which is the same in each cell of a person's body, provides a genetic "blueprint," or "code," for every living organism. DNA fingerprinting is useful in criminal

Ballistics The study of firearms, including the firing of the weapon and the flight of the bullet.

DNA Fingerprinting The identification of a person based on a sample of her or his DNA, the genetic material found in the cells of all living things.

Describe how forensic experts use DNA fingerprinting to solve crimes.

LEARNING **3** OBJECTIVE

investigations because no two people, save for identical twins, have the same genetic code. Therefore, lab technicians, using the process described in Figure 5.3 that follows, can compare the DNA sample of a suspect to the evidence found at the crime scene. If the match is negative, it is certain that the two samples did not come from the same source. If the match is positive, the lab will determine the odds that the DNA sample could have come from someone other than the suspect. Those odds are so high—sometimes reaching 30 billion to one—that a match is practically conclusive.[27]

The process begins when forensic technicians gather blood, semen, skin, saliva, or hair from the scene of a crime. Blood cells and sperm are rich in DNA, making them particularly useful in murder and rape cases, but DNA has also been extracted from sweat on dirty laundry, skin cells on eyeglasses, and saliva on used envelope seals. Once a suspect is identified, her or his DNA can be used to determine whether she or he can be placed at the crime scene. In 2013, for example, investigators from the Wasatch County (Utah) Sheriff's Department connected Joseph M. Simpson to the bludgeoning death of a teenage prostitute by obtaining Simpson's DNA sample from a discarded cigarette.

DNA IN ACTION The ability to "dust" for genetic information on such a wide variety of evidence, as well as that evidence's longevity and accuracy, greatly increases the chances that a crime will be solved. Indeed, police no longer need a witness or even a suspect in custody to solve crimes. What they do need is a piece of evidence and a database.

In 1985, for example, Saba Girmai was found strangled to death in a dumpster in Mountain View, California. For nearly three decades, police were unable to establish any useful leads concerning Girmai's murderer. This changed when technicians at the Santa Clara County District Attorney's Crime Laboratory developed a DNA profile of the suspect using evidence found underneath Girmai's fingerprints. Checking these results against the state's crime database, the technicians found a match with Daniel Garcia,

FIGURE 5.3 Unlocking Evidence in DNA

Deoxyribonucleic acid, or DNA, is the genetic material that carries the code for all living cells. Through DNA profiling, a process explained here, forensic scientists test DNA samples to see if they match the DNA profile of a known criminal or other test subject.

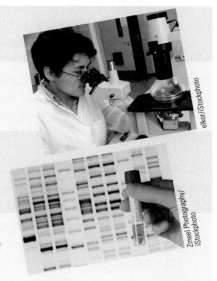

1. DNA samples can be taken from a number of sources, including saliva, blood, hair, and skin. These samples are labeled and shipped to a forensic lab.

2. The DNA is extracted from the cells of the sample using complex proteins known as enzymes. An electrical charge is then sent through the resulting DNA fragments to separate them according to size.

3. Another set of enzymes is added to the now separate DNA fragments. These enzymes attach themselves to different categories of genetic material within the DNA fragments and become distinct when exposed to photographic film. The "photograph" of this visible pattern is the DNA fingerprint.

4. Crime lab technicians will look for thirteen points on the DNA fingerprint called "markers." These thirteen markers are then compared with a suspect's DNA or with DNA found at a crime scene. If a match is found for each of the thirteen markers, there is almost no chance that the two DNA samples came from different persons.

who had been previously convicted of a different crime. Twenty-eight years after the fact, in 2013, Garcia finally was arrested in connection with Girmai's death.

Databases and Cold Hits The identification of Daniel Garcia is an example of what police call a **cold hit,** which occurs when law enforcement finds a suspect "out of nowhere" by comparing DNA evidence from a crime scene against the contents of a database. The largest and most important database is the national Combined DNA Index System (CODIS). Operated by the FBI since 1998, CODIS gives local and state law enforcement agencies access to the DNA profiles of those who have been convicted of various crimes. CODIS contains DNA records of over 10.7 million people, and as of January 2014, the database had produced 230,900 cold hits nationwide.[28]

Cold Hit The establishment of a connection between a suspect and a crime, often through the use of DNA evidence, in the absence of an ongoing criminal investigation.

New Developments DNA fingerprinting has only been available since the late 1980s, and the scope of its investigative uses continues to expand rapidly. At present, for example, the process of DNA profiling takes between two and three weeks. The U.S. military, however, is in the final stages of creating a system that will cut that time to ninety minutes, which will aid law enforcement immensely by quickly matching suspects to crimes.[29] Other new developments involving this technology include the following:

1. *Touch DNA,* which allows investigators to test for the presence of DNA by scraping items such as a piece of food or an article of clothing for microscopic cells left behind by the suspect.
2. *Familial searches,* based on the premise that parents, siblings, and other relatives have similar DNA to suspects whose identity might be unknown or who might be unavailable for testing.
3. *DNA fog,* a security system that, when triggered by an alarm, marks intruders with genetic material derived from plants that is almost impossible to remove and links suspects to crime scenes.
4. The possible use of DNA as a *genetic witness,* by providing law enforcement with a physical description of a suspect, including her or his age or eye, skin, and hair color.[30]

Because of its cost, DNA fingerprinting has traditionally been used mostly in conjunction with "important" violent crime investigations. A recent study by the National Institute of Justice found, however, that not only was using DNA testing in property crimes cost effective, but it also dramatically increased the police's ability to identify burglary and theft suspects.[31] Because many property offenders commit violent crimes as well, it seems logical that apprehending "unimportant" burglars and thieves would prevent a significant amount of serious criminal activity.[32] (Another use of DNA to prevent crime is the subject of the feature *CJ Controversy—DNA Fingerprinting of Arrestees* that follows.)

////**SELF** ASSESSMENT

Fill in the blanks, and check your answers on page 165.

_____ officers make up the backbone of a police department. One of their primary functions is to _____ crime by maintaining a visible _____ in the community. _____, in contrast, investigate crimes that have already occurred. In the past two decades, _____, or the science of crime investigation, has been revolutionized by the technique of _____ _____, in which crime labs use samples of a person's genetic material to match suspects to crimes.

DNA FINGERPRINTING OF ARRESTEES

All fifty states collect DNA from offenders convicted of felonies. Twenty-eight states and the federal government go one step further by collecting DNA from those who have only been arrested for committing a violent crime. Maryland is one of those states, and several years ago police in Wicomico County took a DNA sample of Alonzo King after arresting him on assault charges. After the sample connected King to an unsolved rape case from six years earlier, King challenged Maryland's law before the U.S. Supreme Court. His lawyers argued that it is unfair to "punish" those not yet proven guilty of a committing any crime by extracting their DNA.

POLICE SHOULD TAKE DNA FROM ARRESTEES BECAUSE . . .

- By increasing the number of DNA samples in law enforcement databases, we increase the likelihood of cold hits and of preventing future crimes by unidentified offenders who would otherwise remain free.

- Society's interest in preventing violent crimes is more important than the rights of people who have been arrested for violent, criminal behavior.

POLICE SHOULD NOT TAKE DNA FROM ARRESTEES BECAUSE . . .

- Our criminal justice system is based on the premise that someone is innocent until proven guilty. A person should not suffer the consequences of a guilty verdict until his or her guilt has been proven in court.

- DNA samples provide a wealth of personal information about suspects, including genetic conditions and predisposition to disease. The government should not have access to this information based on a mere arrest.

Your Assignment

In 2013, the Supreme Court upheld the government's ability to take DNA samples from arrestees. You can learn the reasoning behind this decision by searching for *Maryland v. King* online. Justice Antonin Scalia disagreed with the Court's ruling, stating that it would have the "beneficial effect of solving more crimes; then again, so would the taking of DNA samples from anyone who flies on an airplane, applies for a driver's license, or attends a public school." What point is Scalia trying to make? Do you agree with him? Your answer should include at least two full paragraphs.

POLICE STRATEGIES: WHAT WORKS

How important are police when it comes to preventing crime? According to the RAND Institute, a 10 percent increase in police staffing in an average city lowers the annual murder rate by 9 percent, the annual robbery rate by 6 percent, and the annual vehicle theft rate by 4 percent.[33] Using the RAND study to argue that her city should hire more law enforcement agents, Oakland, California, city councilwoman Libby Schaaf concluded, "Police are expensive, but worth it."[34]

The reality, however, is that budget cuts are commonplace in today's law enforcement environment, and many police departments find themselves having to do more with less.[35] In this section, we will examine the most important strategies presently being used to improve police efficiency regardless of limitations placed on police resources.

Calls for Service

Incident-Driven Policing
A reactive approach to policing that emphasizes a speedy response to calls for service.

While law enforcement officers do not like to think of themselves as being at the "beck and call" of citizens, that is the operational basis of much police work. All police departments practice **incident-driven policing**, in which calls for service are the primary instigators of action. Between 40 and 60 percent of police activity is the result of 911 calls or other citizen requests, which means that police officers in the field initiate only about half of such activity.[36]

Response Time The rapidity with which calls for service are answered.

Differential Response A strategy for answering calls for service in which response time is adapted to the seriousness of the call.

RESPONSE TIME AND EFFICIENCY The speed with which the police respond to calls for service has traditionally been seen as a crucial aspect of crime fighting and crime prevention. In incident-driven policing, the ideal scenario is as follows: a citizen sees a person committing a crime and calls 911, and the police arrive quickly and catch the perpetrator in the act. Alternatively, a citizen who is the victim of a crime, such as a mugging, calls 911 as soon as possible, and the police arrive to catch the mugger before she or he can flee the immediate area of the crime. Although such scenarios are quite rare in real life, **response time,** or the time elapsed between the instant a call for service is received and the instant the police arrive on the scene, has become a benchmark for police efficiency.

IMPROVING RESPONSE TIME EFFICIENCY Many police departments have come to realize that overall response time is not as critical as response time for the most important calls. For this reason, a number of metropolitan areas have introduced 311 nonemergency call systems to reduce the strain on 911 operations.[37] Another popular method of improving performance in this area is a **differential response** strategy, in which the police distinguish among different calls for service so that they can respond more quickly to the most serious incidents.

LEARNING **4** OBJECTIVE Explain why differential response strategies enable police departments to respond more efficiently to 911 calls.

Suppose, for example, that a police department receives two calls for service at the same time. The first caller reports that a burglar is in her house, and the second says that he has returned home from work to find his automobile missing. If the department employs differential response, the burglary in progress—a "hot" crime—will receive immediate attention. The missing automobile—a "cold" crime that could have been committed several hours earlier—will receive attention "as time permits," and the caller may even be asked to make an appointment to come to the police station to formally report the theft.

NEXT GENERATION 911 The most pressing shortcomings of America's 911 systems are not organizational, but rather technological. These systems were developed more than forty years ago, when copper-wire landlines ran between telephones and a central switch. Today, most emergency calls for service come from mobile phones, and increasing numbers of consumers are taking advantage of VoIP (voice-over-Internet protocol) technology to turn their computers into telephones. Furthermore, by 2013, about 40 percent of American households were wireless only—a percentage that is certain to increase in the near future.[38]

This situation presents a problem for law enforcement. Standard 911 systems cannot pinpoint the exact location of a mobile phone or a computer. If a caller is unable to provide that information, then it can prove very difficult for police officers to determine the site of the emergency. To resolve this issue, law enforcement is making the transition to Next Generation 911 (NG911). This new system will rely on the Internet and will make it possible for officers to receive text messages, videos, photos, and location data about crime incidents. Unfortunately, given that 911 systems are operated by state and local governments, the rollout of NG911 promises to be slow and uneven. Some observers estimate that the technology will not be available nationwide until the end of the present decade.[39]

For reasons ranging from disinterest to fear to laziness, the general public fails to report about 80 percent of gunfire incidents to police. Now, thanks to ShotSpotter, a gunshot detection system, law enforcement has the means to overcome this civic shortcoming. Placed on a rooftop, a ShotSpotter sensor unit, which is about the size of a watermelon, uses microphones, computer software, a clock, and satellite positioning technology to pinpoint the precise time and location of gunfire.

When a unit detects gunfire, it sends an image of the sound wave to the local police department, where a specialist confirms that a weapon has been fired. (The sound wave of a gun blast looks something like a Christmas tree.) Ideally, police officers are dispatched to the scene within forty seconds of the initial shot. Between 2006 and 2014, ShotSpotter detected 39,000 shooting incidents in Washington, D.C., helping the police fight violent crime and providing valuable information about gun use in the city.

The Washington Post/Getty Images

Thinking about Gunshot Detection Systems

As you will see in the next chapter, many cities have placed surveillance cameras in high-crime neighborhoods. How can ShotSpotter be linked with these cameras to provide further evidence of criminal activity?

Patrol Strategies

Many experts believe that, in the words of former Grand Rapids, Michigan, police chief Kevin Belk, an overreliance on calls for service "tends to make you a reactive department," rather than a police force that prevents crimes from happening in the first place.[40] Similarly, another traditional police strategy, *random patrol,* is increasingly felt to be an inefficient use of law enforcement resources.[41] **Random patrol** refers to police officers making the rounds of a specific area with the general goal of detecting and preventing crime. Every police department in the United States randomly patrols its jurisdiction using automobiles. In addition, 53 percent utilize foot patrols, 32 percent bicycle patrols, 16 percent motorcycle patrols, 4 percent boat patrols, and 1 percent horse patrols.[42]

TESTING RANDOM PATROL Police researchers have been questioning the effectiveness of random patrols since the influential Kansas City Preventive Patrol Experiment of the early 1970s. As part of this experiment, different neighborhoods in the city were subjected to three different levels of patrol: random patrol by a single police car, random patrol by multiple police cars, and no random patrol whatsoever. The results of the Kansas City experiment were somewhat shocking. Researchers found that increasing or decreasing preventive patrol had little or no impact on crimes, public opinion of law enforcement, the effectiveness of the police, police response time, traffic accidents, or reports of crime to police.[43]

For some, the Kansas City experiment and other, similar data prove that patrol officers, after a certain threshold, are not effective in preventing crime and that scarce law enforcement resources should therefore be diverted to other areas. "It makes about as much sense to have police patrol routinely in cars to fight crime as it does to have

Random Patrol A patrol strategy that relies on police officers monitoring a certain area with the goal of detecting crimes in progress or preventing crime due to their presence.

firemen patrol routinely in fire trucks to fight fire," said University of Delaware professor Carl Klockars.[44] Still, random patrols are important for maintaining community relations, and they have been shown to reduce fear of crime in areas where police have an obvious presence.[45]

DIRECTED PATROLS In contrast to random patrols, **directed patrols** target specific areas of a city and often attempt to prevent a specific type of crime. Directed patrols have found favor among law enforcement experts as being a more efficient use of police resources than random patrols, as indicated by the recent Philadelphia Foot Patrol Experiment. During this experiment, extra foot patrols were utilized in sixty Philadelphia locations plagued by high levels of violent crime. During three months of directed patrols, arrests increased by 13 percent in the targeted areas, and violent crime decreased by 23 percent. In addition, an estimated fifty-three violent crimes were prevented over the three-month period.[46]

Homeland Security Photo/Alamy

During Project Razor's Edge in August 2013, U.S. Immigration and Customs Enforcement (ICE) agents arrested more than 360 suspects, including this one in Baltimore, Maryland, with ties to the Mara Salvatrucha street gang. How is a nationwide sweep, conducted by federal agents, similar to a local directed patrol, as described in the text?

Predictive Policing and Crime Mapping

When Camden, New Jersey, police chief Scott Thomson learned that his department was about to lose half of its sworn officers due to budget cuts, he knew that, strategically speaking, he needed to get proactive. So, Thomson implemented an Automatic Vehicle Locator system, which tracked his department's patrol cars to make sure that they regularly passed through areas that were marked by high levels of violent crime.[47] With fewer officers, Thomson immediately became more reliant on predictive, or intelligence-led policing, which we first discussed in Chapter 4.

FINDING "HOT SPOTS" As was the case in Camden, New Jersey, predictive policing strategies are strongly linked with directed patrols, which seek to improve on random patrols by targeting specific high-crime areas already known to law enforcement.[48] The target areas for directed patrols are often called **hot spots** because they contain greater numbers of criminals and have higher-than-average levels of victimization. Needless to say, police administrators are no longer sticking pins in maps to determine where hot spots exist. Rather, police departments are using **crime mapping** to locate and identify hot spots, and "cool" them down. Crime mapping uses geographic information systems (GIS) to track criminal acts as they occur in time and space. Once sufficient information has been gathered, it is analyzed to predict future crime patterns.

Why does hot spot policing work? Criminologists Lawrence Sherman and David Weisburd provided a clue more than twenty years ago by observing the anticrime impact of patrol officers. Sherman and Weisburd observed that after a police officer left a certain high-crime area, about fifteen minutes elapsed before criminal activity occurred at

Directed Patrol A patrol strategy that is designed to focus on a specific type of criminal activity at a specific time.

Hot Spots Concentrated areas of high criminal activity that draw a directed police response.

Crime Mapping Technology that allows crime analysts to identify trends and patterns of criminal behavior within a given area.

Reactive Arrests Arrests that come about as part of the ordinary routine of police patrol and responses to calls for service.

that spot.[49] Therefore, a police officer on patrol is most efficient when she or he spends a certain amount of time at a hot spot and then returns after fifteen minutes.

A recent experiment involving the Sacramento Police Department supports this hypothesis. Over a three-month period, twenty-one crime hot spots in the city received fifteen-minute randomized patrols, while another twenty-one crime hot spots received normal random patrols. Using calls for service as a measuring stick, the hot spots subject to fifteen-minute patrols were found to experience much less criminal activity.[50]

THE RISE OF COMPSTAT Computerized crime mapping was popularized when the New York Police Department launched CompStat in the mid-1990s. Still in use, CompStat starts with police officers reporting the exact location of crime and other crime-related information to department officials. These reports are then fed into a computer, which prepares grids of a particular city or neighborhood and highlights areas with a high incidence of serious offenses. (See Figure 5.4 that follows for an example of a GIS crime map.)

In New York and many other cities, the police department holds "Crime Control Strategy Meetings," during which precinct commanders are held accountable for CompStat's data-based reports in their districts. In theory, this system provides the police with accurate information about patterns of crime and gives them the ability to "flood" hot spots with officers at short notice. About two-thirds of large departments now employ some form of computerized crime mapping,[51] and Wesley Skogan, a criminologist at Northwestern University, believes that CompStat and similar technologies are the most likely cause of recent declines in big-city crime.[52]

Arrest Strategies

Like patrol strategies, arrest strategies can be broken into two categories that reflect the intent of police administrators. **Reactive arrests** are those arrests made by police

FIGURE 5.4 A GIS Crime Map for a Neighborhood in New Orleans

This crime map shows the incidence of various crimes during a two-week period in a neighborhood near downtown New Orleans.

officers, usually on general patrol, who observe a criminal act or respond to a call for service. **Proactive arrests** occur when the police take the initiative to target a particular type of criminal or behavior. Proactive arrests are often associated with directed patrols of hot spots and thus are believed by many experts to have a greater influence on an area's crime rates.[53]

QUALITY-OF-LIFE CRIMES The popularity of proactive theories was solidified by a magazine article that James Q. Wilson and George L. Kelling wrote in 1982.[54] In their piece, entitled "Broken Windows," Wilson and Kelling theorized that reform-era policing strategies focused on violent crime to the detriment of the vital police role of promoting the quality of life in neighborhoods. As a result, many communities, particularly in large cities, had fallen into a state of disorder and disrepute, with two very important consequences.

First, these neighborhoods—with their broken windows, dilapidated buildings, and lawless behavior by residents—send out "signals" that criminal activity is tolerated. Second, this disorder spreads fear among law-abiding citizens, dissuading them from leaving their homes or attempting to improve their surroundings. Thus, the **broken windows theory** is based on "order maintenance" of neighborhoods by cracking down on "quality-of-life" crimes. Such offenses include panhandling, public drinking and urinating, loitering, and graffiti painting.

THE BROKEN WINDOWS EFFECT Only by encouraging proactive arrest strategies with regard to quality-of-life crimes, the two professors argued, could American cities be rescued from rising crime rates. Along with CompStat, the implementation of Wilson and Kelling's theory has been given a great of credit for crime decreases in the United States (particularly New York) over the past three decades.[55] It continues to influence police strategy—in January 2013, the Cincinnati Police Department cracked down on traffic accidents in "micro" hot spots of criminal activity such as intersections and street corners. Within a year, the impacted areas experienced a significant decrease in both traffic crashes and crime.[56]

Community Policing

In "Broken Windows," Wilson and Kelling insisted that, to reduce fear and crime in high-risk neighborhoods, police had to rely on the cooperation of citizens. For all its drawbacks, the political era of policing (see Chapter 4) did have characteristics that observers such as Wilson and Kelling have come to see as advantageous. During the nineteenth century, the police were much more involved in the community than they were after the reforms. Officers performed many duties that today are associated with social services, such as operating soup kitchens and providing lodging for homeless people. They also played a more direct role in keeping public order by "running in" drunks and intervening in minor disturbances.[57] To a certain extent, **community policing** advocates a return to this understanding of the police mission.

RETURN TO THE COMMUNITY Community policing can be defined as an approach that promotes community-police partnerships, proactive problem solving, and community engagement to address issues such as fear of crime and the causes of such fear in a particular area. Neighborhood watch programs, in which police officers and citizens work together to prevent local crime and disorder, are a popular version of a community policing initiative. Under community policing, patrol officers have the freedom to improvise.

Proactive Arrests Arrests that occur because of concerted efforts by law enforcement agencies to respond to a particular type of criminal or criminal behavior.

Broken Windows Theory Wilson and Kelling's theory that a neighborhood in disrepair signals that criminal activity is tolerated in the area. By cracking down on quality-of-life crimes, police can reclaim the neighborhood and encourage law-abiding citizens to live and work there.

Community Policing A policing philosophy that emphasizes community support for and cooperation with the police in preventing crime.

They are expected to develop personal relationships with residents and to encourage those residents to become involved in making the community a safer place. As part of Operation Heat Wave, for instance, Dallas detectives go door-to-door in neighborhoods plagued by burglary and auto theft. During these face-to-face meetings, the detectives are able to gather information concerning recent victimizations and encourage attendance at community crime-watch meetings.[58]

THE QUIET REVOLUTION The strategy of increasing police presence in the community has been part of, in the words of George Kelling, a "quiet revolution" in American law enforcement.[59] Today, nearly two-thirds of police departments mention community policing in their mission statements, and a majority of the departments in large cities offer community police training for employees.[60] Furthermore, the idea seems to be popular among law enforcement agents. A recent survey of more than 1,200 officers in eleven police departments found that between 60 and 95 percent agreed with the idea that "police officers should try to solve non-crime problems on their beat."[61] A majority of the officers also reported having positive relations with members of the public, who they felt generally appreciated community policing efforts.[62]

Two Washington, D.C., police officers offer suggestions to a six-year-old during the annual "Shop with a Cop" event in the nation's capital. How can establishing friendly relations with citizens help law enforcement agencies reduce crime?

Problem-Oriented Policing

Several years ago, the city of Glendale, Arizona, was experiencing property crime levels that were 63 percent above the national average. Using crime mapping, the Glendale police found that a disproportionate amount of the city's property offenses were taking place at ten Circle K convenience stores. After analyzing the situation, the police determined that Circle K management practices such as inadequate staffing, failure to respond to panhandling, and poor lighting were making the stores breeding grounds of property crime.

By working with Circle K to resolve these issues, as well as putting a proactive arrest strategy into effect in the stores, the Glendale police reduced property crime at the stores by 42 percent in a single year.[63] These efforts are an example of **problem-oriented policing,** a strategy based on the premise that police departments devote too many of their resources to reacting to calls for service and too few to "acting on their own initiative to prevent or reduce community problems."[64] To rectify this situation, problem-oriented policing moves beyond simply responding to incidents and attempts instead to control or even solve the root causes of criminal behavior.

Problem-oriented policing encourages police officers to stop looking at their work as a day-to-day proposition. Rather, they should try to shift the patterns of criminal behavior in a positive direction. For example, instead of responding to a 911 call concerning illegal drug use by simply arresting the offender—a short-term response—the patrol officers should also look at the long-term implications of the situation. They should analyze the pattern of similar arrests in the area and interview the arrestee to determine the

Explain why reactive arrest strategies might be incompatible with problem-oriented policing. **LEARNING** **5** **OBJECTIVE**

Problem-Oriented Policing
A policing philosophy that requires police to identify potential criminal activity and develop strategies to prevent or respond to that activity.

reasons, if any, that the site was selected for drug activity.[65] Then additional police action should be taken to prevent further drug sales at the identified location. Research shows that, when properly implemented, problem-oriented policing can be even more effective than directed patrols in reducing "hot spot" crime.[66]

//// SELF ASSESSMENT

Fill in the blanks, and check your answers on page 165.

Without exception, modern police departments practice _____-driven policing, in which officers respond to calls for _____ such as 911 phone calls after a crime has occurred. Along the same lines, most patrol officers work _____ patrols, in which they cover designated areas and react to the incidents they encounter. _____ patrols, which often focus on "hot spots" of crime, and _____ arrest policies, which target a particular type of criminal behavior, have both been shown to be very effective. _____ policing is a popular strategy in which officers are encouraged to develop partnerships with citizens to prevent and combat crime.

"US VERSUS THEM": ISSUES IN MODERN POLICING

After a Nassau County, New York, police officer received criticism for accidentally killing Hofstra student Andrea Rebello, described in the opening to this chapter, local law enforcement felt they were in a "damned if you do, damned if you don't" situation. "As bad an ending as this [was] for the police, imagine how bad it would have been if they were outside and something terrible was happening inside," said one former police officer.[67] In fact, several years earlier, Nassau County officers had been heavily criticized for waiting outside a home while inside a man abused and eventually killed his girlfriend.

The question of when and how to use force is one of many on-the-job issues that make law enforcement such a challenging and often dangerous career. When faced with a scenario in which a masked man is holding a gun to a young woman's head and threatening to kill her, sometimes police officers make the right decisions, and sometimes they make the wrong ones. Often, it is difficult to tell the two apart.

Police Subculture

As a rule, police officers do not appreciate being second-guessed when it comes to their split-second shooting decisions. To officers, it seems that civilians believe that suspects with weapons should be given a "free shot" before being fired at by law enforcement.[68] Feelings of frustration and mistrust toward civilians are hallmarks of the **police subculture,** a broad term used to describe the basic assumptions and values that permeate law enforcement agencies and are taught to new members of a law enforcement agency as the proper way to think, perceive, and act. Every organization has a subculture, with values shaped by the particular aspects and pressures of that organization. In the police subculture, those values are formed in an environment characterized by danger, stress, boredom, and violence.

From their first day on the job, rookies begin the process of **socialization,** in which they are taught the values and rules of police work. This process is aided by a number of rituals that are common to the law enforcement experience. Police theorist Harry J. Mullins believes that the following rituals are critical to a police officer's acceptance, and even embrace, of police subculture:

Police Subculture The values and perceptions that are shared by members of a police department and, to a certain extent, by all law enforcement agents.

Socialization The process through which a police officer is taught the values and expected behavior of the police subculture.

1. Attending a police academy.
2. Working with a senior officer, who passes on the "lessons" of police work and life to the younger officer.
3. Making the initial felony arrest.
4. Using force to make an arrest for the first time.
5. Using or witnessing deadly force for the first time.
6. Witnessing major traumatic incidents for the first time.[69]

Each of these rituals makes it clear to the police officer that this is not a "normal" job. The only other people who can understand the stresses of police work are fellow officers, and consequently law enforcement officers tend to insulate themselves from civilians. Eventually, the insulation breeds mistrust, and the police officer develops an "us versus them" outlook toward those outside the force. In turn, this outlook creates what sociologist William Westly called the **blue curtain,** also known as the "blue wall of silence" or, simply, "the code."[70] This curtain separates the police from the civilians they are meant to protect.

The Physical Dangers of Police Work

Shortly after 11:00 P.M. on the night of February 11, 2014, Orange County, Florida, deputy sheriff Jonathan Scott Pine responded to a report of car break-ins in an Orlando gated community. One of the suspects, before fleeing, opened fire on Pine, killing him. According to the Officer Down Memorial Page, Pine was one of 126 law enforcement agents who died in the line of duty from January 2013 to February 2014, and one of thirty-four who were killed by hostile gunfire.[71] In addition, about 53,000 assaults were committed against police officers in 2012, with 28 percent of these assaults resulting in an injury.[72]

These numbers are hardly surprising. As police experts John S. Dempsey and Linda S. Forst point out, police "deal constantly with what may be the most dangerous species on this planet—the human being."[73] At the same time, Dempsey and Forst note that according to data compiled by the federal government, citizens and the police come into contact about 40 million times a year.[74] Given this figure, the police have relatively low death and injury rates.

Stress and the Mental Dangers of Police Work

In addition to physical dangers, police work entails considerable mental pressure and stress. Professor John Violanti and his colleagues at the University at Buffalo have determined that police officers experience unusually high levels of *cortisol,* otherwise known as the "stress hormone," which is associated with serious health problems such as diabetes and heart disease.[75] "Intervention is necessary to help officers deal with this difficult and stressful occupation," says Violanti. "[Police officers] need to learn how to relax, how to think differently about things they experience as a cop."[76]

POLICE STRESSORS The conditions that cause stress—such as worries over finances or relationships—are known as **stressors.** Each profession has its own set of stressors, but police are particularly vulnerable to occupational pressures and stress factors such as the following:

1. The constant fear of being a victim of violent crime.
2. Exposure to violent crime and its victims.
3. The need to comply with the law in nearly every job action.

4. Lack of community support.

5. Negative media coverage.

Police face a number of internal pressures as well, including limited opportunities for career advancement, excessive paperwork, and low wages and benefits.[77] The unconventional hours of shift work can also interfere with an officer's private life and contribute to lack of sleep. Each of these is a primary stressor associated with police work.[78]

THE CONSEQUENCES OF POLICE STRESS Police stress can manifest itself in different ways. The University at Buffalo study cited above found that the stresses of law enforcement often lead to high blood pressure and heart problems.[79] Other research shows that police officers are three times more likely to suffer from alcoholism than the average American.[80] If stress becomes overwhelming, an officer may suffer from **burnout,** becoming listless and ineffective as a result of mental and physical exhaustion.

Another problem related to stress is *post-traumatic stress disorder (PTSD)*. Often recognized in war veterans and rape victims, PTSD is a reaction to a stressor that evokes significant trauma. For police officers, such stressors might include the death of a fellow agent or the shooting of a civilian. An officer suffering from PTSD will

George Frey/Reuters/Landov

1. Re-experience the traumatic event through nightmares and flashbacks.

2. Become less and less involved in the outside world by withdrawing from others and refusing to participate in normal social interactions.

3. Experience "survival guilt," which may lead to loss of sleep and memory impairment.[81]

In 2013, Columbia, South Carolina, police chief Randy Scott resigned after struggling with PTSD related to the fatal automobile crash of a fellow officer eight years earlier.

To put it bluntly, law enforcement officers are exposed to more disturbing images—of violent death, bloody crime scenes, horrible accidents, and human cruelty—in their first few years on the job than most people will see in a lifetime. Though some studies suggest that police officers have higher rates of suicide than the general population, it appears that most develop an extraordinary ability to handle the difficulties of the profession and persevere.[82]

Authority and the Use of Force

If the police subculture is shaped by the dangers of the job, it often finds expression through authority. The various symbols of authority that decorate a police officer—including the uniform, badge, nightstick, and firearm—establish the power she or he

Fellow officers escort the casket of Ogden City, Utah, police officer Jared Francom, who was shot and killed while trying to apprehend a suspect. ■ Besides physical violence, what are some of the occupational threats that police officers face on a daily basis?

Burnout A mental state that occurs when a person suffers from exhaustion and has difficulty functioning normally as a result of overwork and stress.

holds over civilians. For better or for worse, both police officers and civilians tend to equate terms such as *authority* and *respect* with the ability to use force.

Near the beginning of the twentieth century, a police officer stated that his job was to "protect the good people and treat the crooks rough."[83] Implicit in the officer's statement is the idea that to do the protecting, he had to do some roughing up as well. This attitude toward the use of force is still with us today. Indeed, it is generally accepted that not only is police use of force inevitable, but also that police officers who are unwilling to use force in certain circumstances cannot do their jobs effectively.

USE OF FORCE IN LAW ENFORCEMENT In general, the use of physical force by law enforcement personnel is very rare, occurring in only about 1.4 percent of the 40 million annual police-public encounters mentioned earlier. Still, the Department of Justice estimates that law enforcement officers threaten to use force or use force in encounters with 770,000 civilians a year, and nearly 14 percent of those incidents result in an injury.[84] Federal authorities also report that about 690 deaths occur in the process of an arrest on an annual basis.[85] Of course, police officers are often justified in using force to protect themselves and other citizens. As we noted earlier, they are the targets of tens of thousands of assaults each year. Law enforcement agents are also usually justified in using force to make an arrest, to prevent suspects from escaping, to restrain suspects or other individuals for their own safety, or to protect property.[86]

At the same time, few observers would be naïve enough to believe that the police are *always* justified in the use of force. A survey of emergency room physicians found that 98 percent believed that they had treated patients who were victims of excessive police force.[87] How, then, is "misuse" of force to be defined? To provide guidance for officers in this tricky area, nearly every law enforcement agency designs a *use of force matrix*. As the example in Figure 5.5 that follows shows, such a matrix presents officers with the proper force options for different levels of contact with a civilian.

TYPES OF FORCE To comply with the various, and not always consistent, laws concerning the use of force, a police officer must understand that there are two kinds of force: *nondeadly force* and *deadly force*. Most force used by law enforcement is nondeadly force. In most states, the use of nondeadly force is regulated by the concept of **reasonable force,** which allows the use of nondeadly force when a reasonable person would assume that such force was necessary. In contrast, **deadly force** is force that an objective police officer realizes will place the subject in direct threat of serious injury or death.

THE UNITED STATES SUPREME COURT AND USE OF FORCE The United States Supreme Court set the limits for the use of deadly force by law enforcement officers in *Tennessee v. Garner* (1985).[88] The case involved an incident in which Memphis police officer Elton Hymon shot and killed a suspect who was trying to climb over a fence after stealing ten dollars from a residence. Hymon testified that he had been trained to shoot to keep a suspect from escaping, and indeed Tennessee law at the time allowed police officers to apprehend fleeing suspects in this manner.

POLICY.CJ

Officers at more than 15,000 law enforcement agencies employ Tasers as a less lethal alternative to firearms. Search for the term **Taser** on the Internet, and make a list of several ways that this technology leads to fewer injuries for both police officers and suspects. Then, search for **Taser safety issues** and write a full paragraph in which you explain the dangers of Taser use by the police.

FIGURE 5.5 The Orlando (Florida) Police Department's Use of Force Matrix

Like most local law enforcement agencies, the Orlando Police Department has a policy to guide its officers' use of force. These policies instruct an officer on how to react to an escalating series of confrontations with a civilian and are often expressed visually, as shown here.

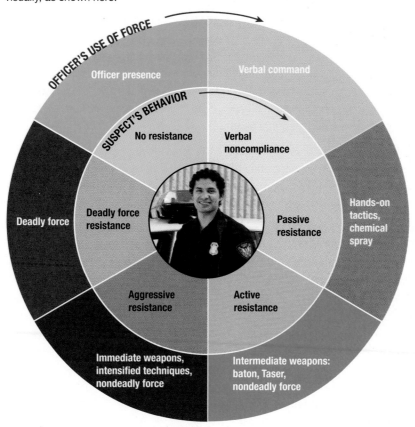

Source: Michael E. Miller, "Taser Use and the Use-of-Force Continuum," *The Police Chief* (September 2010), 72. Photo credit: iStockphoto.com/Mie Ahmt

In reviewing the case, the Supreme Court focused not on Hymon's action but on the Tennessee statute itself, ultimately finding it unconstitutional:

> When the suspect poses no immediate threat to the officer and no threat to others, the use of deadly force is unjustified. . . . It is not better that all felony suspects die than that they escape.[89]

The Court's decision forced twenty-three states to change their fleeing felon rules, but it did not completely eliminate police discretion in such situations. Police officers still may use deadly force if they have probable cause to believe that the fleeing suspect poses a threat of serious injury or death to the officers or others. (We will discuss the concept of probable cause in the next chapter.)

In essence, the Court recognized that police officers must be able to make split-second decisions without worrying about the legal ramifications. Four years after the *Garner* case, the Court tried to clarify this concept in *Graham v. Connor* (1989), stating that the use of any force should be judged by the "reasonableness of the moment."[90] In 2004, the Court modified this rule by suggesting that an officer's use of force could be "reasonable" even if, by objective measures, the force was not needed to protect the officer or others in the area.[91] (See the feature *Discretion in Action—High-Speed Force* that follows.)

HIGH-SPEED FORCE

THE SITUATION You are a police officer who, late at night, clocks a car traveling 73 miles per hour on a road with a 55-mile-per-hour speed limit. You follow the car, activating your blue flashing lights to indicate that the driver, a young man named Victor, should pull over. Instead, Victor speeds up to 85 miles per hour and proceeds to lead you on a chase that seems right out of a Hollywood movie. Going down a narrow, two-lane street, Victor swerves through traffic, forcing numerous other cars off the road, and runs several red lights. You mimic these dangerous maneuvers, and, about six minutes after the chase began, you find yourself directly behind Victor's bumper, both of you speeding at 90 miles per hour. For a short period, there are no other cars nearby.

THE LAW The use of force—including deadly force—by a law enforcement agent is linked to the concept of reasonableness. That is, in this case, is it reasonable for the officer to believe that the fleeing suspect poses a threat of serious injury or death to anybody involved in the chase, including innocent bystanders?

WHAT WOULD YOU DO? Use your discretion to consider your various options. You can abandon the chase as too dangerous and allow Victor to escape. You can continue the pursuit. Or, you can attempt to force Victor off the road, thereby exposing both of you to possible injury or even death. What will you do?

To see how a police officer in rural Georgia reacted in a similar situation, go to Example 5.1 in Appendix B.

 SELF ASSESSMENT

Fill in the blanks, and check your answers on page 165.

Like any organization, a police department has a _____ that determines the values of its employees. In law enforcement, these values are shaped by the _____ dangers, such as assault, and mental dangers, such as high levels of _____, that officers face every day. Laws regulating police use of force rely on two concepts: _____ force, which is the amount of force that a rational person would consider necessary in a given situation, and _____ force, which is a level of force that will place the subject in grave bodily danger.

POLICE MISCONDUCT AND ETHICS

As the two deadly force cases highlighted at the end of the previous section show, American courts generally will uphold a police officer's freedom to decide "what law to enforce, how much to enforce it, against whom, and on what occasions."[92] This judicial support of police discretion is based on the following factors:

1. Police officers are generally considered trustworthy and are therefore assumed to make honest decisions, regardless of contradictory testimony by a suspect.
2. Experience and training give officers the ability to determine whether certain activity poses a threat to society and to take any reasonable action necessary to investigate or prevent such activity.
3. Due to the nature of their jobs, police officers are extremely knowledgeable about human—and, by extension criminal—behaviors.
4. Police officers may find themselves in danger of personal physical harm and must be allowed to take reasonable and necessary steps to protect themselves.[93]

At the same time, as we noted during our discussion of discretion in Chapter 1, freedom to make decisions can mean freedom to make the wrong decisions. Too often, the enormous amount of discretion afforded to police officers, when mixed with the temptations inherent in the law enforcement working environment, can lead to excessive force and other forms of police misconduct, which we will address in this section.

Police Corruption

Police *corruption* has been a concern since the first organized American police departments. As you will recall from Chapter 4, a desire to eradicate, or at least limit, corruption was one of the motivating factors behind the reform movement of policing. For general purposes, **police corruption** can be defined as the misuse of authority by a law enforcement officer "in a manner designed to produce personal gain." The Knapp Commission, set up to investigate the behavior of "dirty cops" in New York City in the 1970s, identified three basic, traditional types of police corruption:

1. *Bribery,* in which the police officer accepts money or other forms of payment in exchange for "favors," which may include allowing a certain criminal activity to continue or misplacing a key piece of evidence before a trial. Related to bribery are *payoffs,* in which an officer demands payment from an individual or a business in return for certain services.
2. *Shakedowns,* in which an officer attempts to coerce money or goods from a citizen or criminal.
3. *Mooching,* in which the police officer accepts free "gifts" such as cigarettes, liquor, or services in return for favorable treatment of the gift giver.[94]

Additionally, corrupt police officers have many opportunities to engage in theft or burglary by taking money or property in the course of their duties. Vice investigations, for example, often uncover temptingly large amounts of illegal drugs and cash. In 2013, for example, a former Chicago police sergeant was sentenced to twenty-two months in prison for "confiscating" thousands of ill-gotten dollars from a drug dealer (who was, in fact, an FBI informant).

Another scenario involves police misconduct that becomes pervasive, infecting a group of officers. Several years ago, dozens of Baltimore police officers were implicated in a $1 million kickback scheme (see photo that follows). For years, the officers had been

In the wake of the Majestic Body Shop scandal, then–Baltimore police commissioner Frederick H. Bealefeld III, left, hired former federal counternarcotics chief Grayling G. Williams, right, to run the Baltimore City Police Department's anticorruption division. What steps can police administrators take to lessen the likelihood of such scandals?

Matt Roth/The New York Times

diverting autos damaged in traffic accidents to the Majestic Body Shop in return for a payoff of several hundred dollars per car. Sometimes, the officers themselves would cause further damage to the cars to increase the portion of the insurance payout that went into their own pockets.

Police Accountability

Given the seeming inevitability of excessive force, corruption, and other misconduct among a small number of law enforcement agents, an important question necessarily arises—*who shall police the police?*

INTERNAL INVESTIGATIONS "The minute the public feels that the police department is not investigating its own alleged wrongdoing well, the police department will not be able to function credibly in even the most routine of matters," says Sheldon Greenberg, a professor of public safety at Johns Hopkins University.[95] The mechanism for these investigations within a police department is the **internal affairs unit (IAU).** In many smaller police departments, the police chief conducts internal affairs investigations, while midsized and large departments have a team of internal affairs officers. The New York Police Department's IAU has an annual budget of about $70 million and consists of 675 officers.

As much as police officers may resent internal affairs units, most realize that it is preferable to settle disciplinary matters in house. The alternatives may be worse. Police officers are criminally responsible for any crimes they might commit, and city and state governments can be held civilly liable for wrongdoing by their law enforcement employees. In 2013 alone, the city of Los Angeles spent $20 million on excessive-force lawsuits involving the L.A. County Sheriff's Department.[96]

CITIZEN OVERSIGHT Many communities also rely on an external procedure for handling citizen complaints against the police, known as **citizen oversight.** In this process, citizens—people who are not sworn officers and, by inference, not biased in favor of law enforcement officers—review allegations of police misconduct or brutality. For the most part, citizen review boards can only recommend action to the police chief or other executive. They do not have the power to discipline officers directly. Police officers generally resent this intrusion by civilians, and most studies have shown that civilian review boards are not widely successful in their efforts to convince police chiefs to take action against their subordinate officers.[97]

SURVEILLANCE AND POLICE MISCONDUCT One form of citizen oversight that has placed police misconduct under a spotlight is cheap digital video. Several years ago, for example, a Philadelphia police lieutenant lost his job when a cell phone camera captured him punching a woman in the face during the city's annual Puerto Rican Day parade. Four days after the incident, 1.3 million people had viewed video of the incident online.

The vast majority of all smartphone videos taken by members of the public portray law enforcement agents unfavorably. At the same time, hundreds of police agencies in the United States are using video technology to *protect* their officers from charges of misconduct.[98] With cameras mounted on patrol cars or on body armor, or with head-worn

Dennis Kenney, a professor at New York's John Jay College of Criminal Justice, warns that self-surveillance devices such as this CopVu chest-mounted video camera raise "tremendous privacy concerns." What might be some of these concerns?

AP Images

systems that see what the wearer sees, police officers are monitoring their own behavior. The resulting video images act as unbiased witnesses to traffic stops, arrests, and other law enforcement encounters with suspects. Furthermore, evidence shows that when police officers know that their actions are being videotaped, they are much less likely to engage in behavior that could lead to sanctions.[99]

Ethics in Law Enforcement

Police corruption is intricately connected with the ethics of law enforcement officers. As you saw in Chapter 1, ethics has to do with fundamental questions of the fairness, justice, rightness, or wrongness of any action. Given the significant power that police officers hold, society expects very high standards of ethical behavior from them. These expectations are summed up in the "Police Code of Conduct," which was developed by the International Association of Chiefs of Police in 1989.

To some extent, the "Police Code of Conduct" is self-evident: "A police officer will not engage in acts of corruption or bribery." In other aspects, it is idealistic, perhaps unreasonably so: "Officers will never allow personal feelings, animosities, or friendships to influence official conduct." The police working environment—rife with lying, cheating, lawbreaking, and violence—often does not allow for such ethical absolutes.

ETHICAL DILEMMAS Some police actions are obviously unethical, such as the behavior of the police officers who received kickbacks from the Baltimore auto body shop, described in a previous section. The majority of ethical dilemmas that a police officer will face are not so clear cut. Criminologists Joycelyn M. Pollock and Ronald F. Becker define an ethical dilemma as a situation in which law enforcement officers

1. Do not know the right course of action,
2. Have difficulty doing what they consider to be right, and/or
3. Find the wrong choice very tempting.[100]

LEARNING **8** OBJECTIVE Explain what an ethical dilemma is, and name four categories of ethical dilemmas that a police officer typically may face.

Because of the many rules that govern policing—the subject of the next chapter—police officers often find themselves tempted by a phenomenon called **noble cause corruption**. This type of corruption occurs when, in the words of John P. Crank and Michael A. Caldero, "officers do bad things because they believe the outcomes will be good."[101] Examples include planting evidence or lying in court to help convict someone the officer knows to be guilty as well as the situation discussed in the feature *A Question of Ethics—The "Dirty Harry" Problem* that follows.

ELEMENTS OF ETHICS Pollock and Becker, both of whom have extensive experience as ethics instructors for police departments, further identify four categories of ethical dilemmas, involving discretion, duty, honesty, and loyalty.[102]

1. *Discretion.* The law provides rigid guidelines for how police officers must act and how they cannot act, but it does not offer guidelines for how officers *should act* in many circumstances. As mentioned at the beginning of this section, police officers often use discretion to determine how they should act, and ethics plays an important role in guiding discretionary actions.

2. *Duty.* The concept of discretion is linked with **duty,** or the moral or legal obligation to act in a certain manner. Society, by passing laws, can make a police officer's duty clearer and, in the process, help eliminate discretion from the

Noble Cause Corruption
Knowing misconduct by a police officer with the goal of attaining what the officer believes is a "just" result.

Duty The legal obligation or moral sense of a police officer that she or he should behave in a certain manner.

A QUESTION OF ETHICS: The "Dirty Harry" PROBLEM

THE SITUATION A young girl has been kidnapped by a psychotic killer named Scorpio. Demanding a $200,000 ransom, Scorpio has buried the girl alive, leaving her with just enough oxygen to survive for a few hours. Detective Harry Callahan manages to find Scorpio, but the kidnapper stubbornly refuses to reveal the location of the girl. Callahan comes to the conclusion that the only way he can get this information from Scorpio in time is to beat it out of him.

THE ETHICAL DILEMMA The U.S. Constitution, as interpreted by the United States Supreme Court, forbids the torture of criminal suspects. Following proper procedure, Callahan should arrest Scorpio and advise him of his constitutional rights. If Scorpio requests an attorney, Callahan must comply. If the attorney then advises Scorpio to remain silent, there is nothing Callahan can do. Of course, after all this time, the girl will certainly be dead.*

WHAT IS THE SOLUTION? What should Detective Callahan do? According to the late Carl B. Klockars of the University of Delaware, "Each time a police officer considers deceiving a suspect into confessing by telling him

that his [or her] fingerprints were found at the scene or that a conspirator has already confessed, each time a police officer considers adding some untrue details to his [or her] account of a probable cause to legitimate a crucial stop or search [that police officer] faces" the same problem as Detective Callahan. Are police ever justified in using unlawful methods, no matter what good may ultimately be achieved?

*This scenario is taken from *Dirty Harry* (1971), one of the most popular police dramas of all time. In the film, Detective Callahan, played by Clint Eastwood, shoots Scorpio and then tortures him. Although Callahan eventually gets the information he needs, it is too late to save the girl.

On February 20, 2013, Vice President Joseph Biden presented Kitsap County, Washington, deputy sheriff Krista McDonald with the Public Safety Officer Medal of Valor. McDonald earned the honor for placing herself in the line of fire to rescue two fellow deputies who had been wounded in a shootout with a suspected sex offender. What role does the concept of duty play in a law enforcement agent's decision, regardless of her or his own safety, to protect the life of another person?

Mandel Ngan/AFP/Getty Images

decision-making process. But an officer's duty will not always be obvious, and ethical considerations can often supplement "the rules" of being a law enforcement agent.

3. *Honesty.* Of course, honesty is a critical attribute for an ethical police officer. A law enforcement agent must make hundreds of decisions in a day, and most of them require him or her to be honest in order to properly do the job.

4. *Loyalty.* What should a police officer do if he or she witnesses a partner using excessive force on a suspect? The choice often sets loyalty against ethics, especially if the officer does not condone the violence.

Although an individual's ethical makeup is determined by a multitude of personal factors, police departments can create an atmosphere that is conducive to professionalism. Brandon V. Zuidema and H. Wayne Duff, both captains with the Lynchburg (Virginia) Police Department, believe that law enforcement administrators can encourage ethical policing by

1. Incorporating ethics into the department's mission statement.
2. Conducting internal training sessions in ethics.
3. Accepting "honest mistakes" and helping the officer learn from those mistakes.
4. Adopting a zero-tolerance policy toward unethical decisions when the mistakes are not so honest.[103]

////SELF ASSESSMENT

Fill in the blanks, and check your answers on page 165.

In general, a law enforcement officer has a great deal of _____ when it comes to her or his duties. Misconduct such as accepting bribes or shaking down citizens is known as _____, and such behavior is investigated by _____ _____ units within police departments. In matters of ethics, a police officer is often guided by his or her sense of _____, or the obligation to act in a certain manner, and a feeling of _____ toward fellow officers.

CHAPTER SUMMARY

For more information on these concepts, look back to the Learning Objective icons throughout the chapter.

 List the three primary purposes of police patrol. (a) The deterrence of crime, (b) the maintenance of public order, and (c) the provision of services that are not related to crime.

 Indicate some investigation strategies that are considered aggressive. Using undercover officers is considered an aggressive (and often dangerous) investigative technique. The use of informants is also aggressive but involves danger for those who inform.

 Describe how forensic experts use DNA fingerprinting to solve crimes. Law enforcement agents gather trace evidence such as blood, semen, skin, or hair from the crime scene. Because these items are rich in DNA, which provides a unique genetic blueprint for every living organism, crime labs can create a DNA profile of the suspect and test it against other such profiles stored in databases. If the profiles match, then law enforcement agents have found a strong suspect for the crime.

 Explain why differential response strategies enable police departments to respond more efficiently to 911 calls. A differential response strategy allows a police department to distinguish among calls for service so that officers may respond to important calls more quickly. Therefore, a "hot" crime, such as a burglary in progress, will receive more immediate attention than a "cold" crime, such as a missing automobile that disappeared several days earlier.

 Explain why reactive arrest strategies might be incompatible with problem-oriented policing. Problem-oriented policing requires that law enforcement try to shift the patterns of criminal behavior rather than react to it by making arrests. That is, instead of simply apprehending offenders after they have offended, problem-oriented policing relies on police officers analyzing the root causes of crime in a particular area and working toward removing those negative influences from the environment.

 Determine when police officers are justified in using deadly force. Police officers must make a reasonable judgment in determining when to use force that will place the suspect in threat of injury or death. That is, given the circumstances, the officer must reasonably assume that the use of such force is necessary to avoid serious injury or death to the officer or someone else.

 Explain why police officers are allowed discretionary powers. The general acceptance of police discretion in the criminal justice system is based on factors such as (a) the general trustworthiness of police officers, (b) police training and experience, (c) police knowledge of criminal behavior, and (d) the need for police officers to make quick decisions to protect themselves against physical harm.

 Explain what an ethical dilemma is, and name four categories of ethical dilemmas that a police officer typically may face. An ethical dilemma is a situation in which police officers (a) do not know the right course of action, (b) have difficulty doing what they consider to be right, and/or (c) find the wrong choice very tempting. The four types of ethical dilemmas involve (a) discretion, (b) duty, (c) honesty, and (d) loyalty.

QUESTIONS FOR CRITICAL ANALYSIS

1. In speaking with a domestic terrorism suspect, a paid FBI informant said, "Allah has more work for you to do," adding, "Revelation is going to come in your dreams that you have to do this thing." The "thing" was to shoot down American military airplanes with handheld missiles. If you were defending the terrorism suspect in court, how would you use this evidence? Why would your efforts be likely to fail?

2. What might be some of the drawbacks of relying on text messaging as part of Next Generation 911?

3. Criminologists John and Emily Beck suggest that crime reduction strategies should treat crime as if it were a form of pollution. How does this comparison make sense in the context of predictive policing and crime mapping?

4. Suppose that a high-crime neighborhood is plagued by numerous abandoned homes and malfunctioning streetlights. Applying the "broken windows" theory, what steps should local politicians take to reduce crime in the area?

5. Nearly every police department in the country has a policy that limits its officers' discretion to engage in high-speed automobile pursuits of fleeing suspects. Why do you think such policies are so popular among police administrators?

KEY TERMS

ballistics 143
blue curtain 154
broken windows theory 151
bureaucracy 137
burnout 155
citizen oversight 160
clearance rate 142
cold case 142
cold hit 145
community policing 151
confidential informant (CI) 141
crime mapping 149

deadly force 156
delegation of authority 137
detective 140
differential response 147
directed patrol 149
DNA fingerprinting 143
duty 162
forensics 142
hot spots 149
incident-driven policing 146
internal affairs unit (IAU) 160
noble cause corruption 162

police corruption 159
police subculture 153
proactive arrests 151
problem-oriented policing 152
random patrol 148
reactive arrests 150
reasonable force 156
response time 147
socialization 153
stressors 154
trace evidence 142

SELF-ASSESSMENT ANSWER KEY

Page 145: i. Patrol; **ii.** deter; **iii.** presence; **iv.** Detectives; **v.** forensics; **vi.** DNA fingerprinting

Page 153: i. incident; **ii.** service; **iii.** random; **iv.** Directed; **v.** proactive; **vi.** Community

Page 158: i. subculture; **ii.** physical; **iii.** stress; **iv.** reasonable; **v.** deadly

Page 163: i. discretion; **ii.** corruption; **iii.** internal affairs; **iv.** duty; **v.** loyalty

NOTES

1. Peter K. Manning, *Police Work: The Social Organization of Policing,* 2d ed. (Prospect Heights, Ill.: Waveland Press, 1997), 96.

2. Samuel Walker, *The Police in America: An Introduction,* 2d ed. (New York: McGraw-Hill, 1992), 16.

3. George L. Kelling and Mark H. Moore, "From Political to Reform to Community: The Evolving Strategy of Police," in *Community Policing: Rhetoric or Reality,* eds. Jack Greene and Stephen Mastrofski (New York: Praeger Publishers, 1988), 13.

4. John S. Dempsey and Linda S. Forst, *An Introduction to Policing,* 6th ed. (Clifton Park, N.Y.: Delmar Cengage Learning, 2011), 84.

5. Karen Amendola, "Which Shift Is Best?" *The Police Chief* (March 2013), 14.

6. Henry M. Wrobleski and Karen M. Hess, *Introduction to Law Enforcement and Criminal Justice,* 7th ed. (Belmont, Calif.: Wadsworth/Thomson Learning, 2003), 119.

7. Bureau of Justice Statistics, *Local Police Departments, 2007* (Washington, D.C.: U.S. Department of Justice, December 2010), 6.

8. Connie Fletcher, "What Cops Know," *On Patrol* (Summer 1996), 44–45.

9. David H. Bayley, *Police for the Future* (New York: Oxford University Press, 1994), 20.

10. Walker, *op. cit.,* 103.

11. Eric J. Scott, *Calls for Service: Citizens Demand an Initial Police Response* (Washington, D.C.: National Institute of Justice, 1981), 28–30.

12. William G. Gay, Theodore H. Schell, and Stephen Schack, *Routine Patrol: Improving Patrol Productivity,* vol. 1 (Washington, D.C.: National Institute of Justice, 1977), 3–6.

13. Gary W. Cordner, "The Police on Patrol," in *Police and Policing: Contemporary Issues,* ed. Dennis Jay Kenney (New York: Praeger Publishers, 1989), 60–71.

14. Peter W. Greenwood and Joan Petersilia, *The Criminal Investigation Process: Summary and Policy Implications* (Santa Monica, Calif.: RAND Corporation, 1975).

15. Quoted in Sarah Stillman, "The Throwaways," *The New Yorker* (September 3, 2012), 38–39.

16. Center on Law and Security, *Terrorist Trial Report Card: September 11, 2001–September 11, 2009* (New York: New York University School of Law, January 2010), 42–44.

17. Tim Potter, "Was Wichita Airport Bomb Suspect a Victim of Entrapment?" *Wichita Eagle* (December 17, 2013), at **www.kansas.com/2013/12/17/3184791/was-wichita-airport-bomb-suspect.html.**

18. *Ibid.*

19. Federal Bureau of Investigation, *Crime in the United States 2012* (Washington, D.C.: U.S. Department of Justice, 2013), Table 25, at **www.fbi.gov/about-us/cjis/ucr/crime-in-the-u.s/2012/crime-in-the-u.s.-2012/cius_home.**

20. James M. Cronin, Gerard R. Murphy, Lisa L. Spahr, Jessica I. Toliver, and Richard E. Weger, *Promoting Effective Homicide Investigations* (Washington, D.C.: Police Executive Research Forum, August 2007), 102–103.

21. Robert C. Davis, Carl Jenses, and Karin E. Kitchens, *Cold Case Investigations: An Analysis of Current Practices and Factors Associated with Successful Outcomes* (Santa Monica, Calif.: RAND Corporation, 2011), xii.

22. Ronald F. Becker, *Criminal Investigations*, 2d ed. (Sudbury, Mass.: Jones & Bartlett, 2004), 7.

23. Bureau of Justice Statistics, *Census of Publicly Funded Forensic Crime Laboratories, 2009* (Washington, D.C.: U.S. Department of Justice, August 2012), 1.

24. Joseph Peterson, Ira Sommers, Deborah Baskin, and Donald Johnson, *The Role and Impact of Forensic Evidence in the Criminal Justice Process* (Washington, D.C.: National Institute of Justice, September 2010), 8–9.

25. Simon A. Cole, "More Than Zero: Accounting for Error in Latent Fingerprinting Identification," *Journal of Criminal Law and Criminology* (Spring 2005), 985–1078.

26. Quoted in "New DNA Database Helps Crack 1979 N.Y. Murder Case," *Miami Herald* (March 14, 2000), 18A.

27. Judith E. Lewter, "The Use of Forensic DNA in Criminal Cases in Kentucky as Compared with Other Selected States," *Kentucky Law Journal* (1997–1998), 223.

28. "CODIS—NDIS Statistics," at **www.fbi.gov/about-us/lab/biometric-analysis/codis/ndis-statistics.**

29. Ray Locker and Kendall Breitmann, "Rapid DNA Test Could Transform Crime Fight," *USA Today* (January 28, 2014), 1A.

30. Gautam Naik, "To Sketch a Thief: Genes Draw Likeness of Suspects," *Wall Street Journal* (March 29, 2009), A9.

31. Nancy Ritter, "DNA Solves Property Crimes (But Are We Ready for That?)," *NIJ Journal* (October 2008), 2–12.

32. Phil Bulman, "DNA and Property Crimes," *The Police Chief* (April 2013), 16.

33. Paul Heaton, *Hidden in Plain Sight: What Cost-of-Crime Research Can Tell Us about Investing in Police* (Santa Monica, Calif.: RAND Corporation, 2010).

34. "63 Percent of Local Police Departments Are Facing Cuts in Their Total Funding, Survey Shows," Police Executive Research Forum, January 2009, at **www.policeforum.org/library/press-releases/PERF%20Survey%20on%20Policing%20&%20Economy.pdf.**

35. "Policing and the Economic Downturn" (Washington, D.C.: Police Executive Research Forum, February 2013), 1–4.

36. Wrobleski and Hess, *op. cit.,* 173.

37. National Institute of Justice, *Managing Calls to the Police with 911/311 Systems* (Washington, D.C.: U.S. Department of Justice, February 5, 2005).

38. Stephen J. Blumberg and Julian V. Luke, *Wireless Substitution: Early Release of Estimates From the National Health Interview Survey, January–June 2013* (Washington, D.C.: Centers for Disease Control, December 2013), 1.

39. Melina Moraga, "Emergency Upgrade: NG911 Brings Public Safety Communications into the 21st Century," *Law Enforcement Technology* (July 2013), 10–13.

40. Quoted in Carl Bialik, "Detroit Police Response Times No Guide to Effectiveness," *Wall Street Journal* (August 2, 2013), at **online.wsj.com/news/articles/SB10001424127887323997004578642250518125898.**

41. *Ibid.*

42. *Local Police Departments, 2007, op. cit.,* Table 12, page 15.

43. George L. Kelling, Tony Pate, Duane Dieckman, and Charles Brown, *The Kansas City Preventive Patrol Experiment: A Summary Report* (Washington, D.C.: The Police Foundation, 1974), 3–4.

44. Carl B. Klockars and Stephen D. Mastrofski, "The Police and Serious Crime," in *Thinking about Police,* eds. Carl B. Klockars and Stephen Mastrofski (New York: McGraw-Hill, 1990), 130.

45. Anthony M. Pate, "Experimenting with Foot Patrol: The Newark Experience," in *Community Crime Prevention: Does It Work?* ed. Dennis P. Rosenbaum (Newbury Park, Calif.: Sage, 1986).

46. Jerry H. Ratcliffe et al., "The Philadelphia Foot Patrol Experiment: A Randomized Controlled Trial of Police Patrol Effectiveness in Violent Crime Hotspots," *Criminology* (August 2011), 795–830.

47. *How Are Innovations in Technology Transforming Policing?* (Washington, D.C.: Police Executive Research Forum, January 2012), 36–38.

48. Lawrence W. Sherman, "Policing for Crime Prevention," in *Contemporary Policing: Controversies, Challenges, and Solutions,* eds. Quint C. Thurman and Jihong Zhao (Los Angeles: Roxbury Publishing Co., 2004), 62.

49. Lawrence W. Sherman and David Weisburd, "General Deterrent Effects of Police Patrol in Crime 'Hot Spots': A Randomized Controlled Trial," *Justice Quarterly* (December 1995), 625–648.

50. Renée J. Mitchell, "Hot-Spot Randomized Control Works for Sacramento," *The Police Chief* (February 2013), 12.

51. David Weisburd and Cynthia Lum, "The Diffusion of Computerized Crime Mapping in Policing: Linking Research and Practice," *Police Practice and Research* 6 (2005), 419–434.

52. Quoted in "New Model Police," *The Economist* (June 9, 2007), 29.

53. Sherman, *op. cit.,* 63–66.

54. *Ibid.,* 65.

55. William Sousa and George L. Kelling, "Of 'Broken Windows,' Criminology, and Criminal Justice," in *Police Innovation: Contrasting Perspectives,* eds. David L. Weisburd and Anthony A. Braga (New York: Cambridge University Press, 2006), 77–97.

56. Daniel W. Gerard, "Cincinnati HAZARD: A Place-Based Traffic Enforcement and Violent Crime Strategy," *The Police Chief* (July 2013), 44–46.

57. Mark H. Moore and George L. Kelling, "'To Serve and Protect': Learning from Police History," *Public Interest* (Winter 1983), 54–57.

58. Brigitte Gassaway, Steven Armon, and Dana Perez, "Engaging the Community: Operation Heat Wave," *Geography and Public Safety* (October 2011), 8–9.

59. George Kelling, "Police and Community: The Quiet Revolution," in *Perspectives in Policing* (Washington, D.C.: National Institute of Justice, 1988).

60. *Local Police Departments, 2003, op. cit.,* 19.

61. Wesley K. Skogan and Megan Alderden, *Police and the Community* (Washington, D.C.: National Police Research Platform, February 2011), 4.

62. *Ibid.,* 5–6.

63. Michael D. White and Charles M. Katz, "Policing Convenience Store Crime: Lessons from the Glendale, Arizona, Smart Policing Initiative," *Police Quarterly* (September 2013), 305–322.

64. Herman Goldstein, "Improving Policing: A Problem-Oriented Approach," *Crime and Delinquency* 25 (1979), 236–258.

65. Bureau of Justice Assistance, *Problem-Oriented Drug Enforcement: A Community-Based Approach for Effective Policing* (Washington, D.C.: Office of Justice Programs, 1993), 5.

66. Christopher S. Koper, Bruce Taylor, and Jamie Roush, "What Works Best at Violent Crime Hot Spots? A Test of Directed Patrol and Problem-Solving Approaches in Jacksonville, Florida," *The Police Chief* (October 2013), 12–13.

67. Quoted in Frank Eltman and Jim Fitzgerald, "Andrea Rebello's Godfather, Henrique Santos, Blames New York Police for Woman's Death," *Associated Press* (May 20, 2013).

68. J. Pete Blair et al., "Reasonableness and Reaction Time," *Police Quarterly* (December 2011), 327.

69. Harry J. Mullins, "Myth, Tradition, and Ritual," *Law and Order* (September 1995), 197.

70. William Westly, *Violence and the Police: A Sociological Study of Law, Custom, and Morality* (Cambridge, Mass.: MIT Press, 1970).

71. Officer Down Memorial Page, at **www .odmp.org/search/year?year=2014** and **www.odmp.org/search/year?year=2013.**

72. Federal Bureau of Investigation, *Law Enforcement Officers Killed and Assaulted, 2012* (Washington, D.C.: U.S. Department of Justice, 2013), at **www.fbi.gov /about-us/cjis/ucr/leoka/2012/officers -assaulted/assaults_topic_page_-2012.**

73. John S. Dempsey and Linda S. Forst, *An Introduction to Policing*, 6th ed. (Clifton Park, N.Y.: Delmar Cengage Learning, 2011), 170.

74. Bureau of Justice Statistics, *Contacts between Police and the Public, 2008* (Washington, D.C.: U.S. Department of Justice, October 2011), 1.

75. University at Buffalo, "Impact of Stress on Police Officers' Physical and Mental Health," *Science Daily* (September 29, 2008), at **www.sciencedaily.com /releases/2008/09/080926105029.htm.**

76. Quoted in *ibid.*

77. Gail A. Goolsakian et al., *Coping with Police Stress* (Washington, D.C.: National Institute of Justice, 1985).

78. J. L. O'Neil and M. A. Cushing, *The Impact of Shift Work on Police Officers* (Washington, D.C.: Police Executive Research Forum, 1991), 1.

79. "Impact of Stress on Police Officers' Physical and Mental Health," *op. cit.*

80. James Hibberd, "Police Psychology," *On Patrol* (Fall 1996), 26.

81. M. J. Horowitz, N. Wilner, N. B. Kaltreider, and W. Alvarez, "Signs and Symptoms of Post Traumatic Stress Disorder," *Archives of General Psychiatry* 37 (1980), 85–92.

82. Daniel W. Clark, Elizabeth K. White, and John M. Violanti, "Law Enforcement Suicide: Current Knowledge and Future Directions," *The Police Chief* (May 2012), 48.

83. Lawrence M. Friedman, *Crime and Punishment in American History* (New York: Basic Books, 1993), 362.

84. *Contacts between Police and the Public, 2008, op. cit.,* 14.

85. Bureau of Justice Statistics, *Arrest-Related Deaths, 2003–2009, Statistical Tables* (Washington, D.C.: U.S. Department of Justice, November 2011), 1.

86. David J. Spotts, "Reviewing Use-of-Force Practices," *The Police Chief* (August 2012), 12.

87. H. Range Hutson, Deirdre Anglin, Phillip Rice, Demetrious N. Kyriacou, Michael Guirguis, and Jared Strote, "Excessive Use of Force by Police: A Survey of Academic Emergency Physicians," *Emergency Medicine Journal* (January 2009), 20–22.

88. 471 U.S. 1 (1985).

89. 471 U.S. 1, 11 (1985).

90. 490 U.S. 386 (1989).

91. *Brosseau v. Haugen,* 543 U.S. 194 (2004).

92. Kenneth Culp Davis, *Police Discretion* (St. Paul, Minn.: West Publishing Co., 1975).

93. C. E. Pratt, "Police Discretion," *Law and Order* (March 1992), 99–100.

94. Knapp Commission, *Report on Police Corruption* (New York: Brazilier, 1973).

95. Quoted in Jennifer Dukes and Loren Keller, "Can Police Be Police to Selves?" *Omaha World-Herald* (February 22, 1998), 1A.

96. Abby Sewell, "Sheriff's Department Lawsuit Costs Rose to $43 Million Last Year," *Los Angeles Times* (January 9, 2014), at **articles.latimes.com/2014/jan/09 /local/la-me-ln-county-lawsuits-sheriff -20140109.**

97. Hazel Glenn Beh, "Municipal Liability for Failure to Investigate Citizen Complaints against Police," *Fordham Urban Law Journal* 23 (Winter 1998), 209.

98. Carol Moore, "Worth More than a Thousand Words," *Law Enforcement Technology* (March 2013), 26–34.

99. William Farrar, "Operation Candid Camera: Rialto Police Department's Body-Worn Camera Experiment," *The Police Chief* (January 2014), 20–25.

100. Jocelyn M. Pollock and Ronald F. Becker, "Ethics Training Using Officers' Dilemmas," *FBI Law Enforcement Bulletin* (November 1996), 20–28.

101. Quoted in Thomas J. Martinelli, "Dodging the Pitfalls of Noble Cause Corruption and the Intelligence Unit," *The Police Chief* (October 2009), 124.

102. Pollock and Becker, *op. cit.,* 20–28.

103. Brandon V. Zuidema and H. Wayne Duff, "Organizational Ethics through Effective Leadership," *Law Enforcement Bulletin* (March 2009), 8–9.

6

Police and the Constitution:
The Rules of Law Enforcement

CHAPTER OUTLINE		CORRESPONDING LEARNING OBJECTIVES
The Fourth Amendment		Outline the four major sources that may provide probable cause.
		Explain the exclusionary rule and the exceptions to it.
Lawful Searches and Seizures		Explain when searches can be made without a warrant.
		Describe the plain view doctrine, and indicate one of its limitations.
Stops and Frisks		Distinguish between a stop and a frisk, and indicate the importance of the case *Terry v. Ohio*.
Arrests		List the four elements that must be present for an arrest to take place.
The Interrogation Process and *Miranda*		Explain why the U.S. Supreme Court established the *Miranda* warnings.
		Indicate situations in which a *Miranda* warning is unnecessary.

To target your study and review, look for these numbered Learning Objective icons throughout the chapter.

RJ Sangosti/*The Denver Post*/Getty Images

Sniff SEARCH

WHEN THE MIAMI-DADE County (Florida) Police Department received an anonymous tip that Joelis Jardines was growing marijuana in his home, they sent Franky to verify. After circling for a few minutes on Jardines's front porch, Franky, a chocolate Labrador Retriever trained to sniff out illegal drugs, sat down near the front door. This was a signal to the two officers on the scene that the dog smelled something suspicious. Relying on Franky's expertise, the officers obtained permission from a judge to search Jardines's home. They found nearly 180 marijuana plants, with an estimated street value of about $700,000.

Jardines eventually pleaded not guilty to drug trafficking charges. At trial, his lawyers claimed that—by allowing Franky to sniff around the outside of Jardines's home—the Miami police had used improper means to justify their search. In 2013, the United States Supreme Court agreed. To come to its decision, the Court relied on a concept called the *expectation of privacy,* which we will address later in this chapter. Historically, Americans have enjoyed a strong expectation of privacy from government intrusion inside their homes and on their *curtilage,* or the domain of their daily home lives.

Under certain circumstances, the Court recognized, we tolerate the presence of uninvited visitors on our property. Such visitors include Girl Scouts selling cookies, trick-or-treaters, and salespeople. This tolerance does not, however, extend to law enforcement agents with drug-sniffing dogs. "The police cannot . . . hang around on the lawn or in the side garden, trawling for evidence and perhaps peering into the windows of the home," said Justice Antonin Scalia. "And the officers [in the Jardines case] had all four of their feet and all four of their companion's planted firmly on that curtilage—the front porch is the classic example of an area intimately associated with the life of the home."

FOR CRITICAL ANALYSIS

1. Do you agree that the home should receive added protection from police searches under American criminal law? Why or why not?

2. If you were to argue *against* the Supreme Court's decision in this case, how could you use the fact that mail carriers are customarily allowed on private property?

3. What if a police officer had come to Joelis Jardines's front door to get information about a missing child in the neighborhood and noticed a strong smell of marijuana? Why might the Court allow a search based on this scenario?

The United States Supreme Court recently ruled that the U.S. Constitution limits the ability of law enforcement to gather evidence of criminal behavior by using narcotics-sniffing police dogs.

THE FOURTH AMENDMENT

In *Florida v. Jardines,* the United States Supreme Court did not address whether Joelis Jardines was guilty or innocent of the charges against him. That was for the trial court to decide. Rather, the Court ruled that the Miami police officers had overstepped the boundaries of their authority by using a drug-sniffing dog to detect the smell of marijuana from Jardines's front porch.[1] In the previous chapter, we discussed the importance of discretion for police officers. This discretion, as we noted, is not absolute. A law enforcement agent's actions are greatly determined by the rules for policing set down in the U.S. Constitution and enforced by the courts.

To understand these rules, law enforcement officers must understand the Fourth Amendment, which reads as follows:

> The right of the people to be secure in their persons, houses, papers, and effects, against unreasonable searches and seizures, shall not be violated, and no Warrants shall issue, but upon probable cause, supported by Oath or affirmation, and particularly describing the place to be searched, and the persons or things to be seized.

This amendment contains two critical legal concepts: a prohibition against *unreasonable searches and seizures* and the requirement of **probable cause** to issue a warrant.

Reasonableness

Law enforcement personnel use searches and seizures to look for and collect the evidence prosecutors need to convict individuals suspected of crimes. As you have just read, when police are conducting a search or seizure, they must be *reasonable*. Though courts have spent innumerable hours scrutinizing the word, no specific meaning for *reasonable* exists. A thesaurus can provide useful synonyms—logical, practical, sensible, intelligent, plausible—but because each case is different, those terms are relative.

In the *Jardines* case, the Supreme Court accepted the argument that the search had been so unreasonable as to violate the Fourth Amendment's prohibition against unreasonable searches and seizures. That does not mean that such searches are unreasonable under any circumstances. The Court has allowed evidence of illegal drugs uncovered by trained dogs sniffing the exterior of luggage in an airport and the outside of a car that the police have stopped for a traffic violation.[2] According to American case law, searches in such public places are more likely to be found reasonable than searches of the home, "the most private . . . of all the places and things the Fourth Amendment protects."[3]

Probable Cause

The concept of reasonableness is linked to probable cause. The Supreme Court has ruled, for example, that any arrest or seizure is unreasonable unless it is supported by probable cause.[4] The burden of probable cause requires more than mere suspicion on a police officer's part. The officer must know of facts and circumstances that would reasonably lead to "the belief that an offense has been or is being committed."[5]

SOURCES OF PROBABLE CAUSE If no probable cause existed when a police officer took a certain action, it cannot be retroactively applied. If, for example, a police officer stops a person for jaywalking and then finds several ounces of marijuana in that person's pocket,

the arrest for marijuana possession would probably be disallowed. Remember, suspicion does not equal probable cause. If, however, an informant had tipped the officer off that the person was a drug dealer, probable cause might exist and the arrest could be valid. Informants are one of several sources that may provide probable cause. These sources include

Outline the four major sources that may provide probable cause.

LEARNING OBJECTIVE 1

1. *Personal observation.* Police officers may use their personal training, experience, and expertise to infer probable cause from situations that may not be obviously criminal. If, for example, a police officer observes several people in a car slowly circling a certain building in a high-crime area, that officer may infer that the people are "casing" the building in preparation for a burglary. Probable cause could be established for detaining the suspects.

2. *Information.* Law enforcement officers receive information from victims, eyewitnesses, informants, and official sources such as police bulletins or broadcasts. Such information, as long as it is believed to be reliable, is a basis for probable cause.

3. *Evidence.* In certain circumstances, which will be examined later in this chapter, police have probable cause for a search or seizure based on evidence—such as a shotgun—in plain view.

4. *Association.* In some circumstances, if the police see a person with a known criminal background in a place where criminal activity is openly taking place, they have probable cause to stop that person. Generally, however, association is not adequate to establish probable cause.[6]

THE PROBABLE CAUSE FRAMEWORK In a sense, the concept of probable cause allows police officers to do their job effectively. Most arrests are made without prior judicial approval in the form of a *warrant* because most arrests are the result of quick police reaction to the commission of a crime. Indeed, it would not be practical to expect a police officer to obtain a warrant before making an arrest on the street. Thus, probable cause provides a framework that limits the situations in which police officers can make arrests, but also gives officers the freedom to act within that framework. In 2003, the Supreme Court reaffirmed this freedom by ruling that Baltimore, Maryland, police officers acted properly when they arrested all three passengers of a car in which cocaine had been hidden in the back seat. "A reasonable officer," wrote Chief Justice William H. Rehnquist, "could conclude that there was probable cause to believe" that the defendant, who had been sitting in the front seat, was in "possession" of the illicit drug despite his protestations to the contrary.[7]

Once an arrest is made, the arresting officer must prove to a judge that probable cause existed. In *County of Riverside v. McLaughlin* (1991),[8] the Supreme Court ruled that this judicial determination of probable cause must be made within forty-eight hours after the arrest, even if this two-day period includes a weekend or holiday.

The Exclusionary Rule

Historically, the courts have looked to the Fourth Amendment for guidance in regulating the activity of law enforcement officers, as the language of the Constitution does not expressly do so. The courts' most potent legal tool in this endeavor is the **exclusionary rule,** which prohibits the use of illegally seized evidence. According to this rule, any evidence obtained by an unreasonable search or seizure is inadmissible (may not be used) against a defendant in a criminal trial.[9] Even highly incriminating evidence, such as a knife stained with the victim's blood, usually cannot be introduced at a trial if illegally obtained. (Thanks to the Supreme Court's ruling detailed at the beginning of this chapter, evidence of the marijuana plants in Joelis Jardines's house was excluded because of the improper search.)

Furthermore, any physical or verbal evidence that police are able to acquire by using illegally obtained evidence is known as the **fruit of the poisoned tree** and is also inadmissible. For example, if the police use the existence of the bloodstained knife to get a confession out of a suspect, that confession will be excluded as well.

One of the implications of the exclusionary rule is that it forces police to gather evidence properly. If they follow appropriate procedures, they are more likely to be rewarded with a conviction. If they are careless or abuse the rights of the suspect, they are unlikely to get a conviction. A strict application of the exclusionary rule, therefore, will permit guilty people to go free because of police carelessness or innocent errors. In practice, relatively few apparently guilty suspects benefit from the exclusionary rule.

LEARNING **2** OBJECTIVE Explain the exclusionary rule and the exceptions to it.

Suppose that this gun—used by a defendant to murder a victim—was found as the result of an improper police search. Why might the exclusionary rule keep evidence of the gun's existence out of court? What is your opinion of the exclusionary rule?

Gary W. Green/*Orlando Sentinel*/Getty Images

"Inevitable Discovery" Exception The legal principle that illegally obtained evidence can be admissible in court if police using lawful means would have "inevitably" discovered it.

"Good Faith" Exception The legal principle that evidence obtained with the use of a technically invalid search warrant is admissible during trial if the police acted in good faith when they sought the warrant from a judge.

Research shows that about 3 percent of felony arrestees avoid incarceration because of improper police searches and seizures.[10]

THE "INEVITABLE DISCOVERY" EXCEPTION Critics of the exclusionary rule maintain that, regardless of statistics, the rule hampers the police's ability to gather evidence and causes prosecutors to release numerous suspects before their cases make it to court. Several Supreme Court decisions have mirrored this view and provided exceptions to the exclusionary rule.

The **"inevitable discovery" exception** was established in the wake of the disappearance of ten-year-old Pamela Powers of Des Moines, Iowa, on Christmas Eve, 1968. The primary suspect in the case, a religious fanatic named Robert Williams, was tricked by a detective into leading police to the site where he had buried Powers. The detective convinced Williams that if he did not lead police to the body, he would soon forget where it was buried. This would deny his victim a "Christian burial." Initially, in *Brewer v. Williams* (1977),[11] the Court ruled that the evidence (Powers's body) had been obtained illegally because Williams's attorney had not been present during the interrogation that led to his admission. Several years later, in *Nix v. Williams* (1984),[12] the Court reversed itself, ruling that the evidence was admissible because the body would have eventually ("inevitably") been found by lawful means.

THE "GOOD FAITH" EXCEPTION The scope of the exclusionary rule has been further diminished by two cases involving faulty warrants. In the first, *United States v. Leon* (1984),[13] the police seized evidence on authority of a search warrant that had been improperly issued by a judge. In the second, *Arizona v. Evans* (1995),[14] due to a computer error, a police officer detained Isaac Evans on the mistaken belief that he was subject to an arrest warrant. As a result, the officer found a marijuana cigarette on Evans's person and, after a search of his car, discovered a bag of marijuana.

In both cases, the Court allowed the evidence to stand under a **"good faith" exception** to the exclusionary rule. Under this exception, evidence acquired by a police officer using a technically invalid warrant is admissible if the officer was unaware of the error. In these two cases, the Court said that the officers acted in good faith. By the same token, if police officers use a search warrant that they know to be technically incorrect, the "good faith" exception does not apply, and the evidence can be suppressed.

//// SELF ASSESSMENT

Fill in the blanks, and check your answers on page 198.

The Fourth Amendment contains two critically important restrictions on police authority: a prohibition against _____ searches and seizures and a requirement of _____ _____ that a crime has been committed before a warrant for a search or seizure can be issued. Judges rely on the _____ rule to keep _____ that has been improperly obtained by the police out of criminal courts.

LAWFUL SEARCHES AND SEIZURES

How far can law enforcement agents go in searching and seizing private property? Consider the steps taken by Jenny Stracner, an investigator with the Laguna Beach (California) Police Department. After receiving information that a suspect, Greenwood, was engaged in drug trafficking, Stracner enlisted the aid of the local trash collector in procuring evidence. Instead of taking Greenwood's trash bags to be incinerated, the collector agreed to give them to Stracner. The officer found enough drug paraphernalia in the garbage to obtain a warrant to search the suspect's home. Subsequently, Greenwood was arrested and convicted on narcotics charges.[15]

Remember, the Fourth Amendment is quite specific in forbidding unreasonable searches and seizures. Were Stracner's search of Greenwood's garbage and her seizure of its contents "reasonable"? The Supreme Court thought so, holding that Greenwood's garbage was not protected by the Fourth Amendment.[16]

The Role of Privacy in Searches

A crucial concept in understanding search and seizure law is *privacy*. By definition, a **search** is a governmental intrusion on a citizen's reasonable expectation of privacy. The recognized standard for a "reasonable expectation of privacy" was established in *Katz v. United States* (1967).[17] The case dealt with the question of whether the defendant was justified in his expectation of privacy in the calls he made from a public phone booth. The Supreme Court held that "the Fourth Amendment protects people, not places," and Katz prevailed.

In his concurring opinion, Justice John Harlan, Jr., set a two-pronged test for a person's expectation of privacy:

1. The individual must prove that she or he expected privacy, and
2. Society must recognize that expectation as reasonable.[18]

Accordingly, the Court agreed with Katz's claim that he had a reasonable right to privacy in a public phone booth. Even though the phone booth was a public place, accessible to anyone, Katz had taken clear steps to protect his privacy.

A LEGITIMATE PRIVACY INTEREST Despite the *Katz* ruling, simply taking steps to protect one's privacy is not enough to protect against law enforcement intrusion. The steps must be reasonably certain to ensure privacy. If a person is unreasonable or mistaken in expecting privacy, he or she may forfeit that expectation. For instance, in *California v. Greenwood* (1988),[19] described above, the Court did not believe that the suspect had a reasonable expectation of privacy when it came to his garbage bags. The Court noted that when we place our trash on a curb, we expose it to any number of intrusions by "animals, children, scavengers, snoops, and other members of the public."[20] In other words, if Greenwood had truly intended for the contents of his garbage bags to remain private, he would not have left them on the side of the road.

In *Florida v. Jardines,* the Supreme Court case that opened this chapter, four of the nine justices believed that the Court had gone too far in protecting the defendant's expectation of privacy. As recently as 2011, these justices

Should law enforcement be able to use police helicopters such as the one shown here to determine if people are carrying out illegal behavior in their fenced-in back yards? Why or why not?

Ricky Carioti/*The Washington Post*/Getty Images

noted, the Court had found that people have no such expectation regarding smells coming from their homes that can be detected by a human being.[21] Why, they asked, should the nose of a drug-sniffing dog be any different?[22]

PRIVACY AND SATELLITE MONITORING As you can see, a number of factors go into determining whether a reasonable expectation of privacy exists. In *United States v. Jones* (2012),[23] the U.S. Supreme Court emphasized the important roles that time and technology play in this equation. The Court's ruling invalidated the efforts of federal agents who had placed a GPS tracking device on the car of Antoine Jones, a Washington, D.C., nightclub owner suspected of drug trafficking. Using the device, which relies on satellite transmissions to determine location, the agents were able to follow Jones's movements for a month. This evidence helped bring about Jones's conviction for conspiring to distribute cocaine.

The Court found that the government had "physically occupied" private property—Jones's car—for an unreasonably long amount of time. As a result, all evidence gathered by the GPS device was ruled inadmissible. Several Supreme Court justices also pointed out that most citizens do not expect the police to be monitoring every drive they make over the course of twenty-eight days.[24] As one commentator stated, the ruling seemed to acknowledge that just because technology now permits greater levels of surveillance, this "does not mean that society has decided there's no such thing as privacy anymore."[25]

Search and Seizure Warrants

The Supreme Court's ruling in the case of Antoine Jones discussed above does not mean that law enforcement officers can *never* track someone for a month using a GPS device or any other technology. Rather, it means that, to do so, they need to obtain a **search warrant,** a step that the federal agents failed to take before beginning their surveillance of Jones. A search warrant is a written court order that authorizes police to search a certain area. Before a judge or magistrate will issue a search warrant, law enforcement officers must provide

1. Information showing probable cause that a crime has been or will be committed.
2. Specific information on the premises to be searched, the suspects to be found and the illegal activities taking place at those premises, and the items to be seized.

The purpose of a search warrant is to establish, before the search takes place, that a *probable cause to search* justifies infringing on the suspect's reasonable expectation of privacy.

PARTICULARITY OF SEARCH WARRANTS The members of the First Congress specifically did not want law enforcement officers to have the freedom to make "general, exploratory" searches through a person's belongings.[26] Consequently, the Fourth Amendment requires that a warrant describe with "particularity" the place to be searched and the things—either people or objects—to be seized.

This "particularity" requirement places a heavy burden on law enforcement officers. Before going to a judge to ask for a search warrant, the officers must prepare an **affidavit** in which they provide specific, written information on the property that they wish to search and seize. They must know the specific address of any place they wish to search. General addresses of apartment buildings or office complexes are not sufficient. Furthermore, courts generally frown on vague descriptions of goods to be seized.

For example, several years ago, a federal court ruled that a warrant permitting police to search a home for "all handguns, shotguns and rifles" and "evidence showing street gang membership" was too broad. As a result, the seizure of a shotgun was disallowed for lack of a valid search warrant.[27]

Seizure The forcible taking of a person or property in response to a suspected violation of the law.

A **seizure** is the act of taking possession of a person or property by the government because of a (suspected) violation of the law. In general, four categories of items can be seized by use of a search warrant:

1. Items resulting from the crime, such as stolen goods.
2. Items that are inherently illegal for anybody to possess (with certain exceptions), such as narcotics and counterfeit currency.
3. Items that can be called "evidence" of the crime, such as a bloodstained sneaker or a ski mask.
4. Items used in committing the crime, such as an ice pick or a printing press used to make counterfeit bills.[28]

See Figure 6.1 that follows for an example of a search warrant.

REASONABLENESS DURING A SEARCH AND SEIZURE No matter how "particular" a warrant is, it cannot provide for all the conditions that are bound to come up during its service. Consequently, the law gives law enforcement officers the ability to act "reasonably" during a search and seizure in the event of unforeseeable circumstances. For example, if a police officer is searching an apartment for a stolen MacBook Pro laptop computer and notices a vial of crack cocaine sitting on the suspect's bed, that contraband is considered to be in "plain view" and can be seized.

Note that if law enforcement officers have a search warrant that authorizes them to search for a stolen laptop computer, they would not be justified in opening small drawers. Because a computer could not fit in a small drawer, an officer would not have a basis for reasonably searching one. Hence, officers are restricted in terms of where they can look by the items they are searching for.

FIGURE 6.1 Example of a Search Warrant

United States District Court

______ DISTRICT OF ______

In the Matter of the Search of
(Name, address or brief description of person or property to be searched)

SEARCH WARRANT

CASE NUMBER:

TO: ______ and any Authorized Officer of the United States

Affidavit(s) having been made before me by ______ (Affiant) who has reason to believe that ☐ on the person of or ☐ on the premises known as (name, description and/or location)

in the ______ District of ______ there is now concealed a certain person or property, namely (describe the person or property)

I am satisfied that the affidavit(s) and any recorded testimony establish probable cause to believe that the person or property so described is now concealed on the person or premises above-described and establish grounds for the issuance of this warrant.

YOU ARE HEREBY COMMANDED to search on or before ______ (Date)

(not to exceed 10 days) the person or place named above for the person or property specified, serving this warrant and making the search (in the daytime — 6:00 A.M. to 10:00 P.M.) (at any time in the day or night as I find reasonable cause has been established) and if the person or property be found there to seize same, leaving a copy of this warrant and receipt for the person or property taken, and prepare a written inventory of the person or property seized and promptly return this warrant to ______ (U.S. Judge or Magistrate) as required by law.

______ Date and Time Issued at ______ City and State

______ Name and Title of Judicial Officer ______ Signature of Judicial Officer

Searches and Seizures without a Warrant

Although the Supreme Court has established the principle that searches conducted without warrants are *per se* (by definition) unreasonable, it has set "specifically established" exceptions to the rule.[29] In fact, most searches take place in the absence of a judicial order. Warrantless searches and seizures can be lawful when police are in "hot pursuit" of a subject or when they search bags of trash left at the curb for regular collection. Because of the magnitude of smuggling activities in "border areas" such as airports, seaports, and international boundaries, a warrant normally is not needed to search property in those places. Furthermore, in 2006 the Court held unanimously that police officers do not need a warrant to enter a private home in an emergency, such as when they reasonably fear for the safety of the inhabitants.[30]

The two most important circumstances in which a warrant is not needed, though, are (1) searches incidental to an arrest and (2) consent searches.

SEARCHES INCIDENTAL TO AN ARREST The most frequent exception to the warrant requirement involves **searches incidental to arrests,** so called because nearly every time police officers make an arrest (a procedure discussed in detail later in the chapter), they also search the suspect. As long as the original arrest was based on probable cause, these searches are valid for two reasons, established by the Supreme Court in *United States v. Robinson* (1973):

1. The need for a police officer to find and confiscate any weapons a suspect may be carrying.
2. The need to protect any evidence on the suspect's person from being destroyed.[31]

Law enforcement officers are, however, limited in the searches they may make during an arrest. These limits were established by the Supreme Court in *Chimel v. California* (1969).[32] In that case, police arrived at Chimel's home with an arrest warrant but not a search warrant. Even though Chimel refused their request to "look around," the officers searched the entire three-bedroom house for nearly an hour, finding stolen coins in the process. Chimel was convicted of burglary and appealed, arguing that the evidence of the coins should have been suppressed.

The Supreme Court held that the search was unreasonable. In doing so, the Court established guidelines as to the acceptable extent of searches incidental to an arrest. Primarily, the Court ruled that police may search any area within the suspect's "immediate control" to confiscate any weapons or evidence that the suspect could destroy. The Court found, however, that there was no justification

> for routinely searching rooms other than that in which the arrest occurs—or, for that matter, for searching through all desk drawers or other closed or concealed areas in that room itself. Such searches, in the absence of well-recognized exceptions, may be made only under the authority of a search warrant.[33]

The exact interpretation of the "area within immediate control" has been left to individual courts, but in general it has been taken to mean the area within the reach of the arrested person. Thus, the Court is said to have established the "arm's reach doctrine" in its *Chimel* decision.

SEARCHES WITH CONSENT **Consent searches,** the second most common type of warrantless searches, take place when individuals voluntarily give law enforcement officers permission to search their persons, homes, or belongings. The most relevant factors in determining whether consent is voluntary are

1. The age, intelligence, and physical condition of the consenting suspect,
2. Any coercive behavior by the police, such as the language used to request consent, and
3. The length of the questioning and its location.[34]

Searches Incidental to Arrests Searches for weapons and evidence that are conducted on persons who have just been arrested.

Consent Searches Searches by police that are made after the subject of the search has agreed to the action. In these situations, consent, if given of free will, validates a warrantless search.

If a court finds that a person has been physically threatened or otherwise coerced into giving consent, the search is invalid.[35] Furthermore, the search consented to must be reasonable. Several years ago, the North Carolina Supreme Court invalidated a consent search that turned up a packet of cocaine. As part of this search, the police had pulled down the suspect's underwear and shone a flashlight on his groin. The court ruled that a reasonable person in the defendant's position would not consent to such an intrusive examination.[36]

The standard for consent searches was set in *Schneckcloth v. Bustamonte* (1973),[37] in which, after being asked, the defendant told police officers to "go ahead" and search his car. A packet of stolen checks found in the trunk was ruled valid evidence because the driver consented to the search. (See the feature *Myth vs Reality—Consent to Search Automobiles* on the right.)

Numerous court decisions have also supported the "knock and talk" strategy, in which the law enforcement agent simply walks up to the door of a residence, knocks, and asks to come in and talk to the resident.[38] The officer does not need reasonable suspicion or probable cause that a crime has taken place in this situation because the decision to cooperate rests with the civilian.

MYTH VS REALITY
Consent to Search Automobiles

THE MYTH If a police officer pulls over a driver and issues a speeding ticket, and then asks to search the car, the driver must agree to the officer's request and submit to a vehicle search.

THE REALITY In fact, in this scenario, the driver is well within his or her rights to refuse an officer's request to search his or her car. As long as police officers do not improperly coerce a suspect to cooperate, however, they are not required to inform the person that he or she has a choice in the matter. In *Ohio v. Robinette* (1996), the United States Supreme Court held that police officers do not need to notify people that they are "free to go" after an initial stop when no arrest is involved.

This lack of notification has significant consequences. In the two years leading up to the *Robinette* case, four hundred Ohio drivers were convicted of narcotics offenses that resulted directly from search requests that could have been denied but were not.

FOR CRITICAL ANALYSIS
Do you think that police officers should be required to tell drivers that permission to search a vehicle can be denied? Why or why not?

RECENT DEVELOPMENTS Because warrantless searches are relatively commonplace—and crucial for law enforcement—defense attorneys are constantly testing their limits. In recent years, for instance, American courts have determined the constitutionality of warrantless searches and seizures of the following:

1. *Digital devices on the border.* Do the traditional reasons for allowing warrantless searches at entry points—combating smuggling and terrorism—also apply to warrantless searches of laptops and cell phones owned by people crossing the border? A federal court has said no, as the search of a car is not nearly as "comprehensive and intrusive" as the search of data stored in an electronic device.[39]
2. *Blood used as evidence in drunk driving cases.* The natural dissipation of alcohol in the bloodstream is not enough, according to the Supreme Court, for police officers to draw a drunk driving suspect's blood without consent or a warrant. Other factors, however, such as slurred speech and the smell of alcohol, may be enough for such a "bodily intrusion" without a warrant.[40]
3. *Cell phone location data.* Cell phone users are assumed to know that they provide communications carriers with their location every time they make a call or send a text. Consequently, a federal court has ruled that law enforcement can access records of those locations without a warrant to trace the movement of suspects.[41]

In 2014, the Supreme Court agreed to address the issue of whether the arm's reach doctrine, discussed on the previous page, justifies providing law enforcement immediate access to the data in the cell phones of arrestees.[42] (Figure 6.2 that follows provides an overview of the circumstances under which warrantless searches have traditionally been allowed.)

Searches of Automobiles

In *Carroll v. United States* (1925),[43] the Supreme Court ruled that the law could distinguish among automobiles, homes, and persons in questions involving police searches. In the years since its *Carroll* decision, the Court has established that the Fourth Amendment does not require police to obtain a warrant to search automobiles or other movable vehicles when they have probable cause to believe that a vehicle contains contraband or evidence of criminal activity.[44]

The reasoning behind such leniency is straightforward: requiring a warrant to search an automobile places too heavy a burden on police officers. By the time the officer could communicate with a judge and obtain the warrant, the suspect could have driven away and destroyed any evidence. Consequently, the Court has consistently held that someone in a vehicle does not have the same reasonable expectation of privacy as someone at home or even in a phone booth.

WARRANTLESS SEARCHES OF AUTOMOBILES For nearly three decades, police officers believed that if they lawfully arrested the driver of a car, they could legally make a warrantless search of the car's entire front and back compartments. This understanding was based on the Supreme Court's ruling in *New York v. Belton* (1981),[45] which seemed to allow this expansive interpretation of the "area within immediate control" with regard to automobiles.

In *Arizona v. Gant* (2009), however, the Court announced that its *Belton* decision had been misinterpreted. Such warrantless searches are allowed only if

1. The person being arrested is close enough to the car to grab or destroy evidence or a weapon inside the car, or
2. The arresting officer reasonably believes that the car contains evidence pertinent to the same crime for which the arrest took place.[46]

FIGURE 6.2 Exceptions to the Requirement That Officers Have a Search Warrant

In many instances, it would be impractical for police officers to leave a crime scene, go to a judge, and obtain a search warrant before conducting a search. Therefore, under the following circumstances, a search warrant is not required.

INCIDENT TO LAWFUL ARREST
Police officers may search the area within immediate control of a person after they have arrested him or her.

CONSENT
Police officers may search a person without a warrant if that person voluntarily agrees to be searched and has the legal authority to authorize the search.

STOP AND FRISK
Police officers may frisk, or "pat down," a person if they suspect that the person may be involved in criminal activity or pose a danger to those in the immediate area.

HOT PURSUIT
If police officers are in "hot pursuit" of, or chasing, a person they have probable cause to believe committed a crime and that person enters a building, the officers may search the building without a warrant.

AUTOMOBILE EXCEPTION
If police officers have probable cause to believe that an automobile contains evidence of a crime, they may, in most instances, search the vehicle without a warrant.

PLAIN VIEW
If police officers are legally engaged in police work and happen to see evidence of a crime in "plain view," they may seize it without a warrant.

ABANDONED PROPERTY
Any property, such as a hotel room that has been vacated or contraband that has been discarded, may be searched and seized by police officers without a warrant.

BORDER SEARCHES
Law enforcement officers on border patrol do not need a warrant to search vehicles crossing the border.

So, for example, police will no longer be able to search an automobile for contraband if the driver has been arrested for failing to pay previous speeding tickets—unless the officer reasonably believes the suspect has the ability to reach and destroy any such contraband. As you can imagine, the law enforcement community reacted negatively to the new restrictions outlined in the *Gant* decision.[47] Police officers, however, still can conduct a warrantless search of an automobile based on circumstances other than the incidental-to-an-arrest doctrine.

These circumstances include probable cause of criminal activity, consent of the driver, and "protective searches" to search for weapons if police officers have a reasonable suspicion that such weapons exist.[48] In addition, an officer may order passengers as well as the driver out of a car during a traffic stop. The Court has reasoned that the danger to an officer is increased when there is a passenger in the automobile.[49]

PRETEXTUAL STOPS Law enforcement agents also have a great deal of leeway regarding automobile stops. Crucially, as long as an officer has probable cause to believe that a traffic law has been broken, her or his "true" motivation for making a stop is irrelevant.[50] So, even if the police officer does not have a legally sufficient reason to search for evidence of a crime such as drug trafficking, the officer can use a minor traffic violation to pull over the car and investigate his or her "hunch." (To learn more about such "pretextual stops," see the feature *Discretion in Action—A Valid Pretext?* that follows.)

A VALID PRETEXT?

THE SITUATION You are a police officer patrolling an area of Washington, D.C., that is marked by extremely high rates of drug-related crime. You become suspicious of a truck with temporary plates being driven slowly by a young African American male. Although you do not consider yourself as being racially biased, you are well aware, from experience, that in this neighborhood many young black men in these types of cars with temporary plates are drug dealers. These suspicions do not, however, reach the level of probable cause needed to pull over the truck. Then, the driver fails to signal while making a right turn.

THE LAW As far as Fourth Amendment law is concerned, any subjective reasons that a police officer might have for stopping a suspect, including any motives based on racial stereotyping or bias, are irrelevant. As long as the officer has objective probable cause to believe a traffic violation or other wrongdoing has occurred, the stop is valid.

WHAT WOULD YOU DO? You are convinced that the driver of the truck is selling illegal drugs, and you want to stop and search him. The failure to signal gives you a valid pretext to pull over the truck, even though your "real" reasons for the stop would be its slow pace, its temporary plates, the race of its driver, and the level of drug crime in the neighborhood. What do you do?

To see how the United States Supreme Court reacted to an officer's decision in a similar situation, go to Example 6.1 in Appendix B.

New York City police officers search a limousine for explosives at a checkpoint set up in response to a credible terrorist threat. If the officers found a stack of counterfeit $100 bills during this search, would the plain view doctrine allow the seizure of the fake cash? Why or why not?

The Plain View Doctrine

As we have already seen, the Constitution, as interpreted by our courts, provides very little protection to evidence *in plain view.* For example, suppose a traffic officer pulls over a person for speeding, looks in the driver's side window, and clearly sees what appears to be a bag of heroin resting on the passenger seat. In this instance, under the **plain view doctrine,** the officer would be justified in seizing the drugs without a warrant.

The plain view doctrine was first enunciated by the Supreme Court in *Coolidge v. New Hampshire* (1971).[51] The Court ruled that law enforcement officers may make a warrantless seizure of an item if four criteria are met:

1. The item is positioned so as to be detected easily by an officer's sight or some other sense.
2. The officer is legally in a position to notice the item in question.
3. The discovery of the item is inadvertent. That is, the officer had not intended to find the item.
4. The officer immediately recognizes the illegal nature of the item. No interrogation or further investigation is allowed under the plain view doctrine.

Advances in technology that allow law enforcement agents to "see" beyond normal human capabilities have raised new issues in regard to plain view principles. *Thermal imagers,* for example, measure otherwise invisible levels of infrared radiation. These devices are particularly effective in detecting marijuana plants grown indoors because of the heat thrown off by the "grow lights" that the plants need to survive. The question for the courts has been whether a warrantless search of a dwelling through its walls by means of a thermal imager violates Fourth Amendment protections of privacy. According to the Supreme Court, an item is not in plain view if law enforcement agents need the aid of this technology to "see" it.[52] Thus, information from a thermal imager is not by itself justification for a warrantless search.

Electronic Surveillance

During the course of a criminal investigation, law enforcement officers may decide to use **electronic surveillance,** or electronic devices such as wiretaps or hidden microphones ("bugs"), to monitor and record conversations, observe movements, and trace or record telephone calls.

BASIC RULES: CONSENT AND PROBABLE CAUSE Given the invasiveness of electronic surveillance, the Supreme Court has generally held that the practice is prohibited by the Fourth Amendment. In *Burger v. New York* (1967),[53] however, the Court ruled that it was permissible under certain circumstances. That same year, *Katz v. United States* (discussed at the beginning of this section) established that recorded conversations are inadmissible as evidence unless certain procedures are followed.

In general, law enforcement officers can use electronic surveillance only if consent is given by one of the parties to be monitored or, in the absence of such consent, with a warrant.[54] For the warrant to be valid, it must

Describe the plain view doctrine, and indicate one of its limitations.
LEARNING OBJECTIVE **4**

Plain View Doctrine The legal principle that objects in plain view of a law enforcement agent who has the right to be in a position to have that view may be seized without a warrant and introduced as evidence.

Electronic Surveillance The use of electronic equipment by law enforcement agents to record private conversations or observe conduct that is meant to be private.

Justin Sullivan/Getty Images

1. Detail with "particularity" the conversations that are to be overheard.
2. Name the suspects and the places that will be under surveillance.
3. Show probable cause to believe that a specific crime has been or will be committed.[55]

Once the specific information has been gathered, the law enforcement officers must end the electronic surveillance immediately.[56] In any case, the surveillance cannot last more than thirty days without a judicial extension.

FORCE MULTIPLYING Pervasive forms of electronic surveillance are allowed under the theory that people who are in public places have no reasonable expectation of privacy.[57] This theory, generally upheld by American courts, allows for the use of a number of technological *force multipliers,* or devices that allow law enforcement agencies to expand their capabilities with a significant increase in personnel. Perhaps the most pervasive force multiplier is closed-circuit television surveillance (CCTV). This form of surveillance relies on strategically placed video cameras to record and transmit all activities in a targeted area. New York City's CCTV system uses about four thousand cameras to cover much of that city's midtown and downtown areas, and other large cities such as Boston and Los Angeles employ hundreds of public surveillance cameras.[58]

Another popular force multiplier involves computerized infrared cameras that take digital photos of license plates. Usually mounted on police cars, these *automatic license plate recognition (ALPR)* devices convert the images to text. Then the numbers are instantly checked against databases that contain records of the license plates of stolen cars and automobiles driven by a wide variety of targets, from wanted felons to citizens with unpaid parking tickets. In heavy-traffic areas, ALPR units can check thousands of license plates each hour.[59]

CJ & TECHNOLOGY   Law Enforcement Drones

craftvision/iStockphoto.com

Covering and surveying large areas is the attraction of another force multiplier: the unmanned drone. We first discussed unmanned drones in the military context in Chapter 3, but for domestic use such drones would carry cameras rather than weapons. This technology is already operating on American soil. Predator drones, for example, help Customs and Border Protection agents spot smugglers and illegal crossers along the U.S.-Mexico border. In addition, several local law enforcement agencies have been given permission to test unmanned drones. The Mesa County (Colorado) Sheriff's Department has sent the smaller Draganflyer X6 to locate missing persons.

In the near future, unmanned drones could change the face of law enforcement. The possibilities of their deployment are far-ranging, from patrolling high-crime neighborhoods to tracking fleeing felons to acting as aerial backup during hostage and mass-shooting situations.

Thinking about Law Enforcement Drones
Before the federal government will allow widespread use of unmanned drones, it must design guidelines for their operation. How should these guidelines address the issues of (a) protecting citizens' privacy and (b) the possibility of armed police drones?

Homeland Security and the Fourth Amendment

Privacy advocates worry that technologically advanced force multipliers are giving the government—through law enforcement—a "way to track all Americans all the time, regardless of whether they're accused of any crime."[60] Similarly, new laws and strategies designed to protect all Americans from terrorist attacks have led many to ask how much privacy we should be willing to sacrifice for homeland security.

THE PATRIOT ACT AND SEARCH WARRANTS Passed in the wake of the September 11, 2001, terrorist attacks, the Patriot Act (discussed in Chapter 1) has generally made it easier for federal agents to conduct searches. For example, to search a suspect's apartment and examine the contents of his or her computer, federal agents previously needed a warrant based on probable cause that a crime had taken place or was about to take place. The Patriot Act amends the law to allow the Federal Bureau of Investigation (FBI) or other federal agencies to obtain warrants for "terrorism" investigations, "chemical weapons" investigations, or "computer fraud and abuse" investigations as long as agents can prove that such actions have a "significant purpose."[61] In other words, no proof of criminal activity needs to be provided.

THE PATRIOT ACT AND SURVEILLANCE The Patriot Act also gives law enforcement agents more leeway when conducting surveillance. The Foreign Intelligence Surveillance Act of 1978 (FISA) allowed for surveillance of a suspect without a warrant as long as the "primary purpose" of the surveillance was to investigate foreign spying and not to engage in criminal law enforcement.[62] The Patriot Act amends FISA to allow for searches and surveillance if a "significant purpose" of the investigation is intelligence gathering or any other type of antiterrorist strategy.[63] The statute also provides federal agents with "roving surveillance authority," allowing them to continue monitoring a terrorist suspect on the strength of the original warrant even if the suspect moves to an area outside the control of the court that issued the warrant.[64]

Protesting outside the Justice Department in Washington, D.C., this woman believes that the federal government should not be allowed to collect information about the telephone habits of U.S. citizens without first obtaining permission from a court. Do you agree with her? ■ Why or why not?

Getty Images

THE NSA AND SURVEILLANCE Following a series of controversies concerning the ability of the National Security Agency (NSA) to monitor the communications of terrorist suspects, in 2008 Congress passed an amended version of the FISA.[65] The new version was designed to give the supervising FISA court greater control over the NSA, a federal intelligence agency that focuses on foreign communications. There is little evidence, however, that the FISA court acts as much of check on the NSA. In 2012, the federal government made 1,856 applications for electronic surveillance of foreign targets. All were approved.[66]

Disapproval of the government's ability to keep the NSA in check intensified after information concerning two of the agency's "secret" initiatives went public in 2013. As part of the first initiative, supported by an expansive interpretation of the Patriot Act, the NSA collected the telephone records of millions of Americans not suspected of terrorism. As part of this operation, NSA agents did not listen to actual phone conversations. Rather, they used records of calls to retroactively determine patterns of behavior that might raise a "red flag" of terrorist activity.[67]

The NSA's second initiative involved the collection of e-mails, Internet phone calls, social networking data, and other electronic communications made by foreign terrorist suspects. When these suspects came in contact with Americans, NSA agents were able to monitor communications without a warrant.[68] NSA officials claimed that these tactics helped prevent "dozens of terrorist events," while critics denounced programs that needlessly collected massive amounts of data on American citizens.[69] Of the controversy, President Barack Obama said, "You can't have 100 percent security and also then have 100 percent privacy."[70]

///// SELF ASSESSMENT

Fill in the blanks, and check your answers on page 198.

A search is a governmental intrusion on the _____ of an individual. To protect these rights, law enforcement agents must procure a _____ _____ before examining a suspect's home or personal possessions. During a properly executed search, officers may _____ any items that may be used as evidence or that are inherently illegal to possess. Law enforcement agents do not need a judge's prior approval to conduct a search incidental to an _____ or when the subject of the search gives his or her _____. Under the Patriot Act, government agents no longer have to show _____ cause to obtain warrants for terrorist investigations. Rather, they only need to show that their actions have a "_____ purpose."

STOPS AND FRISKS

When *reasonable suspicion* exists that a suspect has committed a crime, police officers are well within their rights to *stop and frisk* that suspect. In a stop and frisk, law enforcement officers (1) briefly detain a person they reasonably believe to be suspicious, and (2) if they believe the person to be armed, proceed to pat down, or "frisk," that person's outer clothing.[71]

Defining Reasonable Suspicion

The precedent for the ever-elusive definition of a "reasonable" suspicion in stop-and-frisk situations was established in *Terry v. Ohio* (1968).[72] In that case, a detective named McFadden observed two men (one of whom was Terry) acting strangely in downtown Cleveland. The men would walk past a certain store, peer into the window, and then stop at a street corner and confer. While they were talking, another man joined the conversation and then left quickly.

LEARNING OBJECTIVE 5 Distinguish between a stop and a frisk, and indicate the importance of the case *Terry v. Ohio.*

Several minutes later, the three men met again at another corner a few blocks away. Detective McFadden believed the trio was planning to break into the store. He approached them, told them who he was, and asked for identification. After receiving a mumbled response, the detective frisked the three men and found handguns on two of them, who were then tried and convicted of carrying concealed weapons.

The Supreme Court upheld the conviction, ruling that Detective McFadden had reasonable cause to believe that the men were armed and dangerous, and that swift action was necessary to protect himself and other citizens in the area.[73] The Court accepted McFadden's interpretation of the unfolding scene as based on objective facts and practical conclusions. It therefore concluded that his suspicion was reasonable.

POLICE DISCRETION For the most part, the judicial system has refrained from placing restrictions on police officers' ability to make stops. In the *Terry* case, the Supreme Court did say that an officer must have "specific and articulable facts" to support the decision to make a stop, but added that the facts may be "taken together with rational inferences."[74] The Court has consistently ruled that because of their practical experience, law enforcement agents are in a unique position to make such inferences and should be given a good deal of freedom in doing so.

"TOTALITY OF THE CIRCUMSTANCES" TEST In the years since the *Terry* case was decided, the Court has settled on a "totality of the circumstances" test to determine whether a stop is based on reasonable suspicion.[75] In 2002, for example, the Court ruled that a U.S. Border Patrol agent's stop of a minivan in Arizona was reasonable.[76] On being approached by the Border Patrol car, the driver had stiffened, slowed down his van, and avoided making eye contact with the agent. Furthermore, the children in the van waved at the officer in a mechanical manner, as if ordered to do so. The agent pulled over the van and found 128 pounds of marijuana.

In his opinion, Chief Justice William Rehnquist pointed out that such conduct might have been unremarkable on a busy city highway, but on an unpaved road thirty miles from the Mexican border it was enough to reasonably arouse the agent's suspicion.[77] The justices also made clear that the need to prevent terrorist attacks is part of the "totality of the circumstances" and, therefore, law enforcement agents will have more leeway to make stops near U.S. borders.

A Stop

The terms *stop* and *frisk* are often used in concert, but they describe two separate acts. A **stop** takes place when a law enforcement officer has reasonable suspicion that a criminal activity is about to take place. Because an investigatory stop is not an arrest, there are limits to the extent police can detain someone who has been stopped. For example, in one situation an airline traveler and his luggage were detained for ninety minutes while the police waited for a drug-sniffing dog to arrive. The Supreme Court ruled that the initial stop of the passenger was constitutional, but that the ninety-minute wait was excessive.[78]

In 2004, the Court held that police officers could require suspects to identify themselves during a stop that is otherwise valid under the *Terry* ruling.[79] The case involved a Nevada rancher who was fined $250 for refusing to give his name to a police officer investigating a possible assault. The defendant argued that such requests force citizens to incriminate themselves against their will, which is prohibited, as we shall see later in the chapter, by the Fifth Amendment. Justice Anthony Kennedy wrote, however, that "asking questions is an essential part of police investigations" that would be made much more difficult if officers could not determine the identity of a suspect.[80] The ruling validated "stop-and-identify" laws in twenty states and numerous cities and towns.

A Frisk

The Supreme Court has stated that a **frisk** should be a protective measure. Police officers cannot conduct a frisk as a "fishing expedition" simply to try to find items besides weapons, such as illegal narcotics, on a suspect.[81] A frisk does not necessarily follow a stop and in fact may occur only when the officer is justified in thinking that the safety of police officers or other citizens may be endangered.

Again, the question of reasonable suspicion is at the heart of determining the legality of frisks. In the *Terry* case, the Court accepted that Detective McFadden reasonably believed that the three suspects posed a threat. The suspects' refusal to answer McFadden's questions, though within their rights because they had not been arrested, provided him with sufficient motive for the frisk. In 2009, the Court extended the "stop and frisk" authority by ruling that a police officer could order a passenger in a car that had been pulled over for a traffic violation to submit to a pat-down.[82] To do so, the officer must have a reasonable suspicion that the passenger may be armed and dangerous.

A police officer frisks a suspect in San Francisco, California. What is the main purpose behind a frisk? When are police justified in frisking someone?

Mark Richard/PhotoEdit

Race and Reasonable Suspicion

By the letter of the law, a person's race or ethnicity alone cannot provide reasonable suspicion for stops and frisks.[83] Some statistical measures, however, seem to show that these factors do, at times, play a troubling role in this area of policing. Over a twelve-month period in Los Angeles, African Americans were 127 percent more likely to be stopped than whites, and Hispanics were 43 percent more likely than whites to be frisked.[84] Nationwide, police officers were almost three times as likely to search members of minority groups than whites after a traffic stop.[85]

RACIAL PROFILING Figures such as those noted above are often seen as proof that police sometimes use **racial profiling** in deciding which suspects to stop. Racial profiling occurs when a police action is based on the race, ethnicity, or national origin of the suspect rather than any reasonable suspicion that he or she has broken the law. As you may recall from our discussion of pretextual stops earlier in the chapter, as long as a police officer can provide a valid reason for a stop, any racial motivation on his or her part is often legally irrelevant. When statistics show that a law enforcement agency is improperly focusing its attention on members of minority groups, the remedies include

1. A civil lawsuit against the law enforcement agency for violating provisions of the U.S. Constitution that require all citizens to be treated fairly and equally by the government, and
2. Law enforcement agency policies designed to stop the practice.

Frisk A pat-down or minimal search by police to discover weapons.

Racial Profiling The practice of targeting people for police action based solely on their race, ethnicity, or national origin.

STOP-AND-FRISK AND THE NYPD Both remedies came into play recently in New York City, where police officials had encouraged aggressive stop and frisks for nearly a decade. Between 2004 and 2012, New York Police Department (NYPD) officers made almost 5 million stops. About 83 percent of those stops involved African Americans and Hispanics, even though those two groups make up only about half the city's residents.[86] In more than 50 percent of all stops involving minorities, the police officer's basis for reasonable suspicion was "furtive movements" on the part of the suspect.[87]

NYPD administrators justified the department's tactics by claiming that because blacks and Hispanics were more likely to be perpetrators and victims of crimes, it was natural to focus law enforcement attention in those communities.[88] In 2013, however, a federal judge found that minorities in New York City were "likely targeted for stops based on a lesser degree of objectively founded suspicion than whites" and therefore NYPD's stop-and-frisk tactics violated the Fourth Amendment.[89] At the same time, the NYPD ordered officers to stop relying on "furtive movements" as a basis for reasonable suspicion, and to provide more concrete details of each stop. Almost immediately, the number of stops in the city dropped by 51 percent.[90] (To better understand the issue of racial profiling as it pertains to immigration law, see the feature *CJ Controversy—"Papers, Please"* that follows.)

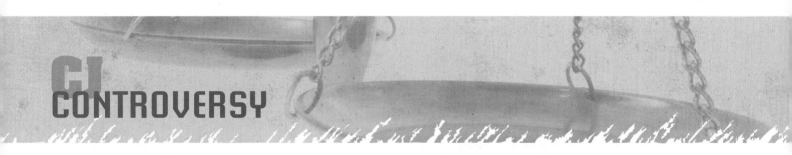

CJ CONTROVERSY

"PAPERS, PLEASE"

About five years ago, the Arizona legislature passed a state law aimed at policing its large number of undocumented immigrants. The legislation, known as S.B. 1070, requires state and local police officers, "when practicable," to check the immigration status of someone they reasonably suspect to be in the country illegally. Much to the disappointment of the law's many critics, in 2012 the United States Supreme Court upheld the so-called "papers, please" provision of S.B. 1070. Thus, law enforcement agents in Arizona have been empowered to check the immigration status of suspects who have been detained for other valid reasons, such as questioning about a crime or receiving a speeding ticket.

THE SUPREME COURT MADE THE RIGHT DECISION BECAUSE . . .

- The law prohibits racial profiling and requires police to check immigration status only *after* the suspect has been stopped for reasons that have nothing to do with immigration law.
- Arizona's S.B. 1070 gives law enforcement another tool to use against violent criminals who happen to be in the United States illegally.

THE SUPREME COURT MADE THE WRONG DECISION BECAUSE . . .

- It is inevitable that police will focus on Arizona's Hispanic population, as determined primarily by skin color, when enforcing S.B. 1070's "papers, please" provision.
- The mistrust caused by the law keeps members of immigrant communities from cooperating with local police, leading to more crime in those communities.

Your Assignment

Since 2008, U.S. Immigration and Customs Enforcement (ICE) has partnered with state and local police to apprehend undocumented immigrants in the United States. To understand how this partnership works, research **Secure Communities** on the Internet. Then, add the term **racial profiling** to your search and write two full paragraphs in which you (1) detail some of the criticisms of Secure Communities and (2) indicate whether those criticisms are justified.

Fill in the blanks, and check your answers on page 198.

A police officer can make a _____, which is not the same as an arrest, if she or he has a _____ suspicion that a criminal act is taking place or is about to take place. Then, the officer has the ability to _____ the suspect for weapons as a protective measure.

ARRESTS

As happened in the *Terry* case discussed earlier, a stop and frisk may lead to an **arrest.** An arrest is the act of apprehending a suspect for the purpose of detaining him or her on a criminal charge. It is important to understand the difference between a stop and an arrest. In the eyes of the law, a stop is a relatively brief intrusion on a citizen's rights, whereas an arrest—which involves a deprivation of liberty—is deserving of a full range of constitutional protections (see *Mastering Concepts—The Difference between a Stop and an Arrest* that follows). Consequently, while a stop can be made based on reasonable suspicion, a law enforcement officer needs probable cause, as defined earlier, to make an arrest.[91]

Elements of an Arrest

When is somebody under arrest? The easy—and incorrect—answer would be whenever the police officer says so. In fact, the state of being under arrest is dependent not only on the actions of the law enforcement officers but also on the perception of the suspect. Suppose Mr. Smith is stopped by plainclothes detectives, driven to the police station, and detained for three hours for questioning. During this time, the police never tell Mr. Smith he is under arrest, and in fact, he is free to leave at any time. But if Mr. Smith or any other reasonable person *believes* he is not free to leave, then, according to the Supreme Court, that person is in fact under arrest and should receive the necessary constitutional protections.[92]

> **Arrest** To deprive the liberty of a person suspected of criminal activity.

MASTERING CONCEPTS
THE DIFFERENCE BETWEEN A STOP AND AN ARREST

Both stops and arrests are considered seizures because both police actions involve the restriction of an individual's freedom to "walk away." Both must be justified by a showing of reasonableness as well. You should be aware, however, of the differences between a stop and an arrest. **During a stop,** police can interrogate the person and make a limited search of his or her outer clothing. If anything occurs during the stop, such as the discovery of an illegal weapon, then officers may arrest the person. **If an arrest is made,** the suspect is now in police custody and is protected by the U.S. Constitution in a number of ways that will be discussed later in the chapter.

	STOP	ARREST
Justification	Reasonable suspicion only	Probable cause
Warrant	None	Required in some, but not all, situations
Intent of Officer	To investigate suspicious activity	To make a formal charge against the suspect
Search	May frisk, or "pat down," for weapons	May conduct a full search for weapons or evidence
Scope of Search	Outer clothing only	Area within the suspect's immediate control or "reach"

Getty Images

List the four elements that must be present for an arrest to take place.

LEARNING 6 OBJECTIVE

Criminal justice professor Rolando V. del Carmen of Sam Houston State University has identified four elements that must be present for an arrest to take place:

1. The *intent* to arrest. In a stop, though it may entail slight inconvenience and a short detention period, there is no intent on the part of the law enforcement officer to take the person into custody. Therefore, there is no arrest. As intent is a subjective term, it is sometimes difficult to determine whether the police officer intended to arrest. In situations when the intent is unclear, courts often rely—as in our hypothetical case of Mr. Smith—on the perception of the arrestee.[93]

2. The *authority* to arrest. State laws give police officers the authority to place citizens under custodial arrest, or take them into custody. Like other state laws, the authorization to arrest varies among the fifty states. Some states, for example, allow off-duty police officers to make arrests, while others do not.

3. *Seizure or detention.* A necessary part of an arrest is the detention of the subject. Detention is considered to have occurred as soon as the arrested individual submits to the control of the officer, whether peacefully or under the threat or use of force.

4. The *understanding* of the person that she or he has been arrested. Through either words—such as "you are now under arrest"—or actions, the person taken into custody must understand that an arrest has taken place. When a suspect has been forcibly subdued by the police, handcuffed, and placed in a patrol car, he or she is believed to understand that an arrest has been made. This understanding may be lacking if the person is intoxicated, insane, or unconscious.[94]

FIGURE 6.3 Example of an Arrest Warrant

United States District Court

DISTRICT OF _____

UNITED STATES OF AMERICA
V.

WARRANT FOR ARREST

CASE NUMBER: _____

To: The United States Marshal
and any Authorized United States Officer

YOU ARE HEREBY COMMANDED to arrest _____
NAME

and bring him or her forthwith to the nearest magistrate to answer a(n)

☐ Indictment ☐ Information ☐ Complaint ☐ Order of Court ☐ Violation Notice ☐ Probation Violation Petition

charging him or her with (brief description of offense)

in violation of Title _____ United States Code, Section(s) _____

Name of Issuing Officer | Title of Issuing Officer

Signature of Issuing Officer | Date and Location

Bail fixed at $ _____ by _____
Name of Judicial Officer

RETURN

This warrant was received and executed with the arrest of the above-named defendant at _____

DATE RECEIVED | NAME AND TITLE OF ARRESTING OFFICER | SIGNATURE OF ARRESTING OFFICER

DATE OF ARREST

Arrests with a Warrant

When law enforcement officers have established probable cause to arrest an individual who is not in police custody, they obtain an **arrest warrant** for that person. An arrest warrant, similar to a search warrant, contains information such as the name of the person suspected and the crime he or she is suspected of having committed. (See Figure 6.3 on the left for an example of an arrest warrant.) Judges or magistrates issue arrest warrants after first determining that the law enforcement officers have indeed established probable cause.

ENTERING A DWELLING There is a perception that an arrest warrant gives law enforcement officers the authority to enter a dwelling without first announcing themselves. This is not accurate. In *Wilson v. Arkansas* (1995),[95] the Supreme Court reiterated the traditionally-recognized requirement that police officers must knock and announce their identity and purpose before entering a dwelling. Under certain conditions, known as **exigent circumstances,** law enforcement officers need not announce themselves. These circumstances include situations in which the officers have a reasonable belief of any of the following:

1. The suspect is armed and poses a strong threat of violence to the officers or others inside the dwelling.

2. Persons inside the dwelling are in the process of destroying evidence or escaping because of the presence of the police.

3. A felony is being committed at the time the officers enter.[96]

Warrantless Arrest An arrest made without first seeking a warrant for the action.

THE WAITING PERIOD The Supreme Court severely weakened the practical impact of the "knock and announce" rule with its decision in *Hudson v. Michigan* (2006).[97] In that case, Detroit police did not knock before entering the defendant's home with a warrant. Instead, they announced themselves and then waited only three to five seconds before making their entrance, not the fifteen to twenty seconds suggested by a prior Court ruling.[98] Hudson argued that the drugs found during the subsequent search were inadmissible because the law enforcement agents did not follow proper procedure.

By a 5–4 margin, the Court disagreed. In his majority opinion, Justice Antonin Scalia stated that an improper "knock and announce" is not unreasonable enough to provide defendants with a "get-out-of-jail-free card" by disqualifying evidence uncovered on the basis of a valid search warrant.[99] Thus, the exclusionary rule, discussed earlier in this chapter, would no longer apply under such circumstances. Legal experts still advise, however, that police observe a reasonable waiting period after knocking and announcing to be certain that any evidence found during the subsequent search will stand up in court.[100]

Arrests without a Warrant

Arrest warrants are not always required, and in fact, most arrests are made on the scene without a warrant. A law enforcement officer may make a **warrantless arrest** if

1. The offense is committed in the presence of the officer,
2. The officer has probable cause to believe that the suspect has committed a particular crime, or
3. The time lost in obtaining a warrant would allow the suspect to escape or destroy evidence, and the officer has probable cause to make an arrest.[101]

The type of crime also comes to bear in questions of arrests without a warrant. As a general rule, officers can make a warrantless arrest for a crime they did not see if they have probable cause to believe that a felony has been committed. For misdemeanors, the crime must have been committed in the presence of the officer for a warrantless arrest to be valid. According to a 2001 Supreme Court ruling, even an arrest for a misdemeanor that involves "gratuitous humiliations" imposed by a police officer "exercising extremely poor judgment" is valid as long as the officer can satisfy probable cause requirements.[102] That case involved a Texas mother who was handcuffed, taken away from her two young children, and placed in jail for failing to wear her seat bet.

In certain situations, warrantless arrests are unlawful even though a police officer can establish probable cause. In *Payton v. New York* (1980),[103] for example, the Supreme Court held that when exigent circumstances do not exist and the suspect does not give consent to enter a dwelling, law enforcement officers cannot force themselves in for the purpose of making a warrantless arrest. A year after the *Payton* ruling, the Court expanded its holding to cover the homes of third parties.[104] So, if police wish to arrest a criminal suspect in another person's home, they cannot enter that home to arrest the suspect without first obtaining a search warrant, a process we discussed earlier in the chapter.

An arrest occurs when a suspect _____ believes that he or she is not free to leave police control. If the officer has prior knowledge of the suspect's criminal activity, she or he must obtain a _____ from a judge or magistrate before making the arrest. Officers can, however, make _____ arrests if an offense is committed in their presence or they have _____ _____ to believe that a crime was committed by the particular subject.

THE INTERROGATION PROCESS AND *MIRANDA*

After the Pledge of Allegiance, there is perhaps no recitation that comes more readily to the American mind than the *Miranda* warning:

> You have the right to remain silent. If you give up that right, anything you say can and will be used against you in a court of law. You have the right to speak with an attorney and to have the attorney present during questioning. If you so desire and cannot afford one, an attorney will be appointed for you without charge before questioning.

The *Miranda* warning is not a mere prop. It strongly affects one of the most important aspects of any criminal investigation—the **interrogation,** or questioning of a suspect from whom the police want to get information concerning a crime and perhaps a confession.

The Legal Basis for *Miranda*

The Fifth Amendment guarantees protection against self-incrimination. In other words, as we shall see again in Chapter 8, a defendant cannot be required to provide information about his or her own criminal activity. A defendant's choice *not* to incriminate himself or herself cannot be interpreted as a sign of guilt by a jury in a criminal trial. A confession, or admission of guilt, is by definition a statement of self-incrimination. How, then, to reconcile the Fifth Amendment with the critical need of law enforcement officers to gain confessions? The answer lies in the concept of **coercion,** or the use of physical or psychological duress to obtain a confession.

When a law enforcement official uses physical force during the interrogation process, it is relatively easy to determine that a suspect's confession has been improperly coerced and is therefore invalid. In handing down its *Miranda* decision,[105] which established the *Miranda* **rights,** the Supreme Court was more concerned with what Columbia Law School professor H. Richard Uviller called *inherent coercion.* This term refers to the assumption that even if a police officer does not lay a hand on a suspect, the general atmosphere of an interrogation is in and of itself coercive.[106]

Though the *Miranda* case is best remembered for the procedural requirement it spurred, at the time the Supreme Court was more concerned about the treatment of suspects during interrogation. (See the feature *Landmark Cases—Miranda v. Arizona* that follows.) The Court found that routine police interrogation strategies, such as leaving suspects alone in a room for several hours before questioning them, were inherently coercive. Therefore, the Court reasoned, every suspect needed protection from coercion, not just those who had been physically coerced. The *Miranda* warning is a result of this

Interrogation The direct questioning of a suspect to gather evidence of criminal activity and to try to gain a confession.

Coercion The use of physical force or mental intimidation to compel a person to do something—such as confess to committing a crime—against her or his will.

Miranda Rights The constitutional rights of accused persons taken into custody by law enforcement officials, such as the right to remain silent and the right to counsel.

need. In theory, if the warning is not given to a suspect before an interrogation, the fruits of that interrogation, including a confession, are invalid.

When a *Miranda* Warning Is Required

As we shall see, a *Miranda* warning is not necessary under several conditions, such as when no questions are asked of the suspect. Generally, *Miranda* requirements apply only when a suspect is in **custody.** In a series of rulings since *Miranda,* the Supreme Court has defined custody as an arrest or a situation in which a reasonable person would not feel free to leave.[107] Consequently, a **custodial interrogation** occurs when a suspect is under

Custody The forceful detention of a person, or the perception that a person is not free to leave the immediate vicinity.

Custodial Interrogation The questioning of a suspect after that person has been taken into custody. In this situation, the suspect must be read his or her *Miranda* rights before interrogation can begin.

LANDMARK CASES:
Miranda v. Arizona

Explain why the U.S. Supreme Court established the *Miranda* warnings. **LEARNING OBJECTIVE 7**

In 1963, a rape and kidnapping victim identified produce worker Ernesto Miranda as her assailant in a lineup. Phoenix, Arizona, detectives questioned Miranda for two hours concerning the crimes, at no time informing him that he had a right to have an attorney present. When the police emerged from the session, they had a signed statement by Miranda confessing to the crimes. He was subsequently convicted and sentenced to twenty to thirty years in prison. After the conviction was confirmed by the Arizona Supreme Court, Miranda appealed to the United States Supreme Court, claiming that he had not been warned that any statement he made could be used against him and that he had a right to counsel during the interrogation.

Miranda v. Arizona
United States Supreme Court
384 U.S. 436 (1966)

IN THE WORDS OF THE COURT . . .
CHIEF JUSTICE WARREN, MAJORITY OPINION

* * * *

The cases before us raise questions which go to the roots of our concepts of American criminal jurisprudence: the restraints society must observe consistent with the Federal Constitution in prosecuting individuals for crime. More specifically, we deal with the admissibility of statements obtained from an individual who is subjected to custodial police interrogation and the necessity for procedures which assure that the individual is accorded his privilege under the Fifth Amendment to the Constitution not to be compelled to incriminate himself.

* * * *

It is obvious that such an interrogation environment is created for no purpose other than to subjugate the individual to the will of his examiner. This atmosphere carries its own badge of intimidation. To be sure, this is not physical intimidation, but it is equally destructive of human dignity. The current practice of incommunicado interrogation is at odds with one of our Nation's most cherished principles— that the individual may not be compelled to incriminate himself. Unless adequate protective devices are employed to dispel the compulsion inherent in custodial surroundings, no statement obtained from the defendant can truly be the product of his free choice.

DECISION
The Court overturned Miranda's conviction, stating that police interrogations are, by their very nature, coercive and therefore deny suspects their constitutional right against self-incrimination by "forcing" them to confess. Consequently, any person who has been arrested and placed in custody must be informed of his or her right to be free from self-incrimination and to be represented by counsel during any interrogation. In other words, suspects must be told that they *do not have to* answer police questions. To accomplish this, the Court established the *Miranda* warning, which must be read prior to questioning a suspect in custody.

FOR CRITICAL ANALYSIS
What is meant by the phrase "coercion can be mental as well as physical"? What role does the concept of "mental coercion" play in Chief Justice Warren's opinion?

Photo by Chris Hondros/Getty Images

Study the details of this photo of an Aspen, Colorado, police officer and a suspect. Why must the officer "Mirandize" the suspect before asking him any questions, even if the officer never formally places the suspect under arrest?

arrest or is deprived of her or his freedom in a significant manner. Remember, a *Miranda* warning is only required before a custodial interrogation takes place. For example, if four police officers enter a suspect's bedroom at 4:00 A.M., wake him, and form a circle around him, then they must give him a *Miranda* warning before questioning. Even though the suspect has not been arrested, he will "not feel free to go where he please[s]."[108]

When a *Miranda* Warning Is Not Required

A *Miranda* warning is not necessary in a number of situations:

1. When the police do not ask the suspect any questions that are *testimonial* in nature. Such questions are designed to elicit information that may be used against the suspect in court. Note that "routine booking questions," such as the suspect's name, address, height, and eye color, do not require a *Miranda* warning. Even though answering these questions may provide incriminating evidence (especially if the person answering is a prime suspect), the Supreme Court has held that they are absolutely necessary if the police are to do their jobs.[109] (Imagine an officer not being able to ask a suspect her or his name.)

2. When the police have not focused on a suspect and are questioning witnesses at the scene of a crime.

3. When a person volunteers information before the police have asked a question.

4. When the suspect has given a private statement to a friend or some other acquaintance. *Miranda* does not apply to these statements so long as the government did not orchestrate the situation.

5. During a stop and frisk, when no arrest has been made.

6. During a traffic stop.[110]

LEARNING
Indicate situations in which a *Miranda* warning is unnecessary.
8
OBJECTIVE

PUBLIC SAFETY EXCEPTION In 1984, the Supreme Court also created a "public-safety exception" to the *Miranda* rule. The case involved a police officer who, after feeling an empty shoulder holster on a man he had just arrested, asked the suspect the location of the gun without informing him of his *Miranda* rights. The Court ruled that the gun was admissible as evidence because the police's duty to protect the public is more important than a suspect's *Miranda* rights.[111] In April 2013, federal law enforcement agents relied on this exception to question Boston Marathon bomber Dzhokhar Tsarnaev from a hospital bed without first "Mirandizing" him. Once the agents were satisfied that Tsarnaev knew of no other active plots or threats to public safety, they read the suspect his *Miranda* rights in the presence of a lawyer.[112]

WAIVING *MIRANDA* Suspects can *waive* their Fifth Amendment rights and speak to a police officer, but only if the waiver is made voluntarily. Silence on the part of a suspect does not mean that his or her *Miranda* protections have been relinquished. To waive their rights, suspects must state—either in writing or orally—that they understand those rights and that they will voluntarily answer questions without the presence of counsel.

To ensure that the suspect's rights are upheld, prosecutors are required to prove by a preponderance of the evidence that the suspect "knowingly and intelligently" waived his or her *Miranda* rights.[113] To make the waiver perfectly clear, police will ask suspects two questions in addition to giving the *Miranda* warning:

1. Do you understand your rights as I have read them to you?
2. Knowing your rights, are you willing to talk to another law enforcement officer or me?

POLICY.CJ

One of the reasons that courts dislike coercion during police interrogations is that it increases the possibility of a *false confession*, which occurs when a suspect admits to a crime that he or she did not actually commit. To learn about a common police interrogation method, go online and search for **The Reid Technique**. Then, research another interrogation technique called **The PEACE Method**. Would PEACE be less likely to produce a false confession than the Reid Technique? Explain your answer in one full paragraph.

If the suspect indicates that she or he does not want to speak to the officer, thereby invoking her or his right to silence, the officer must *immediately* stop any questioning.[114] Similarly, if the suspect requests a lawyer, the police can ask no further questions until an attorney is present.[115]

The Future of *Miranda*

"*Miranda* has become embedded in routine police practice to the point where the warnings have become part of our national culture," wrote Chief Justice William Rehnquist nearly fifteen years ago.[116] This may be true, but, at the same time, many legal scholars believe that a series of Supreme Court rulings have eroded *Miranda*'s protections. "It's death by a thousand cuts," says Jeffrey L. Fisher of the National Association of Criminal Defense Lawyers. Fisher believes the Court is "doing everything it can to ease the admissibility of confessions that police wriggle out of suspects."[117]

VOLUNTARY STATEMENTS One such exception, created by the Supreme Court in 2004, is crucial to understanding the status of *Miranda* rights in current criminal law. The case involved a Colorado defendant who voluntarily told the police the location of his gun (which, being an ex-felon, he was not allowed to possess) without being read his rights.[118] The Court upheld the conviction, finding that the *Miranda* warning is merely *prophylactic*. In other words, it is only intended to prevent violations of the Fifth Amendment. Because only the gun, and not the defendant's testimony, was presented at trial, the police had not violated the defendant's constitutional rights.

In essence, the Court was ruling that the "fruit of the poisoned tree" doctrine, discussed earlier in this chapter, does not bar the admission of physical evidence that is discovered based on voluntary statements by a suspect who has not been "Mirandized." (See Figure 6.4 that follows for a rundown of several other significant Court rulings that have weakened the *Miranda* requirements over the past decades.)

RECORDING CONFESSIONS *Miranda* may eventually find itself obsolete regardless of any decisions made in the courts. A relatively new trend in law enforcement has been for agencies to record interrogations and confessions digitally. Video-recording technology has progressed to the point where it is reasonable to ask law enforcement agents to

FIGURE 6.4 Supreme Court Decisions Eroding *Miranda* Rights

Moran v. Burbine (475 U.S. 412 [1986]). **This case established that police officers are not required to tell suspects undergoing custodial interrogation that their attorney is trying to reach them.** The Court ruled that events that the suspect could have no way of knowing about have no bearing on his ability to waive his *Miranda* rights.

Arizona v. Fulminante (499 U.S. 279 [1991]). **In this very important ruling, the Court held that a conviction is not automatically overturned if the suspect was coerced into making a confession.** If the other evidence introduced at the trial is strong enough to justify a conviction without the confession, then the fact that the confession was illegally gained can be, for all intents and purposes, ignored.

Texas v. Cobb (532 U.S. 162 [2001]). When a suspect refuses to waive his or her *Miranda* rights, a police officer cannot lawfully continue the interrogation until the suspect's attorney arrives on the scene. In this case, however, **the Court held that a suspect may be questioned without having a lawyer present if the interrogation does not focus on the crime for which he or she was arrested,** even though it does touch on another, closely related, offense.

Florida v. Powell (559 U.S. ___ [2010]). Florida's version of the *Miranda* warning informs suspects that they have a right "to talk with an attorney" but does not clearly inform them of their right to a lawyer during any police interrogation. The Court upheld Florida's warning, **ruling that different jurisdictions may use whatever version of the *Miranda* warning they please, as long as it reasonably conveys the essential information about a suspect's rights.**

carry a personal video camera with them at all times.[119] Indeed, as we saw in the previous chapter, many police agencies in the United States now use body-mounted video cameras that record all contacts with suspects.

One of the benefits of recording confessions in this manner would be to lessen suspicions that police officers use verbal techniques like accusation and confrontation to elicit false confessions. Such videos contain clear evidence of how an interview is carried out, and whether law enforcement agents have used improper means to gain the confession. For example, Philadelphia detectives must now video-record interrogations in all homicide cases. This policy change was a reaction to mistreatment of suspects, such as one woman who confessed to murder after being detained and interrogated for forty-one hours. (A judge called the confession involuntary because of "psychological coercion.")[120] Some scholars have suggested that recording all custodial interrogations would satisfy the Fifth Amendment's prohibition against coercion and thus render the *Miranda* warning unnecessary.

//// SELF ASSESSMENT

Fill in the blanks, and check your answers on page 198.

Miranda requirements apply only when law enforcement agents have the suspect in _____. The *Miranda* warning is only required _____ a custodial interrogation takes place. A suspect can _____ his or her *Miranda* rights, but this must be done "knowingly and intentionally." If the suspect indicates that he or she does not wish to speak, the police officer must _____ stop any questioning. The suspect can also end questioning any time by requesting the presence of a/an _____.

CHAPTER SUMMARY

For more information on these concepts, look back to the Learning Objective icons throughout the chapter.

 Outline the four major sources that may provide probable cause. (a) Personal observation, usually due to an officer's personal training, experience, and expertise; (b) information, gathered from informants, eyewitnesses, victims, police bulletins, and other sources; (c) evidence, which often has to be in plain view; and (d) association, which generally must involve a person with a known criminal background who is seen in a place where criminal activity is openly taking place.

 Explain the exclusionary rule and the exceptions to it. This rule prohibits illegally seized evidence, or evidence obtained by an unreasonable search and seizure in an inadmissible way, from being used against the accused in criminal court. Exceptions to the exclusionary rule are the "inevitable discovery" exception established in *Nix v. Williams* and the "good faith" exception established in *United States v. Leon* and *Arizona v. Evans*.

 Explain when searches can be made without a warrant. Searches and seizures can be made without a warrant if they are incidental to an arrest (but they must be reasonable); when they are made with voluntary consent; when they involve the automobile exception; when property has been abandoned; and when items are in plain view, under certain restricted circumstances (see *Coolidge v. New Hampshire*).

 Describe the plain view doctrine, and indicate one of its limitations. Under the plain view doctrine, police officers are justified in seizing an item if (a) the item is easily seen or otherwise identified by an officer; (b) the officer is legally in a position to notice it; (c) the discovery of the item is unintended; and (d) the officer, without further investigation, immediately recognizes the illegal nature of the item. An item is not in plain view if the law enforcement agent needs to use technology such as a thermal imager to "see" it.

 Distinguish between a stop and a frisk, and indicate the importance of the case *Terry v. Ohio.* Though the terms *stop* and *frisk* are often used in concert, a stop is the separate act of detaining a suspect when an officer reasonably believes that a criminal activity is about to take place. A frisk is the physical "pat-down" of a suspect. In *Terry v. Ohio,* the Supreme Court ruled that an officer must have "specific and articulable facts" before making a stop, but those facts may be "taken together with rational inferences."

 List the four elements that must be present for an arrest to take place. (a) Intent, (b) authority, (c) seizure or detention, and (d) the understanding of the person that he or she has been arrested.

 Explain why the U.S. Supreme Court established the *Miranda* warnings. The Supreme Court recognized that police interrogations are, by their nature, coercive. Consequently, to protect a suspect's constitutional rights during interrogation, the Court ruled that the suspect must be informed of those rights before being questioned.

 Indicate situations in which a *Miranda* warning is unnecessary. (a) When no questions that are testimonial in nature are asked of the suspect; (b) when there is no suspect and witnesses in general are being questioned at the scene of a crime; (c) when a person volunteers information before the police ask anything; (d) when a suspect has given a private statement to a friend without the government orchestrating it; (e) during a stop and frisk when no arrests have been made; (f) during a traffic stop; and (g) when a threat to public safety exists.

QUESTIONS FOR CRITICAL ANALYSIS

1. What are the two most significant legal concepts contained in the Fourth Amendment, and why are they important?

2. Should law enforcement agents be required to get a search warrant before accessing records that reveal a cell phone user's location? Those who think a warrant is unnecessary in this situation argue that once users turn their phones on, they have decided to waive their expectations of privacy by "voluntarily" transmitting their locations. What is your opinion of this argument?

3. As described on page 182, the Supreme Court has ruled that the plain view doctrine does permit police to use

thermal imagers to "see" the heat of marijuana "grow lights." How does this ruling support the Court's decision in *Florida v. Jardines,* the case discussed in the opening of the chapter?

4. Suppose that a police officer stops a person who "looks funny." The person acts strangely, so the police officer decides to frisk him. The officer feels a bulge in the suspect's coat pocket, which turns out to be a bag of cocaine. Would the arrest for cocaine possession hold up in court? Why or why not?

5. If, during questioning, a suspect says, "Maybe I should talk to a lawyer," should police immediately stop the interrogation? Why or why not? (To see how the Supreme Court ruled on this matter, search for ***Davis v. United States*** [1994] online.)

KEY TERMS

affidavit   176
arrest   189
arrest warrant   190
coercion   192
consent searches   178
custodial interrogation   193
custody   193
electronic surveillance   182
exclusionary rule   173

exigent circumstances   190
frisk   187
fruit of the poisoned tree   173
"good faith" exception   174
"inevitable discovery" exception   174
interrogation   192
Miranda rights   192
plain view doctrine   182
probable cause   171

racial profiling   187
search   175
searches and seizures   171
searches incidental to arrests   178
search warrant   176
seizure   177
stop   186
warrantless arrest   191

SELF-ASSESSMENT ANSWER KEY

Page 174: i. unreasonable; **ii.** probable cause; **iii.** exclusionary; **iv.** evidence

Page 185: i. privacy; **ii.** search warrant; **iii.** seize; **iv.** arrest; **v.** consent; **vi.** probable; **vii.** significant

Page 189: i. stop; **ii.** reasonable; **iii.** frisk

Page 192: i. reasonably; **ii.** warrant; **iii.** warrantless; **iv.** probable cause

Page 196: i. custody; **ii.** before; **iii.** waive; **iv.** immediately; **v.** lawyer/attorney

NOTES

1. *Florida v. Jardines,* 569 U.S. _____ (2013).
2. *United States v. Place,* 462 U.S. 696 (1983); and *Illinois v. Caballes,* 543 U.S. 405 (2005).
3. *Jardines, op. cit.,* at _____.
4. *Michigan v. Summers,* 452 U.S. 692 (1981).
5. *Brinegar v. United States,* 338 U.S. 160 (1949).
6. Rolando V. del Carmen, *Criminal Procedure for Law Enforcement Personnel* (Monterey, Calif.: Brooks/Cole Publishing Co., 1987), 63–64.
7. *Maryland v. Pringle,* 540 U.S. 366 (2003).
8. 500 U.S. 44 (1991).
9. *United States v. Leon,* 468 U.S. 897 (1984).
10. Thomas Y. Davis, "A Hard Look at What We Know (and Still Need to Learn) about the 'Costs' of the Exclusionary Rule: The NIJ Study and Other Studies of 'Lost' Arrests," *A.B.F. Research Journal* (1983), 680.
11. 430 U.S. 387 (1977).
12. 467 U.S. 431 (1984).
13. 468 U.S. 897 (1984).
14. 514 U.S. 1 (1995).
15. *California v. Greenwood,* 486 U.S. 35 (1988).
16. *Ibid.*
17. 389 U.S. 347 (1967).
18. *Ibid.,* 361.
19. 486 U.S. 35 (1988).
20. *Ibid.*
21. *Kentucky v. King,* 563 U.S. _____ (2011).
22. *Jardines, op cit.,* at ___.
23. 565 U.S. _____ (2012).
24. *Ibid.*
25. Quoted in James Vicini, "Supreme Court Limits Police Use of GPS to Track Suspects," *Reuters* (January 23, 2012).
26. *Coolidge v. New Hampshire,* 403 U.S. 443, 467 (1971).
27. *Millender v. Messerschmidt,* 620 F.3d 1016 (9th Cir. 2010).
28. del Carmen, *op. cit.,* 158.
29. *Katz v. United States,* 389 U.S. 347, 357 (1967).
30. *Brigham City v. Stuart,* 547 U.S. 398 (2006).
31. 414 U.S. 234–235 (1973).
32. 395 U.S. 752 (1969).
33. *Ibid.,* 763.
34. Carl A. Benoit, "Questioning 'Authority': Fourth Amendment Consent Searches," *FBI Law Enforcement Bulletin* (July 2008), 24.
35. *Bumper v. North Carolina,* 391 U.S. 543 (1968).
36. *State v. Stone,* 362 N.C. 50, 653 S.E.2d 414 (2007).

37. 412 U.S. 218 (1973).

38. Jayme W. Holcomb, "Knock and Talks," *FBI Law Enforcement Bulletin* (August 2006), 22–32.

39. *United States v. Cotterman,* 709 F.3d 952 (9th Cir. 2013).

40. *Missouri v. McNeely,* 567 U.S. _____ (2012).

41. *In re: Application of the United States of America for Historical Cell Site Data,* 724 F.3d 600 (5th Cir. 2013).

42. Adam Liptak, "Supreme Court Will Consider Whether Police Need Warrants to Search Cellphones," *New York Times* (January 18, 2014).

43. 267 U.S. 132 (1925).

44. *United States v. Ross,* 456 U.S. 798, 804–809 (1982); and *Chambers v. Maroney,* 399 U.S. 42, 44, 52 (1970).

45. 453 U.S. 454 (1981).

46. *Arizona v. Gant,* 556 U.S. 332 (2009).

47. Adam Liptak, "Justices Significantly Cut Back Officers' Searches of Cars of People They Arrest," *New York Times* (April 22, 2009), A12.

48. Dale Anderson and Dave Cole, "Search and Seizure after *Arizona v. Gant," Arizona Attorney* (October 2009), 15.

49. *Maryland v. Wilson,* 519 U.S. 408 (1997).

50. *Whren v. United States,* 517 U.S. 806 (1996).

51. 403 U.S. 443 (1971).

52. *Kyollo v. United States,* 533 U.S. 27 (2001).

53. 388 U.S. 42 (1967).

54. 18 U.S.C. Sections 2510(7), 2518(1)(a), 2516 (1994).

55. Christopher K. Murphy, "Electronic Surveillance," in "Twenty-Sixth Annual Review of Criminal Procedure," *Georgetown Law Journal* (April 1997), 920.

56. *United States v. Nguyen,* 46 F.3d 781, 783 (8th Cir. 1995).

57. Joseph Siprut, "Privacy through Anonymity: An Economic Argument for Expanding the Right of Privacy in Public Places," *Pepperdine Law Review* 33 (2006), 311, 320.

58. Heather Kelly, "After Boston: The Pros and Cons of Surveillance Cameras," *CNN Tech* (April 26, 2013), at **www.cnn.com/2013/04/26/tech/innovation/security-cameras-boston-bombings.**

59. Craig Beery, "Busted . . . At the Speed of Light," *Law Officer* (December 29, 2007), at **www.lawofficer.com/article/magazine-feature/bustedat-speed-light.**

60. Catherine Crump, quoted in Elizabeth Weise and Greg Toppo, "License Plates Scanners: Love 'Em or Loathe 'Em," *USA Today* (July 19, 2013), 3A.

61. Pub. L. No. 107-56, Section 201-2-2, 115 Stat. 272, 278 (2001).

62. 50 U.S.C. Section 1803 (2000).

63. Patriot Act, Section 203(d)(1), 115 Stat. 272, 280 (2001).

64. Patriot Act, Section 206, amending Section 105(c)(2)(B) of the Foreign Intelligence Surveillance Act.

65. FISA Amendments Act of 2008, Pub. L. No. 110-261, 122 Stat. 2436 (2008).

66. "Look Who's Listening," *The Economist* (June 15, 2013), 24.

67. Michael Isikoff, "FBI Sharply Increases Use of Patriot Act Provision to Collect U.S. Citizens' Records," *NBC.com* (July 11, 2013), at **investigations.nbcnews.com/_news/2013/06/11/18887491-fbi-sharply-increases-use-of-patriot-act-provision-to-collect-us-citizens-records.**

68. Charlie Savage, "N.S.A. Said to Search Content of Messages To and From U.S.," *New York Times* (August 8, 2013), A1.

69. Keith Alexander, quoted in "Look Who's Listening," *op. cit.*

70. Quoted in Anita Kumar and Michael Doyle, "Federal Watching Is Rampant These Days," *Arizona Daily Star* (June 8, 2013), A1.

71. Karen M. Hess and Henry M. Wrobleski, *Police Operation: Theory and Practice* (St. Paul, Minn.: West Publishing Co., 1997), 122.

72. 392 U.S. 1 (1968).

73. *Ibid.,* 20.

74. *Ibid.,* 21.

75. See *United States v. Cortez,* 449 U.S. 411 (1981); and *United States v. Sokolow,* 490 U.S. 1 (1989).

76. *United States v. Arvizu,* 534 U.S. 266 (2002).

77. *Ibid.,* 270.

78. *United States v. Place,* 462 U.S. 696 (1983).

79. *Hibel v. Sixth Judicial District Court,* 542 U.S. 177 (2004).

80. *Ibid.,* 182.

81. *Minnesota v. Dickerson,* 508 U.S. 366 (1993).

82. *Arizona v. Johnson,* 555 U.S. 328 (2009).

83. *United States v. Avery,* 137 F.3d 343, 353 (6th Cir. 1997).

84. Ian Ayres and Jonathan Borowsky, *A Study of Racially Disparate Outcomes in the Los Angeles Police Department* (Los Angeles: ACLU of Southern California, October 2008), i.

85. Lynn Langton and Matthew Durose, *Police Behavior during Traffic and Street Stops* (Washington, D.C.: U.S. Department of Justice, September 2013), Table 7, page 9.

86. Joseph Goldstein, "Judge Rejects New York's Stop-and-Frisk Policy," *New York Times* (August 13, 2013), A1.

87. Jeffrey Toobin, "Rights and Wrongs," *The New Yorker* (May 27, 2013), 39.

88. "Top Cop Defends Stop-Frisk Results," *Associated Press* (August 19, 2013).

89. Goldstein, *op. cit.*

90. Toobin, *op. cit.,* 43.

91. Rolando V. del Carmen and Jeffrey T. Walker, *Briefs of Leading Cases in Law Enforcement,* 2d ed. (Cincinnati, Ohio: Anderson, 1995), 38–40.

92. *Florida v. Royer,* 460 U.S. 491 (1983).

93. See also *United States v. Mendenhall,* 446 U.S. 544 (1980).

94. del Carmen, *op. cit.,* 97–98.

95. 514 U.S. 927 (1995).

96. Linda J. Collier and Deborah D. Rosenbloom, *American Jurisprudence,* 2d ed. (Rochester, N.Y.: Lawyers Cooperative Publishing, 1995), 122.

97. 547 U.S. 586 (2006).

98. *United States v. Banks,* 540 U.S. 31, 41 (2003).

99. *Hudson v. Michigan,* 547 U.S. 586, 593 (2006).

100. Tom Van Dorn, "Violation of Knock-and-Announce Rule Does Not Require Suppression of All Evidence Found in Search," *The Police Chief* (October 2006), 10.

101. "Warrantless Searches and Seizures" in *Georgetown Law Journal Annual Review of Criminal Procedure, 2011* (Washington, D.C.: Georgetown Law Journal, 2011), 955.

102. *Atwater v. City of Lago Vista,* 532 U.S. 318, 346–347 (2001).

103. 445 U.S. 573 (1980).

104. *Steagald v. United States,* 451 U.S. 204 (1981).

105. *Miranda v. Arizona,* 384 U.S. 436 (1966).

106. H. Richard Uviller, *Tempered Zeal* (Chicago: Contemporary Books, 1988), 188–198.

107. *Orozco v. Texas,* 394 U.S. 324 (1969); *Oregon v. Mathiason,* 429 U.S. 492 (1977); and *California v. Beheler,* 463 U.S. 1121 (1983).

108. *Orozco,* 325.

109. *Pennsylvania v. Muniz,* 496 U.S. 582 (1990).

110. del Carmen, *op. cit.,* 267–268.

111. *New York v. Quarles,* 467 U.S. 649 (1984).

112. Ethan Bronner and Michael S. Schmidt, "In Questions at First, No *Miranda* for Suspect," *New York Times* (April 23, 2013), A13.

113. *Moran v. Burbine,* 475 U.S. 412 (1986).

114. *Michigan v. Mosley,* 423 U.S. 96 (1975).

115. *Fare v. Michael C.,* 442 U.S. 707, 723–724 (1979).

116. *Dickerson v. United States,* 530 U.S. 428 (2000).

117. Quoted in Jesse J. Holland, "High Court Trims *Miranda* Warning Rights Bit by Bit," *Associated Press* (August 2, 2010).

118. *United States v. Patane,* 542 U.S. 630 (2004).

119. James Schnabl, "Are Video Police Reports the Answer?" *The Police Chief* (September 2012), 32.

120. Aubrey Whelan and Craig R. McCoy, "Ramsey Orders Changes on Interrogations, Holding Suspects," *Philadelphia Inquirer* (December 20, 2013), A1.

CHAPTER

7 Courts and the Quest for Justice

To target your study and review, look for these numbered Learning Objective icons throughout the chapter.

A Long TIME AGO . . .

ON THE AFTERNOON of March 8, 1975, eight-year-old Karen Smith went to the store to buy a candy bar. Early the next morning, Smith's body was found in the stairwell of the South Bronx, New York, housing project where she lived. She had been raped and stabbed to death. Shortly thereafter, police arrested an eighteen-year-old neighbor, David Bryant, for the crime. Bryant was eventually convicted of murder, and everyone involved in the case expected that he would spend the rest of his life behind bars.

On April 11, 2013, however, Justice Seth L. Marvin of the New York Supreme Court unexpectedly ordered that Bryant be freed from prison. The judge did not take this drastic step because he believed Bryant to be innocent of the terrible acts against Smith. Rather, he did so because an advocacy group convinced him that, thirty-eight years earlier, Bryant's court-appointed defense lawyer had done such a poor job that Bryant had not received a fair trial. Specifically, the lawyer failed to have Bryant's blood tested to see if it matched the blood found at the crime scene. Bryant has type B blood, and a semen stain on Smith's clothing was type O.

Smith's family was surprised and upset at the judge's decision. "We're living the horror of the whole thing again," said Arleen Wolterding, her aunt. "It makes me sick to my stomach." Bryant, who had insisted on his innocence before, during, and after his trial, declared himself to be "in shock" at his sudden freedom. The defense attorney who made the error regarding the blood test nearly four decades earlier, Paul Auerbach, now lives in Florida and had little to offer in support of himself or his ex-client. "I would like to justify the way I handled the case and say [the judge] is wrong," said Auerbach, "but honestly, I can't recall the case."

FOR CRITICAL ANALYSIS

1. Do you agree that Paul Auerbach's failure to have David Bryant's blood tested against crime scene evidence means that Bryant did not receive a fair trial? Explain your answer.

2. Officials have the option of retrying Bryant for Karen Smith's death. What would be some of the difficulties in doing so?

3. Do you think the state of New York should give Bryant a large sum of money to compensate him for his time spent in prison? Why or why not?

I didn't do it

Matthew McDermott/Polaris/Newscom

After spending nearly forty years behind bars for murdering an eight-year-old girl, David Bryant was set free by a New York judge who ruled that Bryant's attorney had provided an inadequate defense.

FUNCTIONS OF THE COURTS

Famed legal scholar Roscoe Pound once characterized "justice" as society's demand "that serious offenders be convicted and punished," while at the same time "the innocent and unfortunate are not oppressed."[1] This somewhat idealistic definition obscures the fact that there are two sides to each court proceeding, and each side has its own idea about what would be a just outcome.

Did the New York court system provide justice for David Bryant, who may or may not have been guilty of murder and spent thirty-eight years behind bars after a flawed trial? Did the court system provide justice for Karen Smith or her family, who must suffer with the knowledge that either the police arrested the wrong man in 1975 or the actual killer has been set free? It seems that justice is often a messy business, and, at best, a criminal court can provide an environment where arguments concerning guilt and innocence can be decided through the fair application of the law.

Courts have extensive powers in our criminal justice system: they can bring the authority of the state to seize property and to restrict individual liberty. Given that the rights to own property and to enjoy personal freedom are enshrined in the U.S. Constitution, a court's *legitimacy* in taking such measures must be unquestioned by society. This legitimacy is based on two factors: impartiality and independence.[2] In theory, each party involved in a courtroom dispute must have an equal chance to present its case and must be secure in the belief that no outside factors are going to influence the decision rendered by the court. In reality, as we shall see over the next three chapters, it does not always work that way.

Due Process and Crime Control in the Courts

As mentioned in Chapter 1, the criminal justice system has two sets of underlying models: due process and crime control. Due process models focus on protecting the rights of the individual, whereas crime control models stress the punishment and repression of criminal conduct. The competing nature of these two models is often evident in the nation's courts.

THE DUE PROCESS FUNCTION The due process function of the courts is to protect individuals from the unfair advantages that the government—with its immense resources— automatically enjoys in legal battles. Seen in this light, constitutional guarantees such as the right to counsel, the right to a jury trial, and protection from self-incrimination are equalizers in the "contest" between the state and the individual. The idea that the two sides in a courtroom dispute are adversaries is, as we shall discuss in the next chapter, fundamental in American courts.

▪ Why is it important that American criminal courtrooms, such as this one in Cape May, New Jersey, are places of impartiality and independence?

AP Images/The Press of Atlantic City, Dale Gerhard

THE CRIME CONTROL FUNCTION Advocates of crime control distinguish between the court's obligation to be fair to the accused and its obligation to be fair to society. The crime control function of the courts emphasizes punishment and retribution—criminals must suffer for the harm they caused society, and it is the courts' responsibility to see that they do so.

Given this responsibility to protect the public, deter criminal behavior, and "get criminals off the streets," the courts should not be concerned solely with giving the accused a fair chance. Rather than using due process rules as "equalizers," the courts should use them as protection against blatantly unconstitutional acts. For example, a detective who beats a suspect with a tire iron to get a confession has obviously infringed on the suspect's constitutional rights. If, however, the detective uses trickery to gain a confession, the court should allow the confession to stand because it is not in society's interest that law enforcement agents be deterred from outwitting criminals.

Define and contrast the four functions of the courts.

LEARNING
1
OBJECTIVE

The Rehabilitation Function

A third view of the court's responsibility is based on the "medical model" of the criminal justice system. In this model, criminals are analogous to patients, and the courts perform the role of physicians who dispense "treatment."[3] The criminal is seen as sick, not evil, and therefore treatment is morally justified. Of course, treatment varies from case to case, and some criminals require harsh treatment such as incarceration. In other cases, however, it may not be in society's best interest for the criminal to be punished according to the formal rules of the justice system. Perhaps the criminal can be rehabilitated to become a productive member of society, thus saving taxpayers the costs of incarceration or other punishment.

The Bureaucratic Function

To a certain extent, the crime control, due process, and rehabilitation functions of a court are secondary to its bureaucratic function. In general, a court may have the goal of protecting society or protecting the rights of the individual, but on a day-to-day basis that court has the more pressing task of dealing with the cases brought before it. Like any bureaucracy, a court is concerned with speed and efficiency, and loftier concepts such as justice can be secondary to a judge's need to wrap up a particular case before six o'clock so that administrative deadlines can be met. Indeed, many observers feel that the primary adversarial relationship in the courts is not between the two parties involved but between the ideal of justice and the reality of bureaucratic limitations.[4]

////SELF ASSESSMENT

Fill in the blanks, and check your answers on page 228.

The _____ _____ function of American courts is to protect _____ from the unfair advantages that the government enjoys during legal proceedings. In contrast, the _____ _____ function of the courts emphasizes punishment—criminals must suffer for the harm they do to _____. A third function of the court system focuses on the need to _____ a criminal, in much the same way as a doctor would treat a patient.

THE BASIC PRINCIPLES OF THE AMERICAN JUDICIAL SYSTEM

One of the most often cited limitations of the American judicial system is its complex nature. In truth, the United States does not have a single judicial system, but fifty-two different systems—one for each state, the District of Columbia, and the federal government. As each state has its own unique judiciary with its own set of rules, some of which may be in conflict with the federal judiciary, it is helpful at this point to discuss some basics—jurisdiction, trial and appellate courts, and the dual court system.

Jurisdiction

In Latin, *juris* means "law," and *diction* means "to speak." Thus, **jurisdiction** literally refers to the power "to speak the law." Before any court can hear a case, it must have jurisdiction over the persons involved in the case or its subject matter. The jurisdiction of every court, even the United States Supreme Court, is limited in some way.

GEOGRAPHIC JURISDICTION One limitation is geographic. Generally, a court can exercise its authority over residents of a certain area. A state trial court, for example, normally has jurisdictional authority over crimes committed in a particular area of the state, such as a county or a district. A state's highest court (often called the state supreme court) has jurisdictional authority over the entire state, and the United States Supreme Court has jurisdiction over the entire country. For the most part, criminal jurisdiction is determined by legislation. The U.S. Congress or a state legislature can determine what acts are illegal within the geographic boundaries it controls, thus giving federal or state courts jurisdiction over those crimes.

One interesting geographic jurisdictional situation involves the 310 Native American reservations in the United States. In general, because of treaties with the federal government, tribes enjoy a considerable amount of self-rule on reservation land. Leaders of the Yakama Nation in Washington, for example, will not adhere to a new state law legalizing marijuana.[5] Furthermore, tribal courts have jurisdiction to prosecute tribal members for crimes committed on tribal property.[6] These courts cannot, however, sentence most convicted defendants to more than three years in prison. Consequently, tribal leaders often ask the U.S. Department of Justice to prosecute in federal court serious crimes, such as murder and rape, that take place on reservations.

INTERNATIONAL JURISDICTION Under international law, each country has the right to create and enact criminal law for its territory. Therefore, the notion that a nation has jurisdiction over any crimes committed within its borders is well established. The situation becomes more delicate when one nation feels the need to go outside its own territory to enforce its criminal law. International precedent does, however, provide several bases for expanding jurisdiction across international borders.

For example, through either treaty-based agreements or case-by-case negotiations, one country may decide to extradite a criminal suspect to another country. **Extradition** is the formal process by which one legal authority, such as a state or a nation, transfers a fugitive or a suspect to another state or country that has a valid claim on that person. In

Jurisdiction The authority of a court to hear and decide cases within an area of the law or a geographic territory.

Extradition The process by which one jurisdiction surrenders a person accused or convicted of violating another jurisdiction's criminal law to the second jurisdiction.

LEARNING **2** OBJECTIVE Define *jurisdiction*, and contrast geographic and subject-matter jurisdiction.

In August 2013, the United States formally requested the extradition of Eric Marques, alleging that the Irish citizen, shown here after being arrested in Dublin, had disseminated "countless" child pornography images to the United States via the Internet. Do you think that ■ the American government should have jurisdiction over suspects such as Marques who commit their crimes on foreign soil?

2013, Colombia extradited Daniel Barrera to the United States to face drug trafficking charges. American officials believe that, through his criminal enterprises, Barrera was responsible for the annual smuggling of about four hundred tons of cocaine into the United States.

For legal and political reasons, some countries will not extradite criminal suspects to the United States. Nevertheless, American authorities have been able to assert jurisdiction in such cases, particularly regarding possible terrorists. They have relied on the principle that our government has jurisdiction over persons who commit crimes against U.S. citizens, even when these suspects live in a foreign country. This principle was cited after the drone attack that killed Anwar al-Awlaki in Yemen, an event discussed in Chapter 3 (see page 96). Yemeni officials had resolutely refused to extradite Awlaki to the United States.[7] Furthermore, some behavior, such as piracy and genocide, is considered a crime against all nations collectively and, according to the principles of *universal jurisdiction,* can be prosecuted by any nation having custody of the wrongdoer.

SUBJECT-MATTER JURISDICTION Jurisdiction over subject matter also acts as a limitation on the types of cases a court can hear. State court systems include courts of *general* (unlimited) *jurisdiction* and courts of *limited jurisdiction.* Courts of general jurisdiction have no restrictions on the subject matter they may address and therefore deal with the most serious felonies and civil cases. Courts of limited jurisdiction, also known as lower courts, handle misdemeanors and civil matters under a certain amount, usually $1,000.

As we will discuss later in the chapter, many states have created special subject-matter courts that only dispose of cases involving a specific crime. For example, a number of jurisdictions have established drug courts to handle an overload of illicit narcotics arrests. Furthermore, under the Uniform Code of Military Justice, the U.S. military has jurisdiction over active personnel who commit crimes, even if those crimes occur outside the course of duty.[8] In such cases, military officials can either attempt to *court-martial* the suspect in military court or allow civilian prosecutors to handle the case in state or federal court.

Trial and Appellate Courts

Explain the difference between trial and appellate courts.
LEARNING
3
OBJECTIVE

Another distinction is between courts of original jurisdiction and courts of appellate, or review, jurisdiction. Courts having *original jurisdiction* are courts of the first instance, or **trial courts.** Almost every case begins in a trial court. It is in this court that a trial (or a guilty plea) takes place, and the judge imposes a sentence if the defendant is found guilty. Trial courts are primarily concerned with *questions of fact.* They are designed to determine exactly what events occurred that are relevant to questions of the defendant's guilt or innocence.

Courts having *appellate jurisdiction* act as reviewing courts, or **appellate courts.** In general, cases can be brought before appellate courts only on appeal by one of the parties in the trial court. (Note that because of constitutional protections against being tried twice for the same crime, prosecutors who lose in criminal trial court *cannot* appeal the verdict.) An appellate court does not use juries or witnesses to reach its decision. Instead,

Trial Courts Courts in which most cases usually begin and in which questions of fact are examined.

Appellate Courts Courts that review decisions made by lower courts, such as trial courts; also known as *courts of appeals.*

its judges make a decision on whether the case should be *reversed* and *remanded,* or sent back to the court of original jurisdiction for a new trial. Appellate judges present written explanations for their decisions, and these **opinions** of the court are the basis for a great deal of the precedent in the criminal justice system.

It is important to understand that appellate courts do not determine the defendant's guilt or innocence—they make judgments only on questions of procedure. In other words, they are concerned with *questions of law* and normally accept the facts as established by the trial court. Only rarely will an appeals court question a jury's decision. Instead, the appellate judges will review the manner in which the facts and evidence were provided to the jury and rule on whether errors were made in the process.

The Dual Court System

As we saw in Chapter 1, America's system of federalism allows the federal government and the governments of the fifty states to hold authority in many areas. As a result, the federal government and each of the fifty states, as well as the District of Columbia, have their own separate court systems. Because of the split between the federal courts and the state courts, this is known as the **dual court system.** (See Figure 7.1 that follows to get a better idea of how federal and state courts operate as distinct yet parallel entities.)

Both federal and state courts are restricted in their jurisdiction. Generally, federal courts preside over cases involving violations of federal law, and state courts preside over cases involving violations of state law. The distinction is not always clear, however. Federal courts have jurisdiction over about 4,500 crimes. Thus, **concurrent jurisdiction,** which occurs when two different court systems have simultaneous jurisdiction over the same case or defendant, is quite common.

For instance, both the federal courts and the Massachusetts state court system have jurisdiction over Dzokhar Tsarnaev, suspected of carrying out the Boston Marathon bombings of April 2013. First, Tsarnaev will face federal terrorism charges in federal court. Then, state officials have the option to try him in state court for the killing of Massachusetts Institute of Technology police officer Sean Collier, even if they must take him from a federal prison cell to do so.

Opinions Written statements by appellate judges expressing the reasons for the court's decision in a case.

Dual Court System The separate but interrelated court system of the United States, made up of the courts on the national level and the courts on the state level.

Concurrent Jurisdiction The situation that occurs when two or more courts have the authority to preside over the same criminal case.

FIGURE 7.1 **The Dual Court System**

SELF ASSESSMENT

Fill in the blanks, and check your answers on page 228.

Before any court can hear a case, it must have _____ over the persons involved or the _____ _____ of the dispute. Almost every case begins in a _____ court, which is primarily concerned with determining the facts of the dispute. After this first trial, the participants can, under some circumstances, ask an _____ court to review the proceedings for errors in applying the law. The American court system is called a _____ court system because _____ courts address violations of federal law and _____ courts address violations of state law.

STATE COURT SYSTEMS

LEARNING
4
OBJECTIVE

Outline the several levels of a typical state court system.

Typically, a state court system includes several levels, or tiers, of courts. State courts may include

1. Lower courts, or local trial courts of limited jurisdiction,
2. Trial courts of general jurisdiction,
3. Appellate courts, and
4. The state's highest court.

As previously mentioned, each state has a different judicial structure, in which different courts have different jurisdictions, but there are enough similarities to allow for a general discussion. Figure 7.2 that follows shows a typical state court system.

Trial Courts of Limited Jurisdiction

Most states have local trial courts that are limited to trying cases involving minor criminal matters, such as traffic violations, prostitution, and drunk and disorderly conduct. Although these minor courts usually keep no written record of the trial proceedings and cases are decided by a judge rather than a jury, defendants have the same rights as those in other trial courts. The majority of all minor criminal cases are decided in these lower courts. Courts of limited jurisdiction can also be responsible for the preliminary stages of felony cases. Arraignments, bail hearings, and preliminary hearings often take place in these lower courts.

MAGISTRATE COURTS One of the earliest courts of limited jurisdiction was the justice court, presided over by a *justice of the peace,* or JP. In the early days of this nation, JPs were found everywhere in the country. Today, more than half the states have abolished justice courts, though JPs still serve a useful function in some cities and rural areas, notably in Texas. The jurisdiction of justice courts is limited to minor disputes between private individuals and to crimes punishable by small fines or short jail terms. The equivalent of a county JP in a city is known as a **magistrate** or, in some states, a municipal court judge. Magistrate courts have the same limited jurisdiction as do justice courts in rural settings. In most jurisdictions, magistrates are responsible for providing law enforcement agents with search and seizure warrants, discussed in Chapter 6.

SPECIALTY COURTS As mentioned earlier, many states have created **problem-solving courts** that have jurisdiction over very narrowly defined areas of criminal justice. Not only do these courts remove many cases from the existing court systems, but they also allow court personnel to become experts in a particular subject. Problem-solving courts include

Magistrate A public civil official with limited judicial authority within a particular geographic area, such as the authority to issue an arrest warrant.

Problem-Solving Courts Lower courts that have jurisdiction over one specific area of criminal activity, such as illegal drugs or domestic violence.

FIGURE 7.2 A Typical State Court System

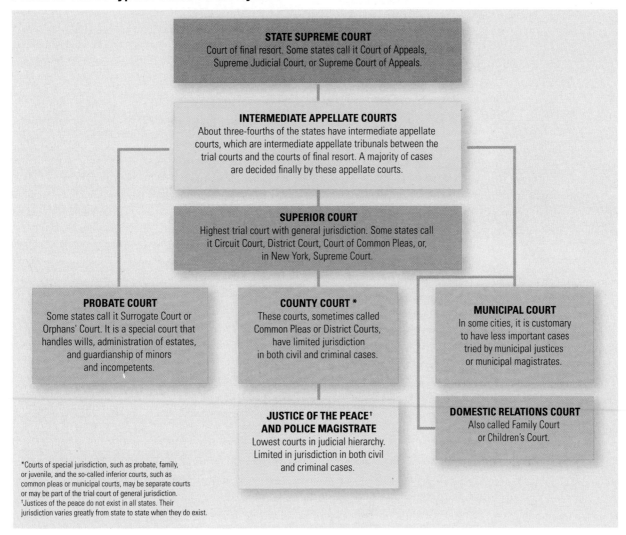

STATE SUPREME COURT
Court of final resort. Some states call it Court of Appeals, Supreme Judicial Court, or Supreme Court of Appeals.

INTERMEDIATE APPELLATE COURTS
About three-fourths of the states have intermediate appellate courts, which are intermediate appellate tribunals between the trial courts and the courts of final resort. A majority of cases are decided finally by these appellate courts.

SUPERIOR COURT
Highest trial court with general jurisdiction. Some states call it Circuit Court, District Court, Court of Common Pleas, or, in New York, Supreme Court.

PROBATE COURT
Some states call it Surrogate Court or Orphans' Court. It is a special court that handles wills, administration of estates, and guardianship of minors and incompetents.

COUNTY COURT *
These courts, sometimes called Common Pleas or District Courts, have limited jurisdiction in both civil and criminal cases.

MUNICIPAL COURT
In some cities, it is customary to have less important cases tried by municipal justices or municipal magistrates.

**JUSTICE OF THE PEACE†
AND POLICE MAGISTRATE**
Lowest courts in judicial hierarchy. Limited in jurisdiction in both civil and criminal cases.

DOMESTIC RELATIONS COURT
Also called Family Court or Children's Court.

*Courts of special jurisdiction, such as probate, family, or juvenile, and the so-called inferior courts, such as common pleas or municipal courts, may be separate courts or may be part of the trial court of general jurisdiction.
†Justices of the peace do not exist in all states. Their jurisdiction varies greatly from state to state when they do exist.

1. Drug courts, which deal only with illegal substance crimes.
2. Gun courts, which have jurisdiction over crimes that involve the illegal use of firearms.
3. Juvenile courts, which specialize in crimes committed by minors. (We will discuss juvenile courts in more detail in Chapter 13.)
4. Domestic courts, which deal with crimes of domestic violence, such as child and spousal abuse.
5. Mental health courts, which focus primarily on the treatment and rehabilitation of offenders with mental health problems.

As we will see in Chapter 10, many state and local governments are searching for cheaper alternatives to locking up nonviolent offenders in prison or jail. Because problem-solving courts offer a range of treatment options for wrongdoers, these courts are becoming increasingly popular in today's more budget-conscious criminal justice system. For example, more than 2,600 drug courts are now operating in the United States, a number that is expected to increase as the financial benefits of diverting drug law violators from correctional facilities become more attractive to politicians.

Judge Sarah Smith, left, talks with an offender at her drug court in downtown Tulsa, Oklahoma. ■ What are some of the benefits of drug courts and other problem-solving courts?

Photo by Adam Wisneski/Tulsa World

Trial Courts of General Jurisdiction

State trial courts that have general jurisdiction may be called county courts, district courts, superior courts, or circuit courts. In Ohio, the name is the court of common pleas and in Massachusetts, the trial court. (The name sometimes does not correspond with the court's functions. For example, in New York the trial court is called the supreme court, whereas in most states the supreme court is the state's highest court.) Courts of general jurisdiction have the authority to hear and decide cases involving many types of subject matter, and they are the setting for criminal trials (discussed in Chapter 8).

State Courts of Appeals

Every state has at least one court of appeals (known as an appellate, or reviewing, court), which may be an intermediate appellate court or the state's highest court. About three-fourths have intermediate appellate courts. The highest appellate court in a state is usually called the supreme court, but in both New York and Maryland, the highest state court is called the court of appeals. The decisions of each state's highest court on all questions of state law are final. Only when issues of federal law or constitutional procedure are involved can the United States Supreme Court overrule a decision made by a state's highest court.

//// SELF ASSESSMENT

Fill in the blanks, and check your answers on page 228.

State court systems include several levels of courts. Lower courts, or courts of _____ jurisdiction, hear only cases involving minor criminal matters or narrowly defined areas of crime such as domestic violence. Trial courts of _____ jurisdiction hear cases involving many different subject matters. The state courts of _____ make the final decisions on all questions of state law.

THE FEDERAL COURT SYSTEM

The federal court system is basically a three-tiered model consisting of (1) U.S. district courts (trial courts of general jurisdiction) and various courts of limited jurisdiction, (2) U.S. courts of appeals (intermediate courts of appeals), and (3) the United States Supreme Court.

Unlike state court judges, who are usually elected, federal court judges—including the justices of the Supreme Court—are appointed by the president of the United States, subject to the approval of the Senate. All federal judges receive lifetime appointments (because under Article III of the Constitution they "hold their offices during Good Behavior").

U.S. District Courts

On the lowest tier of the federal court system are the U.S. district courts, or federal trial courts. These are the courts in which cases involving federal laws begin, and a judge or jury decides the case (if it is a jury trial). Every state has at least one federal district court, and there is one in the District of Columbia. The number of judicial districts varies over time, primarily owing to population changes and corresponding caseloads. At the present time, there are ninety-four judicial districts. The federal system also includes other trial courts of limited jurisdiction, such as the Tax Court and the Court of International Trade.

U.S. Courts of Appeals

In the federal court system, there are thirteen U.S. courts of appeals—also referred to as U.S. circuit courts of appeals. The federal courts of appeals for twelve of the circuits hear appeals from the district courts located within their respective judicial circuits (see Figure 7.3 that follows). The Court of Appeals for the Thirteenth Circuit, called the Federal Circuit, has national appellate jurisdiction over certain types of cases, such as cases in which the U.S. government is a defendant. The decisions of the circuit courts of appeals are final unless a further appeal is pursued and granted. In that case, the matter is brought before the Supreme Court.

The United States Supreme Court

Although it reviews a minuscule percentage of the cases decided in this country each year, the rulings of the United States Supreme Court profoundly affect American society. The impact of Court decisions on the criminal justice system is equally far reaching: *Gideon v. Wainwright* (1963)[9] established every American's right to be represented

FIGURE 7.3 Geographic Boundaries of the Federal Circuit Courts of Appeals

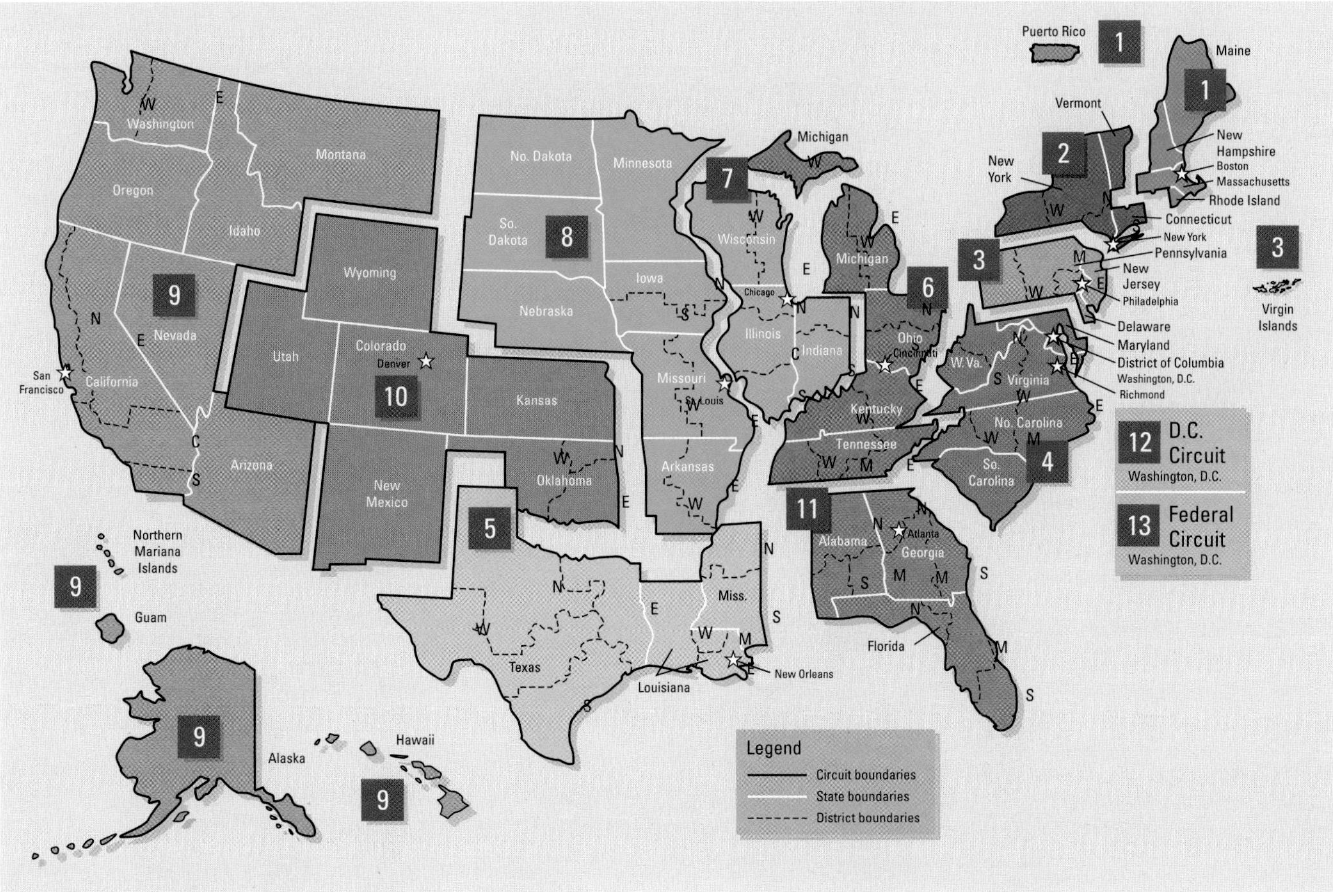

Source: Administrative Office of the United States Courts, January 1994.

by counsel in a criminal trial; *Miranda v. Arizona* (1966)[10] transformed pretrial interrogations; *Furman v. Georgia* (1972)[11] ruled that the death penalty was unconstitutional; and *Gregg v. Georgia* (1976)[12] spelled out the conditions under which it could be allowed. As you have no doubt noticed from references in this textbook, the Court has addressed nearly every important facet of criminal law.

JUDICIAL REVIEW The Supreme Court "makes" criminal justice policy in two important ways: through *judicial review* and through its authority to interpret the law. **Judicial review** refers to the power of the Court to determine whether a law or action by the other branches of the government is constitutional.

In 2005, for example, Congress passed the Stolen Valor Act, which made it a crime punishable by up to six months in prison for someone to falsely claim that he or she had earned military honors or medals.[13] Several years after passage of this legislation, Xavier Alvarez was sentenced to three years of probation and given a $5,000 fine for lying about having received the Medal of Honor. In 2012, the Court overturned Alvarez's conviction and invalidated the federal law on the ground that a false statement that does no obvious harm is protected by the First Amendment's freedom of expression.[14] (In 2013, Congress passed a new version of the Stolen Valor Act that made it a crime to lie about earning military honors "with the intent to obtain money, property, or some other tangible benefit.")[15]

STATUTORY INTERPRETATION As the final interpreter of the Constitution, the Supreme Court must also determine the meaning of certain statutory provisions when applied to specific situations. In the previous chapter, you learned that a law enforcement officer must immediately stop questioning a suspect who invokes her or his *Miranda* rights. In *Maryland v. Shatzer* (2010),[16] the Court considered a situation in which a sexual abuse suspect invoked his *Miranda* rights, spent more than two years in prison (for an unrelated crime), and then waived his *Miranda* rights.

The Court rejected the suspect's claim that due to his much earlier action, the later waiver, although made willingly, "did not count." Instead, the Court decided on a new rule: a *Miranda* invocation is good for only fourteen days. After that, a suspect must clearly reestablish her or his right to silence. (See the feature *CJ Controversy—Under Review* that follows to gain a better understanding of the Supreme Court's role in shaping criminal justice policy.)

JURISDICTION OF THE SUPREME COURT The United States Supreme Court consists of nine justices—a chief justice and eight associate justices. The Supreme Court has original, or trial, jurisdiction only in rare instances (set forth in Article III, Section 2, of the Constitution). In other words, only rarely does a case originate at the Supreme Court level. Most of the Court's work is as an appellate court. It has appellate authority over cases decided by the U.S. courts of appeals, as well as over some cases decided in the state courts when federal questions are at issue.

WHICH CASES REACH THE SUPREME COURT? There is no absolute right to appeal to the United States Supreme Court. Although thousands of cases are filed with the Supreme Court each year, in 2012–2013 the Court heard only seventy-nine. With a **writ of *certiorari*** (pronounced sur-shee-uh-*rah*-ree), the Supreme Court orders a lower court to send it the record of a case for review. A party can petition the Supreme Court to issue a writ of *certiorari*, but whether the Court will do so is entirely within its discretion. More

Explain briefly how a case is brought to the Supreme Court. **LEARNING 5 OBJECTIVE** than 90 percent of the petitions for writs of *certiorari* (or "certs," as they are popularly called) are denied. A denial is not a decision on the merits of a case, nor does it indicate agreement with the lower court's opinion. Therefore, the denial of the writ has no value as a precedent.

The Court will not issue a writ unless at least four justices approve of it. This is called the **rule of four.** Although the justices are not required to give their reasons for refusing to hear a case, most often the discretionary decision is based on whether the legal issue involves a "substantial federal question." Often, such questions arise when lower courts split on a particular issue. For example, in recent years different state courts have produced varying opinions on the question of whether an anonymous tip provides reasonable suspicion for police officers to pull over a driver that the officers themselves do not actually see breaking any traffic laws. To clear up confusion on this question—important because, as we saw in Chapter 6, such stops can lead to warrantless searches—the Court has agreed to hear a case involving the matter.[17] Practical considerations aside, if the justices feel that a case does not address an important federal law or constitutional issue, they will vote to deny the writ of *certiorari*.

> **Rule of Four** A rule of the United States Supreme Court that the Court will not issue a writ of *certiorari* unless at least four justices approve of the decision to hear the case.

CJ CONTROVERSY

UNDER REVIEW

It seems likely that, at some point in this textbook, you have found yourself disagreeing with a U.S. Supreme Court decision regarding the criminal justice system. You are certainly not alone. Given the importance of the subjects on which it is asked to rule—from abortion to gay marriage to affirmative action—the Supreme Court is a lightning rod for controversy. Indeed, there are many who ask whether the Supreme Court should have the authority to overturn laws passed by politicians in this country.

JUDICIAL REVIEW BY THE SUPREME COURT HELPS SOCIETY BECAUSE . . .

- Supreme Court justices are unelected and therefore insulated from the political process. Thus, they are in the best position to decide if legislation, though popular, goes against the Constitution.
- It allows the Court to protect members of minority groups and those with unpopular opinions from the majority, "democratic" viewpoint.

JUDICIAL REVIEW BY THE SUPREME COURT HURTS SOCIETY BECAUSE . . .

- It is undemocratic, as it permits unelected judges to thwart the intent of members of Congress who have been elected by citizens to carry out the wishes of the majority.
- The morals and concerns of Supreme Court justices— wealthy, highly educated lawyers who until recently were primarily white males—are not always in keeping with the morals and concerns of most Americans.

Your Assignment
In the late 1990s, Congress passed a law restricting the sale of videos showing graphic violence against animals. In 2010, the Supreme Court ruled that this law was unconstitutional. Learn more about the Court's decision by searching the Internet for the terms **crush videos** and ***United States v. Stevens***. Do you agree with the Court's decision? Does this decision weaken or strengthen arguments in favor of judicial review? Your answers should include at least two full paragraphs.

Oral Arguments The verbal arguments presented in person by attorneys to an appellate court. Each attorney presents reasons why the court should rule in his or her client's favor.

Concurring Opinions Separate opinions prepared by judges who support the decision of the majority of the court but who want to clarify a particular point or to voice disapproval of the grounds on which the decision was made.

Dissenting Opinions Separate opinions in which judges disagree with the conclusion reached by the majority of the court and expand on their own views about the case.

SUPREME COURT DECISIONS Like all appellate courts, the Supreme Court normally does not hear any evidence. The Court's decision in a particular case is based on the written record of the case and the written arguments (briefs) that the attorneys submit. The attorneys also present **oral arguments**—arguments delivered in person rather than on paper—to the Court, after which the justices discuss the case in *conference*. The conference is strictly private—only the justices are allowed in the room.

Majorities and Pluralities When the Court has reached a decision, the chief justice, if in the majority, assigns the task of writing the Court's opinion to one of the justices. When the chief justice is not in the majority, the most senior justice voting with the majority assigns the writing of the Court's opinion. The opinion outlines the reasons for the Court's decision, the rules of law that apply, and the decision.

From time to time, the justices agree on the outcome of a case, but no single reason for that outcome gains five votes. When this occurs, the rationale that gains the most votes is called the *plurality* opinion. Plurality opinions are problematic, because they do not provide a strong precedent for lower courts to follow. Although still relatively rare, the incidence of plurality opinions has increased over the past fifty years as the Court has become more ideologically fractured.[18]

Concurrence and Dissent Often, one or more justices who agree with the Court's decision may do so for different reasons than those outlined in the majority opinion. These justices may write **concurring opinions** setting forth their own legal reasoning on the issue. Frequently, one or more justices disagree with the Court's conclusion. These justices may write **dissenting opinions** outlining the reasons why they feel the majority erred. Although a dissenting opinion does not affect the outcome of the case before the Court, it may be important later. In a subsequent case concerning the same issue, a justice or attorney may use the legal reasoning in the dissenting opinion as the basis for an argument to reverse the previous decision and establish a new precedent.

///// SELF ASSESSMENT

Fill in the blanks, and check your answers on page 228.

The lowest tier of the federal court system contains U.S. _____ courts, also known as federal trial courts. Appeals from this lower tier are heard in the thirteen U.S. _____ courts of appeals. A decision handed down by a court in this second tier is final unless the United States _____ Court issues a writ of _____, indicating that it has agreed to review the case.

JUDGES IN THE COURT SYSTEM

Supreme Court justices are the most visible and best-known American jurists, but in many ways they are unrepresentative of the profession as a whole. Few judges enjoy three-room office suites fitted with a fireplace and a private bath, as do the Supreme Court justices. Few judges have four clerks to assist them. Few judges get a yearly vacation that stretches from July through September. Most judges, in fact, work at the lowest level of the system, in criminal trial courts, where they are burdened with overflowing caseloads and must deal daily with the pettiest of criminals.

One attribute a Supreme Court justice and a criminal trial judge in any small American city do have in common is the public's expectation that they will be just. Of all the participants in the criminal justice system, no single person is held to the same high standards as the judge. From her or his lofty perch in the courtroom, the judge is counted on to be "above the fray" of the bickering defense attorneys and prosecutors. When the other courtroom contestants rise at the entrance of the judge, they are placing the burden of justice squarely on her or his shoulders.

The Roles and Responsibilities of Trial Judges

One of the reasons that judicial integrity is considered so important is the amount of discretionary power a judge has over the court proceedings. Nearly every stage of the trial process includes a decision or action to be taken by the presiding judge.

BEFORE THE TRIAL A great deal of the work done by a judge takes place before the trial even starts, free from public scrutiny. These duties, some of which you have seen from a different point of view in the section on law enforcement agents, include determining the following:

1. Whether there is sufficient probable cause to issue a search or arrest warrant.
2. Whether there is sufficient probable cause to authorize electronic surveillance of a suspect.
3. Whether enough evidence exists to justify the temporary incarceration of a suspect.
4. Whether a defendant should be released on bail, and if so, the amount of the bail.
5. Whether to accept pretrial motions by prosecutors and defense attorneys.
6. Whether to accept a plea bargain.

During these pretrial activities, the judge takes on the role of the *negotiator*.[19] As most cases are decided through plea bargains rather than through trial proceedings, the judge often offers his or her services as a negotiator to help the prosecution and the defense "make a deal." The amount at which bail is set is often negotiated as well. Throughout the trial process, the judge usually spends a great deal of time in his or her *chambers*, or office, negotiating with the prosecutors and defense attorneys.

DURING THE TRIAL When the trial starts, the judge takes on the role of *referee*. In this role, she or he is responsible for seeing that the trial unfolds according to the dictates of the law and that the participants in the trial do not overstep any legal or ethical bounds. Furthermore, the judge is expected to be neutral, determining the admissibility of testimony and evidence on a completely objective basis.

The judge also acts as a *teacher* during the trial, explaining points of law to the jury. If the trial is not a jury trial, then the judge must also make decisions concerning the guilt or innocence of the defendant. At the

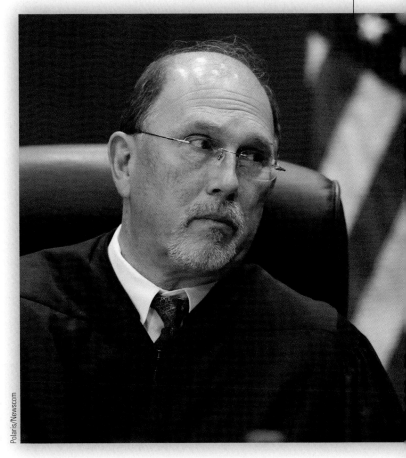

Seminole County, Florida, Circuit Judge Kenneth Lester was disqualified from George Zimmerman's murder trial (see Chapter 3) after he accused the defendant of showing "blatant disregard for the judicial system." Why is it crucial that judges be seen as unbiased against either party in a criminal trial?

Polaris/Newscom

close of the trial, if the defendant is found guilty, the judge must decide on the length of the sentence and the type of sentence. (Different types of sentences, such as incarceration, probation, and other forms of community-based corrections, will be discussed in Chapters 9 and 10.)

THE ADMINISTRATIVE ROLE Judges are also *administrators* and are responsible for the day-to-day functioning of their courts. A primary administrative task of a judge is scheduling. Each courtroom has a **docket,** or calendar of cases, and it is the judge's responsibility to keep the docket current. This entails not only scheduling the trial, but also setting pretrial motion dates and deciding whether to grant attorneys' requests for *continuances,* or additional time to prepare for the trial.

Judges must also keep track of the immense paperwork generated by each case and manage the various employees of the court. In some instances, judges are even responsible for the budgets of their courtrooms. In 1939, Congress, recognizing the burden of such tasks, created the Administrative Office of the United States Courts to provide administrative assistance for federal court judges.[20] Most state court judges, however, do not have the luxury of similar aid, though they are supported by a court staff.

CJ & TECHNOLOGY — Lie Detection in Court

AP Images/Cecil Whig, Matthew Given

During a polygraph test, rubber tubes are placed on a person's chest and abdominal area to record his or her breathing patterns. In addition, two small metal plates are attached to the subject's fingers to measure sweat levels, and a blood pressure cuff indicates her or his heart rate. The examiner asks a series of questions, keeping track of changes in the body's responses to determine if the subject is telling the truth. Law enforcement agents routinely employ polygraphs in the course of criminal investigations, and the technology is widely used by the government to test job applicants and those seeking a security clearance.

In criminal courtrooms, however, polygraph exams are surprisingly absent. The decision to allow evidence of such exams rests primarily with the judge, particularly in federal court. In exercising this discretion, the judge must decide whether the results of the exam are reliable. Even though properly administered polygraphs are, by some measures, accurate about 75 percent of the time, many judges are suspicious of what they believe to be "junk science" and therefore are reluctant to allow it in their courtrooms.

Thinking about Polygraph Exams

In particular, polygraph exams are popular with defendants who want to use the tests to prove their innocence. Assuming that such exams do have 75 percent accuracy rates, are judges justified in keeping the results out of court? Explain your answer.

Selection of Judges

Explain the difference between the selection of judges at the state level and at the federal level. **LEARNING OBJECTIVE 6**

In the federal court system, all judges are nominated by the president and confirmed by the Senate. It is difficult to make a general statement about how judges are selected in state court systems, however, because the procedure varies widely from state to state. In some states, such as New Jersey, all judges are appointed by the governor and confirmed by the upper chamber of the state legislature. In other states, such as Alabama,

partisan elections are used to choose judges. In these elections, a judicial candidate declares allegiance to a political party, usually the Democrats or the Republicans, before the election. States such as Kentucky that conduct **nonpartisan elections** do not require a candidate to affiliate herself or himself with a political party in this manner.

In 1940, Missouri became the first state to combine appointment and election in a single merit selection. When all jurisdiction levels are counted, nineteen states and the District of Columbia now utilize the **Missouri Plan,** as merit selection has been labeled. The Missouri Plan consists of three basic steps:

1. When a vacancy on the bench arises, candidates are nominated by a nonpartisan committee of citizens.
2. The names of the three most qualified candidates are sent to the governor or executive of the state judicial system, and that person chooses who will be the judge.
3. A year after the new judge has been installed, a "retention election" is held so that voters can decide whether the judge deserves to keep the post.[21]

The goal of the Missouri Plan is to eliminate partisan politics from the selection procedure, while at the same time giving the citizens a voice in the process. Regardless of how they are selected, the average term for state judges in this country is about seven years.[22] (See the feature *Comparative Criminal Justice—Back to School* that follows to learn about the French alternative to choosing judges through elections.)

Partisan Elections Elections in which candidates are affiliated with and receive support from political parties.

Nonpartisan Elections Elections in which candidates are presented on the ballot without any party affiliation.

Missouri Plan A method of selecting judges that combines appointment and election.

COMPARATIVE
CRIMINAL JUSTICE

Central Intelligence Agency

Back to School

Elections for judges are extremely rare outside the United States. Indeed, only two nations—Japan and Switzerland—engage in the practice, and then only in very limited situations. To the rest of the world, according to one expert, "American adherence to judicial elections is as incomprehensible as our rejection of the metric system." Much more common, for example, is the French system, crafted to provide extensive training for potential judges.

French judicial candidates must pass two exams. The first, open to law school graduates only, combines oral and written sections and lasts at least four days. In some years, only 5 percent of the applicants overcome this hurdle. Not surprisingly, the pressure is intense. "It gives you nightmares for years afterwards," says Jean-Marc Baissus, a judge in Toulouse. "You come out of [the exam] completely shattered." Those who do survive the first test enter a two-year program at the École Nationale de la Magistrature, a judicial training academy. This school is similar to a police training academy in the United States, in that candidates spend half of their time in the classroom and the other half in the courtroom.

At the end of this program, judicial candidates are subject to a second examination. Only those who pass the exam may become judges. The result, in the words of Mitchel Lasser, a law professor at Cornell University, is that French judges "actually know what the hell they are doing. They've spent years in school taking practical and theoretical courses on how to be a judge." The French also pride themselves on creating judges who are free from the kind of political pressures faced by American judges who must go before the voters.

FOR CRITICAL ANALYSIS

Do you think that the French system of training judges is superior to the American system of electing them? Before explaining your answer, consider that French judges lack the practical courtroom experience of American judges, many of whom served as lawyers earlier in their careers.

New Jersey Governor's Office/Tim Larsen

Before his appointment, New Jersey Superior Court Judge Sohail Mohammed, a native of India, represented nearly three dozen suspects detained following the 9/11 terrorist attacks. He has also trained more than seven thousand law enforcement agents to better understand the Muslim American community. What are the benefits of having judges with a wide range of cultural experiences on the bench?

Diversity on the Bench

According to a recent report by the Brennan Center for Justice in New York City, "Americans who enter the courtroom often face a predictable presence on the bench: a white male."[23] Overall, about two-thirds of all state appellate judges are white males, and women in particular are notably absent from the highest courts of most states.[24] In many states, members of minority groups are underrepresented in comparison to the demographics of the general population. California, for example, is nearly 38 percent Hispanic and 16 percent Asian American. The state judiciary, however, is only 8.3 percent Hispanic and 4.4 percent Asian American.[25]

FEDERAL DIVERSITY Members of minority groups are also underrepresented in the federal judiciary. Of the nearly 1,800 federal judges in this country, about 11 percent are African American, 6 percent are Hispanic, and less than 2 percent are Asian American. Furthermore, only 20 percent are women.[26] Of the 111 justices who have served on the United States Supreme Court, two have been African American: Thurgood Marshall (1970–1991) and Clarence Thomas (1991–present). In 2009, Sonia Sotomayor became the first Hispanic appointed to the Court and the third woman, following Sandra Day O'Connor (1981–2006) and Ruth Bader Ginsburg (1993–present). A year later, Elena Kagan became the fourth woman appointed to the Court.

THE IMPACT OF PAST DISCRIMINATION Edward Chen, a federal judge for the Northern District of California, identifies a number of reasons for the low minority representation on the bench. Past discrimination in law schools has limited the pool of experienced minority attorneys who have the political ties, access to "old boy" networks, and career opportunities that lead to judgeships.[27] Only recently, as increased numbers of minorities have graduated from law schools, have rates of minority judges begun to creep slowly upward. In addition, efforts to diversify American judges by race, ethnicity, and gender have been met with resistance from those who argue that because judges must be impartial, it makes no difference whether a judge is black, Asian, Hispanic, or white.[28]

Sherrilyn A. Ifill of the University of Maryland School of Law rejects this argument. She believes that "diversity on the bench" can only enrich our judiciary by introducing a variety of voices and perspectives into what are perhaps the most powerful positions in the criminal justice system. By the same token, Ifill credits the lack of diversity in many trial and appeals courts with a number of harmful consequences, such as more severe sentences for minority youths than for white youths who have committed similar crimes, disproportionate denial of bail to minority defendants, and the disproportionate imposition of the death penalty on minority defendants accused of killing white victims.[29]

Fill in the blanks, and check your answers on page 228.

In the federal court system, judges are nominated by the _____ and confirmed by the _____. In state court systems, however, the selection process varies. Some states mirror the federal system, with the _____ making judicial appointments with the approval of the legislature. Others conduct either _____ elections, in which political parties openly support judicial candidates, or _____ elections, in which the candidates are not affiliated with any political group. Finally, a number of states rely on _____ selection, which combines appointment and election.

THE COURTROOM WORK GROUP

Television dramas often depict the courtroom as a battlefield, with prosecutors and defense attorneys spitting fire at each other over the loud and insistent protestations of a frustrated judge. Consequently, many people are somewhat disappointed when they witness a real courtroom at work. Rarely does anyone raise his or her voice, and the courtroom professionals appear—to a great extent—to be cooperating with each other. In Chapter 5, we discussed the existence of a police subculture, based on the shared values of law enforcement agents. A courtroom subculture exists as well, centered on the **courtroom work group.**

The most important feature of any work group is that it is a *cooperative* unit, whose members establish shared values and methods that help the group efficiently reach its goals. Though cooperation is not a concept usually associated with criminal courts, it is in fact crucial to the adjudication process.

Members of the Courtroom Work Group

The courtroom work group is made up of those individuals who are involved with the defendant from the time she or he is arrested until sentencing. The most prominent members are the judge, the prosecutor, and the defense attorney. (You will be introduced to the latter two shortly.) Three other court participants complete the work group:

1. The *bailiff of the court* is responsible for maintaining security and order in the judge's chambers and the courtroom. Bailiffs lead the defendant in and out of the courtroom and attend to the needs of the jurors during the trial. A bailiff, often a member of the local sheriff's department but sometimes an employee of the court, also delivers summonses in some jurisdictions.

2. The *clerk of the court* has an exhausting list of responsibilities. Any plea, motion, or other matter to be acted on by the judge must go through the clerk. The large amount of paperwork generated during a trial, including transcripts, photographs, evidence, and any other records, is maintained by the clerk. The clerk also issues subpoenas for jury duty and coordinates the jury selection process. In the federal court system, judges select clerks, while state clerks are either appointed or, in nearly a third of the states, elected.

3. *Court reporters* record every word that is said during the course of the trial. They also record any *depositions,* or pretrial question-and-answer sessions in which a party or a witness answers an attorney's questions under oath.

Courtroom Work Group The collective unit consisting of the judge, prosecutor, defense attorney, and other court workers.

Photo Courtesy of Shawn Davis

FAST FACTS

BAILIFF JOB DESCRIPTION:

- Maintain order and provide security in the courtroom during trials.
- Open and close court, call cases, call witnesses, and the like.
- Escort and guard juries, prevent juries from having contact with the public.

WHAT KIND OF TRAINING IS REQUIRED?

- At a minimum, a high school diploma or GED.

ANNUAL SALARY RANGE?

- $35,000–$43,000

SHAWN DAVIS

BAILIFF

Basically, there are two kinds of bailiffs: administrative bailiffs and criminal bailiffs. An administrative bailiff will handle paperwork, set up court dates, and answer questions about filings that the attorneys may have. A criminal bailiff is responsible for bringing the court to session, directing jurors, and overseeing court security, which involves keeping everybody— judges, attorneys, jurors, spectators, witnesses, and defendants—safe. In my case, I do double duty as an administrative and criminal bailiff.

Violence in the courtroom is rare. Most inmates are on their best behavior in front of the judge. It can flare up in an instant, however, and you have to be constantly on guard. One time, an inmate under my control made a run for it as we were transporting him back to the jail from his court appearance. His leg shackles broke, giving him a short-lived sense of freedom. We were able to tackle him in front of the courthouse just before he could jump into a waiting convertible. We later learned that the accomplice—the inmate's brother— was supposed to bring a handgun and shoot us as part of the escape plan. Another time, a defendant started taking off his shirt and tried to attack the victim, who had just given testimony. He was quickly tackled, cuffed, and carted off to jail.

Social Media Career Tip Networking is crucial. Develop as many useful social media contacts as possible, and cultivate those contacts. Also, reciprocate. If you help others establish online contacts, they are likely to remember you and return the favor. **f** **y**

The Judge in the Courtroom Work Group

The judge is the dominant figure in the courtroom and therefore exerts the most influence over the values and norms of the work group. A judge who runs a "tight ship" follows procedure and restricts the freedom of attorneys to deviate from regulations, while a *"laissez-faire"* judge allows more leeway to members of the work group. A judge's personal philosophy also affects the court proceedings. If a judge has a reputation for being "tough on crime," both prosecutors and defense attorneys will alter their strategies accordingly.

Although preeminent in the work group, a judge must still rely on other members of the group. To a certain extent, the judge is the least informed member of the predominant trio. Like a juror, the judge learns the facts of the case as they are presented by the attorneys. If the attorneys do not properly present the facts, then the judge is hampered in making rulings. Furthermore, a judge's personal opinions need not influence the outcome of criminal proceedings. In 2013, Florida Circuit Court Judge Belvin Perry revealed that he felt "surprise" and "disbelief" when the trial of Casey Anthony for the murder of her two-year-old daughter, over which he had presided two years earlier, resulted in a not guilty verdict.[30]

The Prosecution

If the judge is, as we suggested earlier, the referee of the courtroom, then the prosecutor and the defense attorney are its two main combatants. On the side of the government, acting in the name of "the people," the **public prosecutor** tries cases against criminal defendants. The public prosecutor in federal criminal cases is called a U.S. attorney. In cases tried in state or local courts, the public prosecutor may be referred to as a *prosecuting attorney, state attorney, district attorney, county attorney,* or *city attorney.* Given their great autonomy, prosecutors are generally considered the most dominant figures in the American criminal justice system.

In some jurisdictions, the district attorney is the chief law enforcement officer, with broad powers over police operations. Prosecutors have the power to bring the resources of the state against the individual and hold the legal keys to meting out or withholding punishment. Ideally, this power is balanced by a duty of fairness and a recognition that the prosecutor's ultimate goal is not to win cases, but to see that justice is done. In *Berger v. United States* (1935), Justice George Sutherland called the prosecutor

> in a peculiar and very definite sense the servant of the law, the twofold aim of which is that guilt shall not escape or innocence suffer. He may prosecute with earnestness and vigor—indeed, he should do so. But, while he may strike hard blows, he is not at liberty to strike foul ones. It is as much his duty to refrain from improper methods calculated to produce a wrongful conviction as it is to use every legitimate means to bring about a just one.[31]

In part to lessen the opportunity for "foul" behavior by prosecutors, they are not permitted to keep evidence from the defendant that may be useful in showing his or her innocence.[32] For example, in 2000 former state trooper George Martin was convicted of burning his wife to death in her car in Mobile, Alabama. The only eyewitness to the crime gave conflicting reports to police, including calling the killer "a big man" (Martin is 5 feet, 6 inches tall) and pointing to a different suspect in a photo lineup. Obviously, Martin's defense attorneys could have used this information to create reasonable doubt about their client's guilt. Prosecutors failed to provide the defense with this evidence, however, and consequently, in 2013, a Mobile County judge overturned Martin's conviction and ordered a new trial.[33]

THE OFFICE OF THE PROSECUTOR When he or she is acting as an *officer of the law* during a criminal trial, there are limits on the prosecutor's conduct, as we shall see in the next chapter. During the pretrial process, however, prosecutors hold a great deal of discretion in deciding the following:

1. Whether an individual who has been arrested by the police will be charged with a crime.
2. The level of the charges to be brought against the suspect.
3. If and when to stop the prosecution.[34]

There are more than eight thousand prosecutor's offices around the country, serving state, county, and municipal jurisdictions. Even though the **attorney general** is the chief law enforcement officer in any state, she or he has limited (and in some states, no) control over prosecutors within the state's boundaries.

Each jurisdiction has a chief prosecutor, who is sometimes appointed but more often is elected. As an elected official, he or she typically serves a four-year term, though in some states, such as Alabama, the term is six years. In smaller jurisdictions, the chief prosecutor has several assistants, and they work closely together. In larger ones, the chief prosecutor may have numerous *assistant prosecutors,* many of whom he or she

Public Prosecutors Individuals, acting as trial lawyers, who initiate and conduct cases in the government's name and on behalf of the people.

Attorney General The chief law officer of a state; also, the chief law officer of the nation.

LEARNING OBJECTIVE **7** List the different names given to public prosecutors, and indicate the general powers that they have.

rarely meets. Assistant prosecutors—for the most part, young attorneys recently graduated from law school—may be assigned to particular sections of the organization, such as criminal prosecutions in general or areas of *special prosecution,* such as narcotics or gang crimes. (See Figure 7.4 that follows for the structure of a typical prosecutor's office.)

THE PROSECUTOR AS ELECTED OFFICIAL   The chief prosecutor's autonomy is not absolute. As an elected official, she or he must answer to the voters. (There are exceptions: U.S. attorneys are nominated by the president and approved by the Senate, and chief prosecutors in Alaska, Connecticut, New Jersey, Rhode Island, and the District of Columbia are either appointed or hired as members of the attorney general's office.) The prosecutor may be part of the political machine. In many jurisdictions, the prosecutor must declare a party affiliation and is expected to reward fellow party members with positions in the district attorney's office if elected.

Prosecutorial Politics   The post of prosecutor is also considered a "stepping-stone" to higher political office, and many prosecutors have gone on to serve in legislatures or as judges. Sonia Sotomayor (see the photo on the facing page), the first Hispanic member of the United States Supreme Court, started her legal career in 1979 as an assistant district attorney in New York City. While at that job, she first came to public attention by helping to prosecute the "Tarzan Murderer," an athletic criminal responsible for at least twenty burglaries and four killings.

Prosecutorial Pressures   Like judges, who are often the other elected members of the courtroom work group, prosecutors are subject to community pressures. Such pressures were evident in a case involving a high school senior and the alleged rape of a fourteen-year-old girl in Maryville, Missouri. When, in January 2012, Matt Barnett, the senior, was arrested for having sex with the girl, who was too drunk to consent, the local sheriff said the evidence gathered would "absolutely" result in a prosecution.[35] Two months later, however, Nodaway County prosecutor Robert Rice dropped all charges against Barnett, calling the incident nothing more than a case of "incorrigible teenagers" getting drunk and having sex.[36]

Maryville residents suspected that Rice's decision had been influenced by the fact that Barnett, besides being a popular football player, was the grandson of a prominent local political figure. After the *Kansas City Star* ran an article on the situation—which included such details as the suspect's leaving the lightly dressed alleged victim passed out on her front lawn in freezing weather[37]—Rice began to receive a great deal of criticism for his actions. In October 2013, he relented and asked a judge to appoint a special prosecutor to reopen the case. Finally,

FIGURE 7.4 **The Baltimore City State's Attorney's Office**

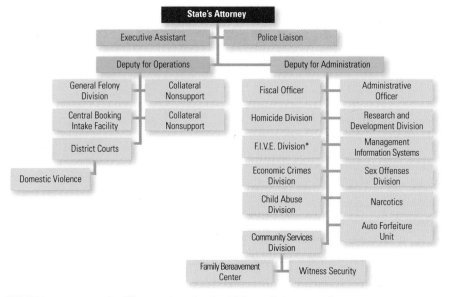

*F.I.V.E. is an acronym for "Firearms Investigation Violence Enforcement."

Source: Baltimore City State's Attorney's Office.

in January 2014, the special prosecutor declined to bring sexual assault charges against Barnett, saying that there was "insufficient evidence" to support such charges.[38]

PROSECUTORS AND VICTIMS Because prosecutors have the responsibility of trying and convicting offenders, crime victims often see themselves as being on "the same side" as the prosecution. In fact, prosecutors do not represent crime victims. Understandably, most victims are focused primarily on the fate of the defendant who caused them harm. Prosecutors, in contrast, must balance the rights of the victims with those of the accused and the best interests of the public at large. Indeed, if a prosecutor becomes too involved in the personal tragedies of crime victims, he or she runs the risk of losing the neutrality that is the hallmark of the office.[39]

A prosecutor's duty of neutrality does not mean that he or she should ignore crime victims or their wishes. Practically, prosecutors rely on victims as sources of information and valuable witnesses. Believable victims are also quite helpful if a case goes to trial, as they may be able to elicit a sympathetic response from the jury.[40] Furthermore, as we saw in Chapter 3, federal and state victims' rights legislation requires the prosecutor to confer with victims at various stages of the criminal justice process.

In keeping with the spirit of these laws, former Brooklyn district attorney Charles Hynes would send a letter to victims of crimes that were being prosecuted by his office. The letter contained information regarding victims' rights under state law, possible victim compensation, and the victims' services unit operated by Hynes's office. It began, "What happened to you was wrong, and I want you to know that my staff will do everything it can to assist you."[41]

Pablo Martinez Monsivais/AP Images

■ Why might experience as a prosecutor make someone such as United States Supreme Court justice Sonia Sotomayor a more effective judge?

The Defense Attorney

The media provide most people's perception of defense counsel: the idealistic public defender who nobly serves the poor, the "ambulance chaser," or the celebrity attorney in the expensive suit. These stereotypes, though not entirely fictional, tend to obscure the crucial role that the **defense attorney** plays in the criminal justice system. Most persons charged with crimes have little or no knowledge of criminal procedure. Without assistance, they would be helpless in court. By acting as a staunch advocate for her or his client, the defense attorney (ideally) ensures that the government proves every point against that client beyond a reasonable doubt, even for cases that do not go to trial. In sum, the defense attorney provides a counterweight against the state in our adversarial system.

THE RESPONSIBILITIES OF THE DEFENSE ATTORNEY The Sixth Amendment right to counsel is not limited to the actual criminal trial. In a number of instances, the United States Supreme Court has held that defendants are entitled to representation as soon as their rights may be denied, which, as we have seen, includes the custodial interrogation and lineup identification procedures.[42] Therefore, an important responsibility of the defense attorney is to represent the defendant at the various stages of the custodial process, such as arrest, interrogation, lineup, and arraignment. Other responsibilities include

1. Investigating the incident for which the defendant has been charged.
2. Communicating with the prosecutor, which includes negotiating plea bargains.

Defense Attorney The lawyer representing the defendant.

3. Preparing the case for trial.
4. Submitting defense motions, including motions to suppress evidence.
5. Representing the defendant at trial.
6. Negotiating a sentence, if the client has been convicted.
7. Determining whether to appeal a guilty verdict.[43]

DEFENDING THE GUILTY At one time or another in their careers, all defense attorneys will face a difficult question: Must I defend a client whom I know to be guilty? According to the American Bar Association's code of legal ethics, the answer is almost always, "yes."[44] The most important responsibility of the criminal defense attorney is to be an advocate for her or his client. As such, the attorney is obligated to use all ethical and legal means to achieve the client's desired goal, which is usually to avoid or lessen punishment for the charged crime.

As Supreme Court justice Byron White once noted, defense counsel has no "obligation to ascertain or present the truth." Rather, our adversarial system insists that the defense attorney "defend the client whether he is innocent or guilty."[45] Indeed, if defense attorneys refused to represent clients whom they believed to be guilty, the Sixth Amendment guarantee of a criminal trial for all accused persons would be rendered meaningless. (To learn more about the difficult situations that can arise with a guilty defendant, see the feature *A Question of Ethics—The Right Decision?* that follows.)

THE PUBLIC DEFENDER Generally speaking, there are two different types of defense attorneys: (1) private attorneys, who are hired by individuals, and (2) **public defenders,** who work for the government. The distinction is not absolute, as many private attorneys accept employment as public defenders, too. The modern role of the public defender was established by the Supreme Court's interpretation of the Sixth Amendment in *Gideon v. Wainwright* (1963).[46]

In that case, the Court ruled that no defendant can be "assured a fair trial unless counsel is provided for him" and therefore the state must provide a public defender for those who cannot afford to hire one for themselves. Subsequently, the Court extended this protection to juveniles in *In re Gault* (1967)[47] and those faced with imprisonment for committing misdemeanors in *Argersinger v. Hamlin* (1972).[48] The impact of these decisions has been substantial: about 90 percent of all criminal defendants in the United States are represented by public defenders or other appointed counsel.[49]

Eligibility Issues Although the Supreme Court's *Gideon* decision obligated the government to provide attorneys for poor defendants, it offered no guidance on just how poor the defendant needs to be to qualify for a public defender. In theory, counsel should be provided for those who are unable to hire an attorney themselves without "substantial hardship."[50] In reality, each jurisdiction has its own guidelines, and a defendant refused counsel in one area might be entitled to it in another. A judge in Kittitas County, Washington, to give an extreme example, frequently denies public counsel for college student defendants. This judge believes that any person who chooses to go to school rather than work automatically falls outside the *Gideon* case's definition of indigence.[51]

Public Defenders Court-appointed attorneys who are paid by the state to represent defendants who cannot afford private counsel.

Effectiveness of Public Defenders Under the U.S. Constitution, a defendant who is paying for her or his defense attorney has a right to choose that attorney without interference from the court. This right of choice does not extend to indigent defendants. According to the United States Supreme Court, "a defendant may not insist on an attorney he cannot afford."[52] In other words, an indigent defendant must accept the public defender provided by the court system. (Note that, unless the presiding judge rules otherwise, a person can waive her or his Sixth Amendment rights and act as her or his own defense attorney.) This lack of control contributes to the widespread belief that public defenders do not provide an acceptable level of defense to indigents. The defense attorney whose mistakes led to David Bryant being freed from prison, as described at the beginning of the chapter, was a public defender.

Statistics show, however, that conviction rates of defendants with private counsel and those represented by publicly funded attorneys are generally the same.[53] The main difference seems to be between private attorneys who are assigned indigent clients and full-time public defenders. A recent study of 3,412 Philadelphia indigent murder defendants found that, compared with private appointed counsel, public defenders reduce the conviction rate by 19 percent and the overall expected time served in prison by 24 percent.[54]

A QUESTION OF ETHICS: The Right DECISION?

LEARNING OBJECTIVE 8
Explain why defense attorneys must often defend clients they know to be guilty.

THE SITUATION
Gerard Marrone is the defense attorney for Levi Aron, charged with kidnapping, murdering, and dismembering eight-year-old Leiby Kletzky in Brooklyn, New York. There is little question of Aron's guilt, as he provided the police with a signed confession and has no alibi for his whereabouts at the time of the crime. Marrone is uncertain about whether he wants to continue representing this "horrific" client. "You can't look at your kids and then look at yourself in the mirror, knowing that a little boy, who's close in age to my eldest son, was murdered so brutally," Marrone said about his conflicting feelings.

THE ETHICAL DILEMMA The criminal justice system would not be able to function if lawyers refused to represent clients they knew to be guilty. At the same time, a lawyer must be guided by his or her own conscience. If a client is so repugnant to the lawyer as to impair the quality of representation, then perhaps the lawyer should drop the case.

WHAT IS THE SOLUTION? What would you do in Marrone's shoes? He decided that his conscience prevented him from representing Aron, and he withdrew from the case. His replacement, Jennifer McCann, criticized Marrone's actions. "To sit there and say, 'This is a hard case, I don't want to take it.'" McCann said. "That's for somebody else, that's not who I am." She added, "It's not about defending [Aron's] actions. It's about defending his rights."

Jesse Ward/The New York Times/Redux Pictures

Defense attorneys Pierre Bazile, right, and Jennifer McCann appear with their client Levi Aron at the State Supreme Court in Brooklyn, New York.

The main reason for this discrepancy, at least in Philadelphia, appears to be financial. Court-appointed defense attorneys in that city receive a flat fee for each client, which essentially works out to an average of $2 an hour. Furthermore, they are afforded limited public funds to investigate their client's innocence. Philadelphia's public defenders, by contrast, are paid an annual salary and supported by a staff of investigators and various experts.

Pat Greenhouse/The Boston Globe/Getty Images

ATTORNEY-CLIENT PRIVILEGE To defend a client effectively, a defense attorney must have access to all the facts concerning the case, even those that may be harmful to the defendant. To promote the unrestrained flow of information between the two parties, legislatures and lawyers themselves have constructed rules of **attorney-client privilege**. These rules require that communications between a client and his or her attorney be kept confidential, unless the client consents to the disclosure.

Defense attorney Jill Corey appears in Quincy, Massachusetts, District Court with her client, Andrew Fanguiaire, who was charged with possession of child pornography. Why are the rules of attorney-client privilege necessary for a defense attorney to properly do his or her job?

Attorney-Client Privilege
A rule of evidence requiring that communications between a client and his or her attorney be kept confidential, unless the client consents to disclosure.

The Privilege and Confessions Attorney-client privilege does not stop short of confessions. Indeed, if, on hearing any statement that points toward guilt, the defense attorney could alert the prosecution or try to resign from the case, attorney-client privilege would be rendered meaningless. Even if the client says, "I have just killed seventeen women. I selected only pregnant women so I could torture them and kill two people at once. I did it. I liked it. I enjoyed it," the defense attorney must continue to do his or her utmost to serve that client.[55]

Without attorney-client privilege, observes legal expert John Kaplan, lawyers would be forced to give their clients the equivalent of the *Miranda* warning before representing them.[56] In other words, lawyers would have to make clear what clients could or could not say in the course of preparing for trial, because any incriminating statement might be used against the client in court. Such a development would have serious ramifications for the criminal justice system.

The Exception to the Privilege The scope of attorney-client privilege is not all encompassing. In *United States v. Zolin* (1989),[57] the Supreme Court ruled that lawyers may disclose the contents of a conversation with a client if the client has provided information concerning a crime that has yet to be committed. This exception applies only to communications involving a crime that is ongoing or will occur in the future. If the client reveals a past crime, the privilege is still in effect, and the attorney may not reveal any details of that particular criminal act.

///SELF ASSESSMENT

Fill in the blanks, and check your answers on page 228.

If the courtroom work group can be said to have a dominant figure, it is the _____. Public _____ are employed by the government and try cases on behalf of "the people." There are two types of defense attorneys: (1) _____ attorneys hired by individuals and (2) _____ defenders, provided to _____ defendants by the government.

CHAPTER SUMMARY

For more information on these concepts, look back to the Learning Objective icons throughout the chapter.

 Define and contrast the four functions of the courts. The four functions are (a) due process, (b) crime control, (c) rehabilitation, and (d) bureaucratic. The most obvious contrast is between the due process and crime control functions. The former is mainly concerned with the procedural rules that allow each accused individual to have a "fair chance" against the government in a criminal proceeding. For crime control, the courts are supposed to impose enough "pain" on convicted criminals to deter criminal behavior. For the rehabilitation function, the courts serve as "doctors" who dispense "treatment." In their bureaucratic function, courts are more concerned with speed and efficiency.

 Define *jurisdiction*, and contrast geographic and subject-matter jurisdiction. Jurisdiction relates to the power of a court to hear a particular case. Courts are typically limited in geographic jurisdiction—for example, to a particular state. Some courts are restricted in subject matter, such as a small claims court, which can hear only cases involving civil matters under a certain monetary limit.

 Explain the difference between trial and appellate courts. Trial courts are courts of the first instance, where a case is first heard. Appellate courts review the proceedings of a lower court. Appellate courts do not have juries.

 Outline the several levels of a typical state court system. (a) At the lowest level are courts of limited jurisdiction, (b) next are trial courts of general jurisdiction, (c) then appellate courts, and (d) finally, the state's highest court.

 Explain briefly how a case is brought to the Supreme Court. Cases decided in U.S. courts of appeals, as well as cases decided in the highest state courts (when federal questions arise), can be appealed to the Supreme Court. If at least four justices approve of a case filed with the Supreme Court, the Court will issue a writ of *certiorari,* ordering the lower court to send the Supreme Court the record of the case for review.

 Explain the difference between the selection of judges at the state level and at the federal level. The president nominates all judges at the federal level, and the Senate must approve the nominations. A similar procedure is used in some states. In other states, all judges are elected on a partisan ballot or on a nonpartisan ballot. Some states use merit selection, or the Missouri Plan, in which a citizen committee nominates judicial candidates, the governor or executive of the state judicial system chooses among the top three nominees, and a year later a "retention election" is held.

 List the different names given to public prosecutors, and indicate the general powers that they have. At the federal level, the prosecutor is called the U.S. attorney. In state and local courts, the prosecutor may be referred to as the prosecuting attorney, state attorney, district attorney, county attorney, or city attorney. Prosecutors in general have the power to decide when and how the state will pursue an individual suspected of criminal wrongdoing. In some jurisdictions, the district attorney is also the chief law enforcement officer, holding broad powers over police operations.

 Explain why defense attorneys must often defend clients they know to be guilty. In our criminal justice system, the most important responsibility of a defense attorney is to be an advocate for her or his client. This means ensuring that the client's constitutional rights are protected during criminal justice proceedings, regardless of whether the client is guilty or innocent.

QUESTIONS FOR CRITICAL ANALYSIS

1. In 2010, authorities in Thailand extradited Russian citizen and alleged international arms dealer Viktor Bout to the United States. The evidence against Bout included an audio recording of a conversation he had with American agents posing as Colombian rebels. During this conversation, Bout agreed to furnish the "revolutionaries" with weapons for the purpose of killing American pilots. How does this evidence give the United States jurisdiction over Bout?

2. Several years ago, the United States Supreme Court "denied cert" in the case of Joel Tenenbaum, who had been ordered to pay a recording company $675,000 in fines for illegally downloading thirty-one songs using a file-sharing Web site. Tenebaum claimed that the fine was excessive and unfair. What does it mean for the Court to "deny cert"? In this instance, what might have been some reasons for the Court's refusal to consider Tenenbaum's case?

3. The United States Supreme Court does not allow its proceedings to be televised. Do you think that doing so would increase or diminish public confidence in the Court? Why or why not?

4. Prosecutors cannot face civil lawsuits for misconduct, even if they have deliberately sent an innocent person to prison. In practical terms, why do you think prosecutors are protected in this manner? Do you agree with a policy of blanket immunity for prosecutors? Explain your answers.

5. Government agencies can charge fees for "free" legal counsel when the fees will not impose a "significant legal hardship" on the defendant. Why might this practice go against the Supreme Court's ruling in *Gideon v. Wainwright* (see page 224)?

KEY TERMS

appellate courts   206
attorney-client privilege   226
attorney general   221
concurrent jurisdiction   207
concurring opinions   214
courtroom work group   219
defense attorney   223
dissenting opinions   214
docket   216

dual court system   207
extradition   205
judicial review   212
jurisdiction   205
magistrate   208
Missouri Plan   217
nonpartisan elections   217
opinions   207
oral arguments   214

partisan elections   217
problem-solving courts   208
public defenders   224
public prosecutors   221
rule of four   213
trial courts   206
writ of *certiorari*   212

SELF-ASSESSMENT ANSWER KEY

Page 204: **i.** due process; **ii.** individuals; **iii.** crime control; **iv.** society; **v.** rehabilitate

Page 208: **i.** jurisdiction; **ii.** subject matter; **iii.** trial; **iv.** appellate; **v.** dual; **vi.** federal; **vii.** state

Page 210: **i.** limited; **ii.** general; **iii.** appeals

Page 214: **i.** district; **ii.** circuit; **iii.** Supreme; **iv.** *certiorari*

Page 219: **i.** president; **ii.** Senate; **iii.** governor; **iv.** partisan; **v.** nonpartisan; **vi.** merit

Page 226: **i.** judge; **ii.** prosecutors; **iii.** private; **iv.** public; **v.** poor/indigent

NOTES

1. Roscoe Pound, "The Administration of Justice in American Cities," *Harvard Law Review* 12 (1912).

2. Russell Wheeler and Howard Whitcomb, *Judicial Administration: Text and Readings* (Englewood Cliffs, N.J.: Prentice Hall, 1977), 3.

3. Larry J. Siegel, *Criminology: Instructor's Manual,* 6th ed. (Belmont, Calif.: West/Wadsworth Publishing Co., 1998), 440.

4. Gerald F. Velman, "Federal Sentencing Guidelines: A Cure Worse Than the Disease," *American Criminal Law Review* 29 (Spring 1992), 904.

5. Maria L. La Ganga, "Tribe Just Says No to Legal Pot," *Los Angeles Times* (December 22, 2013), A1.

6. Pub. L. No. 111-211, 124 Stat. 2258, 2279 (2010).

7. Eli Lake, "Yemen Refuses to Let U.S. Try Cleric," *Washington Times* (May 12, 2010), A1.

8. 18 U.S.C. Section 3231; and *Solorio v. United States,* 483 U.S. 435 (1987).

9. 372 U.S. 335 (1963).

10. 384 U.S. 436 (1966).

11. 408 U.S. 238 (1972).

12. 428 U.S. 153 (1976).

13. 18 U.S.C.A. Section 704.

14. *U.S. v. Alvarez,* 132 S.Ct. 2537 (2012).

15. 18 U.S.C.A. Section 704(a).

16. 559 U.S. 98 (2010).

17. Sherry F. Colb, "The U.S. Supreme Court Considers Anonymous Tips," *Verdict* (October 16, 2013), at **verdict.justia.com/2013 /10/16/u-s-supreme-court-considers -anonymous-tips.**

18. David R. Stras and James F. Spriggs II, "Explaining Plurality Opinions," *Georgetown Law Journal* 99 (March 2010), 519.

19. Barry R. Schaller, *A Vision of American Law: Judging Law, Literature, and the Stories We Tell* (Westport, Conn.: Praeger, 1997).

20. Pub. L. No. 76-299, 53 Stat. 1223, codified as amended at 28 U.S.C. Sections 601–610 (1988 & Supp. V 1993).

21. James E. Lozier, "The Missouri Plan a.k.a. Merit Selection Is the Best Solution for Selecting Michigan's Judges," *Michigan Bar Journal* 75 (September 1996), 918.

22. Ron Malega and Thomas H. Cohen, *State Court Organization, 2011* (Washington, D.C.: U.S. Department of Justice, November 2013), 8.

23. Ciara Torres-Spelliscy, Monique Chase, and Emma Greenman, *Improving Judicial Diversity,* 2d ed. (New York: Brennan Center for Justice, 2010), 1.

24. *Ibid.*

25. Maura Dolan, "Diversity Rises among California Judges," *Los Angeles Times* (February 28, 2013), at **articles.latimes.com/2013 /feb/28/local/la-me-judges-20130301.**

26. Federal Judicial Center, "Diversity on the Bench," at **www.fjc.gov/history/home.nsf /page/judges_diversity.html.**

27. Edward M. Chen, "The Judiciary, Diversity, and Justice for All," *California Law Review* (July 2003), 1109.

28. Theresa B. Beiner, "The Elusive (but Worthwhile) Quest for a Diverse Bench in the New Millennium," *University of California at Davis Law Review* (February 2003), 599.

29. Sherrilyn A. Ifill, "Racial Diversity on the Bench: Beyond Role Models and Public Confidence," *Washington and Lee Law Review* (Spring 2000), 405.

30. Quoted in Scott Stump, "Casey Anthony Judge Felt 'Shock, Disbelief' at Not-Guilty Verdict," *Today.com* (May 6, 2013), at **www .today.com/news/casey-anthony-judge -felt-shock-disbelief-not-guilty-verdict -6C9791042.**

31. 295 U.S. 78 (1935).

32. *Brady v. Maryland,* 373 U.S. 83 (1963).

33. Brendan Kirby, "Judge Overturns 13-Year-Old Capital Murder Conviction of Mobile-Based State Trooper," *AL.com* (September 4, 2013), at **blog.al.com/live /2013/09/judge_overturns_13-year-old _ca.html.**

34. Celesta Albonetti, "Prosecutorial Discretion: The Effects of Uncertainty," *Law and Society Review* 21 (1987), 291–313.

35. Quoted in Dugan Arnett, "Nightmare in Maryville: Teens' Sexual Encounter Ignites a Firestorm against Family," *Kansas City Star* (October 24, 2013), at **www.kansascity .com/2013/10/12/4549775/nightmare -in-maryville-teens-sexual.html.**

36. Quoted in *ibid.*

37. *Ibid.*

38. Stephanie Slifer, "Daisy's Mom Disappointed over Charge in Maryville Case," *CBS News* (January 9, 2014), at **www.cbsnews .com/news/daisys-mom-disappointed -over-charge-in-maryville-case.**

39. Bennett L. Gershman, "Prosecutorial Ethics and Victims' Rights: The Prosecutor's Duty of Neutrality," *Lewis & Clark Law Review* 9 (2005), 561.

40. *Ibid.,* 560–561.

41. Susan Herman, *Parallel Justice for Victims of Crime* (Washington, D.C.: National Center for Victims of Crime, 2010), 89.

42. *Gideon v. Wainwright,* 372 U.S. 335 (1963); *Massiah v. United States,* 377 U.S. 201 (1964); *United States v. Wade,* 388 U.S. 218 (1967); *Argersinger v. Hamlin,* 407 U.S. 25 (1972); and *Brewer v. Williams,* 430 U.S. 387 (1977).

43. Larry Siegel, *Criminology,* 6th ed. (Belmont, Calif.: West/Wadsworth Publishing Co., 1998), 487–488.

44. Center for Professional Responsibility, *Model Rules of Professional Conduct* (Washington, D.C.: American Bar Association, 2003), Rules 1.6 and 3.1.

45. *United States v. Wade,* 388 U.S. 218, 256–258 (1967).

46. 372 U.S. 335 (1963).

47. 387 U.S. 1 (1967).

48. 407 U.S. 25 (1972).

49. Laurence A. Benner, "Eliminating Excessive Public Defender Workloads," *Criminal Justice* (Summer 2011), 25.

50. American Bar Association, "Providing Defense Services," Standard 5-7.1, at **www .abanet.org/crimjust/standards/defsvcs _blk.html#7.1.**

51. Robert C. Boruchowitz, "The Right to Counsel: Every Accused Person's Right," *Washington State Bar Association Bar News* (January 2004), at **www.wsba.org /media/publications/barnews/2004 /jan-04-boruchowitz.htm.**

52. *Wheat v. United States,* 486 U.S. 153, 159 (1988).

53. Bureau of Justice Statistics, *Defense Counsel in Criminal Cases* (Washington, D.C.: U.S. Department of Justice, 2000), 3.

54. James M. Anderson and Paul Heaton, *Measuring the Effect of Defense Counsel on Homicide Case Outcomes: Executive Summary* (Santa Monica, Calif.: RAND Corporation, December 2012), 1.

55. Randolph Braccialarghe, "Why Were Perry Mason's Clients Always Innocent?" *Valparaiso University Law Review* (Fall 2004), 65.

56. John Kaplan, "Defending Guilty People," *University of Bridgeport Law Review* (1986), 223.

57. 491 U.S. 554 (1989).

CHAPTER

8

Pretrial Procedures and the Criminal Trial

To target your study and review, look for these numbered Learning Objective icons throughout the chapter.

Ethan Miller/Getty Images

Standing His
GROUND?

THE ALTERCATION began outside a convenience store in Jacksonville, Florida. Michael Dunn, waiting in his car for his fiancée, told seventeen-year-old Jordan Davis and his three friends to turn down the music blaring from their Dodge Durango. Instead, Davis turned up the volume. The two began to argue and, according to Dunn, Davis said, "This is going down," pointed a shotgun at him, and began to get out of his SUV. In response, Dunn reached into his glove box, removed his 9-millimeter pistol from its holster, loaded the weapon, and began firing. When the SUV drove away, Dunn got out of his car, dropped to one knee, and continued shooting at it. Three of Dunn's ten shots hit Davis, killing the high school senior.

"I had no choice but to defend myself," Dunn testified during his murder trial. "It was life or death." In response, prosecutors presented evidence that Davis was sitting down when he was shot. They also told the jury that no shotgun had been found and highlighted Dunn's actions following the shooting: he drove his fiancée back to their hotel, ate some pizza, walked his dog, and went to bed. If Dunn had really feared for his life, asked prosecutor John Guy, "wouldn't he have called the police" to report the incident?

Under Florida law, a person can use lethal force in self-defense without retreating if he or she reasonably believes that his or her life is in danger. Thus, in this case, the important question was not whether Davis actually pointed a shotgun at Dunn. Rather, it was whether Dunn reasonably believed that the teenager had done so. The jury could not make up its mind on this point, and Dunn was not convicted of killing Davis. The jurors did, however, find Dunn guilty of three counts of attempted murder for shooting at the fleeing SUV, leaving him facing a maximum sixty years in prison.

AP Images/ *The Florida Times-Union*, Bob Mack, Pool

FOR CRITICAL ANALYSIS

1. Do you agree with the outcome of Michael Dunn's trial? Why or why not?

2. Dunn is white, and Jordan Davis was African American. What role, if any, could race have played in the jury's view of Dunn's "reasonable" belief that he needed to use lethal force in self-defense?

3. The jury voted 9–3 to convict Dunn of first degree murder, thus failing to achieve the unanimity required to find him guilty of that charge. What is your opinion of the requirement that a jury be unanimous in deciding the innocence or guilt of most criminal defendants?

Michael Dunn, shown here entering a Jacksonville, Florida, courtroom on February 13, 2014, claimed that he fatally shot seventeen-year-old Jordan Davis outside a convenience store in self defense.

PRETRIAL DETENTION

Initial Appearance An accused's first appearance before a judge or magistrate following arrest.

Bail The dollar amount or conditions set by the court to ensure that an individual accused of a crime will appear for further criminal proceedings.

Because it took place relatively soon after the Florida trial of George Zimmerman—which, as we saw in Chapter 3, also featured the killing of an African American youth and a controversial claim of self-defense—Michael Dunn's trial drew nationwide attention. According to the "wedding cake" model of criminal trials, those who followed the proceedings may have gotten a skewed version of how the criminal justice system works.[1] This model suggests that only the top, and smallest, "layer" of trials comes close to meeting our standards of justice. In high-profile trials such as Dunn's, committed attorneys argue minute technicalities for days, and numerous expert witnesses take the stand for both sides.

On the bottom, largest layer of the wedding cake, the vast majority of defendants are dealt with informally, and the end goal seems to be speed rather than justice. Indeed, as you will learn in this chapter, trial by jury is quite rare. The fate of most criminal suspects in this country is decided during pretrial procedures, which start almost as soon as the police have identified a suspect.

The Initial Appearance

After an arrest has been made, the first step toward determining the suspect's guilt or innocence is the **initial appearance** (for an overview of the entire process, see Figure 8.1 that follows). During this brief proceeding, a magistrate (see Chapter 7) informs the defendant of the charges that have been brought against him or her and explains his or her constitutional rights—particularly, the right to remain silent (under the Fifth Amendment) and the right to be represented by counsel (under the Sixth Amendment). At this point, if the defendant cannot afford to hire a private attorney, a public defender may be appointed, or private counsel may be hired by the state to represent the defendant. As the U.S. Constitution does not specify how soon a defendant must be brought before a magistrate after arrest, it has been left to the judicial branch to determine the timing of the initial appearance. The Supreme Court has held that the initial appearance must occur "promptly," which in most cases means within forty-eight hours of booking.[2]

LEARNING **1** OBJECTIVE Identify the steps involved in the pretrial criminal process.

In misdemeanor cases, a defendant may decide to plead guilty and be sentenced during the initial appearance. Otherwise, the magistrate will usually release those charged with misdemeanors on their promise to return at a later date for further proceedings. For felony cases, however, the defendant is not permitted to make a plea at the initial appearance because a magistrate's court does not have jurisdiction to decide felonies.

Bail

At the initial appearance, in most cases the defendant will be released only if she or he posts **bail**—an amount paid by the defendant to the court and retained by the court until the defendant returns for further proceedings. Defendants who cannot afford bail are generally kept in a local jail or lockup until the date of their trial, though many jurisdictions are searching for alternatives to this practice because of overcrowded incarceration facilities. Just under two-thirds of felony defendants in state courts are released before their trials. Not surprisingly, release is more likely for defendants charged with property crimes than for those charged with violent crimes.[3]

FIGURE 8.1 The Steps Leading to a Trial

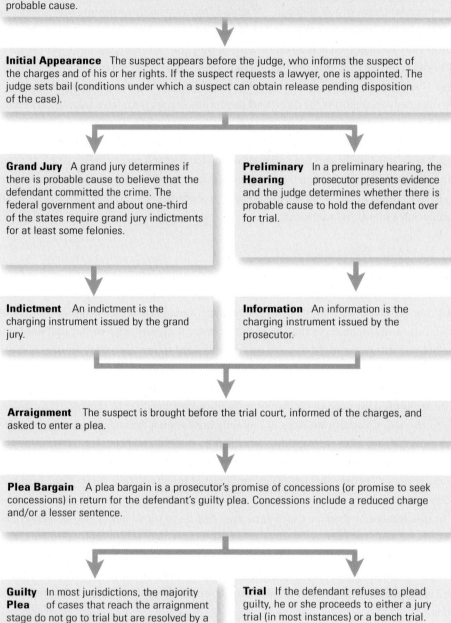

Booking After arrest, at the police station, the suspect is searched, photographed, finger-printed, and allowed at least one telephone call. After the booking, charges are reviewed, and if they are not dropped, a complaint is filed and a judge or magistrate examines the case for probable cause.

Initial Appearance The suspect appears before the judge, who informs the suspect of the charges and of his or her rights. If the suspect requests a lawyer, one is appointed. The judge sets bail (conditions under which a suspect can obtain release pending disposition of the case).

Grand Jury A grand jury determines if there is probable cause to believe that the defendant committed the crime. The federal government and about one-third of the states require grand jury indictments for at least some felonies.

Preliminary Hearing In a preliminary hearing, the prosecutor presents evidence and the judge determines whether there is probable cause to hold the defendant over for trial.

Indictment An indictment is the charging instrument issued by the grand jury.

Information An information is the charging instrument issued by the prosecutor.

Arraignment The suspect is brought before the trial court, informed of the charges, and asked to enter a plea.

Plea Bargain A plea bargain is a prosecutor's promise of concessions (or promise to seek concessions) in return for the defendant's guilty plea. Concessions include a reduced charge and/or a lesser sentence.

Guilty Plea In most jurisdictions, the majority of cases that reach the arraignment stage do not go to trial but are resolved by a guilty plea, often as the result of a plea bargain. The judge sets the case for sentencing.

Trial If the defendant refuses to plead guilty, he or she proceeds to either a jury trial (in most instances) or a bench trial.

THE PURPOSE OF BAIL Bail is provided for under the Eighth Amendment. The amendment does not, however, guarantee the right to bail. Instead, it states that "excessive bail shall not be required." This has come to mean that in all cases except those involving a capital crime (where bail is prohibited), the amount of bail required must be reasonable relative to the seriousness of the wrongdoing. It does *not* mean that the amount of bail must be within the defendant's ability to pay.

SETTING BAIL There is no uniform system for pretrial detention. Each jurisdiction has its own *bail tariffs,* or general guidelines concerning the proper amount of bail. For misdemeanors, the police usually follow a preapproved bail schedule created by local judicial authorities. In felony cases, the primary responsibility to set bail lies with the judge. Figure 8.2 on the right shows typical bail amounts for violent offenses.

Bail guidelines can be quite extensive. In Illinois, for example, a judge is required to take thirty-eight different factors into account when setting bail: fourteen involve the crime itself, two refer to the evidence gathered, four to the defendant's record, nine to the defendant's flight risk and immigration status, and nine to the defendant's general character.[4] For the most part, however, judges are free to use such tariffs as loose guidelines, and they have a great deal of discretion in setting bail according to the circumstances in each case.

PREVENTIVE DETENTION The vagueness of the Eighth Amendment has encouraged judges to use bail to serve another purpose: the protection of the community. That is, if a judge feels that the defendant poses a threat should he or she be released before trial, the judge will set bail at a level the suspect cannot possibly afford. In July 2013, for example, a King County, Washington, district court judge set bail at $2 million for indigent defendant Justin Jasper, accused of planning to firebomb three college campuses in the Seattle area.

Alternatively, more than thirty states and the federal government have passed **preventive detention** legislation to the same effect. These laws allow judges to act "in the best interests of the community" by denying bail to arrestees with prior records of violence, thus keeping them in custody prior to trial.[5] In fact, about 17 percent of released defendants are rearrested before their trials begin, most of them for missing a scheduled court appearance. Only about 8 percent are rearrested for committing a felony while free on bail.[6]

Gaining Pretrial Release

One of the most popular alternatives to bail is **release on recognizance (ROR).** This is used when the judge, based on the advice of trained personnel, decides that the defendant is not at risk to "jump" bail and does not pose a threat to the community. The defendant is then released at no cost with the understanding that he or she will return at the time of the trial. The Vera Institute, a nonprofit organization in New York City, introduced the concept of ROR as part of the Manhattan Bail Project in the 1960s, and such programs are now found in nearly every jurisdiction. When properly administered, ROR programs seem to be successful, with less than 5 percent of the participants failing to show for trial.[7]

POSTING BAIL Those suspected of committing a felony are rarely released on their own recognizance. These defendants may post, or pay, the full amount of the bail in cash to the court. The money will be returned when the suspect appears for trial. Given the large amount of funds required, and the relative lack of wealth of many criminal defendants, a defendant can rarely post bail in cash. Another option is to use real property, such as a house, instead of cash as collateral. These **property bonds** are rare because most

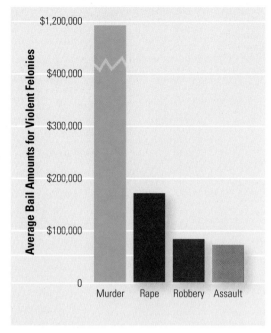

FIGURE 8.2 **Average Bail Amounts for Violent Felonies**

These figures represent the mean bail amounts for the seventy-five largest counties in the nation.

Source: Adapted from Bureau of Justice Statistics, *Felony Defendants in Large Urban Counties, 2009–Statistical Tables* (Washington, D.C.: U.S. Department of Justice, December 2013), Table 16, page 19.

Preventive Detention The retention of an accused person in custody due to fears that she or he will commit a crime if released before trial.

Release on Recognizance (ROR) A judge's order that releases an accused from jail with the understanding that he or she will return of his or her own will for further proceedings.

Property Bond An alternative to posting bail in cash, in which the defendant gains pretrial release by providing the court with property valued at the bail amount as assurance that he or she will return for trial.

courts require property valued at double the bail amount. Thus, if bail is set at $5,000, the defendant (or the defendant's family and friends) will have to produce property valued at $10,000.

BAIL BOND AGENTS If unable to post bail with cash or property, a defendant may arrange for a **bail bond agent** to post a bail bond on the defendant's behalf. The bond agent, in effect, promises the court that he or she will turn over to the court the full amount of bail if the defendant fails to return for further proceedings. The defendant usually must give the bond agent a certain percentage of the bail (frequently 10 percent) in cash. This amount, which is often not returned to the defendant later, is considered payment for the bond agent's assistance and assumption of risk. Depending on the amount of the bail bond, the defendant may also be required to sign over to the bond agent rights to certain property (such as a car, a valuable watch, or other asset) as security for the bond.

///SELF ASSESSMENT

Fill in the blanks, and check your answers on page 266.

During the _____ _____, a magistrate informs the defendant of the charges brought against her or him and explains her or his _____ rights. Following this proceeding, the defendant will be detained until trial unless he or she can post _____, the amount of which is determined by the _____. Even if the defendant can afford to pay this amount, he or she may be kept in jail until trial under a _____ detention statute if the court decides that he or she poses a risk to the community.

ESTABLISHING PROBABLE CAUSE

Once the initial appearance has been completed and bail has been set, the prosecutor must establish *probable cause*. In other words, the prosecutor must show that a crime was committed and link the defendant to that crime. There are two formal procedures for establishing probable cause at this stage of the pretrial process: preliminary hearings and grand juries.

The Preliminary Hearing

During the **preliminary hearing,** the defendant appears before a judge or magistrate who decides whether the evidence presented is sufficient for the case to proceed to trial. Normally, every person arrested has a right to this hearing within a reasonable amount of time after his or her initial arrest—usually, no later than ten days if the defendant is in custody or within thirty days if he or she has gained pretrial release.

THE PRELIMINARY HEARING PROCESS The preliminary hearing is conducted in the manner of a mini-trial. Typically, a police report of the arrest is presented by a law enforcement officer, supplemented with evidence provided by the prosecutor. Because the burden of proving probable cause is relatively light (compared with proving guilt beyond a reasonable doubt), prosecutors rarely call witnesses during the preliminary hearing, saving them for the trial.

During this hearing, the defendant has a right to be represented by counsel, who may cross-examine witnesses and challenge any evidence offered by the prosecutor. In most states, defense attorneys can take advantage of the preliminary hearing to begin the process of **discovery,** in which they are entitled to have access to any evidence in the possession of the prosecution relating to the case. Discovery is considered a keystone in the adversarial process, as it allows the defense to see the evidence against the defendant prior to making a plea.

WAIVING THE HEARING The preliminary hearing often seems rather perfunctory. It usually lasts no longer than five minutes, and the judge or magistrate rarely finds that the prosecutor has not met the burden of showing probable cause that the defendant committed a crime. For this reason, defense attorneys commonly advise their clients to waive their right to a preliminary hearing. Once a judge has ruled affirmatively, in many jurisdictions the defendant is bound over to the **grand jury,** a group of citizens called to decide whether probable cause exists. In other jurisdictions, the prosecutor issues an **information,** which replaces the police complaint as the formal charge against the defendant for the purposes of a trial.

The Grand Jury

The federal government and about one-third of the states require a grand jury to make the decision as to whether a case should go to trial. Grand juries are *impaneled,* or created, for a period of time usually not exceeding three months. During that time, the grand jury sits in closed (secret) session and hears only evidence presented by the prosecutor—the defendant cannot present evidence at this hearing. The prosecutor presents to the grand jury whatever evidence the state has against the defendant, including photographs, documents, tangible objects, the testimony of witnesses, and other items.

If the grand jury finds that probable cause exists, it issues an **indictment** (pronounced in-*dyte*-ment) against the defendant. Like an information in a preliminary hearing, the indictment becomes the formal charge against the defendant. Some states require a grand jury to indict for certain crimes, while in other states a grand jury indictment is optional.

Discovery Formal investigation of evidence by each side prior to trial.

Grand Jury The group of citizens called to decide whether probable cause exists to believe that a suspect committed the crime with which she or he has been charged.

Information The formal charge against the accused issued by the prosecutor after a preliminary hearing has found probable cause.

Indictment A charge or written accusation, issued by a grand jury, that probable cause exists to believe that a named person has committed a crime.

LEARNING OBJECTIVE **2** Identify the main difference between an indictment and an information.

AP Images/*The Missoulian,* Michael Gallacher

In 2013, a federal grand jury indicted Jordan Linn Graham, center, on murder charges for pushing her husband off a cliff to his death in Montana's Glacier National Park. Practically, why does the prosecution hold a major advantage during grand jury proceedings?

Fill in the blanks, and check your answers on page 266.

If a case is to proceed to trial, the prosecutor must establish _____ _____ that the defendant committed the crime in question. One way of doing this involves a _____ hearing, in which a judge or magistrate rules whether the prosecutor has met this burden. In the other method, the decision rests with a group of citizens called a _____ _____, who will hand down an _____ if they believe the evidence is sufficient to support the charges.

THE PROSECUTORIAL SCREENING PROCESS

Some see the high government success rates in pretrial proceedings as proof that prosecutors successfully screen out weak cases before they get to a grand jury or preliminary hearing. Others, however, point out that procedural rules at this stage favor the prosecution and that grand juries rarely, if ever, fail to indict defendants set before them. That being the case, what is to keep prosecutors from using their charging powers indiscriminately? Nothing, say many observers. Once the police have initially charged a defendant with committing a crime, the prosecutor can prosecute the case as it stands, reduce or increase the initial charge, file additional charges, or dismiss the case.

In a system of government and law that relies on checks and balances, asked legal expert Kenneth Culp Davis, why should the prosecutor be "immune to review by other officials and immune to review by the courts?"[8] Though American prosecutors have far-ranging discretionary charging powers, it is not entirely correct to say that they are unrestricted. Controls are indirect and informal, but they do exist.

Case Attrition

Prosecutorial discretion includes the power *not* to prosecute cases. Figure 8.3 that follows depicts the average outcomes of one hundred felony arrests in the United States. As you can see, of the sixty-five adult arrestees brought before the district attorney, only thirty-five are prosecuted, and only eighteen of these prosecutions lead to incarceration. Consequently, fewer than one in three adults arrested for a felony sees the inside of a prison or jail cell. This phenomenon is known as **case attrition,** and it is explained in part by prosecutorial discretion.

About half of those adult felony cases brought to prosecutors by police are dismissed through a *nolle prosequi* (Latin for "unwilling to pursue"). Why are these cases "nolled," or not prosecuted by the district attorney? In the section on law enforcement, you learned that the police do not have the resources to arrest every lawbreaker in the nation. Similarly, district attorneys do not have the means to prosecute every arrest. They must choose how to distribute their scarce resources.

In some cases, the decision is made for prosecutors, such as when police break procedural law and negate important evidence. This happens rarely—less than 1 percent of felony arrests are dropped because of the exclusionary rule, and almost all of these are the result of illegal drug searches.[9]

Screening Factors

Most prosecutors have a *screening* process for deciding when to prosecute and when to "noll." This process varies a bit from jurisdiction to jurisdiction, but prosecutors consider several factors in making the decision:[10]

Case Attrition The process through which prosecutors, by deciding whether to prosecute each person arrested, effect an overall reduction in the number of persons prosecuted.

FIGURE 8.3 **Following One Hundred Felony Arrests: The Criminal Justice Funnel**

100 people arrested

35 juveniles go to juvenile court

65 adults considered for prosecution

30 put on probation or dismissed

35 cases accepted for prosecution

30 cases dropped

5 jump bail

30 cases go to trial

3 acquitted

23 plead guilty

4 found guilty

27 sentenced

9 placed on probation

Incarcerated: 18 adults 5 juveniles

Source: Adapted from Todd R. Clear, George F. Cole, and Michael D. Reisig, *American Corrections,* 9th ed. (Belmont, CA: Wadsworth, 2011), 134.

1. The most important factor in deciding whether to prosecute is not the prosecutor's belief in the guilt of the suspect, but whether there is *sufficient evidence for conviction.* If prosecutors have strong physical evidence and a number of reliable and believable witnesses, they are quite likely to prosecute.

2. Prosecutors also rely heavily on *offense seriousness* to guide their priorities, preferring to take on felony offenses rather than misdemeanors. In other words, everything else being equal, a district attorney will prosecute a rapist instead of a jaywalker because the former presents a greater threat to society than does the latter. A prosecutor will also be more likely to prosecute someone with an extensive record of wrongdoing than a first-time offender.

3. Sometimes a case is dropped even when it involves a serious crime and a wealth of evidence exists against the suspect. These situations usually involve *uncooperative victims.* As you saw in the previous chapter, domestic violence cases are particularly difficult to prosecute because the victims may want to keep the matter private, fear reprisals, or have a strong desire to protect their abuser.

4. *Unreliability of victims* can also affect a charging decision. If the victim in a rape case is a crack addict and a prostitute, while the defendant is a decorated military veteran, prosecutors may be hesitant to have a jury decide which one is more trustworthy.

 LEARNING **3** OBJECTIVE

Explain how a prosecutor screens potential cases.

5. A prosecutor may be willing to drop a case or reduce the charges against *a defendant who is willing to testify against other offenders.* Federal law encourages this kind of behavior by offering sentencing reductions to defendants who provide "substantial assistance in the investigation or prosecution of another person who has committed an offense."[11]

Often, prosecutors are motivated by a sense of doing "the right thing" for their community. This can lead them to establish *case priorities* concerning certain types of crime. In Middlesex County, Massachusetts, for example, the district attorney's office conducts "dangerousness hearings" to determine whether domestic violence offenders pose a risk of murdering their abused partners. If so, the offender can be held without bail until trial.[12] (To get a better idea of the difficulty of making the charging decision, see the feature *Discretion in Action—A Battered Woman* that follows.)

///// SELF ASSESSMENT

Fill in the blanks, and check your answers on page 266.

On average, of sixty-five adult arrestees, a district attorney will prosecute only thirty-five. This process, which is known as case _____, requires that the prosecutor _____ all potential cases and dismiss the ones where the likelihood of _____ is weakest. The most important factor in this decision is whether there is sufficient _____ to find the defendant guilty.

DISCRETION in Action

A BATTERED WOMAN

THE SITUATION For more than twenty years, John regularly beat his wife, Judy. He even put out cigarettes on her skin and slashed her face with glass. John was often unemployed and forced Judy into prostitution to earn a living. He regularly denied her food and threatened to maim or kill her. Judy left home several times, but John always managed to find her, bring her home, and punish her. Finally, Judy took steps to get John put in a psychiatric hospital. He told her that if anybody came for him, he would "see them coming" and cut her throat before they arrived. That night, Judy shot John three times in the back of the head while he was asleep, killing him. You are the prosecutor with authority over Judy.

THE LAW In your jurisdiction, a person can use deadly force in self-defense if it is necessary to kill an unlawful aggressor to save himself or herself from imminent death. (See pages 91–92 for a review of self-defense.) Voluntary manslaughter is the intentional killing of another human being without malice. It covers crimes of passion. First degree murder is premeditated killing, with malice. (See pages 81–83 for a review of the different degrees of murder.)

WHAT WOULD YOU DO? Will you charge Judy with voluntary manslaughter or first degree murder? Alternatively, do you believe she was acting in self-defense, in which case you will not charge her with any crime? Explain your choice.

To see how a Rutherford County, North Carolina, prosecutor decided a case with similar facts, go to Example 8.1 in Appendix B.

PLEADING GUILTY

Based on the information (delivered during the preliminary hearing) or indictment (handed down by the grand jury), the prosecutor submits a motion to the court to order the defendant to appear before the trial court for an **arraignment.** Due process of law, as guaranteed by the Fifth Amendment, requires that a criminal defendant be informed of the charges brought against her or him and be offered an opportunity to respond to those charges. The arraignment is one of the ways in which due process requirements are satisfied by criminal procedure law.

At the arraignment, the defendant is informed of the charges and must respond by pleading not guilty or guilty. In some but not all states, the defendant may also enter a plea of *nolo contendere,* which is Latin for "I will not contest it." The plea of *nolo contendere* is neither an admission nor a denial of guilt. (The consequences for someone who pleads guilty and for someone who pleads *nolo contendere* are the same in a criminal trial, but the latter plea cannot be used in a subsequent civil trial as an admission of guilt.) Most frequently, the defendant pleads guilty to the initial charge or to a lesser charge that has been agreed on through *plea bargaining* between the prosecutor and the defendant. If the defendant pleads guilty, no trial is necessary, and the defendant is sentenced based on the crime he or she has admitted to committing.

Plea Bargaining in the Criminal Justice System

Plea bargaining most often takes place after the arraignment and before the beginning of the trial. In its simplest terms, it is a process by which the accused, represented by the defense counsel, and the prosecutor work out a mutually satisfactory disposition of the case, subject to court approval.

Usually, plea bargaining involves the defendant's pleading guilty to the charges against her or him in return for a lighter sentence, but other variations are possible as well. The defendant can agree to plead guilty in exchange for having the charge against her or him reduced from, say, felony burglary to the lesser offense of breaking and entering. Or a person charged with multiple counts may agree to plead guilty if the prosecutor agrees to drop one or more of the counts. Whatever the particulars, the results of a plea bargain are generally the same: the prosecutor gets a conviction, and the defendant gets a lesser punishment.

In *Santobello v. New York* (1971),[13] the Supreme Court held that plea bargaining "is not only an essential part of the process but a highly desirable part for many reasons." Some observers would agree, but with ambivalence. They understand that plea bargaining offers the practical benefit of saving court resources but question whether it is the best way to achieve justice.[14]

Motivations for Plea Bargaining

Sometimes, it is difficult to perceive criminal court proceedings as anything other than a sort of a contest in which the prosecution and the defense treat each other as adversaries, with a verdict of guilty or not guilty as the "prize" to be won at the conclusion. In many instances, this adversarial system begins in earnest when the two sides try to work out a plea bargain. Given the high rate of plea bargaining—accounting for 97 percent of criminal convictions in state courts[15]—it follows that the prosecutor, defense attorney, and defendant each have strong reasons to engage in the practice.

LEARNING OBJECTIVE **4** Indicate why prosecutors, defense attorneys, and defendants often agree to plea bargains.

PROSECUTORS AND PLEA BARGAINING In most cases, a prosecutor has a single goal after charging a defendant with a crime: conviction. If a case goes to trial, no matter how certain a prosecutor may be that the defendant is guilty, there is always a chance that a jury or judge will disagree. Plea bargaining removes this risk. Furthermore, the prosecutorial screening process described earlier in the chapter is not infallible. Sometimes, a prosecutor will find that the evidence against the accused is weaker than first thought or will uncover new information that changes the complexion of the case. In these situations, the prosecutor may decide to drop the charges or, if he or she still feels that the defendant is guilty, turn to plea bargaining to "save" a questionable case.

The prosecutor's role as an administrator also comes into play. She or he may be interested in the quickest, most efficient manner to dispose of caseloads, and plea bargains reduce the time and money spent on each case. Personal philosophy can affect the proceedings as well. A prosecutor who feels that a mandatory minimum sentence for a particular crime, such as marijuana possession, is too strict may plea bargain in order to lessen the penalty. Similarly, some prosecutors will consider plea bargaining only in certain instances—for burglary and theft, for example, but not for more serious felonies such as rape and murder.

DEFENSE ATTORNEYS AND PLEA BARGAINING Political scientist Milton Heumann has said that the most important lesson a defense attorney learns is that "most of his [or her] clients are guilty."[16] Given this stark reality, favorable plea bargains are often the best a defense attorney can do for clients, aside from helping them to gain acquittals. Some have suggested that defense attorneys have other, less savory motives for convincing a client to plead guilty, such as a desire to increase profit margins by quickly disposing of cases[17] or a wish to ingratiate themselves with the other members of the courtroom work group by showing their "reasonableness."[18]

DEFENDANTS AND PLEA BARGAINING The plea bargain allows the defendant a measure of control over his or her fate. In July 2013, for example, Ariel Castro pleaded guilty to kidnapping, raping, and imprisoning three women for a decade in his Cleveland home (see photo alongside). Had his case gone to trial, Castro risked being convicted of attempted murder—for causing a miscarriage by one his victims—and sentenced to death. Under the terms of his plea agreement, Castro would have spent the rest of his life in prison. (Instead, Castro committed suicide in his jail cell not long after being sentenced.) As Figure 8.4 that follows shows, defendants who plea bargain receive significantly lighter sentences on average than those who are found guilty at trial.

PROTECTING THE DEFENDANT Often, the defendant plays only a minor role in the plea bargaining process, which is dominated by a give-and-take between the prosecutor and the defense attorney. The Supreme Court is aware of the potential for coercion in the process and has taken steps to protect the accused. Until *Boykin v. Alabama* (1969),[19] judges would often accept the defense counsel's word that the defendant wanted to plead guilty. In that case, the Court held that the defendant must make a clear statement that he or she

■ Why did Ariel Castro agree to plead guilty to multiple charges stemming from his kidnapping of three women in Cleveland, Ohio? What incentives might Cuyahoga County prosecutors have had for accepting Castro's guilty plea and declining to seek his execution?

Angelo Merendino/Getty Images

FIGURE 8.4 Sentencing Outcomes for Guilty Pleas

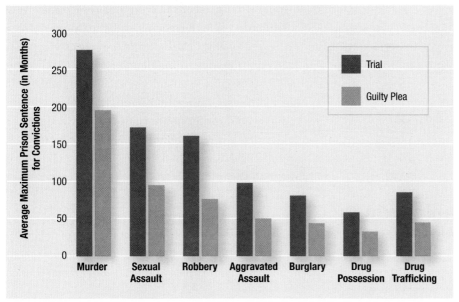

Source: Bureau of Justice Statistics, *Felony Sentences in State Courts, 2006—Statistical Tables* (Washington, D.C.: U.S. Department of Justice, December 2009), Table 4.3.

accepts the plea bargain. As a result, many jurisdictions now ask the accused to sign a *Boykin* **form** waiving his or her right to a trial.

Faulty Advice In 2012, the Supreme Court dramatically affected plea bargaining by ruling that defendants have a constitutional right to effective representation during plea negotiations.[20] That year, the Court considered the plight of Anthony Cooper, who had shot a woman in Detroit. Based on faulty legal advice from his attorney, Cooper rejected a plea bargain that called for a sentence of four to seven years behind bars. Instead, he lost at trial and was sentenced to fifteen to thirty years. After hearing Cooper's appeal, the Court found that, in essence, defendants have a constitutional right to effective counsel during plea bargaining, just as they do during a trial.

A Second Chance to Plead Because of the Supreme Court's ruling, defendants like Cooper now have the opportunity to argue that had they received proper legal advice, they would have accepted the plea bargain rather than risk a trial. If a defendant successfully proves ineffective counsel during plea bargaining, he or she will be given another chance to make a favorable plea.[21]

The four members of the Court who dissented from this decision warned that it would give defendants who lose at trial an unfair opportunity to revisit a rejected plea bargain. "It's going to be tricky," agreed Stephanos Bibas, a law professor at the University of Pennsylvania. "There are going to be a lot of defendants who say after they're convicted that they really would have taken the plea."[22]

Victims and Plea Bargaining

One of the major goals of the victims' rights movement has been to increase the role of victims in the plea bargaining process. In recent years, the movement has had some success in this area. About half of the states now allow for victim participation in plea

Boykin **Form** A form that must be completed by a defendant who pleads guilty. The defendant states that she or he has done so voluntarily and with full comprehension of the consequences.

bargaining. Many have laws similar to North Carolina's statute that requires the district attorney's office to offer victims "the opportunity to consult with the prosecuting attorney" and give their views on "plea possibilities."[23] On the federal level, the Crime Victims' Rights Act grants victims the right to be "reasonably heard" during the process.[24]

Crime victims often have mixed emotions regarding plea bargains. On the one hand, any form of "negotiated justice" that lessens the offender's penalty may add insult to the victim's emotional and physical injuries. On the other hand, trials can bring up events and emotions that some victims would rather not have to re-experience. After Ariel Castro's plea bargain—discussed earlier—was announced, an attorney for Castro's three victims said that his clients were "relieved" and "looking forward to having these legal proceedings draw to a final close in the near future."[25]

Pleading Not Guilty

Despite the large number of defendants who eventually plead guilty, the plea of not guilty is fairly common at the arraignment. This is true even when the facts of the case seem stacked against the defendant. Generally, a not guilty plea in the face of strong evidence is part of a strategy to

1. Gain a more favorable plea bargain,
2. Challenge a crucial part of the evidence on constitutional grounds, or
3. Submit one of the affirmative defenses that we discussed in Chapter 3.

Of course, if either side is confident in the strength of its arguments and evidence, it will obviously be less likely to accept a plea bargain. Both prosecutors and defense attorneys may favor a trial to gain publicity, and sometimes public pressure after an extremely violent or high-profile crime will force a chief prosecutor (who is, remember, normally an elected official) to take a weak case to trial. Also, some defendants may insist on their right to a trial, regardless of their attorneys' advice. In the remainder of this chapter, we will examine what happens to the roughly 3 percent of indictments that do lead to the courtroom.

//// SELF ASSESSMENT

Fill in the blanks, and check your answers on page 266.

A _____ _____ occurs when the prosecution and the defense work out an agreement that resolves the case. Generally, a defendant will plead guilty in exchange for a reduction of the _____ against him or her or a lighter _____, or both. To ensure that the defendant understands the terms of the plea, he or she must sign a _____ form waiving his or her right to a _____.

SPECIAL FEATURES OF CRIMINAL TRIALS

Criminal trial procedures reflect the need to protect criminal defendants against the power of the state by providing them with a number of rights. Many of the most significant rights of the accused are spelled out in the Sixth Amendment, which reads, in part, as follows:

> In all criminal prosecutions, the accused shall enjoy the right to a speedy and public trial, by an impartial jury of the State and the district wherein the crime

shall have been committed, . . . and to be informed of the nature and cause of the accusation; to be confronted with the witnesses against him; to have compulsory process for obtaining witnesses in his favor; and to have the Assistance of Counsel for his defense.

In the last chapter, we discussed the Sixth Amendment's guarantee of the right to counsel. In this section, we start our discussion of the criminal trial by focusing on two protections explicitly guaranteed by the Amendment: the right to a speedy trial by an impartial jury.

A "Speedy" Trial

As you have just read, the Sixth Amendment requires a speedy trial for those accused of a criminal act. The reason for this requirement is obvious: depending on various factors, the defendant may lose his or her right to move freely and may be incarcerated prior to trial. Also, the accusation that a person has committed a crime jeopardizes that person's reputation in the community. If the defendant is innocent, the sooner the trial is held, the sooner his or her innocence can be established in the eyes of the court and the public.

THE DEFINITION OF A SPEEDY TRIAL The Sixth Amendment does not specify what is meant by the term *speedy*. The United States Supreme Court has refused to quantify "speedy" as well, ruling instead in *Barker v. Wingo* (1972)[26] that only in situations in which the delay is unwarranted and proved to be prejudicial can the accused claim a violation of Sixth Amendment rights.

SPEEDY-TRIAL LAWS To meet constitutional requirements, all fifty states have their own speedy-trial statutes. For example, the Illinois Speedy Trial Act holds that a defendant must be tried within 120 days of arrest unless both the prosecution and the defense agree otherwise.[27] Keep in mind, however, that a defendant does not automatically go free if her or his trial is not "speedy" enough. There must be judicial action, which is rare but does occur from time to time. Several years ago, for example, Ernest Burnett spent 106 days in the Schenectady County, New York, jail—sixteen days more than allowed under state law—without prosecutors starting his trial process. As a result of this oversight, a county judge was forced to release Burnett, who had been arrested for kidnapping and trying to kill an ex-girlfriend.

Nearly half of all criminal trials in state courts are settled within three months of the defendant's arrest. About 15 percent take more than a year to adjudicate.[28] At the national level, the Speedy Trial Act of 1974[29] specifies the following time limits for those in the federal court system:

1. No more than thirty days between arrest and indictment.
2. No more than ten days between indictment and arraignment.
3. No more than sixty days between arraignment and trial.

Both federal and state law allow extra time for hearings on pretrial motions, mental competency examinations, and other procedural actions. This extra time can be considerable, particularly when it comes to high-profile trials. For example, in the case that opened this chapter, Michael Dunn's murder trial started fourteen months after he shot Jordan Davis.

STATUTES OF LIMITATIONS The Sixth Amendment's guarantee of a speedy trial does not apply until a person has been accused of a crime. Citizens are protected against unreasonable delays *before* accusation by **statutes of limitations,** which are legislative time limits that require prosecutors to charge a defendant with a crime within a certain amount of time after the illegal act took place. If the statute of limitations on a particular crime is ten years, and the police do not identify a suspect until ten years and one day after the criminal act occurred, then that suspect cannot be charged with that particular offense.

In general, prosecutions for murder and other offenses that carry the death penalty do not have a statute of limitations. This exception provides police with the ability to conduct cold case investigations that last for decades. In 2014, for example, because of a "cold hit" (a DNA-matching process described in Chapter 5), Georgia authorities arrested Lonzo Guthrie for the murder of Eileen Ferro in Shrewsbury, Massachusetts, forty years earlier. The problem with prosecuting such cases, of course, is that so much time has passed since the criminal act that witnesses may be missing or dead, memories may be unreliable, and other evidence may have been lost.

The Role of the Jury

The Sixth Amendment also states that anyone accused of a crime shall be judged by "an impartial jury." In *Duncan v. Louisiana* (1968),[30] the Supreme Court solidified this right by ruling that in all felony cases, the defendant is entitled to a **jury trial.** The Court has, however, left it to the individual states to decide whether juries are required for misdemeanor cases.[31] If the defendant waives her or his right to trial by jury, a **bench trial** takes place in which a judge decides questions of legality and fact, and no jury is involved.

The typical American jury consists of twelve persons. About a dozen states do, under varying circumstances, allow for juries with fewer than twelve members for felony cases. In federal courts, defendants are entitled to have the case heard by a twelve-member jury unless both parties agree in writing to a smaller jury.

In most jurisdictions, jury verdicts in criminal cases must be *unanimous* for **acquittal** or conviction. As will be explained in more detail later, if the jury cannot reach unanimous agreement on whether to acquit or convict the defendant, the result is a *hung jury,* and the judge may order a new trial. The Supreme Court has held that unanimity is not a rigid requirement. It declared that jury verdicts must be unanimous in federal criminal trials but has given states leeway to set their own rules.[32] As a result, Louisiana and Oregon continue to require only ten votes for conviction in criminal cases.

The Privilege against Self-Incrimination

In addition to the Sixth Amendment, which specifies the protections we have just discussed, the Fifth Amendment to the Constitution also provides important safeguards for the defendant. The Fifth Amendment states that no person "shall be compelled in any criminal case to be a witness against himself." Therefore, a defendant has the right not to testify at his or her own trial—in popular parlance, to "take the Fifth." Because defense attorneys often are wary of exposing their clients to prosecutor's questions in court, defendants rarely take the witness stand.

Explain what "taking the Fifth" really means.
LEARNING **5** OBJECTIVE

PREJUDICING THE JURY It is important to note that not only does the defendant have the right to "take the Fifth," but also that the decision to do so should not prejudice the jury in the prosecution's favor. The Supreme Court came to this controversial decision while reviewing *Adamson v. California* (1947),[33] a case involving the convictions of two defendants who had declined to testify in their own defense against charges of robbery, kidnapping, and murder. The prosecutor in the *Adamson* proceedings frequently and insistently brought this silence to the notice of the jury in his closing argument, insinuating that if the pair had been innocent, they would not have been afraid to testify.

The Court ruled that such tactics effectively invalidated the Fifth Amendment by using the defendants' refusal to testify against them. Now judges are required to inform the jury that an accused's decision to remain silent cannot be held against him or her. This protection only covers post-arrest and trial silence, however. In 2013, the Supreme Court ruled that prosecutors can inform a jury that a defendant refused to answer police questions *before* being arrested, a process detailed in Chapter 6.[34]

WITNESSES IN COURT Witnesses are also protected by the Fifth Amendment and may refuse to testify on the ground that such testimony would reveal their own criminal wrongdoing. In practice, such refusals are rare, as witnesses are often granted *immunity* before testifying, meaning that no information they disclose can be used to bring criminal charges against them. Witnesses who have been granted immunity cannot refuse to answer questions in court on the basis of self-incrimination.

During the 2013 trial of alleged mob boss Whitey Bulger, shown here being transported to a Boston courthouse, several criminal associates provided testimony regarding Bulger's illegal activity. Why is it necessary that such witnesses be granted immunity before testifying?

The Presumption of a Defendant's Innocence

The presumption in criminal law is that a defendant is innocent until proved guilty. The burden of proving guilt falls on the state (the public prosecutor). Even if a defendant did in fact commit the crime, she or he will be "innocent" in the eyes of the law unless the prosecutor can substantiate the charge with sufficient evidence to convince a jury (or judge in a bench trial) of the defendant's guilt.[35]

Sometimes, especially when a case involves a high-profile violent crime, pretrial publicity may have convinced many members of the community—including potential jurors—that a defendant is guilty. In these instances, a judge has the authority to change the location of the trial to increase the likelihood of an unbiased jury. In 2014, defense attorneys for Andre Sharpless requested a *change of venue* for their client's murder trial after an article concerning the case appeared in the local newspaper. A judge agreed that the article would influence potential jurors and moved the trial from Wilmington, North Carolina, to Jacksonville, North Carolina, a different media market sixty miles to the north.

A Strict Standard of Proof

In a criminal trial, the defendant is not required to prove his or her innocence. As mentioned earlier, the burden of proving the defendant's guilt lies entirely with the state. Furthermore, the state must prove the defendant's guilt *beyond a reasonable doubt*. In other words, the prosecution must show that, based on all the evidence, the defendant's guilt is clear and unquestionable. In *In re Winship* (1970),[36] a case involving the due process rights

Master Jury List The list of citizens in a court's district from which a jury can be selected; compiled from voter-registration lists, driver's license lists, and other sources.

Venire The group of citizens from which the jury is selected.

of juveniles, the Supreme Court ruled that the Constitution requires the reasonable doubt standard because it reduces the risk of convicting innocent people and therefore reassures Americans of the law's moral force and legitimacy.

This high standard of proof in criminal cases reflects a fundamental social value— the belief that it is worse to convict an innocent individual than to let a guilty one go free. The consequences to the life, liberty, and reputation of an accused person from an erroneous conviction for a crime are substantial, and this has been factored into the process. Placing a high standard of proof on the prosecutor reduces the margin of error in criminal cases (at least in one direction).

//// SELF ASSESSMENT

Fill in the blanks, and check your answers on page 266.

The defendant in any felony case is entitled to a trial by _____. If the defendant waives this right, a _____ trial takes place, in which the _____ decides questions of law and fact. Another benefit for the defendant is the privilege against _____-_____, which gives her or him the right to "take the Fifth." Perhaps the most important protection for the defendant, however, is the presumption in criminal law that she or he is _____ until proved _____. Thus, the burden is on the _____ to prove the defendant's culpability beyond a _____ _____.

JURY SELECTION

The initial step in a criminal trial involves choosing the jury. The main goal of jury selection is to produce a representative cross section of the population of the jurisdiction where the crime was committed. Besides having to live in the jurisdiction where the case is being tried, there are very few restrictions on eligibility to serve on a jury. State legislatures generally set the requirements, and they are similar in most states. For the most part, jurors must be

1. Citizens of the United States.
2. Eighteen years of age or over.
3. Free of felony convictions.
4. Healthy enough to function in a jury setting.
5. Sufficiently intelligent to understand the issues of a trial.
6. Able to read, write, and comprehend the English language (with one exception— New Mexico does not allow non-English-speaking citizens to be eliminated from jury lists simply because of their lack of English-language skills).

The **master jury list,** sometimes called the *jury pool,* is made up of all the eligible jurors in a community. This list is usually drawn from voter-registration lists or driver's license rolls, which have the benefit of being easily available and timely.

The next step in gathering a jury is to draw together the **venire** (Latin for "to come"). The *venire* is composed of all those people who are notified by the clerk of the court that they have been selected for jury duty. Those selected to be part of the *venire* are ordered to report to the courthouse on the date specified by the notice.

Voir Dire

At the courthouse, prospective jurors are gathered, and the process of selecting those who will actually hear the case begins. This selection process is not haphazard. The court ultimately seeks jurors who are free of any biases that may affect their willingness to listen to the facts of the case impartially. To this end, both the prosecutor and the defense attorney have some input into the ultimate makeup of the jury. Each attorney questions prospective jurors in a proceeding known as *voir dire* (French for "to speak the truth"). During *voir dire,* jurors are required to provide the court with a significant amount of personal information, including home address, marital status, employment status, arrest record, and life experiences.

QUESTIONING POTENTIAL JURORS The *voir dire* process involves both written and oral questioning of potential jurors. Attorneys fashion their inquiries in such a manner as to uncover any biases on the parts of prospective jurors and to find persons who might identify with the plights of their respective sides. As one attorney noted, though a lawyer will have many chances to talk to a jury as a whole, *voir dire* is his or her only chance to talk with the individual jurors. (To better understand the specific kinds of questions asked during this process, see Figure 8.5 that follows.) Increasingly, attorneys are also conducting virtual *voir dire* on the Internet, using social networking sites such as Facebook to learn valuable information about potential jurors.

CHALLENGING POTENTIAL JURORS During *voir dire,* the attorney for each side may exercise a certain number of challenges to prevent particular persons from serving on the jury. Both sides can exercise two types of challenges: challenges "for cause" and peremptory challenges.

Challenges for Cause If a defense attorney or prosecutor concludes that a prospective juror is unfit to serve, the attorney may exercise a **challenge for cause** and request that that person not be included on the jury. Attorneys must provide the court with a sound, legally justifiable reason for why potential jurors are "unfit" to serve. For example, jurors can be challenged for cause if they are mentally incompetent, do not understand English, or are proved to have a prior link—be it personal or financial—with the defendant or victim.

Peremptory Challenges Each attorney may also exercise a limited number of **peremptory challenges.** These challenges are based solely on an attorney's subjective reasoning,

Voir Dire The preliminary questions that the trial attorneys ask prospective jurors to determine whether they are biased or have any connection with the defendant or a witness.

Challenge for Cause A *voir dire* challenge for which an attorney states the reason why a prospective juror should not be included on the jury.

Peremptory Challenges *Voir dire* challenges to exclude potential jurors from serving on the jury without any supporting reason or cause.

A Boston jury waits to be dismissed after finding Christian K. Gerhartsreiter guilty of kidnapping his seven-year-old daughter during a supervised visit. Why is it important for a defendant to be tried by a jury of her or his "peers"?

AP Images/CJ Gunther, Pool

FIGURE 8.5 *Sample Juror Questionnaire*

In 2013, former Detroit Mayor Kwame Kilpatrick went on trial for committing numerous corruption-related crimes such as bribery and mail fraud while in office. Kilpatrick, who is African American, claimed that he was being unfairly prosecuted because of his race, and that he had acted with the goal of helping minority businesses in the city. Consequently, as the following excerpt from the juror questionnaire shows, both the prosecution and the defense were interested in potential jurors' views on race.

66. Do you think minorities are generally treated unfairly by the government?
67. What role, if any, do you think race plays in the criminal justice system?
68. Do you think African American defendants are punished more harshly than white defendants in the criminal justice system?
71. Do you believe that African Americans are more likely to commit crimes than whites?

LEARNING OBJECTIVE 6
Contrast challenges for cause and peremptory challenges during *voir dire*.

and the attorney usually is not required to give any legally justifiable reason for wanting to exclude a particular person from the jury. Because of the rather random nature of peremptory challenges, each state limits the number that an attorney may utilize: between five and ten for felony trials (depending on the state) and between ten and twenty for trials that could possibly result in the death penalty (also depending on the state). Once an attorney's peremptory challenges are used up, he or she must accept forthcoming jurors, unless a challenge for cause can be used.

Race and Gender Issues in Jury Selection

For many years, prosecutors used their peremptory challenges as an instrument of segregation in jury selection. Prosecutors were able to keep African Americans off juries in cases in which an African American was the defendant. The argument that African Americans—or members of any other minority group—would be partial toward one of their own was tacitly supported by the Supreme Court. Despite its own assertion, made in *Swain v. Alabama* (1965),[37] that blacks have the same right to appear on a jury as whites, the Court mirrored the apparent racism of society as a whole by protecting the questionable actions of many prosecutors.

THE *BATSON* REVERSAL The Supreme Court reversed this policy in 1986 with *Batson v. Kentucky*.[38] In that case, the Court declared that the Constitution prohibits prosecutors from using peremptory challenges to strike possible jurors on the basis of race. Under the *Batson* ruling, the defendant must prove that the prosecution's use of a peremptory challenge was racially motivated. Doing so requires a number of legal steps:[39]

1. First, the defendant must make a *prima facie* case that there has been discrimination during *venire*. (*Prima facie* is Latin for "at first sight." Legally, it refers to a fact that is presumed to be true unless contradicted by evidence.)
2. To do so, the defendant must show that he or she is a member of a recognizable racial group and that the prosecutor has used peremptory challenges to remove members of this group from the jury pool.
3. Then, the defendant must show that these facts and other relevant circumstances raise the possibility that the prosecutor removed the prospective jurors solely because of their race.
4. If the court accepts the defendant's charges, the burden shifts to the prosecution to prove that its peremptory challenges were race neutral. If the court finds against the prosecution, it rules that a *Batson* violation has occurred.

Photo Courtesy Collins E. Ijoma

COLLINS E. IJOMA

TRIAL COURT ADMINISTRATOR

As the trial court administrator, I serve principally as the chief administrative officer for the largest trial and municipal court system in New Jersey. We provide technical and managerial support to the court (more than sixty superior court judges and thirty-six municipal court judges) on such matters as personnel, program development, case flow, resources, and facilities management. This description may sound "highfalutin" considering that most people can only describe a court in terms of a judge, one or two courtroom staff, and a few other employees associated with the visible activities in the courthouse. Obviously, there is a lot more going on behind the scenes of which the average citizen is not aware.

One thing that keeps me going and enthused about this profession is the resolve and dedication of our judges and staff. The family division embraces a host of issues, and in some cases those who seek help are hurting and desperate. The court may be their only hope.

Social Media Career Tip Many businesses and organizations have their own career Web sites for potential employees. Some have even set up *talent communities* to interact with applicants. Explore these options if you have a specific job in mind.

The Court has revisited the issue of race a number of times in the years since its *Batson* decision. In *Powers v. Ohio* (1991),[40] it ruled that a defendant may contest race-based peremptory challenges even if the defendant is not of the same race as the excluded jurors. In *Georgia v. McCollum* (1992),[41] the Court placed defense attorneys under the same restrictions as prosecutors when making race-based peremptory challenges. Finally, in 2008, the Court, reaffirming its *Batson* decision of twenty-two years earlier, overturned the conviction of an African American death row inmate because a Louisiana prosecutor improperly picked an all-white jury for his murder trial.[42]

These rulings do not mean that a black defendant can never be judged by a jury made up entirely of whites. Rather, they indicate that attorneys cannot use peremptory challenges to reject a prospective juror because of her or his race.

WOMEN ON THE JURY In *J.E.B. v. Alabama ex rel. T.B.* (1994),[43] the Supreme Court extended the principles of the *Batson* ruling to cover gender bias in jury selection. The case was a civil suit for paternity and child support brought by the state of Alabama. Prosecutors used nine of their ten challenges to remove men from the jury, while the defense made similar efforts to remove women. When challenged, the state defended its actions by referring to what it called the rational belief that men and women might have different views on the issues of paternity and child support. The Court disagreed and held this approach to be unconstitutional.

Opening Statements The attorneys' statements to the jury at the beginning of the trial.

Evidence Anything that is used to prove the existence or nonexistence of a fact.

Alternate Jurors

Because unforeseeable circumstances or illness may necessitate that one or more of the sitting jurors be dismissed, the court may also seat several *alternate jurors* who will hear the entire trial. Depending on the rules of the particular jurisdiction, two or three alternate jurors may be present throughout the trial. If a juror has to be excused in the middle of the trial, an alternate may take his or her place without disrupting the proceedings.

//// **SELF** ASSESSMENT

Fill in the blanks, and check your answers on page 266.

The _____ is composed of all those people who have been identified as potential jurors for a particular trial. These people are then gathered for the process of _____ _____, in which the prosecution and defense choose the actual members of the jury. Both sides can remove jurors in two ways: (1) through unlimited challenges for _____, which require the attorney to give a reason for the removal, and (2) through a limited number of _____ challenges, for which no reason is necessary. According to the United States Supreme Court, potential jurors cannot be removed for reasons of _____ or _____.

THE TRIAL

Once the jury members have been selected, the judge swears them in and the trial itself can begin. A rather pessimistic truism among attorneys is that every case "has been won or lost when the jury is sworn." This reflects the belief that a juror's values are the major, if not dominant, factor in the decision of guilt or innocence.[44]

In actuality, it is difficult to predict how a jury will go about reaching a decision. Despite a number of studies on the question, researchers have not been able to identify any definitive consistent patterns of jury behavior. Sometimes, jurors in a criminal trial will follow instructions to find a defendant guilty unless there is a reasonable doubt, and sometimes they seem to follow instinct or prejudice and apply the law in any way they choose.

Opening Statements

Attorneys may decide to open the trial with a statement to the jury, though they are not required to do so. In these **opening statements,** the attorneys give a brief version of the facts and the supporting evidence that they will present during the trial. Because some trials can drag on for weeks or even months, it is extremely helpful for jurors to hear a summary of what will unfold. In short, the opening statement is a kind of "road map" that describes the destination that each attorney hopes to reach and outlines how she or he plans to reach it.

The danger for attorneys is that they will offer evidence during the trial that might contradict an assertion made during the opening statement. This may cause jurors to disregard the evidence or shift their own thinking further away from the narrative being offered by the attorney.[45] (For an example of the opening statement, see Figure 8.6 that follows.)

The Role of Evidence

Once the opening statements have been made, the prosecutor begins the trial proceedings by presenting the state's evidence against the defendant. Courts have complex rules about what types of evidence may be presented and how the evidence may be brought out during the trial. **Evidence** is anything that is used to prove the existence

FIGURE 8.6 The Opening Statement

In the trial of Michael Dunn for the murder of Jordan Davis, which we discussed at the beginning of the chapter, a crucial point was whether Davis pointed a shotgun at the defendant. In their opening statements, prosecutor John Guy (pictured here) and defense attorney Cory Strolla introduced their arguments regarding the shotgun's existence.

Guy: And with two hands, [Dunn] pointed out the window back at Jordan Davis, and pulled the trigger, three times. Every one of the shots in a nice tight little circle, went through the door, and into Davis's body. The only thing [Davis] had on his person was a cell phone and a pocketknife.

Strolla: Jordan Davis threatened Michael Dunn. "You are dead, bitch. This is going down now." With a shotgun barrel sticking out the window, or a lead pipe, whatever it was, it was a deadly weapon. We are not here to say anyone deserved to lose their life. But, under the law [Dunn's actions were] justified.

Getty Images

or nonexistence of a fact. For the most part, evidence can be broken down into two categories: testimony and real evidence. **Testimony** consists of statements by competent witnesses. **Real evidence,** presented to the court in the form of exhibits, includes any physical items—such as the murder weapon or a bloodstained piece of clothing—that affect the case.

Rules of evidence are designed to ensure that testimony and exhibits presented to the jury are relevant, reliable, and not unfairly prejudicial against the defendant. One of the tasks of the defense attorney is to challenge evidence presented by the prosecution by establishing that the evidence is not reliable. Of course, the prosecutor also tries to demonstrate the irrelevance or unreliability of evidence presented by the defense. The final decision on whether evidence is allowed before the jury rests with the judge, in keeping with his or her role as the "referee" of the adversarial system.

TESTIMONIAL EVIDENCE A person without specialized training or knowledge who is called to testify on factual matters that would be understood by the average citizen is referred to as a **lay witness.** If asked about the condition of a victim of an assault, for example, a lay witness could relate certain facts, such as "she was bleeding from her forehead" or "she was unconscious on the ground for several minutes." A lay witness could not, however, give information about the medical extent of the victim's injuries, such as whether she suffered from a fractured skull or internal bleeding. Coming from a lay witness, such testimony would be inadmissible.

When the matter in question requires scientific, medical, or technical skill beyond the scope of the average person, prosecutors and defense attorneys may call an **expert witness** to the stand. The expert witness is an individual who has professional training, advanced knowledge, or substantial experience in a specialized area, such as medicine, computer technology, or ballistics. The rules of evidence state that expert witnesses may base their opinions on three types of information:

1. Facts or data of which they have personal knowledge.
2. Material presented at trial.
3. Secondhand information given to the expert outside the courtroom.[46]

 LEARNING 7 OBJECTIVE Explain the difference between testimony and real evidence, between lay witnesses and expert witnesses, and between direct and circumstantial evidence.

Testimony Verbal evidence given by witnesses under oath.

Real Evidence Evidence that is brought into court and seen by the jury, as opposed to evidence that is described for a jury.

Lay Witness A witness who can truthfully and accurately testify on a fact in question without having specialized training or knowledge.

Expert Witness A witness with professional training or substantial experience qualifying her or him to testify on a certain subject.

DIRECT VERSUS CIRCUMSTANTIAL EVIDENCE Two types of testimonial evidence may be brought into court: direct evidence and circumstantial evidence. **Direct evidence** is evidence that has been witnessed by the person giving testimony. "I saw Bill shoot Chris" is an example of direct evidence. **Circumstantial evidence** is indirect evidence that, even if believed, does not establish the fact in question but only the degree of likelihood of the fact. In other words, circumstantial evidence can create an inference that a fact exists.

Suppose, for example, that the defendant owns a gun that shoots bullets of the type found in the victim's body. This circumstantial evidence, by itself, does not establish that the defendant committed the crime. Combined with other circumstantial evidence, however, it may do just that. For instance, if other circumstantial evidence indicates that the defendant had a motive for harming the victim and was at the scene of the crime when the shooting occurred, the jury might conclude that the defendant committed the crime.

THE "CSI EFFECT" When possible, defense attorneys will almost always make the argument that the state has failed to present any evidence other than circumstantial evidence against their client. Recently, this tactic has been aided by a phenomenon known as the "CSI effect," taking its name from the popular television series *CSI: Crime Scene Investigation* and its spin-offs. According to many prosecutors, these shows have fostered unrealistic notions among jurors as to what high-tech forensic science can accomplish as part of a criminal investigation.

In reality, the kind of physical evidence used to solve crimes on *CSI* is often not available to the prosecution, which must rely instead on witnesses and circumstantial evidence. Several years ago, researchers surveyed more than one thousand jurors in Washtenaw County, Michigan, and found that nearly half "expected the prosecutor to present scientific evidence in every criminal case." This expectation was particularly strong in rape trials and trials lacking direct evidence of a crime.[47]

RELEVANCE Evidence will not be admitted in court unless it is relevant to the case being considered. **Relevant evidence** is evidence that tends to prove or disprove a fact in question. Forensic proof that the bullets found in a victim's body were fired from a gun discovered in the suspect's pocket at the time of arrest, for example, is certainly relevant. The suspect's prior record, showing a conviction for armed robbery ten years earlier, is, as we shall soon see, irrelevant to the case at hand and in most instances will be ruled inadmissible by the judge.

PREJUDICIAL EVIDENCE Evidence may be excluded if it would tend to distract the jury from the main issues of the case, mislead the jury, or cause jurors to decide the issue on an emotional basis. In practice, this rule often precludes prosecutors from using prior purported criminal activities or actual convictions to show that the defendant has criminal propensities or an "evil character." It also can prohibit the defense from portraying the alleged victim in a negative light. For example, before George Zimmerman's murder trial, described in Chapter 3, the judge barred a great deal of evidence concerning Trayvon Martin's past. This evidence included:

1. A photo of Martin showing his gold teeth to the camera while sticking up his middle fingers,
2. School records indicating that Martin had been suspended for marijuana possession,
3. Texts and videos suggesting that Martin was involved in organized fights, and
4. A text from Martin to a friend that read, "U gotta gun?"

Such information, according to the judge, was irrelevant to the altercation between Zimmerman and Martin and would only serve to prejudice the jury against Martin.[48] (See photo alongside.)

These concepts are codified in the Federal Rules of Evidence, which state that evidence of "other crimes, wrongs, or acts is not admissible to prove the character of a person in order to show action in conformity therewith." Such evidence is allowed only when it does not apply to character construction and focuses instead on "motive, opportunity, intent, preparation, plan, knowledge, identity, or absence of mistake or accident."[49]

Although this legal concept has come under a great deal of criticism, it is consistent with the presumption-of-innocence standards discussed earlier. Arguably, if a prosecutor is allowed to establish that the defendant has shown antisocial or even violent traits in the past, this will prejudice the jury against the defendant in the present trial. Even if the judge instructs jurors that this prior evidence is irrelevant, human nature dictates that it will probably have a "warping influence" on the jurors' perception of the defendant.[50] Therefore, whenever possible, defense attorneys will keep such evidence from the jury.

The Prosecution's Case

Because the burden of proof is on the state, the prosecution is generally considered to have a more difficult task than the defense. The prosecutor attempts to establish guilt beyond a reasonable doubt by presenting the *corpus delicti* ("body of the offense" in Latin) of the crime to the jury. The *corpus delicti* is simply a legal term that refers to the substantial facts that show a crime has been committed. By establishing such facts through the presentation of relevant and nonprejudicial evidence, the prosecutor hopes to convince the jury of the defendant's guilt.

DIRECT EXAMINATION OF WITNESSES Witnesses are crucial to establishing the prosecutor's case against the defendant. The prosecutor will call witnesses to the stand and ask them questions pertaining to the sequence of events that the trial is addressing. This form of questioning is known as **direct examination.** During direct examination, the prosecutor will usually not be allowed to ask *leading questions*—questions that might suggest to the witness a particular desired response.

A leading question might be something like "So, Mrs. Williams, you noticed the defendant threatening the victim with a broken beer bottle?" If Mrs. Williams answers "yes" to this question, she has, in effect, been "led" to the conclusion that the defendant was, in fact, threatening with a broken beer bottle. The fundamental purpose behind testimony is to establish what actually happened, not what the trial attorneys would like the jury to believe happened. (A properly worded query would be, "Mrs. Williams, please describe the defendant's manner toward the victim during the incident.")

Ron T. Ennis/Fort Worth Star-Telegram/MCT via Getty Images

Review the list of information concerning Trayvon Martin that was barred by the judge during the murder trial of George Zimmerman. Do you agree that this evidence would have unfairly prejudiced the jury against Martin, whose likeness is reproduced on a tee shirt in this photo? Explain your answer.

Direct Examination The examination of a witness by the attorney who calls the witness to the stand to testify.

COMPETENCE AND RELIABILITY OF WITNESSES The rules of evidence include certain restrictions and qualifications pertaining to witnesses. Witnesses must have sufficient mental competence to understand the significance of testifying under oath. They must also be reliable in the sense that they are able to give a clear and reliable description of the events in question. If not, the prosecutor or defense attorney will make sure that the jury is aware of these shortcomings through *cross-examination*.

Cross-Examination

After the prosecutor has directly examined her or his witnesses, the defense attorney is given the chance to question the same witnesses. The Sixth Amendment states, "In all criminal prosecutions, the accused shall enjoy the right . . . to be confronted with witnesses against him." This **confrontation clause** gives the accused, through his or her attorneys, the right to cross-examine witnesses. **Cross-examination** refers to the questioning of an opposing witness during trial, and both sides of a case are allowed to do so.

QUESTIONING WITNESSES Cross-examination allows the attorneys to test the truthfulness of opposing witnesses and usually entails efforts to create doubt in the jurors' minds that the witness is reliable (see Figure 8.7 that follows). After the defense has cross-examined a prosecution witness, the prosecutor may want to reestablish any reliability that might have been lost. The prosecutor can do so by again questioning the witness, a process known as *redirect examination*. Following the redirect examination, the defense attorney will be given the opportunity to ask further questions of prosecution witnesses, or recross-examination. Thus, each side has two opportunities to question a witness. The attorneys need not do so, but only after each side has been offered the opportunity will the trial move on to the next witness or the next stage.

HEARSAY Cross-examination is also linked to problems presented by *hearsay* evidence. **Hearsay** can be defined as any testimony given about a statement made by someone else. Literally, it is what someone heard someone else say. For the most part, hearsay is not admissible as evidence. When a witness offers hearsay, the person making the original remarks is not in court and therefore cannot be cross-examined. If such testimony were allowed, the defendant's Sixth Amendment right to confront witnesses against him or her would be violated.

FIGURE 8.7 **The Cross-Examination**

During Michael Dunn's trial for the murder of Jordan Davis, a great deal of time was spent trying to determine whether Davis pointed a shotgun at Dunn. As noted earlier in the chapter, no shotgun was found at the crime scene. When Dunn took the stand, the prosecution cross-examined him about what he said to his fiancée, Rhonda Rouer, following the shooting.

Prosecutor: How did you describe the weapon [to her]? Did you say they had a sword? Did you say they had a machete?

Dunn: Gun.

Prosecutor: A gun. You used the word "gun"?

Dunn: Multiple times.

Later in the trial, the prosecution called Rouer (pictured here) as a witness. In her testimony, she stated that Dunn never mentioned that he had been threatened with a shotgun, or any other kind of weapon, during the confrontation.

AP Images/*The Florida Times-Union*, Bob Mack, Pool

There are a number of exceptions to the hearsay rule, and as a result a good deal of hearsay evidence finds its way into criminal trials. For example, a hearsay statement is usually admissible if there seems to be little risk of a lie. Therefore, a statement made by someone who believes that his or her death is imminent—a "dying declaration" or a suicide note—is often allowed in court even though it is hearsay.[51] Similarly, the rules of most states allow hearsay when the statement contains an admission of wrongdoing *and* the speaker is not available to testify in court. The logic behind this exception is that a person generally does not make a statement against her or his own best interests unless it is true.[52]

The Defendant's Case

After the prosecution has finished presenting its evidence, the defense attorney may offer the defendant's case. Because the burden is on the state to prove the accused's guilt, the defense is not required to offer any case at all. It can simply "rest" without calling any witnesses or producing any real evidence, and ask the jury to decide the merits of the case on what it has seen and heard from the prosecution.

CREATING A REASONABLE DOUBT Defense lawyers most commonly defend their clients by attempting to expose weaknesses in the prosecutor's case. Remember that if the defense attorney can create reasonable doubt concerning the client's guilt in the mind of just a single juror, the defendant has a good chance of gaining an acquittal or at least a *hung jury,* a circumstance explained later in the chapter.

Even if the prosecution has presented seemingly strong evidence, a defense attorney may succeed by creating reasonable doubt. In an illustrative case, Jason Korey bragged to his friends that he had shot and killed Joseph Brucker in Pittsburgh, Pennsylvania, and a great deal of circumstantial evidence linked Korey to the killing. The police, however, could find no direct evidence: they could not link Korey to the murder weapon, nor could they match his footprints to those found at the crime scene.

Michael Foglia, Korey's defense attorney, explained his client's bragging as an attempt to gain attention, not a true statement. Though this explanation may strike some as unlikely, in the absence of physical evidence it did create doubt in the jurors' minds, and Korey was acquitted. (Creating reasonable doubt concerning the victim's reliability can be very effective in sexual-assault cases, as explained in the feature *CJ Controversy—Rape Shield Laws* that follows.)

OTHER DEFENSE STRATEGIES The defense can choose among a number of strategies to generate reasonable doubt in the jurors' minds. It can present an *alibi defense,* by submitting evidence that the accused was not at or near the scene of the crime at the time the crime was committed. Another option is to attempt an *affirmative defense,* by presenting additional facts to the ones offered by the prosecution. Possible affirmative defenses, which we discussed in detail in Chapter 3, include (1) self-defense, (2) insanity, (3) duress, and (4) entrapment.

With an affirmative defense strategy, the defense attempts to prove that the defendant should be found not guilty because of certain circumstances surrounding the crime. An affirmative strategy can be difficult to carry out because it forces the defense to prove the reliability of its own evidence, not simply disprove the evidence offered by the prosecution.

The defense is often willing to admit that a certain criminal act took place, especially if the defendant has already confessed. In this case, the primary question of the trial becomes not whether the defendant is guilty, but what the defendant is guilty of. In

RAPE SHIELD LAWS

Historically, the courtroom has been a hostile environment for victims of sexual assault. Because of a pervasive attitude labeled the "chastity requirement" by some experts, rape victims who were perceived to be sexually virtuous were much more likely to be believed by jurors than those who had been sexually active. If a woman had consented to sex before, so the line of thought went, she was more likely to do so again. To protect against this type of prejudicial thinking, almost every jurisdiction in the United States has passed a rape shield law to keep specific evidence, including most evidence about the victim's reputation and previous sexual conduct, out of the courtroom.

RAPE SHIELD LAWS ARE JUST BECAUSE . . .

- Without them, defense attorneys may subject victims of sexual assault to embarrassing and degrading cross-examination concerning their personal lives.
- They ensure that defendants are convicted or acquitted based on the relevant evidence, not the prejudices of jurors more focused on the sexual history of the accuser than on the facts of the case.

RAPE SHIELD LAWS ARE UNJUST BECAUSE . . .

- The Sixth Amendment gives all defendants the right to question their accusers. By limiting this right, rape shield laws leave defendants in sexual assault cases at the mercy of juries who do not know all the facts.
- In many instances, the victim's prior sexual history is relevant to the issue of whether she or he consented to the incident in question and should not be kept from the jury.

Your Assignment

Rape shield laws do contain certain exceptions that allow the defense to use evidence of the accuser's prior sexual conduct in court. To see two examples, search online for **Federal Rule of Evidence 412** and read Exceptions (1)(A) and (1)(B). Do you feel that either or both of these exceptions are necessary to help balance the rights of the accuser and the accused? Explain your answer in two full paragraphs.

---

these situations, the defense strategy focuses on obtaining the lightest possible penalty for the defendant. As we saw earlier, this strategy is responsible for the high percentage of proceedings that end in plea bargains.

Rebuttal and Surrebuttal

After the defense closes its case, the prosecution is permitted to bring new evidence forward that was not used during its initial presentation to the jury. This is called the **rebuttal** stage of the trial. When the rebuttal stage is finished, the defense is given the opportunity to cross-examine the prosecution's new witnesses and introduce new witnesses of its own. This final act is part of the *surrebuttal.* After these stages have been completed, the defense may file a request called a *motion for a directed verdict,* asking the judge to find in the defendant's favor. If this motion is rejected, and it almost always is, the case is closed, and the opposing sides offer their closing arguments.

Closing Arguments

Rebuttal New evidence presented by the prosecution given to counteract or disprove evidence presented by the opposing party.

Closing Arguments Arguments made by each side's attorney after the cases for the plaintiff and defendant have been presented.

In their **closing arguments,** the attorneys summarize their presentations and argue one final time for their respective cases. In most states, the defense attorney goes first, and then the prosecutor. (In Colorado, Kentucky, and Missouri, the order is reversed.) An effective closing argument includes all of the major points that support the government's or the defense's case. It also emphasizes the shortcomings of the opposing party's case.

Jurors will view a closing argument with some skepticism if it merely recites the central points of a party's claim or defense without also responding to the unfavorable facts or issues raised by the other side. Of course, neither attorney wants to focus too much on the other side's position, but the elements of the opposing position do need to be acknowledged and their flaws highlighted. Once both attorneys have completed their remarks, the case is submitted to the jury, and the attorneys' roles in the trial are, for the moment, complete.

Charge The judge's instructions to the jury following the attorneys' closing arguments.

///SELF ASSESSMENT

Fill in the blanks, and check your answers on page 266.

Evidence is any object or spoken _____ that can be used in a criminal trial to prove or disprove a _____ related to the crime. Evidence will not be admitted into the trial unless it is _____ and does not unfairly _____ the jury against the defendant by appealing to emotion rather than fact. The prosecution will usually try to build its case through _____ examination of its witnesses, which the defense will counter with a _____ -examination of its own.

THE FINAL STEPS OF THE TRIAL AND POSTCONVICTION PROCEDURES

After closing arguments, the outcome of the trial is in the hands of the jury. Before the jurors begin discussing what they have heard and seen, the judge gives the jury a **charge,** summing up the case and instructing the jurors on the rules of law that apply to the issues in the case. These charges, also called jury instructions, are usually prepared during a special *charging conference* involving the judge and the trial attorneys. In this conference, the attorneys suggest the instructions they would like to see be sent to the jurors, but the judge makes the final decision as to the charges submitted. If the defense attorney disagrees with the charges sent to the jury, he or she can enter an objection, thereby setting the stage for a possible appeal.

Jury Deliberation

After receiving the charge, the jury begins its deliberations. Jury deliberation is a somewhat mysterious process, as it takes place in complete seclusion. Most of what is known about how a jury deliberates comes from mock trials or interviews with jurors after the verdict has been reached. A general picture of the deliberation process constructed from this research shows that the romantic notion of jurors with high-minded ideals of justice making eloquent speeches is, for the most part, not the reality. In approximately three out of every ten cases, the initial vote by the jury led to a unanimous decision. In 90 percent of the remaining cases, the majority eventually dictated the decision.[53]

One of the most important instructions that a judge normally gives the jurors is that they should seek no outside information during deliberation. The idea is that jurors should base their verdict *only* on the evidence that the judge has deemed admissible. In extreme cases, the judge will order that the jury be *sequestered,* or isolated from the public, during the trial and deliberation stages of the proceedings. Sequestration is used when deliberations are expected to be lengthy, or the trial is attracting a high amount of interest and the judge wants to keep the jury from being unduly influenced. Juries are usually sequestered in hotels and kept under the watch and guard of officers of the court.

iStockphoto.com/Alina555

One former juror, fresh from trial, complained that the members of the courtroom work group had not provided the jury with enough information to render a fair verdict. "We felt deeply frustrated at our inability to fill those gaps in our knowledge," he added. Until recently, frustrated jury members have lacked the means to carry out their own investigations in court. Today, however, jurors with smartphones and tablet computers can easily access news stories and online research tools. With these wireless devices, they can look up legal terms, blog and tweet about their experiences, and sometimes even try to contact other participants in the trial through "friend" requests on social media Web sites.

This access can cause serious problems for judges, whose responsibility it is to ensure that no outside information taints the jury's decision. Following a Vermont trial of an immigrant from the African country of Somalia for the sexual assault of a child, one juror went online to research certain aspects of Somali culture and religion. During deliberation, the juror relied on this research to argue his position that the defendant was guilty. The judge had no choice but to overturn the defendant's eventual conviction, as this juror misconduct could have improperly influenced the final verdict.

Thinking about Wireless Devices in the Courtroom

The Sixth Amendment guarantees the accused the right to trial by an "impartial jury." How does the use of wireless devices in the courtroom threaten this right?

The Verdict

Once it has reached a decision, the jury issues a **verdict.** The most common verdicts are guilty and not guilty, though, as we have seen, juries may signify different degrees of guilt if instructed to do so. Following the announcement of a guilty or not guilty verdict, the jurors are discharged, and the jury trial proceedings are finished.

When a jury in a criminal trial is unable to agree on a unanimous verdict—or a majority in certain states—it returns with no decision. This is known as a **hung jury.** Following a hung jury, the judge will declare a mistrial, and the case will be tried again in front of a different jury if the prosecution decides to pursue the matter a second time. In the case that opened this chapter, prosecutors decided to retry Michael Dunn for the first degree murder of Jordan Davis after a Florida jury could not agree on whether he was guilty of that charge.

A judge can do little to reverse a hung jury, considering that "no decision" is just as legitimate a verdict as guilty or not guilty. In some states, if there are only a few dissenters to the majority view, a judge can send the jury back to the jury room under a set of rules set forth more than a century ago by the Supreme Court in *Allen v. United States* (1896).[54] The ***Allen* Charge,** as this instruction is called, asks the jurors in the minority to reconsider the majority opinion. Many jurisdictions do not allow *Allen* Charges on the ground that they improperly coerce jurors with the minority opinion to change their minds.[55] For all of the attention they receive, hung juries are relatively rare. Juries are unable to come to a decision in only about 6 percent of all cases.[56]

Verdict A formal decision made by the jury.

Hung Jury A jury whose members are so irreconcilably divided in their opinions that they cannot reach a verdict.

***Allen* Charge** An instruction by a judge to a deadlocked jury with only a few dissenters that asks the jurors in the minority to reconsider the majority opinion.

Appeals

Even if a defendant is found guilty, the trial process is not necessarily over. In our criminal justice system, a person convicted of a crime has a right to appeal. An **appeal** is the process of seeking a higher court's review of a lower court's decision for the purpose of correcting or changing the lower court's judgment. A defendant who loses a case in a trial court cannot automatically appeal the conviction. The defendant normally must first be able to show that the trial court acted improperly on a question of law. Common reasons for appeals include the introduction of tainted evidence by the prosecution or faulty jury instructions delivered by the trial judge. In federal courts, about 18 percent of criminal convictions are appealed.[57]

Appeal The process of seeking a higher court's review of a lower court's decision for the purpose of correcting or changing this decision.

Double Jeopardy To twice place at risk (jeopardize) a person's life or liberty. Constitutional law prohibits a second prosecution in the same court for the same criminal offense.

DOUBLE JEOPARDY The appeal process is available only to the defense. If a jury finds the accused not guilty, the prosecution cannot appeal to have the decision reversed. To do so would infringe on the defendant's Fifth Amendment rights against multiple trials for the same offense. This guarantee against being tried a second time for the same crime is known as protection from **double jeopardy.** The prohibition of double jeopardy means that once a criminal defendant is found not guilty of a particular crime, the government may not reindict the person and retry him or her for the same crime. (Some nations allow for such retrials, as explained in the feature *Comparative Criminal Justice—Double Trouble* that follows.)

The American prohibition of double jeopardy is not, however, absolute. There are several circumstances in which, for practical purposes, a defendant can find herself or himself back in court after being found not guilty of committing a particular crime:

LEARNING **8** OBJECTIVE Delineate circumstances in which the constitutional prohibition of double jeopardy does not always apply.

1. One state's prosecution will not prevent a different state or the federal government from prosecuting the same crime.
2. Acquitted defendants can be sued in civil court for circumstances arising from the alleged wrongdoing on the theory that they are not being tried for the same *crime* twice.
3. A hung jury is not an acquittal for purposes of double jeopardy. So, if a jury is deadlocked, the government is free to seek a new trial.

THE APPEAL PROCESS There are two basic reasons for the appeal process. The first is to correct an error made during the initial trial. The second is to review policy. Because of this second function, the appellate courts are an important part of the flexible nature of the criminal justice system. When existing law has ceased to be effective or no longer reflects the values of society, an appellate court can effectively change the law through its decisions and the precedents that it sets.[58] A classic example is the *Miranda v. Arizona* decision (see Chapter 6), which, although it failed to change the fate of the defendant (he was found guilty on retrial), had a far-reaching impact on custodial interrogation of suspects.

It is also important to understand that once the appeal process begins, the defendant is no longer presumed innocent. The burden of proof has shifted, and the defendant is obligated to prove that her or his conviction should be overturned. The method of filing an appeal differs slightly among the fifty states and the federal government, but the five basic steps are similar enough for summarization in Figure 8.8 that follows. For the most part, defendants are not required to exercise their right to appeal. The one exception involves the death sentence. Given the seriousness of capital punishment, the defendant is required to appeal the case, regardless of his or her wishes.

Double Trouble

American college student Amanda Knox's long Italian nightmare began in Perugia on November 6, 2007. That day, she was arrested, along with her boyfriend, for killing her British roommate, Meredith Kercher. In 2009, Knox (pictured at right) was convicted of murder, on the theory that Kercher's death was the result of a drug-fed orgy gone wrong. In 2011, an Italian appellate court overturned this conviction. The court based its ruling on shoddy investigative techniques by Italian law enforcement, which misread DNA evidence at the crime scene that pointed to a drug dealer named Rudy Guede as the obvious wrongdoer. After serving four years of a twenty-six-year prison sentence, Knox was freed and returned home to continue her education at the University of Washington in Seattle.

In March 2013, however, Italy's Court of Cassation reversed Knox's 2011 acquittal and ordered that her case be reviewed. In Italy, prosecutors routinely appeal acquittals. In the United States, because of constitutional protections against double jeopardy, defendants almost never face a second trial for the same crime. On January 30, 2014, an Italian appellate court convicted Knox for a second time of murdering Kercher and sentenced her to twenty-eight-and-a-half years in prison.

AP Images/Mark Lennihan

Following this verdict, Knox vowed that she would "never go willingly back" to Italy.

FOR CRITICAL ANALYSIS

The United States and Italy have a treaty that requires extradition (see Chapter 7) unless there is clear evidence of a miscarriage of justice. Using this standard, should the U.S. government extradite Knox to Italy? Why or why not?

HABEAS CORPUS Even after the appeal process is exhausted, a convict may have access to one final procedure, known as *habeas corpus* (Latin for "you have the body"). *Habeas corpus* is a judicial order that commands a corrections official to bring a prisoner before a federal court so that the court can hear the convict's claim that he or she is being held illegally. A writ of *habeas corpus* differs from an appeal in that it can be filed only by someone who is imprisoned.

Wrongful Convictions

The appeal process is primarily concerned with "legal innocence." That is, appeals courts focus on how the law was applied in a case, rather than on the facts of the case. But what if a defendant who is factually innocent has been found guilty at trial? For the most part, such **wrongful convictions** can be righted only with the aid of new evidence suggesting the defendant's innocence. When such new evidence is uncovered, a prosecutor's office can choose to reopen the case in order to acquit. Or, the defendant's attorneys can use the *habeas corpus* procedure described above to restart court proceedings.

Habeas Corpus An order that requires corrections officials to bring an inmate before a court or a judge to explain why she or he is being held in prison illegally.

Wrongful Conviction The conviction, either by verdict or by guilty plea, of a person who is factually innocent of the charges.

FIGURE 8.8 The Steps of an Appeal

1. The defendant, or *appellant,* files a **notice of appeal**—a short written statement outlining the basis of the appeal.

2. The appellant transfers the trial court record to the appellate court. This record contains items such as evidence and a transcript of the testimony.

3. Both parties file **briefs.** A brief is a written document that presents the party's legal arguments.

4. Attorneys from both sides present **oral arguments** before the appellate court.

5. Having heard from both sides, the judges of the appellate court retire to deliberate the case and make their decision. As described in Chapter 7, this decision is issued as a **written opinion.** Appellate courts generally do one of the following:

   - **Uphold** the decision of the lower court.
   - **Modify** the lower court's decision by changing only a part of it.
   - **Reverse** the decision of the lower court.
   - **Reverse and remand** the case, meaning that the matter is sent back to the lower court for further proceedings.

DNA EXONERATION In Chapter 5, we saw how DNA fingerprinting has been a boon for law enforcement. According to the Innocence Project, a New York–based legal group, as of March 2014, the procedure has also led to the exoneration of 312 convicts in the United States.[59] For example, in 1998, Johnny Williams was wrongly convicted of sexually assaulting a nine-year-old girl in Oakland, California. Williams subsequently spent fourteen years in prison before DNA testing of the girl's clothing showed that Williams was not the rapist. Acting on this new evidence, in March 2013, a superior court judge set Williams free.

THE CAUSES OF WRONGFUL CONVICTIONS Johnny Williams did not match the nine-year-old victim's original description of her attacker. Nonetheless, he was placed in a lineup and eventually identified by the girl. Furthermore, Williams told police more than forty times that he was innocent but eventually confessed after being informed that there were dozens of witnesses who placed him at the scene of the crime.

Williams's case highlights two of the five most common reasons[60] for wrongful convictions later overturned by DNA evidence:

1. *Eyewitness misidentification,* which may occur in as many as one-third of all cases in which it is used to identify criminal suspects.[61]

2. *False confessions,* often as the result of overly coercive police interrogation techniques or a suspect's mental illness.

3. *Faulty forensic evidence* produced by crime labs that analyze evidence from bite marks to handwriting samples to ballistics.

4. *False informant testimony* provided by "jail house snitches" and other offenders who are motivated to lessen their own punishment by incriminating other suspects.

5. *Law enforcement misconduct* by overzealous or corrupt police officers and prosecutors.

POLICY.CJ

Nearly every jurisdiction in the United States allows posttrial DNA testing to prove a convict's innocence under certain circumstances and almost always at the prosecutor's discretion. Should convicts have the right to demand DNA testing to prove their innocence, whether or not a prosecutor agrees? Write one full paragraph explaining your answer to this question. Then, search online for the terms **William Osborne** and **DNA Testing** to see how the Supreme Court decided this issue.

Numerous jurisdictions are taking steps to remedy the problems leading to wrongful convictions. District attorney offices in Cook County, Illinois, and Dallas County, Texas, have formed Conviction Integrity Units to review and reinvestigate questionable convictions. In 2012, the Oregon Supreme Court ruled that state judges must ensure that eyewitness testimony is not unfairly prejudicial, just like any other piece of evidence.[62] A year later, Texas legislators enacted a "Junk Science Writ," which allows inmates to challenge faulty forensic evidence from their prison cells.[63]

//// SELF ASSESSMENT

Fill in the blanks, and check your answers on page 266.

Once both the prosecution and the defense have completed their closing arguments, the judge will give the jury a _____ summing up the case and providing instructions on how to proceed. After the jury has _____ and reached a decision, it will announce a _____ of guilty or not guilty. If the jury cannot do so, a _____ jury occurs, and the judge will call a mistrial. If a defendant is convicted, he or she has the option of _____ this outcome if it can be shown that the trial court acted improperly on a question of _____, not fact, during the proceedings.

CHAPTER SUMMARY

For more information on these concepts, look back to the Learning Objective icons throughout the chapter.

 Identify the steps involved in the pretrial criminal process. (a) Suspect booked at police station after arrest; (b) initial appearance before a magistrate, at which time the defendant is informed of his or her constitutional rights, and a public defender may be appointed or private counsel may be hired by the state to represent the defendant; (c) the posting of bail or release on recognizance; (d) preventive detention, if deemed necessary to ensure the safety of other persons or the community, or regular detention, if the defendant is unable to post bail; (e) a preliminary hearing (mini-trial), at which the judge rules on whether there is probable cause, and the prosecutor issues an information; or a grand jury hearing, after which an indictment is issued against the defendant if the grand jury finds probable cause; (g) the arraignment, at which the defendant is informed of the charges and must respond by pleading not guilty or guilty (or in some cases, *nolo contendere*); (h) plea bargaining. If the defendant refuses to plead guilty, he or she proceeds to either a jury or bench trial.

 Identify the main difference between an indictment and an information. An indictment is the grand jury's declaration that probable cause exists to charge a defendant with a specific crime. In jurisdictions that do not use grand juries, the prosecution issues an information as the formal charge of a crime.

 Explain how a prosecutor screens potential cases. (a) Is there sufficient evidence for conviction? (b) What is the priority of the case? The more serious the alleged crime, the higher the priority. The more extensive the defendant's criminal record, the higher the priority. (c) Are the victims cooperative? (d) Are the victims reliable? (e) Might the defendant be willing to testify against other offenders?

 Indicate why prosecutors, defense attorneys, and defendants often agree to plea bargains. For prosecutors, a plea bargain removes the risk of losing the case at trial, particularly if the evidence against the defendant is weak. For defense attorneys, the plea bargain may be the best deal possible for a potentially guilty client. For defendants, plea bargains give a measure of control over a highly uncertain future.

 Explain what "taking the Fifth" really means. The Fifth Amendment states that no person "shall be compelled in any criminal case to be a witness against himself." Thus, defendants do not have to testify if their testimony would implicate them in the crime. In the United States, silence on the part of a defendant cannot be used by the jury in forming its opinion about guilt or innocence.

 Contrast challenges for cause and peremptory challenges during *voir dire*. A challenge for cause occurs when an attorney provides the court with a legally justifiable reason why a potential juror should be excluded—for example, the juror does not understand English. In contrast, peremptory challenges do not require any justification by the attorney and are usually limited to a small number. They cannot, however, be based, even implicitly, on race or gender.

 Explain the difference between testimony and real evidence, between lay witnesses and expert witnesses, and between direct and circumstantial evidence. Testimony consists of statements by competent witnesses, whereas real evidence includes physical items that affect the case. A lay witness is an "average person," whereas an expert witness speaks with the authority of one who has professional training, advanced knowledge, or substantial experience in a specialized area. Direct evidence is evidence presented by witnesses as opposed to circumstantial evidence, which can create an inference that a fact exists but does not directly establish the fact.

 Delineate circumstances in which the constitutional prohibition of double jeopardy does not always apply. When an act is a crime under both state and federal law, a defendant who is acquitted in state court may be tried in federal court for the same act, and vice versa. He or she may also be tried in a different state. A defendant who is acquitted in a criminal trial may be sued in a civil case for essentially the same act. Also, the government is free to seek a new trial if the jury is deadlocked.

QUESTIONS FOR CRITICAL ANALYSIS

1. In practice, the constitutional right to a lawyer does not cover initial bail hearings. What are the disadvantages for an indigent defendant who is not represented by a lawyer at this point in the pretrial process?

2. Do you think that a prosecutor should offer a favorable plea bargain to a defendant who provides helpful information concerning a different defendant? What are the pros and cons of this practice?

3. During the trial of George Zimmerman (described in Chapter 3), a defense attorney joked, "Knock, knock. Who's there? George Zimmerman. George Zimmerman who? All right, good, you're on the jury." Explain the point behind this attempt at courtroom humor.

4. Why is the appeal process so important to the American criminal justice system? What would be some of the consequences if criminal defendants did not have the ability to appeal questionable convictions?

5. Texas has a law called the Tim Cole Compensation Act, under which people who are wrongfully convicted of crimes may collect $80,000 from the state for each year of unwarranted imprisonment. Do you think this is fair? Why or why not? What are the goals of this kind of legislation?

KEY TERMS

SELF-ASSESSMENT ANSWER KEY

Page 236: i. initial appearance; **ii.** constitutional; **iii.** bail; **iv.** judge; **v.** preventive

Page 238: i. probable cause; **ii.** preliminary; **iii.** grand jury; **iv.** indictment

Page 240: i. attrition; **ii.** screen; **iii.** conviction; **iv.** evidence

Page 244: i. plea bargain; **ii.** charges; **iii.** sentence; **iv.** *Boykin*; **v.** trial

Page 248: i. jury; **ii.** bench; **iii.** judge; **iv.** self-incrimination; **v.** innocent; **vi.** guilty; **vii.** state/prosecutor; **viii.** reasonable doubt

Page 252: i. *venire;* **ii.** *voir dire;* **iii.** cause; **iv.** peremptory; **v.** race; **vi.** gender

Page 259: i. testimony; **ii.** fact; **iii.** relevant; **iv.** prejudice; **v.** direct; **vi.** cross

Page 264: i. charge; **ii.** deliberated; **iii.** verdict; **iv.** hung; **v.** appealing; **vi.** law

1. Lawrence M. Friedman and Robert V. Percival, *The Roots of Justice* (Chapel Hill, N.C.: University of North Carolina Press, 1981), 2–4.

2. *Riverside County, California v. McLaughlin,* 500 U.S. 44 (1991).

3. Bureau of Justice Statistics, *Felony Defendants in Large Urban Counties, 2009—Statistical Tables* (Washington, D.C.: U.S. Department of Justice, December 2013), 15.

4. Illinois Annotated Statutes Chapter 725, Paragraph 5/110-5.

5. 18 U.S.C. Sections 3141-3150 (Supp. III 1985).

6. *Felony Defendants in Large Urban Counties, 2009—Statistical Tables, op. cit.,* Table 18, page 21; and Table 19, page 21.

7. Michael R. Jones, *Unsecured Bonds: The As Effective and Most Efficient Pretrial Release Option* (Washington, D.C.: Pretrial Justice Institute, October 2013), 10–20.

8. Kenneth C. Davis, *Discretionary Justice: A Preliminary Inquiry* (Baton Rouge, La.: Louisiana State University Press, 1969), 189.

9. Milton Hirsh and David Oscar Markus, "Fourth Amendment Forum," *Champion* (December 2002), 42.

10. Bruce Frederick and Don Stemen, *The Anatomy of Discretion: An Analysis of Prosecutorial Decision Making—Summary Report* (New York: Vera Institute of Justice, December 2012), 4–16.

11. 18 U.S.C. Section 3553(e) (2006).

12. Rachel Louise Snyder, "A Raised Hand," *The New Yorker* (July 22, 2013), 36–38.

13. 404 U.S. 257 (1971).

14. Fred C. Zacharias, "Justice in Plea Bargaining," *William and Mary Law Review* 39 (March 1998), 1121.

15. Bureau of Justice Statistics, *Prosecutors in State Courts, 2007—Statistical Tables* (Washington, D.C.: U.S. Department of Justice, December 2011), 2.

16. Milton Heumann, *Plea Bargaining: The Experiences of Prosecutors, Judges, and Defense Attorneys* (Chicago: University of Chicago Press, 1978), 58.

17. Albert W. Alschuler, "The Defense Attorney's Role in Plea Bargaining," *Yale Law Journal* 84 (1975), 1200.

18. Stephen J. Schulhofer, "Plea Bargaining as Disaster," *Yale Law Journal* 101 (1992), 1987.

19. 395 U.S. 238 (1969).

20. *Lafler v. Cooper,* 132 S.Ct. 1376 (2012); and *Missouri v. Frye,* 132 S.Ct. 1399 (2012).

21. Laurence Benner, "Expanding the Right to Effective Counsel at Plea Bargaining," *Criminal Justice* (Fall 2012), 4–11.

22. Quoted in Adam Liptak, "Justices' Ruling Expands Rights of Accused in Plea Bargains," *New York Times* (March 22, 2012), A1.

23. North Carolina General Statutes Section 15A-832(f) (2003).

24. 18 U.S.C. Section 3771 (2004).

25. Quoted in Ashley Fantz, "Ariel Castro Agrees to Plea Deal to Avoid Death Penalty," *CNN Justice* (July 28, 2013), at **www.cnn.com/2013/07/26/justice/ohio-castro.**

26. 407 U.S. 514 (1972).

27. 725 Illinois Compiled Statutes Section 5/103-5 (1992).

28. *Felony Defendants in Large Urban Counties, 2009—Statistical Tables, op. cit.,* Table 20, page 23.

29. 18 U.S.C. Section 3161.

30. 391 U.S. 145 (1968).

31. *Blanton v. Las Vegas,* 489 U.S. 538 (1989).

32. *Apodaca v. Oregon,* 406 U.S. 404 (1972); and *Lee v. Louisiana,* No. 07-1523 (2008).

33. 332 U.S. 46 (1947).

34. *Salinas v. Texas,* 570 U.S. _____ (2013).

35. Barton L. Ingraham, "The Right of Silence, the Presumption of Innocence, the Burden of Proof, and a Modest Proposal," *Journal of Criminal Law and Criminology* 85 (1994), 559–595.

36. 397 U.S. 358 (1970).

37. 380 U.S. 224 (1965).

38. 476 U.S. 79 (1986).

39. Eric L. Muller, "Solving the *Batson* Paradox: Harmless Error, Jury Representation, and the Sixth Amendment," *Yale Law Journal* 106 (October 1996), 93.

40. 499 U.S. 400 (1991).

41. 502 U.S. 1056 (1992).

42. *Snyder v. Louisiana,* 552 U.S. 472 (2008).

43. 511 U.S. 127 (1994).

44. Harry Kalven and Hans Zeisel, *The American Jury* (Boston: Little, Brown, 1966), 163–167.

45. Nancy Pennington and Reid Hastie, "The Story Model for Juror Decision Making," in *Inside the Juror: The Psychology of Juror Decision Making* (Cambridge, Mass.: Harvard University Press, 1983), 192, 194–195.

46. Federal Rule of Evidence 703.

47. Donald E. Shelton, "Juror Expectations for Scientific Evidence in Criminal Cases: Perceptions and Reality about the 'CSI Effect' Myth," *Thomas M. Cooley Law Review* 27 (2010), at **lawreview.tmc.cooley.edu/Resources/Documents/1_27-1%20Shelton%20Article.pdf.**

48. Tracy Connor, "Jury's Look into Travyon Martin's Past Has Its Limits," *NBC News* (June 7, 2013), at **usnews.nbcnews.com/_news/2013/06/07/18832092-jurys-look-into-trayvon-martins-past-has-its-limits?lite.**

49. Thomas J. Reed, "Trial by Propensity: Admission of Other Criminal Acts Evidenced in Federal Criminal Trials," *University of Cincinnati Law Review* 50 (1981), 713.

50. *People v. Zackowitz,* 254 N.Y. 192 (1930).

51. Federal Rules of Procedure, Rule 804(b)(2).

52. Arthur Best, *Evidence: Examples and Explanations,* 4th ed. (New York: Aspen Law & Business, 2001), 89–90.

53. David W. Broeder, "The University of Chicago Jury Project," *Nebraska Law Review* 38 (1959), 744–760.

54. 164 U.S. 492 (1896).

55. *United States v. Fioravanti,* 412 F.2d 407 (3d Cir. 1969).

56. William S. Neilson and Harold Winter, "The Elimination of Hung Juries: Retrials and Nonunanimous Verdicts," *International Review of Law and Economics* (March 2005), 2.

57. Bureau of Justice Statistics, *Federal Justice Statistics, 2009* (Washington, D.C.: U.S. Department of Justice, December 2011), 13, 18.

58. David W. Neubauer, *America's Courts and the Criminal Justice System,* 5th ed. (Belmont, Calif.: Wadsworth Publishing Co. 1996), 254.

59. The Innocence Project, "Know the Cases," at **www.innocenceproject.org/know.**

60. Michigan Law School & Northwestern Law School, "The National Registry of Exonerations," at **www.law.umich.edu/special/exoneration/Pages/browse.aspx.**

61. "When Eyewitnesses Are Mistaken," *The Week* (November 11, 2011), 13.

62. *State v. Lawson,* 291 P.3d 673 (Or. 2012).

63. Rick Jervis, "Texas Leads National Trend in Challenging Forensic Evidence," *USA Today* (December 17, 2013), 3A.

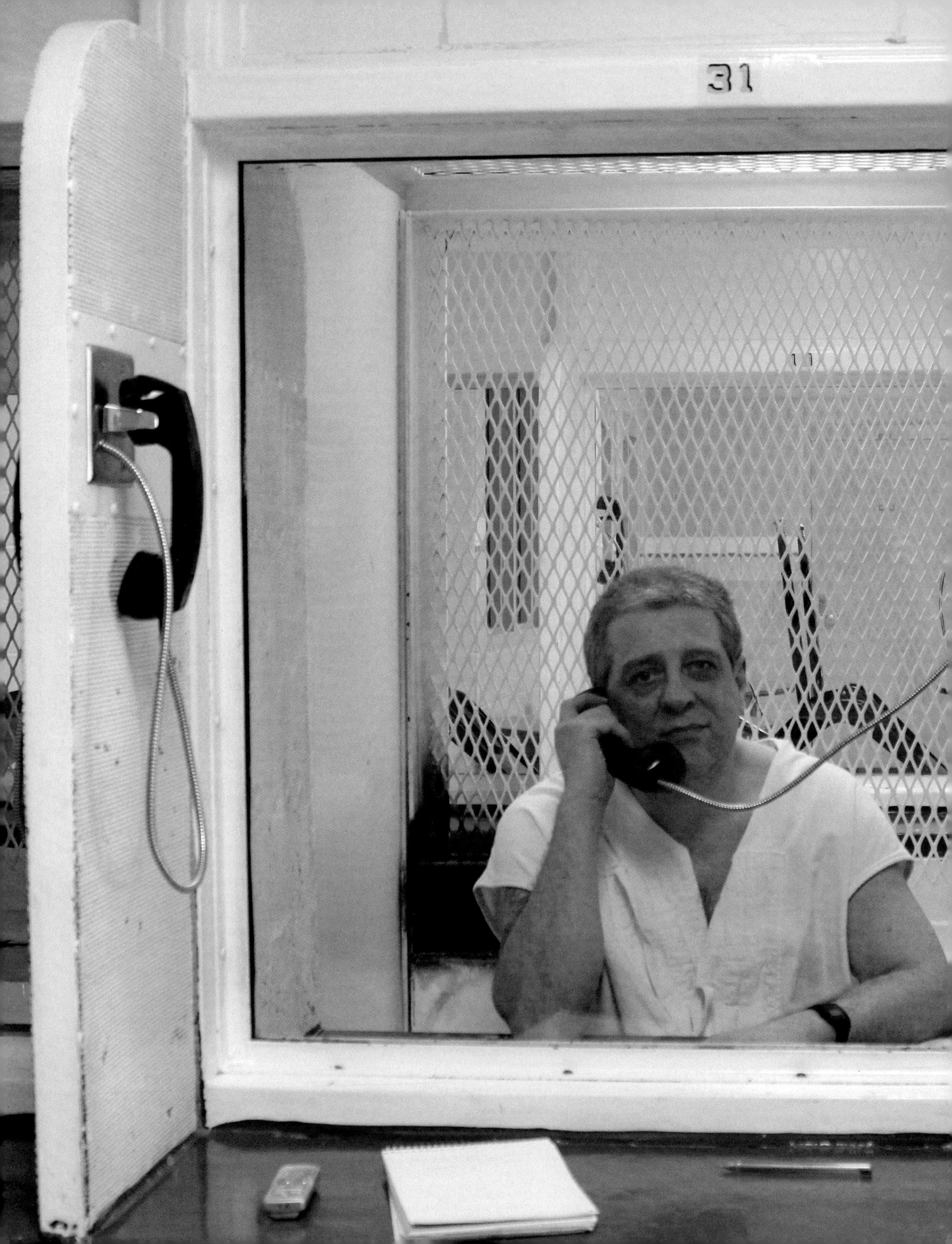
31

CHAPTER

9 Punishment and Sentencing

CHAPTER OUTLINE	CORRESPONDING LEARNING OBJECTIVES
The Purpose of Sentencing	List and contrast the four basic philosophical reasons for sentencing criminals.
The Structure of Sentencing	Contrast indeterminate with determinate sentencing.
	State who has input into the sentencing decision, and list the factors that determine a sentence.
Inconsistencies in Sentencing	Explain some of the reasons underlying the need for sentencing reform.
Sentencing Reform	Identify the arguments for and against the use of victim impact statements during sentencing hearings.
Capital Punishment— The Ultimate Sentence	Identify the two stages that make up the bifurcated process of death penalty sentencing.
	Explain why the U.S. Supreme Court abolished the death penalty for juvenile offenders.
	Describe the main issues of the death penalty debate.

To target your study and review, look for these numbered Learning Objective icons throughout the chapter.

Chantal Valery/AFP/Getty Images

Road RULES

FOLLOWING HER daily routine, on August 21, 2013, fifty-year-old Trish Cunningham decided to bike home after coaching cross-country practice at Annapolis High School in Annapolis, Maryland. As she neared the crest of a hill on a lightly traveled road, a van driven by Whitney Decesaris drove slowly behind her. Although there was no way to see whether traffic was approaching on the other side of the hill, Decesaris decided to pass the bicyclist. When a car did appear coming the other direction, Decesaris swerved back to the right, striking and killing Cunningham. Of the accident, a police officer said, "A little patience by the driver of the van and two lives would not be forever changed."

Under Maryland law, motorists must provide bicyclists with at least three feet of space at all times. Furthermore, state law requires that, before passing, a driver must ensure that the "roadway is clearly visible and is free of approaching traffic." Nonetheless, several months after Cunningham's death an Anne Arundel County grand jury decided that Decesaris deserved a light punishment for her blunder: four traffic citations, with a maximum fine of $500 each. Local bicyclists reacted with outrage, feeling that Decesaris should have been charged with criminally negligent manslaughter, at least. Criminal charges for drivers who kill bicyclists are, however, quite rare in the United States. As one cycling advocate points out, unless a driver is drunk or flees the scene, his or her chances of being punished beyond a fine are "virtually none."

To change this trend, a number of jurisdictions have passed "vulnerable user" laws that provide harsher sanctions for negligent drivers who cause bodily harm to bicyclists or pedestrians. Legal experts do not expect these laws to make much difference. "We as a society have chosen not to criminalize every single small mistake that has a dramatic consequence because you're driving a car," says Joe McCormack, a New York district attorney.

FOR CRITICAL ANALYSIS

1. Do you think Whitney Decesaris should have been punished more severely for killing Trish Cunningham? Why or why not?

2. In general, jurors are unwilling to impose harsh penalties on drivers who accidentally kill bicyclists, regardless of how negligent the driver might have been. Why do you think this is the case?

3. The Dutch legal system automatically places all responsibility for crashes involving motorists and bicyclists on the person driving the car. What might be the consequences of such a law in the United States?

Accidents in which drivers injure or kill bicyclists, such as the one shown here, rarely lead to criminal charges in the United States.

AP Images

THE PURPOSE OF SENTENCING

Professor Herbert Packer said that punishing criminals serves two ultimate purposes: the "deserved infliction of suffering on evil doers" and "the prevention of crime." [1] Even this straightforward assessment raises several questions. How does one determine the sort of punishment that is "deserved"? How can we be sure that certain penalties "prevent" crime? Should criminals be punished solely for the good of society, or should their well-being also be taken into consideration? Would harsher penalties for negligent drivers reduce the annual toll of about 700 cyclists killed and 48,000 injured on American roads? [2] Or would such penalties unfairly punish drivers for accidents that mostly are unintentional and unavoidable?

Sentencing laws indicate how any given group of people answered these questions but do not tell us why they were answered in that manner. To understand why, we must first consider the four basic philosophical reasons for sentencing—retribution, deterrence, incapacitation, and rehabilitation.

Retribution

The oldest and most common justification for punishing someone is that he or she "deserved it"—as the Old Testament states, "an eye for an eye and a tooth for a tooth." Under a system of justice that favors **retribution,** a wrongdoer who has freely chosen to violate society's rules must be punished for the infraction. Retribution relies on the principle of **just deserts,** which holds that the severity of the punishment must be in proportion to the severity of the crime. Retributive justice is not the same as *revenge*. Whereas revenge implies that the wrongdoer is punished only with the aim of satisfying a victim or victims, retribution is more concerned with the needs of society as a whole.

One problem with retributive ideas of justice lies in proportionality. Whether or not one agrees with the death penalty, the principle behind it is easy to fathom: the punishment (death) often fits the crime (murder). But what about the theft of an automobile? How does one fairly determine the amount of time the thief must spend in prison for that crime? Should the type of car or the wealth of the car owner matter? Theories of retribution often have a difficult time providing answers to such questions. [3]

Deterrence

The concept of **deterrence** (as well as incapacitation and rehabilitation) takes a different approach than does retribution. That is, rather than seeking only to punish the wrongdoer, the goal of sentencing should be to prevent future crimes. By "setting an example," society is sending a message to potential criminals that certain actions will not be tolerated. Deterrence can take two forms: general and specific. The basic idea of *general deterrence* is that by punishing one person, others will be discouraged from committing a similar crime. *Specific deterrence* assumes that an individual, after being punished once for a certain act, will be less likely to repeat that act because she or he does not want to be punished again. [4] Those who favor more severe punishments for negligent drivers often express themselves using principles of general deterrence. "Nobody wants to kill a cyclist, but the total absence of consequences [for doing so] does little to focus the mind," said an editorial writer in the *New York Times*. [5]

Both forms of deterrence have proved problematic in practice. General deterrence assumes that a person commits a crime only after a rational decision-making process in which he or she implicitly weighs the benefits of the crime against the possible costs

LEARNING OBJECTIVE

List and contrast the four basic philosophical reasons for sentencing criminals.

OPERATION
FLUSH THE JOHNS

104 Men Charged with
Patronizing a Prostitute
All are presumed innocent until proven guilty.

In June 2013, Nassau County (New York) District Attorney Kathleen Rice released the names and mug shots of more than one hundred men arrested for soliciting prostitutes as part of Operation "Flush the John."
■ How does this shaming strategy rely on the concept of general deterrence to reduce prostitution?

of the punishment. This is not necessarily the case, especially for young offenders who tend to value the immediate rewards of crime over the possible future consequences. The argument for specific deterrence is somewhat weakened by the fact that a relatively small number of habitual offenders are responsible for the majority of certain criminal acts.

Incapacitation

"Wicked people exist," said James Q. Wilson. "Nothing avails except to set them apart from innocent people."[6] Wilson's blunt statement summarizes the justification for **incapacitation** as a form of punishment. As a purely practical matter, incarcerating criminals guarantees that they will not be a danger to society, at least for the length of their prison terms. Such reasoning has increased the popularity of life sentences without the possibility of parole in the criminal justice system. Since 1984, the inmate population serving life-without-parole has quadrupled to nearly 160,000, encompassing one of every nine individuals behind bars in the United States.[7]

Several studies do support incapacitation's efficacy as a crime-fighting tool. Criminologist Isaac Ehrlich of the University at Buffalo estimated that a 1 percent increase in sentence length will produce a 1 percent decrease in the crime rate.[8] More recently, Avinash Singh Bhati of the Urban Institute in Washington, D.C., found that higher levels of incarceration lead to fewer violent crimes but have little impact on property crime rates.[9]

Incapacitation as a theory of punishment does suffer from several weaknesses. Unlike retribution, it offers no proportionality with regard to a particular crime. Giving a burglar a life sentence would certainly ensure that she or he would not commit another burglary. Does that justify such a severe penalty? Furthermore, incarceration protects society only until the criminal is freed. A number of studies have shown that, on release, offenders may actually be more likely to commit crimes than before they were imprisoned.[10] In that case, incapacitation may increase likelihood of crime, rather than diminish it.

Rehabilitation

Incapacitation The philosophy that crime can be prevented by detaining wrongdoers in prison, thereby separating them from the community and reducing criminal opportunities.

Rehabilitation The philosophy that society is best served when wrongdoers are provided the resources needed to eliminate criminality from their behavioral pattern.

For many, **rehabilitation** is the most "humane" goal of punishment. This line of thinking reflects the view that crime is a "social phenomenon" caused not by the inherent criminality of a person, but by factors in that person's surroundings. By removing wrongdoers from their environment and intervening to change their values and antisocial personality traits, the rehabilitative model suggests, criminals can be "treated" and possibly even "cured" of their proclivities toward crime. Although studies of the effectiveness of rehabilitation are too varied to be easily summarized, it does appear that, in most instances, criminals who receive treatment are less likely to reoffend than those who do not.[11]

For the better part of the past three decades, the American criminal justice system has been characterized by a notable rejection of many of the precepts of rehabilitation in favor of retributive, deterrent, and incapacitating sentencing strategies that "get tough on crime." Recently, however, more jurisdictions are turning to rehabilitation as a cost-effective (and, possibly, crime-reducing) alternative to punishment, a topic that we will explore more fully in the next chapter. (The *Mastering Concepts* feature that follows provides a review of the four main sentencing philosophies.)

Restorative Justice An approach to punishment designed to repair the harm done to the victim and the community by the offender's criminal act.

Restitution Monetary compensation for damages done to the victim by the offender's criminal act.

Restorative Justice

Despite the emergence of victim impact statements, which we will discuss later in the chapter, victims have historically been restricted from participating in the punishment process. Such restrictions are supported by the general assumption that victims are focused on vengeance rather than justice. According to criminologists Heather Strang of Australia's Centre for Restorative Justice and Lawrence W. Sherman of the University of Pennsylvania, however, this is not always the case. After the initial shock of the crime has worn off, Strang and Sherman have found, victims are more interested in concessions that have little to do with revenge, such as an opportunity to participate in the process, financial reparations, and an apology from the offender.[12]

Restorative justice strategies focus on these concerns by attempting to repair the damage that a crime does to the victim, the victim's family, and society as a whole. This outlook relies on the efforts of the offender to "undo" the harm caused by the criminal act through an apology and **restitution,** or monetary compensation for losses suffered by the victim(s). Restorative justice has five separate components that differentiate it from the mainstream criminal justice system:

1. *Offender involvement.* Offenders are given the opportunity to take responsibility for and address the reasons behind their behavior in ways that do not involve the corrections system.
2. *Victim involvement.* Victims have a voice in determining how the offender should atone for her or his crime.

MASTERING CONCEPTS

SENTENCING PHILOSOPHIES

In 2013, Judge Vic VanderSchoor sentenced Dennis Huston to sixteen years in prison for embezzling nearly $3 million from government agencies in Franklin County, Washington. Although Huston's defense attorney asked for a lighter punishment because of his client's age (sixty-six years), the judge's decision was in keeping with the four main philosophies of sentencing.

PHILOSOPHY	BASIC PRINCIPLE	EXPLANATION
Retribution	Punishment is society's means of expressing condemnation of illegal acts such as embezzlement.	Dennis Huston "violated the trust of each and every citizen of the county," according to Judge VanderSchoor.
Deterrence	Harsh sentences for embezzlement may convince others not to engage in that illegal behavior.	Prosecutors said that Huston's example would prevent other government employees "from going down that same road."
Incapacitation	Incarcerated criminals are not a threat to the general society for the duration of their time behind bars.	While in prison, Huston will be unable to commit embezzlement or any other white-collar crime.
Rehabilitation	Prison programs can help inmates change their behavior so that they no longer pose a threat to themselves or others.	Huston reportedly used the stolen money to fuel his cocaine and gambling habits. While in prison, he can receive treatment and training to address these problems.

Source: Kristen M. Kraemer, "Huston Sentenced to 16 Years in Franklin County Embezzlement Scandal," *Tri-City Herald* (Kennewick, WA) (March 27, 2013), at **www.tri-cityherald.com/2013/03/27/2331438/huston-sentenced-to-16-years.html**.

3. *Victim-offender interaction.* On a voluntary basis, victims and offenders meet to discuss and better understand the circumstances of the crime. This meeting allows the victim to express her or his feelings related to the offense.

4. *Community involvement.* Community members also affected by the crime can participate in the process, and request an apology and restitution from the offender.

5. *Problem-solving practices.* Participants in the process—including victims, offenders, and community members—can develop strategies for solving the problems that led to the crime in question.[13]

Although restorative justice is theoretically available for all types of criminal behavior, it almost always involves property crime, public order crime, and, particularly, offenses committed by juveniles. Rarely, if ever, will restorative justice principles be applied to violent crime.

COMPENSATING THE VICTIM Programs based on the principles of restorative justice face several obstacles. Primarily, many criminal justice professionals regard these principles as too vague and "touchy-feely" to be useful.[14] Furthermore, federal and state sentencing laws do not address issues such as communication between victims and offenders. So supporters have to rely on sympathetic judges, prosecutors, and defense attorneys to implement restorative justice theories in court. Finally, many courts are unable or unwilling to enforce restitution orders.

On a federal level, the Victims of Crime Act of 1984 established the Crime Victims Fund to provide financial aid for crime victims.[15] This program—financed by fines and penalties assessed on convicted federal offenders—distributes grants to state governments, which in turn pass the funds on to victims. In 2011–2012, through the Crime Victims Fund, states provided nearly $1.2 billion in victim compensation and victim assistance.[16]

VICTIM-OFFENDER DIALOGUE One increasingly popular offshoot of the restorative justice movement is *victim-offender dialogue (VOD).* This practice centers on face-to-face meetings between victims and offenders in a secure setting at the offender's prison. VOD allows the victims to speak directly to offenders about the criminal incident and how it has affected their lives. It also gives the offender a chance to apologize directly to the victim. Today, more than half of state corrections departments support VOD programs within their prisons.[17]

////SELF ASSESSMENT

Fill in the blanks, and check your answers on page 300.

The saying "an eye for an eye and a tooth for a tooth" reflects the concept of _____ as a justification for punishment. The goal of _____ is to prevent future crimes by "setting an example," while _____ purports to prevent crime by keeping offenders behind bars. Models of _____ suggest that criminals can be "treated" and possibly even "cured."

THE STRUCTURE OF SENTENCING

Philosophy not only is integral to explaining *why* we punish criminals, but also influences *how* we do so. The history of criminal sentencing in the United States has been characterized by shifts in institutional power among the different branches of government. When public opinion moves toward more severe strategies of retribution, deterrence, and incapacitation, legislatures have responded by asserting their power over determining sentencing guidelines. In contrast, periods of rehabilitative justice are marked by a transfer of this power to judges.

Legislative Sentencing Authority

Because legislatures are responsible for making laws, these bodies are also initially responsible for passing the criminal codes that determine the length of sentences.

INDETERMINATE SENTENCING Penal codes with **indeterminate sentencing** policies set a minimum and maximum amount of time that a person must spend in prison. For example, the indeterminate sentence for aggravated assault could be three to nine years, or six to twelve years, or twenty years to life. Within these parameters, a judge can prescribe a particular term, after which an administrative body known as the *parole board* decides at what point the offender is to be released. A prisoner is aware that he or she is eligible for *parole* as soon as the minimum time has been served and that good behavior can further shorten the sentence.

LEARNING **2** OBJECTIVE Contrast indeterminate with determinate sentencing.

DETERMINATE SENTENCING Disillusionment with the somewhat vague nature of indeterminate sentencing often leads politicians to support **determinate sentencing,** or fixed sentencing. As the name implies, in determinate sentencing an offender serves exactly the amount of time to which she or he is sentenced (minus "good time," described below). For example, if the legislature deems that the punishment for a first-time armed robber is ten years, then the judge has no choice but to impose a sentence of ten years, and the criminal will serve ten years minus good time before being freed.

"GOOD TIME" AND TRUTH IN SENTENCING Often, the amount of time prescribed by a judge bears little relation to the amount of time the offender actually spends behind bars. In states with indeterminate sentencing, parole boards have broad powers to release prisoners once they have served the minimum portion of their sentence. Furthermore, all but four states offer prisoners the opportunity to reduce their sentences by doing **"good time"**—or behaving well—as determined by prison administrators. (See Figure 9.1 that follows for an idea of the effects of good-time regulations and other early-release programs on state prison sentences.)

Sentence-reduction programs promote discipline within a correctional institution and reduce overcrowding, so many prison officials welcome them. The public, however, may react negatively to news that a violent criminal has served a shorter term than ordered by a judge and pressure elected officials to "do something." In Illinois, for example, some inmates were serving less than half of their sentences by receiving a one-day reduction in their term for each day of "good time." Under pressure from victims' groups, the state legislature passed a **truth-in-sentencing law** in 1995 that requires murderers and others convicted of serious crimes to complete at least 85 percent of their sentences with no time off for good behavior.[18]

As their name suggests, the primary goal of these laws is to provide the public with more accurate information about the actual amount of time an offender will spend behind bars. The laws also keep convicts incapacitated for longer periods of time. Fifteen years after Illinois passed its truth-in-sentencing law, those murderers subject to the legislation were spending an average of seventeen years more in prison than those not subject to the legislation. For sex offenders in the state, the difference was 3.5 years.[19]

Indeterminate Sentencing An indeterminate term of incarceration in which a judge determines the minimum and maximum terms of imprisonment.

Determinate Sentencing A period of incarceration that is fixed by a sentencing authority and cannot be reduced by judges or other corrections officials.

"Good Time" A reduction in time served by prisoners based on good conduct, conformity to rules, and other positive behavior.

Truth-in-Sentencing Laws Legislative attempts to ensure that convicts will serve approximately the terms to which they were initially sentenced.

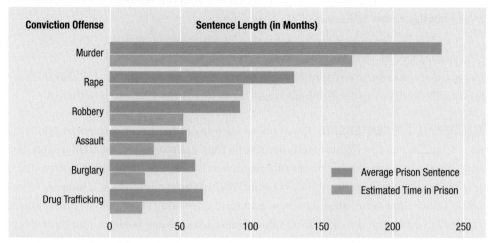

FIGURE 9.1 Average Sentence Length and Estimated Time Actually Served in State Prison

Source: Bureau of Justice Statistics, *National Corrections Reporting Program: Sentence Length of State Prisoners, by Offense, Admission Type, Sex, and Race* (May 5, 2011), "Table 9: First Releases from State Prison, 2009," at **www.bjs.gov/index.cfm?ty=pbdetail&iid=2045.**

Today, forty states have instituted some form of truth-in-sentencing laws, though the future of such statutes is in doubt due to the pressure of overflowing prisons.

Judicial Sentencing Authority

During the pretrial procedures and the trial itself, the judge's role is somewhat passive and reactive. She or he is primarily a "procedural watchdog," ensuring that the rights of the defendant are not infringed while the prosecutor and defense attorney dictate the course of action. At a traditional sentencing hearing, however, the judge is no longer an arbiter between the parties. She or he is now called on to exercise the ultimate authority of the state in determining the defendant's fate.

Just as a physician gives specific treatment to individual patients depending on their particular health needs, the hypothesis goes, a judge considers the specific circumstances of each offender in choosing the best form of punishment. Taking the analogy one step further, just as the diagnosis of a qualified physician should not be questioned, a qualified judge should have absolute discretion in making the sentencing decision. *Judicial discretion* rests on the assumption that a judge should be given ample leeway in determining punishments that fit both the crime and the criminal.[20] As we shall see later in the chapter, the growth of determinate sentencing has severely restricted judicial discretion in many jurisdictions.

JUDICIAL DISPOSITIONS Within whatever legislative restrictions apply, the sentencing judge has a number of options when it comes to choosing the proper form of punishment. These sentences, or *dispositions,* include

1. *Capital punishment.* Reserved normally for those who commit first degree murder—that is, a premeditated killing—capital punishment is a sentencing option in thirty-two states. It is also an option in federal court, where a defendant can be put to death for murder, as well as for trafficking in a large amount of illegal drugs, *espionage* (spying), and *treason* (betraying the United States).

2. *Imprisonment.* Whether for the purpose of retribution, deterrence, incapacitation, or rehabilitation, a common form of punishment in American history has been imprisonment. In fact, it is used so commonly today that judges—and legislators—are having to take factors such as prison overcrowding into consideration when making sentencing decisions. The issues surrounding imprisonment will be discussed in Chapters 11 and 12.

3. *Probation.* One of the effects of prison overcrowding has been a sharp rise in the use of probation, in which an offender is permitted to live in the community under supervision and is not incarcerated. (Probation is covered in Chapter 10.) *Alternative sanctions* (also discussed in Chapter 10) combine probation with other dispositions such as electronic monitoring, house arrest, boot camps, and shock incarceration.

4. *Fines.* Fines can be levied by judges in addition to incarceration and probation or independently of other forms of punishment. When a fine is the only punishment, it usually reflects the judge's belief that the offender is not a threat to the community and does not need to be imprisoned or supervised. In some instances, mostly involving drug offenders, a judge can order the seizure of an offender's property, such as his or her home.

OTHER FORMS OF PUNISHMENT Whereas fines are payable to the government, restitution and community service are seen as reparations to the injured party or to the community. As noted earlier, restitution is a direct payment to the victim or victims of a crime. Community service consists of "good works"—such as cleaning up highway litter or tutoring disadvantaged youths—that benefit the entire community. Along with restitution, *apologies* play an important role in restorative justice, discussed previously in this chapter. An apology is seen as an effort by the offender to recognize the wrongness of her or his conduct and acknowledge the impact that it has had on the victim and the community.

In some jurisdictions, judges have a great deal of discretionary power and can impose sentences that do not fall into any of these categories. This "creative sentencing," as it is sometimes called, has produced some interesting results. A judge in Painesville, Ohio, ordered a man who had stolen from a Salvation Army kettle to pass twenty-four hours as a homeless person. In Broward County, Florida, a man who shoved his wife was sentenced to "take her to Red Lobster," go bowling with her, and then undergo marriage counseling.[21] A Covington, Kentucky, teenager charged with disorderly conduct for falsely yelling "bingo" in a bingo hall was banned from saying that particular word for six months. Though these types of punishments are often ridiculed, many judges see them as a viable alternative to incarceration for less dangerous offenders.

The Sentencing Process

The decision of how to punish a wrongdoer is the end result of what Yale Law School professor Kate Stith and federal appeals court judge José A. Cabranes call the "sentencing ritual."[22] The two main participants in this ritual are the judge and the

After Jason Householder, left, and John Stockum were convicted of criminal damaging for throwing beer bottles at a car, municipal court judge David Hostetler of Coshocton, Ohio, gave them a choice: jail time or a walk down Main Street in women's clothing. As you can see, they chose the dresses. What reasons might a judge have for handing down this sort of "creative" sentence?

AP Images/*Coshocton Tribune*/Dante Smith

Presentence Investigative Report An investigative report on an offender's background that assists a judge in determining the proper sentence.

defendant, but prosecutors, defense attorneys, and probation officers also play a role in the proceedings. Individualized justice requires that the judge consider all the relevant circumstances in making sentencing decisions. Therefore, judicial discretion is often tantamount to *informed* discretion—without the aid of the other members of the courtroom work group, the judge would not have sufficient information to make the proper sentencing choice.

THE PRESENTENCE INVESTIGATIVE REPORT For judges operating under various states' indeterminate sentencing guidelines, information in the **presentence investigative report** is a valuable component of the sentencing ritual. Compiled by a probation officer, the report describes the crime in question, notes the suffering of any victims, and lists the defendant's prior offenses (as well as any alleged but uncharged criminal activity). The report also contains a range of personal data such as family background, work history, education, and community activities—information that is not admissible as evidence during trial. In putting together the presentence investigative report, the probation officer is supposed to gain a "feel" for the defendant and communicate these impressions of the offender to the judge.

The report also includes a sentencing recommendation. This aspect has been criticized as giving probation officers too much power in the sentencing process, because less-diligent judges would simply rely on the recommendation in determining punishment.[23] For the most part, however, judges do not act as if they were bound by the presentence investigative report.

THE PROSECUTOR AND DEFENSE ATTORNEY To a certain extent, the adversarial process does not end when the guilt of the defendant has been established. Both the prosecutor and the defense attorney are interviewed in the process of preparing the presentence investigative report, and both will try to present a version of the facts consistent with their own sentencing goals. The defense attorney in particular has a duty to make sure that the information contained in the report is accurate and not prejudicial toward his or her client. Depending on the norms of any particular courtroom work group, prosecutors and defense attorneys may petition the judge directly for certain sentences.

SENTENCING AND THE JURY Juries also play an important role in the sentencing process. As we will see later in the chapter, it is the jury, and not the judge, who generally decides whether a convict eligible for the death penalty will in fact be executed. Additionally, six states—Arkansas, Kentucky, Missouri, Oklahoma, Texas, and Virginia—allow juries, rather than judges, to make the sentencing decision even when the death penalty is not an option. In these states, the judge gives the jury instructions on the range of penalties available, and then the jury makes the final decision.[24]

Juries have traditionally been assigned a relatively small role in felony sentencing, largely out of concern that jurors' lack of experience and legal expertise leaves them unprepared for the task. When sentencing by juries is allowed, the practice is popular with prosecutors because jurors are more likely than judges to give harsh sentences, particularly for drug crimes, sexual assault, and theft.[25]

Factors of Sentencing

The sentencing ritual strongly lends itself to the concept of individualized justice. With inputs—sometimes conflicting—from the prosecutor, attorney, and probation

State who has input into the sentencing decision, and list the factors that determine a sentence. **LEARNING OBJECTIVE 3**

FASTFACTS

**JUDGE
JOB DESCRIPTION:**

- Preside over trials and hearings in federal, state, and local courts.

WHAT KIND OF TRAINING IS REQUIRED?

- A law degree and several years of legal experience.

- Judges are either appointed or elected.

ANNUAL SALARY RANGE?

- $93,000–$162,000

ELLEN KALAMA CLARK
SUPERIOR COURT JUDGE

Photo Courtesy Ellen Kalama Clark

My favorite thing about my work is making a difference in people's lives. This is especially true in juvenile court, which is my favorite assignment. For example, early one morning I was walking to the juvenile court building when I saw a group of teenage boys heading toward me. Some of them I recognized from being in court, and they recognized me. A couple avoided eye contact, one looked me straight in the eye rather defiantly, and the last one kind of smirked. As we got closer to each other, the last boy—a tall, stocky kid—stopped, and the group just about blocked the sidewalk. It made me nervous.

The boy then leaned forward toward me and said, not in an intimidating manner but certainly meaning to get my attention, "Hey, Judge." I said good morning. He then broke into a big smile and said, "I got my GED [general equivalency diploma]! And I'm staying out of trouble." I didn't remember his name or his offense, but I was absolutely thrilled that he had accomplished those things, that he would want me to know that, and that he was bragging about it in front of his friends. I consider this a great success story.

Social Media Career Tip Think about your online presence as your online personal brand. You create this online personal brand through the sum of all the posts you make on different Web sites and social media tools.

---

officer, the judge can be reasonably sure of getting the "full picture" of the crime and the criminal. In making the final decision, however, most judges consider two factors above all others: the seriousness of the crime and any mitigating or aggravating circumstances.

THE SERIOUSNESS OF THE CRIME As would be expected, the seriousness of the crime is the primary factor in a judge's sentencing decision. The more serious the crime, the harsher the punishment, for society demands no less. Each judge has his or her own methods of determining the seriousness of the offense. Many judges simply consider the "conviction offense," basing their sentence on the crime for which the defendant was convicted.

Other judges—some mandated by statute—focus instead on the **"real offense"** in determining the punishment. The "real offense" is based on the actual behavior of the defendant, regardless of the official conviction. For example, through a plea bargain, a defendant may plead guilty to simple assault when in fact he hit his victim in the face with a baseball bat. A judge, after reading the presentence investigative report, could decide to sentence the defendant as if he had committed aggravated assault, which is the "real" offense. Though many prosecutors and defense attorneys are opposed to "real offense" procedures, which can render a plea bargain meaningless, many criminal justice experts believe that they bring a measure of fairness to the sentencing decision.[26]

MITIGATING AND AGGRAVATING CIRCUMSTANCES When deciding the severity of punishment, judges and juries are often required to evaluate the *mitigating* and *aggravating circumstances* surrounding the case. **Mitigating circumstances** are those

"Real Offense" The actual offense committed, as opposed to the charge levied by a prosecutor as the result of a plea bargain.

Mitigating Circumstances Any circumstances accompanying the commission of a crime that may justify a lighter sentence.

circumstances, such as the fact that the defendant was coerced into committing the crime, that allow a lighter sentence to be handed down. In contrast, **aggravating circumstances,** such as a prior record, blatant disregard for the safety of others, or the use of a weapon, can lead a judge or jury to inflict a harsher penalty than might otherwise be warranted (see Figure 9.2 that follows).

Aggravating circumstances play an important role in a prosecutor's decision to charge a suspect with capital murder. The criminal code of every state that employs the death penalty contains a list of aggravating circumstances that make an offender eligible for execution. Most of these codes require that the murder take place during the commission of felony, create a grave risk of death for multiple victims, or interfere with the duties of law enforcement. (For a comprehensive rundown, go to **www .deathpenaltyinfo.org/aggravating-factors-capital-punishment-state**.) As you will see later in the chapter, mitigating factors such as mental illness and youth can spare an otherwise death-eligible offender from capital punishment.

JUDICIAL PHILOSOPHY Most states and the federal government spell out mitigating and aggravating circumstances in statutes, but there is room for judicial discretion in applying the law to particular cases. Judges are not uniform, or even consistent, in their opinions of which circumstances are mitigating or aggravating. One judge may believe that a fourteen-year-old is not fully responsible for his or her actions, while another may believe that teenagers should be treated as adults by criminal courts.

Sometimes, a judge's personal sentencing philosophy will prove unpopular. In 2013, two state judges came under considerable criticism for handing down relatively light sentences in sexual assault cases. The first, Alabama circuit court judge James W. Woodruff, spared a defendant found guilty of raping his thirteen-year-old neighbor from having to spend any time behind bars. The second, Montana state judge G. Todd Baugh, sentenced a teacher convicted of raping a fourteen-year-old student to only thirty days

FIGURE 9.2 Aggravating and Mitigating Circumstances

Aggravating Circumstances	Mitigating Circumstances
• An offense involved multiple participants, and the offender was the leader of the group.	• An offender acted under strong provocation, or other circumstances in the relationship between the offender and the victim make the offender's behavior less serious and therefore less deserving of punishment.
• A victim was particularly vulnerable.	
• A victim was treated with particular cruelty for which an offender should be held responsible.	• An offender played a minor or passive role in the offense or participated under circumstances of coercion or duress.
• The offense involved injury or threatened violence to others, and was committed to gratify an offender's desire for pleasure or excitement.	• An offender, because of youth or physical impairment, lacked substantial capacity for judgment when the offense was committed.
• The degree of bodily harm caused, attempted, threatened, or foreseen by an offender was substantially greater than average for the given offense.	
• The degree of economic harm caused, attempted, threatened, or foreseen by an offender was substantially greater than average for the given offense.	
• The amount of contraband materials possessed by the offender or under the offender's control was substantially greater than average for the given offense.	

Source: American Bar Association.

in jail, stating that the victim was "older than her chronological age."[27] Despite being heavily criticized by prosecutors and the public, both judges refused to reconsider their decisions.

////// SELF ASSESSMENT

Fill in the blanks, and check your answers on page 300.

_____ sentences set a minimum and a maximum amount of time a convict must spend in prison, whereas _____ sentences reflect the exact length of incapacitation, minus reductions for _____ _____, or behaving well. Judges often rely on information contained in the _____ _____ report when making sentencing decisions. The primary factor in the sentencing process is the _____ of the crime for which the defendant was convicted. _____ circumstances allow a lighter sentence to be handed down, while _____ circumstances can lead to the imposition of a harsher penalty.

INCONSISTENCIES IN SENTENCING

For some, the natural differences in judicial philosophies, when combined with a lack of institutional control, raise important questions. Why should a bank robber in South Carolina and a bank robber in Michigan receive different sentences? Even federal indeterminate sentencing guidelines seem overly vague: a bank robber can receive a prison term from one day to twenty years, depending almost entirely on the judge.[28] Furthermore, if judges have freedom to use their discretion, do they not also have the freedom to misuse it?

Purported improper judicial discretion is often the first reason given for two phenomena that plague the criminal justice system: *sentencing disparity* and *sentencing discrimination*. Though the two terms are often used interchangeably, they describe different statistical occurrences—the causes of which are open to debate.

LEARNING

4 OBJECTIVE

Explain some of the reasons underlying the need for sentencing reform.

Sentencing Disparity

Justice would seem to demand that those who commit similar crimes should receive similar punishments. **Sentencing disparity** occurs when this expectation is not met in one of three ways:

1. Criminals receive similar sentences for different crimes of unequal seriousness.
2. Criminals receive different sentences for similar crimes.
3. Mitigating or aggravating circumstances have a disproportionate effect on sentences.

Most of the blame for sentencing disparities is placed at the feet of the judicial profession. Even with the restrictive presence of the sentencing reforms we will discuss shortly, judges have a great deal of influence over the sentencing decision, whether they are making that decision themselves or instructing the jury on how to do so. Like other members of the criminal justice system, judges are individuals, and their discretionary sentencing decisions reflect that individuality. Besides judicial discretion, several other causes have been offered as explanations for sentencing disparity, including differences between geographic jurisdictions and between federal and state courts.

For offenders, the amount of time spent in prison often depends on where the crime was committed. A comparison of the sentences for drug trafficking reveals that someone convicted of the crime in Oregon faces an average of 65 months in prison, whereas a similar offender in eastern North Carolina can expect an average of 125 months.[29] The average sentences imposed in the Fourth Circuit, which includes North Carolina, South Carolina, Virginia, and West Virginia, are consistently harsher than those in the Ninth Circuit, comprising most of the western states: 52 months longer for convictions related to firearms and 48 months longer for all offenses.[30] Such disparities can be attributed to a number of different factors, including local attitudes toward crime and available financial resources to cover the expenses of incarceration.

Also, because of different sentencing guidelines, which we will discuss later in the chapter, the punishment for the same crime in federal and state courts can be dramatically different. Figure 9.3 that follows shows the sentencing disparities for certain crimes in the two systems.

Sentencing Discrimination

Sentencing discrimination occurs when disparities can be attributed to such extralegal variables as the defendant's gender, race, or economic standing.

RACE AND SENTENCING At first glance, racial discrimination would seem to be rampant in sentencing practices. Research by Cassia Spohn of Arizona State University and David Holleran of the College of New Jersey suggests that minorities pay a "punishment penalty" when it comes to sentencing.[31] In Chicago, Spohn and Holleran found that convicted African Americans were 12.1 percent more likely and convicted Hispanics were 15.3 percent more likely to go to prison than convicted whites. Another report released several years ago by the Illinois Disproportionate Justice Impact Study Commission

FIGURE 9.3 Average Maximum Sentences for Selected Crimes in State and Federal Courts

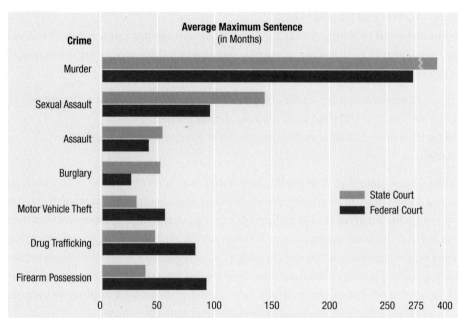

Source: Bureau of Justice Statistics, *Felony Defendants in Large Urban Counties, 2009—Statistical Tables* (Washington, D.C.: U.S. Department of Justice, December 2013), Table 25, page 30; and U.S. Sentencing Commission, "Statistical Information Packet, Fiscal Year 2009, First Circuit," Table 7, at **www.ussc.gov/Data_and_Statistics/Federal_Sentencing_Statistics/State_District_Circuit/2009/1c09.pdf.**

found that African Americans were nearly five times more likely to be sentenced to prison than whites for low-level drug crimes in that state.[32]

Nationwide, about 38 percent of all inmates in state and federal prisons are African American,[33] even though members of that minority group make up only about 13 percent of the country's population and represent 28 percent of those arrested.[34] In federal prisons, nearly seven out of every ten inmates are either African American or Hispanic.[35]

SENTENCING BIAS? Such numbers, while drastic, may not be the result of blatant sentencing bias. For example, the large numbers of Hispanics in federal prison are a direct result of immigration laws, which disproportionately target that demographic. Furthermore, Spohn and Holleran found that the rate of imprisonment rose significantly for minorities who were young and unemployed. This led them to conclude that the disparities between races were not the result of "conscious" discrimination on the part of the sentencing judges. Rather, faced with limited time to make decisions and limited information about the offenders, the judges would resort to stereotypes, considering not just race, but age and unemployment as well.[36]

Another study, published in 2006, found that older judges and judges who were members of minority groups in Pennsylvania were less likely to send offenders to prison, regardless of their race.[37] Such research findings support the argument in favor of diversity among judges, discussed in Chapter 7.

LENGTH OF SENTENCE Further evidence suggests that race has an impact on length of sentences. Several years ago, researchers from the University of Nevada at Reno found that African Americans received "significantly higher" maximum sentences than white defendants for felony convictions and drunk driving in that state.[38] Nationwide, the issue of crack cocaine sentencing has placed a harsh spotlight on racial disparity in the criminal justice system. Powder cocaine and crack, a crystallized form of the drug that is smoked rather than inhaled, are chemically identical. Under federal legislation passed in 1986, however, sentences for crimes involving crack were, in some instances, one hundred times more severe than for crimes involving powder cocaine.[39]

Because blacks are more likely to use crack, with white users favoring powder cocaine, these laws had a disproportionate impact on the African American community in the United States. About 80 percent of federal crack defendants are black and therefore received considerably more severe punishments than their powder-favoring, mostly white, counterparts.[40] In 2010, Congress reduced the crack/powder cocaine disparity,[41] and in 2014 the Obama administration urged federal inmates sentenced under the old guidelines to apply for a reduction in their sentences. "[These are] low-level, nonviolent drug offenders who remain in prison, and who would likely have received a substantially lower sentence if convicted of precisely the same offenses today," said one federal official. "This is not fair, and it harms our criminal justice system."[42]

WOMEN AND SENTENCING Few would argue that race or ethnicity should be a factor in sentencing decisions—the system should be "color-blind." Does the same principle apply to women? In other words, should the system be "gender-blind" as well—at least on a policy level? Congress answered that question in the Sentencing Reform Act of 1984, which emphasized the ideal of gender-neutral sentencing.[43] In practice, however, this

A judge in Pontiac, Michigan, sentenced seventy-five-year-old Sandra Layne to at least twenty-two years in prison for fatally shooting her teenage grandson during an argument. How might a woman's gender work against her in sentencing situations involving family-related violent crimes?

AP Images

has not occurred. Women who are convicted of crimes are less likely to go to prison than are men, and those who are incarcerated tend to serve shorter sentences. According to government data, on average, a woman receives a sentence that is twenty-nine months shorter than that of a man for a violent crime and nine months shorter for a property crime.[44]

When adjusting for comparable arrest offenses, criminal histories, and other pre-sentencing factors, Sonja B. Starr of the University of Michigan Law School found that male convicts receive sentences that are 60 percent more severe than those for women.[45] One study attributes these differences to the elements of female criminality: in property crimes, women are usually accessories, and in violent crimes, women are usually reacting to physical abuse. In both situations, the mitigating circumstances lead to lesser punishment.[46]

///// SELF ASSESSMENT

Fill in the blanks, and check your answers on page 300.

Sentencing _____ occurs when similar crimes are punished with dissimilar sentences, while sentencing _____ is the result of judicial consideration of extralegal variables, such as the defendant's race or gender.

SENTENCING REFORM

Judicial discretion, then, has both positives and negatives. Although it allows judges to impose a wide variety of sentences to fit specific criminal situations, it also fails to rein in a judge's subjective biases, which can lead to disparity and perhaps discrimination. Critics of judicial discretion believe that its costs (the lack of equality) outweigh its benefits (providing individualized justice). As Columbia law professor John C. Coffee noted:

If we wish the sentencing judge to treat "like cases alike," a more inappropriate technique for the presentation could hardly be found than one that stresses a novelistic portrayal of each offender and thereby overloads the decisionmaker in a welter of detail.[47]

In other words, Professor Coffee feels that judges are given too much information in the sentencing process, making it impossible for them to be consistent in their decisions. It follows that limiting judicial discretion would not only simplify the process but lessen the opportunity for disparity or discrimination. This attitude has spread through state and federal legislatures, causing extensive changes in sentencing procedures within the American criminal justice system.

Sentencing Guidelines
Legislatively determined guidelines that judges are required to follow when sentencing those convicted of specific crimes.

Sentencing Guidelines

In an effort to eliminate the inequities of disparity by removing judicial bias from the sentencing process, many states and the federal government have turned to **sentencing guidelines,** which require judges to dispense legislatively determined sentences based on such factors as the seriousness of the crime and the offender's prior record.

STATE SENTENCING GUIDELINES In 1978, Minnesota became the first state to create a Sentencing Guidelines Commission with a mandate to construct and monitor the use of a determinate sentencing structure. The Minnesota Commission left no doubt as to the philosophical justification for the new sentencing statutes, stating unconditionally that retribution was its primary goal.[48] Today, about twenty states employ some form of sentencing guidelines with similar goals.

In general, these guidelines remove discretionary power from state judges by turning sentencing into a mathematical exercise. Members of the courtroom work group are guided by a *grid,* which helps them determine the proper sentence. Figure 9.4 that follows shows the grid established by the Massachusetts sentencing commission. As in the grids used by most states, one axis ranks the type of crime, while the other refers to the offender's criminal history. In the grid for Massachusetts, the red boxes indicate the "incarceration zone." A prison sentence is required for crimes in this zone. The yellow boxes delineate a "discretionary zone," in which the judge can decide between incarceration or intermediate sanctions, which you will learn about in the next chapter.

FEDERAL SENTENCING GUIDELINES In 1984, Congress passed the Sentencing Reform Act (SRA),[49] paving the way for federal sentencing guidelines that went into effect three years later. Similar in many respects to the state guidelines, the SRA also eliminated parole for federal prisoners and severely limited early release from prison due to good behavior.[50] The impact of the SRA and the state guidelines has been dramatic. Sentences have become harsher—by the mid-2000s, the average federal prison sentence was fifty months, more than twice as long as in 1984.[51]

Furthermore, much of the discretion in sentencing has shifted from the judge to the prosecutor. Because the prosecutor chooses the criminal charge, she or he can, in effect, present the judge with the range of sentences. Defendants and their defense attorneys realize this and are more likely to agree to a plea bargain, which is, after all, a "deal" with the prosecutor.

FIGURE 9.4 Massachusetts's Sentencing Guidelines

Sentencing Guidelines Grid

Level	Illustrative Offenses	Sentence Range				
6	Manslaughter (Involuntary) Armed Robbery A&B DW* (Significant Injury)	40–60 Months	45–67 Months	50–75 Months	60–90 Months	80–120 Months
5	Unarmed Robbery Unarmed Burglary Stalking in Violation of Order Larceny ($50,000 and over)	12–36 Months IS-IV IS-III IS-II	24–36 Months IS-IV IS-III IS-II	36–54 Months	48–72 Months	60–90 Months
	Criminal History Scale	A No/Minor Record	B Moderate Record	C Serious Record	D Violent/Repetitive	E Serious Violent

Intermediate Sanction Levels

IS-IV	24-Hour Restriction
IS-III	Daily Accountability
IS-II	Standard Supervision

*A&B DW = Assault and Battery, Dangerous Weapon

The numbers in each cell represent the range from which the judge selects the maximum sentence (Not More Than);

The minimum sentence (Not Less Than) is two-thirds of the maximum sentence and constitutes the initial parole eligibility date.

Source: www.mass.gov/courts/formsandguidelines/sentencing/grid.html.

JUDICIAL DEPARTURES Even in their haste to limit a judge's power, legislators realized that sentencing guidelines could not be expected to cover every possible criminal situation. Therefore, both state and federal sentencing guidelines allow an "escape hatch" of limited judicial discretion known as a **departure.** Judges in Massachusetts can "depart" from the grid in Figure 9.4 if a case involves mitigating or aggravating circumstances.[52]

Much to the disappointment of supporters of sentencing reform, a series of Supreme Court decisions handed down midway though the first decade of the 2000s held that federal sentencing guidelines were advisory only.[53] Federal judges have taken advantage of this discretion, departing from sentencing guidelines in almost half of all cases before them.[54]

A recent study by the Transactional Records Access Clearinghouse found widespread sentencing disparities in federal courts, particularly in drug, weapons, and white-collar cases.[55] Furthermore, the U.S. Sentencing Commission reports that racial disparity in federal courts is again on the rise, with African American male defendants receiving sentences of about 20 percent greater lengths than white males who have been convicted of similar offenses.[56]

Mandatory Sentencing Guidelines

In an attempt to close the loophole of judicial discretion offered by departures, politicians (often urged on by their constituents) have passed sentencing laws even more contrary to the idea of individualized justice. These **mandatory** (minimum) **sentencing guidelines** further limit a judge's power to deviate from determinate sentencing laws by setting firm standards for certain crimes. Forty-six states have mandatory sentencing laws for crimes such as selling illegal drugs, driving under the influence of alcohol, and committing any crime with a dangerous weapon. In Alabama, for example, any person caught selling illegal drugs must spend at least two years in prison, with five years added to the sentence if the sale takes place within three miles of a school or housing project.[57]

Departure A stipulation in many federal and state sentencing guidelines that allows a judge to adjust his or her sentencing decision based on the special circumstances of a particular case.

Mandatory Sentencing Guidelines Statutorily determined punishments that must be applied to those who are convicted of specific crimes.

Similarly, Congress has set mandatory minimum sentences for more than one hundred crimes, mostly drug offenses.

As might be expected, such laws are often unpopular with judges. After being forced to send a defendant to prison for fifty-five years for selling marijuana and illegally possessing a handgun, U.S. district judge Paul Cassell called the sentence "unjust, cruel, and irrational."[58] Furthermore, mandatory minimum sentences perpetuate many of the inconsistencies previously detailed concerning race, ethnicity, and gender. Nearly 70 percent of all convicts subject to mandatory minimum sentences are African American or Hispanic, and 90 percent of such convicts are men.[59]

POLICY.CJ

About half of the 218,000 inmates in U.S. federal prisons are serving time for nonviolent drug crimes, and most of these offenders were sentenced under harsh mandatory minimum guidelines. Criticizing these guidelines, U.S. Attorney General Eric Holder has said that "too many Americans go to too many prisons for too long and for no good law enforcement reason." To learn about bipartisan efforts to remedy this situation, search online for the **Smarter Sentencing Act**. Then, list two ways that this legislation would impact federal mandatory minimum sentences for nonviolent drug offenders.

"THREE-STRIKES" LEGISLATION **Habitual offender laws** are a form of mandatory sentencing found in twenty-six states and used by the federal government. Also known as "three-strikes-and-you're-out" laws, these statutes require that any person convicted of a third felony must serve a lengthy prison sentence. In many cases, the crime does not have to be of a violent or dangerous nature. Under Washington's habitual offender law, for example, a "persistent offender" is automatically sentenced to life even if the third felony offense happens to be "vehicular assault" (an automobile accident that causes injury), unarmed robbery, or attempted arson, among other lesser felonies.[60] Consequently, two-thirds of all inmates serving life-without-parole in that state were sentenced for a third strike.[61] In California, convicts have been sent to prison for life for third offenses that include shoplifting a pair of tube socks, stealing a slice of pizza, and possessing .14 grams of methamphetamine.[62]

"THREE-STRIKES" IN COURT The Supreme Court validated the most draconian aspects of habitual offender laws with its decision in *Lockyer v. Andrade* (2003).[63] That case involved the sentencing under California's "three-strikes" law of Leandro Andrade to fifty years in prison for stealing $153 worth of videotapes. Writing for the majority in a bitterly divided 5–4 decision, Justice Sandra Day O'Connor concluded that Andrade's punishment was not so "objectively" unreasonable that it violated the Constitution.[64] In his dissent, Justice David H. Souter countered that "[i]f Andrade's sentence is not grossly disproportionate, the principle has no meaning."[65] Basically, the justices who upheld the law said that if the California legislature—and by extension the California voters—felt that the law was reasonable, then the judicial branch was in no position to disagree.

Given the Court's *Andrade* decision, it was somewhat ironic when, in 2012, California voters decided that the state's three-strikes law was indeed unreasonable. That year, by a two-thirds vote, Californians passed a ballot initiative revising the law. Now, a life sentence will be imposed only when the third felony conviction is for a serious or violent crime.[66] Furthermore, the measure authorizes judges to resentence those inmates who are serving life prison terms in California prisons because of a nonviolent "third strike." An estimated three thousand state inmates—including Leandro Andrade—became eligible for reduced sentences under the revised law.[67] In Chapter 11, we will see that numerous states are similarly rethinking mandatory minimum sentencing in an effort to reduce their large and costly prison populations.

Habitual Offender Laws
Statutes that require lengthy prison sentences for those who are convicted of multiple felonies.

Victim Impact Statement (VIS) A statement to the sentencing body (judge, jury, or parole board) in which the victim is given the opportunity to describe how the crime has affected her or him.

Victim Impact Evidence

The final piece of the sentencing puzzle involves victims and victims' families. As mentioned in previous chapters, crime victims traditionally were banished to the peripheries of the criminal justice system. This situation has changed dramatically with the emergence of the victims' rights movement over the past few decades. Victims are now given the opportunity to testify—in person or through written testimony—during sentencing hearings about the suffering they have experienced as the result of the crime. These **victim impact statements (VISs)** have proved extremely controversial, however, and even the Supreme Court has had a difficult time determining whether they cause more harm than good.

BALANCING THE PROCESS The Crime Victims' Rights Act provides victims the right to be reasonably heard during the sentencing process,[68] and many state victims' rights laws contain similar provisions.[69] In general, these laws allow a victim (or victims) to tell his or her "side of the story" to the sentencing body, be it a judge, jury, or parole officer. In non-murder cases, the victim can personally describe the physical, financial, and emotional impact of the crime. When the charge is murder or manslaughter, relatives or friends can give personal details about the victim and describe the effects of her or his death. In almost all instances, the goal of the VIS is to increase the harshness of the sentence.

Most of the debate surrounding VISs centers on their use in the sentencing phases of death penalty cases. Supporters point out that the defendant has always been allowed to present character evidence in the hopes of dissuading a judge or jury from capital punishment. According to some, a VIS balances the equation by giving survivors a voice in the process. Presenting a VIS is also said to have psychological benefits for victims, who are no longer forced to sit in silence as decisions that affect their lives are made by others.[70] Finally, on a purely practical level, a VIS may help judges and juries make informed sentencing decisions by providing them with an understanding of all of the consequences of the crime. (For an example of a victim impact statement from a recent death penalty case, see Figure 9.5 that follows.)

THE RISKS OF VICTIM EVIDENCE Opponents of the use of VISs claim that they interject dangerously prejudicial evidence into the sentencing process, which should be governed by reason, not emotion. The inflammatory nature of VISs, they say, may distract judges and juries from the facts of the case, which should be the only basis for a sentence.[71] In fact, research has shown that hearing victim impact evidence makes jurors more likely to impose the death penalty.[72] The Supreme Court, however, has given its approval to the use of VISs, allowing judges to decide whether the statements are unfairly prejudicial on a case-by-case basis, just as they do with any other type of evidence.[73]

////SELF ASSESSMENT

Fill in the blanks, and check your answers on page 300.

With the aim of limiting judicial discretion, many states and the federal government have enacted sentencing _____. These laws have greatly _____ the length of prison sentences in the United States. The trend toward longer prison terms has also been influenced by _____ - _____ laws, a form of mandatory sentencing that requires increased punishment for a person convicted of multiple felonies. According to the United States Supreme Court, _____ _____ statements may be presented at sentencing hearings so long as they are not overly prejudicial.

FIGURE 9.5 Victim Impact Statement (VIS)

In 2013, an Arizona jury found Jodi Arias guilty of first degree murder for killing Travis Alexander, her ex-boyfriend. Arias stabbed Alexander twenty-seven times, slashed his throat, and shot him after he had died. During the sentencing phase of the trial, Steven Alexander, Travis's brother, gave a VIS as part of the prosecution's argument that Arias should receive the death penalty. A portion of that VIS is reprinted here.

AP Images

The nature of my brother's murder has had a major impact on me. It has even invaded my dreams. I have nightmares about someone coming after me with a knife and then going after my wife and my daughter. When I wake up, I cannot establish what is real and what is a dream. . . . It may sound childish, but I cannot sleep alone in the dark anymore. I've had dreams of my brother, all curled up in the shower, thrown in there, left to rot, for days, all alone. I don't want these nightmares anymore. I don't want to have to see my brother's murderer anymore.

Steven Alexander gives a victim impact statement during the penalty phase of Jodi Arias's trial for murdering his brother.

CAPITAL PUNISHMENT— THE ULTIMATE SENTENCE

"You do not know how hard it is to let a human being die," Abraham Lincoln (1809–1865) once said, "when you feel that a stroke of your pen will save him." Despite these misgivings, during his four years in office Lincoln approved the execution of 267 soldiers, including those who had slept at their posts.[74] Our sixteenth president's ambivalence toward **capital punishment** is reflected in America's continuing struggle to reconcile the penalty of death with the morals and values of society. Capital punishment has played a role in sentencing since the earliest days of the Republic and—having survived a brief period of abolition between 1972 and 1976—continues to enjoy public support.

Still, few topics in the criminal justice system inspire such heated debate. Death penalty opponents such as legal expert Stephen Bright wonder whether "there comes a time when a society gets beyond some of the more primitive forms of punishment."[75] They point out that only twenty-three countries still employ the death penalty and that the United States is the sole Western democracy that continues the practice. Critics also claim that a process whose subjects are chosen by "luck and money and race" cannot serve the interests of justice.[76] Proponents believe that the death penalty serves as the ultimate deterrent for violent criminal behavior and that the criminals who are put to death are the "worst of the worst" and deserve their fate.

Capital Punishment The use of the death penalty to punish wrongdoers for certain crimes.

Today, about three thousand convicts are living on "death row" in American prisons, meaning they have been sentenced to death and are awaiting execution. In the 1940s, as many as two hundred people were put to death in the United States in one year. As Figure 9.6 that follows shows, the most recent high-water mark was ninety-eight in 1999. Despite declines since then, state governments are still regularly executing convicts. Consequently, the questions that surround the death penalty—Is it fair? Is it humane? Does it deter crime?—will continue to mobilize both its supporters and its detractors.

Methods of Execution

In its early years, when the United States adopted the practice of capital punishment from England, it also adopted English methods, which included drawing and quartering and boiling the convict alive. By the nineteenth century, these techniques had been deemed "barbaric" and were replaced by hanging. Indeed, the history of capital punishment in America is marked by attempts to make the act more humane. The 1890s saw the introduction of electrocution as a less painful method of execution than hanging, and in 1890 in Auburn Prison, New York, William Kemmler became the first American to die in an electric chair.

The "chair" remained the primary form of execution until 1977, when Oklahoma became the first state to adopt lethal injection. Today, this method dominates executions in all thirty-two states that employ the death penalty. Sixteen states authorize at least two different methods of execution, meaning that electrocution (nine states), lethal gas (three states), hanging (three states), and the firing squad (two states) are still used on rare occasions.[77]

For most of the past three decades, states have used a similar three-drug process to carry out lethal injections. The process—which involves a sedative, a paralyzing agent, and a drug that induces heart failure—was designed to be as painless as possible for the condemned convict. Over the past five years, however, the companies that manufacture these three drugs have increasingly refused to sell them for execution purposes. This has forced state officials to experiment with untested replacement drugs, a development that—as we shall soon see—has added an element of uncertainty to capital punishment in the United States.

FIGURE 9.6 **Executions in the United States, 1976 to 2013**

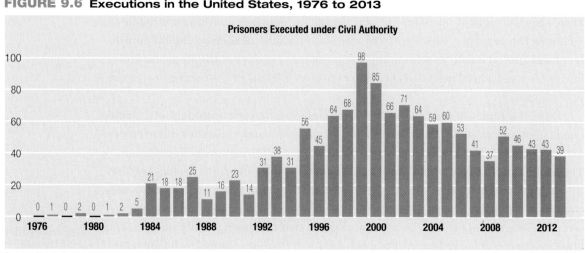

Source: Death Penalty Information Center.

The Death Penalty and the Supreme Court

The United States Supreme Court's attitude toward the death penalty has been shaped by two decisions made more than a century ago. First, in 1890, the Supreme Court established that so long as they are not carried out in an "inhuman" or "barbarous" fashion, executions are not forbidden by the Eighth Amendment.[78] Since then, the Court has never ruled that any *method* of execution is unconstitutionally "cruel and unusual."

In *Weems v. United States* (1910),[79] the Court made a ruling that further clarified the meaning of "cruel and unusual" as defined by the Eighth Amendment, though the facts of the case did not involve capital punishment. The defendant had been sentenced to fifteen years of hard labor, a heavy fine, and a number of other penalties for the relatively minor crime of falsifying official records. The Court overturned the sentence, ruling that the penalty was too harsh considering the nature of the offense. Ultimately, in the *Weems* decision, the Court set three important precedents concerning sentencing:

1. Cruel and unusual punishment is defined by the changing norms and standards of society, and therefore is not based on historical interpretations.
2. Courts may decide whether a punishment is unnecessarily cruel with regard to physical pain.
3. Courts may decide whether a punishment is unnecessarily cruel with regard to psychological pain.[80]

In *Baze v. Rees* (2008),[81] the Supreme Court ruled that the mere possibility of pain "does not establish the sort of 'objectively intolerable risk of harm' that qualifies as cruel and unusual" punishment. That ruling, however, applied to the three-drug process of execution described on the previous page, which has become difficult to implement. Furthermore, there is some evidence that the replacement lethal injection methods used by various states may carry a "risk of harm." On January 9, 2014, Michael Lee Wilson said, "I feel my whole body burning," as he was executed in Oklahoma.[82] A week later, Dennis McGuire, making choking and snorting sounds, took twenty-five minutes to die in an Ohio death chamber. (See photo alongside.) Due to mounting legal challenges by death row inmates over the new methods, the Court may need to revisit the issue of cruel and unusual punishment and lethal injection in the near future.[83]

Death Penalty Sentencing

In the 1960s, the Supreme Court became increasingly concerned about what it saw as serious flaws in the way the states administered capital punishment. Finally, in 1967, the Court put a moratorium on executions until it could "clean up" the process. The chance to do so came with the *Furman v. Georgia* case, decided in 1972.[84]

This photo shows the death chamber at the Southern Ohio Correctional Facility in Lucasville, Ohio, site of the recent prolonged execution of convicted murderer Dennis McGuire. Do you think that offenders convicted of capital crimes are entitled to a pain-free execution? Why or why not?

AP Images

THE BIFURCATED PROCESS In its *Furman* decision, by a 5–4 margin, the Supreme Court essentially held that the death penalty, as administered by the states, violated the Eighth Amendment. Justice Potter Stewart was particularly eloquent in his concurring opinion, stating that the sentence of death was so arbitrary as to be comparable to "being struck by lightning."[85] Although the *Furman* ruling invalidated the death penalty for more than six hundred offenders on death row at the time, it also provided the states with a window to make the process less arbitrary, thereby bringing their death penalty statutes up to constitutional standards.

The result was a two-stage, or *bifurcated,* procedure for capital cases. In the first stage, a jury determines the guilt or innocence of the defendant for a crime that has, by state statute, been determined to be punishable by death. If the defendant is found guilty, the jury reconvenes in the second stage and considers all aggravating and mitigating factors to decide whether the death sentence is in fact warranted. (See *Mastering Concepts—The Bifurcated Death Penalty Process* that follows.) Therefore, even if a jury finds the defendant guilty of a crime, such as first degree murder, that *may be* punishable by death, in the second stage it can decide that the circumstances surrounding the crime justify only a punishment of life in prison.

Today, thirty-two states and the federal government have capital punishment laws based on the bifurcated process. State governments are responsible for almost all executions in this country. The federal government has carried out only three death sentences since 1963 and usually seeks capital punishment only for high-profile defendants such as Dzokhar Tsarnaev, accused of bombing the Boston Marathon in April 2013.

THE JURY'S ROLE The Supreme Court reaffirmed the important role of the jury in death penalties in *Ring v. Arizona* (2002).[86] The case involved Arizona's bifurcated process: after the jury determined a defendant's guilt or innocence, it would be dismissed, and the judge alone would decide whether execution was warranted. The Court found that this procedure violated the defendant's Sixth Amendment right to a jury trial, ruling that juries must be involved in *both* stages of the bifurcated process. The decision invalidated death penalty laws in Arizona, Colorado, Idaho, Montana, and Nebraska, forcing legislatures in those states to hastily revamp their procedures. (To learn how a jury makes this difficult decision, see the feature *Discretion in Action—Life or Death?* that follows.)

Alabama is the only state that routinely allows a measure of judicial discretion when it comes to capital punishment. Alabama juries only *recommend* a sentence of death or life in prison. If the judge feels that the sentence is unreasonable, he or she can override the jury. This unusual policy has

MASTERING CONCEPTS
THE BIFURCATED DEATH PENALTY PROCESS

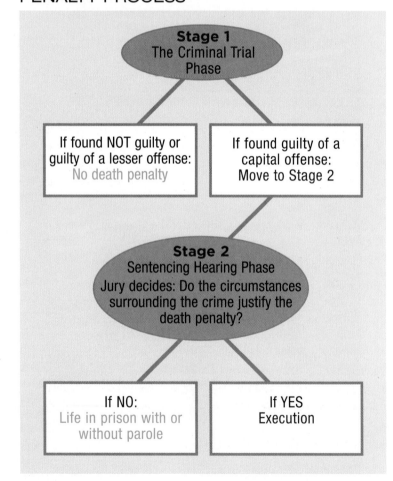

Stage 1
The Criminal Trial Phase

If found NOT guilty or guilty of a lesser offense:
No death penalty

If found guilty of a capital offense:
Move to Stage 2

Stage 2
Sentencing Hearing Phase
Jury decides: Do the circumstances surrounding the crime justify the death penalty?

If NO:
Life in prison with or without parole

If YES
Execution

come under criticism because, since 1976, Alabama judges have rejected a life sentence in favor of execution ninety-five times (compared to only nine overrides in the other direction). The Supreme Court recently refused to accept a case challenging the practice, however, ensuring that it will continue.[87]

MITIGATING CIRCUMSTANCES Several mitigating circumstances will prevent a defendant found guilty of first degree murder from receiving the death penalty. These circumstances include

1. *Insanity.* In 1986, the United States Supreme Court held that the Constitution prohibits the execution of "those who are unaware of the punishment they are about to suffer and why they are to suffer it."[88]
2. *Mental retardation.* In *Atkins v. Virginia* (2002),[89] the Court noted that eighteen states had barred the execution of mentally handicapped persons. Thus, applying the *Weems* test, it decided that the "changing norms of society" prohibited the execution of defendants with I.Q. scores of under "approximately 70."
3. *Age.* In 2005, the Court effectively ended the execution of those who had had committed their capital crimes as juveniles.[90] (See the feature *Landmark Cases—Roper v. Simmons* that follows.)

In 2014, the Court clarified one contentious area of the death penalty process—how to determine if a defendant is "mentally retarded" under the *Atkins* guidelines. In this case, the Court rejected Florida's use of a rigid I.Q. standard of 71 to make such a determination, criticized by opponents as an unfairly subjective cutoff point.[91]

LIFE OR DEATH?

THE SITUATION In a fit of extreme jealousy, twenty-seven-year-old Jodi drove one thousand miles to the home of her thirty-year-old ex-boyfriend, Travis. After the couple had sex, Jodi stabbed Travis twenty-seven times and left him for dead in the shower. You are part of the jury that found Jodi guilty of first degree murder. You and your fellow jurors must now decide whether she should receive the death penalty, or, alternately, life in prison, as punishment for her crime.

THE LAW Jurors must weigh aggravating factors against mitigating factors during the death penalty phase of criminal trials. If you believe that the aggravating factors surrounding Jodi's crime outweigh the mitigating factors, you must vote for her to be executed.

WHAT WOULD YOU DO? In arguing for her client's life, Jodi's attorney raises a number of mitigating factors, including the childhood abuse the Jodi suffered, her borderline personality disorder, and her lack of a prior criminal record. Jodi also addresses the jury, telling you that her death would devastate her family. "I'm asking you, please, please don't do that to them. I've already hurt them so badly," Jodi says. Finally, Jodi describes several volunteer prison programs she would like to participate in and speaks of her desire to bring "people together in a positive and constructive way" behind bars. The prosecutor counters that the violent nature of Jodi's crime outweighs any mitigating factors, and members of Travis's family ask you to sentence her to death (see Figure 9.5 on page 289). Do you think Jodi should receive the death penalty or life in prison? Why?

To see whether an Arizona jury chose the death sentence in similar circumstances, go to Example 9.1 in Appendix B.

LANDMARK CASES:
Roper v. Simmons

Explain why the U.S. Supreme Court abolished the death penalty for juvenile offenders.

LEARNING OBJECTIVE 7

When he was seventeen years old, Christopher Simmons abducted Shirley Cook, used duct tape to cover her eyes and mouth and bind her hands, and threw her to her death in a river. Although he bragged to his friends that he would "get away with it" because he was a minor, he was found guilty of murder and sentenced to death by a Missouri court. After the United States Supreme Court held, in 2002, that "evolving standards of decency" rendered the execution of mentally retarded persons unconstitutional, Simmons appealed his own sentence. His case gave the Court a chance to apply the "evolving standards of decency" test to death sentences involving offenders who were juveniles at the time they committed the underlying capital crime.

Roper v. Simmons
United States Supreme Court
543 U.S. 551 (2005)

IN THE WORDS OF THE COURT . . .
JUSTICE KENNEDY, MAJORITY OPINION

* * * *

The evidence of national consensus against the death penalty for juveniles is similar, and in some respects parallel, to the evidence *Atkins* held sufficient to demonstrate a national consensus against the death penalty for the mentally retarded.

* * * *

Three general differences between juveniles under 18 and adults demonstrate that juvenile offenders cannot with reliability be classified among the worst offenders. First, as any parent knows and as the scientific and sociological studies * * * tend to confirm, "[a] lack of maturity and an underdeveloped sense of responsibility are found in youth more often than in adults and are more understandable among the young. These qualities often result in impetuous and ill-considered actions and decisions." * * * In recognition of the comparative immaturity and irresponsibility of juveniles, almost every State prohibits those under 18 years of age from voting, serving on juries, or marrying without parental consent.

The second area of difference is that juveniles are more vulnerable or susceptible to negative influences and outside pressures, including peer pressure. * * * The third broad difference is that the character of a juvenile is not as well formed as that of an adult. The personality traits of juveniles are more transitory, less fixed.

These differences render suspect any conclusion that a juvenile falls among the worst offenders. * * * Retribution is not proportional if the law's most severe penalty is imposed on one whose culpability or blameworthiness is diminished, to a substantial degree, by reason of youth and immaturity.

DECISION
The Court found that, applying the Eighth Amendment in light of "evolving standards of decency," the execution of offenders who were under the age of eighteen when their crimes were committed was cruel and unusual punishment and therefore unconstitutional.

FOR CRITICAL ANALYSIS
In his majority opinion, Justice Kennedy noted that a number of countries, including China, Iran, and Pakistan, had recently ended the practice of executing juveniles, leaving the United States "alone in a world that has turned its face against the practice." What impact, if any, should international customs have on American criminal law?

Debating the Sentence of Death

Of the topics covered in this textbook, few inspire such passionate argument as the death penalty. Many advocates believe that execution is "just deserts" for those who commit heinous crimes. In the words of legal scholar Ernest van den Haag, death is the "only fitting retribution for murder that I can think of."[92] Opponents worry that retribution is simply another word for vengeance and that "the use of the death penalty by the state will increase the acceptance of revenge in our society and will give official sanction to a climate of violence."[93] As the debate over capital punishment continues, it tends to focus on several key issues: deterrence, fallibility, arbitrariness, and discrimination.

DETERRENCE Those advocates of the death penalty who wish to show that the practice benefits society often turn to the idea of deterrence. In other words, they believe that by executing convicted criminals, the criminal justice system discourages potential criminals from committing similar violent acts. Several reports released in the first decade of the 2000s claim that each convict executed deters between three and eighteen future homicides.[94] More recent research suggests that if the death penalty does have a deterrent effect, it is small and relatively short-lived, influencing behavior only for about a month after an execution takes place.[95]

LEARNING
8
OBJECTIVE

Describe the main issues of the death penalty debate.

The main problem with studies that support the death penalty, say its critics, is that there are too few executions carried out in the United States each year to adequately determine their impact.[96] Furthermore, each study that "proves" the deterrent effect of the death penalty seems be matched by one that "disproves" the same premise.[97] In the end, the deterrence debate follows a familiar pattern. Opponents of the death penalty claim that murderers rarely consider the consequences of their act, and therefore it makes no difference whether capital punishment exists or not. Proponents counter that this proves the death penalty's deterrent value, because if the murderers *had* considered the possibility of execution, they would not have committed their crimes.

FALLIBILITY In a sense, capital punishment acts as the ultimate deterrent by rendering those executed incapable of committing further crimes. Incapacitation as a justification for the death penalty, though, rests on two questionable assumptions: (1) every convicted murderer is likely to recidivate, and (2) the criminal justice system is *infallible*. In other words, the system never convicts someone who is actually not guilty.

Although several executions from the 1980s and 1990s are coming under increased scrutiny,[98] no court has ever found that an innocent person has been executed in the United States. According to the Death Penalty Information Center, however, between 1973, when the Supreme Court had temporarily suspended capital punishment, and March 2014, 144 men and women who had been convicted of capital crimes and sentenced to death—though not executed—were later found to be innocent. Over that same time period, 1,369 executions took place, meaning that for every 9.5 convicts put to death during that period, 1 death row inmate has been found innocent.[99]

ARBITRARINESS As noted earlier, one of the reasons it is so difficult to determine the deterrent effect of the death penalty is that it is rarely meted out. Despite the bifurcated process required by the Supreme Court's *Furman* ruling (discussed earlier in the chapter), a significant amount of arbitrariness appears to remain in the system. Only 2 percent of all defendants convicted of murder are sentenced to death, and, as we have seen, relatively few of those on death row are ever executed.[100]

The chances of a defendant in a capital trial being sentenced to death seem to depend heavily on the quality of the defense counsel and the jurisdiction where the crime was committed. As Figure 9.7 that follows shows, a convict's likelihood of being executed is strongly influenced by geography. Five states (Florida, Missouri, Oklahoma, Texas, and Virginia) account for more than two-thirds of all executions, while eighteen states and the District of Columbia do not provide for capital punishment within their borders. Thus, a person on trial for first degree murder in Idaho has a much better chance of avoiding execution than someone who has committed the same crime in Texas.

DISCRIMINATORY EFFECT Whether or not capital punishment is imposed arbitrarily, some observers claim that it is not done without bias. A disproportionate number of those executed since 1976—just over one-third—have been African American, and today 42 percent of all inmates on death row are black.[101] Another set of statistics also continues to be problematic: in 269 cases involving interracial murders in which the defendant was executed between 1976 and March 2014, the defendant was African American and the victim was white. Over that same time period, only 20 cases involved a white defendant and a black victim.[102] In fact, although slightly less than half of murder victims are white, three out of every four executions involve white victims.[103]

In *McCleskey v. Kemp* (1987),[104] the defense attorney for an African American sentenced to death for killing a white police officer used similar statistics to challenge Georgia's death penalty law. A study of two thousand Georgia murder cases showed

FIGURE 9.7 Executions by State, 1976–2013

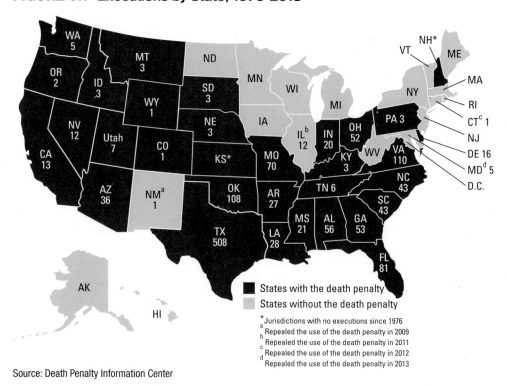

Source: Death Penalty Information Center

that although African Americans were the victims of six out of every ten murders in the state, more than 80 percent of the cases in which death was imposed involved murders of whites.[105] In a 5–4 decision, the United States Supreme Court rejected the defense's claims, ruling that statistical evidence did not prove discriminatory intent on the part of Georgia's lawmakers. (For a discussion of the moral component of the death penalty debate, see the feature *CJ Controversy—The Morality of the Death Penalty* that follows.)

The Immediate Future of the Death Penalty

As noted earlier, the number of executions carried out each year in the United States has decreased dramatically since 1999. Other statistics also indicate a decline in death penalty activity. In 2013, only 80 people were sentenced to death, compared with 277 in 1999.[106] According to James S. Liebman, a law professor at Columbia University, prosecutors in 60 percent of the nation's counties no longer seek the death penalty, even with defendants who have been convicted of capital crimes.[107]

REASONS FOR THE DECLINE IN EXECUTIONS We have already addressed some of the reasons for the diminishing presence of executions in the criminal justice system. With its decisions in the *Atkins* (2002) and *Roper* (2005) cases, the United States Supreme Court

CJ CONTROVERSY

THE MORALITY OF THE DEATH PENALTY

In 2014, Washington governor Jay Inslee announced that no executions would take place in that state during his term in office, even though the death penalty remained legal there. Noting that half of the thirty-two death sentences imposed in Washington since 1981 had been overturned, Inslee said, "There are too many flaws in the system." Inslee's move angered Sherry Shaver, whose twenty-two-year-old daughter had been killed by Washington death row inmate Dewayne Woods in 1996. "I don't want revenge," Shaver said. "I want justice." For Shaver and many others, the death penalty is not a question of "changing norms and standards," but rather an expression of moral judgment on those who commit murder.

THE EXECUTION OF MURDERERS IS A MORAL ACT BECAUSE . . .

- If the death penalty can prevent even a single future murder, then it is morally justifiable and perhaps even required by the government.

- The victim's family members often say that a murderer's execution brings them a sense of "closure" by helping them to come to terms with their grief.

THE EXECUTION OF MURDERERS IS AN IMMORAL ACT BECAUSE . . .

- The death penalty is an inherently cruel and barbaric act, and it is improper for the government of a civilized nation to kill its own citizens.

- Problems of arbitrariness, discrimination, and wrongful convictions rob the death penalty of any moral weight or justification.

Your Assignment

How do arguments concerning the morality of the death penalty apply when the punishment extends to other crimes besides murder? In general, do you think an argument can be made that someone who rapes a child should be executed? To see how the United States Supreme Court views this issue, research the case **Kennedy v. Louisiana** online. Then, write two full paragraphs describing your own opinion of the matter.

removed the possibility that hundreds of mentally handicapped and juvenile offenders could be sentenced to death. Furthermore, nearly all of the states that allow for the death penalty now permit juries to impose a sentence of life in prison without parole as an alternative to death. In Texas, the number of death sentences imposed each year dropped by about 50 percent after jurors were given the life-without-parole option, a trend that has been mirrored throughout the United States.[108]

PUBLIC OPINION AND THE DEATH PENALTY In March 2013, after the Maryland legislature voted to ban the death penalty, state lieutenant governor Anthony Brown said, "Today is a victory for those who believe that fairness and truth and justice, and not retribution or bias, are fundamental to our core beliefs as Marylanders."[109] Maryland became the sixth state in six years to end capital punishment, along with Connecticut, Illinois, New Jersey, New Mexico, and New York.

Does this mean society's "standards of decency" are changing to the point that the death sentence is in danger of being completely abolished in the United States? Probably not. The Supreme Court has shown no interest in holding that the death penalty itself is unconstitutional. In addition to its *Baze* decision (discussed earlier in this section), in 2007 the Court made it easier for prosecutors to seek the death penalty by allowing them to remove potential jurors who express reservations about the practice.[110]

Although public support for the death penalty has been steadily dropping since the mid-1990s, one poll taken in 2013 showed that 60 percent of Americans still favor the practice.[111] (That percentage does, however, drop to about 48 percent when the choice is between execution and a sentence of life in prison without parole.)[112] Another poll found that 58 percent of the respondents favored an official moratorium on executions nationwide to consider the problem of wrongful death sentences.[113] In the early 2000s, then, many Americans seem more interested in making the sentence of death fairer than in doing away with it altogether.

///// SELF ASSESSMENT

Fill in the blanks, and check your answers on page 300.

By a large margin, _____ _____ is the most widespread method of execution in the United States today. According to the United States Supreme Court's *Weems* decision, "cruel and unusual punishment" under the Eighth Amendment is determined by the changing _____ _____ _____ of society. Following these guidelines, in 2002 the Court barred the execution of the _____ _____, and in 2005 it prohibited the execution of persons who were _____ at the time of their crime.

CHAPTER SUMMARY

For more information on these concepts, look back to the Learning Objective icons throughout the chapter.

 List and contrast the four basic philosophical reasons for sentencing criminals. (a) Retribution, (b) deterrence, (c) incapacitation, and (d) rehabilitation. Under the principle of retributive justice, the severity of the punishment is in proportion to the severity of the crime. In contrast, the deterrence approach seeks to prevent future crimes by setting an example. The incapacitation theory of punishment simply argues that a criminal in prison cannot inflict further harm on society. In contrast, the rehabilitation theory asserts that criminals can be rehabilitated in the appropriate prison environment.

 Contrast indeterminate with determinate sentencing. Indeterminate sentencing follows from legislative penal codes that set minimum and maximum amounts of incarceration time. Determinate sentencing carries a fixed amount of time, although this may be reduced for "good time."

 State who has input into the sentencing decision, and list the factors that determine a sentence. The prosecutor, defense attorney, probation officer, and judge provide inputs. The factors considered in sentencing are (a) the seriousness of the crime, (b) mitigating circumstances, (c) aggravating circumstances, and (d) judicial philosophy.

 Explain some of the reasons underlying the need for sentencing reform. One reason is sentencing disparity, which is indicative of a situation in which those convicted of similar crimes receive dissimilar sentences (often due to a particular judge's sentencing philosophy). Sentencing discrimination has also occurred on the basis of defendants' gender, race, or economic standing. An additional reason for sentencing reform has been a general desire to "get tough on crime."

 Identify the arguments for and against the use of victim impact statements during sentencing hearings. Proponents of victim impact statements believe that they allow victims to provide character evidence in the same manner as defendants have always been allowed to do and that they give victims a therapeutic "voice" in the sentencing process. Opponents argue that the statements bring unacceptable levels of emotion into the courtroom.

 Identify the two stages that make up the bifurcated process of death penalty sentencing. The first stage of the bifurcated process requires a jury to find the defendant guilty or not guilty of a crime that is punishable by execution. If the defendant is found guilty, then, in the second stage, the jury reconvenes to decide whether the death sentence is warranted.

 Explain why the U.S. Supreme Court abolished the death penalty for juvenile offenders. In its *Roper v. Simmons* decision, the Supreme Court ruled that national "evolving standards of decency" no longer justified the execution of juvenile offenders. Such offenders are understood to be less blameworthy than adults because of various issues relating to immaturity and irresponsibility.

 Describe the main issues of the death penalty debate. Many of those who favor capital punishment believe that it is "just deserts" for the most violent of criminals. Those who oppose it see the act as little more than revenge. There is also disagreement over whether the death penalty acts as a deterrent. The relatively high number of death row inmates who have been found innocent has raised questions about the fallibility of the process, while certain statistics seem to show that execution is rather arbitrary. Finally, many observers contend that capital punishment is administered unfairly with regard to members of minority groups.

QUESTIONS FOR CRITICAL ANALYSIS

1. Suppose that the U.S. Congress passed a new law that punished shoplifting with a mandatory eighty-five-year prison term. What would be the impact of the new law on shoplifting nationwide? Would such a harsh law be justified by its deterrent effect? What about imposing a similarly extreme punishment on a more serious crime—a mandatory sentence of life in prison for, say, drunk driving? Would such a law be in society's best interest? Why or why not?

2. Why are truth-in-sentencing laws generally popular among victims' rights advocates? Why might these laws not be so popular with prison administrators or government officials charged with balancing a state budget?

3. Harold is convicted of unarmed burglary after a trial in Boston, Massachusetts. He has no prior convictions. According to the grid on page 286, what punishment do the state guidelines require? What would his punishment be if he had a previous conviction for armed robbery, which means that he has a "serious" criminal record?

4. As noted earlier in the chapter, Alabama judges often override capital punishment–related sentencing decisions made by juries in that state. What are the arguments for and against giving judges this power?

5. Some observers believe that, by abolishing the death penalty, officials in states such as Connecticut and Maryland have taken away an important bargaining chip for prosecutors to use during plea negotiations. Why might this be the case?

KEY TERMS

aggravating circumstances   280
capital punishment   289
departure   286
determinate sentencing   275
deterrence   271
"good time"   275
habitual offender laws   287
incapacitation   272

indeterminate sentencing   275
just deserts   271
mandatory sentencing
   guidelines   286
mitigating circumstances   279
presentence investigative report   278
"real offense"   279
rehabilitation   272

restitution   273
restorative justice   273
retribution   271
sentencing discrimination   282
sentencing disparity   281
sentencing guidelines   285
truth-in-sentencing laws   275
victim impact statement (VIS)   288

SELF-ASSESSMENT ANSWER KEY

Page 274: i. retribution; **ii.** deterrence; **iii.** incapacitation; **iv.** rehabilitation

Page 281: i. Indeterminate; **ii.** determinate; **iii.** good time; **iv.** presentence investigative; **v.** seriousness; **vi.** Mitigating; **vii.** aggravating

Page 284: i. disparity; **ii.** discrimination

Page 288: i. guidelines; **ii.** increased; **iii.** three-strikes/habitual offender; **iv.** victim impact

Page 298: i. lethal injection; **ii.** norms and standards; **iii.** mentally handicapped; **iv.** juveniles/minors

NOTES

1. Herbert L. Packer, "Justification for Criminal Punishment," in *The Limits of Criminal Sanction* (Palo Alto, Calif.: Stanford University Press, 1968), 36–37.

2. Pedestrian and Bicycle Information Center, "Pedestrian and Bicyclist Crash Statistics," at **www.pedbikeinfo.org/data/factsheet_crash.cfm#No1.**

3. Harold Pepinsky and Paul Jesilow, *Myths That Cause Crime* (Cabin John, Md.: Seven Locks Press, 1984).

4. Brian Forst, "Prosecution and Sentencing," in *Crime,* eds. James Q. Wilson and Joan Petersilia (San Francisco: ICS Press, 1995), 376.

5. Daniel Duane, "Is It O.K. to Kill Cyclists?" *New York Times* (November 10, 2013), SR6.

6. James Q. Wilson, *Thinking about Crime* (New York: Basic Books, 1975), 235.

7. Ashley Nellis, *Life Goes On: The Historic Rise of Life Sentences in America* (Washington, D.C.: The Sentencing Project, September 2013), 1.

8. Isaac Ehrlich, "Participation in Illegitimate Activities: A Theoretical and Empirical Investigation," *Journal of Political Economy* 81 (May/June 1973), 521–564.

9. Avinash Singh Bhati, *An Information Theoretic Method for Estimating the Number of Crimes Averted by Incapacitation* (Washington, D.C.: Urban Institute, July 2007), 18–33.

10. Martin H. Pritikin, "Is Prison Increasing Crime?" *Wisconsin Law Review* (2008), 1049–1108.

11. Patricia M. Clark, "An Evidence-Based Intervention for Offenders," *Corrections Today* (February/March 2011), 62–64.

12. Heather Strang and Lawrence W. Sherman, "Repairing the Harm: Victims and Restorative Justice," *Utah Law Review* (2003), 15, 18, 20–25.

13. Kimberly S. Burke, *An Inventory and Examination of Restorative Justice Practices for Youth in Illinois* (Chicago: Illinois Criminal Justice Information Authority, April 2013), 6–7.

14. Leena Kurki, "Restorative and Community Justice in the United States," in *Crime and Justice: A Review of Research,* vol. 27, ed. Michael Tonry (Chicago: University of Chicago Press, 2000), 253–303.

15. 42 U.S.C. Section 10601 (2006).

16. Office for Victims of Crime, "Crime Victims Fund" (June 2013), at **www.ovc.gov/pubs/crimevictimsfundfs/intro.html.**

17. Josh Allen, "Jon Wilson Helps Crime Victims Talk with Their Offenders," *The Christian Science Monitor Weekly* (April 9, 2012), 45.

18. Gregory W. O'Reilly, "Truth-in-Sentencing: Illinois Adds Yet Another Layer of 'Reform' to Its Complicated Code of Corrections," *Loyola University of Chicago Law Journal* (Summer 1996), 986, 999–1000.

19. David E. Olson et al., *Final Report: The Impact of Illinois' Truth-in-Sentencing Law on Sentence Lengths, Time to Serve and Disciplinary Incidents of Convicted Murderers and Sex Offenders* (Chicago: Illinois Criminal Justice Information Authority, June 2009), 4–5.

20. Paul W. Keve, *Crime Control and Justice in America: Searching for Facts and Answers* (Chicago: American Library Association, 1995), 77.

21. Danielle A. Alvarez, "Flowers, Dinner, Bowling—and Counseling—Ordered by Broward Judge in Domestic Case," *Sunsentinel.com* (February 7, 2012), at **articles.sun-sentinel.com/2012-02-07/news/fl-flowers-food-bowling-20120207_1_red-lobster-broward-judge-judge-johnjay-hurley.**

22. Kate Stith and José A. Cabranes, "Judging under the Federal Sentencing Guidelines," *Northwestern University Law Review* 91 (Summer 1997), 1247.

23. Mark M. Lanier and Claud H. Miller III, "Attitudes and Practices of Federal Probation Officers towards Pre-Plea/Trial Investigative Report Policy," *Crime & Delinquency* 41 (July 1995), 365–366.

24. Nancy J. King and Rosevelt L. Noble, "Felony Jury Sentencing in Practice: A Three-State Study," *Vanderbilt Law Review* (2004), 1986.

25. Jena Iontcheva, "Jury Sentencing as Democratic Practice," *Virginia Law Review* (April 2003), 325.

26. Julie R. O'Sullivan, "In Defense of the U.S. Sentencing Guidelines Modified Real-Offense System," *Northwestern University Law Review* 91 (1997), 1342.

27. Alan Binder, "Alabama Prosecutor Asking Again for Tougher Rape Sentence," *New York Times* (December 25, 2013), A18; and "Montana Appeals Sentence in Rape of 14-Year-Old Girl," *Associated Press* (December 2, 2013).

28. 18 U.S.C. Section 2113(a) (1994).

29. U.S. Sentencing Commission, "Statistical Information Packet, Fiscal Year 2012, Oregon," Table 7, at **www.ussc.gov/Data_and_Statistics/Federal_Sentencing_Statistics/State_District_Circuit/2012/or12.pdf;** and "Statistical Information Packet, Fiscal Year 2012, Eastern District of North Carolina," Table 7, at **www.ussc.gov/Data_and_Statistics/Federal_Sentencing_Statistics/State_District_Circuit/2012/nce12.pdf.**

30. U.S. Sentencing Commission, "Statistical Information Packet, Fiscal Year 2012, Fourth Circuit," Table 7, at **www.ussc.gov/Data_and_Statistics/Federal_Sentencing_Statistics/State_District_Circuit/2012/4c12.pdf;** and "Statistical Information Packet, Fiscal Year 2012, Ninth Circuit," Table 7, at **www.ussc.gov/Data_and_Statistics/Federal_Sentencing_Statistics/State_District_Circuit/2012/9c12.pdf.**

31. Cassia Spohn and David Holleran, "The Imprisonment Penalty Paid by Young, Unemployed Black and Hispanic Male Offenders," *Criminology* 35 (2000), 281.

32. Illinois Disproportionate Justice Impact Study Commission, "Key Findings and Recommendations" (2011), at **www.senatedem.ilga.gov/phocadownload/PDF/Attachments/2011/djisfactsheet.pdf.**

33. Bureau of Justice Statistics, *Prisoners in 2012—Advance Counts* (Washington, D.C.: U.S. Department of Justice, July 2013), Table 10, page 11.

34. Nellis, *op. cit.,* 10.

35. Bureau of Justice Statistics, *Federal Statistics, 2010* (Washington, D.C.: U.S. Department of Justice, December 2013), Table 14, page 24.

36. Spohn and Holleran, *op. cit.,* 301.

37. Brian Johnson, "The Multilevel Context of Criminal Sentencing: Integrating Judge- and County-Level Influences," *Criminology* (May 2006), 259–298.

38. Jeff German and Cy Ran, "Sentencing Study Finds Disparities You'd Expect," *Las Vegas Sun* (August 13, 2008), 1.

39. Anti-Drug Abuse Act of 1986, Pub. L. No. 99-570, 100 Stat. 3207 (1986).

40. Solomon Moore, "Justice Department Seeks Equity in Sentences for Cocaine," *New York Times* (April 30, 2009), A17.

41. Pub. L. No. 111-220, Section 2, 124 Stat. 2372.

42. Quoted in Matt Apuzzo, "Justice Dept. Starts Quest for Inmates to Be Freed," *New York Times* (January 31, 2014), A13.

43. 28 U.S.C. Section 991 (1994).

44. Bureau of Justice Statistics, *Felony Sentences in State Courts, 2006—Statistical Tables* (Washington, D.C.: U.S. Department of Justice, December 2009), Table 3.5, page 20.

45. Sonja B. Starr, "Estimating Gender Disparities in Federal Criminal Cases," *University of Michigan Law and Economics Research Paper* (August 29, 2012), at **papers.ssrn.com/sol3/papers.cfm?abstract_id=2144002**.

46. Clarice Feinman, *Women in the Criminal Justice System,* 3d ed. (Westport, Conn.: Praeger, 1994), 35.

47. John C. Coffee, "Repressed Issues of Sentencing," *Georgetown Law Journal* 66 (1978), 987.

48. J. S. Bainbridge, Jr., "The Return of Retribution," *ABA Journal* (May 1985), 63.

49. Pub. L. No. 98-473, 98 Stat. 1987, codified as amended at 18 U.S.C. Sections 3551–3742 and 28 U.S.C. Sections 991–998 (1988).

50. Julia L. Black, "The Constitutionality of Federal Sentences Imposed under the Sentencing Reform Act of 1984 after *Mistretta v. United States,*" *Iowa Law Review* 75 (March 1990), 767.

51. U.S. Sentencing Commission, *Fifteen Years of Guidelines Sentencing: An Assessment of How Well the Federal Criminal Justice System Is Achieving the Goals of Sentencing Reform* (Washington, D.C.: U.S. Sentencing Commission, November 2004), 46.

52. Neal B. Kauder and Brian J. Ostrom, *State Sentencing Guidelines: Profiles and Continuum* (Williamsburg, Va.: National Center for State Courts, 2008), 15.

53. *Blakely v. Washington,* 542 U.S. 296 (2004); *United States v. Booker,* 543 U.S. 220 (2005); and *Gall v. United States,* 552 U.S. 38 (2007).

54. U.S. Sentencing Commission, "Table N: National Comparison of Sentence Imposed and Position Relative to the Guideline Range, Fiscal Year 2012," *FY 2012 Sourcebook,* at **www.ussc.gov/Research_and_Statistics/Annual_Reports_and_Sourcebooks/2012/TableN.pdf.**

55. Transactional Records Access Clearinghouse, "Wide Variations Seen in Federal Sentencing" (March 5, 2012), at **trac.syr.edu/whatsnew/email.120305.html**.

56. U.S. Sentencing Commission, *Demographic Differences in Federal Sentencing Practices: An Update of the Booker Report's Multivariate Regression Analysis* (Washington, D.C.: U.S. Sentencing Commission, March 2010), C-3.

57. Alabama Code 1975 Section 20-2-79.

58. Quoted in Melinda Rogers, "Reluctant Utah Judge Orders Man to 57 Years in Prison for Gang Robberies," *Salt Lake Tribune* (December 15, 2011), at **www.sltrib.com/sltrib/mobile/53124012-90/maumauprison-angelos-court.html.csp**.

59. U.S. Sentencing Commission, *Report to Congress: Mandatory Minimum Penalties in the Federal Criminal Justice System* (Washington, D.C.: U.S. Sentencing Commission, October 2011), xxviii.

60. Washington Revised Code Annotated Section 9.94A.030.

61. Nellis, *op. cit.,* 16.

62. Matt Taibbi, "Cruel and Unusual Punishment: The Shame of Three Strikes Laws," *Rolling Stone* (March 27, 2013), at **www.rollingstone.com/politics/news/cruel-and-unusual-punishment-the-shame-of-three-strikes-laws-20130327**.

63. 538 U.S. 63 (2003).

64. *Ibid.,* 76.

65. *Ibid.,* 83.

66. Marisa Lagos and Ellen Huet, "'Three Strikes' Law Changes Approved by Wide Margin," *San Francisco Chronicle* (November 7, 2012), A14.

67. Nicole D. Porter, *The State of Sentencing 2012* (Washington, D.C.: The Sentencing Project, January 2013), 4.

68. Justice for All Act of 2004, Pub. L. No. 108-405, 118 Stat. 2260.

69. Paul G. Cassell, "In Defense of Victim Impact Statements," *Ohio State Journal of Criminal Law* (Spring 2009), 614.

70. Edna Erez, "Victim Voice, Impact Statements, and Sentencing: Integrating Restorative Justice and Therapeutic Jurisprudence Principles in Adversarial Proceedings," *Criminal Law Bulletin* (September/October 2004), 495.

71. Bryan Myers and Edith Greene, "Prejudicial Nature of Impact Statements," *Psychology, Public Policy, and Law* (December 2004), 493.

72. Bryan Myers and Jack Arbuthnot, "The Effects of Victim Impact Evidence on the Verdicts and Sentencing Judgments of Mock Jurors," *Journal of Offender Rehabilitation* (1999), 95–112.

73. *Payne v. Tennessee,* 501 U.S. 808 (1991).

74. Walter Berns, "Abraham Lincoln (Book Review)," *Commentary* (January 1, 1996), 70.

75. Comments made at the Georgetown Law Center, "The Modern View of Capital Punishment," *American Criminal Law Review* 34 (Summer 1997), 1353.

76. David Bruck, quoted in Bill Rankin, "Fairness of the Death Penalty Is Still on Trial," *Atlanta Journal-Constitution* (July 29, 1997), A13.

77. Bureau of Justice Statistics, *Capital Punishment, 2010* (Washington, D.C.: U.S. Department of Justice, December 2011), 2.

78. *In re Kemmler,* 136 U.S. 447 (1890).

79. 217 U.S. 349 (1910).

80. Pamela S. Nagy, "Hang by the Neck until Dead: The Resurgence of Cruel and Unusual Punishment in the 1990s," *Pacific Law Journal* 26 (October 1994), 85.

81. 553 U.S. 35 (2008).

82. Quoted in Dan Frosch and Sabrina Tavernise, "Judge Rejects Execution Delay over Use of Compounded Drug," *New York Times* (January 27, 2014), A11.

83. Erica Goode, "After a Prolonged Execution in Ohio, Questions Over 'Cruel and Unusual,'" *New York Times* (January 18, 2014), A12.

84. 408 U.S. 238 (1972).

85. 408 U.S. 309 (1972) (Stewart, concurring).

86. 536 U.S. 584 (2002).

87. Adam Liptak, "Alabama Judges Retain the Right to Override Juries in Capital Sentencing," *New York Times* (November 19, 2013), A15.

88. *Ford v. Wainwright,* 477 U.S. 399, 433 (1986).

89. 536 U.S. 304 (2002).

90. *Roper v. Simmons,* 543 U.S. 551 (2005).

91. *Hall v. Florida,* 572 U.S. ____ (2014).

92. Ernest van den Haag, "The Ultimate Punishment: A Defense," *Harvard Law Review* 99 (1986), 1669.

93. *The Death Penalty: The Religious Community Calls for Abolition* (pamphlet published by the National Coalition to Abolish the Death Penalty and the National Interreligious Task Force on Criminal Justice, 1988), 48.

94. Hashem Dezhbakhsh, Paul H. Rubin, and Joanna M. Shepherd, "Does Capital Punishment Have a Deterrent Effect? New Evidence from Postmoratorium Panel Data," *American Law and Economics Review* 5 (2003), 344–376; H. Naci Mocan and R. Kaj Gittings, "Getting Off Death Row: Commuted Sentences and the Deterrent Effect of Capital Punishment," *Journal of Law and Economics* 46 (2003), 453–478; Joanna M. Shepherd, "Deterrence versus Brutalization: Capital Punishment's Differing Impact among States," *Michigan Law Review* 104 (2005), 203–255; and Paul R. Zimmerman, "State Executions, Deterrence, and the Incidence of Murder," *Journal of Applied Economics* 7 (2005), 163–193.

95. Kenneth C. Land, Raymond H. C. Teske, Jr., and Hui Zheng, "Overview of: 'The Differential Short-Term Impacts of Executions on Felony and Non-Felony Homicides,'" *Criminology & Public Policy* (August 2012), 539–563.

96. Richard Berk, "Can't Tell: Comments on 'Does the Death Penalty Save Lives?'" *Criminology and Public Policy* (November 2009), 845–851.

97. John J. Donohue and Justin Wolfers, "Uses and Abuses of Empirical Evidence in the Death Penalty Debate," *Stanford Law Review* 58 (2005), 791–845.

98. Roger C. Barnes, "Death Penalty Undermines Justice," *San Antonio Express-News* (July 12, 202), 6B.

99. Death Penalty Information Center, "Innocence and the Death Penalty," at **www.deathpenaltyinfo.org/innocence-and-death-penalty**.

100. Adam Liptak, "Geography and the Machinery of Death," *New York Times* (February 5, 2007), Λ10.

101. Deborah Fins, *Death Row U.S.A.* (New York: NAACP Legal Defense and Educational Fund, Summer 2013), 1.

102. Death Penalty Information Center, "National Statistics on the Death Penalty and Race," at **www.deathpenaltyinfo.org/race-death-row-inmates-executed-1976#defend**.

103. *Ibid.*

104. 481 U.S. 279 (1987).

105. David C. Baldus, George Woodworth, and Charles A. Pulaski, *Equal Justice and the Death Penalty: A Legal and Empirical Analysis* (Boston: Northeastern University Press, 1990), 140–197, 306.

106. *The Death Penalty in 2013: Year End Report* (Washington, D.C.: Death Penalty Information Center, December 2013), 1.

107. Quoted in Ethan Bronner, "Use of Death Sentences Continues to Fall in U.S.," *New York Times* (December 21, 2012), A24.

108. David McCord, "What's Messing with Texas Death Sentences?" *Texas Tech Law Review* (Winter 2011), 601–608.

109. Quoted in Mark Morgenstein, "Maryland Legislature Votes to End Death Penalty," *CNN Justice* (March 15, 2013), at **www.cnn.com/2013/03/15/justice/maryland-death-penalty-ban**.

110. *Uttecht v. Brown,* 551 U.S. 1 (2007).

111. Gallup, "U.S. Death Penalty Support Lowest in More than 40 Years" (October 29, 2013), at **www.gallup.com/poll/165626/death-penalty-support-lowest-years.aspx**.

112. Quinnipiac University, "Hillary Clinton Owns 2016 Dem Nomination, Quinnipiac University National Poll Finds" (May 2, 2013), at **www.quinnipiac.edu/images/polling/us/us05022013.pdf**.

113. Richard C. Dieter, *A Crisis of Confidence: Americans' Doubts about the Death Penalty* (Washington, D.C.: Death Penalty Information Center, June 2007), 5, 9.

10 Probation, Parole, and Intermediate Sanctions

To target your study and review, look for these numbered Learning Objective icons throughout the chapter.

Getty Images

NO JOKE

FORMER PROFESSIONAL football player Chad Johnson's troubles with the criminal justice system began when his ex-wife, reality television star Evelyn Lozada, confronted him about a receipt for a box of condoms. During the ensuing argument, Johnson apparently head-butted Lozada, who was subsequently treated at a nearby hospital. Soon thereafter, authorities in Broward County, Florida, charged Johnson with simple battery, a misdemeanor punishable by up to a year in jail.

After he pleaded no contest to the charge, a judge sentenced Johnson to one year of probation and ordered him to attend domestic violence awareness classes. The resolution "allows him to put this incident behind him and move on with his life," said Adam Swickle, Johnson's lawyer. Eight months later, however, a warrant was issued for Johnson's arrest because he had violated the terms of his probation. Specifically, Johnson did not meet with his probation officer as required and also failed to provide proof that he had enrolled in the domestic violence course.

So, on June 10, 2013, Johnson found himself back in Broward County court, in front of Judge Kathleen McHugh. The hearing was something of a formality, as a plea deal had been worked out between Swickle and the prosecutor that would have spared Johnson from going to jail for his probation violations. When the judge asked Johnson if he was satisfied with his legal representation, however, Johnson said yes and playfully slapped Swickle on the butt. "I don't know that you're taking this whole thing seriously," said an angry McHugh. "This isn't a joke." Proving her displeasure, McHugh rejected the plea deal and sentenced Johnson to thirty days in jail. As it turned out, Johnson spent only a week behind bars before the judge relented and set him free. Apologizing, Johnson said, "I think my time locked up gave me enough time to reflect on some of the sins I made in this courtroom."

AP Images

In June 2013, former professional football player Chad Johnson appeared in Broward County, Florida, court after failing to meet the terms of his probation.

FOR CRITICAL ANALYSIS

1. Do you think that Chad Johnson was sufficiently punished for the domestic violence incident involving his ex-wife? Why or why not?

2. In general, what might be some of the arguments for allowing an offender who does not seem to pose a risk to the community to serve his or her sentence in the community, under supervision, rather than in prison or jail?

3. Did Judge Kathleen McHugh overreact to Johnson's playfulness? Why might a judge punish such courtroom misbehavior with jail time?

THE JUSTIFICATION FOR COMMUNITY CORRECTIONS

LEARNING
1
OBJECTIVE

Explain the justifications for community-based corrections programs.

Chad Johnson's initial sentence sparked skepticism, as many observers felt that he had been "let off easy" because of his fame and high-priced defense attorney. In fact, the judge who decided not to put Johnson behind bars for a domestic violence conviction was hardly acting outside the norm. Today, nearly 4 million offenders are serving their sentences in the community on *probation* rather than behind bars. In addition, approximately 850,000 convicts in the United States have been *paroled,* meaning that they are finishing their prison sentences "on the outside" under the supervision of correctional officers.[1]

America, says University of Minnesota law professor Michael Tonry, is preoccupied with the "absolute severity of punishment" and the "widespread view that only imprisonment counts."[2] Consequently, **community corrections** such as probation and parole are often considered a less severe, and therefore a less worthy, alternative to imprisonment. In reality, community corrections are crucially important. One in fifty adults in this country is living under community supervision,[3] and few criminal justice matters are more pressing than the need to successfully reintegrate these offenders into society.

Reintegration

A very small percentage of all convicted offenders have committed crimes that warrant life imprisonment or capital punishment. Most, at some point, will return to the community. Consequently, according to one group of experts, the task of the corrections system

> includes building or rebuilding solid ties between the offender and the community, integrating or reintegrating the offender into community life—restoring family ties, obtaining employment and an education, securing in the larger sense a place for the offender in the routine functioning of society.[4]

Considering that some studies have shown higher recidivism rates for offenders who are subjected to prison culture, a frequent justification of community-based corrections is that they help to reintegrate the offender into society.

Reintegration has a strong theoretical basis in rehabilitative theories of punishment. An offender is generally considered to be "rehabilitated" when he or she no longer represents a threat to other members of the community and therefore is believed to be fit to live in that community. In the context of this chapter and the two that follow, it will also be helpful to see reintegration as a process through which criminal justice officials such as probation and parole officers provide the offender with incentives to follow the rules of society.

These incentives can be positive, such as enrolling the offender in a drug treatment program. They can also be negative—in particular, the threat of return to prison or jail for failure to comply. In all instances, criminal justice professionals must carefully balance the needs of the individual offender against the rights of law-abiding members of the community.

Diversion

Another justification for community corrections, based on practical considerations, is **diversion.** As you are already aware, many criminal offenses fall into the category of "petty," and it is nearly impossible, as well as unnecessary, to imprison every offender for every offense. Community-based corrections are an important means of diverting some offenders to alternative modes of punishment so that scarce incarceration resources

Community Corrections The correctional supervision of offenders in the community as an alternative to sending them to prison or jail.

Reintegration A goal of corrections that focuses on preparing the offender for a return to the community unmarred by further criminal behavior.

Diversion In the context of corrections, a strategy to divert those offenders who qualify away from prison and jail and toward community-based and intermediate sanctions.

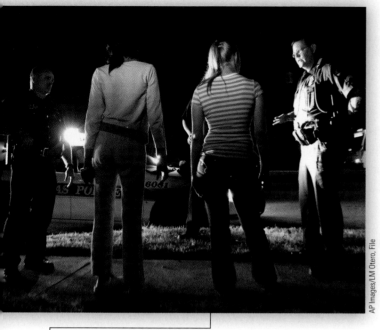

In Dallas, street prostitutes such as the two shown here are often treated as crime victims and offered access to treatment and rehabilitation programs. How might society benefit if such offenders are kept out of jail or prison through these kinds of diversion programs?

AP Images/LM Otero, File

are consumed by only the most dangerous criminals. In his "strainer" analogy, corrections expert Paul H. Hahn likens this process to the workings of a kitchen strainer. With each "shake" of the corrections "strainer," the less-serious offenders are diverted from incarceration. At the end, only the most serious convicts remain in prison.[5]

The diversionary role of community-based punishments has become more pronounced as prisons and jails have filled up over the past four decades. In fact, probationers and parolees now account for about 70 percent of all adults in the American corrections systems.[6]

The "Low-Cost Alternative"

Not all of the recent expansion of community corrections can be attributed to acceptance of its theoretical underpinnings. Many politicians and criminal justice officials who do not look favorably on ideas such as reintegration and diversion have embraced programs to keep nonviolent offenders out of prison. The reason is simple: economics. The cost of constructing and maintaining prisons and jails, as well as housing and caring for inmates, has placed a great deal of pressure on corrections budgets across the country. Indeed, to cut prison operating costs, states are taking such steps as installing windmills and solar panels to save energy, and using medical schools to provide less costly health care.[7]

Community corrections offer an enticing financial alternative to imprisonment. Data compiled by the Center for Economic and Policy Research suggest that for each nonviolent offender shifted from incarceration to community supervision, the federal government saves about $22,700 annually, and state governments save about $23,200 each year.[8] Not surprisingly, many jurisdictions are adopting policies that favor keeping offenders out of prison or jail cells. By diverting significant numbers of nonviolent criminals from state prisons to probation and parole, for example, New Hampshire estimates that it will save about $190 million, including new prison construction and operating costs, by 2021.[9] Officials can also require community-based criminals to finance their own supervision. In Oklahoma, probationers pay a $40 monthly fee to cover part of the costs of community corrections.[10]

//// SELF ASSESSMENT

Fill in the blanks, and check your answers on page 330.

The three basic justifications for community corrections are (1) _____, which focuses on building or rebuilding the offender's ties with the community; (2) _____, a strategy that attempts to allocate scarce jail and prison space to only the most dangerous criminals; and (3) _____ considerations, as community corrections are generally _____ expensive than incarceration.

PROBATION: DOING TIME IN THE COMMUNITY

Probation A criminal sanction in which a convict is allowed to remain in the community rather than be imprisoned.

As Figure 10.1 that follows shows, **probation** is the most common form of punishment in the United States. Although it is administered differently in various jurisdictions, probation can be generally defined as the legal status of an offender who, after being convicted of a crime, has been directed by the sentencing court to remain in the community under the supervision of a probation service for a designated period of time and subject to certain conditions imposed by the court or by law.[11]

The theory behind probation is that certain offenders, having been found guilty of a crime, can be treated more economically and humanely by putting them under controls while still allowing them to live in the community. One of the advantages of probation has been that it provides for the rehabilitation of the offender while saving society the costs of incarceration.

Sentencing and Probation

Probation is basically an arrangement between sentencing authorities and the offender. In traditional probation, the offender agrees to comply with certain terms for a specified amount of time in return for serving the sentence in the community. One of the primary benefits for the offender, besides not getting sent to a correctional facility, is that the length of the probationary period is usually considerably shorter than the length of a prison term (see Figure 10.2 that follows).

The traditional form of probation is not the only arrangement that can be made. A judge can hand down a **suspended sentence,** under which a defendant who has been convicted and sentenced to be incarcerated is not required to serve the sentence. Instead, the judge puts the offender on notice, keeping open the option of reinstating the original sentence and sending the offender to prison or jail if he or she reoffends. In practice, suspended sentences are quite similar to probation.

ALTERNATIVE SENTENCING ARRANGEMENTS Judges can also combine probation with incarceration. Such sentencing arrangements include

1. *Split sentences.* In **split sentence probation,** also known as *shock probation,* the offender is sentenced to a specific amount of time in prison or jail, to be followed by a period of probation.
2. *Shock incarceration.* In this arrangement, an offender is sentenced to prison or jail with the understanding that after a period of time, she or he may petition the court to be released on probation. Shock incarceration is discussed more fully later in the chapter.
3. *Intermittent incarceration.* With intermittent incarceration, the offender spends a certain amount of time each week, usually during the weekend, in a jail, workhouse, or other government institution.

Split sentences are popular with judges, as they combine the "treatment" aspects of probation with the "punishment" aspects of incarceration. According to the U.S. Department of Justice, about a fifth of all probationers are also sentenced to some form of incarceration.[12]

CHOOSING PROBATION Generally, research has shown that offenders are most likely to be denied probation if they

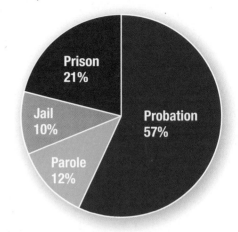

FIGURE 10.1 Probation in American Corrections

As you can see, the majority of convicts under the control of the American corrections system are on probation.

Source: Bureau of Justice Statistics, *Correctional Populations in the United States, 2012* (Washington, D.C.: U.S. Department of Justice, December 2013), Table 2, page 3.

Suspended Sentence A judicially imposed condition in which an offender is sentenced after being convicted of a crime but is not required to begin serving the sentence immediately.

Split Sentence Probation A sentence that consists of incarceration in a prison or jail, followed by a probationary period in the community.

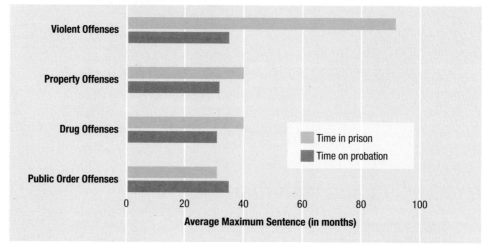

FIGURE 10.2 Average Length of Sentence: Prison versus Probation

As these figures show, the average probation sentence is much shorter than the average prison sentence for most crimes except public order offenses.

Source: Bureau of Justice Statistics, *Felony Defendants in State Courts, 2009—Statistical Tables* (Washington, D.C.: U.S. Department of Justice, December 2013), Table 25, page 30; and Table 27, page 31.

Specify the conditions under which an offender is most likely to be denied probation. LEARNING 2 OBJECTIVE

1. Are convicted on multiple charges.
2. Were on probation or parole at the time of the arrest.
3. Have two or more prior convictions.
4. Are addicted to narcotics.
5. Seriously injured the victim of the crime.
6. Used a weapon during the commission of the crime.[13]

As might be expected, the chances of a felon being sentenced to probation are highly dependent on the seriousness of his or her crime. Only 19 percent of probationers in the United States have committed a violent crime, including domestic violence and sex offenses. The majority of probationers have been convicted of property crimes, drug offenses, or public order crimes such as drunk driving.[14]

PROBATION DEMOGRAPHICS As with other areas of the criminal justice system, African Americans make up a higher percentage of the national probation population (30 percent) than the U.S. population (13 percent). Fifty-four percent of probationers are white, and 13 percent are Hispanic.[15] The percentage of female probationers is significantly higher than female prison inmates (24 percent to 7 percent),[16] which is in keeping with the gender sentencing trends we discussed in the previous chapter. More detailed surveys of probationers reveal that they tend to be between the ages of twenty-one and thirty-nine, single, and high school graduates, and have annual incomes of less than $20,000.[17]

Conditions of Probation

A judge may decide to impose certain conditions as part of a probation sentence. These conditions represent a "contract" between the judge and the offender, in which the latter agrees that if she or he does not follow certain rules, probation may be revoked (see Figure 10.3 that follows). The probation officer usually recommends the conditions of probation, but judges also have the power to set any terms they believe to be necessary.

For example, in the case that opened this chapter, Chad Johnson was ordered to attend domestic violence awareness classes and was prohibited from having any contact with the victim, his ex-wife Evelyn Lozada, as part of his initial probationary sentence.

PRINCIPLES OF PROBATION A judge's personal philosophy is often reflected in the probation conditions that she or he creates for probationers. In *In re Quirk* (1997),[18] for example, the Louisiana Supreme Court upheld the ability of a trial judge to impose church attendance as a condition of probation. Though judges have a great deal of discretion in setting the conditions of probation, they do operate under several guiding principles. First, the conditions must be related to the dual purposes of probation, which most federal and state courts define as the rehabilitation of the probationer and the protection of the community. Second, the conditions must not violate the U.S. Constitution, as probationers are generally entitled to the same constitutional rights as other prisoners.[19]

Of course, probationers do give up certain constitutional rights when they consent to the terms of probation. Most probationers, for example, agree to spot checks of their homes for contraband such as drugs or weapons, and they therefore have a diminished expectation of privacy.

In *United States v. Knights* (2001),[20] the United States Supreme Court upheld the actions of deputy sheriffs in Napa County, California, who searched a probationer's home without a warrant or probable cause. The unanimous decision was based on the premise that because those on probation are more likely to commit crimes, law enforcement agents "may therefore justifiably focus on probationers in a way that [they do] not on the ordinary citizen."[21]

TYPES OF CONDITIONS Obviously, probationers who break the law are very likely to have their probation revoked. Other, less serious infractions may also result in revocation, as we saw with Chad Johnson at the beginning of this chapter. The conditions placed on a probationer fall into three general categories:

1. *Standard conditions,* which are imposed on all probationers. These include reporting regularly to the probation officer, notifying the agency of any change of address, not leaving the jurisdiction without permission, and remaining employed.

FIGURE 10.3 Conditions of Probation

UNITED STATES DISTRICT COURT FOR THE DISTRICT OF COLUMBIA

To: _____ No. 84-417

Address: 1440 N St., N.W., #10, Wash., D.C.

In accordance with authority conferred by the United States Probation Law, you have been placed on probation this date, January 25, 2015 for a period of one year by the Hon. Thomas F. Hogan United States District Judge, sitting in and for this District Court at Washington, D.C.

CONDITIONS OF PROBATION

It is the order of the Court that you shall comply with the following conditions of probation:

(1)-You shall refrain from violation of any law (federal, state, and local). You shall get in touch immediately with your probation officer if arrested or questioned by a law enforcement officer.

(2)-You shall associate only with law-abiding persons and maintain reasonable hours.

(3)-You shall work regularly at a lawful occupation and support your legal dependents, if any, to the best of your ability. When out of work you shall notify your probation officer at once. You shall consult him prior to job changes.

(4)-You shall not leave the judicial district without permission of the probation officer.

(5)-You shall notify your probation officer immediately of any change in your place of residence.

(6)-You shall follow the probation officer's instructions.

(7)-You shall report to the probation officer as directed.

(8)-You shall not possess a firearm (handgun or rifle) for any reason.

The special conditions ordered by the Court are as follows:
    Imposition of sentence suspended, one year probation, Fine of $75 on each count.

I understand that the Court may change the conditions of probation, reduce or extend the period of probation, and at any time during the probation period or within the maximum probation period of 5 years permitted by law, may issue a warrant and revoke probation for a violation occurring during the probation period.

I have read or had read to me the above conditions of probation. I fully understand them and I will abide by them.

_____ Date _____
Probationer

You will report as follows: _____ as directed by your Probation Officer

_____ Date _____
U.S. Probation Officer

Describe the three general categories of conditions placed on a probationer.

LEARNING **3** OBJECTIVE

2. *Punitive conditions,* which usually reflect the seriousness of the offense and are intended to increase the punishment of the offender. Such conditions include fines, community service, restitution, drug testing, and home confinement (discussed later).

3. *Treatment conditions,* which are imposed to reverse patterns of self-destructive behavior. Such treatment generally includes counseling for drug and alcohol abuse, anger management, and mental health issues, and is a component of approximately 27 percent of probation sentences in this country.[22]

Some observers feel that judges have too much discretion in imposing overly restrictive conditions that no person, much less one who has exhibited antisocial tendencies, could meet. Citing prohibitions on drinking liquor, gambling, and associating with "undesirables," as well as requirements such as meeting early curfews, the late University of Delaware professor Carl B. Klockars claimed that if probation rules were taken seriously, "very few probationers would complete their terms without violation."[23]

As almost seven out of ten probationers do complete their terms successfully,[24] Klockars's statement suggests that either probation officers are unable to determine that violations are taking place or many of them are exercising a great deal of discretion in reporting minor probation violations. Perhaps the officers realize that violating probationers for every single "slip-up" is unrealistic and would impose unreasonable burdens on federal and state prison systems and corrections budgets.

The Supervisory Role of the Probation Officer

The probation officer has two basic roles. The first is investigative and consists of conducting the presentence investigation (PSI), which was discussed in Chapter 9. The second is supervisory and begins as soon as the offender has been sentenced to probation. In smaller probation agencies, individual officers perform both tasks. In larger jurisdictions, the trend has been toward separating the responsibilities, with *investigating officers* handling the PSI and *line officers* concentrating on supervision.

One of the most difficult aspects of a probation officer's supervisory duties is an unavoidable *role conflict* in the work. On the one hand, the probation officer has the task of guiding the probationer to a successful completion of the probationary term. On the other hand, the probation officer must protect the community from the probationer, who has already shown that he or she is capable of breaking the law. Operating under vague institutional guidelines, probation officers mostly must rely on their own discretion to navigate the complexities of their profession.[25]

THE USE OF AUTHORITY The ideal probation officer–offender relationship is based on trust. In reality, this trust often does not exist. Any incentive an offender might have to be completely truthful with a line officer is marred by one simple fact: self-reported wrongdoing can be used to revoke probation. Even probation officers whose primary mission is to rehabilitate are under institutional pressure to punish their clients for violating conditions of probation. One officer deals with this situation by telling his clients

> that I'm here to help them, to get them a job, and whatever else I can do. But I tell them too that I have a family to support and that if they get too far off track, I can't afford to put my job on the line for them. I'm going to have to violate them.[26]

Photo Courtesy of Peggy McCarthy

PEGGY McCARTHY

LEAD PROBATION OFFICER

The best thing about my job is that every day is different. I may be in court first thing in the morning, and then in my office meeting with defendants or developing case plans. In the afternoon, I may be at the jail taking statements for court reports or out in the field seeing my defendants. If I work a late shift, I may be visiting counseling agencies or talking to collateral sources or doing surveillance. I may be organizing a search on a defendant's home or making an arrest. I may be working with the police to solve crimes or locate absconders. Or I may simply be completing administrative duties like filing or returning phone calls to defendants and/or their family members. Anything can happen at any time, and I have to be ready to respond. If a probation officer gets bored, something is wrong.

I take a great deal of pride in assisting defendants with the difficult task of making positive change in their lives. The rewards may be few and far between, but when a defendant with a history of substance abuse stays clean and sober for a year, when a gang-affiliated defendant secures a job and no longer associates with negative peers, or when a defendant who admittedly never liked school obtains a GED or diploma, that is when I realize that what I'm doing day in and day out is 100 percent worthwhile.

Social Media Career Tip Manage your online reputation—or someone else will do it for you. Monitor your profile using tools such as Pipl and ZabaSearch. Check BoardTracker, BoardReader, and Omgili for information on what people are saying about you on message boards.

In the absence of trust, most probation officers rely on their **authority** to guide an offender successfully through the sentence. An officer's authority, or ability to influence a person's actions without resorting to force, is based partially on her or his power to revoke probation. It also reflects her or his ability to impose a number of lesser sanctions. For example, if a probationer fails to attend a required alcohol treatment program, the officer can send him or her to a "lockup," or detention center, overnight. To be successful, a probation officer must establish this authority early in the relationship because it is the primary tool for persuading the probationer to behave in an acceptable manner.[27]

THE CASELOAD DILEMMA Even the most balanced, "firm but fair" approach to probation can be defeated by the problem of excessive *caseloads*. A **caseload** is the number of clients a probation officer is responsible for at any one time. Heavy probation caseloads seem inevitable: unlike a prison cell, a probation officer can always take "just one more" client. Furthermore, the ideal caseload size is very difficult to determine because different offenders require different levels of supervision.[28]

The consequences of disproportionate probation officer–probationer ratios are self-evident, however. When burdened with large caseloads, probation officers find it practically impossible to rigorously enforce the conditions imposed on their clients. Lack of surveillance leads to lack of control, which can undermine the very basis of a probationary system. In Sacramento County, California, where probation officers have

Authority The power designated to an agent of the law over a person who has broken the law.

Caseload The number of individual probationers or parolees under the supervision of a probation or parole officer.

caseloads of more than 120 each and more than 90 percent of all probationers are unsupervised, these offenders are responsible for 30 percent of the county's total arrests.[29]

Revocation of Probation

The probation period can end in one of two ways. Either the probationer successfully fulfills the conditions of the sentence, or the probationer misbehaves and probation is revoked, resulting in a prison or jail term. The decision of whether to revoke after a **technical violation**—such as failing to report a change of address or testing positive for drug use—is often a judgment call by the probation officer and therefore the focus of controversy. (See the feature *Discretion in Action—A Judgment Call* that follows to learn more about the issues surrounding revocation.)

As we have seen, probationers do not always enjoy the same protections under the U.S. Constitution as other members of society do. The United States Supreme Court has not stripped these offenders of all rights, however. In *Mempa v. Rhay* (1967),[30] the Court ruled that probationers were entitled to an attorney during the revocation process. Then, in *Morrissey v. Brewer* (1972) and *Gagnon v. Scarpelli* (1973),[31] the Court established a three-stage procedure by which the "limited" due process rights of probationers must be protected in potential revocation situations:

1. *Preliminary hearing.* In this appearance before a "disinterested person" (often a judge), the facts of the violation or arrest are presented, and it is determined whether probable cause for revoking probation exists. This hearing can be waived by the probationer.

DISCRETION in Action

Explain the decision that a probation officer must make regarding a probationer who has violated the terms of her or his probation agreement. **LEARNING OBJECTIVE 4**

A JUDGMENT CALL

THE SITUATION Your client, Alain, was convicted of selling drugs and given a split sentence—three years in prison and three years on probation. You meet Alain for the first time two days after his release, and you are immediately concerned about his mental health. His mother confirms your worries, telling you that Alain needs help. You refer him to a psychiatric hospital, but the officials there determine that he "does not require mental health treatment at this time." Several weeks later, Alain's mother tells you that he is staying out late at night and "hanging out with the wrong crowd," both violations of his probation agreement. After he tests positive for marijuana, you warn Alain that, after one more violation, you will revoke his probation and send him back to prison. He tells you that he is "feeling agitated" and "having intermittent rage." You refer him to a substance abuse and mental health treatment facility, where he tests positive for marijuana once again.

THE LAW For any number of reasons, but particularly for the failed drug tests, you can start revocation proceedings against Alain. These proceedings will almost certainly conclude with his return to prison.

WHAT WOULD YOU DO? On the one hand, Alain has violated the terms of his probation agreement numerous times. On the other hand, he has been convicted of only one crime—a drug violation—and you have no evidence that he is behaving violently or poses a danger to himself or others. Furthermore, Alain has strong family support and is willing to enter treatment for his substance abuse problems. Do Alain's technical violations cause you to begin the revocation process? Why or why not?

To see how a Fairfield County, Connecticut, probation officer dealt with a similar situation, go to Example 10.1 in Appendix B.

2. *Revocation hearing.* During this hearing, the probation agency presents evidence to support its claim of violation, and the probationer can attempt to refute this evidence. The probationer has the right to know the charges being brought against him or her. Furthermore, probationers can testify on their own behalf and present witnesses in their favor, as well as confront and cross-examine adverse witnesses. A "neutral and detached" body must hear the evidence and rule on the validity of the proposed revocation.

3. *Revocation sentencing.* If the presiding body rules against the probationer, then the judge must decide whether to impose incarceration and for what length of time. In a revocation hearing dealing with technical violations, the judge will often reimpose probation with stricter terms or intermediate sanctions.

In effect, this is a "bare-bones" approach to due process. Most of the rules of evidence that govern regular trials do not apply to revocation hearings. Probation officers are not, for example, required to read offenders their *Miranda* rights before questioning them about crimes they may have committed during probation. In *Minnesota v. Murphy* (1984),[32] the Supreme Court ruled that a meeting between probation officer and client does not equal custody and, therefore, the Fifth Amendment protection against self-incrimination does not apply either.

Does Probation Work?

On March 11, 2014, police in Berkeley County, West Virginia, arrested William Jackson for placing a plastic bag over seventy-two-year-old Martha Tyler's head and suffocating her to death. At the time of the murder, Jackson was on probation for drug charges and grand larceny. Indeed, probationers are responsible for a significant amount of crime. According to the most recent data, 11 percent of all suspects arrested for violent crimes (and 13 percent of those arrested for murder) were on probation at the time of their apprehension.[33] Such statistics raise a critical question—is probation worthwhile?

GOALS OF PROBATION To measure the effectiveness of probation, one must first establish its purpose. Generally, as we saw earlier, the goal of probation is to reintegrate and divert as many offenders as possible while at the same time protecting the public. Specifically, probation and other community corrections programs are evaluated by their success in preventing *recidivism*—the eventual rearrest or return to incarceration of the probationer.[34] Given that many probationers are first-time, nonviolent offenders, the system is not designed to prevent relatively rare outbursts of violence.

RISK FACTORS FOR RECIDIVISM About 15 percent of all probationers are returned to prison or jail before the end of their probationary terms.[35] There are several risk factors that make a probationer more likely to recidivate, including

1. *Antisocial personality patterns,* meaning that the probationer is impulsive, pleasure seeking, restlessly aggressive, or irritable.

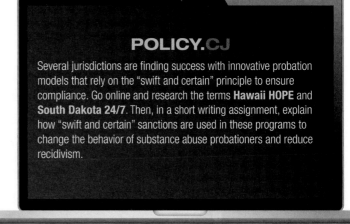

POLICY.CJ

Several jurisdictions are finding success with innovative probation models that rely on the "swift and certain" principle to ensure compliance. Go online and research the terms **Hawaii HOPE** and **South Dakota 24/7**. Then, in a short writing assignment, explain how "swift and certain" sanctions are used in these programs to change the behavior of substance abuse probationers and reduce recidivism.

2. *Procriminal attitudes,* such as negative attitudes toward authority and the law, as well as a tendency to rationalize one's prior criminal behavior.

3. *Social supports for crime,* including friends who are offenders and a living environment lacking in positive role models.[36]

Other important risk factors for recidivism include substance abuse and unemployment. By concentrating resources on those probationers who exhibit these risk factors, probation departments can succeed in lowering overall recidivism rates.[37]

In addition, the most effective supervisory probation strategy for reducing recidivism appears to be a mix of supervision (behavior monitoring) and treatment (behavior change). Researchers have labeled this a "hybrid" approach to probation, and numerous studies attest to the benefits of mixing "tough love" and treatment such as drug counseling and continuing education instead of focusing on one or the other.[38] Also, as noted earlier, caseloads matter. A recent study of probation practices in Iowa and Oklahoma found that the lower the caseload for each individual probation officer, the lower the rates of probationers being arrested for new crimes.[39]

///// SELF ASSESSMENT

Fill in the blanks, and check your answers on page 330.

Offenders sentenced to probation serve their sentence in the _____ under the supervision of a _____ _____. If a probationer commits a _____ _____ by failing to follow the _____ of his or her probation, it may be revoked. If revocation occurs, the offender will be sent to _____. To a large extent, the effectiveness of probation programs is measured by _____, or the rate at which offenders are rearrested. In many instances, this effectiveness is compromised by the heavy _____ carried by probation officers.

THE PAROLE PICTURE

At any given time, about 850,000 Americans are living in the community on **parole,** or the *conditional* release of a prisoner after a portion of his or her sentence has been served behind bars. Parole allows the corrections system to continue to supervise an offender who is no longer incarcerated. As long as parolees follow the conditions of their parole, they are allowed to finish their terms outside the prison. If parolees break the terms of their early release, however, they face the risk of being returned to a penal institution.

Parole is based on three concepts:[40]

1. *Grace.* The prisoner has no right to be given an early release, but the government has granted her or him that privilege.

2. *Contract of consent.* The government and the parolee enter into an arrangement whereby the latter agrees to abide by certain conditions in return for continued freedom.

3. *Custody.* Technically, though no longer incarcerated, the parolee is still the responsibility of the state. Parole is an extension of corrections.

Because of good-time credits and parole, most prisoners do not serve their entire sentence in prison. In fact, the average felon serves only about half of the term handed down by the court.

Comparing Probation and Parole

LEARNING OBJECTIVE 5 Identify the main differences between probation and parole.

Both probation and parole operate under the basic assumption that the offender serves her or his time in the community rather than in a prison or jail. The main differences between the two concepts—which sound confusingly similar—involve their circumstances. Probation is a sentence handed down by a judge following conviction and usually does not include incarceration. Parole is a conditional release from prison and occurs after an offender has already served some time in a correctional facility. (See *Mastering Concepts—Probation versus Parole* that follows for clarification.)

Parole Contract An agreement between the state and the offender that establishes the conditions of parole.

CONDITIONS OF PAROLE In many ways, parole supervision is similar to probation supervision. Like probationers, offenders who are granted parole are placed under the supervision of community corrections officers and required to follow certain conditions. The duties of probation officers and parole officers are so similar that many jurisdictions combine the two posts in a single position. Furthermore, certain parole conditions mirror probation conditions. All parolees, for example, must comply with the law, and they are generally responsible for reporting to their parole officer at certain intervals.

The frequency of these visits, along with the other terms of parole, is spelled out in the **parole contract,** which sets out the agreement between the state and the paroled offender. Under the terms of the contract, the state agrees to conditionally release the inmate, and the future parolee agrees that her or his conditional release will last only as long as she or he abides by the contract. (See Figure 10.4 that follows for a list of standard parole conditions.)

PAROLE REVOCATION About a quarter of parolees return to prison before the end of their parole period, most because they were convicted of a new offense or had their parole revoked.[41] Property crimes are the most common reason that both male and female parolees return to incarceration, and men on parole are twice as likely as their

MASTERING CONCEPTS
PROBATION VERSUS PAROLE

Probation and parole have many aspects in common. In fact, probation and parole are so similar that many jurisdictions combine them into a single agency. There are, however, some important distinctions between the two systems, as noted below.

	PROBATION	PAROLE
Basic Definition	An **alternative to imprisonment** in which a person who has been convicted of a crime is allowed to serve his or her sentence in the community subject to certain conditions and supervision by a probation officer.	An **early release** from a correctional facility, in which the convicted offender is given the chance to spend the remainder of her or his sentence under supervision in the community.
Timing	The offender is sentenced to a probationary term in place of a prison or jail term. If the offender breaks the conditions of probation, he or she is sent to prison or jail. Therefore, **probation generally occurs *before* imprisonment.**	Parole is a form of early release. Therefore, **parole occurs *after* an offender has spent time behind bars.**
Authority	**Probation is under the domain of the judiciary.** A judge decides whether to sentence a convict to probation, and a judge determines whether a probation violation warrants revocation and incarceration.	**Parole often falls under the domain of the parole board.** This administrative body determines whether the prisoner qualifies for early release and the conditions under which the parole must be served.
Characteristics of Offenders	As a number of studies have shown, probationers are normally less involved in the criminal lifestyle. Most of them are **first-time offenders who have committed nonviolent crimes.**	Many parolees have **spent months or even years in prison** and, besides abiding by conditions of parole, must make the difficult transition to "life on the outside."

FIGURE 10.4 Standard Conditions of Parole

The parolee must do the following:

- Stay within a certain area.
- Obtain permission before changing residence or employment.
- Obtain and maintain employment.
- Maintain acceptable, nonthreatening behavior.
- Not possess firearms or weapons.
- Report any arrest within twenty-four hours.
- Not use illegal drugs or alcohol or enter drinking establishments.
- Not break any state or local laws.
- Allow contacts by parole officers at home or employment without obstruction.
- Submit to search of person, residence, or motor vehicle at any time by parole officers.

female counterparts to have their parole revoked for a violent crime.[42] **Parole revocation** is similar in many aspects to probation revocation. If the parolee commits a new crime, then a return to prison is very likely. If, however, the individual commits a technical violation by breaking a condition of parole, then parole authorities have discretion as to whether revocation proceedings should be initiated.

When authorities do attempt to revoke parole for a technical violation, they must provide the parolee with a revocation hearing.[43] Although this hearing does not provide the same due process protections as a criminal trial, the parolee does have the right to be notified of the charges, to present witnesses, to speak in his or her defense, and to question any hostile witnesses (so long as such questioning would not place them in danger). In the first stage of the hearing, the parole authorities determine whether there is probable cause that a violation occurred. Then, they decide whether to return the parolee to prison.

Discretionary Release

As you may recall from Chapter 9, corrections systems are classified by sentencing procedure—indeterminate or determinate. Indeterminate sentencing occurs when the legislature sets a range of punishments for particular crimes, and the judge and the parole board exercise discretion in determining the actual length of the prison term. For that reason, states with indeterminate sentencing are said to have systems of **discretionary release.**

ELIGIBILITY FOR PAROLE Under indeterminate sentencing, parole is not a right but a privilege. This is a crucial point, as it establishes the terms of the relationship between the inmate and the corrections authorities during the parole process. In *Greenholtz v. Inmates of the Nebraska Penal and Correctional Complex* (1979),[44] the Supreme Court ruled that inmates do not have a constitutionally protected right to expect parole, thereby giving states the freedom to set their own standards for determining parole eligibility. In most states that have retained indeterminate sentencing, a prisoner is eligible to be considered for parole release after serving a legislatively determined percentage of the minimum sentence—usually one-half or two-thirds—less any good time or other credits.

Not all convicts are eligible for parole. About one-third of prison inmates serving life sentences have no possibility of parole. Most of these prisoners have committed violent crimes such as first degree murder. According to the American Civil Liberties Union, however, approximately 3,300 "lifers" are nonviolent offenders whose harsh prison terms were regulated by the mandatory sentencing laws we discussed in the previous chapter.[45] Critics believe that life-without-parole is an "outrageous" punishment for nonviolent offenders and have called on the nation's politicians to end the practice in the United States.[46]

PAROLE PROCEDURES A convict does not apply for parole. Rather, different jurisdictions have different procedures for determining discretionary release dates. In many states, the offender is eligible for discretionary release at the end of his or her minimum

Parole Revocation When a parolee breaks the conditions of parole, the process of withdrawing parole and returning the person to prison.

Discretionary Release The release of an inmate into a community supervision program at the discretion of the parole board within limits set by state or federal law.

sentence minus good-time credits (see Chapter 9). For instance, in 2014, Glenwood Carr was sentenced to six to twelve years in prison for fleeing the scene of a fatal accident that he caused by driving drunk in Clay, New York. This means that Carr will become eligible for parole after serving six years, less good time. In other states, parole eligibility is measured at either one-third or one-half of the maximum sentence, or it is a matter of discretion for the parole authorities.

In most states, the responsibility for making the parole decision falls to the **parole board,** whose members are generally appointed by the governor. According to the American Correctional Association, the parole board has four basic roles:

Nancy Stone/MCT/Newscom

1. To decide which offenders should be placed on parole.
2. To determine the conditions of parole and aid in the continuing supervision of the parolee.
3. To discharge the offender when the conditions of parole have been met.
4. If a violation occurs, to determine whether parole privileges should be revoked.[47]

Most parole boards are small, made up of three to seven members. In many jurisdictions, board members' terms are limited to between four and six years. The requirements for board members vary. Nearly half the states have no prerequisites, while others require a bachelor's degree or some expertise in the field of criminal justice.

In January 2014, Reynolds Wintersmith was granted a presidential pardon and released from prison after being sentenced to life behind bars without parole for committing a drug-related crime. What is ■ your opinion of the practice of sentencing nonviolent offenders to life-without-parole?

THE PAROLE DECISION Parole boards use a number of criteria to determine whether a convict should be given discretionary release. These criteria include

1. The nature and circumstances of the underlying offense and the offender's current attitude toward it.
2. The offender's prior criminal record.
3. The offender's attitude toward the victim and the victim's family members.
4. The offender's physical, mental, and emotional health.
5. The offender's behavior behind bars, including his or her participation in programs for self-improvement.[48]

LEARNING
6
OBJECTIVE

Explain which factors influence the decision to grant parole.

In a system that uses discretionary parole, the actual release decision is made at a **parole grant hearing.** During this hearing, the entire board or a subcommittee reviews relevant information on the convict. Sometimes, but not always, the offender is interviewed.

Because the board members have only limited knowledge of each offender, key players in the case are often notified in advance of the parole hearing and asked to provide comments and recommendations. These participants include the sentencing judge, the attorneys at the trial, the victims, and any law enforcement officers who may be involved. After these preparations, the typical parole hearing itself is very short—usually lasting just a few minutes.

Parole Board A body of appointed civilians that decides whether a convict should be granted conditional release before the end of his or her sentence.

Parole Grant Hearing A hearing in which the entire parole board or a subcommittee reviews information, meets the offender, and hears testimony from relevant witnesses to determine whether to grant parole.

PAROLE DENIAL When parole is denied, the reasons usually involve poor prison behavior by the offender and/or the severity of the underlying crime.[49] After a parole denial, the entire process will generally be replayed at the next "action date," which depends on the nature of the offender's crimes and all relevant laws. In February 2014, for example, Herman Bell was denied parole for the sixth time. More than four decades earlier, Bell had been convicted of murder for his involvement in the execution-style killings of two New York City police officers and sentenced to twenty-five years to life in prison. Although Bell was sixty-six years old at the time of his latest parole grant hearing, the state parole board told him that "if released at this time, there is a reasonable probability that you would not live and remain at liberty without again violating the law."[50]

Parole Guidelines

Nearly twenty states have moved away from discretionary release systems to procedures that provide for **mandatory release.** Under mandatory release, offenders leave prison only when their prison terms have expired, minus adjustments for good time. No parole board is involved in this type of release, which is designed to eliminate discretion from the process.

Instead, in mandatory release, corrections officials rely on **parole guidelines** to determine the early release date. Similar to sentencing guidelines (see Chapter 9), parole guidelines determine a potential parolee's risk of recidivism using a mathematical equation. Under this system, inmates and corrections authorities know the *presumptive parole date* soon after the inmate enters prison. So long as the offender does not experience any disciplinary or other problems while incarcerated, he or she can be fairly sure of the time of release.

Note that a number of states and the federal government claim to have officially "abolished" parole through truth-in-sentencing laws. (As described in Chapter 9, this form of legislation requires certain statutorily determined offenders to serve at least 85 percent of their prison terms.) For the most part, however, these laws simply emphasize prison terms that are "truthful," not necessarily "longer." Mechanisms for parole, by whatever name, are crucial to the criminal justice system for several reasons. First, they provide inmates with an incentive to behave properly in the hope of an early release. Second, they reduce the costs related to incarceration by keeping down the inmate population, a critical concern for prison administrators.[51]

Victims' Rights and Parole

Herman Bell's chances of being granted parole, described earlier in this section, were certainly not helped by the sentiments of Diane Piagentini, the widow of one of his victims. According to Piagentini, Bell should remain behind bars "until the end of time."[52] Over the past several decades, the community corrections system has expanded to better

Leslie Van Houten, incarcerated at the California Institution for Women in Chino, California, has been denied parole twenty times for her involvement in two grisly murders that took place more than forty-five years ago. ■ Are some crimes so horrific that the offender should never be granted parole, even if she or he no longer poses a threat to society? Explain your answer.

AP Images

encompass the wants and needs of victims. Many probation and parole departments now have employees responsible for assisting victims in areas such as collecting restitution or compensation and providing information about the status and location of offenders.[53]

Intermediate Sanctions
Sanctions that are more restrictive than probation and less restrictive than imprisonment.

The federal Crime Victims' Rights Act provides victims with the right to be reasonably notified of any parole proceedings and the right to attend and be reasonably heard at such proceedings.[54] A number of states offer similar assurances of victim participation in the parole process. Generally, victim testimony before a parole board focuses on the emotional, physical, and financial hardship experienced by the victim or the victim's family because of the offender's criminal act. Given the moral power of such testimony, it is somewhat surprising to learn that victim input appears to have little effect on the parole decision. Instead, parole boards prefer to rely on the traditional criteria for determining parole, described on page 319.[55]

//// SELF ASSESSMENT

Fill in the blanks, and check your answers on page 330.

Parole refers to the _____ release of an inmate from prison before the end of his or her _____. Once an inmate has been released from prison, the terms of his or her release are spelled out in a parole _____, and a _____ violation of these terms or, especially, the commission of a new crime will almost certainly result in a return to prison. In jurisdictions that have systems of discretionary release, a _____ _____ makes the parole decision. In contrast, with a _____ release, the inmate will not leave prison until her or his sentence has expired, minus good-time credits.

INTERMEDIATE SANCTIONS

Many observers feel that the most widely used sentencing options—imprisonment and probation—fail to reflect the immense diversity of crimes and criminals. **Intermediate sanctions** provide a number of additional sentencing options for those wrongdoers who require stricter supervision than that supplied by probation, but for whom imprisonment would be unduly harsh and counterproductive.[56] The intermediate sanctions discussed in this section are designed to match the specific punishment and treatment of an individual offender with a corrections program that reflects that offender's situation.

Dozens of different variations of intermediate sanctions are handed down each year. To cover the spectrum succinctly, two general categories of such sanctions will be discussed in this section: those administered primarily by the courts and those administered primarily by corrections departments, including day reporting centers, intensive supervision probation, shock incarceration, and home confinement. Remember that none of these sanctions are exclusive. They are often combined with imprisonment and probation and parole, and with each other.

Judicially Administered Sanctions

The lack of sentencing options is most frustrating for the person who, in the majority of cases, does the sentencing—the judge. Consequently, when judges are given the discretion to "color" a punishment with intermediate sanctions, they will often do so. In addition to imprisonment and probation, a judge has five sentencing options:

1. Fines.
2. Community service.

3. Restitution.
4. Pretrial diversion programs.
5. Forfeiture.

Fines, community service, and restitution were discussed in Chapter 9. In the context of intermediate sanctions, it is important to remember that these punishments are generally combined with incarceration or probation. For that reason, some critics feel the retributive or deterrent impact of such punishments is severely limited. Many European countries, in contrast, rely heavily on fines as the sole sanctions for a variety of crimes. (See the feature *Comparative Criminal Justice—Swedish Day-Fines* that follows.)

PRETRIAL DIVERSION PROGRAMS Not every criminal violation requires the courtroom process. Consequently, some judges have the discretion to order an offender into a **pretrial diversion program** during the preliminary hearing. (Prosecutors can also offer

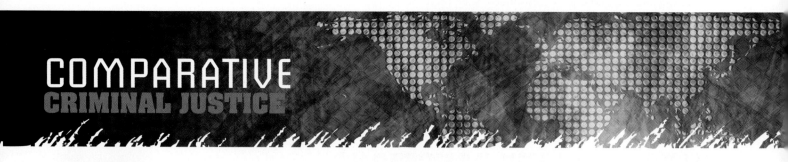

COMPARATIVE
CRIMINAL JUSTICE

Central Intelligence Agency

Swedish Day-Fines

Few ideals are cherished as highly in our criminal justice system as equality. Most Americans take it for granted that individuals guilty of identical crimes should face identical punishments. From an economic perspective, however, this emphasis on equality renders our system decidedly unequal. Take two citizens, one a millionaire investment banker and the other a checkout clerk earning the minimum wage. Driving home from work one afternoon, each is caught by a traffic officer doing 80 miles per hour in a 55-mile-per-hour zone. The fine for this offense is $150. This amount, though equal for both, has different consequences: it represents mere pocket change for the investment banker, but a significant chunk of the checkout clerk's weekly paycheck.

Restricted by a "tariff system" that sets specific amounts for specific crimes, regardless of the financial situation of the convict, American judges often refrain from using fines as a primary sanction. They either assume that poor offenders cannot pay the fine or worry that a fine will allow wealthier offenders to "buy" their way out of a punishment.

PAYING FOR CRIME

In searching for a way to make fines more effective sanctions, many reformers have seized on the concept of the "day-fine,"

as practiced in Sweden and several other European countries. In this system, which was established in the 1920s and 1930s, the fine amount is linked to the monetary value of the offender's daily income. Depending on the seriousness of the crime, a Swedish offender will be sentenced to 1 to 120 day-fines or, as combined punishment for multiple crimes, up to 200 day-fines.

For each day-fine unit assessed, the offender is required to pay one-thousandth of her or his annual gross income (minus a deduction for basic living expenses, as determined by the Prosecutor General's Office) to the court. Consequently, the day-fine system not only reflects the degree of the crime, but also ensures that the economic burden will be equal for those with different incomes.

Swedish police and prosecutors can levy day-fines without court involvement. As a result, plea bargaining is nonexistent, and more than 80 percent of all offenders are sentenced to intermediate sanctions without a trial. The remaining cases receive full trials, with an acquittal rate of only 6 percent, compared with 32 percent in the United States.

FOR CRITICAL ANALYSIS

Do you think a "day-fine" system would be feasible in the United States? Why might it be difficult to implement in this country?

an offender the opportunity to join such a program in return for reducing or dropping the initial charges.) These programs represent an "interruption" of the criminal proceedings and are generally reserved for young or first-time offenders who have been arrested on charges of illegal drug use, child or spousal abuse, or sexual misconduct. Pretrial diversion programs usually include extensive counseling, often in a treatment center. If the offender successfully follows the conditions of the program, the criminal charges are dropped.

PROBLEM-SOLVING COURTS Many judges have found opportunities to divert low-level offenders by presiding over problem-solving courts. In these comparatively informal courtrooms, specially trained judges attempt to address specific problems such as drug addiction, mental illness, and domestic violence that often lead to the eventual rearrest of the offender. About three thousand problem-solving courts are operating in the United States. Although these specialized courts cover a wide variety of subjects, the most common problem-solving courts are drug courts.

The specific procedures of drug courts vary widely. Most, however, follow a general pattern. Either after arrest or on conviction, the offender is given the option of entering a drug court program or continuing through the standard courtroom process. Those who choose the former come under the supervision of a judge who will oversee a mixture of treatment and sanctions designed to cure their addiction. When offenders successfully complete the program, the drug court rewards them by dropping all charges against them. Drug courts operate on the assumption that when a criminal addict's drug use is reduced, his or her drug-fueled criminal activity will also decline. Research shows that drug courts reduce the probability of continued drug abuse and, consequently, lead to a significant reduction in recidivism rates of participants when compared with nonparticipants.[57]

FORFEITURE In 1970, Congress passed the Racketeer Influenced and Corrupt Organizations Act (RICO) in an attempt to prevent the use of legitimate business enterprises as shields for organized crime.[58] As amended, RICO and other statutes give judges the ability to implement forfeiture proceedings in certain criminal cases. **Forfeiture** is a process by which the government seizes property gained from or used in criminal activity. For example, if a person is convicted for smuggling cocaine into the United States from South America, a judge can order the seizure of not only the narcotics, but also the speedboat the offender used to deliver the drugs to a pickup point off the coast of South Florida. In *Bennis v. Michigan* (1996),[59] the Supreme Court ruled that a person's home or car could be forfeited even though the owner was unaware that the property was connected to illegal activity. (In the *CJ Controversy—Civil Forfeiture* feature that follows, we examine the question of whether the government should be able to confiscate property in the *absence* of criminal guilt.)

Once property is forfeited, the government has several options. It can sell the property, with the proceeds going to the state and/or federal law enforcement agencies involved in the seizure. Alternatively, the government agency can use the property directly in further crime-fighting efforts or award it to a third party, such as an informant. Forfeiture can be financially rewarding—the U.S. Marshals Service manages nearly $2 billion worth of contraband and property impounded from criminals and criminal suspects. Each year, the agency shares about $570 million of these funds with state and local law enforcement agencies, with an additional $200 million going to crime victims.[60]

Forfeiture The process by which the government seizes private property attached to criminal activity.

CIVIL FORFEITURE

With criminal forfeiture, as described in the text, a defendant must be convicted of committing a crime before her or his property is confiscated. Under *civil forfeiture,* as implemented by the federal government and almost every state government, law enforcement agencies can confiscate property without the criminal conviction of its owner and can keep that property, even if the owner is ultimately found to be innocent of the crime. The government need only prove a "substantial connection" between the property and underlying crime for civil forfeiture to apply.

CIVIL FORFEITURE IS A GOOD IDEA BECAUSE . . .

- It gives law enforcement a powerful tool to fight drug dealers and white-collar criminals by allowing the police to more easily confiscate the illegal gains of these criminal activities.
- Each year, it raises hundreds of millions of dollars that can be used to better equip and train local police departments and provide restitution for crime victims.

CIVIL FORFEITURE IS A BAD IDEA BECAUSE . . .

- Due process (see Chapter 3) requires that a person be found guilty of committing a crime before he or she can be punished for that crime.
- It introduces the concept of "profit motive" to policing and thus provides law enforcement agents with an incentive to improperly seize property even if no underlying crime has been committed.

Your Assignment

North Carolina is the only state that bans the practice of civil forfeiture by requiring a criminal conviction before a defendant's property can be seized. Should civil forfeiture be banned throughout the United States? As part of your answer, go online and find an example of a **civil forfeiture seizure** that supports your argument either for or against the practice. Your response should include at least two full paragraphs.

Day Reporting Centers

First used in Great Britain, **day reporting centers (DRCs)** are mainly tools to reduce jail and prison overcrowding. Although the offenders are allowed to live in the community rather than jail or prison, they must spend all or part of each day at a reporting center. In general, being sentenced to a DRC is an extreme form of supervision. With offenders under a single roof, they are much more easily monitored and controlled. (According to critics of DRCs, they are also more easily able to "network" with other individuals who have criminal histories and drug and alcohol abuse issues.[61])

DRCs are instruments of rehabilitation as well. They often feature treatment programs for drug and alcohol abusers and provide counseling for a number of psychological problems, such as depression and anger management. Many of those found guilty in the Roanoke (Virginia) Drug Court, for example, are ordered to participate in a yearlong day reporting program. At the center, offenders meet with probation officers, submit to urine tests, and attend counseling and education programs, such as parenting and life-skills classes. After the year has passed, if the offender has completed the program to the satisfaction of the judge and has found employment, the charges will be dropped.[62]

Day Reporting Center (DRC)
A community-based corrections center to which offenders report on a daily basis for treatment, education, and rehabilitation.

Intensive Supervision Probation

Over the past several decades, a number of jurisdictions have turned to **intensive supervision probation (ISP)** to solve the problems associated with the burdensome caseloads we discussed earlier in the chapter. ISP offers a more restrictive alternative to regular probation, with higher levels of face-to-face contact between offenders and officers and with frequent modes of control such as urine tests for drugs. In New Jersey, for example, ISP officers have caseloads of only 20 offenders (compared with 115 for other probation officers in the state) and are provided with additional resources to help them keep tabs on their charges.[63] Different jurisdictions have different methods of determining who is eligible for ISP, but a majority of states limit ISP to offenders who do not have prior probation violations.

The main goal of ISP is to provide prisonlike control of offenders while keeping them out of prison. Critics of ISP believe that it "causes" high failure rates, as more supervision increases the chances that an offender will be caught breaking conditions of probation.[64] A recent comparison of ISP with DRCs, however, found the intensive supervision of ISP to be more effective. In the six months following termination of the program, DRC participants were more likely to be convicted for a new offense and to test positive for drugs than their ISP counterparts. The study suggests that when combined with services such as outpatient drug treatment and educational training, ISP can be effective in producing low rates of recidivism.[65]

Shock Incarceration

As the name suggests, **shock incarceration** is designed to "shock" criminals into compliance with the law. Following conviction, the offender is first sentenced to a prison or jail term. Then, usually within ninety days, he or she is released and resentenced to probation. The theory behind shock incarceration is that by getting a taste of the brutalities of the daily prison grind, the offender will be shocked into a crime-free existence.

In the past, shock incarceration was targeted primarily toward youthful, first-time offenders, who were thought to be more likely to be "scared straight" by a short stint behind bars. Recent data show, however, that 20 percent of all adults sentenced to probation spend some time in jail or prison before being released into the community.[66] Critics of shock incarceration are dismayed by this trend. They argue that the practice needlessly disrupts the lives of low-level offenders who would not otherwise be eligible for incarceration and exposes them to the mental and physical hardships of prison life (which we will discuss in Chapter 12).[67]

The *boot camp* is a variation on traditional shock incarceration. Instead of spending the

LEARNING **7** OBJECTIVE Contrast day reporting centers with intensive supervision probation.

Inmates engage in morning calisthenics at the Impact Incarceration Program in Illinois. ■ In theory, why would boot camps like this one benefit first-time nonviolent offenders more than a jail or prison sentence?

Journal Courier/The Image Works Image

"shock" period of incarceration in prison or jail, offenders are sent to a boot camp. Modeled on military basic training, these camps are generally located within prisons and jails, though some can be found in the community. The programs emphasize strict discipline, manual labor, and physical training. They are designed to instill self-responsibility and self-respect in participants, thereby lessening the chances that offenders will return to a life of crime. More recently, boot camps have also emphasized rehabilitation, incorporating such components as drug and alcohol treatment programs, anger-management courses, and vocational training.[68]

Home Confinement and Electronic Monitoring

Various forms of **home confinement**—in which offenders serve their sentences not in a government institution but at home—have existed for centuries. It has often served, and continues to do so, as a method of political control, used by totalitarian regimes to isolate and silence dissidents. For purposes of general law enforcement, home confinement was impractical until relatively recently. After all, one could not expect offenders to keep their promises to stay at home, and the personnel costs of guarding them were prohibitive. In the 1980s, however, with the advent of **electronic monitoring**, or using technology to guard the prisoner, home confinement became more viable. Today, all fifty states and the federal government have home monitoring programs with about 200,000 offenders, including probationers and parolees, participating at any one time.[69]

List the three levels of home monitoring.

LEARNING
OBJECTIVE

LEVELS OF HOME MONITORING Home monitoring has three general levels of restriction:

1. *Curfew,* which requires offenders to be in their homes at specific hours each day, usually at night.
2. *Home detention,* which requires that offenders remain home at all times, with exceptions being made for education, employment, counseling, or other specified activities such as the purchase of food or, in some instances, attendance at religious ceremonies.
3. *Home incarceration,* which requires the offender to remain home at all times, save for medical emergencies.

Offenders who are confined to their homes are often monitored by electronic devices like this one, which fits around the ankle. ■ What are some of the benefits of electronic monitoring as an intermediate sanction?

Damon Higgins/ZUMA Press/Newscom

Under ideal circumstances, home confinement serves many of the goals of intermediate sanctions. It protects the community. It saves public funds and space in correctional facilities by keeping convicts out of institutional incarceration. It meets public expectations of punishment for criminals. Uniquely, home confinement also recognizes that convicts, despite their crimes, play important roles in the community and allows them to continue in those roles. An offender, for example, may be given permission to leave confinement to care for elderly parents.

Home confinement is also lauded for giving sentencing officials the freedom to match the punishment with the needs of the offender. In 2014, for example, a sixty-four-year-old Maine businessman was sentenced to six months of home confinement for tax fraud. He was, however, allowed to return to his office during the day to earn the money needed to pay nearly $140,000 in court-ordered fines. The offender was also allowed to leave home for doctor appointments and to buy groceries.

TYPES OF ELECTRONIC MONITORING According to some reports, the inspiration for electronic monitoring was a *Spider-Man* comic book in which the hero was tracked by the use of an electronic device on his arm. In 1979, a New Mexico judge named Jack Love, having read the comic, convinced an executive at Honeywell, Inc., to begin developing similar technology to supervise convicts.[70]

Two major types of electronic monitoring have grown out of Love's initial concept. The first is a "programmed contact" program, in which the offender is contacted periodically by telephone or beeper to verify his or her whereabouts. Verification is obtained via a computer that uses voice or visual identification techniques or by requiring the offender to enter a code in an electronic box when called. The second is a "continuously signaling" device, worn around the convict's wrist, ankle, or neck. A transmitter in the device sends out a continuous signal to a "receiver-dialer" device located in the offender's dwelling. If the receiver device does not detect a signal from the transmitter, it informs a central computer, and the police are notified.[71]

CJ & TECHNOLOGY — Global Positioning System (GPS)

AP Images/Jeff T. Green

Global positioning system (GPS) technology is a form of tracking technology that relies on twenty-four military satellites orbiting thousands of miles above the earth. The satellites transmit signals to each other and to a receiver on the ground, allowing a monitoring station to determine the location of a receiving device to within a few feet. GPS provides a much more precise level of supervision than regular electronic monitoring. The offender wears a transmitter, similar to a traditional electronic monitor, around his or her ankle or wrist. This transmitter communicates with a portable tracking device, a small box that uses military satellites to determine the probationer's movements.

GPS technology can be used either "actively," to constantly monitor the subject's whereabouts, or "passively," to ensure that the offender remains within the confines of a limited area determined by a judge or probation officer. Inclusion and exclusion zones are also important to GPS supervision. Inclusion zones are areas such as a home or workplace where the offender is expected to be at certain times. Exclusion zones are areas such as parks, playgrounds, and schools where the offender is not permitted to go. GPS-linked computers can alert officials immediately when an exclusion zone has been breached and create a computerized record of the probationer's movements for review at a later time. Despite the benefits of this technology, it is rarely implemented. According to the Bureau of Justice Statistics, only about eight thousand probationers are currently being tracked by GPS.

Thinking about GPS
How might GPS monitoring be used to improve and overhaul the American bail system, covered in Chapter 8?

Widening the Net

As mentioned above, most of the convicts chosen for intermediate sanctions are low-risk offenders. From the point of view of the corrections official doing the choosing, this makes sense. Such offenders are less likely to commit crimes and attract negative publicity. This selection strategy, however, appears to invalidate one of the primary reasons intermediate sanctions exist: to reduce prison and jail populations. If most of the offenders in intermediate sanctions programs would otherwise have received probation, then the effect on these populations is nullified. Indeed, studies have shown this to be the case.[72]

At the same time, intermediate sanctions broaden the reach of the corrections system. In other words, they increase rather than decrease the amount of control the state exerts over the individual. Suppose a person is arrested for a misdemeanor such as shoplifting and, under normal circumstances, would receive probation. With access to intermediate sanctions, the judge may add a period of home confinement to the sentence. Critics contend that such practices **widen the net** of the corrections system by augmenting the number of citizens who are under the control and surveillance of the state, and also *strengthen the net* by increasing the government's power to intervene in the lives of its citizens.[73] Technological advances, such as the GPS devices mentioned earlier, will only accelerate the trend.

////SELF ASSESSMENT

Fill in the blanks, and check your answers on page 330.

Judicially administered sanctions include fines, restitution, and _____, a process in which the government seizes property connected to illegal activity. Offenders may also be sentenced to spend part of their time at _____ _____ _____, where they receive treatment and are more easily _____ by corrections officials. _____ _____, or militaristic programs designed to instill self-responsibility, are a form of _____ incarceration. Home confinement, another intermediate sanction, has become more effective in recent years, thanks to technology known as _____ _____.

CHAPTER SUMMARY

For more information on these concepts, look back to the Learning Objective icons throughout the chapter.

 Explain the justifications for community-based corrections programs. One justification involves reintegration of the offender into society. Reintegration restores family ties, encourages employment and education, and secures a place for the offender in the routine functioning of society. Other justifications involve diversion and cost savings. By diverting criminals to alternative modes of punishment, further overcrowding of jail and prison facilities can be avoided, as can the costs of incarcerating the offenders.

 Specify the conditions under which an offender is most likely to be denied probation. The offender (a) has been convicted of multiple charges, (b) was on probation or parole when arrested, (c) has two or more prior convictions, (d) is addicted to narcotics, (e) seriously injured the victim of the crime, or (f) used a weapon while committing the crime.

 Describe the three general categories of conditions placed on a probationer. (a) Standard conditions, such as requiring that the probationer notify the agency of a change of address, not leave the jurisdiction without permission, and remain employed; (b) punitive conditions, such as restitution, community service, and home confinement; and (c) treatment conditions, such as required drug or alcohol treatment.

 Explain the decision that a probation officer must make regarding a probationer who has violated the terms of her or his probation agreement. The decision to revoke probation—and probably send the probationer to prison or jail—for either the commission of a crime or a technical violation is often a judgment call by the probation officer. In making this judgment call, the probation officer must weigh the best interests of the probationer against the need to protect the public.

 Identify the main differences between probation and parole. Probation is a sentence handed down by a judge that generally acts as an alternative to incarceration. Parole is a form of early release from prison determined by a parole authority, often a parole board. Probationers are usually first-time offenders who have committed nonviolent crimes, while parolees have often spent significant time in prison.

 Explain which factors influence the decision to grant parole. In deciding whether to grant parole, parole board members consider the severity of the underlying crime, the offender's prior criminal record, and the offender's attitude toward the victim or the victim's family. Other factors include the offender's physical, emotional, and mental well-being, and the offender's behavior behind bars.

 Contrast day reporting centers with intensive supervision probation. In a day reporting center (DRC), the offender is allowed to remain in the community but must spend all or part of each day at the reporting center. While at the center, offenders meet with probation officers, submit to drug tests, and attend counseling and education programs. With intensive supervision probation (ISP), more restrictions are imposed, and there is more face-to-face contact between offenders and probation officers. ISP may also include electronic surveillance.

 List the three levels of home monitoring. (a) Curfew, which requires that the offender be at home during specified hours; (b) home detention, which requires that the offender be at home except for education, employment, counseling, or other specified activities; and (c) home incarceration, which requires that the offender be at home at all times except for medical emergencies.

QUESTIONS FOR CRITICAL ANALYSIS

1. Why might probationers or parolees want to limit their social media activity? Give an example of a circumstance in which a Facebook posting could cause probation or parole to be revoked.

2. Several years ago, an eighty-six-year-old man was found guilty of fatally shooting his eighty-one-year-old wife. The victim was suffering from a painful health condition and had begged her husband to end her life. An Arizona judge sentenced the defendant to two years' probation. Do agree with this punishment? Why or why not?

3. In many jurisdictions, parolees can be stopped and searched by parole or police officers at any time, even if there is no probable cause that the parolee has committed a crime. How can these types of stops and searches be justified?

4. How might technology such as GPS-enhanced electronic monitoring ease the caseload burden of probation and parole officers?

5. In your own words, explain what the phrase "widening the net" means. What might be some of the unintended consequences of increasing the number of offenders who are supervised by corrections officers in the community?

KEY TERMS

SELF-ASSESSMENT ANSWER KEY

Page 308: **i.** reintegration; **ii.** diversion; **iii.** cost; **iv.** less

Page 316: **i.** community; **ii.** probation officer; **iii.** technical violation; **iv.** conditions; **v.** prison or jail; **vi.** recidivism; **vii.** caseloads

Page 321: **i.** conditional; **ii.** sentence; **iii.** contract; **iv.** technical; **v.** parole board; **vi.** mandatory

Page 328: **i.** forfeiture; **ii.** day reporting centers; **iii.** supervised; **iv.** Boot camps; **v.** shock; **vi.** electronic monitoring

NOTES

1. Bureau of Justice Statistics, *Correctional Populations in the United States, 2012* (Washington, D.C.: U.S. Department of Justice, December 2013), Table 2, page 3.

2. Michael Tonry, *Sentencing Matters* (New York: Oxford Press, 1996), 28.

3. Bureau of Justice Statistics, *Probation and Parole in the United States, 2012* (Washington, D.C.: U.S. Department of Justice, December 2013), 1.

4. Corrections Task Force of the President's Commission on Law Enforcement and Administration of Justice (1967).

5. Paul H. Hahn, *Emerging Criminal Justice: Three Pillars for a Proactive Justice System* (Thousand Oaks, Calif.: Sage Publications, 1998), 106–108.

6. *Correctional Populations in the United States, 2012, op. cit.*

7. "Cutting Costs: How States Are Addressing Corrections Budget Shortfalls," *Corrections Directions* (December 2008), 6.

8. John Schmitt, Kris Warner, and Sarika Gupta, *The High Budgetary Cost of Incarceration* (Washington, D.C.: Center for Economic and Policy Research, June 2010), Table 4, page 11.

9. Donna Lyons, "States Are Reshaping Policies to Save Money and Maintain Public Safety with 'Justice Reinvestment' Reforms," *State Legislature Magazine* (January 2013), at **www.ncsl.org/issues -research/justice/high-yield-corrections .aspx.**

10. Nathan Koppel, "Probation Pays Bills for Prosecutors," *Wall Street Journal* (February 12, 2012), A2.

11. Paul W. Keve, *Crime Control and Justice in America* (Chicago: American Library Association, 1995), 183.

12. Bureau of Justice Statistics, *Probation and Parole in the United States, 2010* (Washington, D.C.: U.S. Department of Justice, December 2011), Appendix table 3, page 31.

13. Joan Petersilia and Susan Turner, *Prison versus Probation in California: Implications for Crime and Offender Recidivism* (Santa Monica, Calif.: RAND Corporation, 1986).

14. *Probation and Parole in the United States, 2012, op. cit.*, Appendix table 3, page 18.

15. *Ibid.*

16. *Ibid.*; and Bureau of Justice Statistics, *Prisoners in 2012—Advance Counts* (Washington, D.C.: U.S. Department of Justice, July 2013), Table 1, page 2.

17. Sharyn Adams, Lindsay Bostwick, and Rebecca Campbell, *Examining Illinois Probationer Characteristics and Outcomes* (Chicago: Illinois Criminal Justice Information Authority, September 2011), Table 1, pages 16–17.

18. 705 So.2d 172 (La. 1997).

19. Neil P. Cohen and James J. Gobert, *The Law of Probation and Parole* (Colorado Springs, Colo.: Shepard's/McGraw-Hill, 1983), Section 5.01, 183–184; Section 5.03, 191–192.

20. 534 U.S. 112 (2001).

21. *Ibid.,* 113.

22. Bureau of Justice Statistics, *Felony Defendants in Large Urban Counties, 2009—Statistical Tables* (Washington, D.C.: U.S. Department of Justice, December 2013), Table 28, page 32.

23. Carl B. Klockars, Jr., "A Theory of Probation Supervision," *Journal of Criminal Law, Criminology, and Police Science* 63 (1972), 550–557.

24. *Probation and Parole in the United States, 2012, op. cit.,* Table 4, page 6.

25. Todd R. Clear, George F. Cole, and Michael D. Reisig, *American Corrections,* 10th ed. (Belmont, Calif.: Wadsworth Cengage Learning, 2013), 200.

26. Klockars, *op. cit.,* 551.

27. Hahn, *op. cit.,* 116–118.

28. Matthew T. DeMichele, *Probation and Parole's Growing Caseloads and Workload Allocation: Strategies for Managerial Decision Making* (Lexington, Ky.: American Probation and Parole Association, May 2007).

29. Brad Branna, "Sacramento County Probation Officers Have Highest Caseload in State," *Sacramento Bee* (April 10, 2013), at **www.sacbee.com/2013/04/10/5329755/sacramento-county-probation-officers.html**.

30. 389 U.S. 128 (1967).

31. *Morrissey v. Brewer,* 408 U.S. 471 (1972); and *Gagnon v. Scarpelli,* 411 U.S. 778 (1973).

32. 465 U.S. 420 (1984).

33. *Felony Defendants in Large Urban Counties, 2009—Statistical Tables, op. cit.,* Table 6, page 10.

34. Jennifer L. Skeem and Sarah Manchak, "Back to the Future: From Klockars' Model of Effective Supervision to Evidence-Based Practice in Probation," *Journal of Offender Rehabilitation* 47 (2008), 231.

35. *Probation and Parole in the United States, 2012, op. cit.,* Table 4, page 6.

36. Pamela M. Casey, Roger K. Warren, and Jennifer K. Elek, *Using Offender Risk and Needs Assessment Information at Sentencing* (Williamsburg, Va.: National Center for State Courts, 2011), Table 1, page 5.

37. Nancy Ritter, "Predicting Recidivism Risk: New Tool in Philadelphia Shows Great Promise," *NIJ Journal* (February 2013), 4–13.

38. Skeem and Manchak, *op. cit.,* 226–229.

39. Sarah K. Jalbert et al., *A Multi-Site Evaluation of Reduced Probation Caseload Size in an Evidence-Based Setting* (Cambridge, Mass.: Abt Associates, March 2011), 8–10.

40. Clear, Cole, and Reisig, *op. cit.,* 380.

41. *Probation and Parole in the United States, 2012, op. cit.,* Table 6, page 9.

42. *Ibid.,* Table 7, page 9.

43. *Morrissey v. Brewer,* 408 U.S. 471 (1972).

44. 442 U.S. 1 (1979).

45. *A Living Death: Life with Parole for Nonviolent Offenses* (New York: American Civil Liberties Union, November 2013), 2.

46. "American Oubliette," *The Economist* (November 16, 2013), 16–17.

47. William Parker, *Parole: Origins, Development, Current Practices, and Statutes* (College Park, Md.: American Correctional Association, 1972), 26.

48. Clear, Cole, and Reisig, *op. cit.,* 387.

49. *Ibid.,* 389.

50. Quoted in Thomas Tracy, "Cop-Killer Herman Bell Denied Parole in Murder of Two NYPD Officers in 1971," *New York Daily News* (February 25, 2014), at **www.nydailynews.com/new-york/nyc-crime/cop-killer-herman-bell-denied-parole-article-1.1701111**.

51. Mark P. Rankin, Mark H. Allenbaugh, and Carlton Fields, "Parole's Essential Role in Bailing Out Our Nation's Criminal Justice Systems," *Champion* (January 2009), 47–48.

52. Quoted in Tracy, *op. cit.*

53. Council of State Government/American Probation and Parole Association, "Fact Sheet 1: The Role of Community Corrections in Victim Services" (2012), at **www.appa-net.org/eWeb/docs/APPA/pubs/PVRPPP-FACTSHEET-1.pdf**.

54. 18 U.S.C. Section 3771(a)(4) (2006).

55. Joel M. Caplan, "Parole Release Decisions: Impact of Victim Input on a Representative Sample of Inmates," *Journal of Criminal Justice* (May–June 2010), 291–300.

56. Norval Morris and Michael Tonry, *Between Prison and Probation: Intermediate Punishments in a Rational Sentencing System* (Oxford: Oxford University Press, 1990).

57. Shelli B. Rossman et al., *The Multi-Site Adult Drug Court Evaluation: Executive Summary* (Washington, D.C.: Urban Institute, November 2011), 5.

58. 18 U.S.C. Sections 1961–1968.

59. 516 U.S. 442 (1996).

60. U.S. Marshals, "Facts and Figures 2014," at **www.usmarshals.gov/duties/fact sheets/facts-2014.pdf**.

61. Douglas J. Boyle et al., "Overview of: 'An Evaluation of Day Reporting Centers for Parolees: Outcomes of a Randomized Trial,'" *Criminology & Public Policy* (February 2013), 136.

62. Model State Drug Court Legislation Committee, *Model State Drug Court Legislation: Model Drug Offender Accountability and Treatment Act* (Alexandria, Va.: National Drug Court Institute, May 2004), 42.

63. New Jersey Courts, "ISP Fact Sheet," at **www.judiciary.state.nj.us/probsup/11556_overviewfactsheet.pdf**.

64. Joan Petersilia and Susan Turner, "Intensive Probation and Parole," *Crime and Justice* 17 (1993), 281–335.

65. Douglas J. Boyle et al., *Outcomes of a Randomized Trial of an Intensive Community Corrections Program—Day Reporting Center—for Parolees, Final Report for the National Institute of Justice* (October 2011), 3–4.

66. *Probation and Parole in the United States, 2010,* Appendix table 3, page 31.

67. Clear, Cole, and Reisig, *op. cit.,* 229.

68. Dale Parent, *Correctional Boot Camps: Lessons from a Decade of Research* (Washington, D.C.: U.S. Department of Justice, June 2003), 6.

69. Todd R. Clear et al., *American Corrections in Brief,* 2nd ed. (Belmont, Calif.: Wadsworth Cengage Learning, 2014), 102.

70. Josh Kurtz, "New Growth in a Captive Market," *New York Times* (December 31, 1989), 12.

71. Edna Erez, Peter R. Ibarra, and Norman A. Lurie, "Electronic Monitoring of Domestic Violence Cases—A Study of Two Bilateral Programs," *Federal Probation* (June 2004), 15–20.

72. Michael Tonry and Mary Lynch, "Intermediate Sanctions," in *Crime and Justice,* vol. 20, ed. Michael Tonry (Chicago: University of Chicago Press, 1996), 99.

73. Dennis Palumbo, Mary Clifford, and Zoann K. Snyder-Joy, "From Net Widening to Intermediate Sanctions: The Transformation of Alternatives to Incarceration from Benevolence to Malevolence," in *Smart Sentencing: The Emergence of Intermediate Sanctions,* eds. James M. Byrne, Arthur Lurigio, and Joan Petersilia (Newbury Park, Calif.: Sage, 1992), 231.

To target your study and review, look for these numbered Learning Objective icons throughout the chapter.

Bloomberg via Getty Images

Cost Cutting in
CORRECTIONS

THE ADMINISTRATION of President Barack Obama, a Democrat, recently announced plans to severely lessen the harshness of charges brought against drug offenders in federal courts. Not long ago, Republican politicians in the nation's capital would have roundly criticized such a move as being "soft on crime." Today, however, if there is one thing that both parties can agree on, it is the need to downsize America's corrections system. In 2014, for example, Congress took bipartisan steps to pass two bills aimed at reducing the federal prison population. The first would give federal judges more discretion to depart downward from mandatory minimum sentencing guidelines, while the second proposed an early release from the prison program for nonviolent federal offenders.

This spirit of cooperation is even more evident on the state level. Starting in 2008, nineteen states led by Republicans—along with nine under the control of Democrats—have enacted policies to reduce their incarceration rates. Texas, one of the most conservative states in the nation, saw its prison population decline by nearly six thousand in recent years, mostly by diverting nonviolent offenders to community corrections. Furthermore, in 2012 alone, Florida, under a Republican governor, closed ten correctional facilities, saving the state over $65 million. These policy choices reflect a small but significant trend in American corrections: fewer inmates. In 2010, the total U.S. prison population declined for the first time in nearly four decades. Then, in 2011 and 2012, the number of inmates decreased again.

To be sure, the decreases were slight—totaling about 2.5 percent—and do little to threaten our nation's title as "the globe's leading incarcerator." About 2.3 million Americans are in prison and jail. The United States locks up six times as many of its citizens as Canada does, and seven times as many as most European democracies. Still, the fact that federal and state politicians from both sides of the aisle are willing to work together to lower the number of inmates represents a sea change in the country's corrections strategies. While many supporters of these changes speak of the need to provide "second chances" to offenders through rehabilitation rather than punishment, the motivation behind the shift is primarily financial. "What I think happened," said Republican senator John Cornyn of Texas, "was that we built so many prisons people began to ask the question: 'Can we afford this?'"

FOR CRITICAL ANALYSIS

1. By most measures, the United States imprisons more of its citizens than any other country in the world. Economic considerations aside, what is your opinion of our dramatically high incarceration rates?

2. How do you think declining national crime rates over the past two decades, as discussed in Chapter 2, have contributed to an atmosphere where politicians are less worried about being depicted as "soft on crime"?

3. From 2010 to 2013, the number of drug courts in Georgia nearly tripled. How is the philosophy behind such courts (see page 323) in keeping with policies designed to lower incarceration rates?

Several years ago, thanks to declining inmate populations, Texas was able to close its Central Unit facility, a century-old prison located southwest of Houston.

A SHORT HISTORY OF AMERICAN PRISONS

Penitentiary An early form of correctional facility that emphasized separating inmates from society and from each other.

Today's high rates of imprisonment—often referred to as evidence of "mass incarceration" in the United States—are the result of many criminal justice strategies that we have discussed in this textbook. These include truth-in-sentencing guidelines, relatively long sentences for gun and drug crimes, "three-strikes" habitual offender laws, and judicial freedom to incarcerate convicts for relatively minor criminal behavior. At the base of all these policies is a philosophy that sees prisons primarily as instruments of punishment. The loss of freedom imposed on inmates is the penalty for the crimes they have committed. Punishment has not, however, always been the main reason for incarceration in this country.

English Roots

The prisons of eighteenth-century England, known as "bridewells" after London's Bridewell Palace, had little to do with punishment. These facilities were mainly used to hold debtors or those awaiting trial, execution, or banishment from the community. (In many ways, as will be made clear, these facilities resembled the modern jail.) English courts generally imposed one of two sanctions on convicted felons: they turned them loose, or they executed them.[1] To be sure, most felons were released, pardoned either by the court or by the clergy after receiving a whipping or a branding.

The correctional system in the American colonies differed very little from that of their motherland. If anything, colonial administrators were more likely to use corporal punishment than were their English counterparts, and the death penalty was not uncommon in early America. The one dissenter was William Penn, who adopted the "Great Law" in Pennsylvania in 1682. Based on Quaker ideals of humanity and rehabilitation, this criminal code forbade the use of torture and mutilation as forms of punishment. Instead, felons were ordered to pay restitution of property or goods to their victims. If the offenders did not have sufficient property to make restitution, they were placed in a prison, which was primarily a "workhouse."[2] The death penalty was still allowed under the "Great Law," but only in cases of premeditated murder. Penn proved to be an exception, however, and the path to reform was much slower in the colonies than in England.

Walnut Street Prison: The First Penitentiary

On William Penn's death in 1718, the "Great Law" was rescinded in favor of a harsher criminal code, similar to those of the other colonies. At the time of the American Revolution, however, the Quakers were instrumental in the first broad swing of the incarceration pendulum from punishment to rehabilitation. In 1776, Pennsylvania passed legislation ordering that offenders be reformed through treatment and discipline rather than simply beaten or executed.[3] Several states, including Massachusetts and New York, quickly followed Pennsylvania's example.

Pennsylvania continued its reformist ways by opening the country's first **penitentiary** in a wing of Philadelphia's Walnut Street Jail in 1790. The penitentiary operated on the assumption that silence and labor provided the best hope of rehabilitating the criminal spirit. Remaining silent would force the prisoners to think about their crimes, and eventually the weight of conscience would lead to repentance. At the same time, enforced labor would attack the problem of idleness—regarded as the main cause of crime by penologists of the time.[4] Consequently, inmates at Walnut Street were isolated from one another in solitary rooms and kept busy with constant menial chores.

Contrast the Pennsylvania and the New York penitentiary theories of the 1800s.

LEARNING OBJECTIVE 1

Eventually, the penitentiary at Walnut Street succumbed to the same problems that continue to plague institutions of confinement: overcrowding and excessive costs. As an influx of inmates forced more than one person to be housed in a room, maintaining silence became nearly impossible. By the early 1800s, officials could not find work for all of the convicts, so many were left idle.

The Great Penitentiary Rivalry: Pennsylvania versus New York

The apparent lack of success at Walnut Street did little to dampen enthusiasm for the penitentiary concept. Throughout the first half of the nineteenth century, a number of states reacted to prison overcrowding by constructing new penitentiaries. Each state tended to have its own peculiar twist on the roles of silence and labor, and two such systems—those of Pennsylvania and New York—emerged to shape the debate over the most effective way to run a prison.

THE PENNSYLVANIA SYSTEM After the failure of Walnut Street, Pennsylvania constructed two new prisons: the Western Penitentiary near Pittsburgh (opened in 1826) and the Eastern Penitentiary in Cherry Hill, near Philadelphia (1829). The Pennsylvania system took the concept of silence as a virtue to new extremes. Based on the idea of **separate confinement,** these penitentiaries were constructed with back-to-back cells radiating outward from the center. (See Figure 11.1 that follows for the layout of the original Eastern Penitentiary.) To protect each inmate from the corrupting influence of the others, prisoners worked, slept, and ate alone in their cells. Their primary contact with other human beings came in the form of religious instruction from a visiting clergyman or prison official.[5]

FIGURE 11.1 The Eastern Penitentiary

As you can see, the Eastern Penitentiary was designed in the form of a "wagon wheel," known today as the radial style. The back-to-back cells in each "spoke" of the wheel were arranged in such a way to limit contact between inmates.

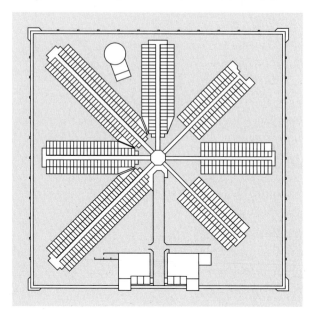

THE NEW YORK SYSTEM If Pennsylvania's prisons were designed to transform wrongdoers into honest citizens, those in New York focused on obedience. When New York's Newgate Prison (built in 1791) became overcrowded, the state authorized the construction of Auburn Prison, which opened in 1816. Auburn initially operated under many of the same assumptions that guided the penitentiary at Walnut Street. Solitary confinement, however, seemed to lead to an inordinate amount of sickness, insanity, and even suicide among inmates, and it was abandoned in 1822. Nine years later, Elam Lynds became warden at Auburn and instilled the **congregate system,** also known as the Auburn system. Like Pennsylvania's separate confinement system, the congregate system was based on silence and labor. At Auburn, however, inmates worked and ate together, with silence enforced by prison guards.[6]

If either state can be said to have "won" the debate, it was New York. The Auburn system proved more popular, and a majority of the new prisons built during the first half of the nineteenth century followed New York's lead, though mainly for economic reasons rather than philosophical ones. New York's penitentiaries were cheaper to build because they did not require so much space. Furthermore, inmates in New York were employed in workshops, whereas those in Pennsylvania toiled alone in their cells.

Consequently, the Auburn system was better positioned to exploit prison labor in the early years of widespread factory production.

The Reformers and the Progressives

The Auburn system did not go unchallenged. In the 1870s, a group of reformers argued that fixed sentences, imposed silence, and isolation did nothing to help prisoners improve their lives. These critics proposed that penal institutions should offer the promise of early release as a prime tool for rehabilitation. Echoing the views of the Quakers a century earlier, the reformers presented an ideology that would heavily influence American corrections for the next century.

This "new penology" was put into practice at New York's Elmira Reformatory in 1876 (see the photo alongside). At Elmira, good behavior was rewarded by early release, and misbehavior was punished with extended time under a three-grade system of classification. On entering the institution, the offender was assigned a grade of 2. If the inmate followed the rules and completed work and school assignments, after six months he was moved up to grade 1, the necessary grade for release. If, however, the inmate broke institutional rules, he was lowered to grade 3. A grade 3 inmate needed to behave properly for three months before he could return to grade 2 and begin to work back toward grade 1 and eventual release.[7]

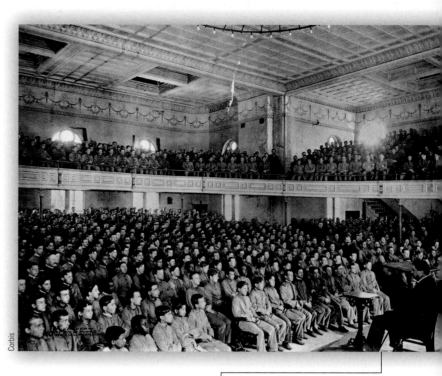

Inmates of the Elmira Reformatory in New York attend a presentation in the prison auditorium. To what extent do you believe that treatment should be a part of the incarceration of criminals?

Although other penal institutions did not adopt the Elmira model, its theories came into prominence in the first two decades of the twentieth century, thanks to the Progressive movement in criminal justice. The Progressives believed that criminal behavior was caused by social, economic, and biological factors and, therefore, a corrections system should have a goal of treatment, not punishment. Consequently, they trumpeted a **medical model** for prisons, which held that institutions should offer a variety of programs and therapies to cure inmates of their "ills," whatever the root causes. The Progressives were largely responsible for the spread of indeterminate sentences (Chapter 9), probation (Chapter 10), intermediate sanctions (Chapter 10), and parole (Chapter 10) in the first half of the twentieth century.

The Reassertion of Punishment

Even though the Progressives had a great influence on the corrections system as a whole, their theories had little impact on the prisons themselves. Many of these facilities had been constructed in the nineteenth century and were impervious to change. More important, prison administrators usually did not agree with the Progressives and their followers, so the day-to-day lives of most inmates varied little from the congregate system of Auburn Prison.

Academic attitudes began to shift toward those of the prison administrators in the mid-1960s. Then, in 1974, the publication of Robert Martinson's famous "What Works?" essay provided opponents of the medical model with statistical evidence that

Medical Model A model of corrections in which the psychological and biological roots of an inmate's criminal behavior are identified and treated.

rehabilitation efforts did nothing to lower recidivism rates.[8] This is not to say that Martinson's findings went unchallenged. A number of critics argued that rehabilitative programs could be successful.[9] In fact, Martinson himself retracted most of his claims in a little-noticed article published five years after his initial report.[10] Attempts by Martinson and others to "set the record straight" were largely ignored, however, as crime rose sharply in the early 1970s. This trend led many criminologists and politicians to champion "get tough" measures to deal with criminals they now considered "incurable." By the end of the 1980s, the legislative, judicial, and administrative strategies that we have discussed throughout this text had positioned the United States for an explosion in inmate populations and prison construction unparalleled in the nation's history.

///// SELF ASSESSMENT

Fill in the blanks, and check your answers on page 359.

In the early 1800s, Pennsylvania's _____ confinement strategy and New York's _____ system were the two dominant methods of managing prisons in the United States. Both were based on _____ and labor, but New York's system proved more popular because its institutions were _____ to construct and exploited the demand for prison _____. In the second half of the century, the Progressive movement rejected both systems and introduced the _____ model for prisons, which focused on rehabilitation rather than punishment.

PRISON ORGANIZATION AND MANAGEMENT

The United States has a dual prison system that parallels its dual court system, which we discussed in Chapter 7. The Federal Bureau of Prisons (BOP) currently operates about one hundred confinement facilities, ranging from prisons to immigration detention centers to community corrections institutions.[11] In the federal corrections system, a national director, appointed by the president, oversees six regional directors and a staff of over 35,000 employees. All fifty states also operate state prisons, which number over 1,700 and make up more than 90 percent of the country's correctional facilities.[12] Governors are responsible for the organization and operation of state corrections systems, which vary widely based on each state's geography, *demographics* (population characteristics), and political culture.

Generally, those offenders sentenced in federal court for breaking federal law serve their time in federal prisons, and those offenders sentenced in state court for breaking state law serve their time in state prisons. As you can see in Figure 11.2 that follows, federal prisons hold relatively few violent felons, because relatively few federal laws involve violent crime. At the same time, federal prisons are much more likely to hold public order offenders, a group that includes violators of federal immigration law.

Prison Administration

Whether the federal government or a state government operates a prison, its administrators have the same general goals, summarized by criminologist Charles Logan as follows:

> The mission of a prison is to keep prisoners—to keep them in, keep them safe, keep them in line, keep them healthy, and keep them busy—and to do it with fairness, without undue suffering and as efficiently as possible.[13]

FIGURE 11.2 Types of Offenses of Federal and State Prison Inmates

As the comparison below shows, state prisoners are most likely to have been convicted of violent crimes, while federal prisoners are most likely to have been convicted of drug and public order offenses.

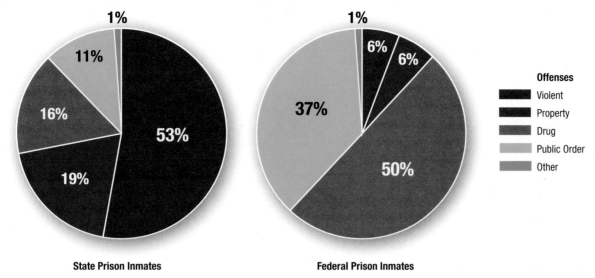

State Prison Inmates

Federal Prison Inmates

Offenses
- Violent
- Property
- Drug
- Public Order
- Other

Source: *Prisoners in 2012: Trends in Admissions and Releases, 1991–2012* (Washington, D.C.: U.S. Department of Justice, December 2013), Table 3, page 5; and Appendix table 10, page 43.

Considering the environment of a prison—an enclosed world inhabited by people who are generally violent and angry, and would rather be anywhere else—Logan's mission statement is somewhat unrealistic. A prison staff must supervise the daily routines of hundreds or thousands of inmates, a duty that includes providing them with meals, education, vocational programs, and different forms of leisure. The smooth operation of this supervision is made more difficult—if not, at times, impossible—by budgetary restrictions, overcrowding, and continual inmate turnover.

FORMAL PRISON MANAGEMENT In some respects, the management structure of a prison is similar to that of a police department, as discussed in Chapter 5. Both systems rely on a hierarchical (top-down) *chain of command* to increase personal responsibility. Both assign different employees to specific tasks, though prison managers have much more direct control over their subordinates than do police managers. The main difference is that police departments have a *continuity of purpose* that is sometimes lacking in prison organizations. All members of a police force are, at least theoretically, working to reduce crime and apprehend criminals. In a prison, an employee who works in the prison laundry service and one who works in the visiting center have little in common. In some instances, employees may even have cross-purposes: a prison guard may want to punish an inmate, while a counselor in the treatment center may want to rehabilitate her or him.

Consequently, a strong hierarchy is crucial for any prison management team that hopes to meet Charles Logan's expectations. As Figure 11.3 that follows shows, the **warden** (also known as a superintendent) is ultimately responsible for the operation of a prison. He or she oversees deputy wardens, who in turn manage the various organizational lines of the institution. The custodial employees, who deal directly with the inmates and make up more than half of a prison's staff, operate under a militaristic hierarchy, with a line of command passing from the deputy warden to the captain to the correctional officer.

LEARNING OBJECTIVE 2 Describe the formal prison management system, and indicate the three most important aspects of prison governance.

Warden The prison official who is ultimately responsible for the organization and performance of a correctional facility.

FIGURE 11.3 Organizational Chart for a Typical Correctional Facility

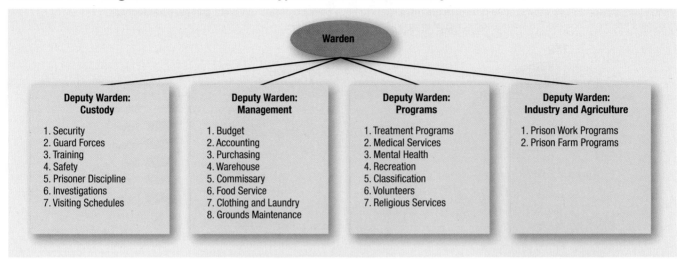

GOVERNING PRISONS Although there is no single "best" form of prison management, political scientist John DiIulio believes that, in general, the sound governance of correctional facilities is a matter of order, amenities, and services:

1. *Order* can be defined as the absence of misconduct such as murder, assault, and rape. Many observers, including DiIulio, believe that, having incarcerated a person, the state has a responsibility to protect that person from disorder in the correctional institution.

2. *Amenities* are those comforts that make life "livable," such as clean living conditions, acceptable food, and entertainment. One theory of incarceration holds that inmates should not enjoy a quality of life comparable to life outside prison. Without the basic amenities, however, prison life becomes unbearable, and inmates are more likely to lapse into disorder.

3. *Services* include programs designed to improve an inmate's prospects on release, such as vocational training, remedial education, and drug treatment. Again, many feel that a person convicted of a crime does not deserve to participate in these kinds of programs, but they have two clear benefits. First, they keep the inmate occupied and focused during her or his sentence. Second, they reduce the chances that the inmate will go back to a life of crime after she or he returns to the community.[14]

According to DiIulio, in the absence of order, amenities, and services, inmates will come to see their imprisonment as not only unpleasant but unfair, and they will become much more difficult to control.[15] Furthermore, weak governance encourages inmates to come up with their own methods of regulating their lives. As we shall see in the next chapter, the result is usually high levels of violence and the expansion of prison gangs and other unsanctioned forms of authority.

Types of Prisons

Classification The process through which prison officials determine which correctional facility is best suited to the individual offender.

One of the most important aspects of prison administration occurs soon after a defendant has been convicted of a crime. In the **classification** process, administrators determine what sort of correctional facility provides the best "fit" for each individual convict. In general, prison administrators rely on three criteria for classification purposes:

1. The seriousness of the crime committed.
2. The risk of future criminal or violent conduct.
3. The need for treatment and rehabilitation programs.[16]

In the federal prison system, this need to classify—and separate—different kinds of offenders has led to six different levels of correctional facilities. Inmates in level 1 facilities are usually nonviolent and require the least amount of security, while inmates in level 6 facilities are the most dangerous and require the harshest security measures. Many states use a similar six-level system, and in both federal and state prisons, a committee headed by a deputy warden usually makes the classification decisions.

Different facilities have different means of separating and classifying inmates. To simplify matters, most observers refer to correctional facilities as being one of three levels—minimum, medium, or maximum. A fourth level—the supermaximum-security prison, known as the "supermax"—is relatively rare and extremely controversial due to its hyperharsh methods of punishing and controlling the most dangerous prisoners.

MAXIMUM-SECURITY PRISONS In a certain sense, the classification of prisoners today owes a debt to the three-grade system developed at the Elmira Reformatory, discussed earlier in the chapter. Once wrongdoers enter a corrections facility, they are constantly graded on behavior. Those who serve "good time," as we have seen, are often rewarded with early release. Those who compile extensive misconduct records are usually housed, along with violent and repeat offenders, in **maximum-security prisons.** The names of these institutions—Folsom, San Quentin, Sing Sing, Attica—conjure up foreboding images of concrete and steel jungles, with good reason.

Maximum-security prisons are designed with full attention to security and surveillance. In these institutions, inmates' lives are programmed in a militaristic fashion to keep them from escaping or from harming themselves, other inmates, or the prison staff. About a quarter of the prisons in the United States are classified as maximum security, and these institutions house about a third of the country's prisoners.

The Design Maximum-security prisons tend to be large—holding more than a thousand inmates—and they have similar features. The entire operation is usually surrounded by concrete walls that stand twenty to thirty feet high and have been sunk deep into the ground to deter tunnel escapes. Fences reinforced with razor-ribbon barbed wire that can be electrically charged may supplement these barriers. The prison walls are studded with watchtowers, from which guards armed with shotguns and rifles survey the movement of prisoners below. The designs of these facilities, though similar, are not uniform. Though correctional facilities built using the radial design pioneered by the Eastern Penitentiary still exist, several other designs have become prominent in more recently constructed institutions.

Inmates live in cells, most of them with similar dimensions to those found in the Topeka Correctional Facility, a maximum-security prison in Topeka, Kansas: eight feet by fourteen feet with cinder block walls.[17] The space contains bunks, a toilet, a sink, and possibly a cabinet or closet. Cells are located in rows of *cell blocks,* each of which forms its own security unit, set off by a series of gates and bars. A maximum-security institution is essentially a collection of numerous cell blocks, each constituting its own prison within a prison.

Regardless of their design, most prisons have cell blocks that open into sprawling prison yards, where the inmates commingle daily. The "prison of the future," however,

Maximum-Security Prison
A correctional institution designed and organized to control and discipline dangerous felons, as well as prevent escape.

LEARNING
3
OBJECTIVE

List and briefly explain the four types of prisons.

Photo Courtesy of Berry Larson

FASTFACTS

**PRISON WARDEN
JOB DESCRIPTION:**

- A prison warden is the chief managing officer of an adult correctional institution.

**WHAT KIND OF
TRAINING IS REQUIRED?**

- Bachelor's degree in criminal justice, corrections, law enforcement, or a related field.
- One or more years of work experience in the management of a major division of a correctional institution.

ANNUAL SALARY RANGE?

- $42,000–$95,000 (depending on size of institution and geographic region)

BERRY LARSON

PRISON WARDEN

Before I began my career as a correctional officer for the Arizona Department of Corrections, I had several people question my desire to work inside a prison. Why would I want to stick myself somewhere so unpleasant and stressful? While at the training academy, however, we were taught that "approach determines response." I found that to be very true during my time as a correctional officer. It is all about the way you carry yourself and the way you relate to the inmates. An inmate can tell if you are trying to be someone you are not. They can also tell if you are afraid. I never had to use physical force once in all the time I was a correctional officer—officer presence and nonverbal/verbal communication is usually sufficient to handle any situation, as long as you keep control of your emotions.

As warden of the Arizona State Prison Complex–Lewis, my duties include touring the units; attending special events such as inmate graduations for GED and vocational programs; managing emergency situations such as power outages, fights and assaults, and staff injuries; and eradicating all criminal activity from the facility. Many, if not most, of our inmates came to us in pretty bad shape—little or no education, a substance abuse history, or mental health or behavioral issues. These young men have spent their lives watching television and playing video games, and simply do not have the skills to be successful in life. We try to remedy the situation by providing them with educational and vocational programs and "life-skills" classes that promote civil and productive behavior.

Social Media Career Tip Regularly reevaluate your social media tools and the methods you use to keep up to date in your fields of interest. If you are still using the same tools as a year ago, you probably aren't keeping up with the latest developments in Internet technology.

rejects this layout. Instead, it relies on a podular design, as evident at the Two Rivers Correctional Institute in Umatilla, Oregon. At Two Rivers, which opened in 2007, fourteen housing pods contain ninety-six inmates each. Each unit has its own yard, so inmates rarely, if ever, interact with members of other pods. This design gives administrators the flexibility to, for example, place violent criminals in pod A and white-collar criminals in pod B without worrying about mixing the two different security levels.[18]

Security Measures Within maximum-security prisons, inmates' lives are dominated by security measures. Whenever they move from one area of the prison to another, they do so in groups and under the watchful eye of armed correctional officers. Television surveillance cameras may be used to monitor their every move, even when sleeping, showering, or using the toilet. They are subject to frequent pat-downs or strip searches at the guards' discretion. Constant "head counts" ensure that every inmate is where he or she should be. Tower guards—many of whom have orders to shoot to kill in the case of a disturbance or escape attempt—constantly look down on the inmates as they move around outdoor areas of the facility.

Technology has added significantly to the overall safety of maximum-security prisons. Walk-through metal detectors and X-ray body scanners, for example, can detect weapons or other contraband hidden on the body of an inmate. The most promising new technology in this field, however, relies on radio frequency identification (RFID). About the size of two grains of rice, an RFID tag consists of a glass capsule that contains a computer chip, a tiny copper antenna, and an electrical device known as a "capacitor" that transmits the data in the chip to an outside scanner. In the prison context, RFID works as a high-tech head count: inmates wear bracelets tagged with the microchips, while correctional officers wear small RFID devices resembling pagers.

Guided by a series of radio transmitters and receivers, the system is able to pinpoint the location of inmates and guards within twenty feet. Every two seconds, radio signals "search out" the location of each inmate and guard, and relay this information to a central computer. On a grid of the prison, an inmate shows up as a yellow dot and a correctional officer as a blue dot. Many RFID systems also store all movements in a database for future reference. "[RFID] completely revolutionizes a prison because you know where everyone is—not approximately but exactly where they are," remarked an official at the National Institute of Justice.

Black Creek/TSI PRISM

Thinking about RFID Tracking

Review the discussion of crime mapping and "hot spots" in Chapter 5. Drawing on your knowledge of crime-mapping technology, discuss how RFID technology can reduce violence and other misconduct such as drug sales in prisons.

SUPERMAX PRISONS About thirty states and the Federal Bureau of Prisons (BOP) operate **supermax** (short for supermaximum security) **prisons,** which are supposedly reserved for the "worst of the worst" of America's corrections population. Many of the inmates in these facilities are deemed high risks to commit murder behind bars—about a quarter of the occupants of the BOP's U.S. Penitentiary Administrative Maximum Facility in Florence, Colorado, have killed other prisoners or assaulted correctional officers elsewhere. Supermax prisons are also used as punishment for offenders who commit serious disciplinary infractions in maximum-security prisons, or for those inmates who become involved with prison gangs.[19] In addition, a growing number of supermax occupants are either high-profile individuals who would be at constant risk of attack in a general prison population or convicted terrorists.

The main purpose of a supermax prison is to strictly control the inmates' movement, thereby limiting (or eliminating) situations that could lead to breakdowns in discipline. The conditions at California's Security Housing Unit (SHU) at Pelican Bay State Prison are representative of most supermax institutions. Prisoners are confined to their one-person cells for twenty-three hours each day under video camera surveillance. They receive meals through a slot in the door. Fluorescent lights are continuously on, day and night, making it difficult for inmates to enjoy any type of privacy or sleep.[20] For the most part, supermax prisons operate in a state of perpetual **lockdown,** in which all inmates are confined to their cells and social activities such as meals, recreational sports, and treatment programs are nonexistent.

Supermax Prison A correctional facility reserved for those inmates who have extensive records of misconduct.

Lockdown A disciplinary action taken by prison officials in which all inmates are ordered to their quarters and nonessential prison activities are suspended.

What security measures can you identify from this photo of a cell block at Arizona State Prison in Florence?

AP Images/Matt York

MEDIUM- AND MINIMUM-SECURITY PRISONS

Medium-security prisons hold about 45 percent of the prison population and minimum-security prisons 20 percent. Inmates at **medium-security prisons** have for the most part committed less-serious crimes than those housed in maximum-security prisons and are not considered high risks for escaping or causing harm. Consequently, medium-security institutions are not designed for control to the same extent as maximum-security prisons and have a more relaxed atmosphere. These facilities also offer more educational and treatment programs and allow for more contact between inmates. Medium-security prisons are rarely walled, relying instead on high fences. Prisoners have more freedom of movement within the structures, and the levels of surveillance are much lower. Living quarters are less restrictive as well—many of the newer medium-security prisons provide dormitory housing.

A **minimum-security prison** seems at first glance to be more like a college campus than an incarceration facility. Most of the inmates at these institutions are first-time offenders who are nonviolent and well behaved. A high percentage are white-collar criminals. Indeed, inmates are often transferred to minimum-security prisons as a reward for good behavior in other facilities. Therefore, security measures are lax compared with even medium-security prisons. Unlike medium-security institutions, minimum-security prisons do not have armed guards. Prisoners are provided with amenities such as television sets and computers in their rooms. They also enjoy freedom of movement and are allowed off prison grounds for educational or employment purposes to a much greater extent than those held in more restrictive facilities.

Some critics have likened minimum-security prisons to "country clubs," but in the corrections system, everything is relative. A minimum-security prison may seem like a vacation spot when compared with the horrors of Sing Sing, but it still represents a restriction of personal freedom and separates the inmate from the outside world. (The feature *Comparative Criminal Justice—Prison Lite* that follows provides a look at Norway's approach to incarceration, in which even the worst offenders are afforded the minimum-security experience.)

////SELF ASSESSMENT

Fill in the blanks, and check your answers on page 359.

The management of a prison is hierarchical, with the _____ (also known as a superintendent) at the top of the power structure. _____ is a crucial component of prison management, as it determines the security requirements needed to safely incarcerate each individual offender. Those offenders who have been convicted of violent crimes and repeat offenders are most likely to be sent to _____-security prisons. If a prisoner assaults another inmate or a correctional officer, prison officials may decide to transfer him or her to a _____ prison.

Medium-Security Prison A correctional institution that houses less dangerous inmates and therefore uses less restrictive measures to prevent violence and escapes.

Minimum-Security Prison A correctional institution designed to allow inmates, most of whom pose low security risks, a great deal of freedom of movement and contact with the outside world.

Central Intelligence Agency

Prison Lite

In Norway, incarceration is based on the premise that loss of liberty is punishment enough for offenders. Consequently, the prisons themselves are made as pleasant as possible. For example, Halden Prison, which houses murderers and rapists, provides amenities such as a recording studio, a "kitchen laboratory" for cooking classes, and a two-bedroom house where inmates can host their families for overnight visits. An inmate at the Skien maximum-security island prison compares his incarceration to "living in a village." He adds, "Everybody has to work. But we have free time so we can do some fishing, or in summer we can swim off the beach. We know we are prisoners but here we feel like people."

Norway's methods have, it appears, created certain expectations among its inmates. After spending several months behind bars following a conviction on multiple counts of murder, one Norwegian prisoner wrote a letter to authorities protesting the conditions of his imprisonment. Among the complaints: not enough butter for his bread, cold coffee, and no skin moisturizer.

FOR CRITICAL ANALYSIS

In the United States, life behind bars has long been predicated on the *principle of least eligibility,* which holds that the least-advantaged members of society outside prison should lead a better existence than any prison or jail inmate. Do you favor the American or the Norwegian approach to prison conditions? Why?

INMATE POPULATION TRENDS

As Figure 11.4 that follows shows, the number of Americans in prison or jail has increased dramatically in the past three decades. This growth can be attributed to a number of factors, starting with the enhancement and stricter enforcement of the nation's illegal drug laws.

Factors in Prison Population Growth

There are more people in prison and jail for drug offenses today than there were for *all* offenses in the early 1970s.[21] In 1980, about 19,000 drug offenders were incarcerated in state prisons and 4,800 drug offenders were in federal prisons. Thirty-two years later, state prisons held about 225,000 inmates who had been arrested for drug offenses, and the number of drug offenders in federal prisons had risen to almost 100,000 (representing about half of all inmates in federal facilities).[22]

LEARNING OBJECTIVE 4 List the factors that have caused the prison population to grow dramatically in the last several decades.

INCREASED PROBABILITY OF INCARCERATION The growth of America's inmate population also reflects the reality that the chance of someone who is arrested going to prison today is much greater than it was thirty years ago. Most of this growth took place in the 1980s, when the likelihood of incarceration in a state prison after arrest increased fivefold for drug offenses, threefold for weapons offenses, and twofold for crimes such as sexual assault, burglary, auto theft, and larceny.[23] For federal crimes, the proportion of convicted defendants being sent to prison rose from 54 percent in 1988 to 87 percent in 2012.[24]

INMATES SERVING MORE TIME In Chapter 9, we discussed a number of "get tough" sentencing laws passed in reaction to the crime wave of the 1970s and 1980s. These measures, including sentencing guidelines, mandatory minimum sentences, and truth-in-sentencing laws, have significantly increased the length of prison terms in the United

FIGURE 11.4 The Inmate Population of the United States

The total number of inmates in the United States has risen from 744,208 in 1985 to about 2.3 million in 2012.

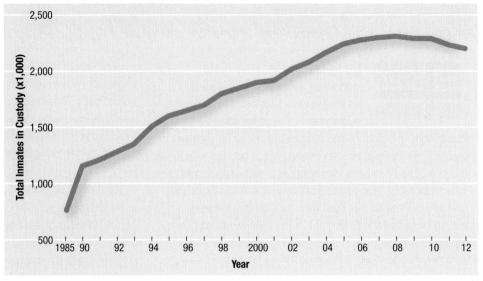

Source: U.S. Department of Justice.

States.[25] Overall, inmates released from state prison in 2009 spent an average of nine months—about 36 percent—longer behind bars than did those inmates released in 1990.[26] On the federal level, in the fifteen years after the passage of the Sentencing Reform Act of 1984, the average time served in federal prison increased more than 50 percent.[27]

FEDERAL PRISON GROWTH Even though the overall prison population of the United States recently has started to decrease, this is not the case for federal prison populations. In 2012, the number of federal prisoners increased by 1 percent.[28] Indeed, between 2000 and 2012, the federal prison population grew 55 percent, from about 134,000 to just over about 208,000.[29]

As already mentioned, an increase in federal drug offenders is largely responsible for the growth of the federal prison population. Because of mandatory minimum sentencing laws, federal drug traffickers spend an average of seventy-four months behind bars, considerably longer than those sentenced to state prisons.[30] Other factors driving federal prison population growth include

1. Starting in 1987, Congress *abolished parole* in the federal corrections system, meaning that federal inmates must serve their entire sentences, minus good-time credits.[31]
2. The number of federal inmates sentenced for *immigration violations* increased more than 50 percent from 2002 to 2012.[32]
3. In 2014, approximately 13,700 *female offenders* were behind bars in federal prison, about double the number in 1995.[33] Indeed, there are more women in federal prison today for drug offenses than there were in 2002 for all offenses.[34]

The Costs of Incarceration

The escalation in the U.S. prison population has been accompanied by increased costs at all levels of government. In 2014, the federal Bureau of Prison's annual budget stood at nearly $7 billion, up about 75 percent from 2000.[35] Today, the states together spend nearly $40 billion a year to operate their corrections systems—up from $12 billion in 1987. Twelve states allocate in excess of $1 billion a year for corrections-related services, often spending more on prisons than on education or health care.[36] Local governments, generally responsible for the costs of operating jails and juvenile detention centers, spend about $26 billion annually on corrections—a number that has held steady for most of the past decade.[37]

Immigration detainees exercise at the federal Adelanto Detention Center in Adelanto, California. Why have efforts to enforce immigration law increased the inmate population at federal prisons, while having little or no impact on the inmate populations of state prisons?

Decarceration

For most states looking to cut correction costs, the focus has been on *decarceration,* or the reduction of inmate populations. As recently as 2007, one expert lamented the unwillingness of corrections authorities to decarcerate, calling the strategy "practically virgin territory."[38] This is no longer the case, as the high cost of imprisonment has caused policymakers to consider several different methods to reduce the number of people in prison. In general, decarceration relies on three strategies:

1. Decreasing the probability that nonviolent offenders will be sentenced to prison.
2. Increasing the rate of release of nonviolent offenders from prison.
3. Decreasing the rate of imprisonment for probation and parole violators.[39]

Many states have adopted one or more of these approaches. In the early 2000s, for example, Michigan's legislature repealed its mandatory minimum-sentencing guidelines for drug offenses and changed the state's parole structure to make discretionary release more likely. As a result, from 2006 to 2010 Michigan's prison population dropped by 14.5 percent, and the state closed twenty corrections facilities.[40] Furthermore, corrections officials in a number of states, including Missouri, New York, and South Carolina, are making a concerted effort to avoid reincarcerating parolees for technical violations.[41]

In response to a U.S. Supreme Court ruling that we will discuss in the next chapter, California has implemented a "realignment" strategy to reduce rates of imprisonment for parole violators. As a result, from 2011 to 2012, the number of offenders admitted to California prisons dropped by 65 percent, from 96,669 to 34,294.[42] Nationwide in 2012, state prison releases exceeded prison admissions by about 27,500.[43] (To better understand the possible consequences of decarceration on crime rates, see the feature *Myth vs Reality—Does Putting Criminals in Prison Reduce Crime?* that follows.)

The Consequences of America's High Rates of Incarceration

Despite the conclusions drawn in the *Myth vs Reality* feature that follows, many observers believe that America's high rate of incarceration has contributed significantly to the drop in the country's crime rates.[44] Putting that particular debate aside, however,

MYTH VS REALITY
Does Putting Criminals in Prison Reduce Crime?

THE MYTH Since the early 1990s, crime rates in the United States have been stable or declining. During most of that same period, as seen in Figure 11.4 earlier in the chapter, the number of imprisoned Americans climbed precipitously. Thus, it seems clear that crime falls when the prison population rises.

This can be attributed to the effects of deterrence and incapacitation, theories of punishment we discussed in Chapter 9. First, the threat of prison deters would-be criminals from committing crimes. Second, a prison inmate is incapable of committing crimes against the public because he or she has been separated from the community.

THE REALITY Numerous statistical examples discredit a direct, sustained link between decreased crime rates and increased prison populations. Canada, for example, experienced a decline in crime rates similar to that of the United States in the 1990s, without any increase in national incarceration levels. Furthermore, by one measurement, New York City has seen crime decrease by a remarkable 80 percent since the early 1990s. Yet, during the early 2000s, the city has been locking up fewer people than it was at the height of its late-1980s crime wave.

According to one theory, mass incarceration accounted for about a quarter of the crime drop of the 1990s, as many of the most violent offenders were removed from society and remain behind bars. Since then, however, a large percentage of new prison admissions have been drug law offenders and probation/parole violators. The data tell us that removing these sorts of criminals from the community has a relatively limited effect on violent and property crime rates. In fact, their absence from their homes may even contribute to criminal activity. As we discussed in Chapter 2, many criminologists believe that widespread family disruption greatly increases the incidence of crime in a community.

Additionally, some experts believe that prisons are "schools of crime" that "teach" low-level offenders to be habitual criminals. If this is true, many inmates are more likely to commit crimes after their release from prison than they would have been if they had never been incarcerated in the first place.

FOR CRITICAL ANALYSIS
How might the new trend of decarceration give criminologists a chance to test theories regarding the correlation between incarceration levels and crime rates?

---

criminologists have noted a number of negative consequences related to this country's immense prison and jail population.

LEARNING
Indicate some of the consequences of our high rates of incarceration. **5**
OBJECTIVE

For one, incarceration can have severe social consequences for communities and the families that make up those communities. About 2.7 million minors in this country—one in twenty-eight—have a parent in prison.[45] These children are at an increased risk of suffering from poverty, depression, and academic problems, as well as higher levels of juvenile delinquency and eventual incarceration themselves.[46] Studies also link high imprisonment rates to increased incidence of sexually transmitted diseases and teenage pregnancy, as the separation caused by incarceration wreaks havoc on interpersonal family relationships.[47]

Incarceration also has a harmful impact on offenders themselves. On release from prison or jail, these men and women suffer from a higher rate of physical and mental health problems than the rest of the population, and are more likely to struggle with addiction, unemployment, and homelessness.[48] Because of the demographics of the U.S. prison population, these problems have a disproportionate impact on members of minority groups. African American males are incarcerated at a rate of more than six times

POLICY.CJ

A felony conviction denies one of the basic rights of American democracy—the right to vote—to about 5.8 million Americans with criminal records. Florida, Iowa, Kentucky, and Virginia permanently deprive those convicted of felonies of their right to vote (*disenfranchisement*). Other states have various requirements, such as an arrest-free waiting period, before the right to vote is reinstated. Go online and research the term **felon voting rights**. Then, write one full paragraph explaining your viewpoint on whether it is fair to deny the vote to criminal offenders in this country.

that of white males and about two and a half times that of Hispanic males.[49] With more black men behind bars than enrolled in the nation's colleges and universities, Marc Mauer of The Sentencing Project, a nonprofit research group in Washington, D.C., believes that the "ripple effect on their communities and on the next generation of kids, growing up with their fathers in prison, will certainly be with us for at least a generation."[50]

//// **SELF** ASSESSMENT

Fill in the blanks, and check your answers on page 359.

Of all the factors in the growth of the prison population in the last several decades, stricter enforcement of the nation's _____ laws has had the greatest impact. Other factors contributing to this growth include (1) increased probability of _____, (2) increased _____ of time served in prison, and (3) the growth of the _____ prison system. Many states are adopting strategies of _____ designed to reduce their inmate populations and the costs associated with their corrections systems.

THE EMERGENCE OF PRIVATE PRISONS

As the prison population soared at the end of the twentieth century, state corrections officials faced a serious problem: too many inmates, not enough prisons. "States couldn't build space fast enough," explains corrections expert Martin Horn. "And so they had to turn to the private sector."[51] With corrections exhibiting all the appearance of "a recession-proof industry," American businesses eagerly entered the market.

Today, **private prisons,** or prisons run by private firms to make a profit, are an important part of the criminal justice system. About two dozen private companies operate more than two hundred facilities across the United States. The two largest corrections firms, Corrections Corporation of America (CCA) and The GEO Group, Inc., manage about 130 correctional facilities and generate about $3.3 billion in annual revenue combined.[52] By 2012, private penal institutions housed nearly 138,000 inmates, representing 8.7 percent of all prisoners in the state and federal corrections systems.[53]

Why Privatize?

It would be a mistake to automatically assume that private prisons are less expensive to run than public ones. Nevertheless, the incentive to privatize is primarily financial.

COST EFFICIENCY According to their proponents, private prisons can often be run more cheaply and efficiently than public ones for the following reasons:

LEARNING **6** OBJECTIVE
List the reasons why private prisons might be run more cheaply than public ones.

1. *Labor costs.* The wages of public employees account for nearly two-thirds of a prison's operating expenses. Although private corrections firms pay base salaries comparable to those enjoyed by public prison employees, their nonunionized staffs receive lower levels of overtime pay, workers' compensation claims, sick leave, and health-care insurance.
2. *Competitive bidding.* Because of the profit motive, private corrections firms have an incentive to buy goods and services at the lowest possible price.
3. *Less red tape.* Private corrections firms are not part of the government bureaucracy and therefore do not have to contend with the massive amount of paperwork that can clog government organizations.[54]

The Saguaro Correctional Facility in Eloy, Arizona—privately operated by the Corrections Corporation of America—has been criticized for only accepting inmates who are in relatively good health. If true, why would this strategy make financial sense for private prisons?

In 2005, the National Institute of Justice released the results of a five-year study comparing low-security public and private prisons in California. The government agency found that private facilities cost taxpayers between 6 and 10 percent less than public ones.[55] More recent research conducted at Vanderbilt University found that states saved about $15 million annually when they supplemented their corrections systems with privately managed institutions.[56]

OVERCROWDING AND OUTSOURCING Private prisons are becoming increasingly attractive to state governments faced with the competing pressures of tight budgets and overcrowded corrections facilities. Lacking the funds to alleviate overcrowding by building more prisons, state officials are turning to the private institutions for help. In Oklahoma, for example, even though the state corrections department continues to build more prison space, more than a quarter of the state's prisoners—about 5,800 inmates—are housed in private facilities.[57] Often, the private prison is out of state, which leads to the "outsourcing" of inmates. California has alleviated its chronic overcrowding problems by sending more than ten thousand inmates to private institutions in Arizona, Mississippi, and Oklahoma.[58]

The Argument against Private Prisons

The assertion that private prisons offer economic benefits is not universally accepted. A number of studies have found that private prisons are no more cost-effective than public ones.[59] Furthermore, opponents of private prisons worry that, despite the assurances of corporate executives, private corrections companies will "cut corners" to save costs, denying inmates important security guarantees in the process.

SAFETY CONCERNS Criticism of private prisons is somewhat supported by the anecdotal evidence. These institutions are the setting for a number of violent incidents each year. In 2012, the Adams County Correctional Center in Natchez, Mississippi—operated by CCA—experienced a riot that ended with the death of a correctional officer and twenty other injuries. During this disturbance, three hundred inmates used broomsticks and other homemade weapons to control the facility for nearly eight hours.[60] In 2014, the federal government launched an investigation into management practices at the Idaho Correctional Center (ICC), another CCA facility. Understaffing had created such a violent atmosphere in the ICC that inmates had nicknamed it "Gladiator School."[61]

Apart from individual incidents, various studies have also uncovered disturbing patterns of misbehavior at private prisons. For example, in the year after CCA took over operations of Ohio's Lake Erie Correctional Institution from the state corrections department, the number of assaults against correctional officers and inmates increased by over 40 percent.[62] In addition, research conducted by Curtis R. Blakely of Truman State University in Missouri and Vic W. Bumphus of the University of Tennessee at Chattanooga found that a prisoner in a private correctional facility was twice as likely to be assaulted by a fellow inmate as a prisoner in a public one.[63]

PHILOSOPHICAL CONCERNS Other critics see private prisons as inherently unjust, even if they do save tax dollars or provide enhanced services. These observers believe that corrections is not simply another industry, like garbage collection or road maintenance, and that only the government has the authority to punish wrongdoers. In the words of John DiIulio:

> It is precisely because corrections involves the deprivation of liberty, precisely because it involves the legally sanctioned exercise of coercion by some citizens over others, that it must remain wholly within public hands.[64]

Furthermore, some observers note, if a private corrections firm receives a fee from the state for each inmate housed in its facility, does that not give management an incentive to increase the amount of time each prisoner serves? Though government parole boards make the final decision on an inmate's release from private prisons, the company could manipulate misconduct and good behavior reports to maximize time served and, by extension, higher profits.[65] "You can put a dollar figure on each inmate that is held at a private prison," says Alex Friedmann of *Prison Legal News*. "They are treated as commodities. And that's very dangerous and troubling when a company sees the people it incarcerates as nothing more than a money stream."[66]

The Future of Private Prisons

Most experts see continued profitability for private prisons, for two reasons. First, shrinking budgets may force states to look for less-costly alternatives to housing inmates in public prisons. Second, as the number of federal prisoners increases, the Federal Bureau of Prisons has turned to private prisons to expand its capacity. Between 2000 and 2012, the number of federal inmates in private prisons more than doubled, from about 15,500 to about 40,500.[67] The current emphasis on imprisoning violators of immigration law seems likely to ensure that this trend will continue.

////SELF ASSESSMENT

Fill in the blanks, and check your answers on page 359.

The incentive for using private prisons is primarily _____. Prison officials also feel pressure to send inmates to private prisons to alleviate _____ of public correctional facilities. Critics of private prisons claim that as a result of their cost-cutting measures, inmates are denied important _____ guarantees and thus may be put in physical danger. The industry's future seems assured, however, because of increased demand for prison beds for immigration law violators on the part of the _____ government.

JAILS

Although prisons and prison issues dominate the public discourse on corrections, there is an argument to be made that jails are the dominant penal institutions in the United States. In general, a prison is a facility designed to house people convicted of felonies for lengthy periods of time, while a **jail** is authorized to hold pretrial detainees and offenders who have committed misdemeanors. On any given day, about 744,000 inmates are in jail in this country, and jails admit almost 12 million persons over the course of an entire year.[68] Nevertheless, jail funding is often the lowest priority for the tight budgets of local governments, leading to severe overcrowding and other dismal conditions.

Many observers see this negligence as having far-reaching consequences for criminal justice. Jail is often the first contact that citizens have with the corrections system.

Jail A facility, usually operated by the county government, used to hold persons awaiting trial or those who have been found guilty of less-serious felonies or misdemeanors.

LEARNING **7** OBJECTIVE Summarize the distinction between jails and prisons, and indicate the importance of jails in the American corrections system.

It is at this point that treatment and counseling have the best chance to deter future criminal behavior.[69] By failing to take advantage of this opportunity, says Professor Franklin Zimring of the University of California at Berkeley School of Law, corrections officials have created a situation in which "today's jail folk are tomorrow's prisoners."[70] (To better understand the role that these two correctional institutions play in the criminal justice system, see *Mastering Concepts—The Main Differences between Prisons and Jails* that follows.)

The Jail Population

Like their counterparts in state prisons, jail inmates are overwhelmingly young male adults. About 46 percent of jail inmates are white, 37 percent are African American, and 15 percent are Hispanic.[71] The main difference between state prison and jail inmates involves their criminal activity. As Figure 11.5 that follows shows, jail inmates are more likely to have been convicted of nonviolent crimes than their counterparts in state prison.

PRETRIAL DETAINEES A significant number of those detained in jails technically are not prisoners. They are **pretrial detainees** who have been arrested by the police and, for a variety of reasons that we discussed in Chapter 8, are unable to post bail. Pretrial detainees are, in many ways, walking legal contradictions. According to the U.S. Constitution, they are innocent until proved guilty. At the same time, by being incarcerated while awaiting trial, they are denied a number of personal freedoms and are subjected to the poor conditions of many jails.

In *Bell v. Wolfish* (1979), the Supreme Court rejected the notion that this situation is inherently unfair by refusing to give pretrial detainees greater legal protections than sentenced jail inmates have.[72] In essence, the Court recognized that treating pretrial detainees differently from convicted jail inmates would place too much of a burden on corrections officials and was therefore impractical.

SENTENCED JAIL INMATES According to the U.S. Department of Justice, about 40 percent of those in jail have been convicted of their current charges.[73] In other words, they have been found guilty of a crime, usually a misdemeanor, and sentenced to time in jail.

MASTERING CONCEPTS

THE MAIN DIFFERENCES BETWEEN PRISONS AND JAILS

	PRISONS	JAILS
1.	. . . are operated by the federal and state governments.	. . . are operated by county and city governments.
2.	. . . hold inmates who may have lived quite far away before being arrested.	. . . hold mostly inmates from the local community.
3.	. . . house only those who have been convicted of a crime.	. . . house those who are awaiting trial or have recently been arrested, in addition to convicts.
4.	. . . generally hold inmates who have been found guilty of serious crimes and received sentences of longer than one year.	. . . generally hold inmates who have been found guilty of minor crimes and are serving sentences of less than a year.
5.	. . . often offer a wide variety of rehabilitation and educational programs for long-term prisoners.	. . . due to smaller budgets, tend to focus only on the necessities of safety, food, and clothing.

FIGURE 11.5 Types of Offenses of Prison and Jail Inmates

As the comparison below shows, jail inmates are more likely than state prisoners to have been convicted of nonviolent crimes. This underscores the main function of jails: to house less-serious offenders for a relatively short period of time.

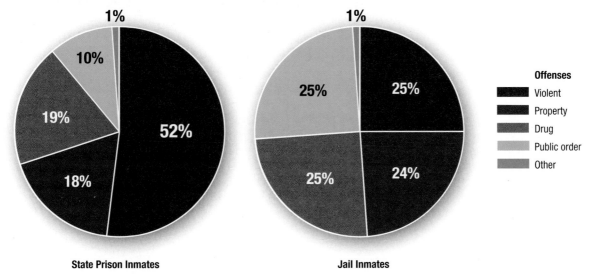

State Prison Inmates

Jail Inmates

Offenses
- Violent
- Property
- Drug
- Public order
- Other

Source: Bureau of Justice Statistics, *Prisoners in 2012—Advance Counts* (Washington, D.C.: U.S. Department of Justice, July 2013), Table 9, page 10; and Bureau of Justice Statistics, *Profile of Jail Inmates, 2002* (Washington, D.C.: U.S. Department of Justice, July 2004), 1.

The typical jail term lasts between thirty and ninety days, and rarely does a prisoner spend more than one year in jail for any single crime. Often, a judge will credit the length of time the convict has spent in detention waiting for trial—known as **time served**—toward his or her sentence. This practice acknowledges two realities of jails:

1. Terms are generally too short to allow the prisoner to gain any benefit (that is, rehabilitation) from the jail's often limited or nonexistent treatment facilities. Therefore, the jail term can serve no purpose except to punish the wrongdoer. (Judges who believe jail time can serve purposes of deterrence and incapacitation may not agree with this line of reasoning.)
2. Jails are chronically overcrowded, and judges need to clear space for new offenders.

OTHER JAIL INMATES Pretrial detainees and those convicted of misdemeanors make up the majority of the jail population. Jail inmates also include probation and parole violators, the mentally ill, juveniles awaiting transfer to juvenile authorities, and immigration law violators being held for the federal government. Increasingly, jails are also called on to handle the overflow from state prisons. To comply with a United States Supreme Court order to reduce its prison population, California corrections officials plan to divert an estimated 75,000 inmates from its prisons to its jails.[74]

Jail Administration

About 3,300 jails are in operation in the United States. The vast majority of these are managed on a county level by an elected sheriff. Most of the remainder are under the control of the federal government or local municipalities. The capacity of jails varies widely. The Los Angeles County Men's Central Jail holds nearly seven thousand people, but jails that large are the exception rather than the rule. Forty percent of all jails in this country house fewer than fifty inmates.[75]

Time Served The period of time a person denied bail (or unable to pay it) has spent in jail prior to his or her trial.

PROBLEMS OF JAIL INMATES Jails are often more difficult to manage than prisons, primarily because of their volatile and diverse inmate populations. According to sociologist John Irwin, the unofficial purpose of jails is to control society's "rabble," or those who are unable to integrate themselves into mainstream society.[76] Certainly, jail inmates have a number of problems, including the following:

1. *Mental illness.* About two-thirds of jail inmates have a history of mental illness, including symptoms of schizophrenia, depression, hallucinations, and suicidal tendencies.[77]

2. *Physical health problems.* More than one-third of jail inmates report having a current medical problem, whether an injury or ailments such as arthritis, asthma, or a sexually transmitted disease.[78]

3. *Substance abuse and dependency.* About two-thirds of jail inmates are dependent on alcohol or other drugs, and half of all convicted jail inmates were under the influence of drugs or alcohol at the time of their arrest.[79]

Given that most jails lack the resources and facilities to properly deal with these problems, the task of managing jail inmate populations falls disproportionately on untrained prison staff. Speaking of mentally ill inmates at Rikers Island, New York City's main jail complex, one corrections official said, "They need medication, treatment, psychological help. They don't need a corrections officer."[80]

THE CHALLENGES OF OVERCROWDING Jail overcrowding exacerbates the problems discussed above. Cells intended to hold one or two people are packed with up to six. Inmates are forced to sleep in hallways. Treatment facilities, when they exist, are overwhelmed. In such stressful situations, tempers flare, leading to violent, aggressive behavior. The jails most likely to suffer from such issues are those in heavily populated metropolitan areas with large numbers of "pass-through" pretrial detainees.[81]

Given the national emphasis on reducing prison populations discussed throughout this chapter, there are concerns that jails will be forced to house more low-level offenders in the future than they have in the past. As most jurisdictions do not have the resources to build new jails, administrators will have to come up with creative ways to alleviate possible overcrowding. Two possible solutions involve pretrial procedures we discussed in Chapter 8: (1) increasing options for pretrial release, and (2) speeding up trials so that detainees do not need to spend as much time waiting in jail for court proceedings to begin.[82] Also, as you can see in Figure 11.6 that follows, community corrections—the subject of the previous chapter—can be useful in reducing jail inmate populations.

New-Generation Jails

For most of our nation's history, jails primarily have been designed for the purpose of keeping inmates safely locked away. Consequently, most jails in the United States continue to resemble those from the days of the Walnut Street Jail in Philadelphia. In this *traditional,* or *linear design,* jail cells are located along a corridor. To supervise the inmates while they are in their cells, custodial officers must walk up and down the corridor, so the number of prisoners they can see at any one time is severely limited. With this limited supervision, inmates can more easily break institutional rules.

PODULAR DESIGN In the 1970s, planners at the Bureau of Federal Prisons decided to upgrade the traditional jail design with the goal of improving conditions for both the

FIGURE 11.6 Community Corrections for Jail Inmates

At midyear 2012, just over 64,000 offenders sentenced to jail terms were serving all or part of their sentences in the community. As you can see from the numbers below, the most common programs include community service, electronic monitoring, and weekend programs that allow inmates to return home for several days each week.

Type of program	Number of participants
Community service	14,761
Electronic monitoring (EM)	13,779
Weekend programs	10,351
Pretrial supervision	7,738
Work programs	7,137
Day reporting	3,890
Treatment programs	2,164
Home detention (without EM)	2,129
Other outside programs	2,149

Source: Bureau of Justice Statistics, *Jail Inmates at Midyear 2012—Statistical Tables* (Washington, D.C.: U.S. Department of Justice, May 2013), Table 9, page 9.

New-Generation Jail A type of jail that is distinguished architecturally from its predecessors by a design that encourages interaction between inmates and jailers and that offers greater opportunities for treatment.

Direct Supervision Approach A process of prison and jail administration in which correctional officers are in continuous visual contact with inmates during the day.

staff and the inmates. The result was the **new-generation jail,** which differs significantly from its predecessors.[83] The layout of the new facilities makes it easier for the staff to monitor cell-confined inmates. The basic structure of the new-generation jail is based on a podular design. Each "pod" contains "living units" for individual prisoners. These units, instead of lining up along a straight corridor, are often situated in a triangle so that a staff member in the center of the triangle has visual access to nearly all the cells.

Daily activities such as eating and showering take place in the pod, which also has an outdoor exercise area. Treatment facilities are also located in the pod, allowing greater access for the inmates. During the day, inmates stay out in the open and are allowed back in their cells only when given permission. The officer locks the door to the cells from his or her control terminal.

DIRECT SUPERVISION APPROACH The podular design also enables a new-generation jail to be managed using a **direct supervision approach.**[84] One or more jail officers are stationed in the living area of the pod and are therefore in constant interaction with all prisoners in that particular pod. Some new-generation jails even provide a desk in the center of the living area, which sends a very different message to the prisoners than the traditional control booth (see photo alongside). Theoretically, jail officials who have constant contact with inmates will be able to stem misconduct quickly and efficiently, and will also be able to recognize "danger signs" from individual inmates and stop outbursts before they occur. (As noted earlier in the chapter, corrections officials are using

■ How does the layout of this direct supervision jail differ from that of the maximum-security prison pictured on page 344? What do these differences tell you about the security precautions needed for jail inmates as opposed to prison inmates?

Photo courtesy Bergen County Sheriff's Office, Bergen, NJ

aspects of podular design when building new prisons, for many of the same reasons that the trend has been popular in jails.)

/// SELF ASSESSMENT

Fill in the blanks, and check your answers on page 359.

A significant number of the people in jail are not prisoners, but rather _____ _____ who are unable to post bail and await trial. About 40 percent have been _____ of their current charges, meaning that the jail sentence is punishment for a crime—usually a _____ and not a felony. Most jails are operated on a local level by the county _____.

THE FUTURE OF MASS INCARCERATION

Even with the growing interest in diversion and decarceration discussed in this chapter, the term mass incarceration remains the most apt descriptor of American corrections. The U.S. prison system is the largest in the world and will remain so for the foreseeable future. Still, many criminal justice experts believe that the recent annual decreases in the prison population, though small, are significant. According to Mark Bauer of The Sentencing Project, "A year or even two years is a blip, but three years starts to look like a trend."[85]

Explain three reasons why the values of the American prison system are being reconsidered by criminal justice officials and the public. — LEARNING OBJECTIVE 8

The primary motivation for reducing prison populations is financial. Because of the recent recession, many states found they simply could not afford a "nail 'em and jail 'em" attitude toward offenders, particularly nonviolent ones. Thus, in 2013 alone, legislators in thirty-one states adopted forty-seven new policies aimed at reducing their prison populations.[86] The federal government, while continuing to experience rising inmate populations, is looking to cut costs, as well. Primarily, federal officials are focused on reducing mandatory minimum sentences for drug crimes. If such sentences were reduced by one-half, the federal government would save an estimated $2.5 billion over the next decade and trim its prison population by approximately 30 percent.[87]

These new efforts to limit mass incarceration are not, however, entirely about "pinching pennies," to use the words of one public safety expert.[88] There is a sense that the values of the American corrections system need to change. It seems unfair, for example, that minority communities have been forced to bear the brunt of the social costs of mass incarceration, as detailed on pages 347–349 of this chapter. It also seems unfair to many that low-level offenders who would benefit from community rehabilitation are instead locked up in prison for the better part of their lives. Governor Nathan Deal of Georgia says that he began supporting legislation to steer nonviolent criminals away from state prison when he realized that "there are so many factors in people's lives we can't simply punish away."[89]

Finally, as the feature *CJ Controversy—Senseless Suffering?* that follows highlights, the severity of the U.S. prison experience is coming under increased scrutiny. In contrast to the prison systems of most other free societies—including Norway, as you saw on page 345—the American prison system is designed to separate and discipline inmates, rather than prepare them for their eventual release. The consequences of this harsher approach, for the inmates and for society at large, will be a recurring theme in the next chapter on life behind bars in the United States.

SENSELESS SUFFERING?

Solitary confinement refers to the disciplinary practice of locking inmates by themselves in small cells for more than twenty-two hours each day over the course of weeks, months, or even years. At any given time, about 81,000 prisoners are "in solitary" in the United States. These inmates are not sentenced to solitary confinement by a judge, and for most of them, the assignment has no connection with the original offense. Rather, solitary confinement is most commonly used as punishment for such disciplinary infractions as failure to obey an order given by a prison official.

SOLITARY CONFINEMENT IS NECESSARILY HARSH BECAUSE . . .

- It is a vital tool in maintaining order and discipline. As human contact is one of the few privileges that inmates enjoy, they have a strong incentive to conform to the rules of the institution rather than risk losing that privilege.

- The practice protects prison staff and inmates alike by removing violent convicts from the general inmate population.

SOLITARY CONFINEMENT IS UNNECESSARILY HARSH BECAUSE . . .

- It causes severe damage to the mental health of prisoners. Researchers have identified a number of resulting symptoms, including intense anxiety, hallucinations, violent fantasies, and reduced impulse control.

- The majority of inmates who suffer these psychological harms will eventually be returned to society, which will have to bear the burden of their mental illnesses.

Your Assignment

Today, no federal law controls the use of solitary confinement in federal prison. If you were to draft such a law, what elements would it contain? Would you give prison officials a "free hand"? Or, would you restrict their discretion in determining who is placed in solitary, the length of the punishment, and the infractions to which it applies? Before answering, research the terms **New York** and **solitary confinement guidelines** to see how one state recently addressed this issue. Your response should include at least two full paragraphs.

CHAPTER SUMMARY

For more information on these concepts, look back to the Learning Objective icons throughout the chapter.

 Contrast the Pennsylvania and the New York penitentiary theories of the 1800s. Basically, the Pennsylvania system imposed total silence on its prisoners. Based on the concept of separate confinement, penitentiaries were constructed with back-to-back cells radiating outward from the center. Prisoners worked, slept, and ate alone in their cells. In contrast, New York used the congregate system: silence was imposed, but inmates worked and ate together.

 Describe the formal prison management system, and indicate the three most important aspects of prison governance. The management structure of a formal system is militaristic, with a hierarchical (top-down) chain of command; the warden (or superintendent) is on top, then deputy wardens, and last, custodial employees. Sound governance of a correctional facility requires officials to provide inmates with a sense of order, amenities such as clean living conditions and acceptable food, and services such as vocational training and remedial education programs.

 List and briefly explain the four types of prisons. (a) Maximum-security prisons are designed mainly with security and surveillance in mind. Such prisons are usually large and consist of cell blocks, each of which is set off by a series of gates and bars. (b) In contrast, medium-security prisons offer considerably more educational and treatment programs, and allow more contact between inmates. Such prisons are usually surrounded by high fences rather than by walls. (c) Minimum-security prisons permit prisoners to have television sets and computers, and often allow them to leave the grounds for educational and employment purposes. (d) In supermaximum-security (supermax) prisons, prisoners are confined to one-person cells for up to twenty-three hours per day under constant video camera surveillance.

 List the factors that have caused the prison population to grow dramatically in the last several decades. (a) The enhancement and stricter enforcement of the nation's drug laws; (b) increased probability of incarceration; (c) inmates serving more time for each crime; and (d) federal prison growth.

 Indicate some of the consequences of high rates of incarceration. Some people believe that the reduction in the country's crime rate is a direct result of increased incarceration rates. Others believe that high incarceration rates are having increasingly negative social consequences, particularly for members of minority groups. These negative consequences include financial hardships, reduced supervision and discipline of children, and a general deterioration of the family structure when one parent is in prison. In addition, upon their release, offenders have a higher rate of physical and mental health problems than the rest of the population, and are more likely to struggle with addiction, unemployment, and homelessness.

 List the reasons why private prisons might be run more cheaply than public ones. (a) Labor costs are lower because private prison employees are nonunionized and receive lower levels of overtime pay, sick leave, and health-care insurance. (b) Competitive bidding requires the operators of private prisons to buy goods and services at the lowest possible prices. (c) There is less bureaucratic paperwork in a private prison facility.

 Summarize the distinction between jails and prisons, and indicate the importance of jails in the American corrections system. Generally, a prison is for those convicted of felonies who will serve lengthy periods of incarceration, whereas a jail is for those who have been convicted of misdemeanors and will serve less than a year of incarceration. Jails also hold individuals awaiting trial, juveniles awaiting transfer to juvenile authorities, probation and parole violators, and the mentally ill. In any given year, approximately 12 million people are admitted to jails, and therefore jails often provide the best chance for treatment or counseling that may deter future criminal behavior by these low-level offenders.

 Explain three reasons why the values of the American prison system are being reconsidered by criminal justice officials and the public. Aside from economic considerations, observers are asking whether it is fair that members of minority communities are bearing the brunt of the social costs of mass incarceration. Also, many find it unfair that nonviolent criminals are denied the chance to rehabilitate themselves in the community. Finally, the harshness of U.S. prison living conditions is coming under increased scrutiny.

QUESTIONS FOR CRITICAL ANALYSIS

1. According to the American Civil Liberties Union, states could save $16 billion a year by releasing low-risk prisoners who are age fifty and older. This estimate is based on the fact that risk of recidivism decreases with age. What are the arguments for and against using age as a primary reason for early release from prison?

2. Supermax prisons operate in a state of perpetual lockdown. Why might a warden institute a lockdown in a maximum-security prison?

3. Do you agree with the argument that private prisons are inherently injust, no matter what costs they may save taxpayers? Why or why not?

4. Why have pretrial detainees been called "walking legal contradictions"? What are the practical reasons why pretrial detainees will continue to be housed in jails prior to trial, regardless of whether their incarceration presents any constitutional irregularities?

5. Experience shows that building new jails does little or nothing to alleviate jail overcrowding. Why might this be the case?

KEY TERMS

classification 340

congregate system 336

direct supervision approach 355

jail 351

lockdown 343

maximum-security prison 341

medical model 337

medium-security prison 344

minimum-security prison 344

new-generation jail 355

penitentiary 335

pretrial detainees 352

private prisons 349

separate confinement 336

supermax prison 343

time served 353

warden 339

SELF-ASSESSMENT ANSWER KEY

Page 338: **i.** separate; **ii.** congregate; **iii.** silence; **iv.** cheaper; **v.** labor; **vi.** medical

Page 344: **i.** warden; **ii.** Classification; **iii.** maximum; **iv.** supermax

Page 349: **i.** drug; **ii.** incarceration/imprisonment; **iii.** length; **iv.** federal; **v.** decarceration

Page 351: **i.** financial; **ii.** overcrowding; **iii.** security/safety; **iv.** federal

Page 356: **i.** pretrial detainees; **ii.** convicted; **iii.** misdemeanor; **iv.** sheriff

NOTES

1. James M. Beattie, *Crime and the Courts in England, 1660–1800* (Princeton, N.J.: Princeton University Press, 1986), 506–507.

2. Samuel Walker, *Popular Justice* (New York: Oxford University Press, 1980), 11.

3. Michael Meranze, *Laboratories of Virtue: Punishment, Revolution, and Authority in Philadelphia, 1760–1835* (Chapel Hill, N.C.: University of North Carolina Press, 1996), 55.

4. Negley K. Teeters, *The Cradle of the Penitentiary: The Walnut Street Jail at Philadelphia,* *1773–1835* (Philadelphia: Pennsylvania Prison Society, 1955), 30.

5. Negley K. Teeters and John D. Shearer, *The Prison at Philadelphia's Cherry Hill* (New York: Columbia University Press, 1957), 142–143.

6. Henry Calvin Mohler, "Convict Labor Policies," *Journal of the American Institute of Criminal Law and Criminology* 15 (1925), 556–557.

7. Zebulon Brockway, *Fifty Years of Prison Service* (Montclair, N.J.: Patterson Smith, 1969), 400–401.

8. Robert Martinson, "What Works? Questions and Answers about Prison Reform," *Public Interest* 35 (Spring 1974), 22.

9. See Ted Palmer, "Martinson Revisited," *Journal of Research on Crime and Delinquency* (1975), 133; and Paul Gendreau and Bob Ross, "Effective Correctional Treatment: Bibliotherapy for Cynics," *Crime & Delinquency* 25 (1979), 499.

10. Robert Martinson, "New Findings, New Views: A Note of Caution Regarding Sentencing Reform," *Hofstra Law Review* 7 (1979), 243.

11. Bureau of Justice Statistics, *Census of State and Federal Correctional Facilities, 2005* (Washington, D.C.: U.S. Department of Justice, October 2008), 2.

12. *Ibid.*

13. Charles H. Logan, "Well Kept: Comparing Quality of Confinement in a Public and Private Prison," *Journal of Criminal Law and Criminology* 83 (1992), 580.

14. John J. DiIulio, *Governing Prisons* (New York: Free Press, 1987), 12.

15. *Ibid.*

16. Todd R. Clear, George F. Cole, and Michael D. Reisig, *American Corrections,* 9th ed. (Belmont, Calif.: Wadsworth Cengage Learning, 2010), 162.

17. Heather Stokes, "The Design to Aging Foundations" (November 13, 2012), at **prezi.com/l3mrp0gvomor/the-design -to-aging-foundations**.

18. Douglas Page, "The Prison of the Future," *Law Enforcement Technology* (January 2012), 11–13.

19. *Madrid v. Gomez,* 889 F.Supp. 1146 (N.D. Cal. 1995).

20. Keramet Reiter, *Parole, Snitch, or Die: California's Supermax Prisons and Prisoners, 1987–2007* (Berkeley, Calif.: University of California Institute for the Study of Social Change, 2010), 1.

21. Steven D. Levitt, "Understanding Why Crime Fell in the 1990s: Four Factors That Explain the Decline and Six That Do Not," *Journal of Economic Perspectives* (Winter 2004), 177.

22. Bureau of Justice Statistics, *Prisoners in 2012—Advance Counts* (Washington, D.C.: U.S. Department of Justice, July 2013), Table 9, page 10; and Bureau of Justice Statistics, *Prisoners in 2012: Trends in Admissions and Releases, 1991–2012* (Washington, D.C.: U.S. Department of Justice, December 2013), Appendix table 10, page 43.

23. Allen J. Beck, "Growth, Change, and Stability in the U.S. Prison Population, 1980–1995," *Corrections Management Quarterly* (Spring 1997), 9–10.

24. U.S. District Courts, "Criminal Defendants Sentenced after Conviction, by Offense, during the 12-Month Period Ending September 30, 2012," at **www.uscourts.gov/uscourts /Statistics/JudicialBusiness/2012 /appendices/D05Sep12.pdf**.

25. Joan Petersilia, "Beyond the Prison Bubble," *Wilson Quarterly* (Winter 2011), 27.

26. *Time Served: The High Cost, Low Return of Longer Prison Terms* (Washington, D.C.: The Pew Center on the States, June 2012), 2.

27. *Fifteen Years of Guidelines Sentencing: An Assessment of How Well the Federal Criminal Justice System Is Achieving the Goals of Sentencing Reform* (Washington, D.C.: U.S. Sentencing Commission, November 2004), 46.

28. Bureau of Justice Statistics, *Correctional Populations in the United States, 2012* (Washington, D.C.: U.S. Department of Justice, December 2013), Appendix table 1, page 10.

29. *Ibid.*

30. Julie Samuels, Nancy La Vigne, and Samuel Taxy, *Stemming the Tide: Strategies to Reduce the Growth and Cut the Cost of the Federal Prison System* (Washington, D.C.: Urban Institute, November 13), 1.

31. Comprehensive Crime Control Act of 1984, Public Law Number 98-473.

32. *Prisoners in 2012: Trends in Admissions and Releases, 1991–2012, op. cit.,* Appendix table 10, page 43.

33. Federal Bureau of Prisons, "Inmate Gender" (February 22, 2014), at **www.bop.gov /about/statistics/statistics_inmate _gender.jsp.**

34. *Prisoners in 2012: Trends in Admissions and Releases, 1991–2012, op. cit.,* Appendix table 10, page 43.

35. Samuels, La Vigne, and Taxy, *op. cit.,* 14–15.

36. Christian Henrichson and Ruth Delaney, *The Price of Prisons: What Incarceration Costs Taxpayers* (New York: Center for Sentencing and Corrections, January 2012), 6, 8.

37. Tracey Kyckelhahn, *Local Government Corrections Expenditures, FY 2005–2011* (Washington, D.C.: Bureau of Justice Statistics, December 2013), 1.

38. James B. Jacobs, "Finding Alternatives to the Carceral State," *Social Research* (Summer 2007), 695.

39. Rosemary Gartner, Anthony N. Doob, and Franklin E. Zimring, "The Past as Prologue? Decarceration in California Then and Now," *Criminology & Public Policy* (May 2011), 294–296.

40. Ram Subramanian and Rebecca Tublitz, *Realigning Justice Resources: A Review of Population and Spending Shifts in Prison and Community Corrections* (New York: Vera Institute of Justice, September 2012), 11.

41. Joseph Walker, "Rules May Help Parolees Avoid Jail for Small Errors," *New York Times* (January 5, 2012), at **cityroom .blogs.nytimes.com/2012/01/05/rating -a-parolees-risk-before-a-return-to -prison**.

42. *Prisoners in 2012: Trends in Admissions and Releases, 1991–2012, op. cit.,* Appendix table 1, page 34.

43. *Ibid.*

44. Dan Seligman, "Lock 'Em Up," *Forbes* (May 23, 2005), 216–217.

45. Bruce Western and Becky Pettit, *Collateral Costs: Incarceration's Effect on Economic Mobility* (Washington, D.C.: The Pew Charitable Trusts, 2010), 4.

46. John Tierney, "Prison and the Poverty Trap," *New York Times* (February 19, 2013), D1.

47. *Ibid.*

48. *Rethinking the Blues: How We Police in the U.S. and at What Cost* (Washington, D.C.: Justice Policy Institute, May 2012), 34.

49. *Prisoners in 2012: Trends in Admissions and Releases, 1991–2012, op. cit.,* Table 18, page 25.

50. Quoted in Fox Butterfield, "Study Finds 2.6% Increase in U.S. Prison Population," *New York Times* (July 28, 2003), A8.

51. Quoted in Scott Cohn, "Private Prison Industry Grows Despite Critics," *cnbc.com* (October 18, 2011), at **www.nbcnews.com /id/44936562/ns/business-cnbc_tv/t /private-prison-industry-grows -despite-critics/#.UW6vC7_zdzU.**

52. Suevon Lee, "By the Numbers: The U.S.'s Growing For-Profit Detention Industry," *ProPublica* (June 20, 2012), at **www .propublica.org/article/by-the -numbers-the-u.s.s-growing-for-profit -detention-industry**.

53. *Prisoners in 2012: Trends in Admissions and Releases, op. cit.,* Appendix table 7, page 40.

54. "A Tale of Two Systems: Cost, Quality, and Accountability in Private Prisons," *Harvard Law Review* (May 2002), 1872.

55. Douglas C. McDonald and Kenneth Carlson, *Contracting for Imprisonment in the Federal Prison System: Cost and Performance of the Privately Operated Taft Correctional Institution* (Cambridge, Mass.: Abt Associates, Inc., October 2005), vii.

56. Vanderbilt University Law School, "New Study Shows Benefits of Having Privately and Publicly Managed Prisons in the Same State" (November 25, 2008), at **law .vanderbilt.edu/article-search/article -detail/index.aspx?nid=213**.

57. Clifton Adcock, "State Weighs Moving More Inmates to Private Prisons, or Buying a Private Prison," *Oklahoma Watch* (January 9, 2014), at **oklahomawatch.org/2014/01/09/with-overcrowded-prisons-state-looks-at-moving-more-inmates-to-private-prisons-or-buying-a-private-prison**.

58. Saki Knafo and Chris Kirkham, "For-Profit Prisons Are Big Winners of California's Overcrowding Crisis," *Huffington Post* (October 25, 2013), at **www.huffingtonpost.com/2013/10/25/california-private-prison_n_4157641.html**.

59. "Behind the Bars: Experts Question Benefits of Private Prisons," *Kentucky Courier Journal* (July 5, 2010), at **www.courier-journal.com/article/20100705/NEWS01/7050312/Behind-Bars-Experts-question-benefitsprivate-prisons**.

60. Robbie Brown, "Mississippi Prison on Lockdown after Guard Dies," *New York Times* (May 23, 2012), A12.

61. "FBI Investigates Company Running 'Gladiator School' Prison," *Associated Press* (March 7, 2014).

62. Gregory Geisler, *CIIC: Lake Erie Correctional Institution* (Columbus, Ohio: Correctional Institution Inspection Committee, January 2013), 16.

63. Curtis R. Blakely and Vic W. Bumphus, "Private and Public Sector Prisons," *Federal Probation* (June 2004), 27.

64. John DiIulio, "Prisons, Profits, and the Public Good: The Privatization of Corrections," in *Criminal Justice Center Bulletin* (Huntsville, Tex.: Sam Houston State University, 1986).

65. Richard L. Lippke, "Thinking about Private Prisons," *Criminal Justice Ethics* (Winter/Spring 1997), 32.

66. Quoted in Cohn, *op. cit.*

67. *Prisoners in 2012: Trends in Admissions and Releases, 1991–2012, op. cit.,* Appendix table 7, page 40.

68. Bureau of Justice Statistics, *Jail Inmates at Midyear 2012—Statistical Tables* (Washington, D.C.: U.S. Department of Justice, May 2013), 1, 4.

69. Arthur Wallenstein, "Jail Crowding: Bringing the Issue to the Corrections Center Stage," *Corrections Today* (December 1996), 76–81.

70. Quoted in Fox Butterfield, "'Defying Gravity,' Inmate Population Climbs," *New York Times* (January 19, 1998), A10.

71. *Jail Inmates at Midyear 2012—Statistical Tables, op. cit.,* Table 12, page 10.

72. 441 U.S. 520 (1979).

73. *Jail Inmates at Midyear 2012—Statistical Tables, op. cit.,* Table 3, page 6.

74. Vauhini Vara and Bobby White, "County Jails Prepare for Extra Guests," *Wall Street Journal* (August 10, 2011), A4.

75. Bureau of Justice Statistics, *Census of Jail Facilities, 2006* (Washington, D.C.: U.S. Department of Justice, December 2011), 14.

76. John Irwin, *The Jail: Managing the Underclass in American Society* (Berkeley, Calif.: University of California Press, 1985), 2.

77. Doris J. James and Lauren E. Glaze, *Bureau of Justice Statistics Special Report: Mental Health Problems of Prison and Jail Inmates* (Washington, D.C.: U.S. Department of Justice, September 2006), 1.

78. Laura M. Maruschak, *Bureau of Justice Statistics Special Report: Medical Problems of Jail Inmates* (Washington, D.C.: U.S. Department of Justice, November 2006), 1.

79. Jennifer C. Karberg and Doris J. James, *Bureau of Justice Statistics Special Report: Substance Dependence, Abuse, and Treatment of Jail Inmates, 2002* (Washington, D.C.: U.S. Department of Justice, July 2005), 1.

80. Quoted in Michael Schwirtz, "Rikers Island Struggles with a Surge in Violence and Mental Illness," *New York Times* (March 19, 2014), A1.

81. Todd R. Clear, George F. Cole, and Michael D. Reisig, *American Corrections,* 10th ed. (Belmont, Calif.: Wadsworth Cengage Learning, 2013), 180.

82. Mark Cuniff, *Jail Crowding: Understanding Jail Population Dynamics* (Washington, D.C.: National Institute of Corrections, January 2002), 36.

83. R. L. Miller, "New Generation Justice Facilities: The Case for Direct Supervision," *Architectural Technology* 12 (1985), 6–7.

84. David Bogard, Virginia A. Hutchinson, and Vicci Persons, *Direct Supervision Jails: The Role of the Administrator* (Washington, D.C.: National Institute of Corrections, February 2010), 1–2.

85. Quoted in Erica Goode, "U.S. Prison Populations Decline, Reflecting New Approach to Crime," *New York Times* (July 26, 2013), A11.

86. *The State of Sentencing 2013: Developments in Policy and Practice* (Washington, D.C.: The Sentencing Project, 2014), 1.

87. Samuels, Vigne, and Taxy, *op. cit.,* 1–3.

88. Quoted in Goode, *op. cit.*

89. Quoted in Neil King, Jr., "As Prisons Squeeze Budgets, GOP Rethinks Crime Focus," *Wall Street Journal* (June 21, 2013), A1.

CHAPTER

12

The Prison Experience and Prisoner Reentry

CHAPTER OUTLINE	CORRESPONDING LEARNING OBJECTIVES	
Prison Culture		Explain the concept of prison as a total institution.
		Describe a consequence of the failure to provide adequate medical care to inmates.
		Indicate some of the reasons for violent behavior in prisons.
Correctional Officers and Discipline		List and briefly explain the six general job categories among correctional officers.
		Describe the hands-off doctrine of prisoner law, and indicate two standards used to determine if prisoners' rights have been violated.
Inside a Women's Prison		Explain the aspects of imprisonment that prove challenging for incarcerated mothers and their children.
Return to Society		Contrast parole, expiration release, pardon, and furlough.
		Explain the goal of prisoner reentry programs.

To target your study and review, look for these numbered Learning Objective icons throughout the chapter.

Khue Bui/*The New York Times*/Redux

Dead HEAT

SEVERAL YEARS AGO, the Texas Department of Criminal Justice announced that it was planning to replace its dilapidated swine-production facilities with new climate-controlled modular barns, at a cost of $750,000. The irony of the situation was not lost on Lance Lowry, a correctional officer at Texas State Penitentiary in Huntsville. It meant that the pigs raised for inmate consumption in Texas were going to be more comfortable than the inmates themselves, and the staff who guarded them. Two-third of the state's 109 correctional facilities lack air-conditioning in their housing units, and during the summer indoor temperatures in these prisons routinely reach 110 degrees. "We don't keep animals in these types of conditions, and that speaks volumes," said Lowry.

Consequently, between 2006 and 2013 at least fourteen Texas inmates died of hyperthermia, a condition that occurs when the body temperature rises above 105 degrees. One of the casualties, Robert Allen Webb, was found lying in his underwear on the concrete floor of his cell, a common practice for inmates trying to stay cool. Several days before his death, Webb told a visitor that "it was so hot he couldn't breathe." As a result of these deaths, the state is facing a number of lawsuits—supported by the correctional officers' union—claiming that the sweltering conditions constitute cruel and unusual punishment.

Despite the deaths, it seems unlikely that Texas legislators are willing to spend the estimated $55 million necessary to cool state prisons. "These people are sex offenders, rapists, murderers," says one state senator. "And we're going to pay for their air-conditioning when I can't go down the street and provide air-conditioning to hard-working, tax-paying citizens?" This attitude is in keeping with the "no frills" movement in American corrections, which has succeeded in removing most amenities from inmates' lives. Many state prisons ban weightlifting, televisions, radios, adult magazines, and conjugal visits. All states and the federal government have limited smoking in their correctional facilities, and some institutions spend less than $2 a day per inmate on meals. Consequently, life in today's penal institutions has been described as "grindingly dull routine interrupted by occasional flashes of violence and brutality."

FOR CRITICAL ANALYSIS

1. What is your opinion of the "no frills" movement in American corrections? Should an inmate's life be nothing more than "dull routine"? Explain your answer.

2. In Texas prisons, the number of violent confrontations between inmates and correctional officers rises during the hotter summer months. What factors might explain the correlation between higher temperatures and increased levels of inmate–staff violence?

3. Most of the inmates who died from heat-related causes in Texas prisons were serving relatively short sentences for nonviolent crimes. Should nonviolent offenders receive better treatment behind bars than violent offenders? Why or why not?

AP Images/Rich Pedroncelli

As part of a "no frills" movement in American corrections, many state prisons limit exercise opportunities for offenders such as these California inmates, shown in the main yard at the Pelican Bay State Prison near Crescent City, California.

PRISON CULTURE

In this chapter, we will look at the life of the imprisoned convict, starting with the realities of an existence behind bars and finishing with the challenges of returning to free society. Along the way, we will discuss violence in prison, correctional officers, women's prisons, different types of release, and several other issues that are at the forefront of American corrections today. To start, we must understand the forces that shape prison culture and how those forces affect the overall operation of the correctional facility.

Any institution, whether a school, a bank, or a police department, has an organizational culture—a set of values that help the people in the organization understand what actions are acceptable and what actions are unacceptable. According to a theory put forth by the influential sociologist Erving Goffman, prison cultures are unique because prisons are **total institutions** that encompass every aspect of an inmate's life. Unlike a student or a bank teller, a prisoner cannot leave the institution or have any meaningful interaction with outside communities. Others arrange every aspect of daily life, and all prisoners are required to follow this schedule in the same manner.[1]

Inmates develop their own argot, or language (see Figure 12.1 that follows). They create their own economy, which, in the absence of currency, is based on the barter of valued items such as food, contraband, and sexual favors. They establish methods of determining power, many of which, as we shall see, involve violence. Isolated and heavily regulated, prisoners create a social existence that is, out of both necessity and design, separate from the outside world.

Adapting to Prison Society

On arriving at prison, each convict attends an orientation session and receives a "Resident's Handbook." The handbook provides information such as meal and official count times, disciplinary regulations, and visitation guidelines. The norms and values of the prison society, however, cannot be communicated by the staff or learned from a handbook. As first described by Donald Clemmer in his classic 1940 work, *The Prison Community,* the process of **prisonization**—or adaptation to the prison culture—advances as the inmate gradually understands what constitutes acceptable behavior in the institution, as defined not by the prison officials but by other inmates.[2]

In studying prisonization, criminologists have focused on two areas: how prisoners change their behavior to adapt to life behind bars, and how life behind bars has changed

Total Institution An institution, such as a prison, that provides all of the necessities for existence to those who live within its boundaries.

Prisonization The socialization process through which a new inmate learns the accepted norms and values of the prison culture.

LEARNING **1** OBJECTIVE

Explain the concept of prison as a total institution.

FIGURE 12.1 **Prison Slang**

Ace Another word for "dollar."

Bang A fight to the death, or shoot to kill.

Base head A cocaine addict.

B.G. "Baby gangster," or someone who has never shot another person.

Booty bandit An incarcerated sexual predator who preys on weaker inmates, called "punks."

Bug A correctional staff member, such as a psychiatrist, who is deemed untrustworthy or unreliable.

Bumpin' titties Fighting.

Catch cold To get killed.

Chiva Heroin.

Dancing on the blacktop Getting stabbed.

Diddler Child molester or pedophile.

Green light Prison gang term for a contract killing.

Hacks Correctional officers.

Jug-up Mealtime.

Lugger An inmate who smuggles in and possesses illegal substances.

Punk An inmate subject to rape, usually more submissive than most inmates.

Ride with To perform favors, including sexual favors, for a convict in return for protection or prison-store goods.

Shank Knife.

Tits-up An inmate who has died.

Topped Committed suicide.

Source: **www.insideprison.com/glossary.asp.**

because of inmate behavior. Sociologist John Irwin identified several patterns of inmate behavior, each one driven by the inmate's personality and values:

1. Professional criminals adapt to prison by "doing time." In other words, they follow the rules and generally do whatever is necessary to speed up their release and return to freedom.

2. Some convicts, mostly state-raised youths or those frequently incarcerated in juvenile detention centers, are more comfortable inside prison than outside. These inmates serve time by "jailing," or establishing themselves in the power structure of prison culture.

3. Other inmates take advantage of prison resources such as libraries or drug treatment programs by "gleaning," or working to improve themselves to prepare for a return to society.

4. Finally, "disorganized" criminals exist on the fringes of prison society. These inmates may have mental impairments or low levels of intelligence and find it impossible to adapt to prison culture on any level.[3]

The process of categorizing prisoners has a theoretical basis, but it serves a practical purpose as well, allowing administrators to reasonably predict how different inmates will act in certain situations. An inmate who is "doing time" generally does not present the same security risk as one who is "jailing."

FIGURE 12.2 The Aging Prison Population

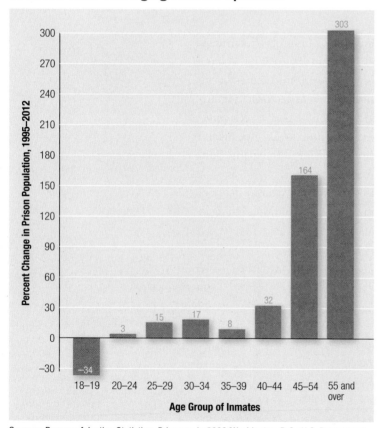

Sources: Bureau of Justice Statistics, *Prisoners in 2003* (Washington, D.C.: U.S. Department of Justice, November 2004), Table 10, page 8; Bureau of Justice Statistics, *Prisoners in 2012—Trends in Admissions and Releases, 1991–2012* (Washington, D.C.: U.S. Department of Justice, December 2013), Appendix table 4, page 37.

Who Is in Prison?

The culture of any prison is heavily influenced by its inmates. Their values, beliefs, and experiences will be reflected in the social order that exists behind bars. As we noted in the last chapter, the past three decades have seen the rise of incarceration rates of women and minority groups. Furthermore, the arrest patterns of inmates have changed over that time period. A prisoner today is much more likely to have been incarcerated on a drug charge or immigration violation than was the case in the 1980s.

AN AGING INMATE POPULATION In recent years, the most significant demographic change in the prison population involves age. Though the majority of inmates are still under thirty-four years old, as you can see in Figure 12.2 alongside, the number of state and federal prisoners over the age of forty has increased dramatically since the mid-1990s. Several factors have contributed to this upsurge, including longer prison terms, mandatory prison terms, recidivism, and higher levels of crimes—particularly violent crimes—committed by older offenders.[4]

AN AILING INMATE POPULATION Overall, about 40 percent of state and federal prisoners suffer from at least one form of illness other than a cold, the most common ailments being arthritis, hypertension, tuberculosis, and asthma.[5] In some areas, the news concerning inmate health is positive. For example, AIDS-related deaths in prisons declined 81 percent between 2001 and 2011.[6] Given the frailties of older inmates, however, prisons and jails are now holding more people with medical issues than in the past. Poor health is the cause of almost nine of ten inmate deaths in state prisons, with heart disease and cancer accounting for nearly half of these fatalities.[7] Not surprisingly, the mortality rates of inmates fifty-five and older from heart disease and cancer are five times higher than for any other age group.[8]

POLICY.CJ

One way to alleviate the financial pressures of aging and ailing inmates on corrections systems would be for jurisdictions to increase the use of medical, or "compassionate," parole. To learn more about this form of discretionary release, go online and search for the term **medical parole**. Then, make a short list describing the types of prisoners who are generally eligible to be granted medical parole.

Corrections budgets are straining under the financial pressures caused by the health-care needs of aging inmates. Generally speaking, an inmate aged fifty years or older is three times more expensive to incarcerate than a younger prisoner.[9] In Georgia, prisoners sixty-five years or older have average annual medical expenses of about $8,500, compared with an average annual medical expense of $961 for inmates under sixty-five.[10] Given the burden of inmate medical costs, state corrections officials may be tempted to cut such services whenever possible. As the feature *Landmark Cases— Brown v. Plata* that follows shows, however, prisoners have a constitutional right to adequate health care.

MENTAL ILLNESS BEHIND BARS Another factor in rising correctional health-care costs is the high incidence of mental illness in American prisons and jails. During the 1950s and 1960s, nearly 600,000 mental patients lived in public hospitals, often against their will. A series of scandals spotlighting the poor medical services and horrendous living conditions in these institutions led to their closure and the elimination of much of the nation's state-run mental health infrastructure.[11] Many mentally ill people now receive no supervision whatsoever, and some inevitably commit deviant or criminal acts.

As a result, in the words of criminal justice experts Katherine Stuart van Wormer and Clemens Bartollas, jails and prisons have become "the dumping grounds for people whose bizarre behavior lands them behind bars."[12] On any given day, for example, the Cook County Jail in Chicago houses between 2,000 and 2,500 inmates who have been diagnosed with a mental illness.[13] As with aging and ailing prisoners, correctional facilities are required by law to provide treatment to mentally ill inmates, thus driving the costs associated with their confinement well above the average.[14] For reasons that should become clear over the course of this chapter, correctional facilities are not designed to foster mental well-being, and inmates with mental illnesses often find that their problems are exacerbated by the prison environment.[15]

Rehabilitation and Prison Programs

In Chapter 9, we saw that rehabilitation is one of the basic theoretical justifications for punishment. **Prison programs,** which include any organized activities designed to foster rehabilitation, benefit inmates in several ways. On a basic level, these programs get prisoners out of their cells and alleviate the boredom that marks prison and jail life. The

Prison Programs Organized activities for inmates that are designed to improve their physical and mental health, provide them with vocational skills, or simply keep them occupied while incarcerated.

LANDMARK CASES:
Brown v. Plata

Describe a consequence LEARNING **2** of the failure to provide adequate medical care to inmates. OBJECTIVE

California's thirty-three prisons are designed to hold 80,000 inmates. For most of the first decade of the 2000s, these facilities housed around 160,000 inmates. "It's an unacceptable working environment for everyone," said a former state corrections official. "It leads to greater violence, more staff overtime, and a total inability to deal with health care and mental illness issues." In 2009, a federal court agreed, ordering the state to reduce its prison population by 30,000 in two years. California officials appealed, giving the United States Supreme Court a chance to rule on the importance of medical care for inmates in this country.

Brown v. Plata
United States Supreme Court
131 S.Ct. 1910 (2011)

IN THE WORDS OF THE COURT . . .
JUSTICE KENNEDY, MAJORITY OPINION

* * * *

For years the medical and mental health care provided by California's prisons has fallen short of minimum constitutional requirements and has failed to meet prisoners' basic health needs. Needless suffering and death have been the well-documented result.

* * * *

Prisoners are crammed into spaces neither designed nor intended to house inmates. As many as 200 prisoners may live in a gymnasium, monitored by as few as two or three correctional officers. * * * The consequences of overcrowding include "increased, substantial risk for transmission of infectious illness" and a suicide rate "approaching an average of one per week." * * * A correctional officer testified that, in one prison, up to 50 sick inmates may be held together in a 12-by 20-foot cage for up to five hours awaiting treatment. The number of staff is inadequate, and prisoners face significant delays in access to care. A prisoner with severe abdominal pain died after a 5-week delay in referral to a specialist; a prisoner with "constant and extreme" chest pain died after an 8-hour delay in evaluation by a doctor; and a prisoner died of testicular cancer after a "failure of MDs to [do a] work up for cancer in a young man with 17 months of testicular pain."

* * * *

A prison that deprives prisoners of basic sustenance, including adequate medical care, is incompatible with the concept of human dignity and has no place in civilized society.

DECISION
The Court found that severe overcrowding in California state prisons denied inmates satisfactory levels of mental and physical health care, and therefore amounted to unconstitutional cruel and unusual punishment. It ordered the state to reduce the prison population to 137.5 percent of capacity—about 110,00 inmates—by June 2013. In 2014, a federal judge extended this deadline for two years to allow various rehabilitation programs to take effect.

FOR CRITICAL ANALYSIS
In his dissent, Justice Alito wrote, "I fear that today's decision will lead to a grim roster of victims." What might be some of the reasons behind this fear? What steps could California corrections officials take to alleviate Alito's worries?

programs also help inmates improve their health and skills, giving them a better chance of reintegration into society after release. Consequently, nearly every federal and state prison in the United States offers some form of rehabilitation.[16]

The primary goal of prison programs, from an administrative standpoint, is to reduce recidivism. Research does demonstrate that offenders who earn a high school equivalency diploma behind bars are more likely to find employment after release and therefore are less likely to be rearrested.[17] Prison drug treatment programs can also be beneficial, reducing the probability of relapse in the "real world."[18] Given their budget constraints, however, prison systems are often forced to limit their vocational, educational, and treatment programs. Many inmates suffering from mental illness would benefit from medication and twenty-four-hour psychiatric care. Yet these services are often inadequate behind bars, mostly due to their high costs.[19]

Violence in Prison Culture

Prisons and jails are dangerous places to live. Prison culture is predicated on violence—one observer calls the modern institution an "unstable and violent jungle."[20] Prison guards use the threat of violence (and, at times, its reality) to control the inmate population. Sometimes, the inmates strike back. Each year, federal correctional officers are subjected to about 80 assaults and 1,500 less serious attacks such as shoving and pushing.[21]

Among the prisoners, violence is used to establish power and dominance. For example, inmates subject to sexual assault are often near the bottom of the prison power structure and, in some instances, may accept rape by one particularly powerful inmate in return for protection from others.[22] According to the federal government, about 4 percent of state and federal prisoners report being victims of sexual assault, with a prison staff member slightly more likely to be the perpetrator than another inmate.[23]

On occasion, violence behind bars leads to death. About sixty-five inmates in state prisons and twenty inmates in local jails are murdered by fellow inmates each year.[24] (Note, though, that this homicide rate is lower than the national murder rate on the "outside.") With nothing but time on their hands, prisoners have been known to fashion deadly weapons out of everyday items such as toothbrushes and mop handles.

EXPLAINING PRISON VIOLENCE As just noted, violence is used primarily to establish the prisoner hierarchy by separating the powerful from the weak. Humboldt State University's Lee H. Bowker has identified several other reasons for violent behavior:

1. It provides a deterrent against being victimized, as a reputation for violence may eliminate an inmate as a target of assault.
2. It enhances self-image in an environment that does not respect other attributes, such as intelligence.
3. In the case of rape, it gives sexual relief.
4. It serves as a means of acquiring material goods through extortion or outright robbery.[25]

The **deprivation model** is also helpful for explaining prison violence. According to this model, the stressful and oppressive conditions of prison life lead to aggressive behavior on the part of inmates. Prison researcher Stephen C. Light found that when conditions such as overcrowding worsen, inmate misconduct often increases.[26] In these circumstances, the violent behavior may not have any express purpose—it may just be a means of relieving tension.

GROUP VIOLENCE IN PRISON Researchers use a variation of the deprivation model to explain group violence behind bars, or *prison riots*. The concept of **relative deprivation** focuses on the gap between what is expected in a certain situation and what is achieved.

LEARNING
3
OBJECTIVE
Indicate some of the reasons for violent behavior in prisons.

Deprivation Model A theory that inmate aggression is the result of the frustration inmates feel at being deprived of freedom, consumer goods, sex, and other staples of life outside the institution.

Relative Deprivation The theory that inmate aggression is caused when freedoms and services that the inmate has come to accept as normal are decreased or eliminated.

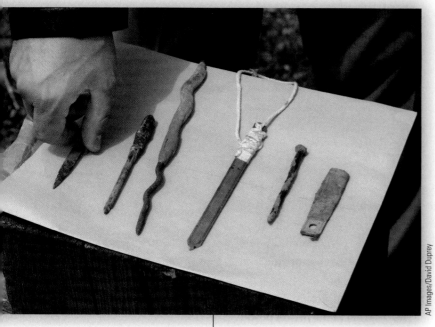

A correctional official displays a set of homemade knives, also known as *shivs,* made by inmates at Attica Correctional Facility in Attica, New York. ■ What technology might help prison officials uncover these weapons?

Criminologist Peter C. Kratcoski has argued that because prisoners enjoy such meager privileges to begin with, any further deprivation can spark disorder.[27] A number of prison experts have noted that group violence often occurs in response to heightened measures of security at corrections facilities.[28] Thus, the violence is primarily a reaction to additional reductions in freedom for inmates, who enjoy very little freedom to begin with.

Prison riots, which have been defined as situations in which a number of prisoners are beyond institutional control for a significant amount of time, are relatively rare. These incidents are marked by extreme levels of inmate-on-inmate violence and can often be attributed, at least in part, to poor living conditions and inadequate prison administration. For example, a recent riot at the Adams County Correctional Center in Natchez, Mississippi, that left one correctional officer dead and twenty others injured was sparked by inmate protests over poor food and lack of medical care. Afterwards, a prisoner said, "The guard that died yesterday was a sad tragedy, but the situation is simple: if you treat a human as an animal for over two years, the response will be as an animal."[29]

ISSUES OF RACE AND ETHNICITY On the morning of March 3, 2013, a huge brawl broke out at the Arizona State Prison Complex in Tucson, with three hundred white and Hispanic inmates battling one hundred African American inmates. Race plays a major role in prison life, and prison violence is often an outlet for racial tension. As prison populations have changed over the past three decades, with African Americans and Hispanics becoming the majority in many penal institutions, issues of race and ethnicity have become increasingly important to prison administrators and researchers.

As early as the 1950s, researchers were noticing different group structures in inmate life. At that time, for example, prisoners at California's Soledad Prison informally segregated themselves according to geography as well as race: Tejanos (Mexicans raised in Texas), Chicanos, blacks from California, blacks from the South and Southwest, and the majority whites all formed separate social worlds.[30]

Leo Carroll, professor of sociology at the University of Rhode Island, has written extensively about how today's prisoners are divided into hostile groups, with race determining nearly every aspect of an inmate's life, including friends, job assignments, and cell location.[31] Carroll's research has also shown how minority groups in prison have seized on race to help form their prison identities.[32]

Prison Gangs and Security Threat Groups (STGs)

Prison Gang A group of inmates who band together within the corrections system to engage in social and criminal activities.

In many instances, racial and ethnic identification is the primary focus of the **prison gang**—a clique of inmates who join together in an organizational structure. Gang affiliation is often the cause of inmate-on-inmate violence. For decades, the California prison system has been plagued by feuds involving various gangs such as the Mexican Mafia, composed of U.S.-born inmates of Mexican descent, and their enemies, a spin-off organization called La Nuestra Familia.

In part, the prison gang is a natural result of life in the modern prison. As one expert says of these gangs:

> Their members have done in prison what many people do elsewhere when they feel personally powerless, threatened, and vulnerable. They align themselves with others, organize to fight back, and enhance their own status and control through their connection to a more powerful group.[33]

In addition to their important role in the social structure of correctional facilities, prison gangs participate in a wide range of illegal economic activities within these institutions, including prostitution, drug selling, gambling, and loan sharking. A study by Alan J. Drury and Matt DeLisi of Iowa State University found that gang members were more likely to be involved in prison misconduct than those inmates who had been convicted of murder.[34]

THE PREVALENCE OF PRISON GANGS The most recent research places the rate of gang membership at 11.7 percent in federal prisons, 13.4 percent in state prisons, and 15.6 percent in jails.[35] When the National Gang Crime Research Center surveyed prison administrators, however, almost 95 percent said that gang recruitment took place at their institutions, so the overall prevalence of gangs is probably much higher. Los Angeles correctional officials believe that eight out of every ten inmates in their city jails are affiliated with a gang.[36]

In many instances, prison gangs are extensions of street gangs. Though the stereotypical gang is composed of African Americans or Hispanics, the majority of large prisons also have white, or "Aryan," gangs. One of the largest federal capital prosecutions in U.S. history, involving thirty-two counts of murder, focused on a major prison gang known as the Aryan Brotherhood.

COMBATING PRISON GANGS In their efforts to combat the influence of prison gangs, over the past decade correctional officials have increasingly turned to the **security threat group (STG)** model. Generally speaking, an STG is an identifiable group of three or more individuals who pose a threat to the safety of other inmates or members of the corrections community. About two-thirds of all prisons have a correctional officer who acts as an STG coordinator.[37] This official is responsible for determining groups of individuals (not necessarily members of a prison gang) that qualify as STGs and then taking appropriate measures to contain them.

In many instances, these measures are punitive. Prison officials, for example, have reduced overall levels of violence significantly by putting gang members in solitary confinement, away from the general prison population. Other punitive measures include restrictions on privileges such as family visits and prison program participation, as well as delays of parole eligibility.[38] Treatment philosophies also have a place in these strategies. New York prison administrators have increased group therapy and anger-management classes for STGs, a decision they credit for low murder rates in their state prisons.[39]

Security Threat Group (STG) A group of three or more inmates who engage in activity that poses a threat to the safety of other inmates or the prison staff.

A member of the Aryan Brotherhood in California's Calipatria State Prison. This particular prison gang espouses white supremacy, but for the most part its leadership focuses on illegal activities such as extortion and drug trafficking. **Why might an inmate join a prison gang?**

Mark Allen Johnson/ZumaPress/Newscom

AP Images

One piece of technology has made the task of controlling prison gangs extremely difficult: the cell phone. Although inmates are prohibited from possessing these devices, cell phones are routinely used to arrange attacks, plan escapes, and operate illegal money-making schemes from behind bars. The phones are usually smuggled in by visitors, who hide them in locations as varied as babies' diapers, food packages, soda cans, and body cavities. Each year, Florida corrections staff confiscate more than four thousand cell phones from prisoners and, as one state official points out, "we know that's not all of them."

In 2013, forty-four inmates and correctional officers at the Baltimore City Detention Center were arrested for helping to operate the Black Guerrilla Family gang from within the prison using cell phones. In response, the state of Maryland started a managed-access program to deal with the problem. "Cellular umbrella" antenna technology analyzes all calls made from the prison and instantly blocks any that originate from a contraband phone. During a test run at a California prison over the course of eleven days, a managed-access system blocked 24,190 call attempts from 2,593 unauthorized devices.

Thinking about Contraband Cell Phones

Prisoner advocates argue that inmates are motivated to use black market cell phones because prison landlines are too expensive, in some states costing $4.99 per call plus $0.89 a minute. What are the arguments for and against charging prisoners such high rates to contact those on the outside?

//// SELF ASSESSMENT

Fill in the blanks, and check your answers on page 389.

Prison culture is different from the culture of schools or workplaces because prison is a _____ _____ that dominates every aspect of the inmate's life. In recent decades, the prison culture has been affected by the increased average _____ of inmates, which has led to skyrocketing _____-_____ costs for federal and state corrections systems. Some researchers rely on the _____ model, which focuses on the stressful and oppressive conditions of incarceration, to explain general prison violence. The concept of _____ _____, based on the gap between an inmate's expectations and reality, is used to explain the conditions that lead to prison riots. Corrections officials will take punitive measures such as solitary confinement to combat prison _____, or cliques of inmates that join together in an organizational structure based, often, on their members' _____ or ethnicity.

CORRECTIONAL OFFICERS AND DISCIPLINE

Ideally, the presence of correctional officers—the standard term used to describe prison guards—has the effect of lessening violence in American correctional institutions. Practically speaking, this is indeed the case. Without correctional officers, the prison would be a place of anarchy. But in the highly regulated, oppressive environment of the prison, correctional officers must use the threat of violence, if not actual violence, to instill discipline and keep order. Thus, the relationship between prison staff and inmates is marked by mutual distrust. Consider the two following statements, the first made by a correctional officer and the second by a prisoner:

> [My job is to] protect, feed, and try to educate scum who raped and brutalized women and children ... who, if I turn my back, will go into their cell, wrap a blanket around their cellmate's legs, and threaten to beat or rape him if he doesn't give sex, carry contraband, or fork over radios, money, or other goods willingly. And they'll stick a shank in me tomorrow if they think they can get away with it.[40]

> The pigs in the state and federal prisons ... treat me so violently, I cannot possibly imagine a time I could ever have anything but the deepest, aching, searing hatred for them. I can't begin to tell you what they do to me. If I were weaker by a hair, they would destroy me.[41]

John Smierciak/MCT/Landov

In high-security prisons, correctional officers such as these two at the supermax prison in Tamms, Illinois, monitor even the most mundane of inmate activities, including working, exercising, eating, and showering. How might this constant surveillance contribute to tension between correctional officers and prisoners?

It may be difficult for an outsider to understand the emotions that fuel such sentiments. French philosopher Michel Foucault points out that discipline, both in prison and in the general community, is a means of social organization as well as punishment.[42] Discipline is imposed when a person behaves in a manner that is contrary to the values of the dominant social group. Correctional officers and inmates have different concepts of the ideal structure of prison society, and as the two quotations just cited demonstrate, this difference generates intense feelings of fear and hatred, which often lead to violence.

Prison Employment

Given the unpleasant working conditions in state prisons described at the beginning of this chapter—along with a starting annual salary of only $27,000—it should come as no surprise that Texas is having a hard time hiring and retaining corrections officers.[43] In general, however, there are numerous benefits to a career as a correctional officer. Because the position is a civil service (government) job, it offers steady benefits and employment security. In some states, such as California and New York, salaries can reach $70,000. Furthermore, because of a professionalism movement in hiring, the standards for correctional officers have risen dramatically in the past few decades.[44]

BECOMING A CORRECTIONAL OFFICER Most prospective correctional officers are required to pass the civil service exam in their state of employment. Furthermore, as with police cadets (see Chapter 4), correctional officers usually go through a military-style training program prior to deployment in a prison. This program incorporates classwork and physical training, including instruction in areas such as self-defense, inmate control, and protection against communicable disease. Like police cadets, correctional officer trainees also go through a period of supervision with an experienced co-worker, in which they learn not only the job's specific techniques and procedures, but also about the prison environment and subculture.[45]

RANK AND DUTIES The custodial staff at most prisons is organized according to four general ranks—captain, lieutenant, sergeant, and officer. In keeping with the militaristic model, captains are primarily administrators who deal directly with the warden on custodial issues. Lieutenants are the disciplinarians of the prison, responsible for policing and transporting the inmates. Sergeants oversee platoons of officers in specific parts of the prison, such as various cell blocks or work spaces.

Lucien X. Lombardo, professor of sociology and criminal justice at Old Dominion University, has identified six general job categories among correctional officers:[46]

LEARNING
List and briefly explain the six general job categories among correctional officers.
4
OBJECTIVE

1. *Block officers.* These employees supervise cell blocks containing as many as four hundred inmates, as well as the correctional officers on block guard duty. In general, the block officer is responsible for the well-being of the inmates. He or she tries to ensure that the inmates do not harm themselves or other prisoners and also acts as something of a camp counselor, dispensing advice and seeing that inmates understand and follow the rules of the facility.

2. *Work detail supervisors.* In many penal institutions, the inmates work in the cafeteria, the prison store, the laundry, and other areas. Work detail supervisors oversee small groups of inmates as they perform their tasks.

3. *Industrial shop and school officers.* These officers perform maintenance and security functions in workshop and educational programs. Their primary responsibility is to make sure that inmates are on time for these programs and do not cause any disturbances during the sessions.

4. *Yard officers.* Officers who work the prison yard usually have the least seniority, befitting the assignment's reputation as dangerous and stressful. These officers must be constantly on alert for breaches in prison discipline or regulations in the relatively unstructured environment of the prison yard.

5. *Tower guards.* These officers spend their entire shifts, which usually last eight hours, in isolated, silent posts high above the grounds of the facility. Although their only means of communication are walkie-talkies or cellular devices, the safety benefits of the position can outweigh the loneliness that comes with the job.

6. *Administrative building assignments.* Officers who hold these positions provide security at prison gates, oversee visitation procedures, act as liaisons for civilians, and handle administrative tasks such as processing the paperwork when an inmate is transferred from another institution.

Discipline

As Erving Goffman noted in his essay on the "total institution," in the general society adults are rarely placed in a position where they are "punished" as a child would be.[47] Therefore, the strict disciplinary measures imposed on prisoners come as something of a shock and can provoke strong defensive reactions. Correctional officers who must deal with these responses often find that disciplining inmates is the most difficult and stressful aspect of their job.

SANCTIONING PRISONERS As mentioned earlier, one of the first things that an inmate receives on entering a correctional facility is a manual that details the rules of the prison or jail, along with the punishment that will result from rule violations. These handbooks can be quite lengthy—running one hundred pages in some instances—and specific. Not only will a prison manual prohibit obvious misconduct such as violent or sexual activity, gambling, and possession of drugs or currency, but it also addresses matters of daily life such as personal hygiene, dress codes, and conduct during meals.

Correctional officers enforce the prison rules in much the same way that a highway patrol officer enforces traffic regulations. For a minor violation, the inmate may be "let off easy" with a verbal warning. More serious infractions will result in a "ticket," or a report forwarded to the institution's disciplinary committee.[48] The disciplinary committee generally includes several correctional officers and, in some instances, outside citizens or even inmates. Although, as we shall see, the United States Supreme Court has ruled that an inmate must be given a "fair hearing" before being disciplined,[49] in reality he or she has very little ability to challenge the committee's decision. Depending on the seriousness of the violation, sanctions can range from a loss of privileges such as visits from family members to the unpleasantness of solitary confinement, discussed in the previous chapter.

USE OF FORCE Generally, courts have been unwilling to put too many restrictions on the use of force by correctional officers. As we saw with police officers in Chapter 5, correctional officers are given great leeway to use their experience to determine when force is warranted. In *Whitley v. Albers* (1986),[50] the Supreme Court held that the use of force by prison officials violates an inmate's Eighth Amendment protections only if the force amounts to "the unnecessary and wanton infliction of pain." Excessive force can be considered "necessary" if the legitimate security interests of the penal institution are at stake. Consequently, an appeals court ruled that when officers at a Maryland prison formed an "extraction team" to remove the leader of a riot from his cell, beating him in the process, the use of force was justified given the situation.[51]

Legitimate Security Interests Courts have found that the "legitimate security interests" of a prison or jail justify the use of force when the correctional officer is

1. Acting in self-defense.
2. Acting to defend the safety of a third person, such as a member of the prison staff or another inmate.
3. Upholding the rules of the institution.
4. Preventing a crime such as assault, destruction of property, or theft.
5. Preventing an escape effort.[52]

In addition, most prisons and jails have written policies that spell out the situations in which their employees may use force against inmates. (Read the feature *Discretion in Action—Spitting Mad* that follows, and then give your opinion about a use-of-force situation involving correctional officers.)

The "Malicious and Sadistic" Standard The judicial system has not, however, given correctional officers total freedom of discretion to apply force. In *Hudson v. McMillan* (1992),[53] the Supreme Court ruled that minor injuries suffered by a convict at the hands of a correctional officer following an argument did violate the inmate's rights, because there was no security concern at the time of the incident. In other words, the issue is not *how much* force was used, but whether the officer used the force as part of a good faith effort to restore discipline or acted "maliciously and sadistically" to cause harm. This "malicious and sadistic" standard has been difficult for aggrieved prisoners to meet: in the ten years

SPITTING MAD

THE SITUATION During a fit of depression caused by the breakup of his marriage, a state prison inmate named Schmidt purposefully tears at a previous wound in his arm. Correctional officers, following the orders of Deputy Warden Wasserman, strap Schmidt into a chair that restricts the inmate's ability to move. As he is being restrained, Schmidt becomes agitated and curses the correctional officers. Then, he spits at a nurse trying to treat his injuries. Wasserman reacts by discharging a can of pepper spray at Schmidt. (When aimed at the face, pepper spray is a nonlethal weapon that causes a sensation similar to having sand or needles in the eyes.) Wasserman then places a spit mask on Schmidt, which traps the chemicals against the offender's skin. Schmidt is not allowed to clean his eyes and nose for nearly half an hour but suffers no lasting physical harm as a result of the pepper spray.

THE LAW In most cases, correctional officers are justified in using force against inmates so long as that force does not cause "unnecessary and wanton" pain. ("Wanton" means "deliberate and unprovoked.")

WHAT WOULD YOU DO? Suppose you are the warden at the prison where this incident took place. Would you discipline Deputy Warden Wasserman for his use of force against Schmidt? Do you think that the steps Wasserman took to restrain Schmidt were justified? What about the use of pepper spray? Keep in mind that a spitting inmate may pose a danger to correctional officers if the inmate has a communicable disease.

To see how state prison officials in Maine handled a similar situation, go to Example 12.1 in Appendix B.

following the *Hudson* decision, only about 20 percent of excessive force lawsuits against correctional officials were successful.[54]

Female Correctional Officers

Security concerns were the main reason that, for many years, prison administrators refused to hire women as correctional officers in men's prisons. The consensus was that women were not physically strong enough to subdue violent male inmates and that their mere presence in the predominantly masculine prison world would cause disciplinary breakdowns.[55] As a result, in the 1970s a number of women brought lawsuits against state corrections systems, claiming that they were being discriminated against on the basis of their gender. For the most part, these legal actions were successful in opening the doors to men's prisons for female correctional officers (and vice versa).[56] Today, more than 150,000 women work in correctional facilities, many of them in constant close contact with male inmates.[57]

As it turns out, female correctional officers have proved just as effective as their male counterparts in maintaining discipline in men's prisons.[58] Furthermore, evidence shows that women prison staff can have a calming influence on male inmates, thus lowering levels of prison violence.[59] The primary problem caused by women working in male prisons, it seems, involves sexual misconduct. According to the federal government, 61 percent of prison staff members who engage in sexual misconduct are female, suggesting a disturbing amount of consensual sex with inmates.[60] Similar issues exist between male correctional officers and female inmates, though in those cases the sexual contact is much more likely to be coerced.[61]

Protecting Prisoners' Rights

The general attitude of the law toward inmates is summed up by the Thirteenth Amendment to the U.S. Constitution:

> Neither slavery nor involuntary servitude, except as a punishment for crime whereof the party shall have been duly convicted, shall exist within the United States.

In other words, inmates do not have the same guaranteed rights as other Americans. For most of the nation's history, courts have followed the spirit of this amendment by applying the **"hands-off" doctrine** of prisoner law. This (unwritten) doctrine assumes that the care of inmates should be left to prison officials and that it is not the place of judges to intervene in penal administrative matters.

At the same time, the United States Supreme Court has stated that "[t]here is no iron curtain between the Constitution and the prisons of this country."[62] Consequently, like so many other areas of the criminal justice system, the treatment of prisoners is based on a balancing act—in this case, between the rights of prisoners and the security needs of the correctional institutions. Of course, as just noted, inmates do not have the same civil rights as other members of society. In 1984, for example, the Supreme Court ruled that arbitrary searches of prison cells are allowed under the Fourth Amendment because inmates have no reasonable expectation of privacy.[63] (See Chapter 6 for a review of this expectation.)

THE "DELIBERATE INDIFFERENCE" STANDARD As for those constitutional rights that inmates do retain, in 1976 the Supreme Court established the **"deliberate indifference"** standard. In the case in question, *Estelle v. Gamble*,[64] an inmate had claimed to be the victim of medical malpractice. In his majority opinion, Justice Thurgood Marshall wrote that prison officials violated a convict's Eighth Amendment rights if they "deliberately" failed to provide him or her with necessary medical care. At the time, the decision was hailed as a victory for prisoners' rights, and it continues to ensure that a certain level of health care is provided. Several years ago, for example, a federal appeals court ruled that Texas prison officials could be found "deliberately indifferent" for allowing soaring temperatures in their facilities, as discussed at the beginning of this chapter.[65]

In general, however, courts have found it difficult to define *deliberate* in this context. Does it mean that prison officials "should have known" that an inmate was placed in harm's way, or does it mean that officials purposefully placed the inmate in that position? The Supreme Court seems to have taken the latter position. In *Wilson v. Seiter* (1991),[66] for example, inmate Pearly L. Wilson filed a lawsuit alleging that certain conditions of his confinement—including overcrowding; excessive noise; inadequate heating, cooling, and ventilation; and unsanitary bathroom and dining facilities—were cruel and unusual. The Court ruled against Wilson, stating that he had failed to prove that

Susan Farley/The New York Times

 About a quarter of the security staff at Sing Sing Correctional Facility in Ossining, New York—shown here—are women. What are some of the challenges that face female correctional officers who work in a men's maximum-security prison?

LEARNING **5** OBJECTIVE Describe the hands-off doctrine of prisoner law, and indicate two standards used to determine if prisoners' rights have been violated.

"Hands-Off" Doctrine The unwritten judicial policy that favors noninterference by the courts in the administration of prisons and jails.

"Deliberate Indifference" A standard for establishing a violation of an inmate's Eighth Amendment rights, requiring that prison officials were aware of harmful conditions in a correctional institution *and* failed to take steps to remedy those conditions.

these conditions, even if they existed, were the result of "deliberate indifference" on the part of prison officials.

THE "IDENTIFIABLE HUMAN NEEDS" STANDARD In its *Wilson* decision, the Supreme Court created the **"identifiable human needs"** standard for determining Eighth Amendment violations. The Court asserted that a prisoner must show that the institution has denied her or him a basic need such as food, warmth, or exercise.[67] The Court mentioned only these three needs, however, forcing the lower courts to determine for themselves what other needs, if any, fall into this category.

Because of the Supreme Court's *Estelle* decision (described earlier), prisoners do have a well-established right to "adequate" medical care. "Adequate" has been interpreted to mean a level of care comparable to what the inmate would receive if he or she were not behind bars.[68] This concept has not always proved popular with the general public. In 2012, a federal judge in Boston commanded Massachusetts to cover the costs of gender reassignment surgery for a male inmate who had murdered his wife twelve years earlier. After numerous complaints from taxpayers, the judge rescinded his order. Furthermore, as noted earlier in the chapter, several years ago the Supreme Court asserted, controversially, that the overcrowding of California's state prisons was so severe that it denied inmates satisfactory levels of health care.[69]

THE FIRST AMENDMENT IN PRISON The First Amendment reads, in part, that the federal government "shall make no law respecting an establishment of religion, or prohibiting the free exercise thereof; or abridging the freedom of speech." In the 1970s, the prisoners' rights movement forced open the "iron curtain" to allow the First Amendment behind bars. In 1974, for example, the Supreme Court held that prison officials can censor inmate mail only if doing so is necessary to maintain prison security.[70] The decade also saw court decisions protecting inmates' access to group worship, instruction by clergy, special dietary requirements, religious publications, and other aspects of both mainstream and nonmainstream religions.[71]

Judges will limit some of these protections when an obvious security interest is at stake. In 2010, for example, a Pennsylvania prison was allowed to continue banning religious headscarves because of legitimate concerns that the scarves could be used to conceal drugs or strangle someone.[72] In general, however, the judicial system's commitment to freedom of speech and religion behind bars remains strong. Such was the case in 2013, when a California appeals court ruled that a supermax inmate had a First Amendment right to read a paperback novel that depicted sex between werewolves and humans. A warden had banned the novel, *The Silver Crown*, as obscene and tending to incite violence.[73]

//// SELF ASSESSMENT

Fill in the blanks, and check your answers on page 389.

Correctional officers known as _____ _____ are responsible for the daily well-being of the inmates in their cells. Perhaps the most stressful and important aspect of a correctional officer's job is enforcing _____ among the inmates. To do so, the officers may use force when a _____ security interest is being served. Courts will not, however, accept any force that is "_____ and sadistic." To prove that prison officials violated the _____ Amendment's prohibitions against cruel and unusual punishment, the inmate must first show that the officials acted with "_____ indifference" in taking or not taking an action.

INSIDE A WOMEN'S PRISON

When the first women's prison in the United States opened in 1839 on the grounds of New York's Sing Sing institution, the focus was on rehabilitation. Prisoners were prepared for a return to society with classes on reading, knitting, and sewing. Early women's reformatories had few locks or bars, and several included nurseries for the inmates' young children. Today, the situation is dramatically different. "Women's institutions are literally men's institutions, only we pull out the urinals," remarks Meda Chesney-Lind, a criminologist at the University of Hawaii.[74] Following a recently concluded decade-long study of conditions in women's prisons, researchers at the University of Cincinnati identified six specific concerns relating to female inmates:

1. They often suffer from lack of *self-efficacy,* meaning that they do not feel able to meet personal goals, and feel that they are not in control of their own lives.

2. Their criminal behavior is linked to *parental stress*—specifically, the financial strain of raising children and the possibility of losing custody of children due to antisocial behavior such as crime and substance abuse.

3. They are more likely than male offenders to suffer from *mental health problems* such as depression, anxiety, and self-injurious behaviors.

4. They are more likely than male offenders to have been *victims of physical and sexual abuse* as children and adults.

5. Before arrest, they were involved in *unhealthy relationships* with family members, spouses, or romantic partners that contributed to their criminal behavior.

6. Their lives are marked by *poverty and homelessness,* often brought on by substance abuse, child care responsibilities, and lack of educational and work skills.[75]

Given the different circumstances surrounding male and female incarceration, the uniformity in treatment of inmates regardless of gender can have serious consequences for the women imprisoned in this country.

Characteristics of Female Inmates

Male inmates outnumber female inmates by approximately nine to one, and there are only about a hundred women's correctional facilities in the United States. Consequently, most research concerning the American corrections system focuses on male inmates and men's prisons. Enough data exist, however, to provide a useful portrait of women behind bars. Female inmates are typically low income and undereducated, and have a history of unemployment. Female offenders are much less likely than male offenders to have committed a violent offense. Most are incarcerated for a nonviolent drug or property crime.[76] As Figure 12.3 on the right shows, the demographics of female prisoners are similar to those of their male counterparts. That is, the majority of female inmates are under the age of forty, and the population is disproportionately African American.

The single factor that most distinguishes female prisoners from their male counterparts is a history of physical or sexual abuse. A self-reported study conducted by the federal government

FIGURE 12.3 Female Prisoners in the United States by Race, Ethnicity, and Age

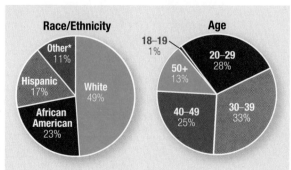

*Includes American Indians, Alaska Natives, Native Hawaiians, other Pacific Islanders, and persons identifying two or more races.

Source: Bureau of Justice Statistics, *Prisoners in 2012—Trends in Admissions and Releases, 1991–2012* (Washington, D.C.: U.S. Department of Justice, December 2013), Appendix table 4, page 37.

indicates that 55 percent of female jail inmates have been abused at some point in their lives, compared with only 13 percent of male jail inmates.[77] Fifty-seven percent of women in state prisons and 40 percent of women in federal prisons report some form of past abuse—both of these percentages are significantly higher than those for male prisoners.[78] Health experts believe that these levels of abuse are related to the significant amount of drug and/or alcohol addiction that plagues the female prison population, as well as to the mental illness problems that such addictions can cause or exacerbate.[79]

The Motherhood Problem

Explain the aspects of imprisonment that prove challenging for incarcerated mothers and their children. LEARNING **6** OBJECTIVE

Drug and alcohol use within a women's prison can be a function of the anger and depression many inmates experience due to being separated from their children. An estimated seven out of every ten female prisoners have at least one minor child. About 1.7 million American children have a mother who is under correctional supervision.[80] Given the scarcity of women's correctional facilities, inmates are often housed at great distances from their children. One study found that almost two-thirds of women in federal prison are more than five hundred miles from their homes.[81]

Further research indicates that an inmate who serves her sentence more than fifty miles from her residence is much less likely to receive phone calls or personal visits from family members. For most inmates and their families, the costs of "staying in touch" are too high.[82] This kind of separation can have serious consequences for the children of inmates. When a father goes to prison, his children are likely to live with their mother. When a mother is incarcerated, however, her children are likely to live with other relatives or, in about 11 percent of the cases, be sent to foster care.[83] Only nine states provide facilities where inmates and their infant children can live together, and even in these facilities nursery privileges generally end once the child is eighteen months old.

The Culture of Women's Prisons

After spending five years visiting female inmates in the Massachusetts Correctional Institution (MCI) at Framingham, journalist Cristina Rathbone observed that the medium-security facility seemed "more like a high school than a prison."[84] The prisoners were older and tougher than high school girls, but they still divided into cliques, with the "lifers" at the top of the hierarchy and "untouchables" such as child abusers at the bottom. Unlike in men's prisons, where the underground economy revolves around drugs and weapons, at MCI-Framingham the most treasured contraband items are clothing, food, and makeup.[85]

Although both men's and women's prisons are organized with the same goals of control and discipline, the cultures within the two institutions are generally very different. As we have seen, male prison society operates primarily on the basis of power. Deprived of the benefits of freedom, male prisoners tend to create a violent environment that bears little relation to life on the outside.[86] In contrast, researchers have found that female prisoners

Female inmates at the Women's Eastern Reception, Diagnostic and Correctional Center in Vandalia, Missouri, visit with their daughters and granddaughters. Why is it difficult for many mothers behind bars to see their children?

AP Images/Whitney Curtis

prefer to re-create their outside identities by forming social networks that resemble, as noted earlier, high school cliques or, more commonly, the traditional family structure.[87] In these pseudo-families, inmates often play specific roles, with the more experienced convicts acting as "mothers" to younger, inexperienced "daughters." As one observer noted, the younger women rely on their "moms" for emotional support, companionship, loans, and even discipline.[88]

////SELF ASSESSMENT

Fill in the blanks, and check your answers on page 389.

The majority of female inmates have been arrested for nonviolent _____ or property crimes. On admission to a correctional facility, women report much higher levels of physical and sexual _____ than their male counterparts, and female inmates often suffer from depression because they are separated from their _____. Researchers have found that women prisoners often form social networks that resemble the traditional _____ structure to deal with the stresses of incarceration.

RETURN TO SOCIETY

With only a few weeks left to serve on his prison sentence for drug charges, John Cadogan was worried. As he explained in a group therapy session at the men's state prison in Chino, California, his meth-addicted ex-girlfriend wanted to see him "on the outside." Cadogan feared that she was going to tempt him to restart his own drug use. The other inmates agreed that the situation was fraught with difficulty. "It's like playing Russian roulette with a loaded gun," said one.[89]

Each year, about 650,000 inmates are released from American prisons. Many, such as Cadogan, face numerous challenges in their efforts to avoid relapse and reincarceration. More so than in the past, however, ex-convicts are not facing these challenges alone. Given the benefits to society of reducing recidivism, corrections officials and community leaders are making unprecedented efforts to help newly released prisoners establish crime-free lives.

Types of Prison Release

The vast majority of all inmates leaving prison—about 65 percent—do so through one of the parole mechanisms discussed in Chapter 10. Of the remaining 35 percent, most are given an **expiration release.**[90] Also known as "maxing out," an expiration release occurs when an inmate has served the maximum amount of time on the initial sentence, minus reductions for good-time credits, and is not subjected to community supervision. Another, quite rare unconditional release is a **pardon,** a form of executive clemency. The president (on the federal level) and the governor (on the state level) can grant a pardon, or forgive a convict's criminal punishment. Most states have a board of pardons—affiliated with the parole board—that makes recommendations to the governor in cases in which it believes a pardon is warranted. Most pardons involve obvious miscarriages of justice, though sometimes a governor will pardon an individual to remove the stain of conviction from her or his criminal record.

LEARNING **7** OBJECTIVE

Contrast parole, expiration release, pardon, and furlough.

Certain temporary releases also exist. Some inmates, who qualify by exhibiting good behavior and generally proving that they do not represent a risk to society, are allowed to leave the prison on **furlough** for a certain amount of time, usually between a day and a week. On occasion, a furlough is granted because of a family emergency, such as a funeral. Furloughs can be particularly helpful for an inmate who is nearing release and can use them to ease the readjustment period. Finally, *probation release* occurs following a short period of incarceration at the back end of shock probation, which we discussed in Chapter 10. As you have seen, however, probationers generally experience community supervision in place of a prison term.

The Challenges of Reentry

What steps can corrections officials take to lessen the possibility that ex-convicts will reoffend following their release? Efforts to answer that question have focused on programs that help inmates make the transition from prison to the outside. In past years, these programs would have come under the general heading of "rehabilitation," but today corrections officials and criminologists refer to them as part of the strategy of **prisoner reentry**.

The concept of reentry has come to mean many things to many people. For our purposes, keep in mind the words of Joan Petersilia of Stanford University, who defines *reentry* as encompassing "all activities and programming conducted to prepare ex-convicts to return safely to the community and to live as law abiding citizens."[91] In other words, whereas rehab is focused on the individual offender, *reentry* encompasses the released convict's relationship with society.

Life on the Outside

Perhaps the largest obstacle to successful prisoner reentry is the simple truth that life behind bars is very different from life on the outside. As one inmate explains, the "rules" of prison survival are hardly compatible with good citizenship:

> An unexpected smile could mean trouble. A man in uniform was not a friend. Being kind was a weakness. Viciousness and recklessness were to be respected and admired.[92]

The prison environment also insulates inmates. They are not required to make the day-to-day decisions that characterize a normal existence beyond prison bars. Depending on the length of incarceration, a released inmate must adjust to an array of economic, technological, and social changes that took place while she or he was behind bars. Common acts such as using an ATM or a smartphone may be completely alien to someone who has just completed a long prison term.

OTHER BARRIERS TO REENTRY Additional obstacles hamper reentry efforts. Housing can be difficult to secure, as many private property owners refuse to rent to someone with a criminal record, and federal and state laws restrict public housing options for ex-convicts. A criminal past also limits the ability to find employment, as does the lack of job skills of someone who has spent a significant portion of his or her life in prison. Felix Mata, who works with ex-convicts in Baltimore, Maryland, estimates that the average male prisoner returning to that city has only $50 in his pocket and owes $8,000 in child support. Furthermore, these men generally have no means of transportation, no place to live, and no ability to gain employment. At best, most ex-prisoners can expect to earn no more than $8,500 annually the first few years after being released.[93]

These economic barriers can be complicated by the physical and mental condition of the freed convict. We have already discussed the high incidence of substance abuse among prisoners and the health-care needs of aging inmates. In addition, one study concluded that as many as one in five Americans leaving jail or prison is seriously mentally ill.[94] (See Figure 12.4 that follows for a list of the hardships commonly faced by former inmates in their first year out of prison.)

THE THREAT OF RELAPSE All of these problems conspire to make successful reentry difficult to achieve. Perhaps it is not surprising that research conducted by the Pew Center on the States found that 43 percent of ex-prisoners are back in prison or jail within three years of their release dates.[95] Such figures highlight the problem of recidivism among those released from incarceration.

Even given the barriers to reentry we have discussed, these rates of recidivism seem improbably high. Regardless of their ability to find a job or housing, many ex-convicts are fated to run afoul of the criminal justice system. Psychologists Edward Zamble and Vernon Quinsey explain the phenomenon as a *relapse process*.[96] Take the hypothetical example of an ex-convict who gets in a minor automobile accident while driving from his home to his job one morning. The person in the other car gets out and starts yelling at the ex-convict, who "relapses" and reacts just as he would have in prison—by punching the other person in the face. The ex-convict is then convicted of assault and battery and given a harsh prison sentence because of his criminal record.

Promoting Desistance

One ex-inmate compared the experience of being released to entering a "dark room, knowing that there are steps in front of you and waiting to fall."[97] The goal of reentry is to act as a flashlight for ex-convicts by promoting **desistance,** a general term used to describe the released inmate's continued abstinence from offending and his or her gradual reintegration into society. Certainly, the most important factor in the process is the individual convict. She or he has to *want* to desist and take steps to do so. In most cases, however, ex-inmates are going to need help—help getting an education, help finding and keeping a job, and help freeing themselves from harmful addictions to drugs and alcohol. Corrections officials are in a good position to offer this assistance, and their efforts in doing so form the backbone of the reentry movement.

> **Desistance** The process through which criminal activity decreases and reintegration into society develops over a period of time.

LEARNING **8** OBJECTIVE Explain the goal of prisoner reentry programs.

FIGURE 12.4 **Prisoner Reentry Issues**

Researchers from the Urban Institute in Washington, D.C., asked nearly three hundred former prisoners (all male) in the Cleveland, Ohio, area about the most pressing issues they faced in their first year after release. The answers provide a useful snapshot of the many challenges of reentry.

1. *Housing.* Nearly two-thirds of the men were living with family members, and about half considered their housing situation "temporary." Many were concerned about their living environment: half said that drug dealing was a major problem in their neighborhoods, and almost 25 percent were living with drug or alcohol abusers.

2. *Employment.* After one year, only about one-third of the former inmates had a full-time job, and another 11 percent were working part-time.

3. *Family and friends.* One in four of the men identified family support as the most important thing keeping them from returning to criminality. Another 16 percent said that avoiding certain people and situations was the most crucial factor in their continued good behavior.

4. *Programs and services.* About two-thirds of the former inmates had taken part in programs and services such as drug treatment and continuing education.

5. *Health.* More than half of the men reported suffering from a chronic health condition, and 29 percent showed symptoms of depression.

6. *Substance use.* About half of the men admitted to weekly drug use or alcohol intoxication. Men who had strong family ties and those who were required to maintain telephone contact with their parole officer were less likely to engage in frequent substance use.

7. *Parole violation and recidivism.* More than half of the former inmates reported that they had violated the conditions of their parole, usually by drug use or having contact with other parolees. Fifteen percent of the men returned to prison in the year after release. Four out of five of the returns were the result of a new crime.

Source: Christy A. Visher and Shannon M. E. Courtney, *One Year Out: Experience of Prisoners Returning to Cleveland* (Washington, D.C.: Urban Institute, April 2007), 2.

Preparation for reentry starts behind bars. In addition to the rehabilitation-oriented prison programs discussed earlier in the chapter, most correctional facilities offer "life skills" classes to inmates. This counseling covers topics such as finding and keeping a job, locating a residence, understanding family responsibilities, and budgeting. After release, however, former inmates often find it difficult to continue with educational programs and counseling as they struggle to readjust to life outside prison. Consequently, parole supervising agencies operate a number of programs to facilitate offenders' desistance efforts while, at the same time, protecting the community to the greatest extent possible.

Homeboy Industries, which operates this bakery in downtown Los Angeles, provides former gang members and recently released ex-convicts with job training opportunities and other reentry programs. Why is finding employment such an important part of the desistance process?

WORK RELEASE AND HALFWAY HOUSES As indicated in Figure 12.4 on the previous page, work and lodging are crucial components of desistance. Corrections officials have several options in helping certain parolees—usually low-risk offenders—find employment and a place to live during the supervision period. Nearly a third of correctional facilities offer **work release programs,** in which prisoners nearing the end of their sentences are given permission to work at paid employment in the community.[98]

Inmates on work release must either return to the correctional facility in the evening or live in community residential facilities known as **halfway houses.** These facilities, also available to other parolees and those who have finished their sentences, are often remodeled hotels or private homes. They provide a less-institutionalized living environment than a prison or jail for a small number of offenders (usually between ten and twenty-five). Halfway houses can be tailored to the needs of former inmates. Many communities, for example, offer substance-free transitional housing for those whose past criminal behavior was linked to drug or alcohol abuse.

WHAT WORKS IN REENTRY Substance abuse treatment can have a significant impact on desistance. Federal prisoners who receive such treatment in the community as a follow-up to prison programs are 16 percent less likely to return to prison and 15 percent less likely to resume drug use than those who do not.[99] Employment aid is also essential. Several years ago, the mayor of Newark, New Jersey, created an Office of Reentry to help ex-inmates find jobs. Of those who are successful, only 10 percent are likely to reoffend.[100]

The incentive to reduce recidivism—thereby holding down inmate populations— has spurred a number of states to implement far-reaching desistance programs. The Michigan Prison Reentry Initiative, for example, establishes an individualized "transition plan" for all released inmates. This plan, which includes not only substance abuse treatment and employment aid but transportation, housing, and life skills counseling, is credited with reducing Michigan's recidivism rate among parolees by 18 percent.[101]

The Special Case of Sex Offenders

Despite the beneficial impact of reentry efforts, one group of wrongdoers has consistently been denied access to such programs: those convicted of sex crimes. The eventual

Work Release Program Temporary release of convicts from prison for purposes of employment. The offenders may spend their days on the job, but must return to the correctional facility at night and during the weekend.

Halfway House A community-based form of early release that places inmates in residential centers and allows them to reintegrate with society.

return of these offenders to society causes such high levels of community anxiety that the criminal justice system has not yet figured out what to do with them.

FEAR OF SEX OFFENDERS According to one poll, 66 percent of Americans are "very concerned" about child molesters, compared with 52 percent who expressed such concern about violent criminals and 36 percent about terrorists.[102] To a large degree, this attitude reflects the widespread belief that convicted sex offenders cannot be "cured" of their criminality and therefore are destined to continue committing sex offenses after their release from prison.[103]

It is true that the medical health profession has had little success in treating the "urges" that lead to sexually deviant or criminal behavior.[104] This has not, however, translated into rampant recidivism among sex offenders when compared to other types of criminals. According to the U.S. Department of Justice, the rearrest rates of rapists (46 percent) and those convicted of other forms of sexual assault (41 percent) are among the lowest for all offenders.[105] Furthermore, after analyzing eighty-two recidivism studies, Canadian researchers R. Karl Hanson and Kelly Morton-Bourgon found that only 14 percent of sex offenders were apprehended for another sex crime after release from prison or jail. On average, such offenders were significantly more likely to be rearrested for nonsexual criminal activity, if they were rearrested at all.[106]

CONDITIONS OF RELEASE Whatever their recidivism rates, sex offenders are subject to extensive community supervision after being released from prison. Generally, they are supervised by parole officers and live under the same threat of revocation as other parolees. Specifically, many sex offenders—particularly child molesters—have the following special conditions of release:

1. No contact with children under the age of eighteen.
2. Psychiatric treatment.
3. Must stay a certain distance from schools or parks where children are present.
4. Cannot own toys that may be used to lure children.
5. Cannot have a job or participate in any activity that involves children.

Also, more than half of the states and hundreds of municipalities have passed laws limiting housing options for convicted sex offenders, which is the subject of the feature *CJ Controversy—Residency Restrictions* that follows.

SEX OFFENDER NOTIFICATION LAWS Perhaps the most dramatic step taken by criminal justice authorities to protect the public from sex crimes involves *sex offender registries,* or databases that contain sex offenders' names, addresses, photographs, and other information. The movement to register sex offenders started about two decades ago, after seven-year-old Megan Kanka of Hamilton Township, New Jersey, was raped and murdered by a twice-convicted pedophile (an adult sexually attracted to children) who had moved into her neighborhood after being released from prison on parole.

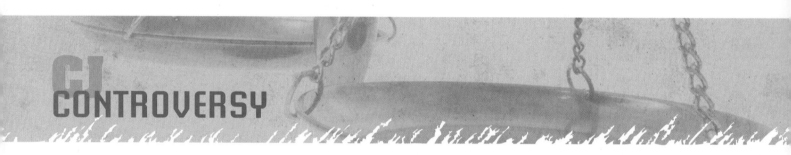

CONTROVERSY

RESIDENCY RESTRICTIONS

In many jurisdictions throughout the United States, residency laws ban sex offenders from living within a certain distance of places where children naturally congregate. In New Jersey, for example, "high-risk" offenders cannot take up residence within 3,000 feet of any school, park or campground, church, theater, bowling alley, library, or convenience store. (For medium- and low-risk offenders, the distances are 2,500 feet and 1,000 feet, respectively.) The overlapping "off-limit zones" created by residency requirements can dramatically restrict where a sex offender is able to find affordable housing.

RESIDENCY RESTRICTIONS SHOULD BE ENCOURAGED BECAUSE . . .

- Forbidding sex offenders from residing near schools and other areas that attract large groups of children decreases their access to these children, thus reducing the risk that they will reoffend.
- The right of convicted sex offenders to choose where they live is less important than the protection of law-abiding citizens.

RESIDENCY RESTRICTIONS SHOULD BE DISCOURAGED BECAUSE . . .

- They push sex offenders into less-populated, rural areas or into homelessness, which makes it much more difficult for law enforcement and corrections agents to stay in contact with them.
- They are inadequate. Strangers commit only about 10 percent of all sexual offenses against children. Sex offenders are much more likely to be family members, friends, or other acquaintances.

Your Assignment
A number of states allow for *civil confinement,* or the indefinite detention of sex offenders in psychiatric hospitals. Go online and, in two separate searches, pair **sex offender** with **residency restrictions** and then with **civil confinement.** Which strategy do you think is more effective in protecting the public from sex offenders? Or, is there a better third way? Your answer should include at least two full paragraphs.

Shortly thereafter, in response to public outrage, the state passed a series of laws known collectively as the New Jersey Sexual Offender Registration Act, or "Megan's Law."[107] Today, all fifty states and the federal government have their own version of Megan's Law, or a **sex offender notification law,** which requires local law authorities to alert the public when a sex offender has been released into the community.

Active and Passive Notification No two sex offender notification laws have exactly the same provisions, but all are designed with the goal of allowing the public to learn the identities of convicted sex offenders living in their midst. In general, the laws demand that a paroled sex offender notify local law enforcement authorities on taking up residence in a state. In Georgia, for example, paroled sex offenders are required to present themselves to both the local sheriff and the superintendent of the public school district where they plan to live.[108] This registration process must be renewed every time the parolee changes address.

The authorities, in turn, notify the community of the sex offender's presence through the use of one of two models. Under the "active" model, the authorities directly notify the community or community representatives. Traditionally, this notification has taken the form of bulletins or posters, distributed and posted within a certain distance from the offender's home. Now, however, a number of states use e-mail alerts to fulfill notification obligations. In the "passive" model, information on sex offenders is made open and available for public scrutiny.

Effectiveness of Sex Offender Registries In 2006, Congress passed the Adam Walsh Child Protection and Safety Act, which established a national registry of sex offenders.[109] In addition, all fifty states operate sex offender registries with data on registered sex offenders in their jurisdictions. (For an idea of how this process works, you can visit the Federal Bureau of Investigation's Sex Offender Registry Web site.) The total number of registered sex offenders in the United States is about 750,000.

Do sex offender registries actually protect the public? Perhaps not. According to Amanda Agan of the University of Chicago, rates of sex offenses have not declined in response to sex offender registries. Agan's research also shows that areas with elevated concentrations of registered sex offenders do not experience elevated levels of sex crimes.[110] One reason for this may be the fact, mentioned earlier, that sex offenders do not have particularly high rates of sex crime recidivism. Furthermore, almost nine of ten sex crimes are committed by people who have no history of such offenses and thus are not registered.[111] Finally, sex offender laws are so broad that many of those registered have been convicted of crimes such as indecent exposure or public urination that do not involve a sexual act or sexual contact.[112]

Sex Offender Notification Law Legislation that requires law enforcement authorities to notify people when convicted sex offenders are released into their neighborhood or community.

////SELF ASSESSMENT

Fill in the blanks, and check your answers on page 389.

Ex-convicts often struggle to succeed after being released from prison because their limited skills make it difficult to find _____. The resulting financial troubles hamper the offender's ability to secure _____, which makes it more likely that he or she will recidivate. One way in which the corrections system tries to reverse this process is by offering _____ programs that include job training and work release opportunities. Corrections officials also promote _____, or the process by which a former inmate stops committing crimes, by allowing certain low-risk offenders to live in _____ houses, where they can receive specialized treatment. Sex offender _____ laws, also known as Megan's Laws, mandate that law enforcement officials alert the public when a sex offender has moved into the community.

CHAPTER SUMMARY

For more information on these concepts, look back to the Learning Objective icons throughout the chapter.

 Explain the concept of prison as a total institution. Though many people spend time in partial institutions—schools, companies where they work, and religious organizations—only in prison is every aspect of an inmate's life controlled, and that is why prisons are called total institutions. Every detail for every prisoner is fully prescribed and managed.

 Describe a consequence of the failure to provide adequate medical care to inmates. In the first decade of the 2000s, medical care for inmates in California's prison system was severely compromised by extreme overcrowding. As a result, the United States Supreme Court ordered state corrections officials to release thirty thousand inmates so that standards of health care in the prison could be more compatible "with the concept of human dignity."

 Indicate some of the reasons for violent behavior in prisons. (a) To separate the powerful from the weak and establish a prisoner hierarchy; (b) to minimize one's own probability of being a target of assault; (c) to enhance one's self-image; (d) to obtain sexual relief; and (e) to obtain material goods through extortion or robbery.

 List and briefly explain the six general job categories among correctional officers. (a) Block officers, who supervise cell blocks or are on block guard duty; (b) work detail supervisors, who oversee the cafeteria, prison store, and laundry, for example; (c) industrial shop and school officers, who generally oversee workshop and educational programs; (d) yard officers, who patrol the prison yard when prisoners are allowed there; (e) tower guards, who work in isolation; and (f) those who hold administrative building assignments, such as prison gate guards and overseers of visitation procedures.

 Describe the hands-off doctrine of prisoner law, and indicate two standards used to determine if prisoners' rights have been violated. The hands-off doctrine assumes that the care of prisoners should be left to prison officials and that it is not the place of judges to intervene. Nonetheless, the Supreme Court has created two standards to be used by the courts in determining whether a prisoner's Eighth Amendment protections against cruel and unusual punishment have been violated. Under the "deliberate indifference" standard, prisoners must show that prison officials were aware of harmful conditions at the facility and failed to remedy them. Under the "identifiable human needs" standard, prisoners must show that they were denied a basic need such as food, warmth, or exercise.

 Explain the aspects of imprisonment that prove challenging for incarcerated mothers and their children. Besides the anxiety that results from any separation of parent and child, incarcerated mothers often find it difficult to stay in contact with their children due to long distances between the prison and home. Furthermore, when a mother is imprisoned, her children are more likely not only to be separated from their father, but also to wind up in foster care.

 Contrast parole, expiration release, pardon, and furlough. Parole is an early release program for those incarcerated. Expiration release occurs when the inmate has served the maximum time for her or his initial sentence minus good-time credits. A pardon can be given only by the president or by one of the fifty governors. Furlough is a temporary release while in jail or prison.

 Explain the goal of prisoner reentry programs. Based on the ideals of promoting desistance, these programs have two main objectives: (a) to prepare a prisoner for a successful return to the community, and (b) to protect the community by reducing the chances that the ex-convict will continue her or his criminal activity after release from prison.

QUESTIONS FOR CRITICAL ANALYSIS

1. Prisoner X is serving fourteen years in prison for robbery. He has fallen ill, and only a $1 million heart transplant will save his life. Are corrections officials *required* to pay for the heart transplant? Should they be required to do so? Explain your answers.

2. Several years ago, an inmate sued the Florida Department of Corrections, claiming that his soy-based diet was cruel and unusual punishment. Under what circumstances, if any, do you think that unpleasant prison food can violate an inmate's constitutional rights?

3. Do you agree with prison policies that prohibit male correctional officers from patting down and strip-searching female inmates? Why or why not? Under what circumstances might such policies be unrealistic?

4. How does the process of prisonization differ between male and female inmates?

5. What is the main justification for legislation that prohibits convicted sex offenders from accessing Facebook and online video games? What is your opinion of such legislation?

KEY TERMS

"deliberate indifference"   377
deprivation model   369
desistance   383
expiration release   381
furlough   381
halfway house   384

"hands-off" doctrine   377
"identifiable human needs"   378
pardon   381
prisoner reentry   382
prison gang   370
prisonization   365

prison programs   367
relative deprivation   369
security threat group (STG)   371
sex offender notification law   387
total institution   365
work release program   384

SELF-ASSESSMENT ANSWER KEY

Page 372: i. total institution; **ii.** age; **iii.** health-care; **iv.** deprivation; **v.** relative deprivation; **vi.** gangs; **vii.** race

Page 378: i. block officers; **ii.** discipline; **iii.** legitimate; **iv.** malicious; **v.** Eighth; **vi.** deliberate

Page 381: i. drug; **ii.** abuse; **iii.** children; **iv.** family

Page 387: i. employment; **ii.** housing; **iii.** reentry; **iv.** desistance; **v.** halfway; **vi.** notification

NOTES

1. Erving Goffman, "On the Characteristics of Total Institutions," in *Asylums: Essays on the Social Situation of Mental Patients and Other Inmates* (New York: Doubleday, 1961), 6.

2. Donald Clemmer, *The Prison Community* (Boston: Christopher, 1940).

3. John Irwin, *Prisons in Turmoil* (Boston: Little, Brown, 1980), 67.

4. *Old Behind Bars: The Aging Prison Population in the United States* (Human Rights Watch, 2012), 24–42.

5. Bureau of Justice Statistics, "Medical Problems of Prisoners," "Highlights" and Table 2 (April 2008), at www.ojp.usdoj.gov/bjs/pub/pdf/mpp.pdf.

6. Bureau of Justice Statistics, *Mortality in Local Jails and State Prisons, 2000–2011—Statistical Tables* (Washington, D.C.: U.S. Department of Justice, August 2013), 3.

7. *Ibid.*, Table 14, page 19.

8. *Ibid.*, 3.

9. Kevin E. McCarthy and Carrie Rose, *State Initiatives to Address Aging Prisoners* (Hartford, Conn.: Connecticut General Assembly, Office of Legislative Research, 2013), 3.

10. *Old Behind Bars: The Aging Prison Population in the United States, op. cit.*, 76.

11. Michael Vitiello, "Addressing the Special Problems of Mentally Ill Prisoners: A Small Piece of the Solution to Our Nation's Prison Crisis," *Denver University Law Review* (Fall 2010), 57–62.

12. Katherine Stuart van Wormer and Clemens Bartollas, *Women and the Criminal Justice System*, 3d ed. (Upper Saddle River, N.J.: Pearson Education, 2011), 143.

13. "Locked In," *The Economist* (August 3, 2013), 24.

14. Fred Osher et al., *Adults with Behavioral Health Needs under Correctional Supervision: A Shared Framework for Reducing Recidivism and Promoting Recovery* (New York: Council of State Governments Justice Center, 2012), 8.

15. William Kanapaux, "Guilty of Mental Illness," *Psychiatric Times* (January 1, 2004), at www.psychiatrictimes.com/forensic-psych/content/article/10168/47631.

16. Bureau of Justice Statistics, *Census of State and Federal Correctional Facilities, 2005* (Washington, D.C.: U.S. Department of Justice, October 2008), 6.

17. Lois M. Davis et al., *Evaluating the Effectiveness of Correctional Education* (Santa Monica, Calif.: RAND Corporation, 2013).

18. Joan Petersilia, "Beyond the Prison Bubble," *Wilson Quarterly* (Winter 2011), 29.

19. Anasseril E. Daniel, "Care of the Mentally Ill in Prisons: Challenges and Solutions," *Journal of the American Academy of Psychiatry and the Law Online* (December 2007), at **www.jaapl.org/content/35/4/406.full.**

20. Robert Johnson, *Hard Time: Understanding and Reforming the Prison,* 2d ed. (Belmont, Calif.: Wadsworth, 1996), 133.

21. Federal Bureau of Prisons report, cited in Kevin Johnson, "Report Points to Prison Security Failures," *USA Today* (June 8, 2009), 3A.

22. James E. Robertson, "The Prison Rape Elimination Act of 2003: A Primer," *Criminal Law Bulletin* (May/June 2004), 270–273.

23. Bureau of Justice Statistics, *Sexual Victimization in Prisons and Jails Reported by Inmates, 2011–12* (Washington, D.C.: U.S. Department of Justice, May 2013), 6.

24. *Mortality in Local Jails and State Prisons, 2000–2011—Statistical Tables, op. cit.,* Table 1, page 7; and Table 14, page 19.

25. Lee H. Bowker, *Prison Victimization* (New York: Elsevier, 1981), 31–33.

26. Stephen C. Light, "The Severity of Assaults on Prison Officers: A Contextual Analysis," *Social Science Quarterly* 71 (1990), 267–284.

27. Randy Martin and Sherwood Zimmerman, "A Typology of the Causes of Prison Riots and an Analytical Extension to the 1986 Virginia Riot," *Justice Quarterly* 7 (1990), 711–737.

28. Bert Useem, "Disorganization and the New Mexico Prison Riot of 1980," *American Sociological Review* 50 (1985), 677–688.

29. Quoted in R. L. Nave, "Private Prisons, Public Problems," *Jackson (MS) Free Press* (June 6, 2012), at **www.jacksonfreepress.com/news/2012/jun/06/private-prisons-public-problems.**

30. Irwin, *op. cit.,* 47.

31. Leo Carroll, "Race, Ethnicity, and the Social Order of the Prison," in *The Pains of Imprisonment,* eds. R. Johnson and H. Toch (Beverly Hills, Calif.: Sage, 1982).

32. Leo Carroll, *Hacks, Blacks, and Cons: Race Relations in a Maximum-Security Prison* (Lexington, Mass.: Lexington Books, 1988), 78.

33. Craig Haney, "Psychology and the Limits of Prison Pain," *Psychology, Public Policy, and Law* (December 1977), 499.

34. Alan J. Drury and Matt DeLisi, "Gangkill: An Exploratory Empirical Assessment of Gang Membership, Homicide Offending, and Prison Misconduct," *Crime & Delinquency* (January 2011), 130–146.

35. *A Study of Gangs and Security Threat Groups in America's Adult Prisons and Jails* (Indianapolis: National Major Gang Task Force, 2002).

36. George W. Knox, *The Problem of Gangs and Security Threat Groups (STGs) in American Prisons Today: Recent Research Findings from the 2004 Prison Gang Survey,* available at **www.ngcrc.com/corr2006.html.**

37. *Ibid.*

38. John Winterdyk and Rick Ruddell, "Managing Prison Gangs: Results from a Survey of U.S. Prison Systems," *Journal of Criminal Justice* 38 (2010), 733–734.

39. Alan Gomez, "States Make Prisons Far Less Deadly," *USA Today* (August 22, 2008), 3A.

40. Quoted in John J. DiIulio, Jr., *No Escape: The Future of American Corrections* (New York: Basic Books, 1991), 268.

41. Jack Henry Abbott, *In the Belly of the Beast* (New York: Vintage Books, 1991), 54.

42. Michel Foucault, *Discipline and Punish: The Birth of the Prison* (New York: Pantheon Books, 1977), 128.

43. Mike Ward, "Prison Population Dip Makes Guard Shortage Bearable in Texas Oil Patch," *Austin American-Statesman* (August 14, 2012), at **www.statesman.com/news/news/state-regional-govt-politics/prison-population-dip-makes-guard-shortage-beara-1/nRNRK.**

44. Todd R. Clear, George F. Cole, and Michael D. Reisig, *American Corrections,* 10th ed. (Belmont, Calif.: Wadsworth Cengage Learning, 2013), 333–334.

45. *Ibid.,* 335.

46. Lucien X. Lombardo, *Guards Imprisoned: Correctional Officers at Work* (Cincinnati, Ohio: Anderson Publishing Co., 1989), 51–71.

47. Goffman, *op. cit.,* 7.

48. Clear, Cole, and Reisig, *op. cit.,* 333.

49. *Wolff v. McDonnell,* 418 U.S. 539 (1974).

50. 475 U.S. 312 (1986).

51. *Stanley v. Hejirika,* 134 F.3d 629 (4th Cir. 1998).

52. Christopher R. Smith, *Law and Contemporary Corrections* (Belmont, Calif.: Wadsworth, 1999), Chapter 6.

53. 503 U.S. 1 (1992).

54. Darrell L. Ross, "Assessing *Hudson v. McMillan* Ten Years Later," *Criminal Law Bulletin* (September/October 2004), 508.

55. Van Wormer and Bartollas, *op. cit.,* 387.

56. Cristina Rathbone, *A World Apart: Women, Prison, and a Life behind Bars* (New York: Random House, 2006), 46.

57. Carl Nink et al., *Women Professionals in Corrections: A Growing Asset* (Centerville, Utah: MTC Institute, August 2008), 1.

58. Denise L. Jenne and Robert C. Kersting, "Aggression and Women Correctional Officers in Male Prisons," *Prison Journal* (1996), 442–460.

59. Nink et al., *op. cit.,* 8–9.

60. Paul Guerino and Allen J. Beck, *Sexual Victimization Reported by Adult Criminal Correctional Authorities, 2007–2008* (Washington, D.C.: U.S. Department of Justice, January 2011), 8.

61. Van Wormer and Bartollas, *op. cit.,* 146–148.

62. *Wolff v. McDonnell, op. cit.,* 539.

63. *Hudson v. Palmer,* 468 U.S. 517 (1984).

64. 429 U.S. 97 (1976).

65. *Blackmon v. Garza,* 484 F. App'x 866 (5th Cir. 2012).

66. 501 U.S. 294 (1991).

67. *Wilson v. Seiter,* 501 U.S. 294, 304 (1991).

68. *Woodall v. Foti,* 648 F.2d, 268, 272 (5th Cir. 1981).

69. *Brown v. Plata,* 563 U.S. ____ (2011).

70. *Procunier v. Martinez,* 416 U.S. 396 (1974).

71. *Cruz v. Beto,* 405 U.S. 319 (1972); *Gittlemacker v. Prasse,* 428 F.2d 1 (3d Cir. 1970); and *Kahane v. Carlson,* 527 F.2d 492 (2d Cir. 1975).

72. Maryclaire Dale, "Court Says Pa. Prison Can Ban Muslim Scarf," *Associated Press* (August 2, 2010).

73. Bob Egelko, "Warden Can't Ban Werewolf Novel, Court Rules," *San Francisco Chronicle* (June 5, 2013), at **www.sfgate.com/crime/article/Warden-can-t-ban-werewolf-novel-court-rules-4581024.php.**

74. Quoted in Alexandra Marks, "Martha Checks in Today," *Seattle Times* (October 8, 2004), A8.

75. Emily M. Wright et al., "Gender-Responsive Lessons Learned and Policy Implications for Women in Prison: A Review," *Criminal Justice and Behavior* (September 2012), 1612–1632.

76. Bureau of Justice Statistics, *Sourcebook of Criminal Justice,* 3d ed. (Washington, D.C.:

U.S. Department of Justice, 2003), Table 6.56, page 519; and Bureau of Justice Statistics, *Prisoners in 2012—Trends in Admissions and Releases, 1991–2012* (Washington, D.C.: U.S. Department of Justice, December 2013), Appendix table 11, page 43.

77. Bureau of Justice Statistics, *Profile of Jail Inmates, 2002* (Washington, D.C.: U.S. Department of Justice, July 2004), 10.

78. Bureau of Justice Statistics, *Prior Abuse Reported by Inmates and Probationers* (Washington, D.C.: U.S. Department of Justice, April 1999), 2.

79. *Caught in the Net: The Impact of Drug Policies on Women and Families* (Washington, D.C.: American Civil Liberties Union, 2004), 18–19.

80. Sarah Schirmer, Ashley Nellis, and Marc Mauer, *Incarcerated Parents and Their Children: Trends 1991–2007* (Washington, D.C.: The Sentencing Project, February 2009), 2.

81. Kelly Bedard and Eric Helland, "Location of Women's Prisons and the Deterrent Effect of 'Harder' Time," *International Review of Law and Economics* (June 2004), 152.

82. *Ibid.*

83. Schirmer, Nellis, and Mauer, *op cit.,* 5.

84. Rathbone, *op. cit.,* 4.

85. *Ibid.,* 158.

86. Van Wormer and Bartollas, *op. cit.,* 137–138.

87. Barbara Bloom and Meda Chesney-Lind, "Women in Prison," in Roslyn Muraskin, ed., *It's a Crime: Women and Justice,* 4th ed. (Upper Saddle River, N.J.: Prentice Hall, 2007), 542–563.

88. Piper Kerman, *Orange Is the New Black: My Year in a Women's Prison* (New York: Spiegal and Grau, 2011), 131.

89. Quoted in Sean J. Miller, "When Prison Doors Swing Open," *Christian Science Monitor Weekly* (May 21, 2012), 29.

90. *Prisoners in 2012—Trends in Admissions and Releases, 1991–2012,* Table 2, page 4.

91. Joan Petersilia, *When Prisoners Come Home: Parole and Prisoner Reentry* (New York: Oxford University Press, 2003), 39.

92. Victor Hassine, *Life without Parole: Living in Prison Today,* eds. Thomas J. Bernard and Richard McCleary (Los Angeles: Roxbury Publishing Co., 1996), 12.

93. Christy A. Visher, Sara A. Debus-Sherrill, and Jennifer Yahner, "Employment after Prison: A Longitudinal Study of Former Prisoners," *Justice Quarterly* 28 (2011), 713.

94. *Ill Equipped: U.S. Prisons and Offenders with Mental Illness* (New York: Human Rights Watch, 2003).

95. Pew Center on the States, *State of Recidivism: The Revolving Door of America's Prisons* (Washington, D.C.: The Pew Charitable Trusts, April 2011), 2.

96. Edward Zamble and Vernon Quinsey, *The Criminal Recidivism Process* (Cambridge, England: Cambridge University Press, 1997).

97. Quoted in Kevin Johnson, "After Years of Solitary, Freedom Is Hard to Grasp," *USA Today* (June 9, 2005), 2A.

98. *Census of State and Federal Correctional Facilities, 2005, op. cit.,* Table 6, page 5.

99. Alan Ellis and Todd Bussert, "Looking at the BOP's Amended RDAP Rules," *Criminal Justice* (Fall 2011), 37.

100. "They All Come Home," *The Economist* (April 23, 2011), 34.

101. Justice Center, *States Report Reductions in Recidivism* (Lexington, Ky.: The Council of State Governments, September 2012), 3.

102. "The Greatest Fear," *The Economist* (August 26, 2006), 25.

103. James F. Quin, Craig J. Forsyth, and Carla Mullen-Quinn, "Societal Reaction to Sex Offenders: A Review of the Origins and Results of the Myths Surrounding Their Crimes and Treatment Amenability," *Deviant Behavior* 25 (2004), 215–232.

104. Belinda Brooks Gordon and Charlotte Bilby, "Psychological Interventions for Treatment of Adult Sex Offenders," *British Medical Journal* (July 2006), 5–6.

105. Bureau of Justice Statistics, *Recidivism of Prisoners Released in 1994* (Washington, D.C.: U.S. Department of Justice, June 2002), Table 9, page 8.

106. R. Karl Hanson and Kelly Morton-Bourgon, "The Characteristics of Persistent Sexual Offenders: A Meta-Analysis of Recidivism Studies," *Journal of Consulting and Clinical Psychology* 73 (2005), 1154–1163.

107. New Jersey Revised Statute Section 2C: 7-8(c) (1995).

108. Georgia Code Annotated Section 42-9-44.1(b)(1).

109. Public Law Number 109-248, Section 116, 120 Statute 595 (2006).

110. Amanda Y. Agan, "Sex Offender Registries: Fear without Function?" *Journal of Law and Economics* (February 2011), 207–239.

111. Jamie Fellner, ed., *No Easy Answers: Sex Offenders Laws in the U.S.* (New York: Human Rights Watch, 2007), 25.

112. Agan, *op. cit.*

13 The Juvenile Justice System

To target your study and review, look for these numbered Learning Objective icons throughout the chapter.

Bob Daemmrich/The Image Works

A Textbook CASE

FOR THE BETTER part of a month, Andy Williams, a fifteen-year-old high school freshman, bragged that he was going take one of his father's guns to school and start shooting. Williams's friends thought he was joking. On March 5, 2001, however, Williams made good on his "joke," killing two classmates and wounding thirteen other people at Santana High School in Santee, California, a suburb of San Diego. Despite his age, prosecutors charged Williams as an adult, and he pleaded guilty to numerous counts of first degree murder and attempted murder. A judge sentenced Williams to fifty years to life in prison.

In 2013, Williams—twelve years into his sentence and twenty-seven years old—gave an interview from his cell at Ironwood State Prison, located near Blythe, California. He described the litany of personal problems he had faced in the weeks leading up to his violent outburst: heavy drug and alcohol use, sexual abuse at the hands of an older friend, and merciless bullying by other students. On the morning of the shootings, Williams said, "I got up and accepted that today I'm going to die. I'm glad it's over." He remembered hiding in a school bathroom stall, clutching his father's loaded .22 handgun, and thinking, "I'm not somebody that's going to hurt people, and I was aware that I was going hurt somebody."

Williams admitted that he felt that he needed to make good on his bragging or face further ridicule from his peers. "I think it's hard to separate what I am from what I've done," he said. "I know that the people I shot did not deserve to be killed or wounded, and I will never stop regretting that." Michele Borba, an expert on juvenile behavior, calls Williams a "sad, textbook case" of a teenage shooter. "There's always a slow trajectory into violence," she says, "and then a final straw in which the youth feels there is no other option."

FOR CRITICAL ANALYSIS

1. Do you think that a fifteen-year-old who commits a violent crime such as murder should receive the same punishment as an adult killer? Why or why not?

2. Andy Williams will become eligible for parole when he is in his mid-60s. How should the fact that he was a juvenile at the time of his crimes influence the parole board's decision to grant or deny him conditional release?

3. Williams said that, because he was small for his age, other students had punched and kicked him and even sprayed his pants with lighter fluid to set him on fire. If you were Williams's defense attorney at the time of his trial, how would you use this bullying to try to lessen your client's punishment?

AFP/Getty Images

In March 2001, Andy Williams, then fifteen years old, pleaded guilty to killing two classmates at Santana High School in Santee, California.

THE EVOLUTION OF AMERICAN JUVENILE JUSTICE

Parens Patriae A doctrine that holds that the state has a responsibility to look after the well-being of children and to assume the role of parent, if necessary.

A difficult question—asked every time a young offender such as Andy Williams commits a heinous act of violence—lies at the heart of the juvenile justice debate: Should such acts by youths be given the same weight as those committed by adults, or should they be seen as "mistakes" that can be corrected by care and counseling? From its earliest days, the American juvenile justice system has operated as an uneasy compromise between "rehabilitation and punishment, treatment and custody."[1]

At the beginning of the 1800s, juvenile offenders were treated the same as adult offenders—they were judged by the same courts and sentenced to the same severe penalties. This situation began to change soon after, as urbanization and industrialization created an immigrant underclass that was, at least in the eyes of many reformers, predisposed to deviant activity. Certain members of the Progressive movement, known as the child savers, began to take steps to "save" children from these circumstances, introducing the idea of rehabilitating delinquents in the process.

The Child-Saving Movement

In general, the child savers favored the doctrine of *parens patriae,* which holds that the state has not only a right but also a duty to care for children who are neglected, delinquent, or in some other way disadvantaged. Juvenile offenders, the child savers believed, required treatment, not punishment, and they were horrified at the thought of placing children in prisons with hardened adult criminals. In 1967, then–Supreme Court justice Abe Fortas said of the child savers:

> They believed that society's role was not to ascertain whether the child was "guilty" or "innocent," but "What is he, how has he become what he is, and what had best be done in his interest and in the interest of the state to save him from a downward career." The child—essentially good, as they saw it—was made "to feel that he is the object of [the government's] care and solicitude," not that he was under arrest or on trial.[2]

Child-saving organizations convinced local legislatures to pass laws that allowed them to take control of children who exhibited criminal tendencies or had been neglected by their parents. To separate these children from the environment in which they were raised, the organizations created a number of institutions, the best known of which was New York's House of Refuge. Opening in 1825, the House of Refuge implemented many of the same reformist measures popular in the penitentiaries of the time, meaning that its charges were subjected to the healthful influences of hard study and labor. Although the House of Refuge was criticized for its harsh discipline (which caused many boys to run away), similar institutions sprang up throughout the Northeast during the middle of the 1800s.

The Illinois Juvenile Court

The efforts of the child savers culminated with the passage of the Illinois Juvenile Court Act in 1899. The Illinois legislature created the first court specifically for juveniles, guided by the principles of *parens patriae* and based on the belief that children are not fully responsible for criminal conduct and are capable of being rehabilitated.[3]

List the four major differences between juvenile courts and adult courts.

LEARNING **1** OBJECTIVE

The Illinois Juvenile Court and those that followed in its path in other states were (and, in many cases, remain) drastically different from adult courts in the following ways:

1. *No juries.* The matter was decided by judges who wore regular clothes instead of black robes and sat at a table with the other participants rather than behind a bench. Because the primary focus of the court was on the child and not the crime, the judge had wide discretion in disposing of each case.

2. *Different terminology.* To reduce the stigma of criminal proceedings, "petitions" were issued instead of "warrants." The children were not "defendants," but "respondents," and they were not "found guilty," but "adjudicated delinquent."

3. *No adversarial relationship.* Instead of trying to determine guilt or innocence, the parties involved in the juvenile court worked together in the best interests of the child, with the emphasis on rehabilitation rather than punishment.

4. *Confidentiality.* To avoid "saddling" the child with a criminal past, juvenile court hearings and records were kept sealed, and the proceedings were closed to the public.

By 1945, every state had a juvenile court system modeled after the first Illinois court. For the most part, these courts were able to operate without interference until the 1960s and the onset of the juvenile rights movement.

Status Offender A juvenile who has engaged in behavior deemed unacceptable for those under a certain statutorily determined age.

Juvenile Delinquency Behavior that is illegal under federal or state law that has been committed by a person who is under an age limit specified by statute.

Status Offending

After the first juvenile court was established in Illinois, the Chicago Bar Association described its purpose as, in part, to "exercise the same tender solicitude and care over its neglected wards that a wise and loving parent would exercise with reference to his [or her] own children under similar circumstances."[4] In other words, the state was given the responsibility of caring for those minors whose behavior seemed to show that they could not be controlled by their parents. As a result, many **status offenders** found themselves in the early houses of refuge and continue to be placed in state-run facilities today. A status offense is an act that, if committed by a juvenile, is considered illegal and grounds for possible state custody. The same act, if committed by an adult, does not warrant law enforcement action. (See Figure 13.1 alongside to see which status offenses are most common.)

FIGURE 13.1 Status Offenses

About 140,000 status offenses are processed by juvenile courts in the United States each year. The most common, as this graph shows, are truancy (skipping school) and alcohol-related offenses.

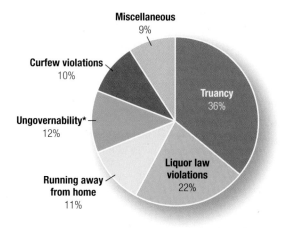

* Being beyond the control of parents, teachers, or other adult authority figures.

Source: Charles Puzzanchera and Sarah Hockenberry, *Juvenile Court Statistics, 2010* (Pittsburgh: National Center for Juvenile Justice, June 2013), 66.

Juvenile Delinquency

In contrast to status offending, **juvenile delinquency** refers to conduct that would also be criminal if committed by an adult. According to federal law and the laws of most states, a juvenile delinquent is someone who has not yet reached his or her eighteenth birthday—the age of adult criminal responsibility—at the time of the offense in question. In two states (New York and North Carolina), persons aged sixteen and older are considered adults, and eleven other states confer adulthood on seventeen-year-olds for purposes of criminal law.

Under certain circumstances, discussed later in this chapter, children under these ages can be tried in adult courts and incarcerated in adult prisons and jails. Remember that Andy Williams was fifteen years old when he was charged as an adult for the shooting rampage at his high school, described in the chapter opening. By contrast, in 2013, high school football players Trent Mays, aged seventeen, and Ma'lik Richmond, aged sixteen, were found to be *delinquent beyond a reasonable doubt* for sexually assaulting an intoxicated sixteen-year-old girl in Steubenville, Ohio (see photo alongside). Because they were adjudicated as juveniles, Mays and Richmond cannot be incarcerated past their twenty-first birthdays. Williams, charged as an adult, faces the possibility of spending his entire life behind bars.

Constitutional Protections and the Juvenile Court

Though the ideal of the juvenile court seemed to offer the "best of both worlds" for juvenile offenders, in reality the lack of procedural protections led to many children being arbitrarily punished not only for crimes, but for status offenses as well. Juvenile judges were treating all violators similarly, which led to many status offenders being incarcerated in the same institutions as violent delinquents. In response to a wave of lawsuits demanding due process rights for juveniles, the United States Supreme Court issued several rulings in the 1960s and 1970s that significantly changed the juvenile justice system.

Depending on the state, juvenile offenders found to be delinquent—such as Trent Mays, left, and Ma'lik Richmond—usually will not be incarcerated past their twenty-first birthdays. ■ Is this a just punishment for juveniles who commit violent crimes? Why or why not?

KENT V. UNITED STATES The first decision to extend due process rights to children in juvenile courts was *Kent v. United States* (1966).[5] The case concerned sixteen-year-old Morris Kent, who had been arrested for breaking into a woman's house, stealing her purse, and raping her. Because Kent was on juvenile probation, the state sought to transfer his trial for the crime to an adult court (a process to be discussed later in the chapter).

Without giving any reasons for his decision, the juvenile judge consented, and Kent was sentenced in the adult court to a thirty- to ninety-year prison term. The Supreme Court overturned the sentence, ruling that juveniles have a right to counsel and a hearing in any instance in which the juvenile judge is considering sending the case to an adult court. The Court stated that, in such instances, a child receives "the worst of both worlds," getting neither the "protections accorded to adults" nor the "solicitous care and regenerative treatment" offered in the juvenile system.[6]

IN RE GAULT The *Kent* decision provided the groundwork for *In re Gault* one year later. Considered by many to be the single most important case concerning juvenile justice, *In re Gault* involved a fifteen-year-old boy who was arrested for allegedly making a lewd phone call while on probation.[7] In its decision, the Supreme Court held that juveniles facing a loss of liberty were entitled to many of the same basic procedural safeguards granted to adult offenders in this country. (See the feature *Landmark Cases: In re Gault* that follows.)

OTHER IMPORTANT COURT DECISIONS During the next decade, the Supreme Court handed down three more important rulings on juvenile court procedure. The ruling in *In re Winship* (1970)[8] required the government to prove "beyond a reasonable doubt" that a juvenile had committed an act of delinquency, raising the burden of proof from a "preponderance of the evidence." In *Breed v. Jones* (1975),[9] the Court held that the Fifth

In re Gault

Identify and briefly describe the single most important U.S. Supreme Court case with respect to juvenile justice. **LEARNING OBJECTIVE 2**

In 1964, fifteen-year-old Gerald Gault and a friend were arrested for making lewd telephone calls to a neighbor in Gila County, Arizona. Gault, who was on probation, was placed under custody with no notice given to his parents. The juvenile court in his district held a series of informal hearings to determine Gault's punishment. During these hearings, no records were kept, Gault was not afforded the right to counsel, and the complaining witness was never made available for questioning. At the close of the hearing, the judge sentenced Gault to remain in Arizona's State Industrial School until the age of twenty-one. Gault's lawyers challenged this punishment, arguing that the proceedings had denied their client his due process rights. Eventually, the matter reached the United States Supreme Court.

In re Gault
United States Supreme Court
387 U.S. 1 (1967)

IN THE WORDS OF THE COURT . . .
JUSTICE FORTAS, MAJORITY OPINION

* * * *

From the inception of the juvenile court system, wide differences have been tolerated—indeed insisted upon—between the procedural rights accorded to adults and those of juveniles. In practically all jurisdictions, there are rights granted to adults which are withheld from juveniles.

* * * *

The absence of substantive standards has not necessarily meant that children receive careful, compassionate, individualized treatment. The absence of procedural rules based upon constitutional principle has not always produced fair, efficient, and effective procedures. Departures from established principles of due process have frequently resulted not in enlightened procedure, but in arbitrariness.

* * * *

Ultimately, however, we confront the reality of that portion of the Juvenile Court process with which we deal in this case. A boy is charged with misconduct. The boy is committed to an institution where he may be restrained of liberty for years.* * * His world becomes "a building with whitewashed walls, regimented routine and institutional hours. . . ." Instead of mother and father and sisters and brothers and friends and classmates, his world is peopled by guards, custodians, state employees, and "delinquents" confined with him for anything from waywardness to rape and homicide. In view of this, it would be extraordinary if our Constitution did not require the procedural regularity and the exercise of care implied in the phrase "due process." Under our Constitution, the condition of being a boy does not justify a kangaroo court.

* * * *

DECISION
The Court held that juveniles were entitled to the basic procedural safeguards afforded by the U.S. Constitution, including the right to advance notice of charges, the right to counsel, the right to confront and cross-examine witnesses, and the privilege against self-incrimination. The decision marked a turning point in juvenile justice in this country: no longer would informality and paternalism be the guiding principles of juvenile courts. Instead, due process would dictate the adjudication process, much as in an adult court.

FOR CRITICAL ANALYSIS
What might be some of the negative consequences of the *In re Gault* decision for juveniles charged with committing delinquent acts? Can you think of any reasons why juveniles should not receive the same due process protections as adult offenders?

Amendment's double jeopardy clause prevented a juvenile from being tried in an adult court for a crime that had already been adjudicated in juvenile court. In contrast, the decision in *McKeiver v. Pennsylvania* (1971)[10] represented an instance in which the Court did not move the juvenile court further toward the adult model. In that case, the Court ruled that the Constitution did not give juveniles the right to a jury trial.

///SELF ASSESSMENT

Fill in the blanks, and check your answers on page 421.

At its inception, the American juvenile justice system was guided by the principles of _____ _____, which holds that the state has a responsibility to look after children when their parents cannot do so. In general, juveniles are involved in two types of wrongdoing: (1) acts that would not be crimes if committed by adults, or _____ _____, and (2) acts that would be crimes if committed by an adult, or juvenile _____.

DETERMINING DELINQUENCY TODAY

In the eyes of many observers, the net effect of the Supreme Court decisions during the 1966–1975 period was to move juvenile justice away from the ideals of the child savers. As a result of these decisions, many young offenders would find themselves in a formalized system that is often indistinguishable from its adult counterpart. Although the Court has recognized that minors charged with crimes possess certain constitutional rights, it has failed to dictate at what age these rights should be granted. Consequently, the legal status of juvenile offenders in the United States varies depending on where they live, with each state making its own policy decisions on the crucial questions of age and competency.

The Age Question

According to his brother, thirteen-year-old Damien Reel often played with knives at his family's home in Englewood, Oregon. On February 11, 2014, after arguing with his parents, Reel grabbed one of his "toys" and randomly slashed the neck of a man who was jogging on a nearby street. In Chapter 3, we saw that early American criminal law recognized infancy as a defense against criminal charges. At that time, on attaining fourteen years of age, a youth was considered an adult and treated accordingly by the criminal justice system. Today, as Figure 13.2 alongside shows, the majority of states, including Oregon (as well as the District of Columbia), allow for the prosecution of juveniles fifteen

FIGURE 13.2 The Minimum Age at Which a Juvenile Can Be Tried as an Adult

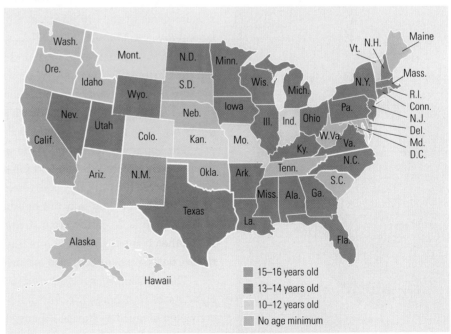

- 15–16 years old
- 13–14 years old
- 10–12 years old
- No age minimum

Source: Patrick Griffin et al., *Trying Juveniles as Adults: An Analysis of State Transfer Laws and Reporting* (Washington, D.C.: Office of Juvenile Justice and Delinquency Prevention, September 2011).

years of age and younger as adults. Thus, Oregon officials had the option of prosecuting Reel for attempted murder as an adult, despite his tender years.

As noted earlier, when juveniles who remain in juvenile court are found guilty, they receive "limited" sentences. Then, depending on the state, they cannot remain incarcerated in juvenile detention centers past their eighteenth or twenty-first birthday.

The Culpability Question

Many researchers believe that by the age of fourteen, an adolescent has the same ability as an adult to make a competent decision. Nevertheless, according to some observers, a juvenile's ability to theoretically understand the difference between "right" and "wrong" does not mean that she or he should be held to the same standards of competency as an adult.

JUVENILE BEHAVIOR A study released in 2003 by the Research Network on Adolescent Development and Juvenile Justice found that 33 percent of juvenile defendants in criminal courts had the same low level of understanding of legal matters as mentally ill adults who had been found incompetent to stand trial.[11] Legal psychologist Richard E. Redding believes that "adolescents' lack of life experience may limit their real-world decision-making ability. Whether we call it wisdom, judgment, or common sense, adolescents may not have nearly enough."[12]

Juveniles are generally more impulsive, more likely to engage in risky behavior, and less likely to calculate the long-term consequences of any particular action. Furthermore, adolescents are far more likely to respond to peer pressure than are adults. The desire for acceptance and approval may drive them to commit crimes: juveniles are arrested as part of a group at much higher rates than adults.[13] Furthermore, juveniles are less likely than adults to display remorse immediately following a violent act. As a result, they are often penalized by the courts for showing "less grief than the system demands."[14]

DIMINISHED GUILT The "diminished culpability" of juveniles was one of the reasons given by the United States Supreme Court as part of its landmark decision in *Roper v. Simmons* (2005).[15] As we saw in Chapter 9, that case forbade the execution of offenders who were under the age of eighteen when they committed their crimes. In his majority opinion, Justice Anthony Kennedy wrote that because minors cannot fully comprehend the consequences of their actions, the two main justifications for the death penalty—retribution and deterrence—do not "work" with juvenile wrongdoers.[16]

The Supreme Court applied the same reasoning in two later cases that have dramatically affected the sentencing of violent juvenile offenders. First, in *Graham v. Florida* (2010),[17] the Court held that juveniles who commit crimes that do not involve murder may not be sentenced to life in prison without the possibility of parole. According to Justice Kennedy, who wrote the majority opinion, state officials must give these inmates "some meaningful opportunity to obtain release based on demonstrated maturity and rehabilitation."[18]

Then, with *Miller v. Alabama* (2012),[19] the Court banned laws in twenty-eight states that made life-without-parole sentences *mandatory* for juveniles convicted of murder. The case focused on the fate of Evan Miller, who was fourteen years old when he killed a neighbor with a baseball bat. The ruling did not signify that juvenile offenders such as Miller could not, under any circumstances,

In 2013, juvenile offender T. J. Lane was sentenced to life in prison without the possibility of parole for killing three students during a shooting spree at Chardon High School in Chardon, Ohio. According to the United States Supreme Court's *Miller* decision, under what circumstances can juveniles receive life-without-parole sentences? Do you agree with the Court's ruling?

AP Images/Mark Duncan

be sentenced to life without parole. Rather, the Court stated that judges must have the discretion to weigh the mitigating factors in each individual case.

For example, Miller had been abused by his stepfather and neglected by his alcoholic and drug-addicted mother, had spent most of his life in foster care, and had tried to commit suicide four times.[20] According to the Court, this type of personal history must be taken into account when determining the proper sentence for a juvenile murderer. Such mitigating factors may indicate that the offender has the potential to be rehabilitated and therefore should be afforded the possibility of parole.

LEARNING **3** OBJECTIVE Describe the reasoning behind recent U.S. Supreme Court decisions that have lessened the harshness of sentencing outcomes for violent juvenile offenders.

///▰SELF ASSESSMENT

Fill in the blanks, and check your answers on page 421.

The age at which a child can be held criminally responsible for his or her actions differs from _____ to _____. Many experts believe that minors should not be held to the same level of competency as adults, partially because they are more _____ and more likely to respond to _____ pressure. This "diminished culpability" was one of the reasons the United States Supreme Court gave in 2005 for prohibiting the _____ _____ for offenders who were under the age of eighteen when they committed their crimes.

TRENDS IN JUVENILE DELINQUENCY

When asked, juveniles will admit to a wide range of illegal or dangerous behavior, including carrying weapons, getting involved in physical fights, driving after drinking alcohol, and stealing or deliberately damaging school property.[21] Has the juvenile justice system been effective in controlling and preventing this kind of misbehavior, as well as more serious acts?

To answer this question, many observers turn to the Federal Bureau of Investigation's Uniform Crime Report (UCR), initially covered in Chapter 2. Because the UCR breaks down arrest statistics by age of the arrestee, it has been considered the primary source of information on the presence of juveniles in America's justice system. This does not mean, however, that the UCR is completely reliable when it comes to measuring juvenile delinquency. The process measures only those juveniles who were caught and therefore does not accurately reflect all delinquent acts in any given year. Furthermore, it measures the number of arrests but not the number of arrestees, meaning that—due to repeat offenders—the number of juveniles actually in the system could be below the number of juvenile arrests.

Delinquency by the Numbers

With these cautions in mind, UCR findings are quite helpful in determining the extent of juvenile delinquency in the United States today. In 2012, juveniles accounted for 11.7 percent of violent crime arrests and 10.8 percent of criminal activity arrests in general.[22] According to the 2012 UCR, juveniles were responsible for

- 7 percent of all murder arrests.
- 9 percent of all aggravated assault arrests.
- 14 percent of all forcible rapes.
- 16 percent of all weapons arrests.
- 21 percent of all robbery arrests.
- 18 percent of all Part I property crimes.
- 9 percent of all drug offenses.

The Rise and Fall of Juvenile Crime

As Figure 13.3 that follows shows, juvenile arrest rates for violent crimes have fluctuated dramatically over the past three decades. In the 2000s, with a few exceptions, juvenile crime in the United States has decreased at a rate similar to that of adult crime, as discussed earlier in this textbook. From 1996 to 2010, juvenile court delinquency caseloads declined by 32 percent.[23] Not surprisingly, the drop in juvenile arrests and court appearances has led to fewer juveniles behind bars. The national population of juvenile inmates decreased 18 percent between 2008 and 2010, allowing officials in some states, including California, Ohio, and Texas, to close juvenile detention facilities.[24]

A number of theories have been put forth to explain this downturn in juvenile offending. Some observers point to the increase in police action against "quality-of-life" crimes such as loitering, which they believe stops juveniles before they have a chance to commit more serious crimes. Similarly, about 80 percent of American municipalities enforce juvenile curfews, which restrict the movement of minors during certain hours, usually after dark.[25] In 2012, law enforcement made about 54,000 arrests for curfew and loitering law violations.[26] Furthermore, hundreds of local programs designed to educate children about the dangers of drugs and crime operate across the country. Though the results of such community-based efforts are difficult, if not impossible, to measure—it cannot be assumed that children would have become delinquent if they had not participated—these programs are generally considered a crucial element of keeping youth crime under control.[27]

Girls in the Juvenile Justice System

Although overall rates of juvenile offending have been dropping, arrest rates for girls are declining more slowly than those for boys. Between 1997 and 2010, the number of cases involving males in delinquency courts declined 31 percent, while the female caseload in such courts declined by 14 percent.[28] Self-reported studies show, however, that there has been little change in girls' violent behavior over the past few decades.[29] Why, then, is the presence of girls in the juvenile and criminal justice system increasing relative to their male counterparts?

A GROWING PRESENCE Although girls have for the most part been treated more harshly than boys for certain status offenses,[30] in the past police were likely to arrest offending boys while allowing girls to go home to the care of their families for similar acts of juvenile delinquency. This is no longer the case. According to the Office of Juvenile Justice and Delinquency Prevention, juvenile courts handled twice as many cases involving girls in 2009 as they did in 1985.[31] A particular problem area for

FIGURE 13.3 Arrest Rates of Juveniles

After rising dramatically in the mid-1990s, juvenile arrest rates for violent crimes have—with a few exceptions—continued to drop steadily in the 2000s.

Source: Office of Juvenile Justice and Delinquency Prevention, *Juvenile Arrests 2011* (Washington, D.C.: U.S. Department of Justice, December 2013), 8.

girls appears to be the crime of assault. In 2012, females accounted for 25 percent of all juvenile arrests for aggravated assault and 37 percent of those arrests for simple assault, higher percentages than for other violent crimes.[32]

FAMILY-BASED DELINQUENCY Criminologists disagree on whether recent arrest rates for female juveniles reflect a change in behavior or a change in law enforcement practices. A significant amount of data supports the latter proposal, especially research showing that police are much more likely to make arrests in situations involving domestic violence than they were even a decade ago. Experts have found that girls are four times more apt to fight with parents or siblings than are boys, who usually engage in violent encounters with strangers. Consequently, a large percentage of female juvenile arrests for assault arise out of family disputes— arrests that until relatively recently would not have been made.[33]

Scott Olson/Getty Images News/Getty Images

■ Why might girls be treated more harshly than boys for certain status offenses such as running away from home?

Evidence also shows that law enforcement agents continue to treat girls more harshly for some status offenses. More girls than boys are arrested for the status offense of running away from home,[34] for example, even though studies show that male and female juveniles run away from home with equal frequency.[35] Criminologists who focus on issues of gender hypothesize that such behavior is considered normal for boys, but is seen as deviant for girls and therefore more deserving of punishment.[36]

LEARNING OBJECTIVE **4** Explain how law enforcement's emphasis on domestic violence has influenced female juvenile arrest patterns.

School Violence and Bullying

One Wednesday morning in April 2014, sixteen-year-old Alex Hribal walked through a hallway at Franklin Regional High School in Murrysville, Pennsylvania, with two large knives. Before being tackled by an assistant principal, Hribal stabbed and slashed twenty students and a security guard, and was later charged with numerous counts of attempted murder and aggravated assault. The incident was every student's (and teacher's and parent's) worst nightmare. Like other episodes of school violence, it received heavy media coverage, fanning fears that our schools are unsafe.

SAFE SCHOOLS Research does show that juvenile victimization and delinquency rates increase during the school day, and the most common juvenile crimes, such as simple assaults, are most likely to take place on school grounds.[37] In spite of well-publicized mass shootings such as the one that took place at Sandy Hook Elementary School in Newtown, Connecticut, in December 2012, however, violent crime is not commonplace in American schools. In fact, school-age youths are about fifty times more likely to be murdered away from school than on a campus.[38] Furthermore, between 1995 and 2012, victimization rates of students for nonfatal crimes at school declined significantly, meaning that, in general, schools are safer today than they were in the recent past.[39]

For the most part, these statistics mirror the downward trend of all criminal activity in the United States since the mid-1990s. In addition, since the fatal shootings of twelve students and a teacher at Columbine High School in Littleton, Colorado, in 1999, many schools have improved security measures. From 1999 to 2011, the percentage of American schools using security cameras to monitor their campuses increased from 19 to 61 percent. Today, 92 percent of public schools control access to school buildings by locking or monitoring their doors.[40]

Furthermore, schools have become less forgiving places. One in nine secondary school students are suspended or expelled each year, reflecting the popularity of "zero tolerance" policies toward behavior involving alcohol, drugs, or violence.[41] About half of all public schools in the United States are patrolled by law enforcement agents known as School Resource Officers, who have the power to arrest unruly students.[42]

BULLIED STUDENTS Andy Williams insisted that he was partially driven to violence, as discussed at the beginning of this chapter, by the angst of being bullied by his fellow students. **Bullying** can be broadly defined as repeated, aggressive behavior that contains at least one of the following elements:

1. *Physical abuse,* such as hitting, punching, or damaging the subject's property.
2. *Verbal abuse,* such as teasing, name calling, intimidation, or homophobic or racist remarks.
3. *Social and emotional abuse,* such as spreading false rumors, social exclusion, or playing jokes designed to humiliate.
4. *Cyber abuse,* which includes any form of bullying that takes place online or through the use of devices such as smartphones.

Bullying has traditionally been seen more as an inevitable rite of passage among adolescents than as potentially criminal behavior. In recent years, however, society has become more aware of the negative consequences of bullying, underscored by a number of high-profile "bullycides." In September 2013, for example, twelve-year-old Rebecca Sedwick jumped to her death at an abandoned concrete plant in Lakeland, Florida. Sedwick had been relentlessly bullied online and face to face by two other girls, who, among other things, told her that she was "ugly" and that she should "drink bleach and die."[43] Furthermore, between 2009 and 2012, at least five American teenage boys committed suicide after being bullied about their sexuality.

According to data gathered by the federal government, 28 percent of students aged twelve to eighteen have been victims of bullying.[44] In particular, gay students are targeted—nine out of ten report being bullied each year.[45] As a response to this problem, every state but Montana has passed anti-bullying legislation. These laws focus mostly on "soft" measures, such as training school personnel how to recognize and respond to bullying.[46] As yet, state legislatures have been reluctant to take "harder" measures such as specifically defining bullying as a crime. For example, in October 2013 Polk County sheriff Grady Judd arrested the two girls who had bullied Rebecca Sedwick prior to her death and charged them with felony aggravated stalking. The state's attorney's office quickly dropped the charges, however, after determining that the girls' behavior, while reprehensible, was not criminal.

Bullying Overt acts taken by students with the goal of intimidating, harassing, or humiliating other students.

Although it is not clear whether bullying in general is more prevalent now than in the past, one form of bullying is definitely on the rise. As the Internet, texting, and social networking sites such as Facebook have become integral parts of youth culture, so, it seems, has cyberbullying. In one recent poll, 85 percent of American and Canadian students said that they had been subject to cyberbullying at least once during the previous year.

To many, cyberbullying can be even more devastating than "old school" bullying. Not only does the anonymity of cyberspace seem to embolden perpetrators, causing them to be more vicious than they might be in person, but, as one expert points out, when bullying occurs online, "you can't get away from it." Still, as the example of Rebecca Sedwick in the text highlights, criminal law does not yet cover most forms of cyberbullying. The consensus seems to be that children should not be charged with a crime for vicious behavior online unless that behavior contains a "specific threat of bodily harm or death." Another suggestion, that parents be held legally responsible for their child's online bullying, has also been ruled out as an impracticable response to the problem.

Cheryl E. Davis/Shutterstock.com

Thinking about Cyberbullying

How should the criminal justice system respond to cyberbullying, if at all?

/// SELF ASSESSMENT

Fill in the blanks, and check your answers on page 421.

The crime rate for juveniles has generally been _____ for more than a decade. Crime rates for _____, however, are declining at a slower rate than for _____ juveniles, possibly because of police attention to domestic violence. _____ violence is another area in which crime rates have dropped since the 1990s, thanks, in part, to greater security measures such as surveillance cameras and locked building doors. _____, in both its traditional and electronic forms, remains a problem, however, and is increasingly being addressed by school administrators and state legislators.

FACTORS IN JUVENILE DELINQUENCY

An influential study conducted by Professor Marvin Wolfgang and several colleagues in the early 1970s introduced the "chronic 6 percent" to criminology. The researchers found that out of one hundred boys, six will become chronic offenders, meaning that they are arrested five or more times before their eighteenth birthdays. Furthermore, Wolfgang and his colleagues determined that these chronic offenders are responsible for half of all crimes and two-thirds of all violent crimes within any given cohort (a group of persons who have similar characteristics).[47] Does this "6 percent rule" mean that no matter what steps society takes, six out of every hundred juveniles are "bad seeds" and will act delinquently? Or does it point to a situation in which a small percentage of children may be more likely to commit crimes under certain circumstances?

Most criminologists favor the second interpretation. In this section, we will examine the four factors that have traditionally been used to explain juvenile criminal behavior and violent crime rates: age, substance abuse, family problems, and gangs. Keep in mind, however, that the factors influencing delinquency are not limited to these topics (see Figure 13.4 that follows). Researchers are constantly interpreting and reinterpreting statistical evidence to provide fresh perspectives on this very important issue.

For example, increased attention to the nationwide problem of bullying led to numerous studies regarding its impact on victims. Generally speaking, research has shown that victims of bullying are at an increased risk of becoming bullies themselves, and of engaging in a variety of other antisocial and criminal behavior.[48] In 2013, Michael Turner, an associate professor of criminal justice and criminology at the University of North Carolina at Charlotte, released data showing that bullied preteens were twice as likely to wind up in prison as those preteens who had not been bullied. Furthermore, Turner found that, regardless of race, exposure to bullying during adolescence correlates strongly with substance abuse and delinquency.[49]

The Age-Crime Relationship

Crime statistics are fairly conclusive on one point: the older a person is, the less likely he or she will exhibit criminal behavior. Self-reported studies confirm that most people are involved in some form of criminal behavior—however "harmless"—during their early years. In fact, Terrie Moffitt of Duke University has said that "it is statistically aberrant to refrain from crime during adolescence."[50] So, why do the vast majority of us not become chronic offenders?

According to many criminologists, particularly Travis Hirschi and Michael Gottfredson, any group of at-risk persons—regardless of gender, race, intelligence, or class—will commit fewer crimes as they grow older.[51] This process is known as **aging out** (or, sometimes, *desistance,* a term we first encountered in the previous chapter). Professor Robert J. Sampson and his colleague John H. Laub believe that this phenomenon is explained by certain events, such as marriage, employment, and military service, which force delinquents to "grow up" and forgo criminal acts.[52]

Another view sees the **age of onset,** or the age at which a youth begins delinquent behavior, as a consistent predictor of future criminal behavior. One study compared recidivism rates between juveniles first judged to be delinquent before the age of fifteen and those first adjudicated delinquent after the age of fifteen. Of the seventy-one subjects who made up the first group, 32 percent became chronic offenders. Of the sixty-five who made up the second group, none became chronic offenders.[53] Furthermore, according to the Office of Juvenile Justice and Delinquency Prevention, the earlier a youth enters the juvenile justice system, the more likely he or she will become a violent offender.[54] This research suggests that juvenile justice resources should be concentrated on the youngest offenders, with the goal of preventing crime and reducing the long-term risks for society.

FIGURE 13.4 Risk Factors for Juvenile Delinquency

The characteristics listed here are generally accepted as "risk factors" for juvenile delinquency. In other words, if one or more of these factors are present in a juvenile's life, he or she has a greater chance of exhibiting delinquent behavior—though such behavior is by no means a certainty.

Family	• Single parent/lack of parental role model • Parental or sibling drug/alcohol abuse • Extreme economic deprivation • Family members in a gang or in prison
School	• Academic frustration/failure • Learning disability • Negative labeling by teachers • Disciplinary problems
Community	• Social disorganization (refer to Chapter 2) • Presence of gangs and obvious drug use in the community • Availability of firearms • High crime/constant feeling of danger • Lack of social and economic opportunities
Peers	• Delinquent friends • Friends who use drugs or who are members of gangs • Lack of "positive" peer pressure
Individual	• Tendency toward aggressive behavior • Inability to concentrate or focus/easily bored/hyperactive • Alcohol or drug use • Fatalistic/pessimistic viewpoint

Substance Abuse

As we have seen throughout this textbook, substance abuse plays a strong role in criminal behavior for adults. The same can certainly be said for juveniles. According to the University of Michigan's Institute for Social Research, 28 percent of American tenth-graders and 42 percent of American twelfth-graders are regular alcohol drinkers, increasing their risks for violent behavior, delinquency, academic problems, and unsafe sexual behavior.[55] Close to 40 percent of high school seniors report using marijuana at least once in the past twelve months, and just under 20 percent admit to using an illegal drug other than marijuana during that time period.[56]

A STRONG CORRELATION As with adults, substance abuse among juveniles seems to play a major role in offending. Drug use is associated with a wide range of antisocial and illegal behaviors by juveniles, from school suspensions to large-scale theft.[57] Nearly all young offenders (94 percent) entering juvenile detention self-report drug use at some point in their lives, and 85 percent have used drugs in the previous six months.[58] According to the Arrestee Drug Abuse Monitoring Program, nearly 60 percent of male juvenile detainees and 46 percent of female juvenile detainees test positive for drug use at the time of their offense.[59] Drug use is a particularly strong risk factor for girls: 75 percent of young women incarcerated in juvenile facilities report regular drug and alcohol use—starting at the age of fourteen—and studies show that 60 percent to 87 percent of female teenage offenders need substance abuse treatment.[60]

STRONG CAUSATION? The correlation between substance abuse and offending for juveniles seems obvious. Does this mean that substance abuse *causes* juvenile offending? Researchers make the point that most youths who become involved in antisocial behavior do so before their first experience with alcohol or drugs. Therefore, it would appear that substance abuse is a form of delinquent behavior rather than its cause.[61] Still, a recent study of adolescent offenders did find that substance abuse treatment reduces criminal behavior in the short term, suggesting that, at the least, the use of illegal drugs is an integral component of the juvenile delinquent lifestyle.[62]

Child Abuse and Neglect

Abuse by parents also plays a substantial role in juvenile delinquency. **Child abuse** can be broadly defined as the infliction of physical or emotional damage on a child. Similar though not the same, **child neglect** refers to deprivations—of love, shelter, food, and proper care—children undergo by their parents. According to the National Survey of Children's Exposure to Violence, one in ten children in the United States experience mistreatment at the hands of a close family member.[63]

Children in homes characterized by violence or neglect suffer from a variety of physical, emotional, and mental health problems at a much greater rate than their peers.[64] This, in turn, increases their chances of engaging in delinquent behavior. One survey of violent juveniles showed that 75 percent had been subjected to severe abuse by a family member and 80 percent had witnessed violence in their homes.[65] Nearly half of all juveniles—and 80 percent of girls—sentenced to life in prison suffered high rates of abuse.[66]

Gangs

When youths cannot find the stability and support they require in the family structure, they will often turn to their peers. This is just one explanation for why juveniles

Child Abuse Mistreatment of children by causing physical, emotional, or sexual damage without any plausible explanation, such as an accident.

Child Neglect A form of child abuse in which the child is denied certain necessities such as shelter, food, care, and love.

join **youth gangs.** Although jurisdictions may have varying definitions, for general purposes a youth gang is viewed as a group of three or more persons who (1) self-identify as an entity separate from the community by special clothing, vocabulary, hand signals, and names and (2) engage in criminal activity. According to an exhaustive survey of law enforcement agencies, there are probably around 30,000 gangs with approximately 785,000 members in the United States.[67]

Juveniles who have experienced the risk factors discussed in this section are more likely to join a gang, and once they have done so, they are more likely to engage in delinquent and violent behavior than nongang members.[68] Statistics show high levels of gang involvement in most violent criminal activities in the United States.[69] About 80 percent of fatal shootings in Chicago are attributed to gangs, and mini-gangs of teenagers known as "crews" account for 30 percent of all shootings in New York City.[70] Furthermore, a study of criminal behavior among juveniles in Seattle found that gang members were considerably more likely to commit crimes than at-risk youths who shared many characteristics with gang members but were not affiliated with any gang (see Figure 13.5 that follows).

WHO JOINS GANGS? The average gang member is seventeen to eighteen years old, though members tend to be older in cities with long traditions of gang activity such as Chicago and Los Angeles. Although it is difficult to determine with any certainty the makeup of gangs as a whole, one recent survey found that 46 percent of all gang members in the United States are Hispanic, 35 percent are African American, and 11 percent are white, with the remaining 8 percent belonging to other racial or ethnic backgrounds.[71]

Though gangs tend to have racial or ethnic characteristics—that is, one group predominates in each gang—many researchers do not believe that race or ethnicity is the dominant factor in gang membership. Instead, gang members seem to come from lower-class or working-class communities, mostly in urban areas but with an increasing number

FIGURE 13.5 Comparison of Gang and Nongang Delinquent Behavior

Taking self-reported surveys of subjects aged thirteen to eighteen in the Seattle area, researchers for the Office of Juvenile Justice and Delinquency Prevention found that gang members were much more likely to exhibit delinquent behavior than nongang members.

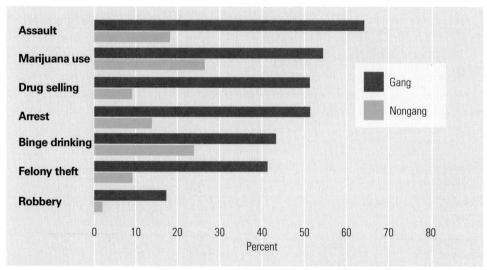

Source: Karl G. Hill, Christina Lui, and J. David Hawkins, *Early Precursors of Gang Membership: A Study of Seattle Youth* (Washington, D.C.: Office of Juvenile Justice and Delinquency Prevention, December 2001), Figure 1, page 2.

from the suburbs and rural counties. In addition, researchers are finding that adolescents who will eventually join a gang display significantly higher levels of delinquent behavior than those who will never become involved in gang activity.[72]

A very small percentage of youth gang members are female. In many instances, girls associate themselves with gangs, even though they are not considered members. Generally, girls assume subordinate gender roles in youth gangs, providing emotional, physical, and sexual support for the dominant males.[73] Still, almost half of all youth gangs report having female members, and, as in other areas of juvenile crime and delinquency, involvement of girls in gangs is increasing.[74]

WHY DO YOUTHS JOIN GANGS? The decision to join a gang, as with the decision to engage in any sort of antisocial or criminal behavior, is a complex one, and the factors that go into it vary depending on the individual. Generally, however, the reasons for gang membership involve one or more of the following:

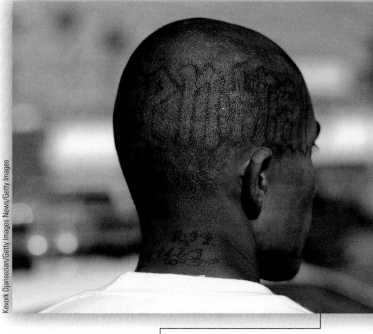

In Los Angeles, a gang member signifies his allegiance to the "Street Villains" through a series of elaborate tattoos. What role does identity play in a juvenile's decision to join a gang?

Kevork Djansezian/Getty Images News/Getty Images

1. *Identity.* Being part of a gang often confers a status that the individual feels he or she could not attain outside the gang.
2. *Protection.* Many gang members live in neighborhoods marked by high levels of crime and violence, and gang membership guarantees support and retaliation in case of an attack.
3. *Fellowship.* The gang often functions as an extension of the family and provides companionship that may not be available at home.
4. *Criminal activity.* Many gang members enjoy financial rewards because of the gang's profits.
5. *Intimidation.* Some youths are pressured or forced to join the gang, often to act as "foot soldiers" in the gang's criminal enterprises.[75]

////SELF ASSESSMENT

Fill in the blanks, and check your answers on page 421.

Criminologists have identified a number of _____ factors that increase the probability of juvenile misbehavior. One is youth. Studies of a process called _____ _____ show that children commit fewer offenses as they grow older. _____ _____ at the hands of parents or guardians increases the chances of life imprisonment, particularly for girls. Youth who become involved in _____ are also more likely to engage in criminal activity than those who do not.

FIRST CONTACT: THE POLICE AND PRETRIAL PROCEDURES

As part of the Juvenile Robbery Intervention Program, New York City detectives spend hours monitoring the Facebook pages and Twitter accounts of teenagers at risk for gang involvement and violent crime. Most commonly, however, contact between juvenile offenders and law enforcement takes place on the streets, initiated by a police officer on patrol who either apprehends the juvenile while he or she is committing a crime or answers a call for service. (See Figure 13.6 that follows for an overview of the juvenile justice process.) The youth is then passed on to an officer of the juvenile court, who must decide how to handle the case.

Police Discretion and Juvenile Crime

Police arrest about 1.1 million youths under the age of eighteen each year. In most states, police officers must have probable cause to believe that the minor has committed an offense, just as they would if the suspect was an adult. Police power with regard to juveniles is greater than with adults, however, because police can take youths into custody for status offenses, such as possession of alcohol or truancy. In these cases, the officer is acting *in loco parentis*, or in the place of the parent. The officer's role is not necessarily to punish the youths, but to protect them from harmful behavior.

Police officers also have a great deal of discretion in deciding what to do with juveniles who have committed crimes or status offenses. Juvenile justice expert Joseph Goldstein labels this discretionary power **low-visibility decision making** because it relies on factors that the public is not generally in a position to understand or criticize. When a grave offense has taken place, a police officer may decide to formally arrest the juvenile, send him or her to juvenile court, or place the youth under the care of a social-service organization. In less serious situations, the officer may simply issue a warning or take the offender to the police station and release the child into the custody of her or his parents.

In making these discretionary decisions, police generally consider the following factors:

LEARNING **6** OBJECTIVE
List the factors that normally determine what police do with juvenile offenders.

1. The nature of the child's offense.
2. The offender's past history of involvement with the juvenile justice system.
3. The setting in which the offense took place.

FIGURE 13.6 The Juvenile Justice Process

This diagram shows the possible tracks that a young person may take after her or his first contact with the juvenile justice system (usually a police officer).

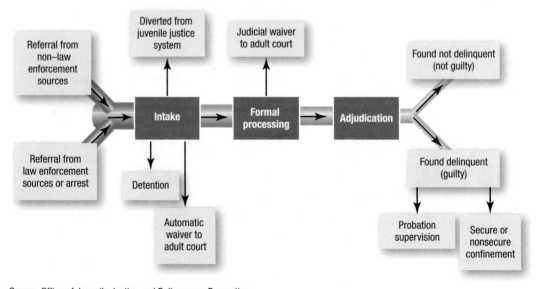

Source: Office of Juvenile Justice and Delinquency Prevention.

4. The ability and willingness of the child's parents to take disciplinary action.

5. The attitude of the offender.

Law enforcement officers notify the juvenile court system that a particular young person requires its attention through a process known as a **referral.** Anyone with a valid reason, including parents, relatives, welfare agencies, and school officials, can refer a juvenile to the juvenile court. The vast majority of cases in juvenile courts, however, are referred by the police.[76]

Intake

As noted earlier, if, following arrest, a police officer feels the offender warrants the attention of the juvenile justice process, the officer will refer the youth to juvenile court. Once this step has been taken, a complaint is filed with a special division of the juvenile court, and the **intake** process begins. Intake may be followed by diversion to a community-based program, transfer to an adult court, or detention to await trial in juvenile court. Thus, intake, diversion, transfer, and detention are the four primary stages of pretrial juvenile justice procedure.

During intake, an official of the juvenile court—usually a probation officer, but sometimes a judge—must decide, in effect, what to do with the offender. The intake officer has several options during intake:

1. Simply dismiss the case, releasing the offender without taking any further action. This occurs in about one in five cases, usually because the judge cannot determine a sufficient reason to continue.[77]

2. Divert the offender to a social-service program, such as drug rehabilitation or anger management.

3. File a **petition** for a formal court hearing. The petition is the formal document outlining the charges against the juvenile.

4. Transfer the case to an adult court, where the offender will be tried as an adult.

With regard to status offenses, judges have sole discretion to decide whether to process the case or to *divert* the youth to another juvenile service agency.

Pretrial Diversion

In the early 1970s, Congress passed the first Juvenile Justice and Delinquency Prevention (JJDP) Act, which ordered the development of methods "to divert juveniles from the traditional juvenile justice system."[78] Within a few years, hundreds of diversion programs had been put into effect. Today, diversion refers to the process of removing low-risk offenders from the formal juvenile justice system by placing them in community-based rehabilitation programs.

Diversion programs vary widely but fall into three general categories:

1. *Probation.* In this program, the juvenile is returned to the community but placed under the supervision of a juvenile probation officer. If the youth breaks the conditions of probation, he or she can be returned to the formal juvenile system.

2. *Treatment and aid.* Many juveniles have behavioral or medical conditions that contribute to their delinquent behavior, and many diversion programs offer remedial education, drug and alcohol treatment, and other forms of counseling to alleviate these problems.

3. *Restitution.* In these programs, the offender "repays" her or his victim, either directly or symbolically through community service.[79]

LEARNING OBJECTIVE **7** Describe the four primary stages of pretrial juvenile justice procedure.

Referral The notification process through which a law enforcement officer or other concerned citizen makes the juvenile court aware of a juvenile's unlawful or unruly conduct.

Intake The process by which an official of the court must decide whether to file a petition, release the juvenile, or place the juvenile under some other form of supervision.

Petition The document filed with a juvenile court alleging that the juvenile is a delinquent or a status offender, and requesting that the court either hear the case or transfer it to an adult court.

Proponents of diversion programs include many labeling theorists, who believe that contact with the formal juvenile justice system "labels" the youth a delinquent, which leads to further delinquent behavior. Increasingly, juvenile justice practitioners are relying on principles of restorative justice (see Chapter 9) to divert adolescents from formal institutions. For example, in Barron County, Wisconsin, delinquents have access to victim-offender conferences, underage drinking and anger-management workshops, and group intervention courses for chronic offenders.[80] Juvenile drug courts, modeled on the adult drug courts we discussed in Chapter 10, have also had some success in this area.[81]

Transfer to Adult Court

One side effect of diversionary programs is that the youths who remain in the juvenile courts are more likely to be seen as "hardened" and thus less amenable to rehabilitation. This, in turn, increases the likelihood that the offender will be transferred to an adult court, a process in which the juvenile court waives jurisdiction over the youth. As the American juvenile justice system has shifted away from ideals of treatment and toward punishment, transfer to adult court has been one of the most popular means of "getting tough" on delinquents. Each year, about six thousand delinquent cases are waived to adult criminal court—approximately 1 percent of all cases that reach juvenile court.[82] (See the feature *CJ Controversy—Juvenile Crime, Adult Time* that follows to get a better understanding of this issue.)

JUDICIAL TRANSFER There are three types of transfer laws, and most states use more than one of them depending on the jurisdiction and the seriousness of the offense. Juveniles are most commonly transferred to adult courts through **judicial waiver,** in which the juvenile judge is given the power to determine whether a young offender's case will be waived to adult court. The judge makes this decision based on the offender's age, the nature of the offense, and any criminal history. All but five states employ judicial waiver.

OTHER METHODS OF TRANSFER Twenty-nine states have taken the waiver responsibility out of judicial hands through **automatic transfer,** also known as *legislative waiver.* In these states, the legislatures have designated certain conditions—usually involving serious crimes such as murder and rape—under which a juvenile case is automatically "kicked up" to adult court. In Rhode Island, for example, a juvenile aged sixteen or older with two prior felony adjudications will automatically be transferred on being accused of a third felony.[83]

Fifteen states also allow for **prosecutorial waiver,** in which prosecutors are allowed to choose whether to initiate proceedings in juvenile or criminal court when certain age and offense conditions are met. In twenty-five states, criminal court judges also have the freedom to send juveniles who were transferred to adult court back to juvenile court. Known as *reverse transfer* statutes, these laws are designed to provide judges with a measure of discretion, even when automatic transfer takes place.

Detention

Once the decision has been made that the offender will face adjudication in a juvenile court, the intake official must decide what to do with him or her until the start of the trial. Generally, the juvenile is released into the custody of parents or a guardian—most

JUVENILE CRIME, ADULT TIME

In the 1980s and 1990s, reacting to the widespread belief that violent and chronic juvenile offenders were "beyond help," most states changed their transfer laws to make it easier to get juvenile offenders into adult courts. Over the past decade, this attitude has changed, as reflected in the Supreme Court cases we discussed earlier in this chapter that recognize the "heightened capacity for change" in young offenders. Consequently—to the consternation of many prosecutors—state politicians have begun to pass laws that reduce the likelihood of juveniles being tried as adults and placed in adult jails and prisons.

VIOLENT JUVENILE OFFENDERS SHOULD BE TRIED AS ADULTS BECAUSE . . .

- Juvenile courts lack the ability to hand down punishments harsher than minimum terms in juvenile corrections facilities. Juveniles who commit violent crimes deserve the more punitive measures available in adult courts.

- Violent juvenile offenders pose a risk to nonviolent offenders in juvenile correctional facilities. Thus, their removal makes the juvenile justice system safer.

VIOLENT JUVENILE OFFENDERS SHOULD NOT BE TRIED AS ADULTS BECAUSE . . .

- Recidivism rates are higher for young offenders incarcerated in adult facilities than for those held in juvenile facilities. One reason for this may be that adult prisons and jails act as "schools of crime" for juveniles.

- The threat of adult punishment has little deterrent effect on juveniles because they do not appreciate the consequences of their actions to the same extent that adults do.

Your Assignment

Should juveniles ever be tried as adults? Or, perhaps, should only certain older, violent juvenile offenders be tried as adults? What limits, if any, do you think should be placed on juvenile transfer to adult court? Before writing your answer, which should include two full paragraphs, go online and read the Supreme Court's *Graham v. Florida* and *Miller v. Alabama* decisions. Focus on the sections of these decisions that deal with the differences between juvenile and adult offenders.

---

jurisdictions favor this practice in lieu of setting money bail for youths. The intake officer may also place the offender in **detention,** or temporary custody in a secure facility, until the disposition process begins. Once a juvenile has been detained, most jurisdictions require that a **detention hearing** be held within twenty-four hours. During this hearing, the offender has several due process safeguards, including the right to counsel, the right against self-incrimination, and the right to cross-examine and confront witnesses.

In justifying its decision to detain, the court will usually address one of three issues:

1. Whether the child poses a danger to the community.
2. Whether the child will return for the adjudication process.
3. Whether detention will provide protection for the child.

The Supreme Court upheld the practice of preventive detention (see Chapter 8) for juveniles in *Schall v. Martin* (1984)[84] by ruling that youths can be detained if they are deemed a "risk" to the safety of the community or to their own welfare. Partly as a result, the number of juveniles detained for acts of violence increased 98 percent between 1985 and 2010.[85]

Detention The temporary custody of a juvenile in a secure facility after a petition has been filed and before the adjudicatory process begins.

Detention Hearing A hearing to determine whether a juvenile should remain detained while waiting for the adjudicatory process to begin.

Fill in the blanks, and check your answers on page 421.

If the circumstances are serious enough, a police officer can formally _____ an offending juvenile. Otherwise, the officer can _____ the juvenile to the juvenile court system or place her or him in the care of a _____-service organization. During the _____ process, a judge or juvenile probation officer decides the immediate fate of the juvenile delinquent. One of the options is _____, in which low-risk offenders are placed in community rehabilitation programs. If the judge believes that the seriousness of the offense so warrants, he or she can transfer the juvenile into the adult court system through a process called judicial _____.

TRYING AND PUNISHING JUVENILES

In about half of all referred cases, the juvenile is eventually subject to formal proceedings in juvenile court.[86] As noted earlier, changes in the juvenile justice system since *In re Gault* (1967) have led many to contend that juvenile courts have become indistinguishable, both theoretically and practically, from adult courts.[87] Just over half of the states, for example, permit juveniles to request a jury trial under certain circumstances. As the *Mastering Concepts* feature that follows explains, however, juvenile justice proceedings may still be distinguished from the adult system of criminal justice, and these differences are evident in the adjudication and disposition of the juvenile trial.

Adjudication

During the adjudication stage of the juvenile justice process, a hearing is held to determine whether the offender is delinquent or in need of some form of court supervision. Most state juvenile codes dictate a specific set of procedures that must be followed during the **adjudicatory hearing,** with the goal of providing the respondent with "the essentials of due process and fair treatment." Consequently, the respondent in an adjudicatory hearing has the right to notice of charges, counsel, and confrontation and cross-examination, as well as the privilege against self-incrimination. Furthermore, "proof beyond a reasonable doubt" must be established to find the child delinquent. When the child admits guilt—that is, admits to the charges of the initial petition—the judge must ensure that the admission was voluntary.

At the close of the adjudicatory hearing, the judge is generally required to rule on the legal issues and evidence that have been presented. Based on this ruling, the judge determines whether the respondent is delinquent or in need of court supervision. Alternatively, the judge can dismiss the case based on a lack of evidence. It is important to remember that finding a child delinquent is *not* the same as convicting an adult of a crime. A delinquent does not face the same restrictions imposed on adult convicts in some states, such as limits on the right to vote (discussed in Chapter 11).

Disposition

Once a juvenile has been adjudicated delinquent, the judge must decide what steps will be taken toward treatment and/or punishment. Most states provide for a *bifurcated* process in which a separate **disposition hearing** follows the adjudicatory hearing. Depending on state law, the juvenile may be entitled to counsel at the disposition hearing.

LEARNING OBJECTIVE 8 Explain the distinction between an adjudicatory hearing and a disposition hearing.

Adjudicatory Hearing The process through which a juvenile court determines whether there is sufficient evidence to support the initial petition.

Disposition Hearing Similar to the sentencing hearing for adults, a hearing in which the juvenile judge or officer decides the appropriate punishment for a youth found to be delinquent or a status offender.

MASTERING CONCEPTS
THE JUVENILE JUSTICE SYSTEM VERSUS THE CRIMINAL JUSTICE SYSTEM

AP Images/Columbus Dispatch/
James D. DeCamp

When the juvenile justice system was first established in the United States, its participants saw it as being separate from the adult criminal justice system. Indeed, the two systems remain separate in many ways. There are, however, a number of similarities between juvenile and adult justice. Here, we summarize both the similarities and the differences.

SIMILARITIES	DIFFERENCES		
		Juvenile System	Adult System
• The right to receive the *Miranda* warnings.	Purpose	Rehabilitation of the offender.	Punishment.
• Procedural protections when making an admission of guilt.	Arrest	Juveniles can be arrested for acts (status offenses) that are not criminal for adults.	Adults can be arrested only for acts made illegal by the relevant criminal code.
• Prosecutors and defense attorneys play equally important roles.	Wrongdoing	Considered a "delinquent act."	A crime.
	Proceedings	Informal; closed to public.	Formal and regimented; open to public.
• The right to be represented by counsel at the crucial stages of the trial process.	Information	Courts may NOT release information to the press.	Courts MUST release information to the press.
	Parents	Play significant role.	Play no role.
• Access to plea bargains.	Release	Into parent/guardian custody.	May post bail when appropriate.
• The right to a hearing and an appeal.	Jury trial	In some states, juveniles do NOT have this right.	All adults have this right.
• The standard of evidence is proof beyond a reasonable doubt.	Searches	Juveniles can be searched in school without probable cause.	No adult can be searched without probable cause.
	Records	Juvenile's record is sealed at age of adult criminal responsibility.	Adult's criminal record is permanent.
• Offenders can be placed on probation by the judge.	Sentencing	Juveniles are placed in separate facilities from adults.	Adults are placed in county jails or state or federal prisons.
• Offenders can be held before adjudication if the judge believes them to be a threat to the community.	Death penalty	No death penalty.	Death penalty for certain serious crimes under certain circumstances.
• Following trial, offenders can be sentenced to community supervision.			

SENTENCING JUVENILES In an adult trial, the sentencing phase is primarily concerned with the need of the community to be protected from the convict. In contrast, a juvenile judge uses the disposition hearing to determine a sentence that will serve the needs of the child. For assistance in this crucial process, the judge will order the probation department to gather information on the juvenile and present it in the form of a **predisposition report.** The report usually contains information concerning the respondent's family background, the facts surrounding the delinquent act, and interviews with social workers, teachers, and other important figures in the child's life.

JUDICIAL DISCRETION In keeping with the rehabilitative tradition of the juvenile justice system, juvenile judges generally have a great deal of discretion in choosing one of several disposition possibilities. A judge can tend toward leniency, delivering only a stern

Predisposition Report A report prepared during the disposition process that provides the judge with relevant background material to aid in the disposition decision.

Graduated Sanctions The practical theory in juvenile corrections that a delinquent or status offender should receive a punishment that matches in seriousness the severity of the wrongdoing.

reprimand or warning before releasing the juvenile into the custody of parents or other legal guardians. Otherwise, the choice is among incarceration in a juvenile correctional facility, probation, or community treatment. In most cases, the seriousness of the offense is the primary factor used in determining whether to incarcerate a juvenile, though history of delinquency, family situation, and the offender's attitude are all relevant.

Juvenile Corrections

In general, juvenile corrections are based on the concept of **graduated sanctions**—that is, the severity of the punishment should fit the crime. Consequently, status and first-time offenders are diverted or placed on probation, repeat offenders find themselves in intensive community supervision or treatment programs, and serious and violent offenders are placed in correctional facilities.[88]

As society's expectations of the juvenile justice system have changed, so have the characteristics of its corrections programs. In some cities, for example, juvenile probation officers join police officers on the beat. Because the former are not bound by the same search and seizure restrictions as other law enforcement officials, this interdepartmental teamwork provides more opportunities to fight youth crime aggressively. Juvenile correctional facilities are also changing their operations to reflect public mandates that they should both reform and punish. Also, note that about 5,400 juveniles are in adult jails and another 45,000 are serving time in adult prisons.[89]

JUVENILE PROBATION The most common form of juvenile corrections is probation—33 percent of all delinquency cases disposed of by juvenile courts result in conditional diversion. The majority of all adjudicated delinquents (60 percent) will never receive a disposition more severe than being placed on probation.[90] These statistics reflect a general understanding among juvenile court judges and other officials that a child should normally be removed from her or his home only as a last resort.

A bailiff tells a juvenile who has just completed his community service to tuck in his shirt at a City of Houston Municipal Court hearing. Why do juvenile court judges favor community service and probation, when appropriate, as sentencing options for juveniles?

The Washington Post/Getty Images

Juvenile inmates prepare to enter a dormitory at Texas's Marlin Orientation and Assessment Unit. What might be some of the reasons that juvenile correctional facilities often operate similarly to adult prisons and jails?

The organization of juvenile probation is very similar to adult probation (see Chapter 10), and juvenile probationers are increasingly subjected to electronic monitoring and other supervisory tactics. The main difference between the two programs lies in the attitude toward the offender. Adult probation officers have an overriding responsibility to protect the community from the probationer, while juvenile probation officers are expected to take the role of a mentor or a concerned relative in looking after the needs of the child.

CONFINING JUVENILES About 70,000 American youths (down from approximately 107,000 in 1995) are incarcerated in public and private juvenile correctional facilities in the United States.[91] Most of these juveniles have committed crimes against people or property, but a significant number (about 16 percent) have been incarcerated for technical violations of their probation or parole agreements.[92] After deciding that a juvenile needs to be confined, the judge has two sentencing options: nonsecure juvenile institutions and secure juvenile institutions.

Nonsecure Confinement Some juvenile delinquents do not require high levels of control and can be placed in **residential treatment programs.** These programs, run by either probation departments or social-service departments, allow their subjects freedom of movement in the community. Generally, this freedom is predicated on the juveniles following certain rules, such as avoiding alcoholic beverages and returning to the facility for curfew. Residential treatment programs can be divided into four categories:

1. *Foster care programs,* in which the juveniles live with a couple who act as surrogate parents.
2. *Group homes,* which generally house between twelve and fifteen youths and provide treatment, counseling, and education services by a professional staff.

Residential Treatment Program A government-run facility for juveniles whose offenses are not deemed serious enough to warrant incarceration in a juvenile correctional facility.

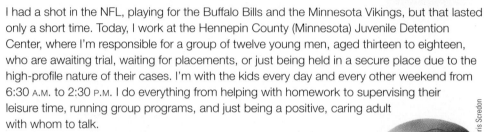

Photo Courtesy of Carl McCullough, Sr.

CARL McCULLOUGH, SR.
RESIDENT YOUTH WORKER

I had a shot in the NFL, playing for the Buffalo Bills and the Minnesota Vikings, but that lasted only a short time. Today, I work at the Hennepin County (Minnesota) Juvenile Detention Center, where I'm responsible for a group of twelve young men, aged thirteen to eighteen, who are awaiting trial, waiting for placements, or just being held in a secure place due to the high-profile nature of their cases. I'm with the kids every day and every other weekend from 6:30 A.M. to 2:30 P.M. I do everything from helping with homework to supervising their leisure time, running group programs, and just being a positive, caring adult with whom to talk.

Having the NFL experience is a huge icebreaker with the residents. "Why are you here?" they always ask me, and I tell them I am here because I care about them, because I want to see a change, and because I'd like to help them believe that something better is possible. To do this job well, you have to be good at building relationships. It helps to know how to work with different cultures as well. Then you have to have patience; without it you won't last long. You know they are going to test you, to see what they can and can't get away with. You also have to be willing to learn a few things from them. You have to be a good listener.

iStockphoto.com/Chris Scredon

Social Media Career Tip Potential employers want information about you, but they do not want your life story. To capitalize on two primary benefits of social media, personalize your message and be concise.

---

3. *Family group homes,* which combine aspects of foster care and group homes, meaning that a single family, rather than a group of professionals, looks after the needs of the young offenders.

4. *Rural programs,* which include wilderness camps, farms, and ranches where between thirty and fifty children are placed in an environment that provides recreational activities and treatment programs.

Secure Confinement Secure facilities are comparable to the adult prisons and jails we discussed in Chapters 11 and 12. These institutions go by a confusing array of names depending on the state in which they are located, but the two best known are boot camps and training schools. A **boot camp** is the juvenile variation of shock probation.

As we noted in Chapter 10, boot camps are modeled after military training for new recruits. Boot camp programs are based on the theory that by giving wayward youths a taste of the "hard life" of military-like training for short periods of time, usually no longer than 180 days, they will be "shocked" out of a life of crime. At a typical youth boot camp, inmates are grouped in platoons and live in dormitories. They spend eight hours a day training, drilling, and doing hard labor, and also participate in programs such as basic adult education and job skills training.

Boot Camp A variation on traditional shock incarceration in which juveniles (and some adults) are sent to secure confinement facilities modeled on military basic training camps instead of prison or jail.

No juvenile correctional facility is called a "prison." This does not mean they lack a strong resemblance to prisons. The facilities that most closely mimic the atmosphere at an adult correctional facility are **training schools,** alternatively known as youth camps, youth development centers, industrial schools, and several other similar titles. Whatever the name, these institutions claim to differ from their adult countparts by offering a variety of programs to treat and rehabilitate the young offenders. In reality, training schools are plagued by many of the same problems as adult prisons and jails, including high levels of inmate-on-inmate violence, substance abuse, gang wars, and overcrowding.

AFTERCARE Juveniles leave correctional facilities through an early-release program or because they have served the length of their sentences. Juvenile corrections officials recognize that many of these children, like adults, need assistance readjusting to the outside world. Consequently, released juveniles are often placed in **aftercare** programs. Based on the same philosophy that drives the prisoner reentry movement (discussed in the previous chapter), aftercare programs are designed to offer services for the juveniles, while at the same time supervising them to reduce the chances of recidivism.

The ideal aftercare program includes community support groups, aid in finding and keeping employment, and continued monitoring to ensure that the juvenile is able to deal with the demands of freedom. Statistics suggest, however, that the aftercare needs of young offenders often go unmet. Nearly 60 percent of those who have been referred to juvenile court are "re-referred" before turning eighteen years old.[93] More troubling is the notion that many juvenile offenders are likely, if not destined, to become adult offenders. A recent report on Illinois's juvenile justice system criticized it as "a 'feeder system' to the adult criminal justice system and a cycle of crime, victimization, and incarceration."[94]

> **Training School** A correctional institution for juveniles found to be delinquent or status offenders.
>
> **Aftercare** The variety of therapeutic, educational, and counseling programs made available to juvenile delinquents (and some adults) after they have been released from a correctional facility.

///SELF ASSESSMENT

Fill in the blanks, and check your answers on page 421.

A juvenile offender's delinquency is determined during the _____ hearing, which is similar in many ways to an adult trial. If the juvenile is found to be delinquent, her or his sentence is determined during the _____ hearing. The most common form of juvenile corrections is _____. If the judge decides that the juvenile needs more stringent supervision, he or she can sentence the offender to a _____ facility such as a residential treatment program. If the juvenile's offense has been particularly serious, she or he will most likely be sent to a secure confinement facility such as a _____ camp or a _____ school.

CHAPTER SUMMARY

For more information on these concepts, look back to the Learning Objective icons throughout the chapter.

 List the four major differences between juvenile courts and adult courts. Juvenile courts (a) have no juries, (b) use different terminology than adult courts, (c) avoid adversarial relationships among the parties involved, and (d) maintain confidentiality.

 Identify and briefly describe the single most important U.S. Supreme Court case with respect to juvenile justice. The case was *In re Gault,* decided by the Supreme Court in 1967. In this case, a minor was arrested for allegedly making an obscene phone call. His parents were not notified and were not present during the juvenile court judge's decision-making process. The Supreme Court held that juveniles are entitled to many of the same due process rights granted to adult offenders, including notice of charges, the right to counsel, the privilege against self-incrimination, and the right to confront and cross-examine witnesses.

Describe the reasoning behind recent U.S. Supreme Court decisions that have lessened the harshness of sentencing outcomes for violent juvenile offenders. In banning capital punishment and limiting the availability of life sentences without parole for offenders who commit their crimes as juveniles, the Supreme Court has focused on the concept of "diminished culpability." This concept is based on the notion that violent juvenile offenders cannot fully comprehend the consequences of their actions and are more deserving of the opportunity for rehabilitation than adult violent offenders.

 Explain how law enforcement's emphasis on domestic violence has influenced female juvenile arrest patterns. Girls are much more likely to fight with parents and siblings than are boys, whose physical confrontations tend to involve strangers. Because police officers have taken a more aggressive stand against domestic violence, they are more likely to arrest female juveniles involved in family disputes now than they were in the past.

 Describe the one variable that always correlates highly with juvenile crime rates. The older a person is, the less likely he or she will exhibit criminal behavior. This process is known as aging out. Thus, persons in any at-risk group will commit fewer crimes as they get older.

 List the factors that normally determine what police do with juvenile offenders. The arresting police officers consider (a) the nature of the offense, (b) the youthful offender's past criminal history, (c) the setting in which the offense took place, (d) whether the parents can and will take disciplinary action, and (e) the attitude of the offender.

 Describe the four primary stages of pretrial juvenile justice procedure. (a) Intake, in which an official of the juvenile court engages in a screening process to determine what to do with the youthful offender; (b) pretrial diversion, which may consist of probation, treatment and aid, and/or restitution; (c) transfer to an adult court, in which case the youth leaves the juvenile justice system; and (d) some type of detention, in which the youth is held until the disposition process begins.

 Explain the distinction between an adjudicatory hearing and a disposition hearing. An adjudicatory hearing is essentially a "trial" to determine whether the offender is delinquent or in need of court supervision. Defense attorneys may be present during the adjudicatory hearing in juvenile courts. In many states, once adjudication has occurred, there is a separate disposition hearing that is similar to the sentencing phase in an adult court. At this point, the court, often aided by a predisposition report, determines the sentence that serves the "needs" of the child.

QUESTIONS FOR CRITICAL ANALYSIS

1. What is the difference between a status offense and a crime? What punishments do you think should be imposed on juveniles who commit status offenses?

2. Do you think that bullying should be punishable as a felony along the same lines as assault? (For the definition of *assault,* go back to Chapter 2.) Why or why not?

3. What role should age play in determining whether a juvenile reasonably believes himself or herself to be "in custody" for purposes of a police interrogation? (See Chapter 6 to review the interrogation process.)

4. Several years ago, eight Florida teenagers ranging in age from fourteen to eighteen beat a classmate so badly that she suffered a concussion. According to law enforcement officials, the teenagers recorded the assault so that they could post it on the Internet. If you were a prosecutor and could either waive these teenagers to adult court or refer them to the juvenile justice system, which option would you choose? What other information would you need to make your decision?

5. Forty-four states have enacted parental responsibility statutes, which make parents responsible for the offenses of their children. Seventeen of these states hold parents criminally liable for their children's actions, punishing the parents with fines, community service, and even incarceration. What is your opinion of these laws—particularly those with criminal sanctions for parents?

KEY TERMS

adjudicatory hearing   414

aftercare   419

age of onset   406

aging out   406

automatic transfer   412

boot camp   418

bullying   404

child abuse   407

child neglect   407

detention   413

detention hearing   413

disposition hearing   414

graduated sanctions   416

intake   411

judicial waiver   412

juvenile delinquency   396

low-visibility decision making   410

parens patriae   395

petition   411

predisposition report   415

prosecutorial waiver   412

referral   411

residential treatment program   417

status offender   396

training school   419

youth gang   408

SELF-ASSESSMENT ANSWER KEY

Page 399: i. *parens patriae;* **ii.** status offenses; **iii.** delinquency

Page 401: i. state; **ii.** state; **iii.** impulsive; **iv.** peer; **v.** death penalty

Page 405: i. declining; **ii.** girls; **iii.** male; **iv.** School; **v.** Bullying

Page 409: i. risk; **ii.** aging out; **iii.** Child abuse; **iv.** gangs

Page 414: i. arrest; **ii.** refer; **iii.** social; **iv.** intake; **v.** diversion; **vi.** waiver

Page 419: i. adjudicatory; **ii.** disposition; **iii.** probation; **iv.** nonsecure; **v.** boot; **vi.** training

1. Jennifer M. O'Connor and Lucinda K. Treat, "Getting Smart about Getting Tough: Juvenile Justice and the Possibility of Progressive Reform," *American Criminal Law Review* 33 (Summer 1996), 1299.

2. *In re Gault*, 387 U.S. 1, at 15 (1967).

3. Samuel Davis, *The Rights of Juveniles: The Juvenile Justice System*, 2d ed. (New York: C. Boardman Co., 1995), Section 1.2.

4. Quoted in Anthony Platt, *The Child Savers* (Chicago: University of Chicago Press, 1969), 119.

5. 383 U.S. 541 (1966).

6. *Ibid.*, 556.

7. 387 U.S. 1 (1967).

8. 397 U.S. 358 (1970).

9. 421 U.S. 519 (1975).

10. 403 U.S. 528 (1971).

11. Research Network on Adolescent Development and Juvenile Justice, *Youth on Trial: A Developmental Perspective on Juvenile Justice* (Chicago: John D. & Catherine T. MacArthur Foundation, 2003), 1.

12. Richard E. Redding, "Juveniles Transferred to Criminal Court: Legal Reform Proposals Based on Social Science Research," *Utah Law Review* (1997), 709.

13. Howard N. Snyder and Melissa Sickmund, *Juvenile Offenders and Victims: A National Report* (Washington, D.C.: U.S. Department of Justice, 1995), 47.

14. Martha Grace Duncan, "'So Young and So Untender': Remorseless Children and the Expectations of the Law," *Columbia Law Review* (October 2002), 1469.

15. 543 U.S. 551 (2005).

16. *Ibid.*, 567.

17. 130 S.Ct. 2011 (2010).

18. *Ibid.*, at 2030.

19. 132 S. Ct. 2455 (2012).

20. *Ibid.*, at 2463.

21. *Surveillance Summaries: Youth Risk Behavior Surveillance—United States, 2011* (Washington, D.C.: Centers for Disease Control and Prevention, June 8, 2012).

22. Federal Bureau of Investigation, *Crime in the United States 2012* (Washington, D.C.: U.S. Department of Justice, 2013), Table 38, at **www.fbi.gov/about-us/cjis/ucr /crime-in-the-u.s/2012/crime-in-the -u.s.-2012/cius_home.**

23. Charles Puzzanchera and Sarah Hockenberry, *Juvenile Court Statistics 2010* (Washington, D.C.: National Center for Juvenile Justice, June 2013), 8.

24. Office of Juvenile Justice and Delinquency Prevention, *Juvenile Residential Facility Census, 2010: Selected Findings* (Washington, D.C.: U.S. Department of Justice, September 2013), 1; and Todd Richmond,

"Fewer Young Criminals Push States to Close Prisons," *Associated Press* (June 7, 2010).

25. David McDowell, "Juvenile Curfew Laws and Their Influence on Crime," *Federal Probation* (December 2006), 58.

26. *Crime in the United States 2012, op. cit.,* Table 38.

27. Office of Juvenile Justice and Delinquency Prevention, "Community Prevention Grants Program," at **www.ojjdp.gov/cpg.**

28. Puzzanchera and Hockenberry, *op. cit.,* 12.

29. Sara Goodkind et al., "Are Girls Really Becoming More Delinquent? Testing the Gender Convergence Hypothesis by Race and Ethnicity, 1976–2005," *Children and Youth Services Review* (August 2009), 885–889.

30. Kimberly Kempf-Leonard and Lisa Sample, "Disparity Based on Sex: Is Gender-Specific Treatment Warranted?" *Justice Quarterly* 17 (2000), 89–128.

31. Crystal Knoll and Melissa Sickmund, *Delinquency Cases in Juvenile Court, 2009* (Washington, D.C.: Office of Juvenile Justice and Delinquency Prevention, October 2012), 2.

32. *Crime in the United States 2012, op. cit.,* Table 33.

33. Margaret A. Zahn et al., "The Girls Study Group—Charting the Way to Delinquency Prevention for Girls," in *Girls Study Group: Understanding and Responding to Girls' Delinquency* (Washington, D.C.: Office of Juvenile Justice and Delinquency Prevention, October 2008), 3.

34. Puzzanchera and Hockenberry, *op. cit.,* 73.

35. Melissa Sickmund and Howard N. Snyder, *Juvenile Offenders and Victims: 1999 National Report* (Washington, D.C.: Office of Juvenile Justice and Delinquency Prevention, 1999), 58.

36. Meda Chesney-Lind, *The Female Offender: Girls, Women, and Crime* (Thousand Oaks, Calif.: Sage Publications, 1997).

37. Denise C. Gottfredson and David A. Soulé, "The Timing of Property Crime, Violent Crime, and Substance Abuse among Juveniles," *Journal of Research in Crime and Delinquency* (February 2005), 110–120.

38. National Center for Education Statistics and Bureau of Justice Statistics, *Indicators of School Crime and Safety: 2012* (Washington, D.C.: U.S. Department of Justice, June 2013), 6.

39. *Ibid.,* Figure 2.1, page 11.

40. *Ibid.,* 85–86.

41. Jacob Kang-Brown et al., *A Generation Later: What We've Learned about Zero-Tolerance in Schools* (New York: Vera Institute of Justice, December 2013), 2.

42. Barbara Raymond, "Assigning Police Officers to Schools," Center for Problem-Oriented Policing, *Response Guide No. 10* (2010), at **www.popcenter.org /Responses/school_police/print.**

43. Quoted in "Online Bullying: Charging Kids with Felonies," *The Week* (November 1, 2013), 14.

44. *Indicators of School Crime and Safety: 2012, op. cit.,* 44.

45. Jessica Bennett, "From Lockers to Lockup," *Newsweek* (October 11, 2010), 39.

46. Adam J. Speraw, "No Bullying Allowed: A Call for a National Anti-Bullying Statute to Promote a Safer Learning Environment in American Public Schools," *Valparaiso University Law Review* (Summer 2010), 1151–1198.

47. Marvin E. Wolfgang, *From Boy to Man, from Delinquency to Crime* (Chicago: University of Chicago Press, 1987).

48. Carlos A. Cuevas et al., *Children's Exposure to Violence and the Intersection between Delinquency and Victimization* (Washington, D.C.: Office of Juvenile Justice and Delinquency Prevention, October 2013), 1–2.

49. Michael Turner, "Repeat Bully Victimization and Legal Outcomes in a National Sample: The Impact over the Life Course" (2013), at **www.apa.org/news/press /releases/2013/08/bully-victimizations .pdf.**

50. Quoted in John H. Laub and Robert J. Sampson, "Understanding Desistance from Crime," in *Crime and Justice: A Review of Research* (Chicago: University of Chicago Press, 2001), 6.

51. Travis Hirschi and Michael Gottfredson, "Age and the Explanation of Crime," *American Journal of Sociology* 89 (1982), 552–584.

52. Robert J. Sampson and John H. Laub, "A Life-Course View on the Development of Crime," *Annals of the American Academy of Political and Social Science* (November 2005), 12.

53. David P. Farrington, "Offending from 10 to 25 Years of Age," in *Prospective Studies of Crime and Delinquency,* eds. Katherine Teilmann Van Dusen and Sarnoff A. Mednick (Boston: Kluwer-Nijhoff Publishers, 1983), 17.

54. Office of Juvenile Justice and Delinquency Prevention, *Juveniles in Court* (Washington, D.C.: U.S. Department of Justice, June 2003), 29.

55. Lloyd D. Johnston et al., *Monitoring the Future: National Results on Adolescent Drug Use—Overview of Key Findings, 2012* (Ann Arbor, Mich.: Institute for Social Research, February 2013), 38.

56. *Ibid.,* 11, 13.

57. Carl McCurley and Howard Snyder, *Co-occurrence of Substance Abuse Behaviors in Youth* (Washington, D.C.: Office of Juvenile Justice and Delinquency Prevention, 2008).

58. Gary McClelland, Linda Teplin, and Karen Abram, "Detection and Prevalence of Substance Abuse among Juvenile Detainees," *Juvenile Justice Bulletin* (Washington, D.C.: Office of Juvenile Justice and Delinquency Prevention, June 2004), 10.

59. Arrestee Drug Abuse Monitoring Program, *Preliminary Data on Drug Use and Related Matters among Adult Arrestees and Juvenile Detainees* (Washington, D.C.: National Institute of Justice, 2003).

60. *Mental Health Treatment for Youth in the Juvenile Justice System* (Alexandria, Va.: National Mental Health Association, 2004), 10.

61. Larry J. Siegel and Brandon C. Welsh, *Juvenile Delinquency: The Core,* 4th ed. (Belmont, Calif.: Wadsworth Cengage Learning, 2011), 268.

62. Edward P. Mulvey, *Highlights from Pathways to Desistance: A Longitudinal Study of Serious Adolescent Offenders* (Washington, D.C.: Office of Juvenile Justice and Delinquency Prevention, March 2011), 1–3.

63. Sherry Hamby et al., *Juvenile Justice Bulletin: Children's Exposure to Intimate Partner Violence and Other Family Violence* (Washington, D.C.: Office of Juvenile Justice and Delinquency Prevention, October 2011), 1.57.

64. Kimberly A. Tyler and Katherine A. Johnson, "A Longitudinal Study of the Effects of Early Abuse on Later Victimization among High-Risk Adolescents," *Violence and Victims* (June 2006), 287–291.

65. Grover Trask, "Defusing the Teenage Time Bombs," *Prosecutor* (March/April 1997), 29.

66. Ashley Nellis, *The Lives of Juvenile Lifers: Findings from a National Survey* (Washington, D.C.: The Sentencing Project, March 2012), 2.

67. Arlen Egley, Jr., and James C. Howell, *Highlights of the 2011 National Youth Gang Survey* (Washington, D.C.: Office of Juvenile Justice and Delinquency Prevention, September 2013), 1.

68. Chris Melde and Finn-Aage Esbensen, "Gang Membership as a Turning Point in the Life Course," *Criminology* (August 2011), 513–546.

69. *2011 National Gang Threat Assessment—Emerging Trends* (Washington, D.C.: National Gang Intelligence Center, 2012), 15–17.

70. Tony Dokoupil, "'Small World of Murder': As Homicides Drop, Chicago Police Focus on Social Network of Gangs," *NBC News* (December 17, 2013), at **www.nbcnews .com/news/other/small-world-murder -homicides-drop-chicago-police-focus -social-networks-f2D11758025;** and Vivian Yeem, "An 8th Grader, a Gun and a Bus Rider in the Way," *New York Times* (March 14, 2014), A1.

71. National Gang Center, "National Youth Gang Survey Analysis: Race/Ethnicity of Gang Members, 1996–2011," at **www .nationalgangcenter.gov/survey -analysis/demographics.**

72. Rachel A. Gordon, Benjamin B. Lahey, Eriko Kawai, Rolf Loeber, and Magda Stouthamer-Loeber, "Antisocial Behavior and Youth Gang Membership: Selection and Socialization," *Criminology* (February 2004), 55–89.

73. National Alliance of Gang Investigators Associates, *2005 National Gang Threat Assessment* (Washington, D.C.: Bureau of Justice Assistance, 2005), 10–11.

74. Angela Wolf and Livier Gutierrez, *It's About Time: Prevention and Intervention Services for Gang-Affiliated Girls* (Washington, D.C.: National Council on Crime and Delinquency, March 2012), 1–2.

75. Los Angeles Police Department, "Why Young People Join Gangs" (2014), at **www .lapdonline.org/top_ten_most_wanted _gang_members/content_basic_view /23473.**

76. Puzzanchera and Hockenberry, *op. cit.,* 31.

77. Knoll and Sickmund, *op. cit.,* 3.

78. 42 U.S.C. Sections 5601–5778 (1974).

79. S'Lee Arthur Hinshaw II, "Juvenile Diversion: An Alternative to Juvenile Court," *Journal of Dispute Resolution* (1993), 305.

80. Ted Gordon Lewis, "Barron County Restorative Justice Programs: A Partnership Model for Balancing Community and Government Resources for Juvenile Justice Services," *Journal of Juvenile Justice* (Fall 2011), 17–32.

81. Audrey Hickert et al., "Impact of Juvenile Drug Courts on Drug Use and Criminal Behavior," *Journal of Juvenile Justice* (Fall 2011), 60–77.

82. Puzzanchera and Hockenberry, *op. cit.,* 52.

83. Rhode Island General Laws Section 14-1-7.1 (1994 and Supp. 1996).

84. 467 U.S. 253 (1984).

85. Puzzanchera and Hockenberry, *op. cit.,* 32.

86. Knoll and Sickmund, *op. cit.,* 3.

87. Barry C. Feld, "Criminalizing the American Juvenile Court," *Crime and Justice* 17 (1993), 227–254.

88. Eric R. Lotke, "Youth Homicide: Keeping Perspective on How Many Children Kill," *Valparaiso University Law Review* 31 (Spring 1997), 395.

89. Bureau of Justice Statistics, *Jail Inmates at Midyear 2012—Statistical Tables* (Washington, D.C.: U.S. Department of Justice, May 2013), 1; and Bureau of Justice Statistics, *Prisoners in 2012—Trends in Admissions and Releases, 1991–2012* (Washington, D.C.: U.S. Department of Justice, December 2013), Appendix table 4, page 37.

90. Knoll and Sickmund, *op. cit.,* 3.

91. *Reducing Youth Incarceration in the United States* (Baltimore, Md.: The Annie E. Casey Foundation, February 2013), 1.

92. *Common Ground: Lessons Learned from Five States That Reduced Juvenile Confinement by More Than Half* (Washington, D.C.: Justice Policy Institute, February 2013), 9–10.

93. Howard N. Snyder and Melissa Sickmund, *Juvenile Offenders and Victims: 2006 National Report* (Washington, D.C.: National Center for Juvenile Justice, March 2006), 235.

94. *Youth Reentry Improvement Report* (Springfield, Ill.: Illinois Juvenile Justice Commission, November 2011), 9.

CHAPTER

14

Today's Challenges in Criminal Justice

CHAPTER OUTLINE	CORRESPONDING LEARNING OBJECTIVES
White-Collar Crime	Indicate some of the ways in which white-collar crime is different from violent or property crime.
	Explain the concept of corporate violence.
Cyber Crime	Distinguish cyber crime from "traditional" crime.
	Describe the three following forms of malware: (a) programs that create botnets, (b) worms, and (c) viruses.
Gun Control Policy	Explain how background checks, in theory, protect the public from firearm-related violence.
The Terror Threat	Describe the concept of *jihad* as practiced by al Qaeda and its followers.
	Identify three important trends in international terrorism.
	Differentiate between enemy combatants and criminal terrorist suspects.

To target your study and review, look for these numbered Learning Objective icons throughout the chapter.

Joe Raedle/Getty Images

425 \\\\\

The future OF CRIME?

MARK, a software programmer, identifies himself as a "libertarian anarchist" and believes that "anything that's not violent should not be criminalized." Unfortunately for Mark, the hallucinogenic drug LSD is criminalized, and purchasing it on the street carries a high risk of arrest and significant prison time. So, Mark decided to take a safer path. He logged onto the Internet and ordered one hundred micrograms of LSD from the online black market Web site Silk Road. Four days later, the drugs, sent from Canada, arrived at his house via the U.S. Postal Service. "It kind of felt like I was in the future," said Mark of the transaction.

Silk Road, which began operations in February 2011, hosted sellers of a wide variety of contraband, using a reputation-based trading system like those favored by legitimate sites such as eBay and Amazon. People shopping at Silk Road could buy illegal drugs such as LSD and heroin, find counterfeit passports and driver's licenses, and even engage the services of a hired assassin. Identities were protected by software known as Tor, which allows users to mask their IP addresses (codes that identify individual computers on the Internet) and the IP addresses of anyone with whom they communicate. Silk Road added another layer of privacy by requiring that all business be conducted using a virtual currency called *bitcoin* that circumvents the involvement of banks and other financial institutions.

As it turned out, Silk Road was too good to be true for the criminal underground. Using an undercover agent posing as a drug dealer, the Federal Bureau of Investigation infiltrated the Web site and eventually uncovered its crucial IP addresses. In October 2013, the federal government shut down Silk Road and seized its alleged founder Ross Ulbricht at a public library in San Francisco. "Your anonymous activity isn't anonymous," one law enforcement official warned online wrongdoers following Ulbricht's arrest. "We know where you are, what you are doing, and we will catch you."

Julia Zakharova/Shutterstock

FOR CRITICAL ANALYSIS

1. How was the anonymity provided by the Internet a win/lose proposition for Silk Road, allowing it to thrive but also leading to its downfall?

2. Should the government outlaw software such as Tor, which essentially hides the tracks of Internet users? Why or why not?

3. What are some terrorism-related homeland security concerns raised by a virtual currency such as bitcoin and a black market Web site such as Silk Road?

Silk Road, the online black market Web site, relied on bitcoin, a virtual currency represented by these golden medals, for all its illegal transactions.

WHITE-COLLAR CRIME

The black market Web site Silk Road could not have existed without the virtual currency bitcoin. As U.S. Attorney Richard Zabel pointed out, instead of needing hard cash, "users were able to purchase [illegal] drugs from anywhere in the world, essentially with the push of a button."[1] Bitcoin is not, however, inherently illegal. It is bought and sold online, just like any other commodity, and is accepted by legitimate Internet businesses such as Overstock.com.

From a law enforcement perspective, the problem with the virtual currency is that there is no way of knowing whether bitcoin online accounts are registered in the user's actual name. Thus, bitcoin is ideal for those who want to engage in *white-collar crime,* an umbrella term for wrongdoing marked by deceit and scandal rather than violence. For example, it is relatively easy to avoid paying taxes on bitcoin transactions. In addition, virtual currencies are well-suited to facilitating *money laundering,* or the process of concealing the source of illegally obtained funds, in this case by converting those funds into bitcoins.

As we mentioned in Chapter 1, white-collar crime has a broad impact on the global economy, costing American businesses hundreds of billions of dollars in losses each year. Despite its global and national importance, however, white-collar crime has consistently challenged a criminal justice system that struggles to define the problem, much less effectively combat it.

What Is White-Collar Crime?

White-collar crime is not an official category of criminal behavior measured by the federal government in the Uniform Crime Report. Rather, it covers a broad range of illegal acts involving "lying, cheating, and stealing," according to the FBI's Web site on the subject.[2] To give a more technical definition, white-collar crimes are financial activities characterized by deceit and concealment that do not involve physical force or violence. Figure 14.1 that follows lists and describes some common types of white-collar crime.

LEARNING OBJECTIVE **1** Indicate some of the ways in which white-collar crime is different from violent or property crime.

DIFFERENT TECHNIQUES To differentiate white-collar crime from "regular" crime, criminologists Michael L. Benson of the University of Cincinnati and Sally S. Simpson of the University of Maryland focus on technique. For example, in an ordinary burglary, a criminal uses physical means, such as picking a lock, to get somewhere he or she should not be—someone else's home—to do something that is clearly illegal. Furthermore, the victim is a specific, identifiable individual—the homeowner. In contrast, white-collar criminals usually (1) have legal access to the place where the crime occurs; (2) are spatially separated from the victim, who is often unknown; and (3) behave in a manner that is, at least superficially, legitimate.[3]

Benson and Simpson also identify three main techniques used by white-collar criminals to carry out their crimes:[4]

1. *Deception.* White-collar crime almost always involves a party who deceives and a party who is deceived. The nation's federal Medicare system, which provides health insurance for those sixty-five years of age and older, is a frequent target of deceptive practices. For example, in 2013, the FBI arrested six in-home health-care providers who recruited dishonest Medicare beneficiaries to request costly and unnecessary nursing services in Detroit. When the federal government

FIGURE 14.1 White-Collar Crimes

Embezzlement

Embezzlement is a form of employee fraud in which an individual uses his or her position within an organization to *embezzle,* or steal, the employer's funds, property, or other assets. Pilferage is a less-serious form of employee fraud in which the individual steals items from the workplace.

Tax Evasion

Tax evasion occurs when taxpayers underreport (or do not report) their taxable income or otherwise purposely attempt to evade a tax liability.

Credit-Card and Check Fraud

Credit-card fraud involves obtaining credit-card numbers through a variety of schemes (such as stealing them from the Internet) and using the numbers for personal gain. Check fraud includes writing checks that are not covered by bank funds, forging checks, and stealing traveler's checks.

Mail and Wire Fraud

This umbrella term covers all schemes that involve the use of mail, radio, television, the Internet, or a telephone to intentionally deceive in a business environment.

Securities Fraud

Securities fraud covers illegal activity in the stock market. Stockbrokers who steal funds from their clients are guilty of securities fraud, as are those who engage in *insider trading,* which involves buying or selling securities on the basis of information that has not been made available to the public.

Bribery

Also known as *influence peddling,* bribery occurs in the business world when somebody within a company or government sells influence, power, or information to a person outside the company or government who can benefit. A county official, for example, could give a construction company a lucrative county contract to build a new jail. In return, the construction company would give some of the proceeds, known as a *kickback,* to the official.

Consumer Fraud

This term covers a wide variety of activities designed to defraud consumers, from selling counterfeit art to offering "free" items, such as electronic devices or vacations, that include a number of hidden charges.

Insurance Fraud

Insurance fraud involves making false claims in order to collect insurance payments. Faking an injury in order to receive payments from a workers' compensation program, for example, is a form of insurance fraud.

reimbursed these health-care providers for the home care—which was never actually performed—the white-collar criminals kept the funds for themselves.

2. *Abuse of trust.* A white-collar criminal often is in a position of trust and misuses that trust for personal benefit. In 2013, for example, the FBI arrested three men for stealing about $6.7 million from a victim by convincing him that they had invested the funds in large blocks of Facebook stock.

3. *Concealment and conspiracy.* To continue their illegal activities, white-collar criminals need to conceal those activities. In *odometer fraud,* for example, an automobile dealership "rolls back" the odometers of used cars so that a higher price can be charged for the vehicles. As soon as the fraud is discovered, the scheme can no longer succeed.

VICTIMS OF WHITE-COLLAR CRIME As the above examples show, sometimes the victim of a white-collar crime is obvious. A fraudulent stockbroker is stealing directly from his or her clients, and odometer fraud denies consumers the actual value of their purchased automobiles. But who was victimized in the fraudulent Medicare benefits scheme? In that instance, the "victims" were the U.S. taxpayers, who collectively had to cover the cost of the unwarranted benefits. Such health-care scams defraud U.S. taxpayers out of at least $70 billion each year.[5] Often, white-collar crime does not target individuals but rather large groups or more abstract concepts such as "society" or "the environment."

Regulating and Policing White-Collar Crime

LEARNING

Explain the concept of corporate violence.

2

OBJECTIVE

For legal purposes, a corporation can be treated as a person capable of forming the intent necessary to commit a crime. Thus, in 2013, the British oil and gas company BP pleaded guilty to fourteen criminal charges, including manslaughter, and agreed to pay a

$4 billion fine after accepting responsibility for the *Deepwater Horizon* oil spill four years earlier. Not only did the spill off the coast of Louisiana cause immense ecological damage and threaten the livelihood of thousands of seafood suppliers, but eleven workers also died in the oil rig explosion that caused the disaster.

The aftermath of the *Deepwater Horizon* oil spill, caused by BP's negligence, is an example of *corporate violence*. In contrast to assaults committed by individual people, **corporate violence** is a result of policies or actions undertaken by a corporation. In the United States, parallel regulatory and criminal systems have evolved to prevent corporate violence and other forms of white-collar crime. (The feature *A Question of Ethics— Buyer Beware* that follows addresses the problematic question of how society should hold corporations responsible for corporate violence.)

THE REGULATORY JUSTICE SYSTEM AND WHITE-COLLAR CRIME Although most white-collar crimes cause harm, these harms are not necessarily covered by criminal statutes. Indeed, more often they are covered by *administrative* laws, which we first encountered in Chapter 3. Such laws make up the backbone of the U.S. regulatory system, through which the government attempts to control the actions of individuals, corporations, and other institutions. The goal of **regulation** is not prevention or punishment as much as **compliance,** or the following of regulatory guidelines.

For example, more than a decade ago the Food and Drug Administration (FDA) approved use of the antipsychotic drug Risperdal—produced by Johnson & Johnson—to

Corporate Violence Physical harm to individuals or the environment that occurs as the result of corporate policies or decision making.

Regulation Governmental control of society, through rules and laws, that is generally carried out by administrative agencies.

Compliance The state of operating in accordance with governmental standards.

A QUESTION OF ETHICS: Buyer BEWARE

THE SITUATION In March 2014, General Motors (GM) recalled 2.6 million Chevrolet Cobalts and other small cars because of a flawed ignition switch. According to internal company documents, in 2009 GM engineers had held a meeting concerning this defect—which caused the cars to lose power and shut down while being driven—but did nothing to warn consumers. From the time of that meeting until the recall, the faulty ignition switch was linked to crashes of GM vehicles that caused at least thirteen deaths.

THE ETHICAL DILEMMA GM's failure to warn motorists about the flawed ignition switch seems to have been based on the company's finances—an earlier recall would have cost hundreds of millions of dollars and left the company open to numerous civil lawsuits—and a desire to safeguard its reputation. Still, GM clearly had an ethical duty to protect the well-being of its clients, regardless of any other considerations.

WHAT IS THE SOLUTION? Documentary filmmaker Michael Moore suggested that GM executives and engineers should face the death penalty for "covering up" the faulty ignition switches. Although such an outcome is highly improbable, it does raise the relevant question of whether the criminal justice system can force corporations to behave ethically.

At the same time GM was recalling millions of its cars, Toyota agreed to pay a $1.2 billion fine for similarly hiding defects that are suspected of having caused more than thirty deaths between 2000 and 2010. No individual Toyota employee was the subject of a criminal inquiry, however, and the fine, though the largest ever levied against an automobile company, represented a small fraction of Toyota's worth. Do you think fines, civil lawsuits, and the financial ramifications of a damaged reputation are enough to ensure that corporations will behave ethically? (GM profits fell 85 percent in the first part of 2014.) If not, what other punishments should be considered? What might be some of the challenges of punishing individuals for corporate misdeeds?

Several years ago, Rita Crundwell was convicted of stealing more than $54 million from the city of Dixon, Illinois, for which she had been working as a financial officer. Why does Crundwell's wrongdoing fall into the category of white-collar crime?

AP Images/Sauk Valley Media/Alex T. Paschal

treat schizophrenia, a condition we discussed in Chapter 2. Violating these guidelines, representatives of Johnson & Johnson marketed Risperdal as a medication for elderly nursing home patients and children who suffered from attention deficit hyperactivity disorder and autism. In 2013, the corporation agreed to pay $2.2 billion in penalties stemming from its lack of compliance, which placed Risperdal users at risk of stroke and other health problems.

The FDA—which protects the public health by regulating food products and a wide variety of drugs and medical practices—is one of the federal administrative agencies whose compliance oversight brings them into contact with white-collar crime. Other important federal regulatory agencies that deal with white-collar crime include

1. The Environmental Protection Agency (EPA), which regulates air quality, water quality, and toxic waste. The EPA was intricately involved in the federal government's response to the *Deepwater Horizon* oil spill, described above.
2. The Occupational Safety and Health Administration (OSHA), which enforces workplace health and safety standards.
3. The Securities and Exchange Commission (SEC), which ensures that financial markets such as the New York Stock Exchange operate in a fair manner.

Many observers believe the virtual currencies such as bitcoin, discussed at the beginning of this chapter, will eventually come under greater regulatory scrutiny because of federal laws designed to prevent financial transactions through anonymous accounts.[6]

LAW ENFORCEMENT AND WHITE-COLLAR CRIME In general, when officials at a regulatory agency find that criminal prosecution is needed to punish a particular violation, they will refer the matter to the U.S. Department of Justice. Either through such referrals or at their own discretion, federal officials prosecute white-collar crime using the investigatory powers of several different federal law enforcement agencies. The FBI has become the lead agency when it comes to white-collar crime, particularly in response to recent financial scandals. The U.S. Postal Inspection Service is also quite active in such investigations, as fraudulent activities often involve the U.S. mail. In addition, the Internal Revenue Service's Criminal Investigation division has jurisdiction over a wide variety of white-collar crimes, including tax fraud, and operates perhaps the most effective white-collar crime lab in the country.[7]

Local and state agencies also investigate white-collar crimes, but because of the complexity and costs of such investigations, most are handled by the federal government. Federal prosecutors are also in a unique position to enforce the federal Racketeer Influenced and Corrupt Organizations Act (RICO), which we discussed briefly in Chapter 10. Originally designed to combat organized crime, RICO makes it illegal to receive income through a pattern of *racketeering*.[8] The definition of **racketeering** is

Racketeering The criminal action of being involved in an organized effort to engage in illegal business transactions.

so inclusive—basically covering any attempt to earn illegal income involving more than one person—that it can be used against a broad range of criminal activity. In 2013, for example, federal prosecutors used RICO to convict twenty-one members of the Hells Angels motorcycle club in South Carolina for drug and firearms trafficking, money laundering, and attempted armed robbery.

White-Collar Crime in the Early 2000s

The decade that ended in 2010 was marked by two periods of financial scandal. First, in 2001 and 2002, fraudulent accounting practices led to the demise of giant corporations such as Enron and Worldcom, costing investors tens of billions of dollars. Then, near the end of the decade, the collapse of the subprime mortgage market caused millions of Americans to lose their homes to foreclosure and led to the collapse of major financial institutions such as Lehman Brothers and Washington Mutual. Headlines focused on widespread *mortgage fraud,* or dishonest practices relating to home loans, along with the misdeeds of Bernard Madoff. Before his 2008 arrest, Madoff managed to defraud thousands of investors out of approximately $65 billion.

As has often occurred in U.S. history, these scandals and the concurrent economic downturns led to greater regulation and criminalization of white-collar crime. In 1934, for example, in the wake of the Great Depression, Congress established the SEC to watch over the American economy.[9] Similarly, in 2002 Congress passed legislation which, among other things, enhanced the penalties for those convicted of white-collar crimes.[10] In response to the "Great Recession" of 2008 and 2009, the FBI created the National Mortgage Fraud Team and began to crack down on a variety of white-collar crimes. Indeed, FBI agents are increasingly using aggressive tactics such as going undercover, planting wiretaps, and raiding offices—tactics previously reserved for drug dealers, mobsters, and terrorists—against white-collar criminals.[11]

///SELF ASSESSMENT

Fill in the blanks, and check your answers on page 452.

According to the FBI, white-collar crimes are economic activities characterized by _____ and concealment that do not involve _____. Administrative agencies such as the _____ Protection Agency make up the backbone of the U.S. regulatory system, which combats white-collar crime by requiring _____ with certain guidelines. A powerful tool for law enforcement in combating white-collar crimes, _____ can be used against groups or organizations that attempt to earn income illegally.

CYBER CRIME

Within months after being shut down by the FBI, as discussed at the beginning of the chapter, the online black market bazaar Silk Road reappeared in much the same form as before. The Web site's revival proved short-lived, however. In February 2014, online thieves stole $2.7 million of bitcoins from Silk Road's customer accounts. The site's new administrators blamed a "glitch" in the system, though some suspected that they stole the bitcoins themselves. Indeed, because bitcoins are traded electronically and are nearly impossible to trace to individuals, the perpetrators of the heist will probably never be identified.

Such is the quandary posed by the Internet for criminals and the law enforcement agents trying to stop them: The same anonymity that makes online activity appealing

Cyber Crime A crime that occurs online, in the virtual community of the Internet, as opposed to in the physical world.

also makes it vulnerable to deception. "In the eighties, if there was a bank robbery, the pool of suspects was limited to the people who were in the vicinity at the time," says Shawn Henry, former head of the FBI's cyber field office in Washington, D.C. "Now when a bank is robbed, the pool of suspects is limited to the number of people in the world with access to a $500 laptop and an Internet connection. Which . . . is two and a half billion people."[12]

Computer Crime and the Internet

Nearly every business in today's economy, including illegal ones, relies on computers to conduct its daily affairs and to provide consumers with easy access to its products and services. Furthermore, more than 500 million American household devices are now connected to the Internet, and the proliferation of handheld Internet devices has made it possible to be online at almost any time or place. In short, the Internet has become a place where large numbers of people interact socially and commercially. In any such environment, wrongdoing has an opportunity to flourish. Throughout this section, we will be using the broad term **cyber crime** to describe any criminal activity occurring via a computer in the virtual community of the Internet.

CYBER ADVANTAGES The example of *child pornography* shows how cyber crime has raised the stakes for the criminal justice system. (Child pornography is the illegal production and sale of material depicting sexually explicit conduct involving a child.) In the late 1970s, about 250 child pornography magazines were circulating in the United States, and it was relatively easy for law enforcement to confiscate these hard copies.[13] With the advent of the Internet, however, child pornography became much easier to disseminate. The reasons for this include the following:

1. *Speed.* The Internet provides a quick means of sending visual material over long distances. Child pornographers can deliver their material faster and more securely online than through regular mail.
2. *Security.* Any illegal material that passes through the hands of a mail carrier is inherently in danger of being discovered. This risk is significantly reduced with e-mail. Furthermore, Internet sites that offer child pornography can protect their customers with passwords, which keep random Web surfers (or law enforcement agents) from stumbling on the site of chat rooms.
3. *Anonymity.* Obviously, anonymity is the most important protection offered by the Internet for sellers and buyers of child pornography, as it is for any person engaged in illegal behavior in cyberspace.[14]

Because of these three factors, courts and lawmakers have had a difficult time controlling not only child pornography, but also a wide variety of other online wrongdoing.

THE INCIDENCE OF CYBER CRIME It is very difficult, if not impossible, to determine how

"You know, you can do this just as easily online."

Peter C. Vey/The New Yorker Collection/The Cartoon Bank

much cyber crime actually takes place. Often, people never know that they have been the victims of this type of criminal activity. Furthermore, businesses sometimes fail to report such crimes for fear of losing customer confidence. Nonetheless, in 2012, the Internet Crime Complaint Center (IC3), operated as a partnership between the FBI and the National White Collar Crime Center, received about 290,000 complaints representing just over $525 million in victim losses.[15] According to the Norton Cybercrime Report, nearly 50 percent of all adults who use the Internet have been victimized by cyber crime, with annual global losses exceeding $113 billion.[16]

Cyber Crimes against Persons and Property

Most cyber crimes are not "new" crimes. Rather, they are existing crimes in which the Internet is the instrument of wrongdoing. The challenge for law enforcement is to apply traditional laws, which were designed to protect persons from physical harm or to safeguard their physical property, to crimes committed in cyberspace. Here, we look at several types of activity that constitute "updated" crimes against persons and property—online consumer fraud, cyber theft, and cyber aggression.

 LEARNING OBJECTIVE 3 Distinguish cyber crime from "traditional" crime.

CYBER CONSUMER FRAUD The expanding world of e-commerce has created many benefits for consumers. It has also led to some challenging problems, including fraud conducted via the Internet. In general, fraud is any misrepresentation knowingly made with the intention of deceiving another person. Furthermore, the victim must reasonably rely on the fraudulent information to her or his detriment. **Cyber fraud,** then, is fraud committed over the Internet. Scams that were once conducted solely by mail or phone can now be found online, and new technology has led to increasingly more creative ways to commit fraud. Online dating scams, for example, have increased dramatically in recent years, with fraudsters creating fake profiles to deceive unwitting romantic partners. According to the IC3, in 2012 online romance scam artists defrauded victims out of more than $55 million.[17] In one case, a Galesburg, Illinois, woman defrauded twenty-three men she met on dating Web sites out of hundreds of thousands of dollars by asking them to help pay for her mother's fictitious medical expenses.

As you can see in Figure 14.2 alongside, fraud accounts for the largest percentage of losses related to consumer cyber crime. Two widely reported forms of cyber crime are *advance fee fraud* and *online auction fraud.* In the simplest form of advance fee fraud, consumers order and pay for items such as automobiles or antiques that are never delivered. Online auction fraud is also fairly straightforward. A person lists an item for auction, on either a legitimate or a fake auction site, and then refuses to send the product after receiving payment. In 2013, for example, U.S. Immigration and Customs Enforcement uncovered a scheme in which a group of Romanians had set up a fraudulent eBay site and convinced five American victims to send them $120,000 for nonexistent items such as boats and cars.

CYBER THEFT In cyberspace, thieves are not subject to the physical limitations of the "real" world. A thief can steal data stored in a networked computer with network access from anywhere on the globe. Only the speed of the connection and the thief's computer equipment limit the quantity of data that can be stolen.

FIGURE 14.2 **The Costs of Cyber Crime**

After polling adults in twenty-four countries, including the United States, researchers associated with the American security software company Symantec estimated that nearly 1.5 million computer users worldwide are victims of cyber crime each day. As the graph below shows, 85 percent of the financial costs associated with cyber crime are the result of fraud, theft, or computer repairs made necessary by the wrongdoing.

Other 15%
Theft 17%
Fraud 42%
Repairs 26%

Source: *2012 Norton Cybercrime Report* (Mountain View, CA: Symantec, 2012), 4, 6.

Identity Theft This freedom from physical limitations has led to a marked increase in **identity theft,** which occurs when the wrongdoer steals a form of identification—such as a name, date of birth, or Social Security number—and uses the information to access the victim's financial resources. According to the federal government, about 7 percent of American households have at least one member who has been the victim of identity theft.[18]

More than half of identity theft involves the misappropriation of an existing credit-card account.[19] In the "real world," this is generally accomplished by stealing an actual credit card. Online, an identity thief can steal financial information by fooling Web sites into thinking that he or she is the actual account holder. For example, important personal information such as one's birthday, hometown, or employer that is available on social media sites such as Facebook can be used to convince a third party to reveal the victim's Social Security or bank account number.

The more personal information a cyber criminal obtains, the easier it is for him or her to find a victim's online user name. Once the online user name has been compromised, the easier it is to steal a victim's password, which is often the last line of defense to financial information. Numerous software programs aid identity thieves in illegally obtaining passwords. A technique called *keystroke logging,* for example, relies on software that embeds itself in a victim's computer and records every keystroke made on that computer. User names and passwords are then recorded and sold to the highest bidder. Internet users should also be wary of any links contained within e-mails sent from an unknown source, as these links can sometimes be used to illegally obtain personal information. (See Figure 14.3 that follows for some hints on how to protect your online passwords.)

Phishing A distinct form of identity theft known as **phishing** adds a different wrinkle to this particular form of cyber crime. In a phishing attack, the perpetrators "fish" for financial data and passwords from consumers by posing as a legitimate business such as a bank or credit-card company. The "phisher" sends an e-mail asking the recipient to "update" or "confirm" vital information, often with the threat that an account or some other service will be discontinued if the information is not provided. Once the unsuspecting target enters the information, the phisher can use it to masquerade as the person or to drain his or her bank

FIGURE 14.3 Protecting Online Passwords

Once an online password has been compromised, the information on the protected Web site is fair game for identity thieves. By following these simple rules, you can strengthen the protection provided by your online passwords.

1. **Don't** use existing words such as your pet's name or your hometown. Such words are easy for computer identity theft programs to decode.
2. **Do** use at least eight characters in your passwords, with a nonsensical combination of upper- and lower-case letters, numbers, and symbols. A weak password is "scout1312." A strong password is "4X$dQ%3Z9j."
3. **Don't** use the same username and password for different Web accounts. If you do, then each account is in danger if one account is compromised.
4. **Do** use a different password for each Web account. If necessary, write down the various passwords and keep the list in a safe place.
5. **Don't** use information that can be easily found online or guessed at in choosing the questions that Web sites use to verify your password. That is, don't select questions such as "What is your birthday?" or "What is your city of birth?" Instead, choose questions with obscure answers that you are certain to remember or can easily look up.
6. **Don't** log on to any Web site if you are connected to the Internet via a wireless network (Wi-Fi) that is not itself password protected.

or credit account. Over the past several years, dozens of companies, including Amazon.com, Zappos.com, and LinkedIn, have been forced to warn consumers that fraudulent e-mails asking for personal and financial information had been sent in the companies' names.

Phishing scams have also spread to other areas, such as text messaging and social-networking sites. Nearly 13 percent of all phishing, for example, takes place using Facebook alerts.[20] A new form of this fraud, called spear phishing, is much more difficult to detect because the messages seem to have come from co-workers, friends, or family workers. "It's a really nasty tactic because it's so personalized," explains security expert Bruce Schneier. "It's an e-mail from your mother saying she needs your Social Security number for the will she's doing."[21]

CYBER AGGRESSION AND THE NEW MEDIA The growing use of mobile devices such as smartphones and tablets has added another outlet for online criminal activity, leading to attacks such as vishing (phishing by phone) and smishing (phishing by SMS/text message). About four in ten mobile phone users, for example, have experienced some form of cyber crime on their devices.[22] In particular, widespread smartphone use seems to have exacerbated cyberbullying, which we discussed in the context of school crime in the previous chapter. According to a recent survey, American teenagers who consider themselves "heavy users" of their cell phones are much more likely to experience cyberbullying than those who consider themselves "normal users" of the devices.[23]

In 2009, the U.S. Department of Justice released a landmark study that shed light on the high incidence of stalking in the United States. Defined as a "credible threat" that puts a person in reasonable fear for her or his safety or the safety of the person's immediate family, stalking, according to the study, affects approximately 3.4 million Americans each year.[24]

About one in four of these victims experiences a form of **cyberstalking,** in which the perpetrator uses e-mail, text messages, or some other form of electronic communication to carry out his or her harassment.[25] Nearly every state and the federal government have passed legislation to combat this criminal behavior. For instance, in April 2014, Adam Savader of Great Neck, New York, was sentenced to thirty months in federal prison for cyberstalking fifteen different women. Besides sending his victims sexually explicit e-mails, Savader stole nude photos of the women by hacking into various social media sites. He then threatened to release the photos to the victims' relatives if they did not provide him with more such images.

Cyber Crimes in the Business World

Just as cyberspace can be a dangerous place for consumers, it presents a number of hazards for businesses that wish to offer their services on the Internet. The same circumstances that enable companies to reach a large number of consumers also leave them vulnerable to cyber crime. For example, several years ago federal law enforcement agents arrested Dutch citizen David Schrooten for infecting the online sales systems of several Seattle businesses with spyware programs. This spyware collected at least 44,000 credit-card numbers, subsequently sold by Schrooten to third parties for fraudulent use.

HACKERS David Schrooten is a particular type of cyber criminal known as a *hacker*. **Hackers** are people who use one computer to illegally access another. The danger posed by hackers has increased significantly because of **botnets,** or networks of computers that

Cyberstalking The crime of stalking, committed in cyberspace through the use of e-mail, text messages, or another form of electronic communication.

Hacker A person who uses one computer to access another.

Botnet A network of computers that have been appropriated without the knowledge of their owners and used to spread harmful programs via the Internet; short for *robot network*.

LEARNING OBJECTIVE 4

Describe the three following forms of malware: (a) programs that create botnets, (b) worms, and (c) viruses.

Worm A computer program that can automatically replicate itself and interfere with the normal use of a computer. A worm does not need to be attached to an existing file to move from one network to another.

Virus A computer program that can replicate itself and interfere with the normal use of a computer. A virus cannot exist as a separate entity and must attach itself to another program to move through a network.

Spam Bulk e-mails, particularly of commercial advertising, sent in large quantities without the consent of the recipient.

Intellectual Property Property resulting from intellectual, creative processes.

have been appropriated by hackers without the knowledge of their owners. A hacker will secretly install a program on thousands, if not millions, of personal computer "robots," or "bots," that allows him or her to forward transmissions to an even larger number of systems. The program attaches itself to the host computer when someone operating the computer opens a fraudulent e-mail.

Malware Programs that create botnets are one of the latest forms of *malware*, a term that refers to any program that is harmful to a computer or, by extension, a computer user. A **worm**, for example, is a software program that is capable of reproducing itself as it spreads from one computer to the next. A **virus**, another form of malware, is also able to reproduce itself but must be attached to an "infected" host file to travel from one computer network to another. Worms and viruses can be programmed to perform a number of functions, such as prompting host computers to continually "crash" and reboot, or otherwise infect the system.

Malware is increasingly being used to target specific companies or organizations. During the 2013 holiday season, for example, a group of Eastern European hackers managed to gain access to the computer system of the retail giant Target. Once "inside," these hackers infected the in-store devices that Target customers use to swipe their credit and debit cards with a "memory scraper" malware nicknamed Kaptoxa. Over the course of several weeks, the malware was used to steal credit- and debit-card data, as well as passwords, phone numbers, and addresses, from at least 70 million Target customers. Experts estimate that the Kaptoxa virus was used to steal more than $4 billion in unrecoverable losses from these unfortunate consumers.[26]

The Spread of Spam Businesses and individuals alike are targets of **spam**, or unsolicited "junk e-mails" that flood virtual mailboxes with advertisements, solicitations, and other messages. Considered relatively harmless in the early days of the Internet, in 2013, an average of 100 billion spam messages were being sent each day. About 970 million of these spam messages contained some form of malware.[27]

Spam is also the preferred method of phishing, the identity theft scam described earlier. By sending millions or even billions of these fraudulent e-mails, phishers need only entice a few users to "take the bait" to ensure a successful and lucrative operation. Finally, "social" spam is becoming more common on social-networking sites such as Facebook. This form of hacking relies on fake messages, such as "hey, check out this free iPad," that appear to be from a friend rather than an unknown company. The message includes a link to download a coupon for the free product. In reality, however, by clicking on the link, the unsuspecting user has allowed malware to infect his or her computer.

PIRATING INTELLECTUAL PROPERTY ONLINE

Most people think of wealth in terms of houses, land, cars, stocks, and bonds. Wealth, however, also includes **intellectual property**, which

Target Corp. executive vice president John Mulligan, right, testifies before the U.S. Congress following a security breach that allowed hackers to steal financial and personal data from tens of millions of consumers. Why does this type of cyber crime fall into the category of identity theft, as described earlier in the section?

Bloomberg via Getty

consists of the products that result from intellectual, creative processes. The government provides various forms of protection for intellectual property, such as copyrights and patents. These protections ensure that a person who writes a book or a song or creates a software program is financially rewarded if that product is sold in the marketplace.

Intellectual property such as books, films, music, and software is vulnerable to "piracy"—the unauthorized copying and use of the property. In the past, copying intellectual products was time consuming, and the quality of the pirated copies was clearly inferior. In today's online world, however, things have changed. Simply clicking a mouse can now reproduce millions of unauthorized copies, and pirated duplicates of copyrighted works obtained via the Internet are often exactly the same as the original, or close to it. The Software Alliance estimates that 42 percent of all business software is pirated, costing software makers more than $63 billion each year.[28]

Encryption The translation of computer data in a secret code with the goal of protecting those data from unauthorized parties.

Fighting Cyber Crime

After Target suffered the extensive hacking attack described earlier, the company brought in private experts to plug its security holes and erase the malware from its compromised systems. Ideally, of course, corporations should have software already in place to prevent hacking operations, and most do. Businesses spend billions of dollars a year to *encrypt* their vital information. **Encryption** is the process of encoding information stored in computers in such a way that only authorized parties have access to it.

Companies will also hire outside experts to act as hackers and attempt to gain access to their systems, a practice known as "penetration testing." Even the most thorough private protection services, however, are often one step behind the ingenuity of the hacker community. In the Target attack, for example, the malware was programmed to constantly erase itself, making it practically impossible to detect. "The dynamics of the Internet and cyberspace are so fast that we have a hard time staying ahead of the adversary," admits former U.S. Secret Service agent Robert D. Rodriguez.[29]

REGULATING THE INTERNET Clearly, private industry needs government help to fight off cyber criminals. As we saw in the previous section, a primary way in which the government protects its citizens is through regulation. With hundreds of millions of users in every corner of the country transferring unimaginable amounts of information almost instantaneously, the Internet has, however, proved resistant to government regulation.

In addition, although a number of countries have tried to "control" the Internet (see the feature *Comparative Criminal Justice—The Great Firewall of China* that follows), the U.S. government has generally adopted a hands-off attitude to better promote the free flow of ideas and encourage the growth of electronic commerce. Thus, in this country cyberspace is unregulated for the most part, making efforts to fight cyber crime all the more difficult. Furthermore, many cyber criminals, such as the ones who launched the cyber attack on Target, operate in foreign countries, beyond the reach of American authorities.

CHALLENGES FOR LAW ENFORCEMENT In trying to describe the complexities of fighting cyber

POLICY.CJ

At the beginning of 2014, only three states—Delaware, Nevada, and New Jersey—allowed online gambling such as Internet poker within state limits. The rest of the country, including the federal government, bans the practice instead of regulating it. Go online and research the topic **legalize online gambling**. Then, come up with one reason in favor of legalizing online gambling in the United States and one reason against it. Finally, write one full paragraph explaining your viewpoint regarding the issue.

The Great Firewall of China

The online anonymity enjoyed by many Americans on the Internet is increasingly hard to come by in China. In 2012, the Chinese government imposed new rules that require Internet users in that country to give their real names to service providers. The regulations also require the service providers to report suspicious online activity, such as viewing pornography or the use of words such as *freedom* or *democracy,* to the authorities. Observers have little doubt that the changes are designed to restrict freedom of speech on the Internet. In the past, Chinese bloggers have been jailed for making politically sensitive comments or accusing local officials of wrongdoing.

In the United States, the issue of whether the government should regulate the Internet—and, if so, how much—is hotly debated. In China, the question was answered long before the Internet was even imagined. Since the 1950s, the Chinese Communist Party has exercised strict control over all forms of information, including newspapers, television, radio, movies, and books. Today, under the auspices of the Ministry of Industry and Information Technology, that control has been extended to the World Wide Web.

Under broad laws that prohibit, among other things, "destroying the order of society" and "making falsehoods or distorting the truth," Chinese censors have free rein to limit the flow of information through government-controlled Internet service providers. The "Great Firewall," as this system is sometimes called, routinely blocks more than a million Web sites. Many of the sites are pornographic, but the obstruction also extends to Facebook, Twitter, YouTube, and Evite. These steps anger many Chinese citizens, and a number of blogs in the country are dedicated to "tearing down the Great Firewall." One bookstore owner refused to install government-mandated monitoring software onto her establishment's Wi-Fi system, instead choosing to disconnect the service. She decried the "Orwellian surveillance system that forces my customers to disclose their identity to a government that wants to monitor how they use the Internet."

FOR CRITICAL ANALYSIS

How would the type of Internet censorship used by the Chinese government affect cyber crime in the United States? Under what circumstances, if any, would Americans accept such levels of Internet control by the government?

---

crime, Michael Vatis, former director of the FBI's National Infrastructure Protection Center, imagines a bank robbery during which the police arrive just as "the demand note and fingerprints are vanishing, the security camera is erasing its own images, and the image of the criminal is being erased from the mind of the teller."[30] The difficulty of gathering evidence is just one of the challenges that law enforcement officers face in dealing with cyber crime.

Cyber Forensics Police officers cannot put yellow tape around a computer screen or dust a Web site for fingerprints. The best, and often the only, way to fight computer crime is with technology that gives law enforcement agencies the ability to "track" hackers and other cyber criminals through the Internet. But, as Michael Vatis observed, these efforts are complicated by the fact that digital evidence can be altered or erased even as the cyber crime is being committed. In Chapter 5, we discussed forensics, or the application of science to find evidence of criminal activity. Within the past two decades, a branch of this science known as **cyber forensics** has evolved to gather evidence of cyber crimes.

The main goal of cyber forensics is to gather **digital evidence,** or information of value to a criminal investigation that is stored on, received by, or transmitted by an electronic device such as a computer. Sometimes, this evidence is not particularly difficult to find. In the Steubenville, Ohio, sexual assault case mentioned in Chapter 13, for example, the two young suspects recorded their crimes on cell phones and then posted

Cyber Forensics The application of computer technology to finding and utilizing evidence of cyber crimes.

Digital Evidence Information or data of value to a criminal investigation that are either stored or transmitted by electronic means.

the evidence on social media. A twelve-minute cell phone video even featured a witness mocking the unconscious victim as "dead" and "so raped."[31] (The growing importance of cyber crime has led a number of universities to offer graduate certificates in cyber forensics. To learn about one, go to the Web site of the Marshall University Forensic Science Center.)

Cyber Sleuthing For more complex investigations, experts in cyber forensics can employ software that retraces a suspect's digital movements. Such software works by creating a digital duplicate of the targeted hard drive, enabling cyber sleuths to break access codes, determine passwords, and search files. "Short of taking your hard drive and having it run over by a Mack truck," says one expert, "you can't be sure that anything is truly deleted from your computer."[32]

The latest challenge to cyber investigators is posed by *cloud computing*, in which data are stored not in a physical location but in a virtual, shared computing platform that is linked simultaneously to a number of different computers. Therefore, law enforcement officers investigating wrongdoing in the "cloud" may not have full control of the "crime scene."[33]

////SELF ASSESSMENT

Fill in the blanks, and check your answers on page 452.

Web thieves have opportunities to practice _____ theft because of the large amount of personal financial information that is stored on the Internet. A _____ is someone who gains illegal access to one computer by using another computer. These wrongdoers sometimes use _____, or networks of hijacked computers, to carry out various improper online activities, including the illegal spread of junk e-mails known as _____. To protect the data on their computer systems, corporations use a process called _____, which encodes digital information in such a way that only authorized parties can access it.

GUN CONTROL POLICY

Federal law regarding firearm sales online is fairly strict. The seller cannot simply mail the gun to the buyer. Instead, the seller must send the gun to a store or dealer that has been licensed by the federal government, and the buyer must pick up the gun in person. In May 2013, however, libertarian activist Cody Wilson uploaded instructions for making a plastic gun (using a 3-D printer) to the Internet. Within forty-eight hours, blueprints for this firearm—which fires .380 caliber bullets and is effective at short range—were downloaded 100,000 times and shared across the expanse of the Web.[34]

Being plastic, this gun can pass through metal detectors at airports, schools, and government buildings without notice. Consequently, some observers called for the federal government to ban it. Others insisted that the plastic gun should be regulated like any other firearm, meaning that it would be widely available to the public. Thus, this new type of weapon became another flashpoint in the debate over *gun control,* the shorthand term for policies that the government implements to regulate firearm ownership.

Firearms in the United States

Gun ownership is widespread in the United States, with about one-third of American households possessing at least one firearm.[35] According to the Congressional Research Service, there are about 310 million guns in the United States, not counting weapons on military bases.[36] Furthermore, there are nearly 130,000 federally licensed firearms dealers in this country, compared with about 144,000 gas stations and 14,000 McDonald's restaurants.[37]

Curtis Reeves, shown here in a Dade City, Florida, courtroom, was charged with second degree murder after fatally shooting another man during an argument over text messaging in a movie theater. How does this sort of incident impact your opinion concerning laws that allow registered gun owners to carry their weapons in public?

Explain how background checks, in theory, protect the public from firearm-related violence.

LEARNING

5

OBJECTIVE

The vast majority of gun owners are law-abiding citizens who use firearms for self-protection or recreational activities. Still, about 31,000 people are killed by gunfire in the United States each year, and firearms are used in 69 percent of the nation's murders and 41 percent of its robberies.[38] Furthermore, illegally obtained firearms are a constant concern for law enforcement officials and, apparently, many citizens. A recent poll showed that about half of Americans favor stricter measures by the government to control gun ownership.[39]

Regulating Gun Ownership

The Second Amendment to the U.S. Constitution states, "A well regulated Militia, being necessary to the security of a free State, the right of the people to keep and bear Arms, shall not be infringed." Because this language is somewhat archaic and vague, the United States Supreme Court has attempted to clarify the amendment's modern meaning. Over the course of two separate rulings, the Court stated that the Second Amendment provides individuals with a constitutional right to bear arms and that this right must be recognized at all levels of government—federal, state, and local.[40]

BACKGROUND CHECK In both its Second Amendment cases, the Supreme Court emphasized that, to promote public safety, the government could continue to prohibit certain individuals—such as criminals and the mentally ill—from legally purchasing firearms. The primary method for doing so involves **background checks** of individuals who purchase firearms from federally licensed gun dealers.

The mechanics of background checks are regulated by the Brady Handgun Violence Prevention Act, enacted in 1993.[41] Known as the Brady Bill, this legislation requires a person wishing to purchase a gun from a licensed firearms dealer to apply for the privilege of doing so. The application process includes a background check by a law enforcement agency, usually the FBI. The applicant can be prohibited from purchasing a firearm if his or her record contains one of a number of "red flags," including a previous felony conviction, evidence of illegal drug addiction, or wrongdoing associated with domestic violence.[42]

The Brady Bill has been criticized for requiring background checks only for those consumers who purchase guns from federally licensed firearms dealers. It does not cover purchases made at gun shows or from private citizens, which make up a significant percentage of the market.

Background Check An investigation of a person's history to determine whether that person should be allowed a certain privilege, such as the ability to possess a firearm.

MENTAL HEALTH ISSUES Crucially, any person who has been involuntarily committed to a "mental institution" or "adjudicated as a mental defective" is also barred from purchasing or possessing firearms. The designation of being "mentally defective" is given to a person whom a court or other legal entity determines

1. Is a danger to herself or himself or others,
2. Lacks the mental capacity to manage her or his own affairs, or
3. Has been found insane or incompetent to stand trial by a criminal or military court.[43]

Though this designation seems fairly broad, it fails to cover a wide range of behavior. For example, about a month before Aaron Alexis fatally shot twelve people at the Washington Naval Yard, an incident covered in Chapter 2, he reported hearing voices from the walls of hotel rooms. As a result, he was voluntarily treated at two separate military hospitals for mental illness. Because voluntary commitments do not fall under the legal definition of being "adjudicated as a mental defective," Alexis was able to legally purchase the shotgun he used for his shooting spree.[44]

Another problem with the background check system is that it relies on states to provide the federal government with mental-health information about their citizens. When states fail to do so, a background check is somewhat meaningless. In one well-known example of a background check failure, in 2005 a Virginia judge declared Virginia Tech student Seung-Hui Cho to be mentally ill. The state did not, however, submit Cho's name to the FBI, as required by federal law. Consequently, Cho was able to pass a background check and purchase several handguns. On April 16, 2007, he used the weapons to kill thirty-two people and injure seventeen others on the Virginia Tech campus in Blacksburg.

RECENT LEGISLATIVE GUN CONTROL EFFORTS On December 14, 2012, Adam Lanza shot and killed twenty first-graders and six staff members at Sandy Hook Elementary School in Newtown, Connecticut. In the aftermath of this tragedy, the U.S. Senate considered a bill to expand background checks for gun buyers beyond those required by the Brady Bill. The proposed legislation would have also banned certain semiautomatic weapons, which can rapidly fire multiple rounds, and the high-capacity ammunition clips that allow them to do so. In April 2013, the Senate defeated these proposed measures, reflecting the power of anti-gun control activists in our political landscape.[45]

Because of federal inaction, it has been left to the individual states to pass stricter gun control measures, if their elected officials choose to do so. In the twelve months following the Sandy Hook shootings, states passed thirty-nine laws tightening gun ownership regulations. The New York Secure Firearms Enforcement Act, for example, requires background checks for private gun transactions and for the sale of ammunition. The law also makes it more difficult to purchase semiautomatic weapons and easier to keep firearms out of the hands of the mentally ill within state limits.[46]

During that same twelve-month period, states passed seventy laws removing restrictions on the sale and use of firearms. Eight of these new laws allow guns on grade school grounds, two allow guns on college campuses, and several others allow people to carry firearms in churches and bars.[47] (To express your own opinion on this divisive issue, see the feature *CJ Controversy—The Debate over Gun Control* that follows.)

///// SELF ASSESSMENT

Fill in the blanks, and check your answers on page 452.

_____ _____ refers to government policies designed to regulate the possession and sale of firearms in the United States. The United States Supreme Court has ruled that, although the _____ Amendment of the Constitution gives citizens the right to bear arms, governments can prohibit certain individuals, such as criminals and the _____ _____, from purchasing firearms. To regulate firearms sales, the government can require individuals to undergo a _____ _____ before purchasing a firearm, to ensure that the person does not have a prior _____ conviction or any other statutorily determined "red flags" in her or his past.

THE DEBATE OVER GUN CONTROL

Critics of our nation's gun laws have been disappointed that high-profile shooting sprees such as those carried out by Adam Lanza and Aaron Alexis, mentioned in the text, have not led to greater gun control in the United States. Opponents of stricter gun control laws point out that firearm massacres are quite rare and, in fact, our gun homicide rates are at historically low levels. They also reject the notion that firearms themselves are to blame for violent crime. Said one gun seller, "That's like pointing a finger at Ford and blaming them for car deaths."

THE U.S. SHOULD MAKE IT HARDER FOR PEOPLE TO OWN GUNS BECAUSE . . .

- The importance of guns for self-protection is overstated. Less than 1 percent of all gun deaths involve self-defense, with the rest being accidents, suicides, and homicides.

- Semiautomatic weapons that can rapidly fire multiple rounds of bullets, such as the .223 Bushmaster used by Lanza, are designed for military use and do not belong in the hands of civilians.

THE U.S. SHOULD NOT MAKE IT HARDER FOR PEOPLE TO OWN GUNS BECAUSE . . .

- Someone who is going to commit a crime with a gun is probably going to obtain that firearm illegally. Consequently, stricter gun control would "prevent only law-abiding citizens from owning handguns."

- Firearms give citizens the ability to protect themselves and their families against criminal attacks when public law enforcement agents are unable to do so.

Your Assignment

To learn more about each side of the gun control debate, visit the Web sites of the **Brady Campaign to Prevent Gun Violence** and the **National Rifle Association (NRA).** Do you think that our government should place greater restrictions on gun ownership and use? Why or why not? Your answer should include at least two full paragraphs.

THE TERROR THREAT

In the first chapter of this textbook, we defined *terrorism* as the use or threat of violence in furtherance of political objectives. Today, the dominant strain of terrorism mixes political goals with very strong religious affiliations. Modern terrorism is also characterized by extreme levels of violence. In September 2013, a four-day raid on a shopping mall in Nairobi, Kenya, left more than sixty dead and almost two hundred wounded. The January 24, 2011, suicide bombing at Russia's busiest airport in Moscow killed at least 35 people and injured 150 more. And, of course, the September 11, 2001, attacks on New York and Washington, D.C., claimed nearly three thousand lives. Indeed, the power of terrorism is a direct result of the fear caused by this violence—not only the fear that such atrocities will be repeated, but also that next time, they will be much worse.

The Global Context of Terrorism

Generally, terrorist acts are not the acts of nations or legally appointed governments. Rather, terror is the realm of **nonstate actors,** free of control by or allegiance to any nation, who use violence to further their own goals. At the same time, as David A. Westbrook of the University at Buffalo Law School (New York) points out, the large scale and financial resources of some modern terrorist organizations make them as powerful as many nations, if not more so.[48]

Nonstate Actor An entity that plays a role in international affairs but does not represent any established state or nation.

In addition, the high body counts associated with the worst terrorist acts seem better described in terms of war than of crime, which in most cases involves two people—the criminal and the victim. Thus, perhaps the most satisfying description of terrorism is as a "supercrime" that incorporates many of the characteristics of international warfare.[49] Indeed, it often seems that the United States is "at war" with al Qaeda, the organization responsible for the September 11, 2001, attacks against this country.

AL QAEDA AND *JIHAD* The al Qaeda organization grew out of a network of volunteers who migrated to Afghanistan in the 1980s to rid that country of foreign occupiers. The group was lead by Osama bin Laden, a young militant from a wealthy family in Saudi Arabia.

A. Majeed/AFP/Getty Images

Bin Laden and his comrades considered their actions to be a form of *jihad,* a controversial term that has been the subject of much confusion. Contrary to what many think, *jihad* does not mean "holy war." Rather, it refers to three kinds of struggle, or exertion, required of the Muslim faithful:

1. The struggle against the evil in oneself,
2. The struggle against the evil outside oneself, and
3. The struggle against nonbelievers.[50]

Many Muslims assert that this can be achieved without violence and denounce the form of *jihad* practiced by al Qaeda. Clearly, however, bin Laden and his followers rejected the notion that *jihad* can be accomplished through peaceable efforts.

In the 1990s, bin Laden began to turn his attention to the United States, and al Qaeda set its sights on American interests abroad. In 1998, for example, the organization bombed two U.S. embassies in Africa, killing 231 people. Two years later, al Qaeda agents launched a suicide attack on the U.S.S. *Cole,* a Navy destroyer docked in Aden, a port in the small Middle Eastern country of Yemen, during which seventeen U.S. sailors died.

About a year after the September 11, 2001, attacks, bin Laden wrote a letter to the American people outlining the reasons behind al Qaeda's opposition to the U.S. government. These included American support for Israel, which is widely seen as an enemy to Muslims, and U.S. exploitation of Islamic countries for their oil. Furthermore, bin Laden criticized the presence of U.S. military forces in the Middle East, "spreading your ideology and thereby polluting the hearts of our people."[51]

A Continuing Threat On May 1, 2011, a team of U.S. Navy Seals killed bin Laden during a shootout with his bodyguards near Islamabad, the capital of Pakistan. A year after bin Laden's death, Matthew Olsen, the director of the National Counterterrorism Center, said that the "core al Qaeda," which operates out of Pakistan, "was at its weakest point in the last ten years."[52] More than half of the group's leaders had been killed

Volunteers search a destroyed vehicle following a suicide bombing that killed nine people in Peshawar, Pakistan, on April 16, 2013. The attack targeted an election campaign rally and was evidently carried out by the Taliban, a group that opposes Pakistan's political process. Explain why such acts of violence are considered "terrorism."

LEARNING OBJECTIVE **6** Describe the concept of *jihad* as practiced by al Qaeda and its followers.

by American military raids and drone strikes, and its members were focused more on survival than on planning large-scale terrorist operations.

Weakened as it may be, al Qaeda is still a formidable organization. It now relies on a loose affiliation of franchises that operate in Iraq, Yemen, Somalia, Nigeria, and other nations—"more of a McDonald's . . . than a General Motors," in the words of one expert.[53] For example, an al Qaeda spinoff operating out of Algeria has been linked with the killings of four Americans in Benghazi, Libya, on September 11, 2012. The September 2013 massacre at the shopping mall in Nairobi, Kenya, discussed earlier, was carried out by the al-Shabaab group, a partner of al Qaeda based in the African country of Somalia. (See Figure 14.4 that follows for a description of some of al Qaeda's "franchises.")

FIGURE 14.4 Al Qaeda's Global Partners

The Islamist groups described in this figure are loosely affiliated with the "original" al Qaeda. They have a number of different goals, showing the diversity of international terrorist groups that base themselves in the Middle East.

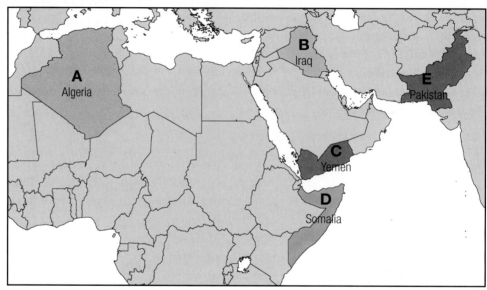

GROUP	GOALS	HIGH-PROFILE ACTIVITY
A. Al Qaeda in Islamic Maghreb (AQIM)	Remove Algeria's government; attack the United States.	In 2007, detonated car bombs outside the Algerian prime minister's office and several police stations—the blasts killed more than 30 and wounded more than 150.
B. Al Qaeda in Iraq (AQI)	Harass American military in Iraq; oust elected Iraqi government.	Destabilizes Iraqi society with numerous suicide bombing attacks on U.S. military personnel and local civilians.
C. Al Qaeda in the Arabian Peninsula (AQAP)	Establish safe haven for like-minded terrorists in Yemen.	Trained underwear suicide bomber who attempted to destroy a Northwest Airlines flight to Detroit in 2009; shipped packages containing bombs to Jewish religious centers in Chicago in 2010.
D. Al-Shabaab	Establish Islamic law in Somalia.	In 2013, laid siege to a shopping mall in Nairobi, Kenya, killing more than sixty people and wounding close to two hundred.
E. Lashkar-e-Taiba	Establish Islamic rule in India; unite Muslims in region.	Launched three days of coordinated attacks in Mumbai, India, in 2008, killing 164 and wounding 308.

Self-Radicalization Despite heavy activity by al Qaeda splinter groups near their home bases in the Middle East, one U.S. official says that is it "really hard to imagine" one of them "gathering together the resources, the talent, and the money to mount another 9/11-type of attack."[54] As an alternative, al Qaeda operations on American soil are largely limited to using propaganda videos and "call to action" messages circulated via social media. Indeed, FBI director James Comey identifies homegrown extremists as the primary terrorist threat facing the United States today.[55]

Such fears were certainly given credence by the actions of Tamerlan Tsarnaev, 26, and his younger brother Dzokhar, 19, who allegedly detonated two bombs near the finish line of the Boston Marathon on April 15, 2013. The Tsarnaevs apparently found instructions for making the explosives, which killed three people and wounded more than 260 others, in the online magazine *Inspire,* which frequently publishes Web articles with titles such as "Make a Bomb in the Kitchen of Your Mom." A year before the bombings, Tamerlan, who was killed during a police chase after the attacks, made a YouTube playlist that indicated a growing interest in Islamic radicalism.

"Self-radicalized" terrorists such as the Tsarnaev brothers have the ability to operate under law enforcement's radar up until the moment they strike. This ability is often used as justification for preventive policing, described in Chapter 5, which relies on informants and undercover agents to stop homegrown terrorist plots before they develop. Such tactics can be effective on the international level as well. Several years ago, for example, a double agent posing as a suicide bomber managed to infiltrate al Qaeda in the Arabian Peninsula. When, in 2012, this agent was given a mission to destroy a U.S.-bound airplane with a bomb to be hidden in his clothing, he delivered the explosive device to American intelligence agents instead.

TERRORISM TRENDS FOR THE FUTURE Smaller operations involving American-born terrorists influenced by international sources reflect several trends identified by homeland security expert Brian M. Jenkins. Each of these trends de-emphasizes the importance of any single, dominant organization such as al Qaeda:[56]

1. *Terrorists have developed more efficient methods of financing their operations,* through avenues such as Internet fund-raising, drug trafficking, and money laundering schemes.

2. *Terrorists have developed more efficient organizations* based on the small-business model, in which individuals are responsible for different tasks including recruiting, planning, propaganda, and social services such as supporting the families of suicide bombers. These "employees" do not answer to a single leader but rather function as a network that is quick to adjust and difficult to infiltrate.

3. *Terrorists have exploited new communications technology to mount global campaigns,* relying on the Internet for immediate, direct communication among operatives and as a crucial recruiting tool. Furthermore, large numbers of "jihobbyists" are operating online, disseminating extremist writings and videos, and using social media to spread the terrorist message in cyberspace.

LEARNING OBJECTIVE **7** Identify three important trends in international terrorism.

As you may have noted, each of these trends favors the global terrorism movement. Indeed, Jenkins finds that today's *jihadists* are dangerous, resilient survivors who have achieved some strategic results and are determined to continue attacking their enemies. "Destroying their terrorist enterprise," he concludes, "will take years."[57]

Keystone/Gaetan Bally/Redux

Without warning, on August 1, 2013, the federal government shut down nineteen U.S. diplomatic missions in the Middle East and north Africa and issued a worldwide travel alert. As it turned out, the National Security Agency (NSA) had intercepted satellite phone calls between Ayman al-Zawahiri, the head of al Qaeda, and other terrorist leaders suggesting that Americans in the region might be targeted for attack.

In Chapter 6, we saw that the NSA has come under a great deal of criticism for collecting data on American citizens in the name of homeland security. Despite this controversy, many experts still consider the agency crucial to protecting the United States against international terrorists. To this end, the NSA is using radio frequency technology, code-named Quantum, that allows it to upload spyware onto computer networks even if those computers are not connected to the Internet. With this spyware, NSA agents can collect and alter data on the infected computer without its owner's knowledge. By 2014, the NSA had implanted Quantum spyware in nearly 100,000 computers worldwide.

Thinking about the Quantum Project

How can the Quantum Project protect Americans from terrorist attacks that originate abroad? How could this spyware be use domestically to fight crime? What concerns if any, do you have about Quantum's potential impact on the privacy of Americans?

Counterterrorism Strategies

On the morning of September 12, 2001, al Qaeda spokesman Sulaiman Abu Ghaith stood by the side of his father-in-law, Osama bin Laden, and celebrated the previous day's attacks against the United States. Almost thirteen years later, in March 2014, a jury in New York convicted Abu Ghaith on numerous counts of plotting to kill Americans, giving a federal judge the option of sentencing the defendant to life in prison.

Despite Abu Ghaith's conviction, a number of politicians criticized the U.S. Department of Justice's decision to try him in criminal court instead of treating him as a military prisoner. These critics believe that by providing Abu Ghaith and other possible terrorists the constitutional protections offered to criminal suspects (discussed in Chapter 6), the government is giving up valuable opportunities to gather intelligence. "A foreign member of al Qaeda should never be treated like a common criminal and should never hear the words 'you have a right to remain silent,'" said a group of Senate Republicans in a press release.[58] The debate over "what to do" with suspected terrorists has divided American lawmakers for more than a decade and appears set to continue well into the future.

THE CRIMINAL JUSTICE MODEL Under the *criminal justice model* of homeland security, terrorism is treated like any other crime. That is, the law enforcement, court, and corrections systems work together to deter terrorist activity through the threat of arrest and punishment, as was the case with Sulaiman Abu Ghaith. Since the September 11, 2001, attacks, the criminal justice system has, as we have seen throughout this textbook, been very active in apprehending, prosecuting, and convicting terrorist suspects.

Photo Courtesy of Paul Morris

PAUL MORRIS

CUSTOMS AND BORDER PROTECTION AGENT

The most memorable day of my career was, without a doubt, September 11, 2001. That morning, as I watched the fall of the Twin Towers, I knew that things were going to be different. Personally, the attacks left me with a resolve to ensure, to the maximum extent possible, that nothing similar ever happens again. Professionally, that day marked a sea change with respect to how the federal border agencies viewed border security. Ever since, our anti-terrorism mission has been elevated above our other responsibilities, such as controlling illegal immigration, protecting our agricultural interests, and stopping the flow of illegal narcotics into this country.

To be sure, as each of these tasks is crucially important, the extra burdens of anti-terrorism pose a significant challenge. With the volume of vehicles, cargo, and persons crossing our borders, there can be no guarantees that a potential terrorist or weapon of mass destruction cannot slip across the border. Nevertheless, with advanced identification technology, increased personnel, and a more efficient infrastructure, I am confident that the possibility of such a breach is low.

www.dhs.gov

Social Media Career Tip Consider setting up personal and career-oriented Facebook pages or Twitter accounts and keeping your posts on each separated. Remember, though, that just because material is on your "personal" page or account, it still may be seen by others outside your network.

Material Support One of the country's most important counterterrorism criminal laws was passed in response to the 1995 truck bombing of the Alfred P. Murrah Federal Building in Oklahoma City, Oklahoma, which killed 168 people. The primary goal of this legislation, the Antiterrorism and Effective Death Penalty Act (AEDPA), was to hamper terrorist organizations by cutting off their funding. The law prohibits persons from "knowingly providing material support or resources" to any group that the United States has designated a "foreign terrorist organization."[59]

Material support is defined very broadly in the legislation, covering funding, financial services, lodging, training, expert advice or assistance, communications equipment, transportation, and other physical assets.[60] For example, several years ago, an American citizen named Tarek Mehanna was convicted under the AEDPA for posting videos and documents on the Internet that, among other things, glorified suicide bombings. Even though Mehanna never planned or attempted to carry out any terrorist activity, he was sentenced to 210 months in prison. Sulaiman Abu Ghaith was similarly convicted of providing material support to terrorists, mainly for appearing in a series of videos lauding al Qaeda's violent goals.

Terrorism Convictions From 2001 to 2014, federal prosecutors have successfully tried more than four hundred defendants on terrorism-related charges in criminal court.[61] Most of these defendants violated the AEDPA, the Patriot Act (see Chapter 1), and other

> **Material Support** An umbrella term for criminal aid to a terrorist organization that covers not only financial support, but also logistical support such as expert advice or assistance.

antiterrorism laws relating to the use of *weapons of mass destruction* and conspiracy to murder Americans in foreign countries. (**Weapons of mass destruction** is an umbrella term used to cover deadly instruments that represent a significant threat to persons or property.)

THE MILITARY MODEL From 2001 to 2009, the administration of President George W. Bush made it clear that, besides the criminal justice model, there was a parallel response to the terrorist threat: the *military model*. Although the scope of this textbook does not include U.S. military actions in Afghanistan, Iraq, and other global "hot spots," the militarization of the fight against terrorists did lead to several developments with repercussions for the criminal justice system.

Under President Bush, the U.S. Department of Defense was authorized to designate certain terrorist suspects detained during the course of military operations as **enemy combatants.** According to the policy at the time, this designation allowed a suspect to be "held indefinitely until the end of America's war on terrorism or until the military determines on a case-by-case basis that the particular detainee no longer poses a threat to the United States or its allies."[62] Although some observers argued that the alleged Boston Marathon bomber Dzokhar Tsarnaev should be considered an enemy combatant, federal officials refused. According to federal law, an enemy combatant must be a (1) foreign national who has (2) provided "substantial assistance" to one of several international terrorist groups, including al Qaeda. Tsarnaev, an American citizen, met neither requirement.[63]

In the several years following September 11, 2001, about eight hundred enemy combatants were transferred to the U.S. Naval Base at Guantánamo Bay, Cuba (GTMO). These detainees were denied access to legal representation and family members, and were subjected to harsh interrogation tactics such as simulated drowning, sleep and food deprivation, physical stress positions, and isolation.[64] As a result of the conditions at GTMO, the U.S. government has come under a great deal of international criticism,

LEARNING **8** OBJECTIVE

Differentiate between enemy combatants and criminal terrorist suspects.

Weapon of Mass Destruction A weapon that has the capacity to cause large number of casualties or significant property damage.

Enemy Combatant A foreign national who has supported foreign terrorist organizations such as al Qaeda that are engaged in hostilities against the military operations of the United States.

particularly from Arab and Muslim countries and from those non-Muslim nations, such as Australia and Great Britain, whose citizens have been held at the detention center.

Political Issues By May 2014, about 150 detainees remained at GTMO, with the rest having been released or repatriated to their home countries. The Obama administration has indicated a strong desire to close down the facility, and no new prisoners have been sent to GTMO since President Obama took office in 2009. Indeed, that year the president proposed moving all GTMO detainees to a supermax prison in Illinois. As a response, the U.S. Congress passed legislation that barred the transfer of any detained enemy combatants onto domestic soil.[65]

Security Issues Regardless of congressional opposition, the president does have the option of using an executive waiver to transfer GTMO detainees to the mainland United States. Despite his misgivings about "keeping individuals in no man's land in perpetuity,"[66] as of the summer of 2014 President Obama had not taken advantage of this waiver. The reason: many homeland security officials believe that these detainees still pose a threat. About one in seven individuals released from GTMO has returned, or is suspected of having returned, to terrorist activities.[67] One former prisoner, Said Ali al-Shihri, became the deputy leader of al Qaeda operations in Yemen.[68]

In 2008, the United States Supreme Court ruled that GTMO detainees should have a "meaningful opportunity" to challenge their incarceration in court.[69] Four years later, however, even though the federal government had provided no such opportunity, the Court refused to revisit the issue.[70] Furthermore, at least fifty GTMO inmates are considered too dangerous for release. Federal officials will review their status periodically, but in theory they could be held indefinitely.[71] In the spring of 2013, frustration over the possibility of indefinite detention led to hunger strikes involving nearly one hundred GTMO detainees that lasted the better part of a year.

MILITARY TRIBUNALS Besides indefinite detention, the other possibility for those who remain incarcerated at GTMO involves **military tribunals,** which are held at the naval base. Such tribunals—also known as *military commissions*—offer more limited protections than those afforded to defendants in civilian courts, as described in Chapter 8. In a tribunal, the accused does not have the right to a trial by jury, as guaranteed by the Sixth Amendment. Instead, a panel of at least five military commissioners acts in place of the judge and jury, and decides questions of both "fact and law."

Only two-thirds of the panel members need to agree for a conviction, in contrast to the unanimous jury required by criminal trials. Furthermore, evidence that would be inadmissible in criminal court, such as some forms of hearsay testimony (discussed in Chapter 8) and "fruit of the poisoned tree" from unreasonable searches and seizures (discussed in Chapter 6), is allowed before these tribunals.[72] (See Figure 14.5 that follows for an overview of the rules that govern military trials.)

TRIBUNAL TROUBLES The track record of military tribunals as an instrument for bringing terrorists to justice is not encouraging. Since September 11, 2001, federal prosecutors operating in civilian criminal courts have obtained convictions of sixty-seven terrorist suspects captured on foreign soil. During that same time period, only six GTMO detainees have been found guilty, and all of these convictions have been the result of plea bargaining.[73]

FIGURE 14.5 Military Trials for Terrorist Suspects

The guidelines for military tribunals can be found in the Military Commissions Act of 2009. Several basic questions concerning the procedures used in such tribunals are answered below.

Who is eligible to appear before a military tribunal?

Only "unprivileged enemy belligerents" can be tried by a military tribunal. A person is considered an "unprivileged enemy belligerent" if he or she

A. Has engaged in hostilities against the United States or one of its military allies;

B. Has purposefully and materially supported hostilities against the United States or one of its military allies; or

C. Was a member of al Qaeda at the time of the offense.

Who decides the suspect's guilt or innocence?

A suspect's fate will be decided by a tribunal of at least five military officers. The vote will be conducted in secret, and a two-thirds majority is necessary to find the suspect guilty.

What procedural protections will the suspect be granted during military tribunals?

The military tribunals provide the following procedural protections:

A. The right of the accused to present witnesses in his or her defense and cross-examine hostile witnesses.

B. Protection against self-incriminating statements (see Chapter 8).

C. A ban on statements obtained through cruel, inhuman, or degrading treatment.

D. The ability to offer the affirmative defense of mental disease or defect (see Chapter 3).

Source: Military Commissions Act of 2009, Public Law No. 111-84, Sections 1801–1807, 123 Stat. 2190 (2009).

Furthermore, military tribunal efforts to prosecute Khalid Sheikh Mohammed, the self-proclaimed mastermind behind the September 11 attacks, and four of his co-conspirators have been plagued by delays. These proceedings commenced in May 2012. By April 2014, after ten pretrial sessions, a trial date still seemed years in the future, as the sides argued over the admissibility of evidence relating to the detainees' treatment by government agents while in custody. "It's one thing to have a fair trial," said Don Arias, whose brother Adam was killed in New York City on September 11, 2001. "It's another to drag it out and drag it out."[74]

////SELF ASSESSMENT

Fill in the blanks, and check your answers on page 452.

Terrorists are _____ actors, meaning that they are not affiliated with any established nation. Under the criminal justice model of homeland security, terrorist acts are treated like _____, and terrorists are prosecuted in _____ courts. Under the military model, suspected terrorists are designated _____ _____ and tried by military _____.

CHAPTER SUMMARY

For more information on these concepts, look back to the Learning Objective icons throughout the chapter.

 Indicate some of the ways in which white-collar crime is different from violent or property crime. A wrongdoer committing a standard crime usually uses physical means to get somewhere he or she legally should not be in order to do something clearly illegal. Also, the victims of violent and property crimes are usually easily identifiable. In contrast, a white-collar criminal generally has legal access to the crime scene where he or she is doing something seemingly legitimate. Furthermore, victims of white-collar crimes are often unknown or unidentifiable.

 Explain the concept of corporate violence. Corporate violence occurs when a corporation implements policies that ultimately cause harm to individuals or the environment.

 Distinguish cyber crime from "traditional" crime. Most cyber crimes are not "new" types of crimes. Rather, they are traditional crimes committed in cyberspace. Perpetrators of cyber crimes are often aided by certain aspects of the Internet, such as its ability to cloak the user's identity and its effectiveness as a conduit for transferring—or stealing—large amounts of information very quickly.

 Describe the three following forms of malware: (a) programs that create botnets, (b) worms, and (c) viruses. (a) Damaging software programs create botnets, or networks of computers that have been hijacked without the knowledge of their owners and used to spread harmful programs across the Internet. (b) A worm is a damaging software program that reproduces itself as it moves from computer to computer. (c) A virus is a damaging software program that must be attached to an "infected" host file to transfer from one computer to the next.

 Explain how background checks, in theory, protect the public from firearm-related violence. Any person who wants to buy a firearm from a federally licensed dealer must go through an application process that includes a background check. This process is designed to keep firearms out of the hands of individuals who are deemed safety risks. Consequently, a person will fail the background check—and have the gun purchase denied—if he or she exhibits any one of a number of dangerous tendencies, including showing signs of mental illness, having a felony conviction, being addicted to illegal drugs, or engaging in domestic violence.

 Describe the concept of *jihad* as practiced by al Qaeda and its followers. *Jihad* is a term for the struggle against evil that the Muslim faith demands of its adherents. As practiced by al Qaeda and other religious extremist groups, the tenets of *jihad* focus on violent action against "evil" nonbelievers, a viewpoint that is rejected by the majority of Muslims.

 Identify three important trends in international terrorism. (a) Terrorists have developed more efficient methods of financing their operations. (b) Terrorists have developed more efficient organizations, based on the small-business model. (c) Terrorists have exploited new communications technology to mount global campaigns.

 Differentiate between enemy combatants and criminal terrorist suspects. Enemy combatants are taken into the custody of the U.S. military and do not enjoy the same level of constitutional protection as do terrorist suspects charged with criminal behavior. For example, enemy combatants have been subjected to indefinite detention, and their cases are adjudicated by military tribunals, not civilian criminal courts.

QUESTIONS FOR CRITICAL ANALYSIS

1. After being found guilty of defrauding thousands of investors out of approximately $65 billion, seventy-one-year-old Bernie Madoff was sentenced to 150 years in prison. Do you think this is a fair punishment for white-collar criminality? Why or why not?

2. According to several studies, someone who is a victim of a cyber crime such as identity theft has a relatively high risk of being a victim of the same crime again. Why do you think this is the case?

3. Consider the following proposed state law: *It is unlawful for any person, with intent to terrify, intimidate, threaten, harass, annoy, or offend, to use ANY ELECTRONIC OR DIGITAL DEVICE and use any obscene, lewd, or profane language.* What is your opinion of this statute? What might be some of its unforeseen consequences?

4. Should someone with a valid license be allowed to carry a concealed weapon on the grounds of a college campus? How about in a college dorm or classroom? Explain your answers.

5. According to Donna Marsh, whose pregnant daughter was killed on September 11, 2001, in New York City, it is "unconscionable" to hold enemy combatants for more than a decade without trial, and it "demeans the United States' justice system" to say these suspects cannot be tried in civilian courts. What is your opinion of these statements?

KEY TERMS

SELF-ASSESSMENT ANSWER KEY

Page 431: i. deceit; **ii.** violence/physical force; **iii.** Environmental; **iv.** compliance; **v.** RICO/antiracketeering laws

Page 439: i. identity; **ii.** hacker; **iii.** botnets; **iv.** spam; **v.** encryption

Page 441: i. Gun control; **ii.** Second; **iii.** mentally ill; **iv.** background check; **v.** felony

Page 450: i. nonstate; **ii.** crimes; **iii.** criminal/civilian; **iv.** enemy combatants; **v.** tribunals/commissions

NOTES

1. Quoted in Tom Hays, "Officials Leery of Virtual Currency," *Arizona Daily Star* (February 17, 2014), A13.

2. The Federal Bureau of Investigation, "White-Collar Crime" at **www.fbi.gov /about-us/investigate/white_collar /whitecollarcrime.**

3. Michael L. Benson and Sally S. Simpson, *White-Collar Crime: An Opportunity Perspective* (New York: Routledge, 2009), 79–80.

4. *Ibid.,* 81–87.

5. "SIRF's Up," *The Economist* (November 30, 2013), 27.

6. Peter J. Henning, "More Bitcoin Regulation Is Inevitable," *Dealbook* (February 3, 2014), at **dealbook.nytimes.com/2014/02/03 /more-bitcoin-regulation-is-inevitable /?_php=true&_type=blogs&_r=0.**

7. David O. Friedrichs, *Trusted Criminals: White Collar Crime in Contemporary Society,* 4th ed. (Belmont, Calif.: Wadsworth Cengage Learning, 2010), 278–283.

8. Lawrence Salinger, *Encyclopedia of White-Collar and Corporate Crime,* 2d ed. (Thousand Oaks, Calif.: Sage, 2004), 361.

9. 15 U.S.C. Sections 78a *et seq.*

10. White-Collar Crime Penalty Enhancement Act of 2002, 18 U.S.C. Sections 1341, 1343, 1349–1350.

11. Peter Lattman and William K. Rashbaum, "A Trader, an F.B.I. Witness, and Then a Suicide," *Reuters* (June 2, 2011).

12. Quoted in John Seabrook, "Network Insecurity," *The New Yorker* (May 20, 2013), 64.

13. Richard Wortley and Stephen Smallbone, "The Problem of Internet Child Pornography," Center for Problem-Oriented Policing (2006), at **www.popcenter.org /problems/child_pornography.**

14. William R. Graham, Jr., "Uncovering and Eliminating Child Pornography Rings on the Internet," *Law Review of Michigan State University Detroit College of Law* (Summer 2000), 466.

15. Internet Crime Complaint Center, *IC3 2012 Internet Crime Report* (Glen Allen, Va.: National White Collar Crime Center, 2013), 4.

16. *2013 Norton Report* (Mountain View, Calif.: Symantec, 2013), 4, 11.

17. Internet Crime Complaint Center, *op. cit.,* 16.

18. Bureau of Justice Statistics, *Identity Theft Reported by Households, 2005–2010* (Washington, D.C.: U.S. Department of Justice, November 2011), 1.

19. *Ibid.*, Table 4, page 5.

20. Benny Evangelista Alejandro Martinez-Cabrera, "Big Jump in Number of People on Twitter," *San Francisco Chronicle* (September 4, 2010), D2.

21. Quoted in Matt Richtel and Verne G. Kopytoff, "E-Mail Fraud Hides behind Friendly Face," *New York Times* (June 3, 2011), A1.

22. *2013 Norton Report, op. cit.,* 7.

23. "Openet-Sponsored Study Reveals 41 Percent of Teenagers Experience Cyberbullying" (January 18, 2012), at **www.openet.com/company/news-events/pressreleases?id=482.**

24. Bureau of Justice Statistics, *Stalking Victimization in the United States* (Washington, D.C.: U.S. Department of Justice, January 2009), 1.

25. *Ibid.*

26. Elizabeth E. Harris et al., "A Sneaky Path into Target Customers' Wallets," *New York Times* (January 18, 2014), A1.

27. "Q1 2013 Report: 973 Million Malware Emails Sent Out Each Day," *Softpedia* (May 2, 2013), at **news.softpedia.com/news/Q1-2013-Report-973-Million-Malware-Emails-Sent-Out-Each-Day-350611.shtml.**

28. *Shadow Market: 2011 BSA Global Software Piracy Study* (Washington, D.C.: Business Software Alliance, May 2012), 1.

29. Quoted in Marc Santora, "In Hours, Thieves Took $45 Million in A.T.M. Scheme," *New York Times* (May 10, 2013), A1.

30. Quoted in Richard Rapaport, "Cyberwars: The Feds Strike Back," *Forbes* (August 23, 1999), 126.

31. "Steubenville: A Very Modern Rape Case," *The Week* (March 29, 2013), 19.

32. Quoted in "Cybersleuths Find Growing Role in Fighting Crime," *HPC Wire,* at **www.hpcwire.com/hpc-bin/artread.pl?direction=Current&articlenumber=19864.**

33. George Grispos and William B. Glisson, "Calm Before the Storm: The Challenges of Cloud Computing in Digital Forensics," *International Journal of Digital Crime and Forensics* (2012), 28–48.

34. "Downloading Guns: Firearms Go Digital," *The Week* (May 24, 2013), 4.

35. James Lindgren, "Fall from Grace: Arming America and the Bellesiles Scandal," *Yale Law Journal* 111 (2002), 2203.

36. Bureau of Alcohol, Tobacco, Firearms and Explosives, *Firearms Commerce in the United States 2011* (Washington, D.C.: U.S. Department of Justice, August 2011), 15.

37. Mathias H. Heck, Jr., "Section Offers Forum for Discussion of Gun Policy," *Criminal Justice* (Winter 2014), 1.

38. Federal Bureau of Investigation, *Crime in the United States 2012* (Washington, D.C.: U.S. Department of Justice, 2013), at **www.fbi.gov/about-us/cjis/ucr/crime-in-the-u.s/2012/crime-in-the-u.s.-2012/cius_home,** Expanded homicide data table 7 and table 15.

39. Lydia Saad, "U.S. Remains Divided over Passing Stricter Gun Laws," *Gallup Politics* (October 25, 2013), at **www.gallup.com/poll/165563/remains-divided-passing-stricter-gun-laws.aspx.**

40. *District of Columbia v. Heller,* 554 U.S. 570 (2008); and *McDonald v. Chicago,* 561 U.S. 3025 (2010).

41. 18 U.S.C. 922(t).

42. Ronald J. Frandsen et al., *Background Checks for Firearm Transfers, 2010—Statistical Tables* (Washington, D.C.: U.S. Department of Justice, February 2013), 1.

43. 27 C.F.R. Section 478.11 (2010).

44. Josh Horowitz, "How Aaron Alexis Passed a Background Check and Bought a Gun," *Huffington Post* (September 19, 2013), at **www.huffingtonpost.com/josh-horwitz/how-aaron-alexis-passed-a_b_3955687.html.**

45. Jonathan Weisman, "Senate Blocks Drive for Gun Control," *New York Times* (April 18, 2013), A1.

46. "Governor Cuomo Signs NY Safe Act in Rochester" (January 16, 2013), at **www.governor.ny.gov/press/12162013cuomo-signs-safe-act-roch.**

47. Herbert Buchsbau, "Amid Wave of Pro-Gun Legislation, Georgia Proposes Sweeping Law," *New York Times* (March 25, 2014), A11.

48. David A. Westbrook, "Bin Laden's War," *Buffalo Law Review* (December 2006), 981–1012.

49. George P. Fletcher, "The Indefinable Concept of Terrorism," *Journal of International Criminal Justice* (November 2006), 894–911.

50. Ahmed S. Hashim, "Al-Qaida: Origins, Goals, and Grand Strategy," in *The McGraw-Hill Homeland Security Handbook,* ed. David G. Kamien (New York: McGraw-Hill, 2006), 24.

51. Quoted in *ibid.,* 9.

52. Quoted in Steve Coll, "Name Calling," *The New Yorker* (March 4, 2013), 17.

53. Quoted in Josh Meyer, "Small Groups Seen as Biggest Threat in U.S.," *Los Angeles Times* (August 16, 2007), 1.

54. Quoted in Siobhan Gorman, "Terror Risk Falls, U.S. Officials Say," *Wall Street Journal* (April 28–29, 2012), A4.

55. Timothy M. Phelps, "Terrorist Threat in U.S. Declining, FBI Director Says," *Arizona Daily Star* (November 15, 2013), A15.

56. Brian Michael Jenkins, "The New Age of Terrorism," in *The McGraw-Hill Homeland Security Handbook, op. cit.,* 117–129.

57. *Ibid.,* 128.

58. Quoted in Peter Finn, "Somali's Case a Template for U.S. as It Seeks to Prosecute Terrorism Suspects in Federal Court," *Washington Post* (March 30, 2013), A1.

59. 18 U.S.C. Section 2339B(a)(1) (1996).

60. 18 U.S.C. Section 2339A(b) (Supp. I 2001).

61. Christopher Matthews, "U.S.'s Shift on Terror Prosecutions Bears Fruit," *Wall Street Journal* (March 28, 2014), at **online.wsj.com/news/articles/SB10001424052702304688104579467533591475394.**

62. *In re Guantánamo Detainee Cases,* 535 F.Supp.2d 443, 447 (D.D.C. 2005).

63. Rachel Weiner, "Experts: 'Enemy Combatant' Designation Makes No Sense in Tsarnaev Case," *Washington Post* (April 22, 2013), at **www.washingtonpost.com/blogs/the-fix/wp/2013/04/22/experts-enemy-combatant-designation-would-make-no-sense-in-tsarnaev-case.**

64. Michael Greenberger, "You Ain't Seen Nothin' Yet: The Inevitable Post-Hamdan Conflict between the Supreme Court and the Political Branches," *Maryland Law Review* 66 (2007), 805, 807.

65. Public Law Number 111-383 (January 7, 2011).

66. Quoted in Charlie Savage, "Obama Renews Push to Close Cuba Prison," *New York Times* (May 1, 2013), A1.

67. "One in 7 Who Leave Guantanamo Involved in Terrorism," *Reuters* (May 26, 2009), at **www.reuters.com/article/2009/05/26/us-usa-guantanamo-idUSTRE54P5RY20090526.**

68. Brian Bennett, "Former Detainees Now Plot in Yemen," *Los Angeles Times* (November 2, 2010), A1.

69. *Boumediene v. Bush,* 553 U.S. 723 (2008).

70. Adam Liptak, "Justices Reject Detainees' Appeal, Leaving Cloud over Earlier Guantánamo Ruling," *New York Times* (June 12, 2012), A14.

71. Charlie Savage, "U.S. Prepares to Lift Ban on Guantanamo Cases," *New York Times* (January 20, 2011), A1.

72. Military Commission Act of 2009, Pub. L. No. 111-84, Sections 1801–1807, 123 Stat. 2190 (2009).

73. Charlie Savage, "Guantanamo Detainee Pleads Guilty in 2002 Attack on Tanker Off Yemen," *New York Times* (February 21, 2014), A17.

74. Quoted in "9/11 Trial Could Be Years Away," *San Francisco Chronicle* (April 18, 2014), A4.

The Constitution of the United States

PREAMBLE

We the People of the United States, in Order to form a more perfect Union, establish Justice, insure domestic Tranquility, provide for the common defence, promote the general Welfare, and secure the Blessings of Liberty to ourselves and our Posterity, do ordain and establish this Constitution for the United States of America.

ARTICLE I

Section 1. All legislative Powers herein granted shall be vested in a Congress of the United States, which shall consist of a Senate and House of Representatives.

Section 2. The House of Representatives shall be composed of Members chosen every second Year by the People of the several States, and the Electors in each State shall have the Qualifications requisite for Electors of the most numerous Branch of the State Legislature.

No Person shall be a Representative who shall not have attained to the Age of twenty five Years, and been seven Years a Citizen of the United States, and who shall not, when elected, be an Inhabitant of that State in which he shall be chosen.

Representatives and direct Taxes shall be apportioned among the several States which may be included within this Union, according to their respective Numbers, which shall be determined by adding to the whole Number of free Persons, including those bound to Service for a Term of Years, and excluding Indians not taxed, three fifths of all other Persons. The actual Enumeration shall be made within three Years after the first Meeting of the Congress of the United States, and within every subsequent Term of ten Years, in such Manner as they shall by Law direct. The Number of Representatives shall not exceed one for every thirty Thousand, but each State shall have at Least one Representative; and until such enumeration shall be made, the State of New Hampshire shall be entitled to chuse three, Massachusetts eight, Rhode Island and Providence Plantations one, Connecticut five, New York six, New Jersey four, Pennsylvania eight, Delaware one, Maryland six, Virginia ten, North Carolina five, South Carolina five, and Georgia three.

When vacancies happen in the Representation from any State, the Executive Authority thereof shall issue Writs of Election to fill such Vacancies.

The House of Representatives shall chuse their Speaker and other Officers; and shall have the sole Power of Impeachment.

Section 3. The Senate of the United States shall be composed of two Senators from each State, chosen by the Legislature thereof, for six Years; and each Senator shall have one Vote.

Immediately after they shall be assembled in Consequence of the first Election, they shall be divided as equally as may be into three Classes. The Seats of the Senators of the first Class shall be vacated at the Expiration of the second Year, of the second Class at the Expiration of the fourth Year, and of the third Class at the Expiration of the sixth Year, so that one third may be chosen every second Year; and if Vacancies happen by Resignation, or otherwise, during the Recess of the Legislature of any State, the Executive thereof may make temporary Appointments until the next Meeting of the Legislature, which shall then fill such Vacancies.

No Person shall be a Senator who shall not have attained to the Age of thirty Years, and been nine Years a Citizen of the United States, and who shall not, when elected, be an Inhabitant of that State for which he shall be chosen.

The Vice President of the United States shall be President of the Senate, but shall have no Vote, unless they be equally divided.

The Senate shall chuse their other Officers, and also a President pro tempore, in the Absence of the Vice President, or when he shall exercise the Office of President of the United States.

The Senate shall have the sole Power to try all Impeachments. When sitting for that Purpose, they shall be on Oath or Affirmation. When the President of the United States is tried, the Chief Justice shall preside: And no Person shall be convicted without the Concurrence of two thirds of the Members present.

Judgment in Cases of Impeachment shall not extend further than to removal from Office, and disqualification to hold and enjoy any Office of honor, Trust, or Profit under the United States: but the Party convicted shall nevertheless be liable and subject to Indictment, Trial, Judgment, and Punishment, according to Law.

Section 4. The Times, Places and Manner of holding Elections for Senators and Representatives, shall be prescribed in each State by the Legislature thereof; but the Congress may at any time by Law make or alter such Regulations, except as to the Places of chusing Senators.

The Congress shall assemble at least once in every Year, and such Meeting shall be on the first Monday in December, unless they shall by Law appoint a different Day.

Section 5. Each House shall be the Judge of the Elections, Returns, and Qualifications of its own Members, and a Majority of each shall constitute a Quorum to do Business; but a smaller Number may adjourn from day to day, and may be authorized to compel the Attendance of absent Members, in such Manner, and under such Penalties as each House may provide.

Each House may determine the Rules of its Proceedings, punish its Members for disorderly Behavior, and, with the Concurrence of two thirds, expel a Member.

Each House shall keep a Journal of its Proceedings, and from time to time publish the same, excepting such Parts as may in their Judgment require Secrecy; and the Yeas and Nays of the Members of either House on any question shall, at the Desire of one fifth of those Present, be entered on the Journal.

Neither House, during the Session of Congress, shall, without the Consent of the other, adjourn for more than three days, nor to any other Place than that in which the two Houses shall be sitting.

Section 6. The Senators and Representatives shall receive a Compensation for their Services, to be ascertained by Law, and paid out of the Treasury of the United States. They shall in all Cases, except Treason, Felony and Breach of the Peace, be privileged from Arrest during their Attendance at the Session of their respective Houses, and in going to and returning from the same; and for any Speech or Debate in either House, they shall not be questioned in any other Place.

No Senator or Representative shall, during the Time for which he was elected, be appointed to any civil Office under the Authority of the United States, which shall have been created, or the Emoluments whereof shall have been increased during such time; and no Person holding any Office under the United States, shall be a Member of either House during his Continuance in Office.

Section 7. All Bills for raising Revenue shall originate in the House of Representatives; but the Senate may propose or concur with Amendments as on other Bills.

Every Bill which shall have passed the House of Representatives and the Senate, shall, before it become a Law, be presented to the President of the United States; If he approve he shall sign it, but if not he shall return it, with his Objections to the House in which it shall have originated, who shall enter the Objections at large on their Journal, and proceed to reconsider it. If after such Reconsideration two thirds of that House shall agree to pass the Bill, it shall be sent together with the Objections, to the other House, by which it shall likewise be reconsidered, and if approved by two thirds of that House, it shall become a Law. But in all such Cases the Votes of both Houses shall be determined by Yeas and Nays, and the Names of the Persons voting for and against the Bill shall be entered on the Journal of each House respectively. If any Bill shall not be returned by the President within ten Days (Sundays excepted) after it shall have been presented to him, the Same shall be a Law, in like Manner as if he had signed it, unless the Congress by their Adjournment prevent its Return in which Case it shall not be a Law.

Every Order, Resolution, or Vote, to which the Concurrence of the Senate and House of Representatives may be necessary (except on a question of Adjournment) shall be presented to the President of the United States; and before the Same shall take Effect, shall be approved by him, or being disapproved by him, shall be repassed by two thirds of the Senate and House of Representatives, according to the Rules and Limitations prescribed in the Case of a Bill.

Section 8. The Congress shall have Power To lay and collect Taxes, Duties, Imposts and Excises, to pay the Debts and provide for the common Defence and general Welfare of the United States; but all Duties, Imposts and Excises shall be uniform throughout the United States;

To borrow Money on the credit of the United States;

To regulate Commerce with foreign Nations, and among the several States, and with the Indian Tribes;

To establish an uniform Rule of Naturalization, and uniform Laws on the subject of Bankruptcies throughout the United States;

To coin Money, regulate the Value thereof, and of foreign Coin, and fix the Standard of Weights and Measures;

To provide for the Punishment of counterfeiting the Securities and current Coin of the United States;

To establish Post Offices and post Roads;

To promote the Progress of Science and useful Arts, by securing for limited Times to Authors and Inventors the exclusive Right to their respective Writings and Discoveries;

To constitute Tribunals inferior to the supreme Court;

To define and punish Piracies and Felonies committed on the high Seas, and Offenses against the Law of Nations;

To declare War, grant Letters of Marque and Reprisal, and make Rules concerning Captures on Land and Water;

To raise and support Armies, but no Appropriation of Money to that Use shall be for a longer Term than two Years;

To provide and maintain a Navy;

To make Rules for the Government and Regulation of the land and naval Forces;

To provide for calling forth the Militia to execute the Laws of the Union, suppress Insurrections and repel Invasions;

To provide for organizing, arming, and disciplining, the Militia, and for governing such Part of them as may be employed in the Service of the United States, reserving to the States respectively, the Appointment of the Officers, and the Authority of training the Militia according to the discipline prescribed by Congress;

To exercise exclusive Legislation in all Cases whatsoever, over such District (not exceeding ten Miles square) as may, by Cession of particular States, and the Acceptance of Congress, become the Seat of the Government of the United States, and to exercise like Authority over all Places purchased by the Consent of the Legislature of the State in which the Same shall be, for the Erection of Forts, Magazines, Arsenals, dock-Yards, and other needful Buildings;—And

To make all Laws which shall be necessary and proper for carrying into Execution the foregoing Powers, and all other Powers vested by this Constitution in the Government of the United States, or in any Department or Officer thereof.

Section 9. The Migration or Importation of such Persons as any of the States now existing shall think proper to admit, shall not be prohibited by the Congress prior to the Year one thousand eight hundred and eight, but a Tax or duty may be imposed on such Importation, not exceeding ten dollars for each Person.

The privilege of the Writ of Habeas Corpus shall not be suspended, unless when in Cases of Rebellion or Invasion the public Safety may require it.

No Bill of Attainder or ex post facto Law shall be passed.

No Capitation, or other direct, Tax shall be laid, unless in Proportion to the Census or Enumeration herein before directed to be taken.

No Tax or Duty shall be laid on Articles exported from any State.

No Preference shall be given by any Regulation of Commerce or Revenue to the Ports of one State over those of another: nor shall Vessels bound to, or from, one State be obliged to enter, clear, or pay Duties in another.

No Money shall be drawn from the Treasury, but in Consequence of Appropriations made by Law; and a regular Statement and Account of the Receipts and Expenditures of all public Money shall be published from time to time.

No Title of Nobility shall be granted by the United States: And no Person holding any Office of Profit or Trust under them, shall, without the Consent of the Congress, accept of any present, Emolument, Office, or Title, of any kind whatever, from any King, Prince, or foreign State.

Section 10. No State shall enter into any Treaty, Alliance, or Confederation; grant Letters of Marque and Reprisal; coin Money; emit Bills of Credit; make any Thing but gold and silver Coin a Tender in Payment of Debts; pass any Bill of Attainder, ex post facto Law, or Law impairing the Obligation of Contracts, or grant any Title of Nobility.

No State shall, without the Consent of the Congress, lay any Imposts or Duties on Imports or Exports, except what may be absolutely necessary for executing its inspection Laws: and the net Produce of all Duties and Imposts, laid by any State on Imports or Exports, shall be for the Use of the Treasury of the United States; and all such Laws shall be subject to the Revision and Controul of the Congress.

No State shall, without the Consent of Congress, lay any Duty of Tonnage, keep Troops, or Ships of War in time of Peace, enter into any Agreement or Compact with another State, or with a foreign Power, or engage in War, unless actually invaded, or in such imminent Danger as will not admit of delay.

ARTICLE II

Section 1. The executive Power shall be vested in a President of the United States of America. He shall hold his Office during the Term of four Years, and, together with the Vice President, chosen for the same Term, be elected, as follows:

Each State shall appoint, in such Manner as the Legislature thereof may direct, a Number of Electors, equal to the whole Number of Senators and Representatives to which the State may be entitled in the Congress; but no Senator or Representative, or Person holding an Office of Trust or Profit under the United States, shall be appointed an Elector.

The Electors shall meet in their respective States, and vote by Ballot for two Persons, of whom one at least shall not be an Inhabitant of the same State with themselves. And they shall make a List of all the Persons voted for, and of the Number of Votes for each; which List they shall sign and certify, and transmit sealed to the Seat of the Government of the United States, directed to the President of the Senate. The President of the Senate shall, in the Presence of the Senate and House of Representatives, open all the Certificates, and the Votes shall then be counted. The Person having the greatest Number of Votes shall be the President, if such Number be a Majority of the whole Number of Electors appointed; and if there be more than one who have such Majority, and have an equal Number of Votes, then the House of Representatives shall immediately chuse by Ballot one of them for President; and if no Person have a Majority, then from the five highest on the List the said House shall in like Manner chuse the President. But in chusing the President, the Votes shall be taken by States, the Representation from each State having one Vote; A quorum for this Purpose shall consist of a Member or Members from two thirds of the States, and a Majority of all the States shall be necessary to a Choice. In every Case, after the Choice of the President, the

Person having the greater Number of Votes of the Electors shall be the Vice President. But if there should remain two or more who have equal Votes, the Senate shall chuse from them by Ballot the Vice President.

The Congress may determine the Time of chusing the Electors, and the Day on which they shall give their Votes; which Day shall be the same throughout the United States.

No person except a natural born Citizen, or a Citizen of the United States, at the time of the Adoption of this Constitution, shall be eligible to the Office of President; neither shall any Person be eligible to that Office who shall not have attained to the Age of thirty five Years, and been fourteen Years a Resident within the United States.

In Case of the Removal of the President from Office, or of his Death, Resignation or Inability to discharge the Powers and Duties of the said Office, the same shall devolve on the Vice President, and the Congress may by Law provide for the Case of Removal, Death, Resignation or Inability, both of the President and Vice President, declaring what Officer shall then act as President, and such Officer shall act accordingly, until the Disability be removed, or a President shall be elected.

The President shall, at stated Times, receive for his Services, a Compensation, which shall neither be increased nor diminished during the Period for which he shall have been elected, and he shall not receive within that Period any other Emolument from the United States, or any of them.

Before he enter on the Execution of his Office, he shall take the following Oath or Affirmation: "I do solemnly swear (or affirm) that I will faithfully execute the Office of President of the United States, and will to the best of my Ability, preserve, protect and defend the Constitution of the United States."

Section 2. The President shall be Commander in Chief of the Army and Navy of the United States, and of the Militia of the several States, when called into the actual Service of the United States; he may require the Opinion, in writing, of the principal Officer in each of the executive Departments, upon any Subject relating to the Duties of their respective Offices, and he shall have Power to grant Reprieves and Pardons for Offenses against the United States, except in Cases of Impeachment.

He shall have Power, by and with the Advice and Consent of the Senate to make Treaties, provided two thirds of the Senators present concur; and he shall nominate, and by and with the Advice and Consent of the Senate, shall appoint Ambassadors, other public Ministers and Consuls, Judges of the supreme Court, and all other Officers of the United States, whose Appointments are not herein otherwise provided for, and which shall be established by Law; but the Congress may by Law vest the Appointment of such inferior Officers, as they think proper, in the President alone, in the Courts of Law, or in the Heads of Departments.

The President shall have Power to fill up all Vacancies that may happen during the Recess of the Senate, by granting Commissions which shall expire at the End of their next Session.

Section 3. He shall from time to time give to the Congress Information of the State of the Union, and recommend to their Consideration such Measures as he shall judge necessary and expedient; he may, on extraordinary Occasions, convene both Houses, or either of them, and in Case of Disagreement between them, with Respect to the Time of Adjournment, he may adjourn them to such Time as he shall think proper; he shall receive Ambassadors and other public Ministers; he shall take Care that the Laws be faithfully executed, and shall Commission all the Officers of the United States.

Section 4. The President, Vice President and all civil Officers of the United States, shall be removed from Office on Impeachment for, and Conviction of, Treason, Bribery, or other high Crimes and Misdemeanors.

ARTICLE III

Section 1. The judicial Power of the United States, shall be vested in one supreme Court, and in such inferior Courts as the Congress may from time to time ordain and establish. The Judges, both of the supreme and inferior Courts, shall hold their Offices during good Behaviour, and shall, at stated Times, receive for their Services a Compensation, which shall not be diminished during their Continuance in Office.

Section 2. The judicial Power shall extend to all Cases, in Law and Equity, arising under this Constitution, the Laws of the United States, and Treaties made, or which shall be made, under their Authority;—to all Cases affecting Ambassadors, other public Ministers and Consuls;—to all Cases of admiralty and maritime Jurisdiction;—to Controversies to which the United States shall be a Party;—to Controversies between two or more States;—between a State and Citizens of another State;—between Citizens of different States;—between Citizens of the same State claiming Lands under Grants of different States, and between a State, or the Citizens thereof, and foreign States, Citizens or Subjects.

In all Cases affecting Ambassadors, other public Ministers and Consuls, and those in which a State shall be a Party, the supreme Court shall have original Jurisdiction. In all the other Cases before mentioned, the supreme Court shall have appellate Jurisdiction, both as to Law and Fact, with such Exceptions, and under such Regulations as the Congress shall make.

The Trial of all Crimes, except in Cases of Impeachment, shall be by Jury; and such Trial shall be held in the State where the said Crimes shall have been committed; but when not committed within any State, the Trial shall be at such Place or Places as the Congress may by Law have directed.

Section 3. Treason against the United States, shall consist only in levying War against them, or, in adhering to their Enemies, giving them Aid and Comfort. No Person shall be convicted of Treason unless on the Testimony of two Witnesses to the same overt Act, or on Confession in open Court.

The Congress shall have Power to declare the Punishment of Treason, but no Attainder of Treason shall work Corruption of Blood, or Forfeiture except during the Life of the Person attainted.

ARTICLE IV

Section 1. Full Faith and Credit shall be given in each State to the public Acts, Records, and judicial Proceedings of every other State. And the Congress may by general Laws prescribe the Manner in which such Acts, Records and Proceedings shall be proved, and the Effect thereof.

Section 2. The Citizens of each State shall be entitled to all Privileges and Immunities of Citizens in the several States.

A Person charged in any State with Treason, Felony, or other Crime, who shall flee from Justice, and be found in another State, shall on Demand of the executive Authority of the State from which he fled, be delivered up, to be removed to the State having Jurisdiction of the Crime.

No Person held to Service or Labour in one State, under the Laws thereof, escaping into another, shall, in Consequence of any Law or Regulation therein, be discharged from such Service or Labour, but shall be delivered up on Claim of the Party to whom such Service or Labour may be due.

Section 3. New States may be admitted by the Congress into this Union; but no new State shall be formed or erected within the Jurisdiction of any other State; nor any State be formed by the Junction of two or more States, or Parts of States, without the Consent of the Legislatures of the States concerned as well as of the Congress.

The Congress shall have Power to dispose of and make all needful Rules and Regulations respecting the Territory or other Property belonging to the United States; and nothing in this Constitution shall be so construed as to Prejudice any Claims of the United States, or of any particular State.

Section 4. The United States shall guarantee to every State in this Union a Republican Form of Government, and shall protect each of them against Invasion; and on Application of the Legislature, or of the Executive (when the Legislature cannot be convened) against domestic Violence.

ARTICLE V

The Congress, whenever two thirds of both Houses shall deem it necessary, shall propose Amendments to this Constitution, or, on the Application of the Legislatures of two thirds of the several States, shall call a Convention for proposing Amendments, which, in either Case, shall be valid to all Intents and Purposes, as part of this Constitution, when ratified by the Legislatures of three fourths of the several States, or by Conventions in three fourths thereof, as the one or the other Mode of Ratification may be proposed by the Congress; Provided that no Amendment which may be made prior to the Year One thousand eight hundred and eight shall in any Manner affect the first and fourth Clauses in the Ninth Section of the first Article; and that no State, without its Consent, shall be deprived of its equal Suffrage in the Senate.

ARTICLE VI

All Debts contracted and Engagements entered into, before the Adoption of this Constitution shall be as valid against the United States under this Constitution, as under the Confederation.

This Constitution, and the Laws of the United States which shall be made in Pursuance thereof; and all Treaties made, or which shall be made, under the Authority of the United States, shall be the supreme Law of the Land; and the Judges in every State shall be bound thereby, any Thing in the Constitution or Laws of any State to the Contrary notwithstanding.

The Senators and Representatives before mentioned, and the Members of the several State Legislatures, and all executive and judicial Officers, both of the United States and of the several States, shall be bound by Oath or Affirmation, to support this Constitution; but no religious Test shall ever be required as a Qualification to any Office or public Trust under the United States.

ARTICLE VII

The Ratification of the Conventions of nine States shall be sufficient for the Establishment of this Constitution between the States so ratifying the Same.

AMENDMENT I [1791]

Congress shall make no law respecting an establishment of religion, or prohibiting the free exercise thereof; or abridging the freedom of speech, or of the press; or the right of the people peaceably to assembly, and to petition the Government for a redress of grievances.

AMENDMENT II [1791]

A well regulated Militia, being necessary to the security of a free State, the right of the people to keep and bear Arms, shall not be infringed.

AMENDMENT III [1791]

No Soldier shall, in time of peace be quartered in any house, without the consent of the Owner, nor in time of war, but in a manner to be prescribed by law.

AMENDMENT IV [1791]

The right of the people to be secure in their persons, houses, papers, and effects, against unreasonable searches and seizures, shall not be violated, and no Warrants shall issue, but upon probable cause, supported by Oath or affirmation, and particularly describing the place to be searched, and the persons or things to be seized.

AMENDMENT V [1791]

No person shall be held to answer for a capital, or otherwise infamous crime, unless on a presentment or indictment of a Grand Jury, except in cases arising in the land or naval forces, or in the Militia, when in actual service in time of War or public danger; nor shall any person be subject for the same offence to be twice put in jeopardy of life or limb; nor shall be compelled in any criminal case to be a witness against himself, nor be deprived of life, liberty, or property, without due process of law; nor shall private property be taken for public use, without just compensation.

AMENDMENT VI [1791]

In all criminal prosecutions, the accused shall enjoy the right to a speedy and public trial, by an impartial jury of the State and district wherein the crime shall have been committed, which district shall have been previously ascertained by law, and to be informed of the nature and cause of the accusation; to be confronted with the witnesses against him; to have compulsory process for obtaining witnesses in his favor, and to have the Assistance of Counsel for his defence.

AMENDMENT VII [1791]

In Suits at common law, where the value in controversy shall exceed twenty dollars, the right of trial by jury shall be preserved, and no fact tried by jury, shall be otherwise reexamined in any Court of the United States, than according to the rules of the common law.

AMENDMENT VIII [1791]

Excessive bail shall not be required, nor excessive fines imposed, nor cruel and unusual punishments inflicted.

AMENDMENT IX [1791]

The enumeration in the Constitution, of certain rights, shall not be construed to deny or disparage others retained by the people.

AMENDMENT X [1791]

The powers not delegated to the United States by the Constitution, nor prohibited by it to the States, are reserved to the States respectively, or to the people.

AMENDMENT XI [1798]

The Judicial power of the United States shall not be construed to extend to any suit in law or equity, commenced or prosecuted against one of the United States by Citizens of another State, or by Citizens or Subjects of any Foreign State.

AMENDMENT XII [1804]

The Electors shall meet in their respective states, and vote by ballot for President and Vice-President, one of whom, at least, shall not be an inhabitant of the same state with themselves; they shall name in their ballots the person voted for as President, and in distinct ballots the person voted for as Vice-President, and they shall make distinct lists of all persons voted for as President, and of all persons voted for as Vice-President, and of the number of votes for each, which lists they shall sign and certify, and transmit sealed to the seat of the government of the United States, directed to the President of the Senate;—The President of the Senate shall, in the presence of the Senate and House of Representatives, open all the certificates and the votes shall then be counted;—The person having the greatest number of votes for President, shall be the President, if such number be a majority of the whole number of Electors appointed; and if no person have such majority, then from the persons having the highest numbers not exceeding three on the list of those voted for as President, the House of Representatives shall choose immediately, by ballot, the President. But in choosing the President, the votes shall be taken by states, the representation from each state having one vote; a quorum for this purpose shall consist of a member or members from two-thirds of the states, and a majority of all states shall be necessary to a choice. And if the House of Representatives shall not choose a President whenever the right of choice shall devolve upon them, before the fourth day of March next following, then the Vice-President shall act as President, as in the case of the death or other constitutional disability of the President.—The person having the greatest number of votes as Vice-President, shall be the Vice-President, if such number be a majority of the whole number of Electors appointed, and if no person have a majority, then from the two highest numbers on the list, the Senate shall choose the Vice-President; a quorum for the purpose shall consist of two-thirds of the whole number of Senators, and a majority of the whole number shall be necessary to a choice. But no person constitutionally ineligible to the office of President shall be eligible to that of Vice-President of the United States.

AMENDMENT XIII [1865]

Section 1. Neither slavery nor involuntary servitude, except as a punishment for crime whereof the party shall have been duly convicted, shall exist within the United States, or any place subject to their jurisdiction.

Section 2. Congress shall have power to enforce this article by appropriate legislation.

AMENDMENT XIV [1868]

Section 1. All persons born or naturalized in the United States, and subject to the jurisdiction thereof, are citizens of the United States and of the State wherein they reside. No State shall make or enforce any law which shall abridge the privileges or immunities of citizens of the United States; nor shall any State deprive any person of life, liberty, or property, without due process of law; nor deny to any person within its jurisdiction the equal protection of the laws.

Section 2. Representatives shall be apportioned among the several States according to their respective numbers, counting the whole number of persons in each State, excluding Indians not taxed. But when the right to vote at any election for the choice of electors for President and Vice President of the United States, Representatives in Congress, the Executive and Judicial officers of a State, or the members of the Legislature thereof, is denied to any of the male inhabitants of such State, being twenty-one years of age, and citizens of the United States, or in any way abridged, except for participation in rebellion, or other crime, the basis of representation therein shall be reduced in the proportion which the number of such male citizens shall bear to the whole number of male citizens twenty-one years of age in such State.

Section 3. No person shall be a Senator or Representative in Congress, or elector of President and Vice President, or hold any office, civil or military, under the United States, or under any State, who having previously taken an oath, as a member of Congress, or as an officer of the United States, or as a member of any State legislature, or as an executive or judicial officer of any State, to support the Constitution of the United States, shall have engaged in insurrection or rebellion against the same, or given aid or comfort to the enemies thereof. But Congress may by a vote of two-thirds of each House, remove such disability.

Section 4. The validity of the public debt of the United States, authorized by law, including debts incurred for payment of pensions and bounties for services in suppressing insurrection or rebellion, shall not be questioned. But neither the United States nor any State shall assume or pay any debt or obligation incurred in aid of insurrection or rebellion against the United States, or any claim for the loss or emancipation of any slave; but all such debts, obligations and claims shall be held illegal and void.

Section 5. The Congress shall have power to enforce, by appropriate legislation, the provisions of this article.

AMENDMENT XV [1870]

Section 1. The right of citizens of the United States to vote shall not be denied or abridged by the United States or by any State on account of race, color, or previous condition of servitude.

Section 2. The Congress shall have power to enforce this article by appropriate legislation.

AMENDMENT XVI [1913]

The Congress shall have power to lay and collect taxes on incomes, from whatever source derived, without apportionment among the several States, and without regard to any census or enumeration.

AMENDMENT XVII [1913]

Section 1. The Senate of the United States shall be composed of two Senators from each State, elected by the people thereof, for six years; and each Senator shall have one vote. The electors in each State shall have the qualifications requisite for electors of the most numerous branch of the State legislatures.

Section 2. When vacancies happen in the representation of any State in the Senate, the executive authority of such State shall issue writs of election to fill such vacancies: *Provided,* That the legislature of any State may empower the executive thereof to make temporary appointments until the people fill the vacancies by election as the legislature may direct.

Section 3. This amendment shall not be so construed as to affect the election or term of any Senator chosen before it becomes valid as part of the Constitution.

AMENDMENT XVIII [1919]

Section 1. After one year from the ratification of this article the manufacture, sale, or transportation of intoxicating liquors within, the importation thereof into, or the exportation thereof from the United States and all territory subject to the jurisdiction thereof for beverage purposes is hereby prohibited.

Section 2. The Congress and the several States shall have concurrent power to enforce this article by appropriate legislation.

Section 3. This article shall be inoperative unless it shall have been ratified as an amendment to the Constitution by the legislatures of the several States, as provided in the Constitution, within seven years from the date of the submission hereof to the States by the Congress.

AMENDMENT XIX [1920]

Section 1. The right of citizens of the United States to vote shall not be denied or abridged by the United States or by any State on account of sex.

Section 2. Congress shall have power to enforce this article by appropriate legislation.

AMENDMENT XX [1933]

Section 1. The terms of the President and Vice President shall end at noon on the 20th day of January, and the terms of Senators and Representatives at noon on the 3d day of January, of the years in which such terms would have ended if this article had not been ratified; and the terms of their successors shall then begin.

Section 2. The Congress shall assemble at least once in every year, and such meeting shall begin at noon on the 3d day of January, unless they shall by law appoint a different day.

Section 3. If, at the time fixed for the beginning of the term of the President, the President elect shall have died, the Vice President elect shall become President. If the President shall not have been chosen before the time fixed for the beginning of his term, or if the President elect shall have failed to qualify, then the Vice President elect shall act as President until a President shall have qualified; and the Congress may by law provide for the case wherein neither a President elect nor a Vice President elect shall have qualified, declaring who shall then act as President, or the manner in which one who is to act shall be selected, and such person shall act accordingly until a President or Vice President shall have qualified.

Section 4. The Congress may by law provide for the case of the death of any of the persons from whom the House of Representatives may choose a President whenever the right of choice shall have devolved upon them, and for the case of the death of any of the persons from whom the Senate may choose a Vice President whenever the right of choice shall have devolved upon them.

Section 5. Sections 1 and 2 shall take effect on the 15th day of October following the ratification of this article.

Section 6. This article shall be inoperative unless it shall have been ratified as an amendment to the Constitution by the legislatures of three-fourths of the several States within seven years from the date of its submission.

AMENDMENT XXI [1933]

Section 1. The eighteenth article of amendment to the Constitution of the United States is hereby repealed.

Section 2. The transportation or importation into any State, Territory, or possession of the United States for delivery or use therein of intoxicating liquors, in violation of the laws thereof, is hereby prohibited.

Section 3. This article shall be inoperative unless it shall have been ratified as an amendment to the Constitution by conventions in the several States, as provided in the Constitution, within seven years from the date of the submission hereof to the States by the Congress.

AMENDMENT XXII [1951]

Section 1. No person shall be elected to the office of the President more than twice, and no person who has held the office of President, or acted as President, for more than two years of a term to which some other person was elected President shall be elected to the office of President more than once. But this Article shall not apply to any person holding the office of President when this Article was proposed by the Congress, and shall not prevent any person who may be holding the office of President, or acting as President, during the term within which this Article becomes operative from holding the office of President or acting as President during the remainder of such term.

Section 2. This article shall be inoperative unless it shall have been ratified as an amendment to the Constitution by the legislatures of three-fourths of the several States within seven years from the date of its submission to the States by the Congress.

AMENDMENT XXIII [1961]

Section 1. The District constituting the seat of Government of the United States shall appoint in such manner as the Congress may direct:

A number of electors of President and Vice President equal to the whole number of Senators and Representatives in Congress to which the District would be entitled if it were a State, but in no event more than the least populous state; they shall be in addition to those appointed by the states, but they shall be considered, for the purposes of the election of President and Vice President, to be electors appointed by a state; and they shall meet in the District and perform such duties as provided by the twelfth article of amendment.

Section 2. The Congress shall have power to enforce this article by appropriate legislation.

AMENDMENT XXIV [1964]

Section 1. The right of citizens of the United States to vote in any primary or other election for President or Vice President, for electors for President or Vice President, or for Senator or Representative in Congress, shall not be denied or abridged by the United States, or any State by reason of failure to pay any poll tax or other tax.

Section 2. The Congress shall have power to enforce this article by appropriate legislation.

AMENDMENT XXV [1967]

Section 1. In case of the removal of the President from office or of his death or resignation, the Vice President shall become President.

Section 2. Whenever there is a vacancy in the office of the Vice President, the President shall nominate a Vice President who shall take office upon confirmation by a majority vote of both Houses of Congress.

Section 3. Whenever the President transmits to the President pro tempore of the Senate and the Speaker of the House of Representatives his written declaration that he is unable to discharge the powers and duties of his office, and until he transmits to them a written declaration to the contrary, such powers and duties shall be discharged by the Vice President as Acting President.

Section 4. Whenever the Vice President and a majority of either the principal officers of the executive departments or of such other body as Congress may by law provide, transmit to the President pro tempore of the Senate and the Speaker of the House of Representatives their written declaration that the President is unable to discharge the powers and duties of his office, the Vice President shall immediately assume the powers and duties of the office as Acting President.

Thereafter, when the President transmits to the President pro tempore of the Senate and the Speaker of the House of Representatives his written declaration that no inability exists, he shall resume the powers and duties of his office unless the Vice President and a majority of either the principal officers of the executive department or of such other body as Congress may by law provide, transmit within four days to the President pro tempore of the Senate and the Speaker of the House of Representatives their written declaration that the President is unable to discharge the powers and duties of his office. Thereupon Congress shall decide the issue, assembling within forty-eight hours for that purpose if not in session. If the Congress, within twenty-one days after receipt of the latter written declaration, or, if Congress is not in session, within twenty-one days after Congress is required to assemble, determines by two-thirds vote of both Houses that the President is unable to discharge the powers and duties of his office, the Vice President shall continue to discharge the same as Acting President; otherwise, the President shall resume the powers and duties of his office.

AMENDMENT XXVI [1971]

Section 1. The right of citizens of the United States, who are eighteen years of age or older, to vote shall not be denied or abridged by the United States or by any State on account of age.

Section 2. The Congress shall have power to enforce this article by appropriate legislation.

AMENDMENT XXVII [1992]

No law, varying the compensation for the services of the Senators and Representatives, shall take effect, until an election of Representatives shall have intervened.

Discretion in Action: What Actually Happened

1.1 When given scenarios in which they are asked how they would react to illegal behavior that directly or indirectly involves a friend or family member, many police officers rely on the concept of impartiality. That is, they believe they are ethically required to treat all civilians the same, regardless of any personal connections. In extreme situations, a police officer might call on a colleague to make the actual arrest of a friend or family member to avoid the appearance of a conflict of interest. In this situation, however, Ray is ethically bound to treat Sally's house—a possible crime scene—the same as any other possible crime scene, and to enforce the law against cocaine use and possession.

3.1 After University of Virginia senior George Huguely was arrested for the death of his twenty-two-year-old ex-girlfriend Yeardley Love in 2010, prosecutors charged him with first degree murder, punishable by life in prison. The prosecutors asserted that Huguely was enraged because Love was dating someone else, and that he intended to kill her in a premeditated act. Huguely's lawyers insisted that, at worst, their client was guilty of involuntary manslaughter. At the time of the crime, they pointed out, he was drunk and had no intent to harm Love, much less kill her. Furthermore, they argued, Love died from suffocation well after Huguely left her apartment. In 2012, a Charlottesville, Virginia, jury found Huguely guilty of second degree murder, reasoning that although he did not intend to kill Love, he did act with malice aforethought and his violent behavior was the cause of her death. A judge later sentenced Huguely to twenty-three years in prison.

5.1 Deputy Timothy Scott ended the pursuit by applying his push bumper to the rear of Victor Harris's car. As a result, Harris lost control of his vehicle and spun off the side of the road. In the crash, Harris was badly injured, losing the ability to use his arms and legs. The question of whether Scott made the right decision eventually reached the United States Supreme Court. Ruling in the police officer's favor, the Court stated that Scott had acted reasonably under the circumstances, given the threat that Harris posed to others. The Court added that Harris intentionally placed himself in danger with his reckless actions and therefore could not blame Scott for injuries suffered in the resulting crash.

6.1 In 1996, two Washington, D.C., police officers pulled over Michael J. Wren—a young African American male who was driving a truck with temporary plates in a high-crime neighborhood—for failing to signal while making a right turn. They found two large bags of crack cocaine in Michael's possession, and arrested him. The United States Supreme Court upheld Michael's conviction, ruling that as long as police officers have probable cause to believe that a traffic violation has occurred, the "real" reason for making the stop is irrelevant. As Justice Antonin Scalia put it, "Subjective intentions play no role in ordinary, probable-cause, Fourth Amendment analysis." In practical terms, this ruling gives law enforcement agents the ability to confirm "hunches" about serious illegal behavior as long as the target of these hunches commits even the most minor traffic violation. Such violations could include failing to properly signal during a turn, or making a rolling stop at a stop sign, or driving five miles over the posted speed limit.

8.1 The North Carolina prosecutor in this case charged Judy Norman with first degree murder, reasoning that self-defense did not apply because Judy did not face any *imminent* danger from her husband, John. Despite his threats and the years of abuse, John was, at the time of his murder, asleep and thus incapable of harming her. A jury in the case, however, found Judy guilty of voluntary manslaughter only, and she was sentenced to six years in prison. This case gained national attention because the trial court refused to allow evidence of *battered woman syndrome (BWS)* to be presented to the jury. The term describes the psychological state a person descends into following a lengthy period of physical abuse. In a courtroom, an expert might argue that anyone suffering from this syndrome is in a constant, and reasonable, fear for her or his life. Some states do allow evidence of BWS to support the defendant's claim of self-defense in these sorts of cases, and it has been effective. A New York woman who shot her abusive husband as he slept, for example, was acquitted after a jury accepted her self-defense claims, bolstered by expert testimony on BWS.

9.1 The same Arizona jury that found Jodi Arias guilty of murdering Travis Alexander with such "exceptional cruelty" that she was eligible for the death penalty was unable to decide whether she should be executed. That is, the twelve jurors were unable to come to a unanimous decision on either execution or a life-in-prison sentence. Under state law, prosecutors were able to seat a second jury to make the sentencing decision, and, therefore, a second sentencing phase for Arias was scheduled to take place sixteen months after the first.

10.1 Alain LeConte's probation officer did not take any steps to revoke his probation. The issue became moot, however, when LeConte was arrested for killing a gas station attendant during an armed robbery in Norwalk, Connecticut. The crime took place between his first and second failed drug tests. LeConte's probation officer came under a great deal of criticism for failing to revoke his probation, but she received support from her supervisor. "We can only do so much," he said. "[LeConte's] probation officer went out of her way to assist this young man, but unfortunately it wasn't successful." The supervisor also pointed out that LeConte had no known history of violent behavior and had been a generally cooperative probationer when it came to getting treatment. This case underscores the difficult aspects of a probation officer's job. A misjudgment, even if it was based on a reasonable evaluation of the situation, can end in tragedy.

12.1 Initially, state prison officials decided to fire a correctional officer named Welch following an incident at the Maine Correctional Center in Windham similar to the one described in the feature. Because of Welch's otherwise unblemished career, however, his punishment was eventually reduced to a thirty-day suspension without pay. Following the incident, the Maine Department of Corrections instituted new guidelines regarding "cutters" (inmates who injure themselves) and "spitters" that promoted the use of pepper spray rather than other types of force by correctional officers. It seems that Welch's mistake was that he grew angry at the inmate's insults, and let his anger influence the level of his response. "It's all right for [inmates] to have the last word, we have the last action," said a state prison official.

Table of Cases

A

acquittal A declaration following a trial that the individual accused of the crime is innocent in the eyes of the law and thus is absolved from the charges.

actus reus (pronounced *ak*-tus *ray*-uhs). A guilty (prohibited) act.

adjudicatory hearing The process through which a juvenile court determines whether there is sufficient evidence to support the initial petition.

administrative law The body of law created by administrative agencies (in the form of rules, regulations, orders, and decisions) in order to carry out their duties and responsibilities.

affidavit A written statement of facts, confirmed by the oath or affirmation of the party making it and made before a person having the authority to administer the oath or affirmation.

affirmative action A hiring or promotion policy favoring those groups, such as women, African Americans, or Hispanics, who have suffered from discrimination in the past or continue to suffer from discrimination.

aftercare The variety of therapeutic, educational, and counseling programs made available to juvenile delinquents (and some adults) after they have been released from a correctional facility.

age of onset The age at which a juvenile first exhibits delinquent behavior.

aggravating circumstances Any circumstances accompanying the commission of a crime that may justify a harsher sentence.

aging out A term used to explain the fact that criminal activity declines with age.

Allen **Charge** An instruction by a judge to a deadlocked jury with only a few dissenters that asks the jurors in the minority to reconsider the majority opinion.

appeal The process of seeking a higher court's review of a lower court's decision for the purpose of correcting or changing this decision.

appellate courts Courts that review decisions made by lower courts, such as trial courts; also known as *courts of appeals.*

arraignment A court proceeding in which the suspect is formally charged with the criminal offense stated in the indictment.

arrest To deprive the liberty of a person suspected of criminal activity.

arrest warrant A written order, based on probable cause and issued by a judge or magistrate, commanding that the person named on the warrant be arrested by the police.

assault A threat or an attempt to do violence to another person that causes that person to fear immediate physical harm.

attempt The act of taking substantial steps toward committing a crime while having the ability and the intent to commit the crime, even if the crime never takes place.

attendant circumstances The facts surrounding a criminal event that must be proved to convict the defendant of the underlying crime.

attorney-client privilege A rule of evidence requiring that communications between a client and his or her attorney be kept confidential, unless the client consents to disclosure.

attorney general The chief law officer of a state; also, the chief law officer of the nation.

authority The power designated to an agent of the law over a person who has broken the law.

automatic transfer The process by which a juvenile is transferred to adult court as a matter of state law.

B

background check An investigation of a person's history to determine whether that person should be allowed a certain privilege, such as the ability to possess a firearm.

bail The dollar amount or conditions set by the court to ensure that an individual accused of a crime will appear for further criminal proceedings.

bail bond agent A businessperson who agrees, for a fee, to pay the bail amount if the accused fails to appear in court as ordered.

ballistics The study of firearms, including the firing of the weapon and the flight of the bullet.

ballot initiative A procedure through which the citizens of a state, by collecting enough signatures, can force a public vote on a proposed change to state law.

battery The act of physically contacting another person with the intent to do harm, even if the resulting injury is insubstantial.

bench trial A trial conducted without a jury, in which a judge makes the determination of the defendant's guilt or innocence.

beyond a reasonable doubt The degree of proof required to find the defendant in a criminal trial guilty of committing the crime. The defendant's guilt must be the only reasonable explanation for the criminal act before the court.

Bill of Rights The first ten amendments to the U.S. Constitution.

biology The science of living organisms, including their structure, function, growth, and origin.

biometrics Methods to identify a person based on his or her unique physical characteristics, such as fingerprints or facial configuration.

blue curtain A metaphorical term used to refer to the value placed on secrecy and the general mistrust of the outside world shared by many police officers.

boot camp A variation on traditional shock incarceration in which juveniles (and some adults) are sent to secure confinement facilities modeled on military basic training camps instead of prison or jail.

botnet A network of computers that have been appropriated without the knowledge of their owners and used to spread harmful programs via the Internet; short for *robot network*.

***Boykin* form** A form that must be completed by a defendant who pleads guilty. The defendant states that she or he has done so voluntarily and with full comprehension of the consequences.

broken windows theory Wilson and Kelling's theory that a neighborhood in disrepair signals that criminal activity is tolerated in the area. By cracking down on quality-of-life crimes, police can reclaim the neighborhood and encourage law-abiding citizens to live and work there.

bullying Overt acts taken by students with the goal of intimidating, harassing, or humiliating other students.

bureaucracy A hierarchically structured administrative organization that carries out specific functions.

burglary The act of breaking into or entering a structure (such as a home or office) without permission for the purpose of committing a felony.

burnout A mental state that occurs when a person suffers from exhaustion and has difficulty functioning normally as a result of overwork and stress.

C

capital crime A criminal act that makes the offender eligible to receive the death penalty.

capital punishment The use of the death penalty to punish wrongdoers for certain crimes.

case attrition The process through which prosecutors, by deciding whether to prosecute each person arrested, effect an overall reduction in the number of persons prosecuted.

case law The rules of law announced in court decisions.

caseload The number of individual probationers or parolees under the supervision of a probation or parole officer.

causation The relationship in which a change in one measurement or behavior creates a recognizable change in another measurement or behavior.

challenge for cause A *voir dire* challenge for which an attorney states the reason why a prospective juror should not be included on the jury.

charge The judge's instructions to the jury following the attorneys' closing arguments.

child abuse Mistreatment of children by causing physical, emotional, or sexual damage without any plausible explanation, such as an accident.

child neglect A form of child abuse in which the child is denied certain necessities such as shelter, food, care, and love.

circumstantial evidence Indirect evidence that is offered to establish, by inference, the likelihood of a fact that is in question.

citizen oversight The process by which citizens review complaints brought against individual police officers or police departments.

civil law The branch of law dealing with the definition and enforcement of all private or public rights, as opposed to criminal matters.

civil liberties The basic rights and freedoms of American citizens as guaranteed by the U.S. Constitution, particularly the Bill of Rights.

classification The process through which prison officials determine which correctional facility is best suited to the individual offender.

clearance rate A comparison of the number of crimes cleared by arrest and prosecution with the number of crimes reported during any given time period.

closing arguments Arguments made by each side's attorney after the cases for the plaintiff and defendant have been presented.

coercion The use of physical force or mental intimidation to compel a person to do something—such as confess to committing a crime—against her or his will.

cold case A criminal investigation that has not been solved after a certain amount of time.

cold hit The establishment of a connection between a suspect and a crime, often through the use of DNA evidence, in the absence of an ongoing criminal investigation.

community corrections The correctional supervision of offenders in the community as an alternative to sending them to prison or jail.

community policing A policing philosophy that emphasizes community support for and cooperation with the police in preventing crime.

competency hearing A court proceeding to determine whether the defendant is mentally well enough to understand the charges filed against him or her and cooperate with a lawyer in presenting a defense.

compliance The state of operating in accordance with governmental standards.

concurrent jurisdiction The situation that occurs when two or more courts have the authority to preside over the same criminal case.

concurring opinions Separate opinions prepared by judges who support the decision of the majority of the court but who want to clarify a particular point or to voice disapproval of the grounds on which the decision was made.

confidential informant (CI) A person who provides police with information concerning illegal activity in which he or she is involved.

conflict model A criminal justice model in which the content of criminal law is determined by the groups that hold political power in a community.

confrontation clause The part of the Sixth Amendment that guarantees all defendants the right to confront witnesses testifying against them during the criminal trial.

congregate system A nineteenth-century penitentiary system developed in New York in which inmates were kept in separate cells during the night but worked together in the daytime under a code of enforced silence.

consensus model A criminal justice model in which the majority of citizens in a society share the same values and beliefs. Criminal acts are acts that conflict with these values and beliefs and that are deemed harmful to society.

consent searches Searches by police that are made after the subject of the search has agreed to the action. In these situations, consent, if given of free will, validates a warrantless search.

conspiracy A plot by two or more people to carry out an illegal or harmful act.

constitutional law Law based on the U.S. Constitution and the constitutions of the various states.

control theory A theory that assumes that all individuals have the potential for criminal behavior but are restrained by the damage that such actions would do to their relationships with family, friends, and members of the community.

coroner The medical examiner of a county, usually elected by popular vote.

corporate violence Physical harm to individuals or the environment that occurs as the result of corporate policies or decision making.

corpus delicti The body of circumstances that must exist for a criminal act to have occurred.

correlation The relationship between two measurements or behaviors that tend to move together in the same direction.

courtroom work group The collective unit consisting of the judge, prosecutor, defense attorney, and other court workers.

crime An act that violates criminal law and is punishable by criminal sanctions.

crime control model A criminal justice model that places primary emphasis on the right of society to be protected from crime and violent criminals.

crime mapping Technology that allows crime analysts to identify trends and patterns of criminal behavior within a given area.

criminal justice system The interlocking network of law enforcement agencies, courts, and corrections institutions designed to enforce criminal laws and protect society from criminal behavior.

criminology The scientific study of crime and the causes of criminal behavior.

cross-examination The questioning of an opposing witness during trial.

custodial interrogation The questioning of a suspect after that person has been taken into custody. In this situation, the suspect must be read his or her *Miranda* rights before interrogation can begin.

custody The forceful detention of a person, or the perception that a person is not free to leave the immediate vicinity.

cyber crime A crime that occurs online, in the virtual community of the Internet, as opposed to in the physical world.

cyber forensics The application of computer technology to finding and utilizing evidence of cyber crimes.

cyber fraud Any misrepresentation knowingly made over the Internet with the intention of deceiving another and on which a reasonable person would and does rely to his or her detriment.

cyberstalking The crime of stalking, committed in cyberspace through the use of e-mail, text messages, or another form of electronic communication.

D

dark figure of crime A term used to describe the actual amount of crime that takes place. The "figure" is "dark," or impossible to detect, because a great number of crimes are never reported to the police.

day reporting center (DRC) A community-based corrections center to which offenders report on a daily basis for treatment, education, and rehabilitation.

deadly force Force applied by a police officer that is likely or intended to cause death.

defendant In a civil court, the person or institution against whom an action is brought. In a criminal court, the person or entity who has been formally accused of violating a criminal law.

defense attorney The lawyer representing the defendant.

delegation of authority The principles of command on which most police departments are based, in which personnel take orders from and are responsible to those in positions of power directly above them.

"deliberate indifference" A standard for establishing a violation of an inmate's Eighth Amendment rights, requiring that prison officials were aware of harmful conditions in a correctional institution *and* failed to take steps to remedy those conditions.

departure A stipulation in many federal and state sentencing guidelines that allows a judge to adjust his or her sentencing decision based on the special circumstances of a particular case.

deprivation model A theory that inmate aggression is the result of the frustration inmates feel at being deprived of freedom, consumer goods, sex, and other staples of life outside the institution.

desistance The process through which criminal activity decreases and reintegration into society develops over a period of time.

detective The primary police investigator of crimes.

detention The temporary custody of a juvenile in a secure facility after a petition has been filed and before the adjudicatory process begins.

detention hearing A hearing to determine whether a juvenile should remain detained while waiting for the adjudicatory process to begin.

determinate sentencing A period of incarceration that is fixed by a sentencing authority and cannot be reduced by judges or other corrections officials.

deterrence The philosophy that crime can be prevented through the threat of punishment.

deviance Behavior that is considered to go against the norms established by society.

differential response A strategy for answering calls for service in which response time is adapted to the seriousness of the call.

digital evidence Information or data of value to a criminal investigation that are either stored or transmitted by electronic means.

directed patrol A patrol strategy that is designed to focus on a specific type of criminal activity at a specific time.

direct evidence Evidence that establishes the existence of a fact that is in question without relying on inference.

direct examination The examination of a witness by the attorney who calls the witness to the stand to testify.

direct supervision approach A process of prison and jail administration in which correctional officers are in continuous visual contact with inmates during the day.

discovery Formal investigation of evidence by each side prior to trial.

discretion The ability of individuals in the criminal justice system to make operational decisions based on personal judgment instead of formal rules or official information.

discretionary release The release of an inmate into a community supervision program at the discretion of the parole board within limits set by state or federal law.

discrimination The illegal use of characteristics such as gender or race by employers when making hiring or promotion decisions.

disposition hearing Similar to the sentencing hearing for adults, a hearing in which the juvenile judge or officer decides the appropriate punishment for a youth found to be delinquent or a status offender.

dissenting opinions Separate opinions in which judges disagree with the conclusion reached by the majority of the court and expand on their own views about the case.

diversion In the context of corrections, a strategy to divert those offenders who qualify away from prison and jail and toward community-based and intermediate sanctions.

DNA fingerprinting The identification of a person based on a sample of her or his DNA, the genetic material found in the cells of all living things.

docket The list of cases entered on a court's calendar and thus scheduled to be heard by the court.

domestic terrorism Acts of terrorism that take place on U.S. soil without direct foreign involvement.

domestic violence Maltreatment, including physical violence and psychological abuse, that occurs within a familial or other intimate relationship.

double jeopardy To twice place at risk (jeopardize) a person's life or liberty. Constitutional law prohibits a second prosecution in the same court for the same criminal offense.

double marginality The suspicion that minority law enforcement officers face from both their white colleagues and members of the minority community to which they belong.

drug Any substance that modifies biological, psychological, or social behavior. In particular, an illegal substance with those properties.

drug abuse The use of drugs that results in physical or psychological problems for the user, as well as disruption of personal relationships and employment.

Drug Enforcement Administration (DEA) The federal agency responsible for enforcing the nation's laws and regulations regarding narcotics and other controlled substances.

dual court system The separate but interrelated court system of the United States, made up of the courts on the national level and the courts on the state level.

due process clause The provisions of the Fifth and Fourteenth Amendments to the Constitution that guarantee that no person shall be deprived of life, liberty, or property without due process of law.

due process model A criminal justice model that places primacy on the right of the individual to be protected from the power of the government.

duress Unlawful pressure brought to bear on a person, causing the person to perform an act that he or she would not otherwise perform.

duty The legal obligation or moral sense of a police officer that she or he should behave in a certain manner.

duty to retreat The requirement that a person claiming self-defense prove that she or he first took reasonable steps to avoid the conflict that resulted in the use of deadly force.

E

electronic monitoring A technique of probation supervision in which the offender's whereabouts are kept under surveillance by an electronic device.

electronic surveillance The use of electronic equipment by law enforcement agents to record private conversations or observe conduct that is meant to be private.

encryption The translation of computer data in a secret code with the goal of protecting those data from unauthorized parties.

enemy combatant A foreign national who has supported foreign terrorist organizations such as al Qaeda that are engaged in hostilities against the military operations of the United States.

entrapment A defense in which the defendant claims that he or she was induced by a public official—usually an undercover agent or police officer—to commit a crime that he or she would otherwise not have committed.

ethics A system of moral principles that governs a person's perception of right and wrong.

evidence Anything that is used to prove the existence or nonexistence of a fact.

exclusionary rule A rule under which any evidence that is obtained in violation of the accused's rights, as well as any evidence derived from illegally obtained evidence, will not be admissible in criminal court.

exigent circumstances Situations that require extralegal or exceptional actions by the police.

expert witness A witness with professional training or substantial experience qualifying her or him to testify on a certain subject.

expiration release The release of an inmate from prison at the end of his or her sentence without any further correctional supervision.

extradition The process by which one jurisdiction surrenders a person accused or convicted of violating another jurisdiction's criminal law to the second jurisdiction.

F

Federal Bureau of Investigation (FBI) The branch of the Department of Justice responsible for investigating violations of federal law.

federalism A form of government in which a written constitution provides for a division of powers between a central government and regional governments.

felony A serious crime, usually punishable by death or imprisonment for a year or longer.

felony-murder An unlawful homicide that occurs during the attempted commission of a felony.

field training The segment of a police recruit's training in which he or she is removed from the classroom and placed on the beat, under the supervision of a senior officer.

forensics The application of science to establish facts and evidence during the investigation of crimes.

forfeiture The process by which the government seizes private property attached to criminal activity.

formal criminal justice process The model of the criminal justice process in which participants follow formal rules to create a smoothly functioning disposition of cases from arrest to punishment.

frisk A pat-down or minimal search by police to discover weapons.

fruit of the poisoned tree Evidence that is acquired through the use of illegally obtained evidence and is therefore inadmissible in court.

furlough Temporary release from a prison for vocational or educational training, to ease the shock of release, or for personal reasons.

G

genetics The study of how certain traits or qualities are transmitted from parents to their offspring.

"good faith" exception The legal principle that evidence obtained with the use of a technically invalid search warrant is admissible during trial if the police acted in good faith when they sought the warrant from a judge.

"good time" A reduction in time served by prisoners based on good conduct, conformity to rules, and other positive behavior.

graduated sanctions The practical theory in juvenile corrections that a delinquent or status offender should receive a punishment that matches in seriousness the severity of the wrongdoing.

grand jury The group of citizens called to decide whether probable cause exists to believe that a suspect committed the crime with which she or he has been charged.

gun control Efforts by a government to regulate or control the sale of guns.

H

habeas corpus An order that requires corrections officials to bring an inmate before a court or a judge to explain why she or he is being held in prison illegally.

habitual offender laws Statutes that require lengthy prison sentences for those who are convicted of multiple felonies.

hacker A person who uses one computer to access another.

halfway house A community-based form of early release that places inmates in residential centers and allows them to reintegrate with society.

"hands-off" doctrine The unwritten judicial policy that favors noninterference by the courts in the administration of prisons and jails.

hate crime law A statute that provides for greater sanctions against those who commit crimes motivated by bias against an individual or a group based on race, ethnicity, religion, gender, sexual orientation, disability, or age.

hearsay An oral or written statement made by an out-of-court speaker that is later offered in court by a witness (not the speaker) concerning a matter before the court.

home confinement A community-based sanction in which offenders serve their terms of incarceration in their homes.

homeland security A concerted national effort to prevent terrorist attacks within the United States and reduce the country's vulnerability to terrorism.

hormone A chemical substance, produced in tissue and conveyed in the bloodstream, that controls certain cellular and body functions such as growth and reproduction.

hot spots Concentrated areas of high criminal activity that draw a directed police response.

hung jury A jury whose members are so irreconcilably divided in their opinions that they cannot reach a verdict.

hypothesis A possible explanation for an observed occurrence that can be tested by further investigation.

I

"identifiable human needs" A standard for establishing a violation of an inmate's Eighth Amendment rights, requiring that correctional facilities provide basic human necessities to inmates.

identity theft The theft of personal information, such as a person's name, driver's license number, or Social Security number.

incapacitation The philosophy that crime can be prevented by detaining wrongdoers in prison, thereby separating them from the community and reducing criminal opportunities.

inchoate offenses Conduct deemed criminal without actual harm being done, provided that the harm that would have occurred is one the law tries to prevent.

incident-driven policing A reactive approach to policing that emphasizes a speedy response to calls for service.

indeterminate sentencing An indeterminate term of incarceration in which a judge determines the minimum and maximum terms of imprisonment.

indictment A charge or written accusation, issued by a grand jury, that probable cause exists to believe that a named person has committed a crime.

"inevitable discovery" exception The legal principle that illegally obtained evidence can be admissible in court if police using lawful means would have "inevitably" discovered it.

infancy A condition that, under early American law, excused young wrongdoers of criminal behavior because presumably they could not understand the consequences of their actions.

informal criminal justice process A model of the criminal justice system that recognizes the informal authority exercised by individuals at each step of the criminal justice process.

information The formal charge against the accused issued by the prosecutor after a preliminary hearing has found probable cause.

infraction In most jurisdictions, a noncriminal offense for which the penalty is a fine rather than incarceration.

infrastructure The services and facilities that support the day-to-day needs of modern life, such as electricity, food, transportation, and water.

initial appearance An accused's first appearance before a judge or magistrate following arrest.

insanity A defense for criminal liability that asserts a lack of criminal responsibility due to mental instability

intake The process by which an official of the court must decide whether to file a petition, release the juvenile, or place the juvenile under some other form of supervision.

intellectual property Property resulting from intellectual, creative processes.

intelligence-led policing An approach that measures the risk of criminal behavior associated with certain individuals or locations so as to predict when and where such criminal behavior is most likely to occur in the future.

intensive supervision probation (ISP) A punishment-oriented form of probation in which the offender is placed under stricter and more frequent surveillance and control than in conventional probation.

intermediate sanctions Sanctions that are more restrictive than probation and less restrictive than imprisonment.

internal affairs unit (IAU) A division within a police department that receives and investigates complaints of wrongdoing by police officers.

interrogation The direct questioning of a suspect to gather evidence of criminal activity and to try to gain a confession.

intoxication A defense for criminal liability in which the defendant claims that the taking of intoxicants rendered him or her unable to form the requisite intent to commit a criminal act.

involuntary manslaughter A homicide in which the offender had no intent to kill her or his victim.

irresistible-impulse test A test for the insanity defense under which a defendant who knew his or her action was wrong may still be found insane if he or she was unable, as a result of a mental deficiency, to control the urge to complete the act.

J

jail A facility, usually operated by the county government, used to hold persons awaiting trial or those who have been found guilty of less-serious felonies or misdemeanors.

judicial review The power of a court—particularly the United States Supreme Court—to review the actions of the executive and legislative branches and, if necessary, declare those actions unconstitutional.

judicial waiver The process in which the juvenile court judge, based on the facts of the case at hand, decides that the alleged offender should be transferred to adult court.

jurisdiction The authority of a court to hear and decide cases within an area of the law or a geographic territory.

jury trial A trial before a judge and a jury.

just deserts A sanctioning philosophy based on the assertion that criminals deserve to be punished for breaking society's rules.

justice The quality of fairness that must exist in the processes designed to determine whether individuals are guilty of criminal wrongdoing.

juvenile delinquency Behavior that is illegal under federal or state law that has been committed by a person who is under an age limit specified by statute.

L

larceny The act of taking property from another person without the use of force with the intent of keeping that property.

lay witness A witness who can truthfully and accurately testify on a fact in question without having specialized training or knowledge.

learning theory The theory that delinquents and criminals must be taught both the practical and the emotional skills necessary to participate in illegal activity.

liability In a civil court, legal responsibility for one's own or another's actions.

life course criminology The study of crime based on the belief that behavioral patterns developed in childhood can predict delinquent and criminal behavior later in life.

lockdown A disciplinary action taken by prison officials in which all inmates are ordered to their quarters and nonessential prison activities are suspended.

low-visibility decision making A term used to describe the discretionary power police have in determining what to do with misbehaving juveniles.

M

magistrate A public civil official with limited judicial authority within a particular geographic area, such as the authority to issue an arrest warrant.

mala in se A descriptive term for acts that are inherently wrong, regardless of whether they are prohibited by law.

mala prohibita A descriptive term for acts that are made illegal by criminal statute and are not necessarily wrong in and of themselves.

mandatory release Release from prison that occurs when an offender has served the full length of his or her sentence, minus any adjustments for good time.

mandatory sentencing guidelines Statutorily determined punishments that must be applied to those who are convicted of specific crimes.

master jury list The list of citizens in a court's district from which a jury can be selected; compiled from voter-registration lists, driver's license lists, and other sources.

material support An umbrella term for criminal aid to a terrorist organization that covers not only financial support, but also logistical support such as expert advice or assistance.

maximum-security prison A correctional institution designed and organized to control and discipline dangerous felons, as well as prevent escape.

medical model A model of corrections in which the psychological and biological roots of an inmate's criminal behavior are identified and treated.

medium-security prison A correctional institution that houses less dangerous inmates and therefore uses less restrictive measures to prevent violence and escapes.

mens rea (pronounced mehns *ray*-uh). A wrongful mental state or intent, which is usually as necessary as a wrongful act to establish criminal liability.

military tribunal A court that is operated by the military rather than the criminal justice system and is presided over by military officers rather than judges.

minimum-security prison A correctional institution designed to allow inmates, most of whom pose low security risks, a great deal of freedom of movement and contact with the outside world.

Miranda **rights** The constitutional rights of accused persons taken into custody by law enforcement officials, such as the right to remain silent and the right to counsel.

misdemeanor A criminal offense that is not a felony; usually punishable by a fine and/or a jail term of up to one year.

Missouri Plan A method of selecting judges that combines appointment and election.

mitigating circumstances Any circumstances accompanying the commission of a crime that may justify a lighter sentence.

M'Naghten **rule** A test of criminal responsibility, derived from *M'Naghten's* Case in 1843, that relies on the defendant's inability to distinguish right from wrong.

morals Principles of right and wrong behavior, as practiced by individuals or by society.

murder The unlawful killing of one human being by another.

N

necessity A defense against criminal liability in which the defendant asserts that circumstances required her or him to commit an illegal act.

negligence A failure to exercise the standard of care that a reasonable person would exercise in similar circumstances.

new-generation jail A type of jail that is distinguished architecturally from its predecessors by a design that encourages interaction between inmates and jailers and that offers greater opportunities for treatment.

night watch system An early form of American law enforcement in which volunteers patrolled their community from dusk to dawn to keep the peace.

noble cause corruption Knowing misconduct by a police officer with the goal of attaining what the officer believes is a "just" result.

nolo contendere Latin for "I will not contest it." A criminal defendant's plea, in which he or she chooses not to challenge, or contest, the charges brought by the government.

nonpartisan elections Elections in which candidates are presented on the ballot without any party affiliation.

nonstate actor An entity that plays a role in international affairs but does not represent any established state or nation.

O

opening statements The attorneys' statements to the jury at the beginning of the trial.

opinions Written statements by appellate judges expressing the reasons for the court's decision in a case.

oral arguments The verbal arguments presented in person by attorneys to an appellate court. Each attorney presents reasons why the court should rule in his or her client's favor.

organized crime Illegal acts carried out by illegal organizations engaged in the market for illegal goods or services, such as illicit drugs or firearms.

P

pardon An act of executive clemency that overturns a conviction and erases mention of the crime from the person's criminal record.

parens patriae A doctrine that holds that the state has a responsibility to look after the well-being of children and to assume the role of parent, if necessary.

parole The conditional release of an inmate before his or her sentence has expired.

parole board A body of appointed civilians that decides whether a convict should be granted conditional release before the end of his or her sentence.

parole contract An agreement between the state and the offender that establishes the conditions of parole.

parole grant hearing A hearing in which the entire parole board or a subcommittee reviews information, meets the offender, and hears testimony from relevant witnesses to determine whether to grant parole.

parole guidelines Standards that are used in the parole process to measure the risk that a potential parolee will recidivate.

parole revocation When a parolee breaks the conditions of parole, the process of withdrawing parole and returning the person to prison.

Part I offenses Crimes reported annually by the FBI in its Uniform Crime Report. Part I offenses include murder, rape, robbery, aggravated assault, burglary, larceny, and motor vehicle theft.

Part II offenses All crimes recorded by the FBI that do not fall into the category of Part I offenses. These crimes include both misdemeanors and felonies.

partisan elections Elections in which candidates are affiliated with and receive support from political parties.

patronage system A form of corruption in which the political party in power hires and promotes police officers and receives job-related "favors" in return.

penitentiary An early form of correctional facility that emphasized separating inmates from society and from each other.

peremptory challenges *Voir dire* challenges to exclude potential jurors from serving on the jury without any supporting reason or cause.

petition The document filed with a juvenile court alleging that the juvenile is a delinquent or a status offender, and requesting that the court either hear the case or transfer it to an adult court.

phishing Sending an unsolicited e-mail that falsely claims to be from a legitimate organization in an attempt to acquire sensitive information from the recipient.

plaintiff The person or institution that initiates a lawsuit in civil court proceedings by filing a complaint.

plain view doctrine The legal principle that objects in plain view of a law enforcement agent who has the right to be in a position to have that view may be seized without a warrant and introduced as evidence.

plea bargaining The process by which the accused and the prosecutor work out a mutually satisfactory conclusion to the case, subject to court approval.

police corruption The abuse of authority by a law enforcement officer for personal gain.

police subculture The values and perceptions that are shared by members of a police department and, to a certain extent, by all law enforcement agents.

precedent A court decision that furnishes an example of authority for deciding subsequent cases involving similar facts.

predisposition report A report prepared during the disposition process that provides the judge with relevant background material to aid in the disposition decision.

preliminary hearing An initial hearing in which a magistrate decides if there is probable cause to believe that the defendant committed the crime with which he or she is charged.

preponderance of the evidence The degree of proof required to decide in favor of one side or the other in a civil case. In general, this requirement is met when a plaintiff proves that an explanation more likely than not is true.

prescription drugs Medical drugs that require a physician's permission for purchase.

presentence investigative report An investigative report on an offender's background that assists a judge in determining the proper sentence.

pretrial detainees Individuals who cannot post bail after arrest and are therefore forced to spend the time prior to their trial incarcerated in jail.

pretrial diversion program An alternative to trial offered by a judge or prosecutor, in which the offender agrees to participate in a specified counseling or treatment program in return for withdrawal of the charges.

preventive detention The retention of an accused person in custody due to fears that she or he will commit a crime if released before trial.

prisoner reentry A corrections strategy designed to prepare inmates for a successful return to the community and to lessen the possibility that they will reoffend after release.

prison gang A group of inmates who band together within the corrections system to engage in social and criminal activities.

prisonization The socialization process through which a new inmate learns the accepted norms and values of the prison culture.

prison programs Organized activities for inmates that are designed to improve their physical and mental health, provide them with vocational skills, or simply keep them occupied while incarcerated.

private prisons Correctional facilities operated by private corporations instead of the government and, therefore, reliant on profits for survival.

private security The practice of private corporations or individuals offering services traditionally performed by police officers.

proactive arrests Arrests that occur because of concerted efforts by law enforcement agencies to respond to a particular type of criminal or criminal behavior.

probable cause Reasonable grounds to believe the existence of facts warranting certain actions, such as the search or arrest of a person.

probation A criminal sanction in which a convict is allowed to remain in the community rather than be imprisoned.

probationary period A period of time at the beginning of a police officer's career during which she or he may be fired without cause.

problem-oriented policing A policing philosophy that requires police to identify potential criminal activity and develop strategies to prevent or respond to that activity.

problem-solving courts Lower courts that have jurisdiction over one specific area of criminal activity, such as illegal drugs or domestic violence.

procedural criminal law Law that defines the manner in which the rights and duties of individuals may be enforced.

procedural due process A provision in the Constitution that states the law must be carried out in a fair and orderly manner.

professional model A style of policing advocated by August Vollmer and O. W. Wilson that emphasizes centralized police organizations, increased use of the patrol car, and a limitation of police discretion through regulations and guidelines.

property bond An alternative to posting bail in cash, in which the defendant gains pretrial release by providing the court with property valued at the bail amount as assurance that he or she will return for trial.

prosecutorial waiver A procedure used in situations where the prosecutor has discretion to decide whether a case will be heard by a juvenile court or an adult court.

psychoactive drugs Chemicals that affect the brain, causing changes in emotions, perceptions, and behavior.

psychology The scientific study of mental processes and behavior.

public defenders Court-appointed attorneys who are paid by the state to represent defendants who cannot afford private counsel.

public order crime Behavior that has been labeled criminal because it is contrary to shared social values, customs, and norms.

public prosecutors Individuals, acting as trial lawyers, who initiate and conduct cases in the government's name and on behalf of the people.

R

racial profiling The practice of targeting people for police action based solely on their race, ethnicity, or national origin.

racketeering The criminal action of being involved in an organized effort to engage in illegal business transactions.

random patrol A patrol strategy that relies on police officers monitoring a certain area with the goal of detecting crimes in progress or preventing crime due to their presence.

rational choice theory A school of criminology that holds that wrongdoers weigh the possible benefits of criminal or delinquent activity against the expected costs of being apprehended.

reactive arrests Arrests that come about as part of the ordinary routine of police patrol and responses to calls for service.

real evidence Evidence that is brought into court and seen by the jury, as opposed to evidence that is described for a jury.

"real offense" The actual offense committed, as opposed to the charge levied by a prosecutor as the result of a plea bargain.

reasonable force The degree of force that is appropriate to protect the police officer or other citizens and is not excessive.

rebuttal New evidence presented by the prosecution given to counteract or disprove evidence presented by the opposing party.

recidivism Commission of a new crime by a person who has already been convicted of a previous crime and sent to jail or prison.

recklessness The state of being aware that a risk does or will exist and nevertheless acting in a way that consciously disregards this risk.

recruitment The process by which law enforcement agencies develop a pool of qualified applicants from which to select new employees.

referral The notification process through which a law enforcement officer or other concerned citizen makes the juvenile court aware of a juvenile's unlawful or unruly conduct.

regulation Governmental control of society, through rules and laws, that is generally carried out by administrative agencies.

rehabilitation The philosophy that society is best served when wrongdoers are provided the resources needed to eliminate criminality from their behavioral pattern.

reintegration A goal of corrections that focuses on preparing the offender for a return to the community unmarred by further criminal behavior.

relative deprivation The theory that inmate aggression is caused when freedoms and services that the inmate has come to accept as normal are decreased or eliminated.

release on recognizance (ROR) A judge's order that releases an accused from jail with the understanding that he or she will return of his or her own will for further proceedings.

relevant evidence Evidence tending to make a fact in question more or less probable than it would be without the evidence. Only relevant evidence is admissible in court.

repeat victimization The theory that certain people and places are more likely to be subject to repeated criminal activity and that past victimization is a strong indicator of future victimization.

residential treatment program A government-run facility for juveniles whose offenses are not deemed serious enough to warrant incarceration in a juvenile correctional facility.

response time The rapidity with which calls for service are answered.

restitution Monetary compensation for damages done to the victim by the offender's criminal act.

restorative justice An approach to punishment designed to repair the harm done to the victim and the community by the offender's criminal act.

retribution The philosophy that those who commit criminal acts should be punished based on the severity of the crime and that no other factors need be considered.

robbery The act of taking property from another person through force, threat of force, or intimidation.

rule of four A rule of the United States Supreme Court that the Court will not issue a writ of *certiorari* unless at least four justices approve of the decision to hear the case.

S

search The process by which police examine a person or property to find evidence that will be used to prove guilt in a criminal trial.

searches and seizures The legal term, as found in the Fourth Amendment to the U.S. Constitution, that generally refers to the searching for and the confiscating of evidence by law enforcement agents.

searches incidental to arrests Searches for weapons and evidence that are conducted on persons who have just been arrested.

search warrant A written order, based on probable cause and issued by a judge or magistrate, commanding that police officers or criminal investigators search a specific person, place, or property to obtain evidence.

security threat group (STG) A group of three or more inmates who engage in activity that poses a threat to the safety of other inmates or the prison staff.

seizure The forcible taking of a person or property in response to a suspected violation of the law.

self-defense The legally recognized privilege to protect one's self or property from injury by another.

self-reported survey A method of gathering crime data from offenders that relies on participants to reveal and detail their own criminal or delinquent behavior.

sentencing discrimination A situation in which the length of a sentence appears to be influenced by a defendant's race, gender, economic status, or other factor not directly related to the crime he or she committed.

sentencing disparity A situation in which those convicted of similar crimes do not receive similar sentences.

sentencing guidelines Legislatively determined guidelines that judges are required to follow when sentencing those convicted of specific crimes.

separate confinement A nineteenth-century penitentiary system developed in Pennsylvania in which inmates were kept separate from each other at all times, with daily activities taking place in individual cells.

sex offender notification law Legislation that requires law enforcement authorities to notify people when convicted sex offenders are released into their neighborhood or community.

sexual assault Forced or coerced sexual intercourse or other sexual acts.

sheriff The primary law enforcement officer in a county, usually elected to the post by a popular vote.

shock incarceration A short period of incarceration that is designed to deter further criminal activity by "shocking" the offender with the hardships of imprisonment.

social conflict theories A school of criminology that views criminal behavior as the result of class conflict.

social disorganization theory The theory that deviant behavior is more likely in communities where social institutions such as the family, schools, and the criminal justice system fail to exert control over the population.

socialization The process through which a police officer is taught the values and expected behavior of the police subculture.

social process theories A school of criminology that considers criminal behavior to be the predictable result of a person's interaction with his or her environment.

sociology The study of the development and functioning of groups of people who live together within a society.

spam Bulk e-mails, particularly of commercial advertising, sent in large quantities without the consent of the recipient.

split sentence probation A sentence that consists of incarceration in a prison or jail, followed by a probationary period in the community.

stalking The criminal act of causing fear in a person by repeatedly subjecting that person to unwanted or threatening attention.

status offender A juvenile who has engaged in behavior deemed unacceptable for those under a certain statutorily determined age.

statute of limitations A law limiting the amount of time prosecutors have to bring criminal charges against a suspect after the crime has occurred.

statutory law The body of law enacted by legislative bodies.

statutory rape A strict liability crime in which an adult engages in a sexual act with a minor.

stop A brief detention of a person for questioning by law enforcement agents.

strain theory The theory that crime is the result of frustration and anger felt by individuals who cannot reach their financial and personal goals through legitimate means.

street gang A group of people, usually three or more, who share a common identity and engage in illegal activities.

stressors The aspects of police work and life that lead to feelings of stress.

strict liability crimes Certain crimes, such as traffic violations, in which the defendant is guilty regardless of her or his state of mind at the time of the act.

substantial-capacity test (ALI/MPC test) A test for the insanity defense that states that a person is not responsible for criminal behavior when he or she "lacks substantial capacity" to understand that the behavior is wrong or to know how to behave properly.

substantive criminal law Law that defines the rights and duties of individuals with respect to one another.

substantive due process The constitutional requirement that laws used in accusing and convicting persons of crimes must be fair.

supermax prison A correctional facility reserved for those inmates who have extensive records of misconduct.

supremacy clause A clause in the U.S. Constitution establishing that federal law is the "supreme law of the land" and shall prevail when in conflict with state constitutions or statutes.

suspended sentence A judicially imposed condition in which an offender is sentenced after being convicted of a crime but is not required to begin serving the sentence immediately.

T

technical violation An action taken by a probationer or parolee that, although not criminal, breaks the terms of probation or parole as designated by the court.

terrorism The use or threat of violence to achieve political objectives.

testimony Verbal evidence given by witnesses under oath.

testosterone The hormone primarily responsible for the production of sperm and the development of male secondary sex characteristics, such as the growth of facial and pubic hair and the change of voice pitch.

theory An explanation of a happening or circumstance that is based on observation, experimentation, and reasoning.

time served The period of time a person denied bail (or unable to pay it) has spent in jail prior to his or her trial.

total institution An institution, such as a prison, that provides all of the necessities for existence to those who live within its boundaries.

trace evidence Evidence such as a fingerprint, blood, or hair found in small amounts at a crime scene.

training school A correctional institution for juveniles found to be delinquent or status offenders.

trial courts Courts in which most cases usually begin and in which questions of fact are examined.

truth-in-sentencing laws Legislative attempts to ensure that convicts will serve approximately the terms to which they were initially sentenced.

U

Uniform Crime Report (UCR) An annual report compiled by the FBI to give an indication of criminal activity in the United States.

U.S. Customs and Border Protection (CBP) The federal agency responsible for protecting U.S. borders and facilitating legal trade and travel across those borders.

U.S. Immigration and Customs Enforcement (ICE) The federal agency that enforces the nation's immigration and customs laws.

U.S. Secret Service A federal law enforcement organization with the primary responsibility of protecting the president, the president's family, the vice president, and other important political figures.

V

venire The group of citizens from which the jury is selected.

verdict A formal decision made by the jury.

victim Any person who suffers physical, emotional, or financial harm as the result of a criminal act.

victim impact statement (VIS) A statement to the sentencing body (judge, jury, or parole board) in which the victim is given the opportunity to describe how the crime has affected her or him.

victimology A school of criminology that studies why certain people are the victims of crimes and the optimal role for victims in the criminal justice system.

victim surveys A method of gathering crime data that directly surveys participants to determine their experiences as victims of crime.

virus A computer program that can replicate itself and interfere with the normal use of a computer. A virus cannot exist as a separate entity and must attach itself to another program to move through a network.

visa Official authorization allowing a person to travel to and within the issuing country.

voir dire The preliminary questions that the trial attorneys ask prospective jurors to determine whether they are biased or have any connection with the defendant or a witness.

voluntary manslaughter A homicide in which the intent to kill was present in the mind of the offender, but malice was lacking.

weapon of mass destruction A weapon that has the capacity to cause large number of casualties or significant property damage.

white-collar crime Nonviolent crimes committed by business entities or individuals to gain a personal or business advantage.

widen the net The criticism that intermediate sanctions designed to divert offenders from prison actually increase the number of citizens who are under the control and surveillance of the American corrections system.

work release program Temporary release of convicts from prison for purposes of employment. The offenders may spend their days on the job, but must return to the correctional facility at night and during the weekend.

worm A computer program that can automatically replicate itself and interfere with the normal use of a computer. A worm does not need to be attached to an existing file to move from one network to another.

writ of *certiorari* A request from a higher court asking a lower court for the record of a case. In essence, the request signals the higher court's willingness to review the case.

wrongful conviction The conviction, either by verdict or by guilty plea, of a person who is factually innocent of the charges.

W

warden The prison official who is ultimately responsible for the organization and performance of a correctional facility.

warrantless arrest An arrest made without first seeking a warrant for the action.

Y

youth gang A self-formed group of youths with several identifiable characteristics, including a gang name and other recognizable symbols, a geographic territory, and participation in illegal activities.